First Edition

Managing the Inland Search Function

Written and Edited
by
Brett C. Stoffel
Robert C. "Skip" Stoffel

Artwork by Richard Pargeter
and Robert C. "Skip" Stoffel

Published By:

Emergency Response
International, Inc.

PO Box 434
Monitor, WA. 98836
(509) 888-0427
eri-online.com

Emergency Response International, Inc.- 2016

National Association for
Search And Rescue

PO Box 232020,
Centreville, VA 20120-2020
(877)-893-0702
nasar.org

National Association For Search And Rescue- 2016

DISCLAIMER: This Text is not the complete instructional manual for search management or lost/missing person response. The materials are not meant to replace practical training by competent search, and/or emergency response leaders or to replace actual experience. Emergency Response International, Inc., the author and contributors to this manual do not endorse any specific equipment mentioned in this publication. The author, contributors and Emergency Response International, Inc., take no responsibility for the use of this manual or any information contained therein. Emergency Response International, Inc. and the National Association For Search And Rescue take no responsibility and cannot be held liable for statements made by instructors who utilize this manual. The purchaser or recipient of this textbook agrees to protect, save and hold forever harmless Emergency Response International, Inc., The National Association For Search And Rescue, the author and contributors to this book, against and from all loss, cost, damage, liability or expense arising from, or out of the use of this publication. Emergency Response International, Inc., The National Association For Search And Rescue the author and contributors to this book, may not be held liable in any way for any occurrence in connection with an individual's utilization of the materials and instructions set forth in this text which may result in injury, death or other damages to the purchaser or receiver of this manual, his family, heirs or assigns. **It is the duty of every law enforcement organization, volunteer group, and government agency with responsibilities in searching for lost or missing people to obtain the knowledge and proficiency to perform and maintain effective, efficient search and/or rescue, management skills and operational capability.** The information presented in this publication, serves as an overview outline of basic search management and planning tenets for managers at the local response level.

Copyright © 2017 by Brett C. Stoffel, Robert C. Stoffel and The National Association for Search and Rescue

All rights reserved. No part of this publication may be reproduced, distributed, or transmitted in any form or by any means, including photocopying, recording, or other electronic or mechanical methods, without the prior written permission of the publisher, except in the case of brief quotations embodied in critical reviews and certain other noncommercial uses permitted by copyright law. For permission requests, write to the publisher, at the address below.

First Edition, U.S. Version - January, 2017
ISBN Number: 0-9988557-1-5 and
978-0-9988557-1-4

Emergency Response International, Inc.
dba ERI Publications & Training
319 Olive Street
Cashmere, WA 98815
www.eri-online.com

The Publishers would like to thank the following individuals for their assistance and contributions to the publication of this text book and their tireless contributions to the Search and Rescue community:

Chris Boyer
Cole Brown
Ross Gordon
Robert Koester
David Kovar
John Mckently
Jeff Mitchell
Mike Murray
Sara Rubrecht
Matt Scharper
Mareen Stoffel
Shannon Stoffel
Clive G. Swambow
Tony Wells
Chris Young

Notes:

Since 1973, NASAR has been at the forefront of supporting SAR responders. We recognize the life-saving skills required by agency and volunteer responders and have worked to develop education, standards and certifications to support those that serve that others may live.

In 2015 NASAR and ERI began discussing the history of search management and realized that consolidating their two textbooks into a single, state-of-the-art textbook would be in the best interests of the SAR community. The publication of the *Managing the Inland Search Function* is the result of the partnership between NASAR and ERI.

CMC Rescue provided critical financial support for this project and we would like to thank them for their partnership and continued support of the emergency first responder community.

NASAR wants to thank ERI and the subject matter experts that contributed their time and knowledge in making this the world-class product that you expect from us.

Chris Boyer
Executive Director

Foreword

In 1978, Jim Frank recognized the need to ensure rescue professionals had adequate equipment to perform rescue operations more safely and effectively, thus founding California Mountain Company – now CMC Rescue.

In our forty-year history as a globally recognized provider of rescue and life-safety equipment, CMC Rescue has long supported the education, safety standards and organizations that help make search and rescue a world-class volunteer profession.

CMC Rescue employee-owners also serve as active volunteer members of emergency response teams across the country.

Our mission is to protect professionals working in high-risk environments by providing trusted life safety equipment and education. Whether through our own innovation, or through partnerships that seek to evolve better resources for rescuers, we're committed to advancing industry-wide progression. Since 1972, NASAR has provided fundamental educational tools for the SAR community, and it is an honor to support their efforts.

www.cmcrescue.com • info@cmcrescue.com • 800.235.5741 • 805.562.9120

Table of Contents

Pre-Operations and Planning

Page

1 - SAR Management Introduction 1
2 - A National and International Perspective on Land Search Management & Training 5
3 - Changing Concepts in Search Management & Planning 25
4 - Legal Issues and Public Expectations 37
5 - Search Manager: The Job of Managing a Search 45
6 - SAR Vulnerability Assessment & The Importance of Statistics 55
7 - Preplanning: Developing a Functional Documented Preplan 65
8 - SAR Resources 75
9 - SAR Strategies and Tactical Procedures 89

Operational Response

10 - The Kim Family Search Incident 141
11 - The First Notice & Determining Urgency 175
12 - Planning Data/Searching Data 185
13 - Investigation, Interviewing and Callout 203
14 - Missing and Lost Person Behavior 217
15 - Organization: Incident Command & Functional Mgmt. 243
16 - On-Scene Planning 263
17 - Introduction to Search Theory and Applied Probability 275
18 - Establishing the Search Area 289
19 - Probability of Detection (POD) 343
20 - Applied Search Theory and Planning - POA × POD = POS 365
21 - Clue Orientation 387
22 - Briefing and Debriefing 399
23 - Searching in the Urban Environment 409
24 - Suspending the Search 423

Management and Base Operations

25 - Documentation 429
26 - Search Base Operations 431
27 - External Influences 439
28 - Considerations for Rescue & Recovery 451
29 - Managing Psychology and Stress Reactions in Operations Personnel 457

Post Operations and Administration

30 - Demobilization & Post Mission 477
31 - Acronyms Used In Search and Rescue 483
32 - Bibliography 485

Notes:

SAR Management Introduction 1

Objectives:

- Discuss the course content and topics
- List the course objectives
- Examine objectives for attending the course and potential application in home jurisdictions

Why Search Management?

Reduced to simplest terms, three elements influence the success of a search: resources; strategy and tactics; and most critically the function of **management**. Management describes the function of coordinating the efforts of individuals to accomplish goals and objectives by using available resources efficiently and effectively. Effective managers define the problem at hand, set objectives to solve that problem and apply available resources to those objectives. The right people and equipment *(dogs, electronic technology, aircraft, etc.)* increases the chances for a successful search. Next, managers apply strategy and tactics with appropriate resources in the right order, according to their capabilities for specific environments. Finally, the function of management coordinates the entire myriad of functions, responsibilities, resources, investigative efforts, and personal interaction to create a successful search.

Basic Search management courses focus on those who maintain the responsibility and authority to plan, physically prepare for, and manage search operations in wilderness, rural and urban environments for the appropriate jurisdiction. These courses also provide a framework for conducting consistent search operations for missing persons in repeatable and scientifically defendable ways.

Basic search management training targets any agency or organization, whether professional or volunteer, with search related interests, responsibilities, or capabilities. Participants learn both the rudiments of incident management through accepted systems such as *ICS* and the *Six Step Process,* practical search planning and effort allocation to achieve success in the least amount of time.

The small group discussions and tabletop map exercises presented later, emphasize practical use of these concepts in real search operations.

Terms, Applications and the need for Search Management

The term SAR denotes two separate functions: Search, to locate persons in distress, and the function of Rescue. Rescue utilizes proven procedures to provide for the initial medical or other needs along with a high degree of technical skill for victim retrieval. When responders locate victims in known locations, the principle problem involves the quickest method of removing that individual from danger and moving them to a place of safety and pre-hospital care. On the other hand, search for the lost, missing or injured subject encompasses a sophisticated science using modern investigative techniques, interviewing, statistics and statistical analysis, probability theory, human behavior, terrain evaluation and tracking.

SAR also refers to national and regional emergency situations including providing relief to persons in distress. SAR programs, equipment and personnel vary geographically in accordance with local needs and legislation.

For example, Hurricane Katrina (2005), one of the US's most catastrophic disasters, also included an incredibly large search operation for missing people. Similarly, when tornadoes strike a large metropolitan area like Oklahoma City (2013), responders mobilized to search for and provide rescue operations for affected residents. Likewise, the decades old explosion and crash of Pan American Flight 103 in Lockerbie, Scotland (1988), ended up one of the largest search operations for evidence and human remains in European history. Search operations draw together extremely diverse organizations in a time critical, life threatening situation. All search and rescue incidents generate a commonality of purpose similar to the circumstances found during a community wide disaster. Often, large search incidents, like those mentioned above, involve several jurisdictions and the coordination of both air and ground search resources. Statistics, behavior, probability mapping and the other lessons of *Search Theory* all help to resolve those disasters effectively.

More and more law enforcement agencies and organizations apply the basic material contained in search management training to situations concerning missing people. Therefore, this text and the recommended courses accompanying it, form a *standard* in numerous countries and provide methods used for evidence searches in both small and large-scale police operations as well.

Search management emphasizes planning, organizing, leading and controlling. Good management of search operations targets successful conclusions (finding a missing subject or rescuing a person before they succumb to the effects of injuries or the environment). Over time, basic search management training impacts and adds to future training, planning efforts, and the cooperation expected by Incident Commanders (and indirectly the public) in a fully integrated all hazard emergency response system.

Search mission objectives target finding the missing person quickly and in the best possible condition. A combination of factors, such as legislation, standard of care, circumstances, *public expectations*, liability issues, intense scrutiny by the media and even professional ethics influence the incident outcome. All of these dictate effective and efficient management. Efficient operations use well-trained resources and up-to-date strategy and tactics. Effective operations allocate well-trained resources to maximize success in the least amount of time. Understanding the basics of *search theory* and *effort allocation* generate effective and efficient operations. Good management, good leadership and good investigative skills pull all of it together and make things run smoothly.

What you learn here potentially saves lives!

In management training, a continual focus on improving techniques ultimately increases the chances of finding the subject. **Good management creates opportunities and causes things to happen in a productive and goal oriented way.**

Unfortunately, many searches (and search teams) still lack good management. People make a commendable effort, but many problems remain right alongside unrealistic approaches and solutions. Good intentions alone simply fall short.

Good management consists of capable people who know what to take care of first *(given a set of circumstances)* and carry out an action plan through other people. Knowing what needs to take place and when, as a leader, obviously sets the stage for a successful operation. Outside of direct experience, training courses offer one of the best ways to develop competence in management.

This text emphasizes investigation early, particularly in the law enforcement context. Early publications focused on and referenced the term *lost person* as the center of search efforts. The term *missing person* more aptly describes the subject in today's search operations around the world, regardless of the environment. Initial actions taken by law enforcement often determine whether or not to search. Where to search also depends on very basic law enforcement investigative concepts and protocols. This holds especially true when it comes to abductions but also pertains to other types of missing person incidents both in the rural and urban environments.

Dramatic and rapid changes in technology provide managers and searchers with better resources to conduct a search. Portable computers, statistical analysis, and international missing person behavior data all apply directly to land search. Current experiments in the field provide accurate sweep width determination and accurate POD values for varying environments. The new Personal Locator Beacons *(PLBs) and* ELT's *(Emergency Locator Transmitters),* carried on aircraft for years, save individual lives regularly in the outdoors today. Smart phones and ubiquitous GPS help to narrow potential search areas as well.

In the litigious (large numbers of lawsuits) atmosphere of virtually every society, a Search Manager coordinates the use of varied resources as effectively as possible. This involves a wide range of tasks and the capability to absorb and analyze investigative information quickly, as well as providing leadership, direction and management priorities. The skill requires maintaining flexibility, with a focused approach toward working with and through diverse groups of volunteer and paid professionals.

The principles and helpful tools discussed in this text apply to all search situations, regardless of the number of people, geographic terrain or specific circumstances of an incident.

Experienced search managers consistently identify a number of very important functions in effectively managing search operations. Their experience tells us that the effectiveness of each of the functions performed on a search, directly influences the outcome of the situation.

The key functions:

- Preplanning and Vulnerability Assessments
- Initial Response and Reflex Tasking
- Investigation and Interviewing
- Target Orientation and the Basics of Visual Search
- Confinement and Proper Application of Missing Person Data
- Efficient Strategy and Tactics with Trained Resources
- Application of Scientifically Accepted Search Planning Principles
- Effective use of a command system (*like ICS*)

Mission reports and case studies continue to show that management deficiencies occur on a regular basis.

Some of the more common shortfalls:

- Failure to assume responsibility, *take charge* and provide positive leadership
- Unfamiliarity with accepted state-of-the-art strategy and tactics
- Lack of familiarity with search planning and principles of search theory
- Unfamiliarity with resources, their capabilities, and field application
- No consistent, repeatable, tasks assigned after first notice
- Failure to delegate functions and responsibilities using established benchmarks
- Lack of documentation for decisions made
- Failure to follow an established command system (*like ICS*)

Although these *short falls* continue to occur, we know that search management training makes a difference. For the most part, when search managers apply concepts properly, searches take place more expeditiously. Documentation of these missions show considerable improvements in terms of effectiveness. Which, undoubtedly translates to more lives saved.

Scope of SAR Management Training

Good search management courses provide an information rich environment. The utilization of current texts, articles, research documents, plus the combined experience and knowledge of the instructors and course participants, creates an excellent learning environment. This environment and information sharing define the hallmarks of good search management training.

> *"The mind is like a parachute, it only works when it is open."*
> -Sir James Dewar

Ultimately good search management training leads to better search management. Managers who study state-of-the-art search methods bring more capabilities, provide better coordination, usually communicate better and use pre-planning as a hedge against poor results and failure.

Progressive teaching techniques maximize the use of case studies and practical problem solving exercises. These experiences will serve as the basis for decision making in similar situations encountered by participants after they attend management courses.

This book describes the search management tenets generically for land search with the intent of making the widest possible application of the principles and recommendations. Regardless of the environment *(flat land, mountains, rivers, air search, etc.)* all elements of good land search management stay the same.

This training uses search focused research and case studies to identify past experiences with the expectation that lessons learned aid in preventing similar problems in the future.

This textbook discusses and builds on a logical, disciplined, and organized way of approaching and thinking about finding a missing person. Let your own common sense, experience and professional needs provide both direction and value to the content.

Objectives of Good Search Management Courses

After successful completion of a training course, participants will see the basic tenets of land search management in addition to:

- Describe the functions and responsibilities within the Incident Command System related to SAR
- Identify the role and specific functions of the Incident Commander for a missing or lost person incident
- Describe the most productive and efficient tactics used in searching for lost or missing persons in wilderness, rural, suburban and urban environments
- Explain the functions of vision, target orientation, search image and briefing as they relate to search, detection and recognition
- Identify the key factors involved in deciding to suspend a mission
- Implement the essential elements of a written search preplan and describe its importance for successful missions
- Apply the sequence of initial actions and SAR resources to locate missing or lost subjects
- Demonstrate sound management techniques as an overhead team member in a search for a missing or lost person
- Demonstrate the ability to establish a workable and realistic probable search area and searchable subdivisions in a map exercise
- Relate the basic types of search resources and discuss their functions and limitations

GUIDELINES for taking Search Management Courses

- Active participation enhances learning
- Focus on your needs, seek solutions and strive to create a positive learning environment
- Share your knowledge and learn from other participants by establishing trusted relationships
- Take risks, especially by admitting that you lack knowledge and constructively seek answers
- Participate in small group activities (map exercises) and embrace the chance to experiment and make mistakes. No lives hang in the balance; so, try new or innovative things

A National and International Perspective on Land Search Management & Training

Objectives:

- To understand the origins of current approaches to search management
- To describe the U.S. SAR system, the international SAR System and the SARSAT program
- To outline the various federal agencies and state agencies and define their roles in a SAR operation

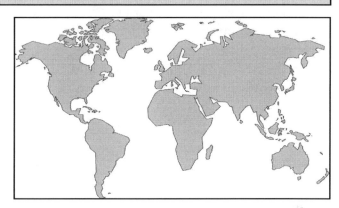

Search and Rescue: An Overview

Traditionally, search and rescue systems provide the response for missing, overdue, lost, injured, or stranded people; most, closely associated with outdoor activities, and wilderness environments. However, rural and urban settings also present problems encountered today in SAR, and more specifically the function of search.

Search - To identify and locate potentially distressed or interested persons or injured who are unable to return to a place of safety on their own.

Rescue - Rescue is to access, stabilize, and evacuate distressed or injured persons by whatever means necessary to ensure their timely transfer to an appropriate care facility or to a familiar environment.

Search and Rescue – *(definitions vary from State to State)* Search and Rescue employs available personnel and facilities to find and render aid to persons and properties in distress or potential distress in the air, on water, or on land.

Responsible Authority - The Responsible Authority serves as the government agency or agencies with legal responsibility and jurisdiction for finding missing persons in the area where a person ends up missing. Due to the potential criminal nature of missing persons search and rescue operations, the responsible authority usually resides with the Law Enforcement Agency of that jurisdiction.

Wilderness takes on several meanings in SAR. For instance, most consider *wilderness* an area generally uninhabited and devoid of any man-made amenities. While this certainly describes natural areas such as large parks and open countryside, it also describes urban areas devastated by a disaster such as the tsunami in Indonesia or hurricanes hitting the coast of the United States. Nearly every disaster involves SAR at some level. Since the majority of the North American population resides in urban areas, emergency responders in general, including SAR personnel, increasingly encounter more urban situations.

The skills and resources needed for managing and conducting SAR Operations need to plug seemlessly into comprehensive emergency management for other emergency scenarios. They provide a training ground and experience building for disaster response capabilities. Management concepts used in SAR Operations scale up to assist in response capability for larger scale emergencies and disasters. Nearly every type of hazard mentioned in the Comprehensive

Emergency Management Plans *(local and state disaster coordination)* also usually contain references to the functions of search and rescue. These scalable SAR operations range from directing the actions of a few responders in a small community impacted by earthquakes, to managing an effort involving hundreds and even thousands of searchers in larger urban calamities, all with numerous threats to human safety. Local governments and any other agencies or organizations participating in SAR response cooperate and coordinate among diverse multi-skilled responders.

Search vs Rescue

Traditionally, planners consider both elements of search and rescue together. For example, when a middle-aged hunter fails to return to a trailhead, local law enforcement initiates a preliminary investigation and launches a search for the person. Subsequent searching locates the hunter's camp, clues and ultimately the hunter in a precarious position after a fall. Rescue operations start to extricate the individual from his position and eventually the wilderness setting.

Land SAR management training in North America strives to provide comprehensive search methods consistent and useful for local, state, federal, tribal and territorial government agencies as well as private organizations to conduct SAR missions for lost, missing or stranded persons.

Four Phases of a SAR Incident

Every search and rescue incident consists of a series of four consecutive phases, each progressing to the next:

- Locate
- Access
- Stabilize, and
- Transport

These four steps form the common acronym L.A.S.T

Locate - The first step in addressing a SAR incident starts with locating the subject. Locating the subject ranges from simply checking an address to launching an extended search in urban or wilderness areas. The quicker responders find the missing or lost person, the sooner rescuers advance onto the next phase. However, the locate phase potentially turns into a major operational effort and often takes the most time to accomplish.

Access - When rescuers find a missing person they need access them in order to assess the situation, look for injuries and prevent further complications or problems. Accomplishing these objectives range from as simple as locating a child in the room of a house, to managing a confined space access and high angle rescue.

Search responders refer to assessing as *size-up*. Size-up consists of identifying hazards to the subject and rescuers, then developing a strategy to deal with the problems found. For instance, imagine a missing climber trapped by a winter storm in a high mountain environment. Safety considerations surrounding rescuers entering such a hostile and dangerous environment certainly impact further actions.

Stabilize - Once the responders gain access to the subject, medical stabilization commences. This process follows pre-hospital care standards starting with primary and secondary physical examinations then basic/advanced life support as indicated. Medical stabilization prepares the subject for transportation to a definitive care facility.

Transport - In the fourth phase of SAR, transportation of the subject provides for pre hospital care. Transportation requires *packaging* the person for movement in a safe and efficient manner while stabilization continues. Packaging consists of preparing the stabilized person for safe transport while simultaneously attending to their ongoing medical needs and their comfort during travel. Weather, nature of injuries, urgency, terrain, available resources, and other related factors determine the type and rate of transportation.

Data Bases - The Application of Data from North America.

Consistently over the years, student comments related to the Missing Person Behavior section of the text, reflect some skepticism. Students tend to question the validity of statistical data gathered in other countries and then used in their countries. Instructors worried that the data used represented only the U.S., Canada, the U.K., or in some cases only regionally specific data (See Chapter 14 on Missing and Lost Person Behavior). Currently research expert Robert Koester continues to collate statistical data on over 150,000 case studies of missing person incidents from all over the world. As discussed in Chapter 14, the collection process separates data by the distinct Eco-Regions of the world rather than by political affiliation. While experts continue to gather evidence supporting this statistical hypothesis, it certainly provides a viable criterion for analyzing behavioral data.

In our estimation, the use of this data and the results from using it, form an added incentive for police organizations around the globe to gather data from their own archives. In some cases, SAR units even create their own systems for gathering and collating this type of information.

Roles of Police, Volunteers, Military and Other Organizations

Initially, police organizations felt it appropriate to handle the function of search by themselves without the help of volunteers. Technical skills in rescue and recovery from hazardous environments, manpower demands, and long off-duty hours contribute to a modification of this type of thinking. Major searches need intense manpower and most law enforcement agencies simply lack personnel; especially trained officers with the ability to manage searches.

In many jurisdictions, in the U.S. and Canada, volunteers conduct search operations while the police organization monitors and oversees the incident from start to finish. This highlights the need for volunteer search crews to attend search management training.

Those volunteers also form a convenient core of dedicated professionals to maintain knowledge while paid agency personnel move into and out of the SAR arena.

Emergent volunteers present a unique challenge to SAR management, especially as an operation grows in scale. The untrained public often wants to assist with high profile or well known incidents and others want to help out when they perceive a need for help. The jurisdiction with operational command needs a solid plan in place ahead of time to help manage these volunteers without overwhelming SAR operations or reducing their effectiveness.

Local legislation and policy usually define the use of military assets for SAR Operations.

Changing World Political Situations

In light of the fluid political and security issues surfacing as a result of September 11th, 2001, combined with previously world conflicts, the role of the trained Incident Commander continues to change. Police professionals active in the fields of missing persons *(particularly children)* and those involved in gathering evidence about war crimes victims, attend search management courses offered around the world. Currently, the benefits of writings and application of the learning objectives and skills from courses in the field continues to yield a tremendous amount of success.

A large number of corporate organizations, especially in third world countries, employ civilians in exploratory efforts for petroleum and mineral deposits. Many of these operations involve both aviation and ground based resources working remote areas, lacking people and transportation resources. Therefore, they often depend on the host country's government to conduct search and/or rescue efforts if accidents or incidents occur. More and more these corporate entities seek information regarding search management, both from their own perspective and to provide technical knowledge to the host countries' officials.

Comments and Recommendations

Effective search operations always include investigation and basic information gathering. Documentation and data collection provide law enforcement departments, or other responsible agencies, with institutional memory and valuable insight into future incidents of a similar nature.

Mission reports and *case studies* show that management deficiencies commonly occur everyday in the search community. Fortunately for many, luck prevails and search operations end quickly. Running a search by pushing resources *(even the right ones)* out the door does not always end up like you want it to. Often managers overlook the effort allocation, in addition to the tactical planning knowledge of how to get the job done in the least amount of time.

Search managers start with a fairly independent relationship with their resources that steadily evolves on any extended operation into a strictly dependent connection. Search resources start with their own ideas of where to look based on past experiences and the initial scarcity of information gathered. However, as those efforts fail to produce results the resource needs more and more guidance from management (e.g. "Where do we look now?"). Even if a Search Manager agrees with the assumption that the majority of searches end quickly, failure to implement numerical assessments and failure to track the changes in those values, negate their use later if the incident happens to extend beyond the first operational period. Reconstructing the appropriate numbers is essentially impossible. The Search Management function not only requires study and expertise, but some aspects (planning) require the same degree of technical knowledge found in professional disciplines like engineering or electronics.

Good search management ultimately strives to find people faster and after safety of responders, always puts the welfare of the *missing subject* first. We need to ask ourselves: "Do the tools and systems we use give us the most options to get the job done right?" "Do the tools and systems adopted provide the professional integrity and assurances for our law enforcement personnel?" And last, but not least . . . "Did we act truly on the missing person's behalf and in their best interest?"

The best training materials, programs and approaches developed in any country consist of those fashioned from the most experienced resources within the country. It only makes sense to adopt the pieces and parts of *exemplary* plans and the *best practices* existing in progressive programs from around the globe.

Through after action review processes people with field experience in search need to ask some serious questions. First, of the strategies and approaches used, which proved most successful over time? We recommend not only asking the advice of developers of programs or publishers of training materials; but, also asking police and volunteer organizations using recognized systems and training standards. Usually, the answers shed light on the value or advantages of one approach over another.

Many land search operations around the world now use Missing and Lost Subject Behavior based on statistical data gathered over the last thirty-five years. Search planners use probability zones *(priority areas and distances); however,* there is no silver bullet in search. Particularly when legal oversight and complex environments cloud the issues of assessing effectiveness and accountability for it.

Eliminating the probabilities and numerical assessments involved in solving search problems works in a significant number of cases. However, since Murphy's law applies to SAR, the extended search rises up and bites us. Many unanswered questions and unproven concepts will continue to be tested as the land SAR community collectively explores the next steps in adopting standardized methods for land search.

Bill Syrotuck said it best in the conclusion to his book *An Introduction to Land Search Probabilities & Calculations.*

> "Search and rescue is both an art and a science. There are theoretical approaches and practical ones... Search directors should never become slaves to the computers, nor should they be slaves to tradition. Search probabilities and calculations are intended as an aid to search planning and decision-making. It *(the process)* introduces formulas and calculations that are a means to measuring optimum planning, compromise, or progress under the reality of any particular mission."

The International SAR System

The international SAR System, used extensively worldwide since the 1950s, was first institutionalized under the International Civil Aviation Organization's (ICAO) Chicago Convention for international civil aviation, and later for maritime SAR by IMO, *(International Maritime Organization)* with associated guidance and standards provided in the IAMSAR *(International Aeronautical and Maritime Search and Rescue)* Manual. Today, most nations use and supplement the international SAR system for their own use as practicable for civil SAR within their own boundaries. The U.S. has used the international SAR system for decades and continues to provide for its use via the U.S. National SAR Plan.

The Chicago Convention's Annex 12 (Search and Rescue) applies to the establishment, maintenance, and operation of SAR services in the territories of States or nations adhering to the Convention, over the high seas, and for coordination of SAR operations between nations.

IMO's 1979 International Convention on Maritime Search and Rescue (SAR Convention) provides that parties follow relevant IMO guidelines for SAR, which incorporate into the IAMSAR Manual. The U.S. is signatory to both the Chicago and Maritime SAR Conventions.

Annex 12 (Search and Rescue) and the SAR Convention provide the basis for developing and implementing international SAR plans so that no matter where a distress situation occurs, SAR organizations rescue persons in distress, and when appropriate, by cooperating SAR organizations of neighboring countries.

Parties to these conventions ensure effective arrangements and provide adequate SAR Services. Neighboring nations need agreements involving the establishment of SAR regions, pooling of SAR facilities, establishment of common procedures, training and liaison, as well as implementing measures to expedite entry of SAR facilities into the territory of other parties.

Plans developed under both conventions divide the globe into Search and Rescue Regions, each with a Rescue Coordination Center, to help ensure the provision of adequate shore-based communication infrastructure, efficient distress alert routing, and operational coordination to support SAR services. Under this geographically-based scheme, RCC's respond to persons in distress without regard to the nationality or status of the persons or the circumstances.

IAMSAR Manual

Jointly published by IMO and the International Civil Aviation Organization (ICAO), the three-volume IAMSAR Manual provides guidelines for a common aviation and maritime approach to organizing and providing search and rescue (SAR) services. To attain a full view of the SAR system, use each volume (available separately in loose-leaf form, binder included) as a standalone document or, in conjunction with the other two volumes.

The IAMSAR manual is divided into three volumes:

Volume I Organization and Management, discusses the global SAR system concept, establishment and improvement of national and regional SAR systems and cooperation with neighboring States to provide effective and economical SAR services.

Volume II Mission Coordination, assists personnel who plan and coordinate SAR operations and exercises.

Volume III Mobile Facilities, is intended to be carried aboard rescue units, aircraft and vessels to help with performance of a search, rescue or on-scene coordinator function, and with aspects of SAR that pertain to their own emergencies.

The Land Search and Rescue Addendum

The Land Search and Rescue Addendum presents the standardization of land-based SAR operations. Many sources compiled information regarding best SAR practices, and lessons learned from tragedies, mishaps and successes. The manual provides a foundational resource for the National Search and Rescue Committee on identifying key agencies and organizations that support land-based SAR operations. It provides guidance on how to plan and organize the implementation of successful lifesaving SAR operations.

Search in the United States

The National Search and Rescue Plan

> "Search and Rescue *(SAR)* is the use of available resources to assist persons and property in potential or actual distress." - U.S. National SAR Plan.

Very few individuals know or understand the national search and rescue *(SAR)* systems providing response and assistance for overdue, missing or stranded people throughout the U.S. Even though many agencies and volunteers involve themselves with SAR across the nation, the federal government assumes some responsibility for the coordination of SAR services to meet domestic needs and specific international commitments, including the coordination of any federal or military resources requested by local or state agencies.

The National Search and Rescue Plan specifies federal roles and responsibilities and creates the basis for the National Search and Rescue Manual. The National SAR Manual discusses search and rescue organization, resources, methods, and techniques used in diverse federal agencies. The overall objective of the plan provides a cooperative network between SAR organizations and resources coordinated by a single federal agency.

The network provides greater protection of life and property while at the same time giving better efficiency and economy. The intended plan offers guidance and coordination to all signatory federal agencies *(see participating agencies at the end of this chapter)*, and State SAR organizations retain their established responsibilities within their boundaries. Federal and state SAR organizations make and sign agreements appropriately

In summary, local and state government agencies assume the responsibilities for initial SAR response commensurate with their capabilities, and within their boundaries. Also, coordination and intermediary between local, state, and federal agencies; thereby creating a cooperative national SAR network defines the federal role.

Key U.S. Federal Land SAR Agencies and Organizations

National SAR Committee (NSARC)

NSARC oversees matters at the Federal level related to the National Search and Rescue Plan. The committee member agencies include the following:

- Department of Commerce (DOC)
- Department of Defense (DoD)
- Department of Homeland Security (DHS)
- Department of Interior (DOI)
- Department of Transportation (DOT)
- Federal Communication Commission (FCC)
- National Aeronautics & Space Administration (NASA).

The National Search and Rescue Plan and the NSARC membership agreement describe general responsibilities of NSARC Member Agencies. At the end of this chapter is a brief overview of each NSARC Member Agency, as well as other Federal Agencies that assist in the conduct of land SAR. Further information concerning the National SAR Committee can be found at: www.uscg.mil/nsarc

Organization and Coordination for the National SAR Plan

The territories of the United State fall into three geographic Search and Rescue Regions (SRRs) with specific SAR coordinators identified in the National SAR Plan:

United States Air Force: A recognized SAR Coordinator for the United States aeronautical SRR corresponding to the continental United States and Alaska.

United States Coast Guard: A recognized SAR Coordinator for all other United States aeronautical and maritime SRRs. Including the State of Hawaii as well as waters over which the United States has jurisdiction, such as navigable waters of the United States.

A *SAR Coordinator* or agency responsible for SAR in the specified region provides administration in their respective regions. The United States Air Force *(USAF)* coordinates the Continental United States and Alaska, and the USCG the Maritime Regions. Each SAR Coordinator establishes agreements with, and maintains files for, military agencies; civilian agencies; plus state, local, and private agencies in order to provide for the fullest practical cooperation and utilization in SAR missions. Further, according to the National SAR Plan, the U.S. Coast Guard coordinates all federal assets in all maritime or navigable waterways. Coordination of all federal assets in the inland regions of the U.S. falls to the U.S. Air Force. More simply, these two agencies coordinate for all federal resources responding to SAR incidents within the United States.

Air Force Rescue Coordination Center Tyndall (AFRCC) Co-located with NORTHCOM

RCC Tyndall resides with the 601st Air and Space Operations Center (601 AOC) at Tyndall Air Force Base, Panama City, Florida. The AFRCC coordinates SAR services for aeronautical and other types of land-based SAR within the U.S. continental aeronautical SRR and Alaska. The AFRCC seeks to encourage a cooperative SAR network with other Federal, State, Tribal, Territorial and local SAR authorities to help coordinate assistance for persons in distress.

AFRCC derives missions from the International Civil Aviation Organization's (ICAO's) Chicago Convention and the International Aeronautical and Maritime SAR Manual. These documents provide the U.S. with a national plan for coordinating SAR services to meet U.S. domestic needs as well as international commitments. The AFRCC lacks responsibility for SAR command and control authority, but supports domestic civil authorities by coordinating DoD civil SAR services to the fullest extent practicable. The AFRCC also lacks tasking authority, SAR facilities, and other assigned SAR resources.

AFRCC acts as the SAR Mission Coordinator (SMC) for incidents and missions involving:

- Overdue general aviation interstate flights
- DoD aircraft; commercial aircraft
- Missions of national concern (e.g. National Special Security Events - NSSEs)

As SAR Mission Controller, the AFRCC operates with the full operational authority of the Federal SAR Coordinator for the continental U.S. (Commander, U.S. Northern Command)

AFRCC receives all:

- Aircraft ELT and personal locator beacon (PLBs) distress beacon alerts registered in the U. S.
- Any distress beacons registered in other countries both geographically located and activated in the Tyndall SAR Region (continental U.S.)
- All U.S. registered distress beacon alerts geographically located outside the U.S.

If located in the continental U.S., the AFRCC works closely with other SAR authorities to:

- Respond to aeronautical and ground distress beacon reports
- Investigate the reports in coordination with Federal, State, Tribal, Territorial, and local SAR authorities
- Determine the required type and scope of response

Through SAR agreements with States, the AFRCC coordinates specific land SAR incidents other than those related to aircraft. These incidents include patient transport, search, rescue, and even SAR unit transport.

Each State in the contiguous U.S. possesses SAR agreements on file with the AFRCC to delineate a responsible SAR Coordinator/SAR coordinating agency and coordinating requirements for all SAR missions in each state.

The AFRCC coordinates Federal SAR capabilities at the request of other designated RCCs, as well as other Federal and State Search Coordinators in support of ongoing civil SAR operations. Three sections administratively divided the center: an Operations Section to prosecute individual SAR missions; a Directorship to provide overall management and formulate SAR plans, agreements, and policy; and a Reports Section to maintain data and records.

AFRCC contact information:

- Toll free: 1-800-851-3051
- Local (both emergency and non-emergency): 850-283-5955.

Four basic types of AFRCC missions:

- Search
- Rescue
- Medivac
- Mercy

- **Search** - When a missing or lost person situation occurs, federal SAR assets activate to assist local jurisdictions in their search efforts.

- **Rescue** - If units find a person or persons in distress in a remote or hard to access location, the possible use of federal SAR assets exists.

- **Medi-vac** - Aero-medical evacuations call for transport from one medical facility to another. When no other transportation option exists, medi-vac deploys.

- **Mercy** - Specific time-critical life threatening situations such as transportation of blood, organs, medical equipment, serum or personnel call for these services.

Any agency possesses the right to request a search and rescue resource belonging to the federal government; however the AFRCC considers, time, distance, location, equipment requirements and urgency before deploying resources. AFRCC personnel also evaluates if any other asset might accomplish the task. Remember, federal resources may in no way compete with local private assets charging for the same service or interfere with any primary military mission.

The State's Role: Coordination and Support

Each state established legislation providing for direct support to local government entities during times of emergency and during life threatening situations. Currently, a responsible state agency for overall coordination and support to local SAR programs reside in approximately 36 out of the 50 states. This support takes many forms, but most often settles in the area of coordination and *one-stop shopping* for resources. Each state establishes a central location or agency familiar with all aspects of emergency management and the available resources in life threatening situations. Many of the resources belong to the state, but exist specifically to aid local jurisdictions.

A number of states, especially in the Northwest, designate a responsible state agency by law for directing and coordinating air based SAR activities. These State Departments (or Divisions) of Aeronautics develop and maintain their aviation search and rescue response programs with cooperation and support from both local and federal agencies. This system improves efficiency by allowing state or local expertise and resources to initiate and carry out aircraft related SAR activities.

If a local emergency manager, sheriff or SAR Coordinator requests outside assistance in the form of specialized teams, search dogs, air support or enhanced communications, the state agency for Emergency Management locates the nearest resources available and coordinates the response in most cases. When local agencies need any federal resources, the state agency provides a direct liaison to that resource.

For instance, the AFRCC maintains working agreements with every state and updates them annually. Technically, responders must exhaust local and state government resources and fail in an attempt to perform a task before seeking federal support. However, policy provides for immediate aid under certain circumstances including time critical threats and life or death situations. Military installation commanders receive some discretion to aid civilian authorities, as long as they avoid impairing the resource's primary military mission. The AFRCC, along with the state authorities, forge and maintain access to these resources.

A good example of this coordination and relationship often takes place during a major search effort for a missing or lost person *(child or adult)*. For discussion, a local law enforcement officer coordinating a search desperately needs air support for transporting searchers into higher altitude areas and to search some very difficult terrain. Limited access to these areas exists coupled with a time critical situation, the Deputy wants to press military assets into service. In addition, the Deputy feels that several search dog teams pay high dividends in specified difficult to reach areas, so transport for those teams also requires arrangements.

Generally, a local coordinator's request for helicopter support runs through the State's Department of Emergency Management or a similar coordinating agency. When presented with no private or commercial helicopter resources available in the surrounding area, federal assets then get tasked. *Remember, military aircraft cannot fly a mission of this type if it takes business away from a private enterprise.* Therefore with a lack of resources, a state's coordinating agency then makes a call to the AFRCC and requests support from the closest military resource.

Every state's emergency management agency maintains responsibility for support, guidance, training and coordination with the local political subdivisions (i.e., counties, municipalities etc.). As such, they provide a vital behind-the-scenes effort in helping local jurisdictions prepare for emergencies, including SAR. The state also initiates laws enhancing effective actions for SAR response. Such legislation often indemnifies volunteer SAR teams, provides for their medical coverage and insurance, and in some cases replaces personal property lost during volunteer SAR work. Although most volunteers willingly work to get the job done, this recognition and coverage by the state often provides additional incentives for volunteer participation.

In many states, SAR mission reporting requirements exist. Contact both local and state authorities to obtain up to date information, forms and guidance documents.

The Local Response

States generally delegate the response for missing persons in the wilderness to a geographic (political) subdivision within the state. Most commonly, the legal responsibility for search functions vests with the county sheriff or local chief law enforcement officer; however,

> **One State's Statutory Definition of SAR**
>
> Search and Rescue means the acts of searching for, rescuing or recovering by means of ground, marine or air activity any person who becomes lost, injured or is killed while outdoors or as a result of natural or man-made disaster, including instances involving searches for downed or missing aircraft.

this varies from state to state. In some cases, state police agencies retain the responsibility, while in other areas, land management agencies or even the fire department assumes those functions. The specific SAR response for any jurisdiction differs greatly from another by virtue of training, resources, and how often they mobilize. For instance, some national parks have jurisdiction to respond and handle all of their own SAR incidents. In others, they jointly manage the function, and in the smallest parks they rely on outside resources entirely. Forest service personnel manage national forest lands entirely; however, this federal agency subsidizes local sheriff's departments for SAR and other law enforcement services on forest service lands.

In urban areas, police, firemen, paramedics, and other emergency management organizations maintain some degree of disaster/emergency readiness through missions involving search and rescue work. Historically, fire department organizations take care of rescue and response to emergencies within their districts. Many volunteers also augment their local fire districts. Law enforcement agencies also maintain full time, efficient response systems designed for their own particular SAR requirements.

Searching for lost or missing persons, especially in urban environments, presents a unique police oriented component. That component specializes in a function essential in all search operations: investigation. Growing numbers of missions in suburban and urban areas for Dementia patients, despondent, runaways and potential abductees require more orientation and training for multifaceted environments. Traditionally rural SAR teams respond to search in urban or urban/rural interface areas with increasing regularity. Comprehensive emergency response planning and coordination, allow these responders to incorporate into both training and tactical applications for search in residential and urban settings. And all of this takes place under the auspices of the local law enforcement agencies.

Many rural areas establish county sheriff reserve deputies; volunteer fire departments; and a variety of volunteer and rescue units to specific local emergency problems. Delivery of search or rescue aid to rural and wilderness areas often presents special logistical challenges compounded by distance, terrain, and weather.

Wilderness or rural SAR demands present units with seasonal incidents and numerous unpredictable situations. Volunteer Mountain Rescue Units, Explorer Scout Search and Rescue Groups, Search and Rescue Dog Teams, Civil Air Patrol Squadrons, Motorized Units, and many types of Volunteer Composite Teams *(with a variety of capabilities)*, usually form as a result of the type and nature of recurring SAR problems in the area. Regardless of the type of subject, or the nature of the SAR emergency occurring, local authorities must develop resources if for no other reason than their proximity to the problem. Time lag, distance, weather and logistics all serve to confound State and federal resources. The same storm or disaster that incapacitates a local area potentially prohibits outside emergency response and resupply deliveries.

Although official agency response differs greatly around the country, one major factor remains constant: the dedication and unfailing willingness of volunteers to respond and work until finishing the job. The volunteer effort in SAR nationwide provides the backbone of aiding people in distress so poignantly stated in a portion of the rescue service motto, "These Things We Do, so That Others May Live." Volunteer response always proves crucial to both wilderness and urban situations. No *official agency* capability in the world replaces volunteer organizations, communications and special skills.

The U.S. SARSAT Program

In the 1980s the United States, Canada, and France developed the SARSAT (Search And Rescue Satellite-Aided Tracking) system and the Soviet Union developed a similar satellite system called the COSPAS (*COSPAS* a Russian acronym translating loosely into Space System for the Search of Vessels in Distress) at roughly the same time. The basic concept involves the use of distress beacons, satellites, and ground equipment to relay distress location and identification information to SAR authorities. In the system, SAR sensors fly on Low-Earth orbiting (LEO) polar and Geostationary Earth Orbiting (GEO) satellites provided by the United States, Russia, India and the Europeans. As an aside, Canada and France provide the SAR *instruments* for the U.S. LEO satellites. These sensitive instruments detect signals transmitted from distress beacons anywhere on the Earth's surface. The four original member nations (U.S. France, Canada and Russia) now enjoy the company of 36 other nations and two regional organizations operating 76 ground stations and 30 mission control centers worldwide. The international COSPAS-SARSAT program stopped monitoring 121.5 MHz signals as of 01 February 2009. Currently the satellites exclusively monitor the 406 MHz frequency. Older 121.5 MHz transmitters only used an analog signal without any information about the distress beacon or the user. Alternatively, the 406 MHz distress beacons transmit a digital code that contains information about the type of beacon and possibly the beacon's exact location (derived from doppler calculation, Global Positioning System (GPS), or vehicle navigation system). Additionally, worldwide, individual 406 MHz distress beacons come with a unique identifier. The unique identifier allows the individual users registration information to link with each distress beacon independently.

After a SAR satellite receives signals from an Emergency Locator Transmitter (ELT), Emergency Position Indicating Radio Beacon (EPIRB) or Personal Locator Beacon (PLB), it relays the signals to earthbound stations referred to as Local User Terminals (LUTs).

The LUT, computes the location of the distress signal and transmits it to the proper Mission Control Center (MCC). The MCC researches and matches the beacon signal to the registered user and transmits the data to an appropriate Rescue Coordination Center (RCC) or foreign country SAR Point Of Contact (SPOC). The RCC then dispatches to the geographically appropriate SAR Jurisdiction. All of this taking place in a matter of minutes.

COSPAS-SARSAT System Satellites

The U.S. operates two distinct types of satellites and LUTs to relay distress beacon signals. NOAA Polar Orbiting Environmental Satellites (POES) and Geostationary Operational Environmental Satellites (GOES), both carry SAR instruments on board.

The system's Polar satellites orbit at an altitude of approximately 850 kilometers and circle the planet once every 102 minutes. The relative motion between the satellites and a distress beacon on the surface allows ground based processors to use the doppler effect and signal timing to determine the distress beacon's location.

The geosynchronous satellites travel along the equatorial plane of the Earth at a speed matching the Earth's rotation allowing the satellites to *hover* continuously over one position on the surface. These geosynchronous points stand at approximately 36,000 kilometers, high enough to allow the satellites to view approximately 1/3 of the Earth's surface. Because these satellites stay above a fixed position relative to the surface, they provide a constant vigil for distress beacons activated anywhere within their footprint.

Distress Alerting Satellite System - DASS

NASA pioneered technology used for the satellite-aided search and rescue capability saving more than 27,000 lives worldwide since its inception nearly three decades ago. Recently, NASA developed new technology which quickly identifies the location of people in distress and reduces the risk of rescuers. The Search and Rescue Mission Office at NASA's Goddard Space Flight Center in Greenbelt, Md., in collaboration with several government agencies, developed a next-generation search and rescue system, called the **Distress Alerting Satellite System (DASS)**. NASA, the National Oceanic and Atmospheric Administration (NOAA), the U.S. Air Force, the U.S. Coast Guard and other agencies, are now completing the development and testing of the new system expecting to make it fully operational in the coming years after a complete constellation of DASS-equipped satellites launches.

When completed, DASS instantaneously detects and locates distress signals generated by 406 MHz beacons installed on aircraft and vessels or carried by individuals. The new technology greatly enhances the international community's ability to rescue people in distress. When NASA installs the satellite-based instruments used to relay the emergency signals on the U.S. military's Global Position System (GPS), a constellation of 24 spacecraft operating in mid-Earth orbit (MEO) rescue capabilities improve tremendously around the world.

Under the current system, (first operational in the mid-1980's as part of the COSPAS-SARSAT system) the so-called *repeaters* placed on NOAA weather satellites operating in low-Earth (LEO) and geostationary (GEO) orbits, although effective, as evidenced by the number of persons rescued, obvious limitations exist.

The LEO satellites orbit the Earth 14 times a day and using the Doppler effect to help pinpoint the location of the signal. However, the satellites continuous motion makes picking up a distress signal the moment a user activates a beacon difficult.

NOAA's geosynchronous (GEO) weather satellites, on the other hand, orbit above the Earth in a fixed location over the equator. Although they provide constant visibility of much of the Earth, they fail to independently locate a beacon unless it contains a navigation receiver encoding and transmitting its position. Emergency beacons come with or without GPS location data. Furthermore, the beacon-to-satellite link tends to get obstructed by terrain.

DASS overcomes these limitations. With a mid-Earth orbit search and rescue capability provided by GPS, six satellites view every emergency signal that goes off. Almost instantly, the system begins processing the signal to determine its precise location. Right now, it takes about an hour or more before the system even acts on a beacon signal.

Although the U.S. currently uses mid-Earth orbiting satellites for its search and rescue instruments. Europe through the use of its Galileo system began development on new search and rescue capabilities, Russia, its GLONASS system, and China, its Compass system. All systems modeled after the NASA-developed DASS.

LEOLUTs and GEOLUTs

NOAA manages and operates Local User Terminals to track, receive, and process alerts from the U.S., European, and Russian Low Earth Orbit satellites. Dual LEO Local User Terminals reside at:

- Andersen Air Force Base, Guam
- USCG Communication Station, Hawaii
- NOAA Command and Data Acquisition Station, Alaska
- Vandenberg Air Force Base, California
- USCG Communication Station, Florida

Dual LEO Local User Terminals at each site allow NOAA to resolve satellite tracking conflicts and provide redundancy in case of failure.

NOAA also manages and operates two local user terminals in Suitland, Maryland, to track, receive, and process distress alerts through the two U.S. geosynchronous satellites. Both sets of Local User Terminals perform error detection and correction on 406 MHz distress beacon messages and automatically generate alert messages to the U.S. MCC (US Mission Control Center). Additionally, one low earth satellite LUT and one geosynchronous satellite LUT in Maryland serve as backup equipment and test beds for the entire system.

U.S. Mission Control Center

The U.S. Mission Control Center receives alert data from other international LUTs and MCCs. It matches distress beacon signals to identify those coming from the same source and merges all received data to help accuracy.

The USMCC appends 406 MHz distress beacon registration information for beacons registered in the U.S., then geographically sorts the data to determine the appropriate recipient (national RCC, Air Force or USCG, foreign SPOC, or other international MCC).

The USMCC also filters redundant data and performs system support and monitoring functions.

Wireless Communications (Cell Phones – Smart Phones)

Our society uses wireless communication technologies more and more every year. The publics increasing reliance on cell phone calls for emergency assistance often causes difficulties for responders. However, in some cases, the cell phone infrastructure provides an additional means of notifying the SAR system of possible persons in distress and eventually locating them.

Due to the limitations of cell phones, SAR checklists should include the following additional items for incidents involving cell phone use:

- Caller's complete cellular telephone number including area code
- Type of cell phone
- User's cellular service provider or carrier
- Whether or not other means of communications exist
- Remaining battery strength in the subject's cell phone
- Establish a communications schedule or require the caller to call back at a regular scheduled time if possible
- Make sure the subject understands that the cell phone, if sufficient battery strength exists, must not turn off the cell phone in order to establish further communications
- Ask the subject if alternate power sources exist (extra battery, charger, etc.)
- Ask the subject if they posses text messaging capabilities to conserve battery life
- Obtain a good alternative point of contact.

Most cellular service providers offer some of the following services (through appropriate authority) to assist in locating the origin of cellular calls:

- **Call Trace/Cellular Tower Locator** - As long as the phone stays connected to the network with power and antenna height, a cell phone carrier determines which cell tower received the call, and the angle from the tower figures out the cell sector location of the phone. Accuracy also depends on the technology placed on the tower.

- **Call Trace Modified** - After initiating a call and notifying a technician, a caller may call back at a specified time to allow the technician to look at the timing advance for estimating distance from the tower.

- **Cell Traffic Recording** - A carrier determines the cell location of the last call placed by a subscriber given the cellular telephone number.

- **Tap** - Provides notification when anyone makes a call from a particular phone. Overdue subject cases benefit the most from this service.

Other personal devices also show up in the marketplace, but usually fail to meet the standard set for 406 MHz devices.

Satellite Emergency Notification Devices (SEND)

The emergence of several non COSPAS-SARSAT type Satellite Emergency Notification Devices (**SEND**) warrants awareness by SAR authorities. The general public readily accesses these devices which require an annual subscription to enable all the features. Their *911* or emergency function lacks the ability to alert traditional Federal SAR services. These alerts forward to a commercial call center which uses a Public Safety Answering Point (PSAP) database to alert police, fire stations and ambulance services in the alert area. The agencies receiving the calls may or may not possess jurisdictional authority for SAR in that area.

U.S. Government SAR Resources and Agencies

The following functions and agency descriptions come from the *Land Search and Rescue Addendum* and the *National Search and Rescue Supplement* to the *International Aeronautical and Maritime Search and Rescue Manual*, published by the National Search and Rescue Committee in 2011.

Within the Department of Homeland Security (DHS), the Federal Emergency Management Agency (FEMA) maintains the National Response Framework (NRF). The NRF provides the guiding principles enabling all government agencies to prepare for and provide a unified national response to disasters and emergencies – from the smallest incident to the largest catastrophe. As part of the NRF, Emergency Support Functions (ESFs) make up the primary mechanisms at the operational level used to organize and provide assistance. Federal Emergency Support Function (ESF) #9 covers Search and Rescue.

Federal Emergency Management Agency (FEMA)

In addition to the stewardship of the NRF and ESFs, FEMA coordinates Federal resources during Catastrophic Incident SAR and as well as involves itself in SAR operations not covered by the National Response Framework. FEMA itself falls under ESF #9 as a Primary Agency with responsibility under the NRF for urban SAR (US&R).

US&R includes structural collapse SAR, as well as operations for natural and man made disasters and catastrophic incidents.

FEMA coordinates Federal US&R planning activities, and each of the ten FEMA regions produce supplemental response plans, including sections on US&R based upon known resources, capabilities, and State, Tribal, Territorial, and local authorities in their areas of responsibility.

FEMA develops national US&R policy, provides planning guidance and coordination assistance, standardizes task force procedures, evaluates task force operational readiness, funds special equipment and training within available appropriations, and reimburses, as appropriate, task force costs incurred as a result of ESF #9 deployment.

FEMA activates the National Urban Search and Rescue Response System for incidents requiring a coordinated Federal US&R response. Upon activation under the NRF, US&R task forces are considered Federal assets under the Robert T. Stafford Disaster Relief and Emergency Assistance Act and other applicable authorities. The System integrates US&R task forces, Incident Support Teams (ISTs), and technical specialists in support of unified SAR operations conducted in accordance with the National SAR Plan. The task forces support State, Tribal, Territorial, and local response efforts to locate survivors and manage recovery operations.

FEMA reimburses for authorized US&R deployments to Stafford Act declaration sites, but lacks the authority or funding to reimburse activities absent a Stafford Act declaration. Non-Stafford Act US&R deployments get reimbursed by the Federal authority requesting US&R assistance in accordance with provisions contained in the Financial Management Support Annex to the NRF. For FEMA US&R information go to:

http://www.fema.gov/emergency/usr

Department of Defense (DoD)

Based on the National Search and Rescue Plan and the National Response Framework, the Secretary of Defense directs all Services and other components of the U.S. Department of Defense to support civil SAR services, including Catastrophic Incident Search and Rescue. As established by the National Search and Rescue Plan, DoD's roles in civil SAR carry out on a not-to-interfere basis with DoD's primary military duties. The DoD's capabilities suit land SAR operations very well. From a single helicopter to large-scale mass rescue operations, DoD operates two internationally recognized Rescue Coordination Centers for civil SAR:

- RCC Tyndall (Air Force Rescue Coordination Center), Tyndall Air Force Base, Panama City, Florida, for SAR operations in the continental U.S. other than Alaska under CDRUSNORTHCOM (Commander, U.S. Northern Command) acting as the Search Coordinator for the continental United States
- RCC Elmendorf (Alaska Rescue Coordination Center), Elmendorf AFB. Anchorage, Alaska for SAR operations in Alaska

Two key DoD references concerning civil SAR include:

- DoD Directive (DoDD) **3025.18,** Defense Support of Civil Authorities (DSCA)
- DoD Instruction (DoDI) **3003.01,** DoD Support to Civil SAR.

DSCA refers to DoD support provided by Federal military forces. DoD civilians and contract personnel, and DoD agencies and components, all respond to civil SAR authorities by request in emergencies for law enforcement support or for other domestic activities. Requests for Defense Support of Civil Authorities come through established procedures from recognized civil authorities.

CDRUSNORTHCOM (Commander, U.S. Northern Command) has responsibility for homeland defense (HD) and providing DSCA with its assigned Area Of Responsibility, including Alaska. CDRUSPACOM (Commander, U.S. Pacific Command) has responsibility for Homeland Defense, and Defense Support to Civil Authorities for Hawaii, U.S. Territories and other areas assigned in its area of responsibility.

For more DSCA information refer to the *Catastrophic Incident SAR Addendum* to the *National Search and Rescue Supplement.*

The DoD is a primary agency under the National Response Framework, Emergency Support Function #9. They respond when a State requests Federal SAR resources for disaster operations.

U.S. Coast Guard (USCG)

The USCG, operating under the Department of Homeland Security (DHS), acts as Federal Search Coordinator for U.S. aeronautical and maritime Search and Rescue Regions, including the oceanic environment, the Great Lakes, and all U.S. navigable waters. For more information, refer to the USCG SAR policy located in the *Coast Guard Addendum* to the *National SAR Supplement.*

USCG conducts land and Catastrophic Incident SAR operations as required. USCG is the Primary Agency for Maritime/Coastal/ Waterborne SAR under the National Response Framework's Emergency Support Function #9 as well. These operations include response to natural and man-made disasters and primarily require USCG air, ship, boat, and response team activities in support of unified SAR operations (as directed by the National SAR Plan). USCG also sponsors and chairs the National Search and Rescue Committee which oversees the national SAR system and U. S. involvement in international SAR.

Obtain additional Coast Guard SAR information go to the Office of Search and Rescue, Coast Guard Headquarters website:

http://www.uscg.mil/hq/cg5/cg534/

National Park Service (NPS)

NPS, operating under the Department of Interior (DOI), provides SAR services on lands and waters administered by NPS and aids authorities in neighboring jurisdictions. The NPS conducts civil SAR operations, including emergency medical aid, in a wide variety of environments such as remote rural and roadless areas, lakes, rivers and oceans, and deserts, mountains and caves, and often requires extended response times and the use of specialized equipment. NPS works closely with Federal, State, Tribal, Territorial, and local SAR organizations.

Most National Parks establish local SAR plans providing park managers with direction and guidance in establishing and managing SAR operations. They also provide visitor protection services, including varying levels of SAR, and provide aid and assistance to visitors, such as search, rescue, and medical assistance.

Qualified SAR services in local communities get utilized if they provide a timely response to SAR incidents within an NPS area. When not available, the NPS makes a reasonable effort to provide a level of SAR service commensurate with park needs. The NPS Branch of Emergency Services, provides oversight, direction, and coordinates their Service-wide SAR Program.

NPS considers search to involve finding lost persons in a wide variety of environments and transporting them to safety. They also consider rescue to involve accessing, stabilizing, extricating and transporting stranded or injured persons using available resources ranging from hand-carried litters to hoist capable helicopters.

The agency cooperates with and supports State, Tribal, Territorial and local governments from its various locations. Interestingly, States may not regulate the NPS without specific congressional consent; however, park areas may adopt all or part of the State SAR policies and guidelines as long as they don't conflict with the NPS Director's Orders. NPS and DOI, along with DoD, are Primary Agencies under the NRF's ESF #9. The DOI also coordinates and utilizes other assets to enhance the NPS capabilities.

NPS - Emergency Incident Coordination Center

While the NPS does not operate a Federal RCC, it maintains a national Emergency Incident Coordination Center (EICC) that coordinates response resources throughout the NPS system. The location of National Parks throughout the U.S., presents diverse physical environments and a diverse visiting public. The challenges associated with each park require varying levels of SAR services. Highly trained Park Rangers normally conduct park SAR operations. Each Park develops SAR plans that identify possible scenarios and response procedures. As one of the three Federal Agencies responsible for conducting SAR operations (USCG and DoD mentioned above are the other two), NPS works closely with Federal RCCs and other authorities and volunteers to provide mutual support.

NPS operates and staffs the EICC located in Luray, Virginia and operates it on a 24 hour basis, 365 days a year. Although each Park often maintains sufficient resources to accomplish SAR missions, the EICC when possible coordinates the movement and mobilization of supplemental personnel, or specialized resources including, aircraft, and small boats.

Find more information on the NPS at:

http://www.nps.gov/index.htm

U.S. Forest Service (USFS)

USFS, operating under the U.S. Department of Agriculture (USDA), manages the national forests and grasslands of the United States. Law enforcement personnel and other staff help the USFS ensure the safety of persons using any of the national forests. USFS personnel respond to emergencies in those locations, using resources applicable to specific areas throughout the country. Agreements between the USFS and local authorities exist in many areas to facilitate mutual assistance. For more information on the USFS go to:

http://www.fs.fed.us/

National Oceanic and Atmospheric Administration (NOAA)

NOAA, operating under the Department of Commerce (DOC), is the lead U.S. agency for the U.S. Search and Rescue Satellite Aided Tracking (SARSAT) Program, as a primary component of the International COSPAS-SARSAT Program. NOAA operates the U.S. Mission Control Center (USMCC) as part of the U.S. SARSAT program ground system, and maintains the U.S. 406 MHz Beacon Registration Database. As previously mentioned, the COSPAS-SARSAT system automatically forwards distress beacon alerts and registration data to RCCs and other SAR Points of Contact (SPOCs).

For more Beacon Registration Database information go to:

> http://www.beaconregistration.noaa.gov

For more information on the U.S. SARSAT program go to:

> http://www.sarsat.noaa.gov/usmcc.html

For information on the International Cospas-Sarsat program go to:

> http://www.cospas-sarsat.org/index.php

Customs and Border Protection (CBP)

Along with FEMA and the USCG, CBP operates under DHS. CBP as an agency operates the world's largest aviation and maritime law enforcement organization. The Office of Air and Marine (OAM) utilizes over 1200 Federal Agents, operating from 80 air and marine locations, with more than 290 aircraft of 22 different types, and more than 250 maritime vessels. As such they wield a wide variety of resources, and just like the DOD, respond to support local civilian authorities for SAR operations, as long as no conflicting situations exist with accomplishing their primary missions.

Within CBP several highly specialized units called Border Patrol, Search, Trauma, and Rescue (BORSTAR) teams respond to emergency search and rescue situations anywhere in the United States. Border Patrol agents make up these teams on a voluntary basis and go far beyond the duties of regular agents. BORSTAR agents undergo a highly specialized regimen consisting of intense training in physical fitness and other disciplines, including medical skills, technical rescue, navigation, communication, swift water rescue, and air operations.

BORSTAR teams primarily respond to incidents involving distressed Government agents and migrants along the border. These rescued individuals are predominantly undocumented aliens but also include agents and border residents. The teams conduct SAR operations throughout the year in varying climates and topographies. Their missions vary in difficulty from locating distressed persons to extremely complex rescue operations in remote locations.

For more information on CBP go to:

> http://www.cbp.gov/xp/cgov/border_security/

Immigration and Customs Enforcement (ICE)

ICE handles investigations for DHS and helps to eliminate vulnerabilities in the nation's border and problems with economic transportation and infrastructure security. Four law enforcement divisions and several support divisions make up the ICE organization. They provide investigation, interdiction and security services to the public and law enforcement partners in federal and local sectors. Several ICE units utilize helicopters and fixed wing aircraft when available, in searches. ICE's aviation mission centers on finding out when, why, and if aircraft cross or intend to cross the US border. For more information on ICE go to:

> http://www.ice.gov/

Bureau of Indian Affairs (BIA)

The BIA, which operates under DOI, manages land held in trust by the U.S. for American Indians, Indian tribes, and Alaska Natives. Over 560 Federally recognized tribal governments exist in the U.S. The U.S. considers tribal lands domestic dependent nations by the Federal Government. The responsible authority for SAR on tribal lands belongs to local tribal governments. Responsible tribal authorities request assistance from Federal, State, other Tribal, and local SAR authorities. To request Emergency Support Function #9 SAR assistance under the national response framework, tribes get included in a State's request for Federal disaster assistance. After approval of a disaster declaration, the tribe(s) work directly with the Federal Government to obtain SAR resources and assistance.

For more information on the BIA go to:

http://www.BIA.gov/

Department of State (DOS)

DOS designates the particular Federal Agencies responsible for civil SAR to represent the U.S. in the following international forums:

- The USCG leads and coordinates U.S. participation in SAR-related initiatives at the International Maritime Organization (IMO)
- The FAA, with support of National Search and Rescue Committee Member Agencies, leads and coordinates U.S. participation in SAR-related initiatives at International Civil Aviation Organization (ICAO)
- NOAA leads and coordinates U.S. participation in the International COSPAS-SARSAT Program and associated international programs
- The US Air Force and US Coast Guard each provide a SAR expert to serve as a member of the International Civil Aviation Organization / International Maritime Organization (ICAO/IMO) Joint SAR Working Group
- The United States Agency for International Development (USAID)/Office of Foreign Disaster Assistance (OFDA) leads and coordinates national participation in international urban SAR activities, particularly with the United Nations

Further, as discussed in the NSP, any SAR related international treaty or agreement or any type, or its implementation, gets subjected to DOS oversight.

For more information on DOS go to:

http://www.state.gov/

Federal Aviation Administration (FAA)

The Federal Aviation Administration *(FAA)* through its Air Route Traffic Control Centers *(ARTCC)* and Flight Service Stations *(FSS)*, monitor and flight-follow aircraft filing flight plans in the U.S. inland region. In some cases, individual citizens contact an FAA facility when knowledge of a probable SAR situation involving aircraft exists. Therefore, the FAA usually becomes the first agency to alert the AFRCC concerning an emergency or overdue aircraft.

Once alerted, the RCC and FAA work together to locate the aircraft, reviewing radio communication (if available) and radar data to ascertain a good last known position (LKP) for the aircraft. Concurrently, other FAA facilities conduct "ramp" checks at airports.

The FAA recalls recorded radar data and identifies and traces aircraft that maintain sufficient altitude to radar track. RCCs regularly seek radar data from the FAA, which greatly assists in aircraft searches, as well as providing route and last radar position data. The FAA requires most aircraft to carry emergency locator transmitters (ELTs).

For more information about the FAA and its SAR capabilities go to:

http://www.faa.gov/airtraffic/publications
and FAA Order JO 7110.10 series (Flight).

Federal Communications Commission (FCC)

The FCC, an independent Federal Agency established by the Communications Act of 1934, regulates interstate and international communications by radio, television, wire, satellite and cable throughout the United States. FCC regulations cover the communications equipment and frequencies used for distress alerting and SAR operations. The FCC also maintains vessel and aircraft radio licensing information helpful to SAR personnel (different from the distress beacon registration information database maintained by NOAA). The FCC has statutory administrative authority for communications violations, including radio related abuse violations (e.g. repeat false alerts or hoaxes). The FCC also provides radio direction-finding support.

RCCs work closely with the FCC to report unauthorized use of emergency frequencies, which subjects violators to administrative actions (including forfeitures) by the FCC under Title 47, United States Code. Violators of the FCC rules and regulations receive imprisonment of up to one year and/or seizure of the offending radio equipment. In addition, Title 14 U. S.C.88(c) (under the United States Coast Guard) makes it a Federal felony, punishable by significant imprisonment and/or monetary fine, for anyone knowingly and willfully communicating a false distress signal.

For more information on the FCC go to:

http://www.fcc.gov/

National Aeronautics and Space Administration (NASA)

NASA in its role as an independent Federal Agency under the National SAR Plan, supports SAR through research and development or applications of technology to search, rescue, survival, and recovery systems and equipment. They develop and test equipment such as location tracking systems, transmitters, receivers, and antennas capable of locating aircraft, ships, spacecraft, or individuals in potential or actual distress.

For more Information on NASA go to:

http://searchandrescue.gsfc.nasa.gov/

National Transportation Safety Board (NTSB)

Congress charges the NTSB with investigating and determining the probable causes of every civil aviation accident in the U.S. and significant accidents in the other modes of transportation (e.g., railroad, highway, marine and pipelines) and in issuing safety recommendations aimed at preventing future accidents.

NTSB maintains a Go Team that begins investigation of a major accident at the scene of the accident as quickly as possible. They assemble a broad spectrum of technical expertise to solve complex transportation safety problems.

NTSB maintains an accident database that helps identify previous wreckage locations.

For more information on the NTSB go to:

http://www.ntsb.gov/

Other Relevant Federal Agencies

SAR sometimes requires the services of other Federal agencies. While each agency's involvement in SAR varies with their primary mission and availability of resources, all are integral to the National SAR System.

Volunteer Auxiliaries

The USCG Auxiliary (CGAUX) and the Civil Air Patrol (CAP) consist of volunteer civilian organizations functioning as supplements to the USCG and USAF, respectively, and extend their capabilities to support SAR missions.

Civil Air Patrol (CAP)

A congressionally chartered, nonprofit organization of experienced aviation-trained volunteers located in every State (and Puerto Rico) serving as a USAF auxiliary. The Civil Air Patrol provides the majority of the response to downed or missing aircraft situations throughout the United States. CAP operates approximately 550 light civil aircraft utilizing land-based SAR and other capabilities including specialized sensors for direction finding and airborne digital imaging. A small number of strategically located aircraft even operate a hyper-spectral enhanced reconnaissance imaging system.

Hyper-spectral systems link many sensors across many *bands* of the electromagnetic spectrum to allow the integrated system to scan well beyond the capabilities of the human eye, or even simpler sensing systems like infra-red or radar alone. CAP operates a nationwide communications system in support of its air and ground operations. CAP averages 80 to 100 saved lives per year and flies 90 percent of the land SAR missions approved by the AFRCC.

Upon request the Civil Air Patrol provides to the appropriate authority in charge of the air search or rescue efforts: mission coordinators; aircraft, pilots, and observers; ground search teams; base camp support; and communications networks. When officially tasked and involved in a search or rescue mission, the U.S. Air Force reimburses for communication expenses, and fuel and oil expenses incurred by aircraft or ground vehicles. Due to the fact that CAP exists as an official auxiliary of the Air Force, all Civil Air Patrol members receive coverage from the Federal Workman's Compensation Act in the event of an injury. Current statistics show that Civil Air Patrol members respond to three-fourths of all air SAR missions.

For more information on CAP go to:

http://www.cap.gov

Coast Guard Auxiliary (CGAUX)

Established by Congress, the CGAUX mission centers on the safety and security of persons, ports, waterways and coastal regions of the United States. The CGAUX balances the missions of recreational boating safety with homeland security. As with all USCG resources, requests for and tasking of CGAUX resources get conducted through the appropriate USCG RCC.

For more information on the CGAUX go to:

http://www.nws.cgaux.org

Changing Concepts in Search Management & Planning   3

Objectives:

- Explain the 'crucials' of search operations

- Describe how and why the crucials of search management have dramatically evolved in the last two decades

- Relate the fundamental principles of effective search management to effective operations

Who are We Searching For?

This simple question gets to the crux of how search operations evolve throughout the world. Early documents in land search, such as Dennis Kelly's *Mountain Search for the Lost Victim* (1973), referred to an almost exclusive orientation to someone lost in a rural or wilderness setting. The National Park Service also clearly oriented their search efforts toward lost people, in the traditional sense, somewhere in the wilderness or perhaps in a rural environment. Bill Syrotuck's initial study also referred to "*Analysis of Lost Person Behavior.*"

However, in the context of emergency response at the local level, and the nature of searching for a missing person or persons, a lost victim in the traditional sense fails to constitute the majority of search incidents. This boils down to:

> **"Most lost persons are also missing, but most missing persons are not lost."**

The statement above shifts our focus and necessitates changes to the way we handle SAR, especially in the early stages of an incident. Additional reasons why persons go missing include: illness, dementia, despondency, psychotic breaks, mental disability, runaways, victims of crime, accidents, or even natural disasters. Obviously, some also end up missing because they get lost in the traditional sense.

To reflect the evolution in who we search for, the Lost Person Questionnaire changed, more appropriately, into the Missing Person Report. It happened because the new form gets used when looking for someone other than a lost person. A missing person report more aptly addresses the needs and required information in traditional law enforcement contexts, including urban environments and the myriad of technological resources available to help locate a person in that environment.

Search and Rescue - How Important?

If someone were to ask, "What is the total demand for search in the U.S. and Canada?" the answer resides purely in speculation. We really don't possess data on how many missing person incidents occur in these countries every year. There is neither a national reporting system or, in most cases, even a thorough or semi-comprehensive local data base to record and report the data. The same holds true throughout the world. While improvements in information technology continue and databases now exist, it will be a number of years *(and perhaps decades)* before we possess actual numbers of missing person cases in a comprehensive sense.

In the U.S., some estimates place the number of cases in the neighborhood of a hundred thousand plus search operations a year. Maybe even more . . . and what about the international number?

Managing a land search deals with the function of search. It focuses solely on searching for, and locating missing persons at risk, abducted, overdue, lost, incapacitated, injured, and additionally, cannot return to a place of safety on their own. The settings for missing individuals vary from an outdoor or rural settings, an urban/suburban environment, a combination of these or as a result of natural or man-caused disaster.

The function of *rescue* denotes a known location with a known individual and situation. Technical Rescue falls outside the scope of this text. Search almost never proceeds straight forward and usually includes pure speculation because of the missing person's unknown whereabouts. Good search management principles provide a comprehensive methodology for applying locally trained resources to an emergency incident in a logical and efficient manner. In addition, more and more law enforcement agencies apply the concepts contained in search management to criminal or terrorist search situations which involve subject evasion as well.

> ***Search & Rescue are BOTH Time Critical!***
>
> *A successful search ends in a successful rescue.*

Successful Searches Stem from Strong Fundamentals

Instructors presuppose readers and course participants possess an academic or practical knowledge base to help form a foundation for the disciplines of search theory and it's field management. An individual needs a basic working knowledge of resources, tactics and skills to adequately direct search operations with any degree of competence. At a minimum, we suggest accompanying this text with *SAR Skills for the Emergency Responder, and The Fundamentals of Search and Rescue* plus extra study of the reference list at the end of this chapter.

Decades Old Guiding Principles in Land Search

In the early stages of Land Search, people like Dennis Kelly *(Mountain Search for the Lost Victim)* wrote down *common sense* recommendations and what they deemed *crucial rules* that proved successful during search operations. Decades ago, the National Park Service not only admitted they were not managing searches well; they began to develop a comprehensive course to teach their personnel how to effectively apply and use resources to find missing or lost persons. Early efforts by the U.S. Park Service helped establish the basic versions of this search management text and its accompanying course of study.

Collective *best practice* recommendations from field practitioners over time, resulted in what we refer to today as the *CRUCIALS*, or undisputed basic principles, of good land search management. The initial land search crucials for search management follow:

> **The Original Crucials of Land Search Management:**
>
> - Search is an Emergency
> - Search is a Classic Mystery
> - Search for Clues and the Subject
> - Concentrate on aspects that are:
>   - Important to search success
>   - Under control of the Search Manager
> - Know if the subject leaves the search area
> - Grid search only as a last resort

While these principles essentially drove search management in the U.S. and Canada for the next thirty years, we now know that despite providing sound guidance and a good foundation for early search efforts, they lacked a number of the essential factors for search planning in the inland environment.

For example, they fail to mention or reference effort allocation, detection capability values *(sweep width)* or measuring any type of success in the least amount of time. The science of search or *search theory* focusses on a number of the concepts conspicuously absent in the early crucials. That does not imply that they fail to provide a good foundation from which to begin. More importantly, progress with our capabilities and improving results during search operations also rests on the basic principles derived through the science of search and their eventual incorporation into land search methods. Progress in any discipline results from change, and change follows inevitably after the discovery of new things.

> *"If you are doing things the same way you did them ten years ago, then you're doing them wrong!"*
> -Winston Churchill -

A Revised and *Improved* Set of Crucials for Search Management:

- Search is an Emergency
- Search is Inexorably Tied to Law Enforcement Investigation
- Search for Clues and the Missing Person
- Concentrate on factors that are:
  - Important to search success
  - Controlled by the Search Manager
- Confine the Search Area
- Gather Good Information
- Apply Trained Appropriate Resources in a Definite Order
- Use Thorough Grid Search (close spacing) Only as a Last Resort
- Document Decisions and Assignments Early with Numerical Assessments for Justification
- Detection Capability Variables must be included in Effective Search Planning
- Allocation of Effort Combined with Detection Capability can Maximize Probability of Success
- Success in the Shortest Time Possible is the Ultimate Goal in Search

These represent the foundation blocks of effective land search. Experience and history tells us that to do otherwise could be fatal to the missing person!

Discussion: The Crucials in Detail:

Search is an Emergency

Why do we call it an emergency?

- The missing person needs emergency care
- The missing person may need protection from themselves and the environment
- Time and weather destroy clues and evidence
- Urgent response generally means a smaller search area and permits the use of more efficient search techniques
- The subject may only respond or remain conscious for a few hours/days

Sometimes people find it hard to *justify* urgency because common sense tells us that a certain percentage of missing people, if left on their own, survive or make their own way to safety. However, in the early stages of a missing person incident, a distinct lack of information abounds with no guaranteed way to determine the status of the potential victim. A quick response helps to minimize search area size and also provides better opportunity to detect visual clues. The Search Area size also strongly links to the potential maximum distance traveled by the missing person (*The time it takes for response to occur influences how far the subject travels in the intervening time*).

A stated goal of good search planning attempts to

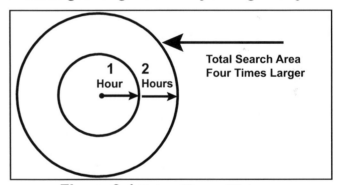

Figure 3-1 Rate × Time = Distance

achieve the most success in the shortest period of time; plus, the time needed for search success directly relates to search area size (*Getting on scene quickly while the missing person is still responsive, without a chance to travel too far*).

Nighttime also gives searchers a unique opportunity to confine the missing person. Under normal circumstances, lost or missing individuals in most categories stop or dramatically reduce their travel at night. Interestingly, resources such as trackers and dog teams work better at night because of visibility or atmospheric conditions or both.

Suggested actions to satisfy the first Crucial (*Search is an Emergency*):

- Respond urgently with trained resources and search at night
- Aid searchers any way possible *(i.e. transport resources to higher ground - plan areas with few or no internal barriers, etc.)*
- Create an atmosphere of positive urgency *(Rapid movement with control, not frenzy)*
- Include noncontiguous areas of search with appropriate investigation *(Include residences of friends, relatives, virtual locations etc.)*
- Use initial strategies that insure maximum chance of locating a responsive, conscious subject. *(Involve the use of sound and sound/light line tactics while missing or lost persons still maintain the capability to respond)*

Search Ties Inexorably to Law Enforcement Investigation

The initial crucials simply stated, "Search was a Classic Mystery." This brings to mind intriguing plots out of a Sherlock Holmes novel, but fails to really address the myriad of typical police functions used in successful searches. Law enforcement agencies regularly deal with interviewing, investigation of scenes, accessing personal data, processing of information, sentinal systems and using networks for expanded inquiries into behavior of specific types of people. Police possess the resources, training and orientation to follow through on information gathered about any particular category of missing person in differing environments *(rural or urban/suburban locations)*. Years of practical operations yield the conclusion that search success often hinges on investigation. Conversely, the search as a whole often benefits when the investigating/interviewing officer knows about the basic concepts of search management and planning.

The goal of investigation in the search context is to develop a body of information and evidence which helps determine the missing person's location. It involves gathering four distinct types of data or evidence.

1. **Physical Evidence** – *processing scenes properly using track and clue awareness skills as well as understanding the chain of evidence in law enforcement.*
2. **Testimonial Evidence** – *apply appropriate skills in interviewing to specifically uncover relevant information.*
3. **Records** (written chronology) – *Logs, registration documents, attendance rosters, bank card activity, and receipts, etc. need to be investigated, tracked and verified.*
4. **Analysis of Statistical Data** – *Lost or missing person behavior data in the form of distances, patterns of consistent characteristics, clues to look for or general subject behavior indicating likely locations.*

First of all, investigators need to determine what clues to look for. Certain categories of subjects *(i.e. hunters, hikers, etc.)* tend to do the same things given similar circumstances. Investigation/interviewing determines potential or possible destinations, intended routes and alternative actions, as well as a specific point last seen or a recreation of the circumstances potentially leading to the missing person's real situation.

Search for Clues *as well as* the Missing Person

- Construct a *subject profile* that deals specifically with the missing individual.

  - Simultaneously trying to run a search and while conducting an investigation *(one person)* leads to failure.

- Establish a boundary and prevent missing persons from passing it undetected.

  - Use confinement and continue to gather reliable information from bystanders or *unknowing witnesses (someone who witnessed something without realizing its importance)*.

- Untrained search resources often damage or destroy good sign or clues.

- Train all team members on track and clue awareness and how to maintain the chain of evidence.

• In addition, consult with friends, relatives and acquaintances to see if the missing person turned up.

It is virtually impossible to pass through the environment without leaving some trace or evidence. Tracks, scent, disturbances, discarded articles all mark the presence of humans in an area. Some estimates state that a single person traveling through the environment leaves approximately 2000 signs, scuffs, impressions or indications of passage for every mile walked (*or 1,200 per kilometer walked*). These clues often give direction of travel, time and positive identification for a subject and thus reduce the potential search area and search difficulty.

• Search for clues, sign or evidence and the missing person.
• The very nature of the search problem indicates many more clues than missing persons in the environment.

Concentrate on Factors that are:

• Important to Search Success
• Controllable in the Context of Management and Planning

What factors drive search success? To answer that question, good students of search management seek to understand the essential elements involved in the discipline of search. Are there sufficient resources to effectively search the identified high probability area in the given time, as well as consistent with survival/safety in that environment? Effective search in a set time frame hinges on allocation of available effort, knowledge of search resource capabilities, and the ability to apply the most efficient tactics to on-scene environmental and terrain conditions. These elements form a very complex problem to solve.

Optimum effort allocations which achieve success in the least amount of time entail not only an understanding of resource capabilities and weaknesses, but how to determine and evaluate effort and detection probability in the field. Planners and command staff control some factors and cannot control others. Things like planning for anticipated operational periods, using the right resources in the right order and continually looking for clues as a priority, all contribute to search success.

If limited visibility influences detection during a search for a missing backpacker, then perhaps the incident requires more personnel to adequately cover the intended search area. Reduced detection range of individual searchers because of fog or storm conditions necessitates more people to search the same area in the same amount of time *(Success in less time)*. By the same token, functions like proper application of specific resources to specialized environments, assigning personnel to continue investigative efforts and making sure that all field personnel get briefed and debriefed in detail form controllable keys to success within the purview of the Search Manager.

Confine the Search Area and Gather Reliable Information

To the extent possible, an initial effort assures that the missing person remains in the search area. To do this, develop and employ quick action strategies to confine the area *(Monitoring and closing any exits or choke points)*. As mentioned previously, establish a boundary and prevent missing persons from passing it undetected. Effective managers know if the subject leaves the search area.

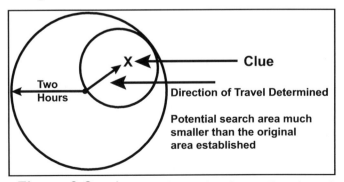

Figure 3-2 Direction of travel reduces the size of the potential search area

Search and in some cases re-search prominent non-contiguous areas like the missing person's home, a friend's house, a relative's house, etc. Someone assigned to investigation needs to carry out these assignments.

- Confinement works in coordination with ongoing active or passive tactics in the field to determine if the missing person left any clues or remains in the search area.

  - Use confinement resources and continue to gather information with cursory interviews from bystanders, group members, *unknowing witnesses*, neighbors, relatives, camp ground residents, utility workers, service and delivery personnel, or anyone else with specific facts about the incident.

Apply Trained Appropriate Resources in a Definite Order

Trained searchers are clue conscious and look for entirely different things than untrained searchers. We generally classify resources as those looking for just clues; those looking for both clues and the missing person; and those only looking for the missing person. Each of these key in on different types of clues and/or visual indicators to make a find. For this reason, knowledge of how resources work provides very clear guidance on the correct priority and order for applying resources during a search for a missing person.

As an example, it makes no sense to ask a track and clue aware hasty team to check an area for sign after hundreds of other searchers walked through first. The task would overwhelm even a seasoned tracker. Also, one would never task an air-scent search dog and handler to search directly behind a hasty team moving through the area checking likely spots, with no thought of wind direction.

Another example reflects the use of sound and light. These tactics assume a living and responsive subject. Use sound and sound/light lines in a search to attract the attention of the missing person. As time passes, responders use this tactic less and less because the probability of a responsive subject decreases with time.

Use Thorough Grid Search (close spacing) Only as a Last Resort

- The cost in terms of manpower and time compared to the benefit significantly offsets to the negative compared with other techniques.
- Close grid searches virtually erase all existing clues or evidence in the suspected area once completed.
- Normally, available manpower precludes close grid searching in all but the most unusual of circumstances e.g. when an incident develops with extensive available manpower, emergent volunteers etc.
- Knowledge of current research in detection ranges and vision mechanisms also excludes close space grid searching in most circumstances.

Document Decisions and Assignments Early with Numerical Assessments for Justification

Searching for missing persons, in the early stages of an incident usually involves inadequate information about either the missing person or the circumstances of the incident. Managers usually make decisions

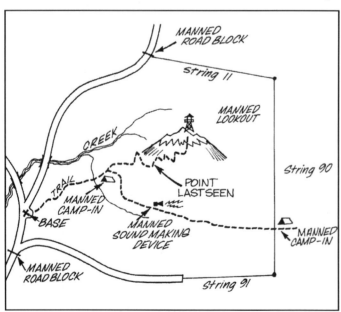

Figure 3-3 Containment

about probable scenarios and applying resources or specific tactics based upon very sketchy, but compelling information. *Urgency*, the level of response derived from that urgency and the Urgency Form, also represents a clear use of numerical assesments to help guide and justify decisions *(See Chapter 11)*.

Much of what we use today as an indicator about where to search initially comes from Incident Databases *(e.g. the International Search and Rescue Incident Database)* for distances and characteristics of subject categories. In some cases, statistical data provides the only clear indication about high probability areas and where to look *(See Chapter 18 on Establishing the Search Area)*. Although this process initially uses subjective decisions based on limited information, the decisions still need to be documented along with everything available from the database used.

In Chapters 14 and 16, the text explicitly defines and explains on-scene planning using *Reflex Tasks* consistently in the early stages of every search. However, sometimes circumstances call for unique strategies or tactical approaches. Those situations require even more documentation of those decisions, probable areas and resources committed. In addition to this documentation, managers need to make assessments about how well likely spots, trails, campgrounds, areas, neighborhoods or other geographic areas were initially covered or searched and the effectiveness of those searches.

Simply providing descriptive adjectives for search effectiveness such as "thorough," "complete," "all most all of it," or "that area's been done" will not suffice. Some type of numerical assessment for these early efforts enable search planning, if necessary, further on in the search. Reconstructing assessments after the fact without documentation proves difficult.

Clearly, if the initial efforts to find a missing person *(the first and sometimes even the second operational periods)* fail, then the initially completed tasks will undoubtedly form the basis for planning the follow-on operational tactics and assignments. As any search progresses, the resources used grow increasingly more and more dependent on search planning for direction and priority. Try to ignore the voices that say: "Much of these early assessments are subjective in nature anyway and not really important in the early context of the search." As will be explained later, very specific procedures will help establish these numerical assessments, and they provide the search planner with an incredible array of options concerning effort allocation and maximizing success in the shortest amount of time. Plus, with proper documentation, decision makers can reconstruct the incident circumstances to later justify their actions.

Include Detection Capability Variables in Search Planning.

Detection of a specified target or search object *(anything from a person to a very small clue)* depends upon many factors, which include proper briefing or programming. A later discussion on Probability of Detection covers a whole series of factors that directly affect whether or not a searcher will detect something given specific conditions in any environment.

Common sense tells us that searchers see less in heavy fog or falling snow as opposed to clear conditions. We also know that searchers see less while concentrating on keeping their feet in rough, steep terrain. These kinds of capability adjustments, gleaned from the debrief process, help develop realistic planning assessments for future operational periods. Research and field experiments conducted for decades on spacing, environment, color, size, terrain, searcher capabilities and other factors involved in search show that there are both mental and physiological factors in human vision that affect what we recognize and detect.

Sweep Width, or a measured detection index, forms a central pillar in search and search theory. Effort allocation and evaluation of all search effort in any environment follows from this basic measurement. In other words, for every resource committed to a specific environment *(searcher, dog and handler, aircraft, etc.)* there is a finite range on both sides

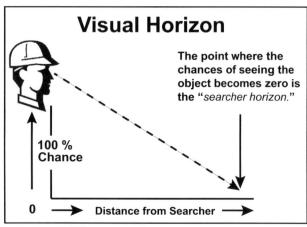

Figure 3-4 Visual Horizon

of the resource where we expect a given chance of detection during a search. Not with a 100% certainty, but with realistic (*objectively determined*) expectations of detection. That detection range has a length that varies depending on environmental conditions, terrain, object size, and other local factors.

Allocation of Effort Combined with Detection Capability Maximizes Probability of Success

As mentioned above, a detection range or *sweep width* which relates to Probability of Detection also links directly to the number of resources needed to cover an area and to the time needed for searching it. A narrow detection range in a segment, because of the vegetation for example, will take a small number of searchers longer to search that segment. An alternative puts more searchers in the area to compensate for the narrower detection range. The more searchers, the quicker the job gets finished. Analysis and comparison of different alternatives form the basis of *Effort Allocation (See Chapter 20 on Probability of Success)*. Changing the detection index *(sweep width)*, speed of advance, numbers of searchers, and time spent in the search segment all affect the effort necessary to search a specific segment or even the entire search area within a set period of time. A knowledgable search planner manipulates these variables and controls them to maximize success in the shortest amount of time.

Chapter 19 *(Probability of Detection)* provides some conservative techniques to determine detection ranges in any local terrain and to establish search team benchmarks for search planners to use in their analysis of effort and success.

The Ultimate Goal in Search - Success in the Shortest Time Possible

The mathematical basis and foundation of searching for objects and/or people forms the core of serious study in Search since World War II. Both formal search theory, developed in the maritime environment in the 1940s, and land search management across the U.S. and Canada for the last thirty years, advocate the conventional formula of POA × POD = POS and its use for search planning. Unfortunately, many land searches and the agencies responsible for them in this country and around the world simply do not utilize this powerful formula and its accompanying protocols.

Conventional Search Planning Formula:

POA × POD = POS

In the formula *POA* stands for Probability of Area and *POD* stands for Probability of Detection. Giving each of those designations a numerical value based on established criteria, then those numerical values together determine a Probability of Success or *POS*. As a planning and evaluation tool, this provides insight and perspective on the development of any search for a missing person. The ultimate goal of search planning *(Using the conventional formula of POA × POD = POS)* maximizes the value of POS in the shortest possible time. The criterion for success in a search for someone who may be in danger or suffering the affects of environmental extremes is measured in time *(minutes, hours, days, etc.)*. The quicker responders get to the person in distress, the better the of chances finding them alive.

Terminology, Definitions and Statistical Data

In the collective blending of concepts, terms, methods and databases in formal search theory and land search management, a common vocabulary serves to make the still changing and growing discipline of land search a little easier to comprehend. Though not terribly difficult or complex, these terms need clarification and a reference for their practical use during real searches. In order to keep continuity throughout this text, a brief introduction of some of these concepts familiarizes the readers with the terms and how effective search managers use them.

The Basic Introduction to Land Search Theory provides very clear definitions and gives practical examples of how to use these tools in operational search planning. Participants in this Search Management Course will then actually use these tools in a number of tabletop map exercises. Like anything reasonably technical in nature, the more a person works with the concepts, the more they develop an ability to actually put them to use in a practical way.

Our measure of effective coverage and success is a product of effort allocation, and a detection index called *sweep width*, not searcher spacing. We also know that the subjective creation of scenarios (*based on investigation*) forms the basis for establishing regions of probability that ultimately determine where to search. These new concepts and more, briefly introduced here, get defined in greater detail in chapters 17 through 20.

For decades, Syrotuck's *Analysis of Lost Person Behavior* published in 1976, provided the only practical database of missing person behavior characteristics and distances traveled by lost subjects. Since then, individuals like Robert Koester, Kenneth Hill, Edward Cornell, Donald Heth, Pete Roberts and Dave Perkins expanded their own research into lost and missing person behavior. As more data comes in, the more refined our capabilities grow at predicting where people in certain categories likely turn up when lost *(See Chapter 14 on Missing and Lost Person Behavior)*. The *International Search and Rescue Incident Database (ISRID)* compiled by Robert Koester assimilated well over 50,000 missing person cases in 2008 and the next iteration promises well over 150,000 cases. Undoubtedly, previous assumptions, conclusions and/or deductions change as that database matures and the community collects and evaluates pertinent information.

Planning Concepts and Terms

The following definitions lay the groundwork for our discussion of search theory.

Region of Probability

Early in any search, managers speculate about the reasons for the missing person's absence. To accomplish this, search planners deduce scenarios and speculate what happened to the missing person based on available information. Each of these hypothetical scenarios links to a specific area(s) of geographic terrain. These scenarios each constitute region(s) of consistent probability and weight according to planners thoughts on the most likely scenario.

Regions of Probability answer the question:

"Where in the search area is the subject more likely and less likely to be?"

Segments answer the question:

"How can the search area be subdivided into manageable pieces for searching by the available resources?"

Sweep Width

As mentioned before, *sweep width*, defined as a detection index used for determining probability of detection in a specific environment under very specific conditions consists of a finite range, measured objectively and varying depending on environmental conditions, terrain, object size, etc. Not with a 100% certainty, but with realistic expectations of the chances of detection. Usually, measures used in sweep width include feet, yards, or meters.

Trackline and Track Line Length

A *Trackline* describes the path or route taken by a search resource as it moves through a segment. *Track Line Length* measures the length of that resource's path while searching in a designated segment. Planners also calculate Track Line Length by multiplying the speed of the resource by the time spent searching in the segment *(e.g. One mile per hour X 4 hours = A four mile Track Line Length)*. It is usually measured in yards, meters, miles or kilometers.

Total Track Line Length

The sum of all resource's Track Line Length's in a segment. Planners sometimes use established benchmarks multiplied by the number of resources or people searching in a segment for a given time, to determine this value.

Area Effectively Swept

An area to help compute coverage when looking for resource probability of detection *(POD)*. This concept represents an area, expressed as square feet, square yards, square meters, square miles or square kilometers. For a resource, Sweep Width and Total Track Line Length multiplied together give an *area effectively swept*. In simple terms, how much of the segment did a particular resource look at?

Effort

Of primary concern in any search operation is *"How long is it going to take to search that area?"* Planners measure effort in searcher hours. The effort required to search a portion of the search area stems from a number of different variables. With *effort allocation, (or where do we spend our searcher hours?)* a number of variables determine success in the shortest time.

Variables for Effort Allocation

- Time spent by searchers
- Number of searchers
- Speed of Searchers
- Different Resources
- Sweep Widths of Different Resources
- Multiple Searches - Same Resource
- Multiple Searches - Different Resources

Optimal Resource Allocation

A process where planners assign and deploy available resources in such a way as to maximize probability of success (POS) in the least amount of time.

Coverage

A search segment contains a specific area based upon its dimensions *(length x width)*. Planners calculate area using square yards, square meters, square miles, square kilometers, acres, or even hectares. Comparing this total segment area to the area effectively swept, we get a ratio that describes how much of the search segment was covered *(or searched)* by the resource(s) deployed to it. Or, more simply, coverage is a ratio comparing the size of the segment to the area effectively swept. With this ratio or coverage factor, we determine probability of detection using a relationship developed through long years of research in search theory.

Average Range of Detection (AROD) (R_d) Range of Detection (Average)

Previous research demonstrated that trained searchers usually fail to predict or accurately evaluate their Probability of Detection (POD) values in the field. Recently, Robert Koester completed research that specifies field procedures which determine reasonably accurate effective sweep width values and as a result, help to develop meaningful POD values for any searchers deployed in the field. The goal of Koester's research and published paper was to develop a simple, objective procedure that obtains effective sweep width (**ESW**) values without conducting full-blown detection experiments.

R_d = The average range of linear distances that a search object is first detected when moving towards it from multiple angles.

Probability Distribution

A probability distribution assigns a probability to each measurable value of a particular factor for comparison with all the other values for that factor *(for example distances traveled by people in a database for a specific category of missing persons).*

Statistical Probability Loading

After identifying regions of probability on a map based on suspected scenarios, planners consult statistical missing person data to find out distances traveled for a particular category of subject. These databases also provide additional information about clues, likely spots and other pertinent subject behavior. Using this information along with facts and circumstances gathered at the scene, planners identify specific geographic areas of probability on the map and assign values about the chances locating that missing person in any particular region of the search area. While this process uses some subjective analysis, it rests on the best information available at the time and establishes the foundation for the rest of the search planning process.

Probability of Area and Probability Density Distributions

POA *(Probability of Area)* in the standard notation formula, is a numerical value that represents the chances or probability that a defined geographic area contains the object or missing person. As mentioned above, planners define regions of probability using facts and information that relate to specific deduced scenarios. It makes sense that a more likely scenario leads to more probability within the area connected to that scenario.

Primarily, search planning determines not only where to search in general, but how to apply the available resources *(allocation of effort)* in such a manner as to achieve the maximum probability of success in the least amount of time *(as efficient as possible).* If a search planner has to decide how much effort to devote to each portion of the total search area, then it is important to know how to estimate probability density distributions. Where in the search area is the highest concentration of probability? Normally, search managers have too few resources to search the entire area all at once. Planners divide regions of probability into searchable segments and allocate numerical values that represent the chances a specific segment contains the subject or object.

Shifting or Shifted Probability of Area

As mentioned just above, POA represents the chances or probability that a defined geographic area contains an object or missing person. While initially these values come from subjective analysis, their initial accuracy pales in comparison to their relationship to other segment probabilities and changes in those values over the course of the incident. If a specific portion of a search area potentially contains the missing person, planners give that segment a probability value and that assessment starts the planning process. When a resource or multiple resources commit to that portion of the search area, and no missing person or clues turn up, then the question is "Will the probability remain the same in that portion of the search area?" The answer to that is no, because that portion was just searched with no result. That segment probability reduces in relation to the other portions of the search area. This describes one way that probability shifts in the context of a search and why planners track it during search planning activities.

Cumulative Probabilities of Detection and Success

Each time a resource searches in a segment planners need to determine a reasonably accurate value for detecting the object. One search by a single resource results in a single probability of detection value. If sending in additional resources or the same resource into the area again, planners need the cumulative affect of these multiple searches. The values are not simply added, but accumulate through set mathematical protocols. Search planners and managers have several choices about the methods that provide cumulative values. Managers can run simultaneously with different resources, one following another using different resources, or by even using the same resource to search the same segment multiple times.

Standard search theory notation *(POA × POD = POS)* provides a value for POS after every search of a specific segment. All SEGMENT values for POS add together to determine an overall POS value for the entire search area *(See Chapter 20)*.

Predictive Probability of Success

Given established protocols for determining *sweep width*, and by applying the principles of *effort allocation* in search planning, good planners speculate potential success based on variable resources, speeds, times and other constraints applied to searching a specific segment. While conditions in the field ultimately dictate the success of a search, the planner can manipulate factors on paper before that operational period to see which tactics or resources in speculated conditions might produce the best results. In this way, a search manager tackles the challenge with the best of several options at hand based on the resources available, terrain and the environmental conditions.

> "Next to creating life, the next most important thing a man can do is to save one."
> - Abraham Lincoln

Recommended Reading List for Search Managers (ICs) and Planners

- Koester, R.J. *Lost Person Behavior - A Search and Rescue Guide on Where to Look - for Land, Air and Water*, dbS Productions LLC, P.O. Box 94, Charlottesville, Virginia USA 22903. ISBN 978-1-879471-39-9
- Speiden, Robert 2009. *Foundations for Awareness, Signcutting and Tracking.* Natural Awareness Tracking School, LLC, 657 Coal Hollow Road, Christiansburg, Virginia 24073. U.S.A.
- Stoffel, R., & Stoffel, B. C. (2013). *SAR Skills for the Emergency Responder*. Cashmere, WA: Emergency Response International, Inc. ISBN: 0-9709583-2-3
- Koester, R. J. (2014). *Incident Command System Field Operations Guide for Search & Rescue: (ICS-FOGSAR)*. Charlottesville, VA: DbS Productions. ISBN 978-1879471320.
- Cooper, D. C., (2005). *Fundamentals of Search and Rescue*. Sudbury, MA: Jones and Bartlett and the National Association for Search and Rescue.

See reference list in the back of this text.

Legal Issues and Public Expectations

4

Objectives:

- Discuss the basic issues of liability in SAR response.

- Relate the essential elements of negligence to prove liability in court.

- Understand the most common causes of lawsuits against emergency responders.

Legal Outlook and Considerations

This chapter in no way provides legal advice for specific situations, rather it describes the common causes of lawsuits and situations that increase the likelihood of liability or troubles in court. Always consult an attorney for advice concerning specific situations or circumstances.

Bad News: Litigation always looms when injury occurs or families suffer the loss of a loved one. Blame comes naturally for people suffering from an injury or loss and they commonly search for a responsible party.

Better News: Litigation costs a lot of money and the legal system requires time to handle the volume of cases waiting for court time.

Good News: Plaintiffs need a legitimate reason to win in court. The competent implementation of a plan according to an established *standard of care* for emergency response significantly reduces the threat and impact of unjustified litigation.

Basic Questions:

Will a court hold a government agency *(Sheriff's Office, Police Department, National Park, etc.)* liable for injury or death caused *(or made likely)* by a failure to eliminate or reduce known SAR hazards or a failure to respond to SAR incidents quickly and efficiently?

Will a court hold a non-paid (i.e. volunteer) SAR organization liable for a failure to respond quickly, efficiently, and deliver according to an established *standard of care*?

Will a court hold a volunteer organization responsible for injuries that occur during a SAR operation *(subject or responder)*?

Depending on where you live in the world, or the interpretation of legal precedent, these questions create complex answers.

Keep the following in mind:

- People think of the emergency response agencies as a *deep pocket with very little distinction between agencies and volunteer groups and non-profits*
- The media, the public and the courts document recurring SAR response mistakes
- The number of SAR incidents in all environments continue to increase with increasing populations, and usually gain immediate media attention
- An *Act of God* almost never provides a blanket defense for natural occurrences
- The media and the general public realize the government's role(s) in SAR, and expect positive results

  - The public expects the government to *know what it is doing*

- Previous cases, television, movies and the internet condition the public to expect positive results from searches and rescue missions. These outlets rarely portray unsuccessful operations

- Non-paid *(volunteer)* SAR organizations often act as agents for the responsible government agency.
- The potential exists for individual responders to incur personal liability for improper actions

> **The public and courts expect professionals *(whether paid or not)* to use an accepted *standard of care*.**

- The possibility also exists for SAR organizations and their officers to incur liability for the acts or omissions of those they supervise. Through the doctrine of *vicarious liability*, organizations and their officers end up responsible for damages caused by the bad actions of members of the organization when the members act on behalf of the parent organization.

Understanding the Law of Negligence related to SAR

Plaintiffs, who claim some harm, bring private legal action to court, called a *Civil Law Suit*, against the person or entity they believe harmed them *(the defendant)*.

Goal of a civil suit:

Monetary compensation for the harm, or the forced implementation of an action or set of actions in the future.

Was There a Duty?

Merriam-Webster online defines duty as an obligatory task.

The provision of SAR services by an agency or organization brings a duty for that agency to actually search and attempt rescue in many areas of the world.

In some cases the duty also encompasses:

- Easily contacted and reachable by phone and radio
- Performing a timely response
- Adequately respond when needed
- Act *reasonably* in specific situations

Some state statutes assign the duty to provide SAR services to the sheriff or some other agency/officer. The specific statutes create an *entitlement* or right to SAR services. The resulting entitlements create an additional burden on the person or organization named to provide those services under the law.

Generally speaking, average citizens lack an obligation to intervene and help third parties, absent some special relationship *(e.g. parent to child)*. Even government personnel like police and fire-fighters, need not to act outside of their official capacity. However, once a party or entity intervenes in a situation, a duty to continue providing aid arises. The victim then relies on the aid provider for help.

The concept of reliance relates very closely to the voluntary undertaking of a duty. Courts often find a duty where the *defendant (accused of causing the harm)* caused the *plaintiff, (victim of the harm)*, to

Beware of implied promises:

> *Same Day Search and Rescue Team*
> *We can do the Job! - Just Call Us!*

directly rely on a promise, or an implied promise of aid. For example, a SAR group advertises its function and capabilities through fund-raisers, or advertisement-like posting of logos on bulletin boards or web sites. This information then *engenders reliance,* by the public, on the services provided by these groups. The public, logically, assumes that group will provide some form of protection when an emergency arrives.

Once a court determines the existence of a duty, they then focus on the actions and inactions of those with the duty to respond. The legal process focuses on whether an average individual or organization with the same skills and resources would act in the same fashion given the same circumstances.

A Standard of Care - the average level of care expected of individuals or organizations in the spectrum of all similarly situated individuals and organizations. The definition of *reasonable* action stems from the specific circumstances and an established *standard of care* based on a generic person with the same training in a similar situation.

The next step in the process requires a reasonable connection between the events causing someone injury and the actions of the defendant(s). The court looks at foreseeability of injury and the chain of events leading to the injury. The law defines the limits of the connection between actions and the results of those actions in a very technical legal fashion including:

- Foreseeability of injury
- Causation of injury
- Cost/benefit of action versus inaction

A court determines these factors <u>after</u> injury or death occurs.

In the U.S. legal system, the plaintiff always holds the burden of proof and must demonstrate:

FAULT (of the defendant) CAUSED DAMAGE (to the plaintiff)

Good News: Burden of proof means each and every element of a particular tort *(harm)* under the law needs to be proven to prevail in court. If the plaintiff(s) *(or their lawyer)* fails to prove one element, then the whole case falls apart.

A plaintiff's lawyer tries to justify the following elements in a Negligence Suit:

- A duty to the plaintiff
- A standard of care
- Violation or Breach of that duty or standard by the defendant
- An act legally caused by the defendant(*If a statute or regulation sets a standard which must be obeyed, then different standard of causation applies*)
- Resulting Injury to the plaintiff

Types of Fault *(Degrees of Negligence)*
Basic Negligence:

- An act which a reasonable and prudent person would not undertake
- Failure to act or render aid when a duty or special relationship exists
- The creation of an unreasonable risk of harm toward a third person

A reasonable and prudent responder in a SAR situation simply needs to act in accordance with their level of training, assuming the organization provides and requires proper training. Thus, a standard first aid trained responder rendering first aid must act as well as the average person trained to the same level of standard first aid, an EMT to the level of an average EMT, etc.

Gross Negligence:

A great departure from the standard of care

Recklessness:

A deliberate act or omission, counter to the standard of care completed with knowledge of the standard

Negligence Per Se:

An act or omission committed in violation of a statute or regulation which results in harm to a person or property. In this case the statute sets the standard of care alone and violating the given statute proves the negligence without any other standard for liability

Res Ipsa Loquitur:

Translation: The thing speaks for itself. Certain situations only occur because of negligence, even without specific evidence

Mal-Intent:

Malicious conduct, willful or wanton behavior *(hurting someone on purpose)*

Remember, in a law suit, juries usually lack SAR expertise; instead you get a jury of average citizens not familiar with the functions of SAR. They will investigate your prior experience, your knowledge, and why you did not know of existing methods, or techniques.

Questions that court actions always attempt to answer:

- Was there a duty?
- In the process, did you injure the victim?
- Were there improper techniques?
- Did you act in good faith?
- Were you working for the victim?
- Were the victim's best interests always the goal?
- Did you do all that you could reasonably do? And, did you document it?

How and Why Lawsuits Occur

These factors all served as the primary cause for negligence in previous SAR cases around the world:

- **Appointment.** Failure to check a person's background and qualifications prior to employment, membership, or assignment to a task *(Check qualifications!)*
- **Retention.** Keeping a person in a job or position which he or she proves unable to accomplish, after you discover *(or should discover)* an inability *(You must get rid of those unable to perform the job!)*.
- **Assignment.** Assignment of an untrained person to a job where they carry no qualification *(Don't let unqualified persons perform functions requiring special skills)*.
- **Entrustment.** Permitting a person to use some piece of equipment or perform some task for which he or she never received training, lacks operational knowledge, or performs improperly *(Provide adequate training and keep track of who possesses the most skill)*.
- **Training.** Not providing training for personnel according to their duties, assignment, work task, rank, equipment used, or otherwise. Providing sloppy or inadequate training *(Train and train right)!*
- **Supervision.** Permitting personnel to act in an unsupervised manner at any time or under any condition which requires supervision *(Provide the supervision)!*
- **Direction.** Failure to use rules and regulations, standard operating procedures, instructions, guidelines, and the enforcement of the same, which relate to the operation of the organization and the conduct of its activities *(Provide direction)!*
- **Documentation.** Failure to properly or completely document all activities such as searches, training, equipment inspections, etc. *(Document everything completely)!*
- **Operation of Emergency Vehicles.** This causes more lawsuits than actual emergency operations. Drive carefully! Follow emergency vehicle laws *(Remember that lights and sirens do not provide the right-of-way, they just ask for it)!*
- **Selection, Maintenance and Use of Equipment.** Use of damaged or defective equipment, failure to create a program for inspecting equipment and monitoring damaged or defective parts. Failure to procure required equipment *(Develop a program to inspect and maintain all equipment. Demand proper training on how to use all equipment)*.

All of the above cause liability!

Government officials, and responders stay liability free if:

- They followed the *standard of care*
- They acted properly and in their official capacity
- They acted within their scope of authority
- They acted *reasonably* and *prudently* based on the *established standard*

What About Trespass During a Search?

Inevitably these questions come up during search operations. Should searchers ask a property owner to search their own property? What rights does a civilian searcher have to enter *private property*? What rights does a police officer have to enter private property? And finally, will a *warrant* for search help?

Jurisdictions vary but most allow emergency responders to act in ways which generate liability in other situations.

> *Caution!* *The descriptions of the following areas of the law do not provide an excuse to act in a cavalier or unprofessional manner, rather they serve to protect and assist responders to help save lives. When confronted with an unusual situation, always consult with SAR management or uniformed law enforcement for guidance.*

Trespass:

An unlawful interference with another's personal or property rights. Trespass, related to SAR, usually describes the entry to another's property without right or permission; or, any unauthorized intrusion or invasion of private premises owned by another.

Necessity:

The legal concept of *Necessity* allows a party to interfere with the property of a third person to avoid a greater harm or injury. *Public Necessity* occurs when a party or entity appropriates or injures private property to protect the entire community. For example a public necessity might require tearing down a building to create a firebreak during an urban fire-storm. The public necessity provides a complete defense, meaning no liability attaches for the harm to the property in a public necessity situation.

Private necessity arises when an individual injures or damages private property to protect a private interest with a higher value than the property. In private necessity situations the defendant incurs liability for the damage caused to the property.

Exigent Circumstances:

Exigent circumstances describe situations which require immediate or unusual action and circumvent the usual protective procedures. For example; when a member of the police department breaks into a residence without a warrant because he hears screaming or other sounds of distress from inside. This almost never applies to search and rescue. Leave decisions about exigent circumstances to trained law enforcement personnel.

What About a Warrant?

A Judge issues warrants to direct law enforcement officers to make an arrest, a search, or a seizure. The issue of this special document requires very strict procedures and a law enforcement concept called *probable cause (beyond the scope of this text)*. A warrant normally comes into play with suspected criminal activity rather than with search for missing persons.

Bottom Line on Private Property

Remember the new crucial from Chapter 3: Search ties inexorably to law enforcement.

When it comes to entering private property, always ask permission. When unable to contact the property owner for permission. Leave decisions about exigent circumstances to those trained and responsible for handling exigent scenarios. Any decisions concerning trespass must meet the *reasonable person* test (i.e. would a generic individual with the same level *of training act the same way?)*. Every situation brings unique decision criteria.

Uniformed police personnel on search teams assigned to cross private or posted property usually minimize difficulties. However, if a landowner asks searchers to leave, searchers need to leave immediately and document the circumstances.

Some Thoughts about the Use of Non-Paid (*Volunteer*) Responders

NOTE: Most non-paid SAR units consist of highly trained and organized members, but from a law enforcement or land management agency viewpoint, consider the following:

- Delegation of responsibility to non-paid *(volunteer)* groups means the loss of some direct control
- Some volunteer teams lack experienced leadership
- Response time by non-paid *(volunteer)* groups varies, plan for it
- Who provides the liability coverage for volunteers? What happens when responders get injured or killed?

We use the term *emergent volunteers* to describe members of the public who wish to help with SAR operations when they *perceive* the operation needs help. As an incident grows in scope and time, more and more emergent volunteers will arrive. Plan for their arrival ahead of time to avoid overwhelming the organization with managing these people. Consult your jurisdiction's emergency responder *(worker)* program and understand what actions qualify a volunteer for liability coverage. Develop clear policies for tracking volunteers and assigning them tasks which both help the situation while preventing unintended harm *(see Chapter 15 on Incident management)*.

Liability Summary:

The public and courts expect officials and responders to respond *reasonably* and *effectively*. The difference between proper response and sloppy response correlates directly to pre-planning and response development.

Prevent future legal problems by:

- Developing and implementing an established *standard of care* through planning and training. Don't force courts to search outside your jurisdiction *define your own standard of care!*
- Consider shortages of time, space, equipment, supplies, manpower inherent in emergencies everywhere.
- Don't make promises you cannot keep in terms of mission statements, standard operating procedures, equipment lists, or other official documents.

What About *Good Samaritan* Laws?

Generally, SAR responders lose this protection when they volunteer their time and efforts as part of a *planned response* under the *color of the law* such as an official SAR mission.

Many state *(or country)* Good Samaritan laws protect generic citizens, not responders. They usually protect persons who accidentally encounter someone needing assistance, not individuals involved in an official SAR effort. Many of these laws also change protections when responders request payment or victims pay for services rendered, or in cases of wanton or willful conduct. Check to see when and how your jurisdiction's Good Samaritan laws work. Most Good Samaritan laws do not prevent law suits. The statutes simply reduce the standard of care to the level of the average person.

By volunteering to go to the scene of an emergency, SAR responders assume a legal duty to give the victim reasonable care and not to increase the risk of harm or cause further harm. If a responder breaches that duty, they may incur personal liability for civil damages. The *standard of care* always serves to protect the responders in those situations. Follow it!

Reasons for Litigation

Note: Special Thanks to Norm Lawson, Esq. for the following list of scenarios.

The following list illustrates the most common causes for litigation involving searchers, rescuers, medics, team leaders, and organizations. Other reasons for litigation exist but the more common and of most interest follow:

Accidents with emergency vehicles. The leading cause of lawsuits against emergency agencies and personnel.

- **Dropping the casualty.** This ranges from dropping the victim off the litter, dropping the victim while hoisting into a helicopter, the victim falls from litter during a helicopter lift, or to accidents during hoisting or lowering operations which injure or kill the victim.

- **Not starting the search or rescue effort soon enough.** Generally in this scenario, delay causes the victim to die, sustain further injury, or otherwise suffer from the delayed response. Victims claim that if responders found the victim or rescued them promptly, the injury or death would not have occurred.

- **Lacking the ability to rescue a victim immediately, not providing at least something for a known victim in a known location.** In this situation, responders found the victim generally by air, but the rescuers lacked the ability to access him promptly, they failed to airdrop survival equipment or personnel to assist the victim. Victim claims increased injuries, or the victim dies.

- **Improper medical treatment for victim.** Responders further injure the victim or victim dies because of the medical care given, or not given. Typical causes of action center on unrecognized or improperly treated neck, head, or spine injuries, heat and cold problems, dehydration, etc.

- **Authorities in charge of the rescue refuse to call or deny participation to properly qualified rescuers.** In this situation, due to false pride, organizational jealously, or other reasons, authorities reject the services of properly qualified personnel or teams or fail to call them even though available and they actually volunteer to assist. The victim dies or suffers injury because those in charge cannot accomplish the search or rescue *(or both)* in a timely and efficient manner.

- **Equipment failures and other problems.** The rope breaks, the ascender, descender, litter, or some other piece of equipment fails and the victim sustains injury or death. Generally such situations include no adequate backup built into the system used, thus contributing to the problem.

- **Failure to follow the plan or SOP of record.** In this situation the plan calls for set actions or using a certain procedure. Responders fail to implement said procedure and the victim receives an injury or dies. US government agencies and the military usually suffer from this cause of action i.e. failure to utilize the National Search and Rescue Plan or they violate it. In cases where the plan or SOP establishes the standard of care, and if the agency used a lowered standard and caused injury, then liability attaches.

- **Lack of communication and general foul-up's.** In one case the rescue agency involved in a mountain SAR incident thought that the people rescued themselves and came off the mountain ...they hadn't. The rescue agency allegedly suffered miscommunication in the incident, thus calling off the search, worsening the plight of the victims.

- **Record keeping problems.** In many cases the rescuers acted properly but failed to properly document what they accomplished, thus placing them in the position of later having to defend against something which they may or may not have done. In one case an intoxicated individual fell off a cliff. His friends *(also tipsy)* climbed down the cliff to the unconscious victim and placed him in a sitting position, thus causing paralysis. The rescue team treated the victim properly but failed to note in their report the position in which they found the victim. Since the victim remained unconscious during the rescue the court applied a legal doctrine called *res ipsa loquitur (absent other evidence, negligence is the only explanation for the injury)* to allow a suit against the rescue team for negligence. The court dismissed the suit only after the partners admitted to moving the victim, who had been moving prior to the arrival of his *friends*. The court determined this movement caused the additional injury, and not the actions of the rescue team.

- **Failure to follow the existing Standard of Care**

Establish your own STANDARD OF CARE. Don't let the courts define it for you!

Search Manager: The Job of Managing a Search

Objectives:

- List the common attributes of a professional search manager.

- Discuss solutions to the common mistakes made on searches.

- Describe the key elements of managing a search.

- List and discuss common practices for motivating and keeping positive attitudes in searchers.

Major Responsibilities of a Search Manager

> Search Management training helps provide the management and leadership skills necessary to effectively coordinate the work efforts of personnel when trying to find a lost or missing person.

The Search Manager's *(or Incident Commander's)* responsibilities include:

- Overall coordination of search efforts
- Safety
- Personnel support
- Providing the equipment involved in operations

Managers need to exhibit knowledge of all phases of search operations, available resources, policies and guidelines controlling local search incident response. Essentially, the Incident Commander gets the right things done at the right time, while utilizing the right members of the search organization.

By definition, a manager's responsibilities consist of planning and directing the work of groups, monitoring their work, and taking corrective action when necessary. Search managers handle searchers directly or as the incident grows, provide direction for supervisors. The Search IC familiarizes himself or herself with all tasks supervised, but need not master each functional area. More importantly, search managers need to know how to manage workers, and motivate them to get their jobs done correctly, and protect them.

Realistically, searching for missing people usually means a person's life depends on the outcome. The days of gathering friends and neighbors to comb an area no longer exist. While we still employ those tactics, the standards for conducting searches continuously increase in the face of expanded media, maturing standards and rapid access to information. The combination of public expectations and growing liability issues, related to government agencies, initiated a new set of standards. Today's society automatically assumes and expects government and responders to know how to run a search, and that accountability lies within the law enforcement agencies. The public's viewpoint: "My loved one went missing, go find them!"

Local governments, particularly law enforcement, train everyday on a myriad of emergency situations. Some of the exercises consist of preparation for very low frequency events but with drastic consequences. The drastic consequences translate to a high risk outcome, hence the training focus. For example, police train on using their issued firearms. The decisions in a situation involving a firearm incorporate whether someone lives or dies; therefore, law enforcement officers all over the world practice with their firearms on a regular basis. They prepare themselves for the relatively infrequent disputes requiring a firearm.

Similarly, a significant number of SAR professionals from around the world admit, the majority of searches end quickly and on a positive note. Searches that end differently represent a relatively low frequency event, but with drastic and life threatening ramifications. Probabilities inevitability show that not all searches go perfectly, consequently leaving someone's life dependent on how the search effort unfolds. When the search ends up complex instead of simple a good working knowledge of both the principles of management and search planning become essential.

> Law enforcement officers and investigators tend to describe **Search Management** as a technical subject area, requiring the use of electronics, basic algebra, statistics, lost subject behavior data, probability theory and a healthy dose of leadership and management skills. They also say search Management comes across: . . . "as technical and difficult a discipline as any other in the law enforcement field."

The same principles describe effective emergency management, regardless of the response level involved. When using efficient search and rescue systems for finding small numbers of people, individuals, or responding to emergencies on a larger scale, the same management guidelines work for planning and responding. Search management capabilities and knowledge provide the basic foundation for more complex emergency operations.

Importance and Consequences of Search Management

Search management, by definition, demands leadership. Without someone in charge and *managing* the overall function, teams display confusion, and misdirected, disjointed efforts.

The function of management remains one of the most important parts of a search. So why, in many jurisdictions, does it fail to work? Lack of planing, organization, coordination and execution, describes the breakdown of the management function. Often, those in charge receive the blame.

Failure occurs from:

- Misunderstanding the nature of the job
- Inability to perform due to lack of knowledge and misinformation
- Lack of ambition or someone gets *assigned* by default
- Insufficient experience
- Shortfalls in understanding the responsibilities or liabilities that come with the job

Professionalism of the Incident Commander *(IC)* or Search Manager

In the emergency response system, what makes a good IC or Search Manager and what characteristics do executive managing other units look for? In other words, what constitutes a professional in search management?

Professionalism in any occupation continually grows through constant effort in meeting recognized professional standards. The job carries the *accepted marks* of a profession. Consider the *accepted marks* of a profession or professional worth while and instructive.

- Specialized terminology
- Specialized knowledge or technical skills
- Recognized education and training standards
- Practices based on study and research
- Sharing and networking information among peers
- High degree of personal responsibility
- Commitment to a specialized field
- Ethical practice standards
- . . . and the list goes on

Local perceptions on what makes a professional search manager or search incident IC reveals some interesting descriptions. Some characterized a Search Manager *(or IC)* as occupying a fairly unique position, both humanitarian and technical in nature. Adjectives like integrator, mediator or designer of compromise described good search ICs. Also, a person with specialized knowledge, commitment and tenacity despite adversity, or distracting social handicaps.

Chief law enforcement officers, when asked, also use words like sincerity, reliability, persistence, and follow through. The final mark, recognition by peers and fellow workers in the SAR community, set an individual apart from others. Obviously, search managers, or SAR coordinators, full time, paid or volunteer, endure an incredible demand for their time in today's busy world.

Networking with peers in other jurisdictions, at national and regional conferences, or even within their own jurisdiction seems to enhance a search manager's credibility. Networking and the exchange of information adds to the growth and credibility of a local search manager.

Dr. Thomas Drabek *(University of Colorado)* said: "a professional is a person who has knowledge that is not commonly shared." Conversely, some say professionalism is largely a state of mind! Professionalism means different things to different people, and managers sometimes successfully complete a job unprofessionally. Consensus among those who recognize professional behavior, state that professionals know their limitations and constantly try to reduce or minimize shortfalls. They exhibit self confidence, enjoy their work, and appear good at what they do. Professionals posses the familiar tools above and know how to use them to the best advantage.

Common Mistakes Made During Searches, and How to Avoid Them:

A heavy load of responsibility rests on the shoulders of the on-scene Search Manager and the people around them look for their support and direction. Observers expect them to act like a professional. The overall success or failure of a mission depends on search managers judgment, leadership capabilities and SAR experience. Therefore a list of common mistakes and how to avoid them follows:

COMMON MISTAKE #1

- No established written protocols or *standards of care* for the jurisdiction concerning the conduct of search operations for missing persons. Written SAR Plans exist, but personnel fail to follow the recommended procedures. They appear optimistic *(rather than pragmatic)* and neglect to plan for the worst case scenario, or catastrophic disaster. When emergencies arise, they expect the force of the moment to pull responders and management through.
- ***Better.*** Devise a preplan and stick to it! Training on *what if* possibilities before an emergency occurs, gives you an advantage in the event of an emergency. If you stick to the plan, you act, rather than think, first. Adopt a *standard of care* and train to it.

COMMON MISTAKE #2

- Using resources in the wrong order. Classic example: the first team responding for a missing person, rushes to find him, trampling over the clues. Then first responder resources *(such as dogs and trackers)*, try to pick up the pieces later.
- ***Better.*** Establish training standards based on operational protocols. Obtain a working knowledge of available resources and the specific advantages of using each one. Train on the proper resources *(and the order)* used in different search scenarios. Training creates the backbone of a good mission and provides discipline and direction. Know your resources by observing them train.

COMMON MISTAKE #3

- Failure to provide visible leadership using a standard, accepted management structure. Usually, this occurs in large missions with multiple agencies involved, or when a new type of emergency develops. In situations like this possible confusion often exists over command structure, who provides leadership and who provides courses of action.
- ***Better.*** Set up an effective organization. Obtain a good *(broad)* perspective of the incident. Clearly identify yourself, as the *Incident Commander*. Choose a visible location and STAY THERE. Good communication between headquarters and field operations allows for control of the whole operation.

COMMON MISTAKE #4

- No adequate system for relief of fatigued leaders on long missions. After hours in the field, the pressures of the job bring on mental fatigue long before noticeable physical fatigue. No scheduled and informed replacements further complicate the situation.
- **Better**. Ensure adequate depth of overhead staff by scheduling backup personnel for multiple shift operations from the start. Never try to run a *one-man show*. Properly document the entire incident and continuously brief staff as you go, making it easier for replacements stepping in as the mission progresses.

COMMON MISTAKE #5

- Failure to implement the system, e.g. plan for future operational time periods *(Why spend the effort planning, after all: "it will be over soon!")*.
- **Better**. Appoint a Plans Chief early in the operation, rather than later *(or not at all)*.

COMMON MISTAKE #6

- Not picking managers, e.g. failure to select people with good management qualities. Friendship longevity or founder status in an organization present unsuitable criteria for selecting individuals to fill management positions.
- **Better**. Designate knowledgeable, trained, and experienced personnel as functional managers.

COMMON MISTAKE #7

- Lack of training, education, and exercising.
- **Better**. Read research and study previous cases. Conduct regular training. Practice and exercise. Train with others.

COMMON MISTAKE #8

- Failure to plan for inter-organizational communications.
- **Better**. Consider all the *players* and complete your planning homework. Regulate communications flow with innovative options. Don't just buy more radios.

Other Common Mistakes:

- Compromising responder safety
- Poor management of specialized resources
- Unwillingness to expand the command structure and organization *(Increasing the size and scope of the search area as well as bringing in additional resources.)*

The above problems all produce the same results. They increase the risk of accidents, lead to reduced effectiveness of the mission force, and increase the possibility of failure for the search effort as a whole.

For a search manager, pre-planning, communications, staff and training, swing the balance of success toward the positive. While at the same time improving efficiency, limiting liability and making the job easier in the long run. In other words, put the incident SAR Manager in the proper position ahead of time to get the job done...and save lives.

Job Responsibilities of Managing a Search

Highly qualified Search Managers posses specific search skills and background in relevant areas, such as:

- Communications
- Air Operations
- Planning
- Running search patterns and/or related areas of specialization

In large complex search operations, search managers sometimes assume their job entails specific search skills *(unique to them)*. However, their responsibilities consist of multiple core management skills outside of their own personal repertoire, such as:

- Coordination among agencies
- Planning - *(Immediate & long term)*
- Decision-making *(In a timely manner)*
- Supervision - *(Making sure tasks get completed)*
- Evaluation - *(Time & effort expended for search success)*

- Leadership - *(Skills for different situations)*
- Logistics - *(Know where to get the right resources)*
- Communications - *(Not more, just better control & coordination)*
- Ground Operations - *(The first and best for the environment)*
- Air Operations - *(Coordinated with ground ops)*
- Knowledge of Laws, Policies - *(Local, State, and Federal)*
- Strategy/Tactics - *(Constant collaboration with SAR units in different jurisdictions and around the world)*
- People tend to question the *actions* taken by managers, rather than the functions of search involved. Result oriented search management relies heavily on the search managers ability to effectively direct other personnel

Consider: As search manager, your product consists of energy released by other people and your performance *(as search manager)* gets measured by their accomplishments, not your own.

Effectively dealing with people depends on a manager's communication skill and ability. People need to know the what, where, when, how, and why of their search responsibilities.

In addition, a competent search manager *(or SAR IC)* possesses a storehouse of in-depth knowledge. A Search Manager needs working knowledge of the following:

- The differences and similarities between wilderness, rural and urban searches for missing persons
- Responsibilities, functions and phases of government at all levels for SAR
- Resource capabilities, limitations and special considerations
- Vocabulary of terminologies and acronyms from a variety of professions involved in response
- Search planning and principles of *theory* that provide the foundation for effective search operations
- Current research on all aspects of search, vision, probability of detection, and mental programming for detection
- Legal considerations and constraints for search in wilderness, urban and rural settings
- Media organization and priorities according to media type
- Record keeping, statistics and data collection.
- Stress management and its affects on search operations
- Ad infinitum

Who Fills the Search Manager Role?

Organizations with search responsibilities need to identify, select, train, and otherwise prepare Search Managers as well as an overhead *(management)* team, who train and work well together, in advance of the anticipated missions. Use of the overhead search team concept prepares team members for future management positions and enhances the overall ability of the organization to manage more complex search operations.

Regardless of how someone got the job—appointed, selected, or volunteered, - a search manager's job demands taking responsibility for results.

Good Search Managers Apply a Mix of Leadership and Management

Search Management involves adopting different styles of leadership to save lives. One of the more significant styles, Situational Leadership as developed by professor Paul Hershey in his book *The Situational Leader*, involves recognizing all the components of a situation, the abilities of subordinates and adjusting the leadership required to most effectively get the job done.

Leadership - The Activating Ingredient

Situational Leadership. Some people possess a natural ability to *lead,* but someone needs to teach people *management*. Experience helps to create an effective manager.

> "Never tell people how to do things. Tell them what to do and they will surprise you with their ingenuity."
> - General George S. Patton.

Characteristics of the missing person, terrain, available resources, and the skill level of the search personnel varies *(often dramatically)* from search to search.

Situational Leadership works best when applying four basic components to the management equation:

1. Characteristics of the **leader**? *(Strongest attributes to best advantage.*
2. Characteristics of the **followers**? *(Trained or untrained.)*
3. Characteristics of the **organization**? *(Autonomous, dependent, independent?*
4. Characteristics of the **environment**? *(Political, isolated, community oriented?)*

Strategically, each component requires a collective mix of experience, judgment and forethought. Just as the political climate changes with new officials, policies, groups and community focus change as a result of specific occurrences. Search Managers need to stay in tune with changes and adapt their leadership styles accordingly. A knowledgeable IC lacking good interactive skills, needs to delegate that essential function. Incident Commanders with extraordinary communication skills and a good rapport with people, but lacking in-depth knowledge about search planning, need to delegate that particular function. Team effort drives successful missions.

Managing Volunteers

Managing staff from a recognized paid emergency service like police or fire requires a unique set of skills, as opposed to managing volunteers from a wide variety of professions and motivations, which involves a much clearer understanding of basic management principles. Volunteers offer value to every community. Volunteers come from all segments of society and provide services not available in the paid professional ranks. To coordinate efforts and maximize the benefits of volunteer involvement in search, managers need special planning, information sharing and a universally accepted management structure. For example, managers need consistency in terminology and acronyms to avoid misunderstandings or lack of communication during debriefing at the end of an operational period.

Any successful volunteer organization maintains flexibility, independence, acceptance of risks and a willingness to coordinate with a recognized Incident Commander and the other authorities in the jurisdiction. Expectations exist on both sides of the organization (*managers vs. members*), therefore it helps to properly verbalize those expectations so everyone operates at the same level of understanding. Successful management of volunteer organizations needs clear, consistent, and timely communication. Utilize a variety of training opportunities and regular communication to educate members, minimize confusion and clarify expectations. As a matter of course, searchers in Urban/suburban environments need even more clear-cut procedures and functions, to accomplish tasks successfully (see Chapter 23). Especially when possible criminal behavior, abductions, or other evidence issues arise.

Managing Paid Emergency Services

Managing paid uniformed emergency service personnel, *(fire, police, EMS, etc.)* while at times different than volunteers, involves some complexities of its own. Search Managers need to acknowledge these conditions to insure coordination and cooperation among agencies and organizations during a major search operation. If any multi-organizational response at the local level meets the following conditions, chances for mission success grow substantially.

Consensus of Responsibility and Role Specification

All personnel, no matter which agency, need to know their specific job requirements and where they fit into the multi-organizational structure. Shared knowledge increases coordination and enhances the integration of tasks across organizations, facilitating clear lines of authority and eliminating conflict.

Network Integration

Network with paid emergency response services, agency representatives, and specialized resources ahead of time, not when you show up on-scene for a search. Use pre-planning meetings to meet the players, and participate in specialized training,

Communication

Effective response and management requires communication within and among diverse organizations before and during search incidents. Organizations need to communicate what specialized roles and capabilities they perform and subsequently accomplish when tasked. Changing conditions, status of other resources, or critical information affecting decisions needs immediate communication back to the management team. When adrenaline flows, SAR personnel from all disciplines tend to use their own service acronyms and terminology, thus leading to confusion and/or misunderstandings during planning or in briefings/debriefings.

Simply getting the facts straight and delivering them accurately falls far short of describing good communication. Good communication consists of common sense, an awareness of the audience and the implications of decisions made, as well as a willingness to accept responsibility for their impact on people and the life saving functions performed during the incident. The IC creates and communicates a vision of success.

Flexibility and Capability to Improvise

Sometimes the situation dictates a change in plans, elements, standardization of procedures, or tasks. Inexperienced *(or ineffective)* managers view plans as rigid and unyielding. However, effective response to SAR operations requires a degree of flexibility, adaptive thinking, and the ability to improvise. Especially in the urban environment. When new scenarios present themselves, adapt the plan.

Establish and Keep Ground Rules

Leaders and a managers need to create and keep ground rules, as well as establish expectations. Set boundaries and let subordinates know their limits from the beginning.

Some Specific Leadership Considerations for Search Management

- Identify key people in the management team. Always identify and obviously mark specific ICS roles (Hats, vests, shirts, etc.).
- Everyone needs to know the designated IC i.e. *Who's in charge.*
- Exert authority, take action and assume responsibility for decisions, in a nonthreatening manner.
- Delegate and use subordinates when the organization/search efforts increase
- Identify key function locations within base camp

Providing Motivation and Incentive to Overhead Team Members and Searchers

Behavioral scientists discovered long ago that social acceptance in a group and belonging to a prestigious group provide important motivating factors for sustained difficult tasks. Also, conscientious search managers pay close attention to the people carrying out difficult search functions in the field. Basic needs such as nutritious food, warm or functional clothing and adequate, comfortable shelter help in keeping the positive attitude necessary for effective search. The best search managers frequently inquire about these and other basic needs for all the personnel working in the SAR incident. The following sound practices insure motivation, positive attitude and incentives for all team members:

- When appropriate, give people praise
- Never take all the credit, share it with everyone involved
- Show that you care about team members in the organization
- Avoid playing favorites and never criticize someone in front of others
- Recognize prejudices and bias of personnel

- Take responsibility for other's actions
- Build independent thinking and actions
- Mentor members and help them grow
- Diligently keep track of people and tasks
- Let people use every moment as a learning moment
- Exhibit confidence, not ego or egotism
- Develop the capability to improvise and show ingenuity
- Delegate important tasks and let people carry them through

What Do SAR Volunteers Expect from Search Managers?

- An awareness and understanding of their capabilities and expertise
- To clearly identify their mission and expectations
- An estimation of the duration of services
- A briefing on the overall plan of action
- An opportunity to provide input into search planning sessions
- To provide adequate briefings and current information
- Adequately debrief members
- Involve members by providing them with constructive critiques
- Ability to read a topographical map

What Should the On-scene Search Manager Expect from SAR Volunteers?

- Organization and structure of functional positions
- Discipline to accomplish assigned tasks and debrief accordingly
- Reliability
- Cooperation with responding agencies and organizations
- Advice about optimum deployment
- High performance standards directly related to high training standards
- Proper clothing and equipment for any climatic conditions
- Self-sufficiency for at least 72 hours
- Ability to navigate accurately and record it on a map precisely

Continuing Operational Problems in Search

- No assessment of the real scope of local SAR incidents in the planning process
- Failure to use the right resources in the right order
- No visible leadership
- No proper immediate action after the first notice
- Failure to delegate key functions
- Poor interagency communication
- Failure to properly document search activities
- No plan for the use of unexpected high numbers of volunteers
- Adversarial, or negative relationships with the media
- No backup or relief for overhead management team members
- Poor management of specialized resources
- Lack of education and training about new search management concepts and tactics

---

From the Research:

Dr. Thomas Drabek's research on *Emergent Search and Rescue Networks (1979, 1982)* at the University of Colorado Natural Hazards Research Center:

The five most common operational problems encountered during emergency response are well documented:

1. Ambiguity of authority
2. Poor utilization of specialized resources
3. Lack of good interagency communications
4. Unplanned media relations
5. Inability to deal with unplanned volunteer response

Establish a Search Management Kit

Consider including the following:

- Standard Operating Procedures *(SOPs)*
- Checklists for contacts & resource designation *(Directory)*
- Maps *(The larger scale and laminated if possible) Topographical of jurisdictional areas or aerial photos (if available)*
- State, Provincial, county, or borough road maps- State, Provincial or Sectional Aeronautical Chart(s)
- Map board with clear plastic or acetate overlay for current map sizes
- Tools *(straight edge, compass, protractor, map scale converter, grease pencils, dry erase pens, etc.)*
- 8 color fine point overhead projection markers *(water soluble) - black, brown, green, purple, red, blue, yellow, orange.* 4 color fine point overhead projection markers *(permanent/alcohol soluble)*
- 4 color highlighters *(pink, green, yellow, orange)*
- Ball point pens, #2 pencils and writing pads
- Roll of scotch tape with dispenser, roll of duct tape and roll of masking tape
- Overlays or acetates for operational period designation. Minimum size should be 18"X18", or better yet, the size of the topographical map
- Mgmt. position indicators. *(vests, arm bands, hats, etc.)*
- Multicolored file folders *(some pre-labeled - TO BE DONE - TASKS IN PROGRESS - TASKS COMPLETED, etc)*
- Flipchart and/or briefing board
- Laptop *(if available)* and software for incident mgmt. and resource tracking software
- Portable radios or cell phones
- Area estimator from land management agency or scaled template for the search area size *(Romer)*
- LAT-LONG and UTM plotters
- Hazard vulnerability analysis
- Jurisdiction's Search Management Preplan
- SAR Management Handbooks, Lost Person Behavior etc.
- Nurse's or physician's guide on prescription drugs and/or a contact pharmacist name and phone number
- Laptop computer(s) and software (PowerPoint, Word processor, spreadsheets etc.)
- ICS and/or other locally used organizational structure forms
- Clipboards
- Digital voice recorder/cellphone app.
- Stapler and extra staples plus staple remover
- Personal activity log, notebook, and recorder
- Milk crates or small plastic containers to organize/store files
- Resource status and management board for T-Cards or other tracking systems

Conclusion

A Search Manager's responsibilities include management and leadership. Both consist of complicated decisions, non-intuitive solutions, difficult choices and certainly exposure to liability. The job requires both personal skills and knowledge about people, management and search planning. Experienced Search Managers develop knowledge not commonly shared. Many factors determine the level of professionalism a search manger possesses; not, whether or not the missing person turns up during the search. The bottom line: a person's life may very well depend on how a Search Manager pulls all of this together. Personalizing key elements of leadership and effective management then using individual attributes combined with the basic principles of search planning really make a difference.

Let People Know your Expectations and Capabilities

Notes:

SAR Vulnerability Assessment & The Importance of Statistics

Objectives:

- Explain the importance and specific components of a search and rescue vulnerability assessment for a local area or jurisdiction.

- Explain the utility of a vulnerability assessment in the planning process.

- Apply the concept of visual perception of environmental risks encountered by the general population in the community, (risk mapping) to selling SAR program capability and the planning process.

What makes up a *Vulnerability Assessment* and why bother with it?

Search managers need an accurate assessment of the local SAR problems occurring in an area before crafting a SAR preplan. A SAR Hazard Assessment determines the operational capabilities and deficiencies of an organization, agency or program. Local jurisdictions need to evaluate capabilities for locating missing or lost persons, rescuing stranded or injured individuals, finding victims of abduction, recovering remains, and assisting law enforcement in locating crime scene evidence. To accomplish this, counties, cities or SAR organizations develop comprehensive plans addressing the following:

- Numbers, types, and frequencies of current and potential local SAR incidents
- Identification of equipment, human and informational resources, as well as training requirements
- An assessment of current capabilities and requirements versus future potentials
- An assessment of the current jurisdictional SAR PrePlan
- An annual review and assessment of operational capabilities or SAR exercise activities

Proper documentation forms the foundation for a Vulnerability Assessment:

- **Mitigation of risks**. If a local jurisdiction experiences ongoing, or recurring incidents, then studying them formally pinpoints those issues for the record. The document needs to identify preventive strategies or measures, and when unforeseen circumstances affect response.

- **Vulnerability based training activities**. Jurisdictions or local organizations often train on what they think constitutes the most likely occurrences, with little or no formal basis for that decision. A complete vulnerability assessment identifies: mission types, frequency of call-outs, types of injuries, equipment utilized, and numbers of personnel in a comprehensive report. This allows jurisdictions to use that vital information for needed justification *(e.g. funding, additional skills, community outreach)* and the focus of SAR team, organization and/or individual training requirements.

- **Response SOPs and resource allocation**. SAR teams usually use previous incidents to develop standard operating procedures. This foundation for SOPs presents a realm of possibilities based on local history coupled with likely future events. Usually, jurisdictions deal with locally available resources and anything outside that capability responds when called upon at the State/Provincial and national level. For quick and easy notification or alert responses, SAR teams need to identify their regularly needed capabilities for resources at the local, regional, state/provincial and national levels.

- **Rescue and recovery procedures and identification of resources.** Hazardous environmental conditions require specialized resources. Smaller communities or even those with less frequent search activity, often lack specialized resources for immediate deployment or for backup in protracted operations. Individual SAR teams need to identify these special resources ahead of time and coordinate with them for notification and call-out when needed. Preestablished protocols defined in the SAR assessment, deal with any associated costs, responsibilities, call-out procedures and financial arrangements.

The SAR Assessment consists of a systematic investigation of search and/or rescue situations that occur regularly in an area. Jurisdictions then append this report/analysis to a SAR Preplan.

Establishing an Assessment consists of analyzing the following factors:

- History of the area, including:
  - Size of the jurisdiction, land ownership, primary land use in the area.
  - Analysis of past incident reports.
  - Probable and possible types of incidents based on past or projected activities
  - Geographic factors
  - Weather, altitude, length of seasons, specific Eco-region, vegetation, precipitation
- Demographic information such as:
  - Growing, stable, or declining population.
  - Development of retiree or senior accommodations
  - Changes and developments in leisure and recreational activities
  - Changes in seasonal or tourist populations
  - Developments based on local attractions
- Availability of resources used to solve potential problems such as:
  - Specialized skills located within the jurisdiction
  - Mutual aid from adjacent jurisdictions
  - Training standards for basic and specialized skills

> **IMPORTANT NOTE:**
> In unique, unusual, or particularly dangerous situations, when pointing to resource or training shortfalls, the SAR Vulnerability Assessment *(SVA)* report needs continuous updating. In other words, update the SVA after fixing a discovered shortfall! It also justifies any additional training requirements, backs up liability safeguards and serves to help with purchasing or acquiring new tools and equipment. While the SVA fails to provide a full safeguard from liability, it shows that the jurisdiction recognized the hazard and plans to make changes accordingly.

The Biggest Benefits of the SVA include:

- Justification for management decisions altering programming and staffing assignments
- Identification of potential trends, future funding needs, resource allocation and training

Using your Vulnerability Assessment During a Search Incident

Identification of search and/or rescue incident types:

- If the incident lies within my jurisdictional assessment then the information in the SVA lays out the resources and issues identified to complete an adequate response.
- If the incident presents a unique situation *(first time occurrence)*. What makes it unique?
- If a unique situation presents itself, review the key factors to aid in planning. What special resources need considering to complete the task?
  - Environmental hazards for the searchers *(e.g. steep terrain, dense brush, snakes, animal traps)*
  - Resource access to the area
  - Geographic features that funnel, impede or attract the missing subject

REMEMBER: Use the SVA as a valuable tool in the information gathering phase of any search. It contains a synopsis of what occurred in the jurisdiction previously and what might occur in the future. The SVA includes demographic information reflecting people at risk not only in the community, but also people involved in seasonal outdoor activities. It contains geographic information *(maps, aerial photographs or sources of digital data)* on locations for equipment caches, communications dead-spots, hazardous areas such as cliffs, elevations, steep terrain and locations used for specific activities, etc. Additional data usually includes the availability of resources, time frame for response, time on-scene and potential shortfalls in local capabilities. The usefulness of the SVA directly relates to the effort and the number of people involved in preparing it.

Look for information or data helpful in planning the search or in the investigation.

Geographic Information:

- Key locations and/or logistical routes

Demographic Information:

- Numbers of people using area - specific activities, general experience level and/or competence in the outdoors

Location of Activity (Visual Information):

- Terrain analysis and location of hazards in the area *(Hazard risk map)*

Example Components of a Potential SAR Vulnerability Assessment:

- Access routes into remote areas or private property
- Lists and locations of city open spaces and parks *(and services available)*
- Specialized training required to respond for unique situations
- Normal populations and seasonal fluctuations that generate SAR activity
- Locations and detail of senior care centers or assisted living facilities, skilled nursing facilities and other health care facilities
- Lists and locations of city, town and rural walking or cycle trails
- Location and detail of boarding and care facilities, including shelters, hospitals and halfway houses
- Location and detail of day care centers *(both child and adult)*
- Lists of local transit depots, routes and contacts
- Attraction areas for subjects of all ages *(e.g. playgrounds, community centers, skateboard parks, arcades or computer internet access locations)*
- Lists of agencies, organizations or facilities dealing with lost children
- Locations and mapping of high crime zones
- Hazardous areas such as industrial complexes, construction sites or manufacturing facilities
- Statistical data comparing run-a-way and lost children in the area *(e.g. numbers, circumstances, local influences, etc.)*
- Annual numbers of incidents by category and location
- Communications dead spots and locations for relays or repeaters
- Shortest, longest and average length of incidents.
- Nearest volunteer support SAR teams to the local area
- Annual training conducted for SAR in the jurisdiction
- Training needed to answer the SAR mission load
- Annual cost of SAR in the jurisdiction - how much volunteers contribute *(equivalent work hours)*
- Types of injuries or first aid problems, and/or deaths
- Numbers of volunteers and responders for SAR

Example from local SVA:

Example terrain & search mission analysis

> After researching all prior searches in this area for the last six years, as a SAR team, we discovered that the PLS frequently fell on or near SR-165 between milepost #6 or #7 *(Note: A well known DOT gravel pit at milepost 6.8)*. To the west of SR-165 a steep hill drops down into the Voights Creek drainage. If a lost subject follows the hill down into the drainage, he/she may locate the Voights Creek Road, which parallels Voights Creek . . . In the last

> six years, the Sheriff Department, located the lost persons on or near the Voights Creek Road over half of the time.
> **Pierce County, Washington SAR Preplan**

Clear Benefits of this Assessment for a Local Jurisdiction Include:

- Realistic and vital pre-planning for any search and/or rescue incident
- A comprehensive assessment establishes both search and rescue resource needs
- Direction and emphasis for preventive and mitigative programs in both search and/or rescue incidents
- An organized and clearly articulated incentive for local SAR recruitment and response efforts
- Enables SAR coordinators to set priorities and goals appropriate for the local need
- Provides a written tool to raise the level of understanding for key public officials controlling budgetary emphasis for SAR response
- Organized properly, the document justifies management decisions altering programming and staffing assignments
- Reducing exposure to liability
- Potential trends and future needs for funding, resource allocation and training

Developing A Vulnerability Assessment

Step 1
Identification of Incident types:

Compile a list of mission types known to occur or likely to occur. Some incidents readily identify themselves due to past history or recent missions, but others prove more elusive. For example, some unique rescue situations may seem irrelevant at first, but with population and activity increasing in the area, they grow more realistic.

Consult with neighboring jurisdictions for maximum benefit in this initial step.

Step 2
Collection of Information:

Research and gather all the necessary information for the assessment. If possible, use all the agencies and organizations involved in local SAR operations. Online newspaper archives and older hard copy files present an incredible source of information.

Types of information to collect and compile:

Geographic Information. Show the physical impact of missions on logistics, communications, and operations in general, by identifying the size of the jurisdiction, location in the state, region, province or country with respect to outside resources, climate, terrain features, possible environments, etc. This provides a base of information for the rest of the assessment.

Demographic Information. This provides vital information for determining the potential risk to populations or outdoor users encountered in the pursuit of certain activities. How many people frequent these environments, and what kinds of activities occupy them? How many people visit the local jurisdiction every year from outside the area? How many missions come from defined numbers of outdoor users? In addition, information about the local area also helps.

Examples:

- Number of senior citizen / convalescent facility incidents per year
- Population fluctuations due to seasons, celebrations, holidays, etc.
- Future incentives for more outdoor users in the area *(Developments, recreational areas, new parks, new sports, unique outdoor activities)*
- Mental health or other institution incidents per year and unusual recreational attractions in the area

Step 3

Location of Activities *(Visual Information):*

Every jurisdiction consists of a mix of factors for describing and analyzing vulnerability. As a final information gathering step in putting together your assessment, develop a comprehensive risk map visually depicting the total mission potential for your area *(sometimes called a measle or data point map)*. This accomplishes several important functions:

- Identifies potential high incident areas
- Provides the basis for resource allocation and backup support
- Identifies potential high activity seasons in specific geographic areas
- Identifies the geographic need for public education and information
- Presents a useful tool for orienting and motivating executive policy makers

Start with a plain map of the area. Reproduce the outline of your jurisdiction on numerous transparent sheets and attach them together so that they overlap. Each overlay identifies an incident type and the location of the missions or anticipated mission *(Use this process based on time of year as well)*. The combination of all missions on all the transparencies, one upon the other depicts the total risk *(Note: GIS technology, SMART boards® and mapping software etc. all help tremendously in creating risk maps, if available)*.

Step 4

Development of the SAR Vulnerability Report:

After gathering the information and analyzing it, write a report and distribute it to the appropriate individuals in the jurisdiction hierarchy. Make this report a part of the Search and Rescue Operational PrePlan.

We suggest the following format for discussion areas as a guide for the Vulnerability Report:

Assumptions:

This section describes the status of the local, state/provincial/territorial and federal response capabilities in the area. It also describes time frames for response and assistance from outside resources. Thus, setting the stage for local response.

Program emphasis and justification:

A section describing the current status of the SAR program at the local level. This includes anything relating to local capabilities. Training, volunteer organizations and status, numbers of incidents per year, trends in the local area, and response times for outside resources. It even presents SAR teams with anticipated incident numbers based on current activities.

Facts bearing on the SAR problem:

This section presents any extenuating circumstances existing in the local area. For example: jurisdictional issues related to federal lands, high use of local areas for recreational purposes, protected areas, First Nation Lands/Reservations, or even impending development of recreation or retirement living facilities.

Discussion:

The discussion section of the document examines both positive and negative aspects of the SAR program in the area. This portion of the report needs to include a frank and honest assessment of the local SAR capability, including both the training and response skills of all responding resources. Key issues include things like tourist impact creating the majority of SAR situations, increasing budgetary expenditures for a growing number of SAR incidents or lack of time and money for technical training. Explain these issues in a clear, candid manner. Create detailed documentation charting all possible options, and the potential repercussions of those options.

Conclusions:

The vulnerability assessment needs to keep away from finger pointing or presenting an opportunity to lay blame on personnel for past problems. Systematically lay out all the facts, building logical conclusions and rationales for the course of action that the jurisdiction, agency or organization intends to embark upon. Possible responses to the assessment range from, more training, additional personnel, changes in policy, no change from the current programs, or a host of justifiable strategies including more comprehensive planning.

Recommendations:

While annual budgetary funds spread thinner and thinner at the local level, the liability of responding to emergency situations still falls on the responsible jurisdictions. This assessment will logically set the stage with facts and conclusions for realistic planning, entirely based on research instead of supposition. As an integral part of the recommendation, the assessment needs to include, a cost/benefit analysis including issues of liability, legal responsibility and public expectations.

Why Keep Statistical Data?

- Tracking the total amount of money spent on Search and Rescue annually.
- Tracking the total number of Search and Rescue missions each year.
- Who represents typical SAR subjects in the jurisdiction? The 14 year old boy or the 54 year old hunter?
- What type of activities repeatedly activate SAR responses?
- What prevents a SAR response? When a person goes missing, what path of actions follow? Distances traveled, etc.?

Individuals involved in Search and Rescue constantly develop new tools and techniques to help save lives. For example, research in everything from hypothermia to better rescue techniques and equipment, all form an effort to raise the *effectiveness* of SAR. Others research areas which require gathering and comparing a cross-section of Search and Rescue data.

Experts in the field of search, such as Ken Hill, Bill Syrotuck and Robert Koester graphically illustrate the value of this research in their works. They show what happens when they gather and analyze helpful information.

As early as 1975, The National Association For Search And Rescue asked Bob Mattson *(National SAR School)*, committee chair for the specific purpose of designing a SAR Data Collection System which served the needs of various organizations from local teams to researchers. At first glance the task seemed relatively simple: it consisted of obtaining a large, broad based sampling of mission report forms used at the time; perhaps an abbreviated form of 20-30 items most commonly used on a search and consolidated into one form for use by all interested parties. The word went out, the sample forms came in and problems started.

Surprisingly, nobody agreed on what made up the right essential information. Each form looked completely different, not only in appearance and format but more importantly in specific areas of information requested. In fact, the date appeared on each form making it the only common piece of information, and even the date caused trouble. Groups argued on whether they wanted the date of the mission or the date they filled out the form. Obviously the need for a different approach prevailed.

Conversations and communication with experts in the field of data collection all echoed the same message:

- Determine how you use each item of information *before* you decide to collect it.
- To design a proper collection system *(the form)* you need to know what questions you want answered.
- In short, determine what purpose the data serves.

With these principles in mind, the committee developed a questionnaire designed to ask knowledgeable SAR staff what kind of information they find most useful to overall Search and Rescue efforts. Then, hoping to receive feedback from a representative body of the SAR community, they distributed the four page questionnaire to over 100 personnel which resulted in 66 responses.

The questionnaire identified specific items of information as *useful* and some as *essential* but more importantly, five major areas of interest in types of data emerged:

The Magnitude of the SAR problem:

The desire for this type of information allows for budgeting, funding, legislative program assistance and grants. Incident data in particular, numbers of incidents, budgets and efforts aid in defining problems and soliciting support from the local county commissioners or representatives at the State/Provincial and national levels. Convincing someone to give you help usually fails if you neglect to tell them a problem exists in the first place. We need answers to questions such as: How many SAR incidents occur annually? How many hours each incident lasts? How much each individual mission and the items needed for each one cost? How many resources each mission uses *(manpower and equipment)*? If search personnel gain a better understanding of these unknown quantities then they possess the ability to grasp the scope of any Search and Rescue situation across the nation or even around the world.

Preventative Education (PSAR) - Preventive Search and Rescue:

Fortunately, dedicated people work hard to put Search and Rescue out of business. Traditionally, mitigation or prevention programs help to reduce injuries and suffering for outdoor enthusiasts. However, as previously mentioned, the listed categories of missing and lost people continues to grow. Mountain bikers, autistic individuals, dementia patients, child and or adult abductions, etc. Answering a few questions will potentially allow the community to reduce potential incidents. But just who is this *potential* missing or lost subject? What caused the incident in the first place, and can we prevent it from happening again? Land management agencies, volunteer groups and dedicated individuals constantly work on prevention, but as responding SAR personnel gain more knowledge about specific subjects and their natural tendencies or behaviors, their abilities to act in response to future incidents improves.

Subject Behavior:

If, in spite of our preventive efforts, people get lost or continue to go missing, what happens? What decisions evolve in response to a lost subject's situation. In what direction and to what distance will subjects travel in different behavioral categories? Will victims travel shorter or longer distances in the urban environment? In short, what datum provides the best chance of finding these missing persons? Until his death, Bill Syrotuck led the way in demonstrating the value of using historical subject behavior as a tool in search planning. Through statistical analysis of case histories, we obtain the ability to define high probability areas in which to locate missing or lost subjects. After Syrotuck's initial work, researchers expanded the field of lost person behavior dramatically. Robert Koester's ISRID *(International Search and Rescue Incident Database)* presents an excellent example of ongoing international collection and collation of behavior data from around the world (Reference *www.dbs-sar.com*). Koester's book and ISRID database (Lost Subject Behavior) created a window for search managers to predict the behavior of similarly situated people. By accurately and faithfully recording the necessary information we contribute to this ever growing capability.

SARCAT - The Search and Rescue Data Collection and Analysis Tool

The latest tool in Robert Koester's research and development efforts for SAR involves a web hosted computer application that simplifies the collection and analysis of any team's or agencies' SAR data. The the new application strives to make the collection of search subject behavior data easy, accurate and standardized.

The application is still under development at this writing, but in its final form, it will posses a world wide map interface with topographic, street and aerial imagery with drag and drop icons to mark key locations like the Initial Planning Point, find location, PLS, LKP, as well as intended and actual routes. The data collected by the program will upload into other programs and most importantly, into the International Search and Rescue Incident Database (ISRID) (*See Chapter 8 on SAR Resources for further information*).

Preplanning:

The most essential aspects of any Search and Rescue team's organizational structure. A preplan improves the effectiveness of a team by making certain critical decisions in advance of the actual mission. This conserves time, effort and resources for a more efficient operation. To improve, we need data about how incidents run. For example: problems usually occur in what areas? This means on a regional or national level as well as in our own county or area of operation. The answers help us recognize and possibly reduce certain objective hazards, as well as determine what types of resources we need and where to locate the resources.

Organizations also use this information to find out if local notification procedures and response times work effectively. Unusual types of incidents, tend to need specialized training to increase effectiveness. Or, perhaps specialized medical training to address more prevalent injuries or problems? Do we need to acquire special equipment or to develop specific skills? Every SAR team needs to ask themselves: *What makes our SAR response more effective?*

Historical Record:

A the end of every SAR incident when the dust settles, retain a record of the entire operation. Keeping records of each incident provides SAR teams with a historical perspective and forms a possible basis of comparison for new SAR methods and techniques. Mission critiques provide very valuable information for future reference if questions about the incident happen to arise.

With the increasing emphasis on legal and liability issues, no single form records all the necessary information. Therefore any forms filled out during an incident, interview notes, regions of probability, segments, team assignments, rational for strategy, operational period maps, radio logs, newspaper clippings, and any other relevant items to the search need safe storage. In addition, SAR teams need to keep forms with a clear, accurate and concise synopses of the mission for future reference and review. To eliminate confusion, use standard forms, for example via ASTM at https://www.astm.org/Standards/F1767.htm or as identified by the emergency response system in the jurisdiction.

For free examples and templates download the PDF versions of the 2nd edition of the *Threat Hazard Identification and Risk Assessment Guide* and the associated *Supplement1: Toolkit*, respectively at:

https://www.fema.gov/media-library/assets/documents/26335
and
https://www.fema.gov/media-library/assets/documents/26338.
.

Chapter 6   The SAR Vulnerability Assessment

SAR Vulnerability Assessment Flowchart

Figure 6-1 SAR Vulnerability Assessment Overview Flowchart

Figure 6-2 The Threat and Hazard Identification and Risk Assessment (THIRA) Process as outlined by the FEMA Comprehensive Preparedness Guide 201.

Notes:

Preplanning: Developing a Functional Documented Preplan

Objectives:

- Discuss the Relevance, Benefits, and Steps in Preparation of a documented SAR Preplan

- Discuss the Importance of Preplanning to the Success of a Search Mission

- List the Elements of a Preplan

- Develop the skills and knowledge to create a Functional SAR Preplan

A Plan:

In SAR a plan represents the local jurisdiction's or organization's preparation in a uniquely defined area to meet a specific event or situation. Responsible parties develop plans in writing and use them as an institutional record, and although based on assumptions about specific conditions, the best plans tend to change over time. Strong response units continuously estimate, analyze and review plans, then refine them to keep abreast of changing circumstances and current requirements. The planning process outlined in the Community Preparedness Guide *(CPG 101 published by FEMA)* lists Search and Rescue under ESF#9 using the Emergency Support Function format to plug into the jurisdictions's emergency operations plan *(EOP)*. While the CPG 101 document outlines the over-arching EOP process suggested by the U.S. government, the following outlines the specifics of the Search and Rescue portions of an EOP specific to ESF #9: Search and Rescue.

NOTE: Although many jurisdictions follow the planning requirements of ESF #9 to deal with catastrophic incidents (i.e. flooding, hurricanes, earthquakes, building collapse etc.), some leave the day to day missing person search to local law enforcement without addressing day to day search operations in the Preplan. From the Federal level all the way through the local response the ESF#9 framework provides the enabling requirements and structure for *all* Search and Rescue activities, including law enforcement or any other agency. This requires coordination between Emergency Management and that agency in the creation of the Preplan.

Three categories of planning documents for SAR

Management Documents

The umbrella under which preparation of the operational preplan evolves, containing policies, authorities, responsibilities, legal constraints and requirements.

Standard Operating Procedures *(S.O.P's)*

Explicit instructions such as what to carry, how to run search patterns, how to tie knots, etc. Resources utilize these references regularly in order to develop a proficiency in certain skills or abilities.

The Preplan

The preplan outlines an overall approach to search operations, indicates guidelines for actions taken at each stage of a search, and recommends standard procedures followed in carrying out various options. It also, clearly defines the responsibilities of all staff positions identified in the SAR organization.

The Documented Plan for Search and Rescue:

When a search incident activates the system, reality and practical experience tells us very few individuals consult a written plan, let alone follow one. Most preplans lack sufficient content to get the job done on-scene. Preplans represent a written record of intentions and agreements. It serves as a set of rules designed for conducting an operation for a lost or missing person.

Preplans outline an overall approach to search and rescue operations. They indicate guidelines for particular actions taken at each stage of a search, and recommend standard procedures to follow when carrying out various options. It clearly defines responsibilities for all personnel involved.

Those responsible for the incident need the management constraints of the jurisdiction entrenched in their minds *before* the incident occurs. Responders need the skills professed by the *How To* manuals well learned and rehearsed ahead of time to respond effectively. The written preplans for SAR operations represent the *standard of care* in document form, to provide key personnel with reminders about policy, procedures, guidelines and technical data during the actual process of the search operations. If properly maintained, SAR Preplans consist of the SAR vulnerability assessment, resource listings and other informational tools appended for easy reference.

Preplanning, an Essential function of Management:

Pre-planning focuses on future decisions. It deals with two major aspects of search management:

- The future *(i.e. What if and when?)*
- Maintaining a consistent policy of *state of the art* protocols to ensure missing subject orientation

Why Plan for Search and Rescue?

Pre-planning makes a unit more *effective, efficient* and *economical.* Remember, someone's life depends on the effectiveness of your search or rescue efforts. Realistically, planning creates good management and decision making under pressure. SAR operations demand correct decisions prior to the incident and operate with the smallest amounts possible of money, human resources, and *time.*

NOTE: When a crises forces people to choose alternative courses of action, people sometimes choose based on incorrect assumptions or worse yet, guess. To prevent this, develop preplans, Standard Operating Procedures *(SOPs)*, and checklists.

"SAR preparedness and preplanning involves more than fancy paraphernalia and a notebook of telephone numbers. . . . The preplan is an operational guide that, if designed and implemented correctly, will help introduce order to the chaos and furor accompanying the initial notification for help."

- Tim J. Setnicka, *Wilderness Search and Rescue,* 1980

A Revisit to the How and Why of Lawsuits

A written plan establishes a *standard of care*, as described in Chapter 4. Here, we list again, a few of the primary factors causing negligence in many SAR cases around the world:

- **Assignment:** Assigning a person to a job he or she lacks training, skill, and qualifications for *(All Personnel qualifications to get the job done).*
- **Entrustment:** Ordering or permitting personnel to use a piece of equipment or device with which they lack training.
- **Training:** Not providing training for personnel according to their duties, assignment, work task, rank, equipment used, or otherwise. Providing sloppy or inadequate training.
- **Direction:** Failure to provide standard operating procedures, rules and regulations, instructions, guidelines, and enforcement of the same, which relate to the operation of the organization and the conduct of its activities.
- **Documentation:** Failure to properly or completely document all activities such as searches, training, equipment inspections, etc.

All of the above cause liability!

Government officials and responders help to free themselves and the unit from potential liability if:

- The unit wrote a reasonable *standard of care* and followed through with it. No deviations *(That means the written PrePlan)*.
- The organization acted properly in their official capacity.
- The entity operated within their scope of authority.
- Personnel executed the plan reasonably and prudently based on the established standard.

Tangible Benefits of a Preplan

- Preplans identify all probable resources needed *(Try not to get carried away!)*.
- Describes the capabilities of all resources.
- Preplans provide a central repository for information, identify potential hazards and problems as well as eliminate inefficiencies.
- Mitigates possible hazards.
- Takes advantage of resources *(prior agreements, funding, etc.)*.
- Ensures proper mobilization and deployment of resources.
- Guides new personnel with recommendations and checklists.
- Allows for development and change of procedures.
- Prevents omissions through redundant checks and balances.
- Aids in prevention by identifying the major causes of SAR incidents.
- Establishes a means to gather and disseminate information *(i.e. forms, reports etc.)*.
- Assigns responsibilities and tasks.
- Establishes the chain of command and organizational structure.
- Identifies a need for training and operational practice with regular review.
- Provides for common terminology and definitions.

REMEMBER

Use the Preplan as a management tool. It provides information, guidelines, and technical data during a mission.

- When preparing a preplan, evaluate it based upon the following factors:
  - Completeness
  - Simplicity
  - Adaptability
  - Well defined authority

- Making a plan work depends on the ability to vividly paint clear mental images of the plan in the minds of the personnel who use it.
- Preplans produce the blueprint that establishes responses to SAR situation
- All key leaders need a familiarity with the contents
- Clearly establish legal responsibilities and areas of responsibility
  - Know your neighboring jurisdictions and emergency services *(capabilities etc.)*
  - Federal and state/provincial/territorial SAR plans
  - Local organizations and responsibilities

- Mutual Aid Agreements *(MAAs)*

  - Put everything in writing
  - Clearly state who is in charge
  - Prepare a list of those available to assist
  - Describe money/liability arrangements
  - Designate who handles the media
  - Practice working together *(training)*
  - Review by legal counsel

- In the final analysis, an EOP's format is acceptable if users understand it, are comfortable with it, and can extract the information they need. Focus on a usable format, making it easy to reference.

- Keep the document **simple:**

  - Limit excessive words, make it clear and to the point
  - No duplication of other documents, use references instead
  - Short, simple explanations
  - As the plan writer, put yourself in the place of the intended user

- Keep the plan **flexible:**
  - Continually review and update
  - Make it applicable to all situations
  - Easily adapted to other situations, not emergency specific
  - Try not to use specific names
  - **Flexible, but substantive enough to complete the job**

Consider these Major Influences When Developing a Preplan

The following subjects need consideration in the actual preparation of a Plan. Multiple sources need to contribute the critical information necessary to make a plan functional and realistic. Try to gather input from all appropriate sources.

NEVER PLAN ALONE

General components of a comprehensive Preplan include:

- **SAR Vulnerability Assessment (SVA) and Risk Analysis** - Records what occurred in the past. What kinds of people used the area. Where they went. What kind of activities they involved themselves in, and how they got in trouble. The environment constantly changes and new types of activities evolve. So, something that never happened in the past, might happen in the future. Consider all likely possibilities and how the organization will respond to each one. Look at individual scenarios seriously, but reasonably. Simply including every remote possibility creates a more complex and less useful plan. The plans need some flexibility plus definitive instructions for practical guidance.
- **The Area** - Consider all aspects and influences, to include; terrain, weather, hazards, attractions, facilities, etc.
- **The Management Constraints** - The Preplan needs to avoid conflict with legal constraints, authorities, policies, etc. The Preplan refers to these constraints, and supplements them with operational details. It provides for the implementation of those policies and procedures.
- **External Influences** - Landowners, cooperating agencies, politics, the media, etc.
- **The Organization** - Internal chain of command, personnel capabilities, etc.
- **Emergent Conditions** - The most important consideration of all based on past experience and observations. This section dictates the types of processes used to complete the job, all of the management constraints, past Preplans, organizational structure, etc. When an incident breaks, the chances of things happening outside the plan increase. Instead of focusing on the IDEAL plan focus instead on REALITY. Good plans strive to overcome what actually happens, the undesirable, and build upon that which contributes to effectiveness and efficiency

Consider the following:

- What an actual chain of command looks like in an emergency.
- What informal communication links emerge?
- Who takes control; and makes decisions?
- Response time of resources; their actual capabilities.

The operational Preplan tends not to address each of these influences directly. In other words, the Preplan becomes more cumbersome by including an extensive history of missions, or repeating the management constraints. These influences, collectively provide the parameters and determine the ingredients for the Preplan.

But it needs CONTROL! Compare actual activity with the Predetermined plans. If the plan fails to account for the factors present during operations, then modify it or write a new one.

A good plan today beats a perfect plan tomorrow

Characteristics of a Good Preplan

- **Format** - If your agency uses a prescribed format, use it, of course. The quality of an operational Preplan runs independent of its format. Format consists of convenience and style; but, content

adapts to any format. One serious consideration, though, the format needs to allow for easy updating and revision *(See Flexibility below)*.
- **Simplicity** - Unless required, duplicating detailed information from other documents wastes time, and complicates the document. Put yourself in the place of the user.

> *If the Preplan gets stuck away in a drawer, and rarely, if ever, gets referred to - even during a mission - then it is not worth the time it took to prepare it.*

In the overall body structure of a SAR organization, the Preplan functions like the brain and memory. All the other components make up the skeleton, muscles and vital organs to keep the organization alive.
- **Flexibility** - An effective Preplan needs constant reviewing and updating. Influencing conditions change, so a Preplan demands regular and frequent evaluation, and appropriate revisions. We strongly suggest evaluating your preplan during an *ongoing mission*, and critiquing it in detail immediately afterward.

Distribute the hard copies of a written Preplan in a thin three ring binder. This allows substitution of individually revised, updated or added pages without redoing the entire plan.

What about a Combination Preplan? What if Preplans consist of a combination of all emergencies *(search, rescue, disaster)*? The prevailing accepted philosophy states that, with the right components, a single plan works in any emergency. It needs flexibility, and a provision of the basic tenets necessary for professionals to use their own judgement in applying current conditions to the situation. It depends on many factors, including:

- Responsibility and authority
- The relationship between the area's types of missions
- Frequency of each incident type
- Complexity of response

Separate plans for each type of incident or emergency usually provide unnecessary redundancy.

Emergency Support Function #9 as an Important Foundation

Local, State and Federal laws require local jurisdictions *(cities of a specific size and counties)* to have emergency management plans in place for unexpected emergencies or disasters. This requirement holds for every state in the U.S. An integral part of all of jurisdictional plans in the U.S. resides in a required section called Emergency Support Function number 9 *(ESF#9)*. ESF #9 relates to and deals with search and rescue and provides the foundation and rationale for the SAR Operational PrePlan.

A Good Preplan Contains:

- Checklists: Itemized descriptions of sequences for performance.
- Resource Lists: Phone numbers, pagers, radio call signs, etc. for acquiring personnel, vehicles, equipment or other supplies.
- Reference Documents: Basis of authority, or guide for procedures with documents listed or hyperlinked but not included.
- Standard Operating Procedures: Standard protocol procedures relating to SAR activities not explicitly described in other documents
- Memoranda of Agreement *(MOA)* or Understanding *(MOU)*: Any cooperative agreements that pertain to SAR activities *(typically the who...and how to...of SAR)*. The Plan need not contain the document, only a reference to it
- Operational Information: Reference to or access to information like missing/lost person statistics, map quad designations, or supply sources

Preplan Details

Include the following components in the Preplan:

The order and the specific elaboration of each section depends on existing circumstances. This list pertains directly to the components of a Preplan for search.

Plan Purpose and Objectives - A concise statement about the document's intended use and purpose.

- The why and what of the plan

Priority of Mission - How SAR emergencies stack up against other types of emergencies, in terms of priority of effort.

- The jurisdictions priorities of response concerning search

Preparation and Planning - Training, standards and minimum staffing for incidents.

Organizational Structure - Specific jobs accomplished during an incident. Make note of volunteer, reserve and regular staff.
- Responsibilities of each individual
- Don't forget dealing with the media!

First Notice - Notification procedures for all personnel to include responders and policy personnel.

- Notification procedures and guidelines for determining the urgency and hence, the level of response
- First notice procedures and personnel notification details
- Establishing urgency with the use of a standard like the Search Urgency Form based on:
  - Planning and searching data - Initially, what type of information needs gathering
  - Missing person questionnaire with protocols for passing information

Criteria and procedures for conducting an investigation - Who investigates? This section needs organizational guidelines.

- Guidelines and protocols for how the investigation unit interfaces with overall mission management *(Who and how?)*
- Investigation procedures and responsibilities
- Protocols for inclusion of clues and investigative *subject profile* information into overall search strategy and tactics *(The clue log for assimilation or follow-up)*

Relative Urgency Guidelines - Considering terrain, subject, weather, any other relevant factors.

Strategy - Considerations for defining the scope of the problem and determining a course of action.

Tactics - Specific considerations regarding the methods and actions carried out to find a lost person, rescuing an injured subject, etc.

- Specific considerations and field procedure options recommended to find and/or rescue lost, injured, overdue and stranded people *(Detailed descriptions for institutional memory)*

Representative examples of operational objectives:

- **S**pecific
- **M**easurable
- **A**chievable
- **R**elevant
- **T**ime related
- **E**valuated
- **R**eviewed and documented

Priorities for Resource Allocation - Determines the order in which to allocate available resources to the mission.

Inventory of Resources - Available resources?

- Human Resources
  - Availability
  - Qualifications
  - Limitations
  - Response time
  - Where and to whom to report

- Physical Resources
  - Availability
  - Obtaining the resources & contact

- Response time
- Any restrictions

- Informational Resources
- Special Resources

Emergent Authorities and Responsibilities

Specific conditions expected.

- Conditions requiring changes in management structure or strategies *(i.e. jurisdictional boundaries, criminal implications, federal/national involvement etc.)*

Knowledge of the Environment - Documents to include maps and other imagery to identify:

- Hazards
- Points of attraction
- Access routes - roads, trails & tracks
- Location of previous incidents
- Communications dead spots

Callout Procedures - Specific information about resources and contacts.

- Procedures for calling out human and equipment resources and what type of information those resources require.

Functional Organization - Management structures for a search incident and the functional positions required.

- Typical management structures for missions at basic and expanded levels *(Only list actual names in the appendix and not in the body of the plan)*.

Method for Collection and Analysis of data from past Incidents

- Case histories
- Missing person behavior - Both local and international data *(ISRID)*

Base Camp Considerations - Preplan locations and layouts for base camps or set-up of mobile command posts

Clue Management - Procedures and guidelines for logging, tracking and following up on clues during the search

Communications Protocols - Procedures, protocols and frequencies for internal, external, command and control as well as tactical communications

Briefing and Debriefing Procedures - Include specific forms in an appendix.

Medical Considerations - Procedures for dealing with injuries *(the subject or search personnel)*.

Fatalities - Provide for the possibility of criminal involvement; investigator and coroner responsibilities.

Rescue/Evacuation Considerations - Consider special rescue problems.

Mission Suspension/De-escalation - How to determine suspension of a mission.

- Lists of possible criteria

Demobilization Procedures -

- The recall of personnel from the field
- Replenishment of equipment/material
- Replace damaged equipment

Documentation/Reporting Requirements - Attach appropriate documents as appendices.

Post Incident Activities - Procedures for constructively reviewing the mission.

- Critique of the operation
- After-action paperwork, Change or update plan, procedures, accidents, claims for injuries, loss of equipment

Methods for Prevention of Future Incidents

- Preventive SAR *(PSAR)* education
- Some way to tell the public why these missions occur

Special Problems - Depending on circumstances, other considerations include:

- Downed Aircraft

    - Restricting airspace
    - Aircraft crash (private, commercial, military)
    - Safeguarding victim valuables
    - Resource protection

- Cost accounting procedures
- Resource tracking, timekeeping, etc.
- Prevention actions
- Dealing with the subject's *(victim's)* relatives
- Physical fitness for SAR Team members
- Press briefings and media spokesperson identification

APPENDICES - Include the following in the operational Preplan as appendices:

- SAR Vulnerability Assessment
- Resource lists
- Phone lists
- Equipment lists
- Organizational chart *(positions)*
- Memorandums of Understanding (MOUs)/and Agreements
- Form

The SAR Planning Process

The process of developing local preplans adds more value to the organization than the plan itself. The process enables individuals and organizations to examine their roles and responsibilities in relation to everyone else and to evaluate the response system as a whole. If done properly, the process elevates SAR awareness and any associated issues/programs on the local priority list.

The following list outlines the step by step process of putting an operational preplan in place:

1. Define the hazards and potential problems *(both search related and rescue related)*; include all historical occurrences.
2. Establish who responds, and with what resources.
3. Obtain chief law enforcement officer support *(or legislatively mandated responsible agency executive)*.
4. Talk to your resources on a first visit *(meet and greet)*.
5. Draft the basic plan and SOPs.
6. Make a second visit to obtain comments on draft plan, clarify responsibilities, and eliminate duplication or conflicts
7. Conduct a training mission or run an actual missing or lost person incident using the plan.
8. Critique the incident, with the goal of improving the plan.
9. Finalize the basic plan, based on critique comments.
10. Maintain the plan and repeat the process as needed.

The key to making a plan work lies within the ability to vividly paint clear mental images in both the process and in the document for the people who need to know and react.

Summary

As a standard rule, it takes two hours of planning for every one hour of performing an activity. Sadly, most units fail to preplan in search at all. Too often, if a unit creates an operational Preplan, they create it because higher authority requires it, or they find something created under other circumstances. As such, these documents rarely really serve as a true operational plan but rather as an administrative burden.

A good operational Preplan is not a problem solving document, rather it avoids problems.

Good Preplans make a real difference.

Good planning results in a substantial savings of time, effort and cost on a search - and in the Search and rescue business, time saves lives!

VITAL PLANNING QUESTIONS

What do we want upon completion of the plan?

ANSWER: Successful SAR Missions.

What needs to be done in order to make the plan reality?

ANSWER: Follow it! Use proper resources and techniques!

What steps avoid embarrassment and inefficiency?

ANSWER: Rehearse! Train! Hold briefings and debriefings! Critique! Follow the Plan! Develop S.O.P.'s!

Notes:

SAR Resources 8

Objectives:

- Identify the basic types of search and rescue resources, and discuss their functions, limitations, and possible locations
- Discuss the importance of identifying, evaluating and cataloging SAR Resources as part of the pre-planning process
- List and discuss the reason why knowledge of resources and their capabilities inextricably link to the application of assets during field operations
- Relate why search planners and managers need to observe diverse SAR resource training

Resources Commonly Used in Search

Meeting and Greeting all the resources in the preplan, while not a written requirement, is a fundamental task for the SAR Manager. A letter or phone call often substitutes for a personal visit. Knowing who the other person or group is, what it can do, and how it operates often means the difference between successfully putting these resources into play or not.
— Tim J. Setnicka, *Wilderness Search and Rescue*, 1980.

A SAR resource consists of anything a search manager acquires, to assist in finding or rescuing a missing or lost person, or a trapped individual or group of people.

Example types of SAR Resources include:

- Human *(searchers, dog handlers, mountain rescue teams)*
- Animal *(air scent, trailing or tracking dogs, horses)*
- Equipment *(vehicles, aircraft, UAVs, radios, lights, GPS units)*
- Information *(media, weather reports, investigations, medical data)*
- Combinations *(dog & handler, aircraft & observers)*

In general SAR Resource classifications fall under either operational or support roles. In other words, assets committed to the field or used to support the operation.

All SAR Preplans need to include a Categorized List of Resources

An integral part of any jurisdiction's written preplan encompasses a comprehensive SAR Resource list, coupled with locator information for those resources. Units need to *produce* an up-to-date directory of SAR Resources for use in their jurisdiction. A SAR directory, a *living* document *(potentially changing on a monthly basis),* consists of an easily revisable format for constant changes by the people charged with using it. Local, state, federal or provincial government agencies with responsibility in SAR sometimes publish their own SAR Resource Directories. Use them, if available, to fill out local directories. Upon request, national volunteer and professional organizations often provide those who ask with lists of helpful resources to aid in filling out local resource directories too.

Types of SAR Resource Categories:

When categorizing resources, take into consideration the strategic or tactical capabilities of the resource. Meaning, a specific application in the field.

- The types of SAR environments need consideration as well.
- When categorizing SAR resources, each situation uses a set of specialized skills, equipment and even personnel.

Example SAR environments include:

- Air search
- Ground search
- Water/lake/river or white water search
- Technical rock
- Snow/ice
- Restricted land search
- Open land
- Desert search
- Specialized search - confined spaces
- Urban/Inner City

List human resources by the following:

- Name
- Phone number, pager number or contact person
- Experience or capability / certification
- Availability
- Call out agency

List resources by generic type:

- Examples: *(aircraft, dogs, horses, scuba, mountain rescue, technology)*
- Cross-reference all lists by tying into all potential applications for each resource *(e.g. Type 1 or Type II resources, management team or field resources, etc.)*

Resource Evaluation

To evaluate a resource's usefulness for a given mission ask yourself **six** basic questions:

1. Availability?

- Number of resources and time to a given location
- Readiness? Immediately available? Time lag for arrival
- Special requesting procedures or conditions
- Measured response or Emergency response *(Remember that search area size depends on time, the area grows larger as time moves forward)*

2. How long on-scene?

- Weekends only
- Professional jobs or obligations
- Full time paid resources only available during a normal work week

3. Capabilities and Qualifications?

- Is the resource able to perform the task quickly, safely, efficiently? Most search resources function far more effectively if deployed rapidly with a good chance of a responsive subject.
- Training, past performance and work record

4. Limitations?

- Corporate/private vs public/agency primary mission
- Mental, or physical condition?
- Proficiency or effectiveness of the resource?
- Competition - ego?
- Team players?
- Special considerations - communications? *(spoken and transmitted)*

5. Past Record?

- Hard working, dedicated resources during extreme conditions or circumstances pay huge dividends
- Task and detail oriented, debriefing skills, navigation skills, attitude

Back-Up Resources?

- Consider more than one source for any resource

Preparing a Resource List

All resource lists need to include every source of manpower, equipment and supplies used in SAR. Organize resources in a variety of ways.

Primary resource types: At the highest level, primary resources divide into two types.

1. Human Resources:

Some resources include pre-organized structures with a variety of skills and knowledge, who also fit into the SAR management strategy directly, such as:

- SAR trained volunteers
- Military
- Police
- Technical or specialized teams

Human resources also include:

- Untrained civilians *(manpower near the scene)*
- Private business

2. Physical Resources:

- Material items *(sleeping cots, portable toilets, etc.)*
- Specialized equipment
- Specific facilities

Primary Mission: (other than SAR) another division of resources to help determine availability.

- **Dedicated emergency** - Assets used just for emergency conditions *(e.g., air ambulance, MAST military helicopter.)*
- **Non-emergency** - Assets that provide valuable services, aid or capabilities not associated with emergency response *(e.g., lighting equipment, logging company assets, public utility assets)*

Resource Funding Base:

Another set of categories established to help define availability.

- **Public sector** - those owned and controlled by the government at local, state and federal levels
- **Private sector** - those provided by business or industry *(e.g., snow machines, transportation vehicles, heavy lift equipment etc.)*
- **Volunteer sector** - those provided by volunteer groups including food, shelter, equipment and communications. Also known as *Non-Paid Professionals*!

In terms of availability, resources dedicated as emergency from the public sector usually respond first and fastest. The least available, non dedicated emergency assets, comprises the volunteer. When exploring strategy and tactics, consider these additional categories as well.

- **Initial response** - quick responders; committed immediately
- **Backup resources** - slower responding due to distance; reliable for shift change and support functions
- **Specialized resources** - technical or specialized skills for specific tasks. *(e.g., divers, satellite communications, lighting systems etc.)*
- **Logistical, supply or maintenance resources** - to keep other resources going in the field
- **Informational** - *(e.g., weather service, databases, pharmaceutical businesses, poison centers, etc)*

Search Resources

Aircraft

Helicopters - useful for movement of manpower, supplies and equipment, search area evaluation *(planning)*, aerial photos, and for actual searching in certain terrain and vegetation.

Limitations *(depending on helicopter):*

- Endurance and need for refueling
- Elevation
- Searching effectiveness *(crew training and experience)*
- Weather and time of day
- Known hazards *(terrain, weather and wind currents, power lines, etc.)*
- Cost

Sources:

- Military - primarily through a Rescue Coordination Center or local base
- Government or Government contract *(land management agencies, police organizations)*
- Civilian private industry *(oil companies, news organizations, corporate executive aircraft)*
- Aeromedical units, public and private

Fixed wing - useful for search area evaluation *(planning)*, searching certain kinds of terrain, high resolution photography for specific sites, infrared search, radio communication relays, downed aircraft search.

Limitations:

- Searching effectiveness, or crew skill level for air search
- Accessibility to search area *(landing strips and/ or fuel)*
- Weather
- Limited fixed orbit on scene

Sources:

- Military - primarily through Rescue Coordination Centers *(RCC)* or local bases
- Civil Air Patrol - through RCC or local CAP unit *(CASARA in Canada)*
- Government or government contract *(police)*
- Private Industry or private aircraft such as air ambulance
- State agency assets through DOT Aeronautics as well as volunteers.

Use of Fixed Wing Aircraft in Support of SAR Operations

General

Although exceptionally useful in many situations, they are not the ultimate answer to the Search Manager's problems. While some fixed wing aircraft provide low, slow flight if equipped with short take off and landing *(STOL)* modifications, they lack the slow-flight/hover capabilities of a helicopter.

What Aircraft Cannot Do

Search Managers need to consider aircraft when conducting any ground SAR activities, but not count on aircraft to solve all situations. On numerous occasions weather, mechanical difficulties, fuel supply, logistical problems and even pilot qualification preclude the use of aircraft resources.

Aircraft Capabilities and Limitations

Many factors affect an aircraft's capabilities and limitations. Temperature, operational altitude, availability, high wing, low wing, payload capability and fuel consumption rates all impact the decision to use a particular airborne resource. By the same token, eventually people ask about cost factors. Who pays for the air time during a search? How much will extended operations cost and what about free (*Military, Federal Law Enforcement - Homeland Security?*) resources?

Even experienced pilots with high hours sometimes lack qualifications to fly search missions. Search and rescue flying demands an exceptionally well trained and qualified pilot. For air operations, trained and experienced spotters/observers in the aircraft provide an invaluable resource. Spotter/observers work very closely as a team with their assigned pilot. Each possesses a cooperative function and need to work together, not separately to get the job done efficiently and effectively.

Once managers request that an aircraft assist in the search effort then consider establishing an air operations branch under the ICS structure. When only one aircraft receives a request and activates, the Operations Chief may simply assume that position. When the need for several aircraft arises, then the unit needs a specialized branch to manage the following functions:

- Establishing and operating helibases or helispots
- Maintaining records on both fixed-wing and helicopter aircraft
- Maintaining required liaison with fixed-wing aircraft using off-scene facilities
- Maintaining all timekeeping for aircraft assigned to the search
- Logistical and supply needs for air operations
- Air safety briefings and oversight for both helicopter and fixed wing operations

Although a single person generally performs these functions during a search incident, the IC needs to delegate these jobs and more if the situation escalates. *(See Chapter 15 on Organization.)*

Air Operations Base *(airfield, air strip, heliport or helipad)*

Locate the air operations base(s) as close to the search area as possible while maintaining needed support functions. Establish and maintain solid communications between the staff at Search Base and aircrews. This helps to ensure fewer communication gaps in the overall operation.

Unmanned Aerial Systems (UAS) or Unmanned Aerial Vehicles (UAVs)

In recent years military and paramilitary organizations drastically increased their use of unmanned aerial vehicles (UAVs) in surveillance and even in combat. Unfortunately, uninformed opinion and national media presently serve to hinder widespread adoption of UAS infrastructure in civilian and law enforcement situations. These small and relatively inexpensive flying machines provide real-time visual information and data to first responders to find or to help find missing subjects. Emergency responders require information and real-time imagery to help make better decisions. UASs provide situational awareness over large areas quickly, reducing the time and the number of searchers required to locate an injured or missing person, and greatly reducing the cost, in dollars and manpower, of search and rescue missions. They let first responders know precisely where to direct further resources, and they serve as communications relays.

UASs potentially operate day or night, in challenging conditions and without risk to personnel. These devices deploy a host of sensing technology to aid in the search for missing persons. In addition to their viewpoint and speed, infrared (IR) or thermal imaging cameras detect body heat; low light television and high resolution cameras enhance human vision, laser range finding, RADAR and embedded GPS together offer tremendous force multiplication capability and accuracy to the information provided. The sensors carried by these platforms usually transmit their data via line of sight or via ad-hoc digital networking.

Common applications link fairly easily with tablet computers and in some cases even cell phones for real-time control, mapping, programming, navigation and observation. These capabilities greatly increase the ability to find people or objects at night, hidden in brush or shadows and even during daytime operations. Current battery powered devices usually provide about 20 to 30 minutes of airborne time before needing a fresh battery. Self contained conventional fuel driven models weigh significantly more, cost more, but offer much expanded time on station. These devices cover massive amounts of territory quickly and provide valuable information for follow on ground teams.

UAS vary from small hobby sized devices to multimillion dollar sensor platforms used by federal agencies like the Air Force and Customs and Border Protection.

As of the time of this writing the FAA authorizes public aircraft as defined by Title 49 U.S.C. section 40102(a)11. The agency grants Certificates of Waiver or Certificates of Authorization (COAs) on a continuous basis for periods of approximately two years to allow these machines to operate in the complicated airspace of the United States for the designated purposes covered by the certificate.

Civil *(commercial)* and hobby operations round out the other possibilities for UASs in the current structure of the FAA regime. Commercial aircraft require a relatively low level of risk as well as a Special Airworthiness Certificate *(SAC)*. The Hobby arena depends upon weight *(less than 55 lbs)* and staying under 400 feet above ground level while maintaining more than 5 miles clearance from established airfields. However, users who receive pay for the use of their UAS fall under the commercial regime regardless of vehicle weight.

Recent legal battles *(all the way to the US Supreme Court)* center on the lack of or extent of, FAA control over UAS platforms. The original drafters of U.S. and international airspace regulations failed to consider unmanned and remote controlled drones' capabilities and prevalence. Anticipate a new regime of regulations within the next decade to more accurately cover the safe operation and expansion of UAS platforms.

Dogs

Tracking or Trailing - dogs of this type search by following the route taken by a person from a last known position. A scent-article from the subject generates the search capability for a trailing dog.

Advantages:

- Trailing dogs effectively discriminate lost subjects from other persons when provided a good scent article
- Highly efficient *(high detection per hour of effort)*

Limitations:

- Less effective after searchers or weather contaminates or destroys scent clues
- Dog team *(dog and handler)* proficiency varies widely

Sources:

- Local, state, district or provincial law enforcement agencies and correctional facilities
- Volunteer units
- Coordination through RCCs

Air-scenting - With the dog's head held high, it uses airborne scenting for locating lost subject.

Advantages:

- Search large areas efficiently
- Use after *airing out* or letting a search segment blow clean from a previous search by other ground resources that possibly contaminated the area with scent

Limitations:

- In general, these dogs lack the capability to discriminate between a lost subject and someone being in the search area
- Relatively ineffective during hot, dry, low humidity and low wind conditions

Sources:

- Volunteer units
- Coordination through RCC
- Local, county, district and state or provincial law enforcement agencies

> **NOTE:** As first responders, search dogs provide a highly efficient and effective resource to the search. Dogs train to locate subjects and clues buried in snow, rubble or submerged in water. In the U.S. the National Association for Search and Rescue provides a comprehensive directory of available SAR dog units. Contact the NASAR Bookstore at PO Box 232020, Centreville, VA 20120-2020, phone: 877-893-0702 info@nasar.org The Mountain Rescue Council Handbook in Great Britain, lists the available Search and Rescue Dog Associations.

Trackers and Track and Clue Aware Searchers

Human Trackers - Follow the route taken by the missing person from a Last Known Position (*LKP*) or (*PLS*) by locating tracks, sign and *disturbances* in the environment left by the subject.

Track and Clue Aware Searchers - Track and Clue Awareness (TCA) forms a method and skill set for effectively and efficiently processing all sign *(or evidence)* and clues relevant to a specific SAR incident or to particular sites (*See page 101 for more information on TCA*). This philosophy and set of methods essentially encompasses scene processing. Adherents of TCA ultimately focus on finding people faster by maximizing opportunities to detect meaningful clues and from those clues, deduce travel vectors *(direction of travel)*.

Advantages:

- Highly efficient if good sign exists at the LKP
- *Eliminates* large portions of the search area
- Determines direction of travel early in a search
- Identifies corroborating evidence
- Processes clue rich areas

Limitations:

- Less effective after time passes and clues get destroyed
- Skill levels of *trackers* or track and clue aware searchers vary widely

Sources:

- Man-tracking or Track & Clue Awareness trained volunteer units
- Border Patrol or police trained tracking units
- Trained military personnel

Trained Field Searchers

Hasty teams - Small *(2 to 3 person)* preestablished, ready to respond, highly mobile, track and clue aware teams.

Advantages:

- Quickly check *high probability* locations, *likely spots*, hazardous areas, etc.
- Locate clues for use in establishing a search area

Sources:

- Local agency or volunteer units

Grid teams - Explorer Search & Rescue and other well trained units. NOT, the general public or large numbers of agency or department personnel.

Advantages:

- Provide thorough searching, especially if trained on concepts like average range of detection *(Rd)*, sweep width, track and clue awareness and similar skills

Limitations:

- Destroy clues if not properly trained
- Very low efficiency *(probability of detection per hour of effort expended)* - use as last resort

Sources:

- Local units, such as rescue squads, Explorer SAR units, and other well trained agency or volunteer units

Special Competence Resources

Rough Terrain Responders - Characterized by units with skills and special equipment for operating effectively in mountainous, steep, fast water, inclement, confined space, urban or even remote environments.

Sources:

- Specially trained units in the local area such as Mountain Rescue Association Units, rescue squads, Ski Patrol Rescue Teams *(SPART)*, etc.

Water responders - Units or individuals with skills and equipment to search, rescue or recover in surf, swift water or deep water environments

Sources:

- Local units or individuals from rescue squads, police dive-rescue units, the Coast Guard or organized divers organizations *(e.g. Diver's Alert Network, National Association of Underwater Instructors, SCUBA Clubs, Rescue 3 International Certified Technicians, etc.)*

Winter environment responders - Units with skills and equipment to search for or rescue in snow, ice, avalanches, etc.

Sources:

- Local units or individuals such as members of National Ski Patrol, Ski area pro-patrol, Mountain Rescue Association Units, Ski Patrol Rescue Teams-*(SPART)*

Specialized Vehicle Responders - Local units or individuals with vehicles capable of responding in special terrain/environmental conditions; such as:

- Over-snow vehicles
- Four-wheel drive vehicles
- All-terrain vehicles
- Mountain bikes

Sources:

- Many ski areas and power supply companies own special snow cats or snow machines used in winter environments with excessive snow.
- Back country Rangers with Land Management Agencies

Confined Space responders *(cavers/industrial rescuers)* - units with skills and equipment to search for or rescue in caves, caverns and mines, tunnels, shafts, tanks or other confined spaces.

Sources:

- Local units or individuals such as members of National Cave Rescue Commission or National Speleological Society, the Mine Safety and Health Administration, and the Office of Surface Mining, Industrial Rescue Teams and some fire department and/or public utility personnel

Collapsed Structures - units that provide expertise in finding, access and extricating people from collapsed structures.

Sources:

- Search dog units
- Urban Rescue Teams *(local fire and rescue or law enforcement agencies)* Urban Search and Rescue *(US&R)* Task Forces available through the Federal Emergency Management Agency *(FEMA)* in the U.S.
- Remote video
- Listening devices
- Robotics and remote control units used to find people in collapsed structures

Mounted Responders - Preferably trained searchers mounted on horses. *(e.g. independent volunteer groups, sheriff's posse, mounted police units, park patrols.)* Also, individuals with riding or pack animals, and skilled handlers for searching remote or rough terrain or for transporting supplies, bodies *(remains)* or equipment.

Sources:

- Organized mounted SAR units
- Sheriff's posse's or auxiliary units
- Mounted police or park rangers
- Ranchers, outfitters, wilderness guides, Local *dude ranch*, guides
- Local riding clubs or individual riders

Management and Support Resources

Hasty Teams

Management or Overhead - Well trained pre-established and equipped, fast reaction 2 to 3 person team to set up a command post and manage the *Reflex Tasking* at a search incident site. The team maintains thorough familiarity and capability with all six functional task groups for *Reflex Tasking*:

- Investigation
- Initial Planning Point
- Containment
- Hub/Immediate Area
- Travel Corridors
- High Probability Tasks

Other - Well trained pre-established and equipped, fast reaction team to accomplish tasks as designated by the IC or Overhead staff.

Search Management Team - The specific functions required to effectively manage a search for a missing person often require highly trained individuals. In particular, the following functions need staffing by specialists:

- Incident Commander *(Search Manager)*.
- Plans Chief *(Planning for Incident & Op Periods)*.
- Search Planner *(Planning during the Search)*
- Operations Chief *(IC's Executive Officer)*
- Investigation Unit Leader *(Investigations Liaison - making sure the right questions get asked)*
- External Influences Officer *(Media, Family)*

Preplan the use of these source specialists, in the same way as planning for tactical resources, due to the fact that availability issues quickly arise within the immediate area or jurisdiction.

Logistical Support - Civic organizations, American Red Cross, Salvation Army, Church groups, Auxiliaries *(e.g., USCG Aux.)*, Military, and private vendors, often provide food and shelter.

Weather Information - Flight Service Stations, Air Traffic Control Centers, radio and T.V. news, F.A.A. centers, and military bases provide weather information. If available, use a local office *Upstream* to check on current as well as predicted weather.

Communications Support - In addition to the internal communications systems of responsible and support agencies/organizations, look for additional and specialized communication from:

- Radio Emergency Associated Communication Teams *(REACT)*
- Radio Amateur Civil Emergency Services units *(RACES)*
- General Mobile Radio Service *(GMRS)*
- HAM operators
- Amateur Radio Emergency Communications Services
- CB Emergency Radio 9

Facility Equipment - The preplan needs to identify sources for the following types of special equipment which help manage and support a large search:

- Extra cellphones and internet access
- Computer equipment
- Photocopy equipment
- Transportation *(buses, vans, trucks, ORVs)*
- Sanitation Facilities *(dumpsters [-skips-] and portable toilets)*
- Temporary shelter *(small circus tents, funeral canopies, military tents or shelters, etc.)*
- Portable heaters
- Generators and/or a power supply

Summary of Regular Search Resources

- Aircraft - Helicopters and Fixed Wing
- Dogs - Trailing/Tracking and Airscent
- Trackers
- Track and Clue Aware Searchers
- Trained Ground Searchers and Hasty Teams
- Special Environment Resources
- Management and Support Personnel
- Informational Sources
- Communications Networks & Personnel
- Logistics and Facility Equipment Resources

Special Resources

Every search and rescue mission involves special resources of some kind. Generally speaking, special resources in the SAR community refer to those resources called upon to solve unique or highly specialized problems. Although used infrequently in general SAR activities, a search manager uses them as a last ditch effort or a time critical maneuver, in conjunction with regular search resources.

Special SAR resources usually include:

- Attraction devices
- Mine Detectors
- Noise Sensitive Equipment
- Prophets, Diviners and Seers
- Photo Interpretation
- Sniffers (mechanical)
- Thermistor Detectors
- Witchers
- Omni Directional Infrared *(IR)*
- Night Vision Goggles *(NVGs)*

- Linguist / Interpreter
- Low Light Level Tracking Cameras for Video

Attraction Devices: Generally discussed in the passive mode of search under Tactics:

- Lights
- Sirens and/or Horns
- Flags or ground signals
- Lines, ropes, strings or tags
- Signs
- Gun shots or flares
- Loud speakers with a PA system
- Balloons
- Search Lights *(trailer mounted)*
- Strobe Lights

Interviewers: Specialized, but most likely a very important regular resource skill a SAR Manager might use. Interviewer's provide expert questioning.

- Different types of questions produce different information
    - All witnesses and casual observers need questioning
    - Never assume anything
    - An interviewer goes from general to more specific
    - Consider specialists for immigrants *(cultural values, priorities etc.)*

Good interviewing yields both planning and searching information.

Magnetometers: Work on deviations in earth's magnetic lines:

- Primarily used in avalanche work
- Locate rocks or pieces of metal in the area

Mine Detectors: An obvious military resource:

- Not readily available
- Sensitive to medium density, not metal
- Primarily used in avalanche search and rescue

Noise Sensitive Equipment: Another military resource:

- Usually not practical
- Used in the past but with not much success
- With very noisy outdoor areas problems arise
- Directional microphones resolve muffled shouts to discernible words

Prophets, Diviners and Seers: On average, they provide a success rate of 3% above pure chance (*Syrotuck*):

- A major search generally brings out these types of people
- Watch out for those that want to charge a fee
- Take them seriously, millions of people believe in them and they may provide help
- Handled by the search director or his aide
- Even if a charlatan, they deserve consideration in order to provide appeasement to the family and loved ones of the victim
- Escort them into the field

Consider them into the overall search strategy.

Photo - Interpretation: Although a good resource, a qualified person needs to analyze the photos.

- Simple black and white aerial photos yield the following:
    - Tracks or signals
    - Evidence of any kind *(wreckage, litter, debris)*

- Infrared photos sense heat and detect warm bodies or warmth of any kind:
    - Animals
    - Springs
    - Campfires

- Camouflage penetrating photos
- Special skills to detect man-made structures

Remember: Depending on the source and availability, possible interpretation problems arise as well as map transfer problems for the search manager on-scene

Underwater Cameras and Detection Equipment:

- Often found in the private sector; needs special liaison and coordination for use

Sniffers - Mechanical:

- Primarily a military resource
- Sensitive to odors
- Application good for finding bodies in disaster type incidents

Thermistor: A device sensitive to the changes in temperature of the medium below.

- Primary use is in avalanche search
- A military resource

Witchers: Approximately 15% effective on the average (*Syrotuck*):

- Slightly different than prophets, diviners and seers
- Good in avalanche search
- Used to search for missing children with some success

Crisis Intervention Specialists:

- Primarily for the family and friends of the missing subject
- Critical Incident Stress Debriefing Teams for SAR personnel themselves

Grief Reaction Specialists:

- Clergy and Funeral Directors *(deal with grief on a regular basis)*

Seismic Equipment:

- Noise and movement sensitive equipment

Remote TV Equipment:

- For collapsed structures as well as surveillance in wilderness areas

Infrared - Omni Directional:

- Detects movement or the presence of a life form in the environment *(Primary law enforcement resource used mostly at night).*

Night Vision Goggles *(NVGs)*:

- Observation equipment used primarily to see images and movement in low light or darkness

GPS *(Global Positioning System)*:

- Tracking of resources, radios, vehicles
- Basic Searcher Navigation

Quick Reference Listing for SAR Resources

List Resources: Every jurisdiction with a responsibility for SAR response should complete an inventory of all the resources that are available both locally and out of the area.

Resource Types: Some resources such as helicopters can be very useful with a number of different capabilities in the search operation. Most search resources, however, can be catalogued in one of the following general types. Make certain that requirements for a search can be satisfied in each of the following areas.

Strategy	Tactics	Method	Name of Resource	Phone #
A. Initial Response Reflex Tasks	Investigation	Field-experienced Sheriff's Dept. Liaison for Investigation		
	Initial Planning Point	Initial arriving Hasty Team members preserve site		
	Containment	Hasty Team members or local volunteer SAR Team members		
	Hub/ Immediate Area	Local law enforcement SAR liaison staff member		
	Travel Corridors	Local volunteer staff - Law Enforcement on-duty officers		
	High Probability Tasks	Local SAR Coordinator - Incident IC or Team Leaders		
	Likely Spots	Local SAR Team member Hasty Teams - Initial Responders		

Figure 8-1a

Strategy	Tactics	Method	Name of Resource	Phone #
B. Management	Operations	Local field-experienced search IC or Team Leader		
	Planning	Local staff trained volunteer overhead team		
	Logistics	Local staff trained volunteer overhead team		
	Interview/ Ask questions	Local staff law enforcement trained overhead team		
	Liaison	Local staff - PIO trained on overhead team		
	Comms	Local staff trained by RACES, REACT, or HAM operators on radio protocols		
	Support	Local staff from Red Cross, volunteer catering Orgs and local volunteer food vendors		

Figure 8-1b

Quick Reference Listing for SAR Resources - continued

Strategy	Tactics	Method	Name of Resource	Phone #
C. Containment	Road Blocks	Law Enforcement, Posse (auxiliary police)		
	Road Patrols	Two and 4 wheel vehicles manned by volunteer SAR		
	Trail Blocks	Law enforcement, volunteer SAR Team members, Climbing Club, unplanned manpower		
	Trail Patrols	Hikers, horse riders, motorbikes, skiers, snowmobiles, ATVs, dune buggies		
	Lookouts	Volunteers, untrained manpower		
	Camp-Ins	Local volunteers - SAR Unit		
	String or Flag Lines	Explorer Scout Units, trained manpower familiar with protocols		
D. Attraction	Sight	Fire, smoke, search lights, aircraft, weather balloons		
	Sound	Sirens, fog horn, guns, power megaphone, aircraft		
E. Clue Finding	Interviewing	Law enforcement, volunteer SAR Team members, Climbing Club, unplanned manpower		
	Visual Tracking	Hikers, horse riders, motorbikes, skiers, snowmobiles, ATVs, dune buggies		
	Tracking Dogs	Volunteers, untrained manpower		
F. Clue / subject Finding	Hasty Search	Local volunteers - SAR Unit		
	Sign cutting	Explorer Scout Units, trained manpower familiar with protocols		
G. Subject Finding	Sweep Team	Thorough, sound/light line sweeps, Type I search		
	AROD (Rd) Search	Trained, familiar with Rd Procedure, Sweep width		
	Water Search	Boats, kayakers, rubber rafts, divers, air scent dogs		
	Special Hazard Search	MRA teams, avalanche teams cavers, mine experts, swiftwater rescue teams, Fire Dept personnel		
	Air Search	Helicopters, fixed wing		

Figure 8-1c

Quick Reference Listing for SAR Resources - continued

Strategy	Tactics	Method	Name of Resource	Phone #
H. Communication	Radio	VHF, UHF, amateur radio		
	Phones	Public & cell phones, field phones, FTS, Autovon, Satellite phones		
I. Transportation	Land	Bus, truck, two wheel vehicle, 4 wheel drive, snowmobile, ATVs, jet skis		
	Air	Helicopter, fixed wing		
	Water	Boats - jet & prop, hovercraft, landing craft		
J. Support	Food/Water	Volunteers, Salvation Army, Red Cross, field kitchen, catering service - private		
	Shelter	Volunteers, Red Cross, Emergency Mgmt., Military		
	Medical	First Aid, EMTs, nurses, Doctors		
	Sanitary	Port-a-potty, field latrines, Land Mgmt. Agency fire camp supplier		
K. Rescue / Recovery	Non-technical	Litter teams, 4 X 4 vehicles, snowmobile sleds, helicopter, ambulance		
	Technical	Rock rescue teams, mine rescue, cave rescue, avalanche, crevasse rescue, helicopter, underwater recovery, side scan sonar		
L. Other	UAV	Etc.		

Figure 8-1d

SAR Strategies and Tactical Procedures 9

Objectives:

- Discuss why proper application of SAR resources comprises the foundation for effective SAR Planning
- Be able to apply a combination of strategies for resources in a given situation
- Relate why track and clue awareness plays a major factor in reducing a probable search area
- Relate possible conflicts between resources applied in the same or adjacent search areas
- Describe the possible sequence of initial attack resources in a specific area

The Reality of Applying Resources

Due to scarce SAR resources, most local jurisdictions lack the luxury of applying multiple resources in any order. They apply the only resources available BUT, with deployed local resources, there is a need to call in outside resources on a priority or ordered basis. **Search is an Emergency.** The ultimate reason for quick, efficient application of SAR resources. During the initial response phase of any search a great number of unknowns compared to known facts exist. Because an individual's life depends on time, constantly consider the following unknowns:

- The missing person possibly needs immediate emergency care
- The person may need protection from the environment, himself/herself or even someone else
- The responsiveness of the missing person may only last for a few hours or days
- Time and weather tend to destroy valuable clues
- Urgent response to a missing person incident reduces the uncertainty of large search areas
- Urgent response permits more efficient search techniques

Again, lack of excess to SAR resources, requires utilizing available assets to everyone's advantage. Particularly the missing or lost person's.

Basic Principles for Applying Resources in Field Operations

- Respond urgently, even at night

  - Aid searchers any way possible
  - Create an atmosphere of positive urgency
  - Include noncontiguous areas of search in proper perspective *(i.e. a friends house, previous home, etc)*

- Use initial strategies that insure maximum chance of locating a responsive, conscious subject

Organizing Resources - An Essential First Step

Any human or physical assets committed to on-scene support of search operations needs to consider the use of that resource appropriately. Committing essential resources to the field when searching for a missing person rates as equally important to the proper personnel and equipment and to the function of providing management simultaneously. To run the entire effort smoothly, establish this control function early on.

Search and/or rescue volunteers tend to get frustrated when they arrive at search base ready to immediately depart for the field and stand around for several hours waiting for someone to sort out tasks and specific field assignments. In other words, get organized as quickly as possible!

Even though we discuss organization in Chapter 15, the initial planning process on-scene consists of developing a Search Action Plan and essentially laying out a blueprint for what happens next. In order to properly manage standard or specialized resources on-scene or due to arrive, the Search Manager needs to immediately assume or assign the responsibilities of organizing the arriving or soon to arrive resources *(See Reflex Tasking in Chapter 14)*.

This function accounts for resources ready for field assignments and able to respond within minutes of management assignments.

Resource Priority and Categories

In Chapter 18, we explore the concept of establishing where to look and the parameters that define a piece of terrain called *the search area*. At some point the Search Manager or an appointed staff member makes a decision about which resources to commit to the field, and in which order. Countless case histories prove the importance of this critical step in the management of search operations.

This decision process requires a full understanding of resource capabilities and limitations. An effective Search Manger knows this valuable information ahead of time, applies it accordingly, and creates a successfully managed mission.

Strategy & Tactics - The Difference and How They Apply to Resources

STRATEGY: Placing resources in the most advantageous location to find a missing person. As well as and scheduling specific functions which give the greatest chance of locating the individual. These activities constitute the overall plan of action.

Example Operational Strategies:

- Establish and segment the search area
- Initiate an investigation
- Develop a subject profile
- Determine the urgency of the situation
- Search for clues
- Determine point last seen or last known position and establish initial planning point
- Confine subject to the search area
- Conduct night searches
- Identify and prioritize high probability areas
- Identify and prioritize high hazard areas
- Establish an operations overhead management team
- Prevent search area contamination by the general public
- Establish a rescue and recovery plan
- Prioritize available resources and assignments

TACTICS: Techniques, procedures and methods used by resources to actually find the missing person or clues.

Example Operational Tactics:

- Use search dogs first in the high priority areas
- Sweep search with whistles and lights every 200 feet
- Run all trails and ridges for tracks and signs, plus 100 feet on either side
- Establish track traps in 4 specific areas
- Re-search two areas with different resources
- Interview hunting partner for favorite area information
- Interview all hikers in the area
- Detail three personnel to follow-up on all physical clues
- Sound patrol vehicle sirens once every hour from the same location
- The helicopter concentrates on two open drainages twice a day at low altitude
- Fixed wing aircraft in Grid 62 flies 500 foot contour patterns in the steep terrain

Committing Resources to the Field

The initiation of search efforts *(tactics)* normally takes place very soon after the first notice about the missing person. These initial efforts, while unique to an incident site, consistently match *(in terms of strategy)* every search. As examples, available resources get tasked to interview people, look for and isolate clues, and determine likely spots and possible destinations. Always accomplish these tasks first. *(See Reflex Tasking in Chapter 14)*

Searching in the field normally involves a definite progression of techniques, methods and procedures. Experience and case studies continually point out the necessity for using the right resources in the right order.

Initial Action Strategies

Confinement: Resource Application to Limit the Search Area

Why Limit the Search Area? The smaller the search area, the less time needed to effectively cover it. In addition, reducing the number of searchers required increases the chances of quickly recovering the missing person. Limited resources, presents an effective search planner with two options. Search areas with the highest chance for success and reduce the size of the area searched.

Confinement - Shutting the Doors

- Remember, the most critical piece to any search, always establish a search area with specific boundaries beyond which the missing subject has not passed

Most importantly, make sure the missing person is in the designated search area.

- Once you define the search area, numerous methods exist for detecting if the person passes through the perimeter

- Mobile missing subjects, require prompt reaction combined with an accurate assessment or analysis of the surrounding terrain. Rapid confinement presents no conflict with other search methods and dramatically reduces the chance of an expanded massive search area

NOTE: In some cases confinement proves difficult, if not impossible.

Confinement:

- No conflict with active search methods
- Starts at the perimeter
- Decreases the chances of a massive search
- Requires prompt initial reaction

Establish a search perimeter encompassing possible missing person locations and beyond which the subject unlikely passed without detection.

Confinement Methods

Road Blocks, Trail Blocks, Camp-ins. Watch any roads or clear pathways, providing routes for a missing person to depart the area in some way. Many lost persons walked out on a road, caught a ride with the first vehicle contacted and completely left the area. Establish road blocks and patrols on all roads leading into and out of the confinement perimeter. In the case of wilderness areas, both trail blocks, patrols, and camp-ins *(in a specified drainage)* serve to identify and preserve perimeter boundaries.

Lookouts. Where National Forest and Park Service lookout stations exist, notify these sites of the missing subject and ask for observation assistance. In many cases lookout towers get replaced by aircraft overflights. Specific posting of individuals in strategic locations on high ground provides a viable method of establishing a perimeter. In urban areas, individuals on street corners, building tops, water tanks, radio towers or overpasses aid in much needed oversight on perimeter boundaries.

Track Traps. A method of strategically placing track traps by first response resources used by the U.S. Border Patrol for years . This involves brushing off bare areas, and dragging road edges, or lightly traveled back roads. This strategy consists of checking for footprints in the brushed areas at regular intervals for an indication that the person moved through the perimeter. It also means checking out natural areas conducive to showing prints or other signs on patches of mud, soft ground, open areas at the tops of ridges, or voids in vegetation along roadways.

String Lines. An ingenious method of confinement developed by the Explorer Search and Rescue *(ESAR)* organization in Washington State. Spools of biodegradable string mounted in a rucksack gets carried by a team member walking through the area on a compass bearing, and the string unrolls leaving a very visible trail. Other ESAR members following along tie the string waist high on brush and other vegetation while placing paper arrows on the string pointing toward a road or base camp. Team members hope the lost subject finds the string and follows the arrows, or at the very least, the string serves as a visible perimeter during search efforts.

A Combination of confinement techniques also work in the Urban Environment. Key locations in cities and along highways use traffic and security cameras to successfully survey activity. These in combination with road or path blocks *(rolling blocks - not totally stopped traffic but moving slow enough for observation)* offer very useful confinement tactics.

Passive Mode versus Active Mode

Generally managers use two approaches in finding a missing person. They apply in rural or wilderness settings as well as in urban neighborhoods. Based on available information, the search manager chooses from one of the basic categories, ACTIVE mode or PASSIVE mode, to use his or her resources, or even a combination of the two.

In the passive mode, without searchers in the field searching, but in set locations instead, managers use special tactics to encourage the missing person to walk out or seek safety at a specific location. **Confinement Mode along with Attraction, describes a combination of two PASSIVE tactics.** When more information needs gathering through investigation or insufficient cause for a search exists, mangers use this method. Tactics in the field call for more waiting, and application of confinement or perhaps some type of attraction.

Detection, means committing resources into the field and describes the ACTIVE mode. Use this mode when acting on the subject's intentions, location, and likely actions of the missing person or in time critical situations. Likely spots consist of intended destinations, campgrounds, a friend's house, nearby brushy or forested areas, or anywhere initial efforts may logically locate the missing person.

The use of **ACTIVE** or **PASSIVE** mode largely depends on factors encompassing any of the following:

- A high urgency factor assigned to the incident due to critical subject conditions
- Quantity, quality and/or availability of search resources
- Existing hazards *(weather, man-made or natural hazards)*

Passive Mode Tactics

Attraction:

In many jurisdictions, historical data defines common areas of confusion or terrain that funnels a subject into a specific location. In general, within a certain period of time the subject walks out or shows up at that location. These cases call for the use of passive tactics. Allow the subject to come to you *(walk out)* or provide attraction points to guide and encourage mobile subjects to move to a certain location. Additionally, passive efforts provide mental encouragement to immobile victims.

Use caution when attracting missing or lost persons in some environments due to extremely dangerous situations. Encouraging people to walk out or make their way to a specific location possibly sets them up to walk into hazardous terrain or dangerous obstacles. Weigh all implications very carefully.

Visual Attraction: Includes search lights, rotating beacons, flares, strobes, balloons, fires, smoke or anything else visually attractive such as bright colored ribbon or clothing

- Attraction used effectively with *Confinement* techniques, takes specific resources and assigns them from the same point

Sound Attraction: Includes horns, P.A. systems, sirens, a discharging firearm, loud whistles, shouting, yelling names, or even beating on the surface of something metal and hollow

- When using noise, remember to **listen** *(for a response from the missing person)* for a period of time after making noise. *(See Sound Sweeps later in this Chapter.)* Also, remember that in valleys, canyons, and mountains, noises reflect and echo, which adds to confusion for the missing or lost person. For example, a bowl at the end of a canyon creates very confusing directional sounds.

Investigation: *(by phone)* Contacting friends, schools, employers, family, nurses, associates, doctors, clergy, business contacts or anyone with possible information. *(See Chapter 13 on Investigation)*

Wait: The choice here comes down to wait until a person walks out or shows up somewhere. But, we need to ask ourselves, how long to wait? In a majority of cases: "Not very long!" Even if you choose to wait for a short time, some planning needs to occur, in case a search begins.

Use the Media: A very productive tactic. Radio bulletins or TV along with requests for information in newspapers or radio, as well as posted fliers distributed in local areas all prove very effective.

Aircraft Fly overs: Local government agencies such as police, private organizations and general aviation pilots often request to divert slightly when returning from regularly scheduled flights or routes. These diversions aren't search flights, but a matter of keeping possibilities open with overflights and sharp eyes. Aircraft owners in the local area usually find no problems in scheduling this type of activity.

Active Mode Tactics

Committing First Resources to the Field

As mentioned above, initial efforts focus on areas where chances of locating the individual *(or clues)* take a minimal amount of effort and abundant resources. Although the most effective initial response resources need clue awareness, possible conflicts may arise.

A search planner or manager needs the ability to spontaneously determine how resources function without thinking about it. This entails an understanding of both the resource's attributes as well as it's shortfalls. Therefore search managers need to observe the training that local resources undertake on a regular basis to see first hand their capabilities and what they bring to a search.

A tracking team relies on subtle physical clues left behind by the subject, such as tracks, broken twigs, crushed leaves, and other visible signs. Take light and time of day into consideration when deploying them as a resource. An air scent dog relies on a cone of scent emanating from the subject in the field and humidity, wind currents, and temperature play a huge part in their success. Using a team of tracking dogs after a tracking team or numerous members of a ground search party systematically worked an area wastes valuable resources.

Some terrain and conditions call for the use of fixed wing aircraft as opposed to a helicopter. Consider the advantages of each type of initial response team, and apply them to areas that best suit their expertise positively adding to a search. The backbone of effective search planning and management comes from properly applying SAR resources to field operations.

Clue aware resources perform the most effective initial response. They consist of:

- Human Trackers as well as Track and Clue Aware Searchers
- Tracking or air scenting dogs *(dependent on humidity, wind and temperature)*
- Trailing Dogs *(depending on weather, temperature and wind)*
- Trained Hasty Teams *(track and clue aware)*
- Aircraft *(looking for tracks, debris or broken vegetation)*

Effective initial tactics include:

- Sign cutting and perimeter cutting
- Hasty Search
- Confinement
- Attraction

Use initial response resources in the following order if possible, realizing of course that their effectiveness depends on the planning and control of the search manager.

Clue Finders

These resources:

- Called first and respond quickly
- Usually small in number and skilled *(Logistic needs are less and they are very independent.)*
- Main function consists of looking in likely spots to find clues

Examples:

- Tracker or track and clue aware searcher
- Tracking or trailing dog
- Interviewing and investigation team
- Direction finding *(DF)* equipment

Clue / Subject Finders

These resources:

- Search areas indicated by Clue Finders
- Provide on-going information or corroborate initial clues
- Investigate possible routes or barriers to missing person travel, check incentives or attractions for further clues left by subject *(this helps to further reduce search area size)*

Examples:

- Air scent search dogs
- Track and clue aware hasty teams
- DF equipment
- Sweep search teams *(clue aware)*

Subject Finders

These resources include:

- Deployed into segmented areas as per high probability or clue indications
- Able to search in the most effective, rapid and efficient manner for the environment

Examples:

- Sweep and grid search teams *(sweep width oriented and trained)*
- Aircraft - equipped with IR - Omnidirectional and/or high resolution cameras

Untrained Volunteers

Not the normal response for search under anything but abnormal or extenuating circumstances. When using untrained searchers simply follow a few basic guidelines to maximize their effectiveness. Virtually all over the world spontaneous volunteers appear ready and willing to search. We address this issue in Chapter 23 under Urban Search where this problem surfaces the most. The search manager considers a number of important points in applying untrained volunteer resources:

- Consider all available initial resources *(be sure to include them in a good preplan)* and their capabilities, even in neighboring communities or other jurisdictions before using untrained volunteers.
- Ask if the volunteers possess any type of search training or emergency management training. What kind of specialized training and how much? Unfortunately, with large amounts of untrained volunteers any trained resources in the jurisdiction take on the responsibility of managing and not searching.
- What can the resources provide in relation to what the operation needs? *(Another set of eyes searching, technical expertise, clue awareness, or support type functions)* Often well meaning, dedicated people fulfill functions such as confinement.
- If using an untrained resource, think about what feedback information they provide to the search planning effort for the next operational period. *(If a resource simply reports that "they failed to find the subject" they lacked any relevant information*

[clues] that lessened the search difficulty and, in fact, destroyed evidence.)

Hasty Teams

Developed originally by Washington State Explorer Search and Rescue, the Hasty Team concept developed into an initial response team of three well trained, self-sufficient and highly mobile searchers. The responsibility of the team consisted of checking out areas most likely to produce the subject *(e.g. trails, trail and road heads, roads, campsites, lakes, clearings, and similar locations)*. A Hasty teams speed of response coupled with accuracy of firsthand information assimilated at the scene, makes them very efficient and useful.

In more recent years, local jurisdictions changed this concept, developing and training quick response teams able to respond to any type of SAR related incident. Teams carry equipment and resources 24 hours a day in the trunks of vehicles and when assigned, they respond 24 hours a day on their respective duty days. A search manager uses Hasty teams for management, recon, search, investigation and even communications.

Optimum Skills:

- Track and clue awareness, *(tracking skills)*
- Clue and subject behavior orientation
- Ability to interview accurately
- Familiarity with the local terrain and inherent dangers of the immediate area
- Complete self-sufficiency in the outdoors
- Advanced first-aid skills or better
- Very good navigation skills

Equipment:

- **Minimum:** 48 to 72 hour pack:

  - Radio communications
  - First-aid supplies
  - Compass, GPS *(and altimeter in some areas)*
  - Maps of the area
  - Essential basic climbing gear *(if near mountainous terrain)*
  - Whistle or signal device

- **Optimum:** 72 hour pack. All of the above plus:

  - Ground to air communications
  - Paramedic supplies
  - Lensatic or silva type compasses or GPS
  - 7.5 minute, or 1:50,000, or 1:25,000 topo maps of the area

Some jurisdictions took these fast response teams and developed them into very specialized and cross trained, three person units.

An Example from One County

- **One Member - Terrain Analysis.** Responsible for map reconnaissance, compass anomalies, altimeter settings and identification of key locations, likely spots, and geographic influences that might affect the missing subject.

- **One Member - Sign Cutting and Clue Detection.** Responsible to check likely spots, physical recon, identification of potential clues, tracks and physical evidence of human travel in the area.

- **One Member - Investigator/Interviewer.** Responsible to recreate the scene, contact eyewitnesses, protect the IPP/PLS/LKP, make contact with dispatch, ask for further investigation, set up initial C.P.

Types of Searches Conducted by Resources - Detection Mode (e.g. looking for anything related to the missing person)

Washington State Explorer Search and Rescue experimented with a system in the late 1980s addressing a simple description or nomenclature for types of searches they wanted ESAR members to accomplish when deployed to the field. These search types provided detection mode procedures designed to seek out the subject or clues in the assigned areas.

For the purposes of briefing, debriefing and common management terminology, the types represented classifications of search effort, and became accepted terms for both field and management related assignments. Search management and planning continues to use these procedures today.

Keep in mind that the priority given to a search dictates the strategy. In general, as elapsed time increases, the relative urgency of the situation also increases. In the initial stages, with a low urgency, search managers use more passive methods. As the search progresses, the need for more active methods increases. The best initial action plan combines the two modes commensurate with the needs of the search at hand.

The methods used maximize the probability of success in the highest priority areas with the most capable resources looking for clues and the subject. High priority *(i.e., time critical)* usually dictates more active measures and larger numbers of resources. Resource application depends on what designation the search manager gives the initial strategy. *Active, passive, or a combination of the two.*

Three Types of Search Detection Modes

Type I - Rapid response to areas of high probability by immediately available resources.

TYPE I CRITERION - *SPEED*

Type I - Considerations:

- The search team assumes *(depending on elapsed time between when subject went missing and when reported)* a RESPONSIVE subject resides in the search area
- Provides an immediate show of effort
- Helps define a search area by gathering intelligence or locating clues, and in follow up after finding a clue
- Very critical to use track and clue aware resources in this type of search

- Searches often result in determining where NOT to search further
- The availability and effective use of Type 1 resources depends on preplanning

Type I - Techniques:

- Investigation *(personal via phone)*
- Thorough checks of last known position *(for clues, tracks, direction of travel, etc.)*
- Follow known *(or suspected)* route
- Trail running using sound and visual searching
- Perimeter check *(possibly used in conjunction with confinement)*
- Sign cutting
- Road patrols
- Check attractions or incentives
- Check hazardous areas
- Check drainages
- Ridge running
- The "bastard" search
- Locating any clues
- ELT/Direction Finder Search

Type I - Most Effective Resources:

- Interviewers and investigators
- Trained *(clue-conscious)* composite hasty teams
- Human trackers *(for both tracking and sign cutting)*
- Dogs
- Aircraft
- Horse responders
- Other, very mobile, trained resources

Type II - A fast, systematic search of a high probability segment of the search area using techniques producing high probabilities of detection per searcher-hour of effort.

TYPE II CRITERION - EFFICIENCY

Type II - Considerations:

- Often employed after Type I efforts in some segments, especially if Type I tactics found clues

- The initial search tactic used when searching in heavily vegetated areas
- Use if the subject RESPONSIVENESS is assumed to still be high
- Large area identified but no particular areas identified and there is insufficient manpower to cover it more thoroughly

Type II efforts effectively locate clues.

Type II - Techniques:

- Used in a specifically defined segment of the search area
- When you find a clue use this technique to follow up in the segment
- Uses an open grid, with wide spacing between searchers. *(Sound/light lines or sound sweeps)*
- Follows search routes using compass bearings

Type II - Most Effective Resources:

- Interviewers and investigators
- Track and clue awareness trained teams
- Dogs
- Horse responders
- Trackers and sign cutters
- Aircraft - both fixed wing and rotor wing
- Trained sound and visual sweep teams
- Other trained teams

Type III - A slower, highly systematic search, using thorough techniques.

TYPE III CRITERION - THOROUGHNESS

Type III - Considerations:

- Use only as last resort
- Use with a limited search area or segment a large amount of manpower
- If searchers lack a keen eye for clues, or when efforts aim at finding extremely small items of an evidentiary nature *(an evidence search)* Type III searches tend to damage clues

Type III - Techniques:

- Closed visual grid or sweep search
- Evidence searches

Type III - Most Effective Resources:

- Trained sweep and grid search teams

Summary of the Three Search Types

Type I: Ridge running, area, trail, and drainage investigation, structure inspection. *(likely spots)*

Type II: Fast, open *(wide spaced)* grid and sound as well as sound/light sweeps. Average Range of Detection.

Type III: Area saturation, close visual grid *(evidence type search)*.

Type I Search. When a report for a missing person comes through, a search manager uses this type of method after arriving on scene. Search Managers quickly brief Team leaders while distributing maps and radios. Small teams of searchers dispatch to check adjacent trails, ridges, drainages, ponds and all known structures in the area such as abandoned cabins, barns, sheds, or lookouts. Some roads require continuous patrolling by vehicles, but many unused logging and fire roads, impassable for vehicles, need patrolling as well, usually on foot or by horse mounted patrols. Apply the Bike Wheel Model for application of resources as described in Chapter 14

Type II Search - Planning. Upon finishing a *Type I* search, meaning all trails, ridges, drainages and structures received thorough checks and with negative results, follow up with a *Type II* search pattern covering the sectors or geographical areas rapidly and efficiently. A *Type II* search pattern assumes the lost person, if not injured, and other than an elderly person or small child, is alive and moving and will respond to a shout or sound sweep whistle blast if within earshot.

The general search area brakes down into search segments consisting of geographical areas bounded by roads, trails, streams, power lines or prominent ridges easily identified on a map. Search teams of 6 to 12 members setup, each with a qualified team leader and select specialty personnel, to search the various segments. In open country using larger search teams often proves advantageous. In dense, brushy areas, reducing teams to 3 - 9 members maintains efficient control and coverage. Several 3 to 9 member teams working the same sector covers an area faster and more efficiently than a larger team which tends to function slowly and often proves difficult to control.

Type II Search - Personnel. Adding additional personnel to a team operating in fairly open country helps but, large teams all spread out often grows difficult to control.

An effective sensor defines an individual searcher's main job, *(primarily eyes and ears)* which contributes to efficient functioning of the whole team. On a Type II search, cover a large area as rapidly as possible, keeping in mind that the team acts as the eyes and ears of the search effort.

A TYPE II TECHNIQUE

Use a three (3) person team, with one compass-bearer. This team works independently from other teams.

The responsibility of determining how and where to establish a search pattern falls on the Search Manager and his staff, while the search team carries out those plans.

Ordinarily, a search for a lost person consists merely of a process of area elimination. Cover the prime areas first, if unsuccessful, cover the secondary areas in a widening scope until locating the missing person. How quickly the team finds the lost person depends on the staffs skill in applying past experience to analyze the situation and make correct decisions regarding proper effort allocation and search area priorities.

Field Methods and Tactical Resource Application

Lost or Missing Outdoor Group Members

Based on the advice from long time search coordinators and managers, Dr. Paul Green, Professor of Outdoor Recreation Leadership at Eastern Washington University, developed a number of field techniques for finding lost members of recreational outings. These initial action, quick response tactics, intended for leaders in charge of an outdoor group, help to successfully locate a missing person in this type of situation.

Professor Green is not advocating for his outdoor leaders to conduct extensive search operations for a missing party member. Instead, this method intends to provide outdoor leaders with some quick action

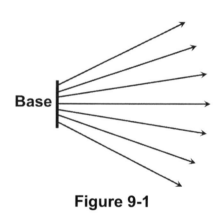

Figure 9-1

strategies for locating the missing group member without calling in an official SAR response team. The techniques described provide good initial strategies to use with limited resources.

Shotgun Search Pattern

The shotgun search technique deploys searchers out of a camp site or base on a pattern similar to firing a shotgun *(See Figure 9-1)*.

The search pattern spreads wider the further the searchers travel from the campsite. This technique, developed for inexperienced searchers, limits the searcher to about a half mile in distance, necessitates

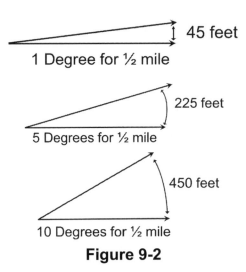

Figure 9-2

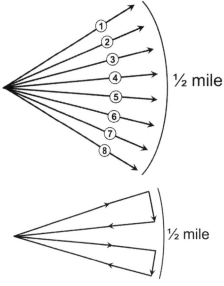

Figure 9-3

a compass and depends heavily on good navigation skills. It also works best when aimed at a road or trail in order to regroup the searchers. In theory, the shotgun search pattern states that a one-degree difference in compass headings *(bearing)* results in a 45-foot separation between searchers at 1/2-mile distances from the camp or starting point and a 90-foot separation at 1 mile *(See Figure 9-2)*. The intended goal, try to saturate the area out to a half mile as quickly as possible.

When starting the search, deploy each searcher on a compass heading 5 degrees different than the person next to them. The searchers begin close together but spread out as they travel, a 1/2 mile of separation between searchers equates to 225 feet *(5 x 45 Ft)*. See Figure 9-3. The searchers then return to the campsite on a reverse bearing *(heading)*. While hiking on the compass headings, searchers looking for clues, blowing their whistles, shouting the camper's name and listening. This easy to deploy search technique gets searchers into the field quickly.

The deployment of the shotgun pattern includes several limitations in the search for a missing group member. One, each participant needs a compass and a knowledge of how to use it. Essentially, knowing the rudiments of navigation such as pace count. Searchers need to know their pace rate for 100 feet. One pace amounts to every time the left foot strikes the ground. The second limitation, the searcher's need to use a reverse heading or back azimuth to return to base or the camp area. This slows their deployment into other priority pieces of terrain in the suspected search area. The pattern's predictable separation between searchers limits it's effectiveness to a maximum distance of 1/2-mile.

The Wagon Wheel Search Pattern

The wagon wheel search pattern, similar to the shotgun technique, differs in that the method used returns the searchers to the campsite or base while at the same time accomplishing the task of searching *new* areas. The actual search pattern looks like the spokes on an old wagon wheel (See Figure 9-4). The same proven separation technique applies to the deployment; a one-degree difference in compass

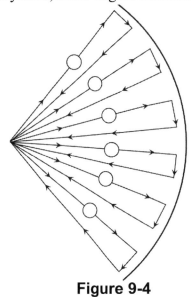

Figure 9-4

headings *(bearings)* results in a 45-foot separation between searchers at 1/2-mile distance from the initial point. Deploy your searchers on a heading 10 degrees different than the person next to them. When they reach a 1/2 mile, a 450 foot (45 x 10 = 450) separation between searchers exists. Each searcher then turns right 96 degrees and walks 225 feet. Another 96 degree turn to the right moves the searchers on a heading to the campsite or base *(See Figure 9-5)*.

Of course, this technique possesses some limitations of its own. Similar to the shotgun pattern, the wagon wheel returns the searchers to the point of origin, but searches new areas at the same time. It also limits the distance on the first turn to 225 feet or less in order to make the correct return angle that brings the searchers back to the campsite or base.

In remote wilderness areas of Montana and Washington State, these techniques effectively locate participants missing from camp or group outings. Therefore, some recommend that SAR groups practice searches of this type with members of the local SAR organization. If practiced, teams develop the techniques and the rapid deployment capability they produce.

SHOTGUN AND WAGON WHEEL SEARCH PATTERNS (96 degree turns) INSTRUCTIONS

Shotgun and wagon wheel search pattern initial bearings for search azimuth, turn right at ½ mile *(96 degrees)* continue for 225 feet or less, make another right turn (96 degrees) and follow return headings. Bearings are in 10-degree increments. These bearings should bring searchers back to base (or initial point).

Bearing	Turn	Return
360	96	192
10	106	202
20	116	212
30	126	222
40	136	232
50	146	242
60	156	252
70	166	262
80	176	272
90	186	282
100	196	292
110	206	302
120	216	312
130	226	322
140	236	332
150	246	342
160	256	352
170	266	362
180	276	12
190	286	22
200	296	32
210	306	42
220	316	52
230	326	62
240	336	72
250	346	82
260	356	92
270	6	98
280	16	112
290	26	122
300	36	132
310	46	142
320	56	152
330	66	162
340	76	172
350	86	182

Figure 9-5

Track & Clue Awareness (TCA)

Ross Gordon and Tony Wells, from the Search And Rescue Institute New Zealand (SARINZ) greatly influenced and helped develop all the information set forth in this section of the chapter. Their vision of all field searchers possessing a Track and Clue Awareness (TCA trained) shaped the progressive cutting edge approach to field search, scene processing and clue awareness that elevated New Zealand to the top of this skill capability. This portion of the chapter involves more than just man-tracking. The concept of TCA covers more than normally addressed in a basic man tracking course.

Finding people fast remains the ultimate goal of all SAR missions. TCA allows responders to maximize opportunities to detect clues and interpret them to determine likely Direction of Travel (DoT) and behaviors - thus continually refining the search area. TCA consists of two integrated functions; man tracking skills and clue/scene processing, which means knowing where to search and what to search for (*clues, sign and evidence*) in addition to analyzing each thing discovered. This skill offers both an investigative (*strategy*) and an operational (*tactic*) search tool.

TCA also includes discovering what activities occurred at a specific site (*point of departure, crime scene, trail junction, campsite, etc*). SAR individuals accomplished in track and clue awareness develop a more holistic skill than just man-tracking. TCA consists of two important and complimentary components:

1. Field searchers who find, analyze and report sign or evidence; and

2. The incident management team (IMT) who follows up on these reports as well as communicating information about the subject and their activities into the field to assist the field searchers with better in-field analysis.

In this manner, field searchers and search mangers work together to prove or disprove likely scenarios, enhance search planning, help in determining probability of area (POA) and future resource allocation in an integrated team approach.

An understanding of the importance of TCA in the planning and management arena promotes the integrating of field reports with key search planning data. Clues, the Initial Planning Point (IPP), Point Last Seen (PLS), Last Known Position (LKP) and Direction of Travel (DoT) each give added credibility when supported by evidence from TCA trained responders. Incident Commanders and Search Planners trained in the concepts of TCA tend to make more efficient and effective assignments for initial responders in the Reflex Tasking phase of the incident.

Never get led blindly into the assumption that the application of track and clue aware searchers to a search, always ends in finding every lost person or persons. Instead, think of track and clue awareness as making searchers aware of both subtle and blatant evidence which provides a much better chance to locate the missing person. TCA also proves *(or disproves)* that a missing person passed through a designated area and what type of activities they took part in while there.

TCA Defined

TCA trained searchers, possess tracking and sign cutting knowledge and skills, but differ from skilled and experienced trackers. Learning to man-track takes hundreds of hours of practicing skill development and hundreds more to reach proficiency. TCA creates field searchers skilled in key aspects of sign detection from which they use to record facts. The teams use sign analysis and interpretation to make informed decisions which, if viable, get reported to the IMT and then integrated into the search planning process.

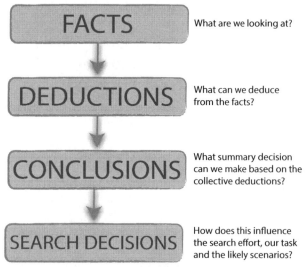

Figure 9-6

SIGN. The term sign includes any disturbance in the baseline environment. It ranges from a vague scuff mark, compression, imprint, vehicle tire pattern, animal marks etc. The sign may be conclusively or inconclusively human. Some sign offers evidence also.

TRACKING: Tracking involves following the evidence or *sign* left by someone or something.

SIGN CUTTING: Sign cutting consists of looking for sign in order to determine a starting point from which to begin tracking. Usually performed perpendicular to the suspected direction of travel of the missing person in order to intercept their track/trail.

TRACK AND CLUE AWARENESS: Track and Clue Awareness includes basic tracking and sign cutting skills, integrated with sign protection and recording skills. This then combines with a high degree of sign interpretation skills to maximize the value of the sign located and assist in directing the SAR effort through recommendations made by the field team to SAR management.

When and Where to Use Track and Clue Awareness Skills

TCA offers management a great deal of information, however success depends on specific conditions and the skill level of the responders.

The acronym CDNA helps to remember this information:

- **Characteristics** including;
  - Pattern/features of prints/sign
  - Size, shape of objects/sign
  - Likely physical state
    - load carrying?
    - injury?
  - Subjects likely mental state
    - disorientation?
    - confusion/panic?
    - dehydration?
    - LPB strategies?
  - Unique identifiers of the sign
- **Direction** of travel (DOT)
  - Missing subject DOT
  - Others present (witnesses?)
- **Number** of persons including;
  - Number in subject's party
  - Others persons/vehicles (witnesses?)
  - Sex/gender (corroborative evidence)
- **Age** of the sign/clues located (time frame)
  - Missing party sign
  - Others persons/vehicles (witnesses?)

TCA, tracking and sign cutting needs to occur in the early stages of a search before well-meaning but unaware searchers or other people in the search area contaminate any evidence *(sign/clues)*. Early application of trackers or track and clue aware searchers also allows preservation of some clues, sign or track *(time and weather-sensitive)* components of evidence.

Can finding clues and also tracking be useful in all environments? What about while its raining? How about at night? What about heavily used areas? Yes, but no one blanket statement covers all situations where searchers use TCA. **Let the TCA specialist decide when and where to effectively use this skill.** Skilled TCA responders look for, and often find, sign, evidence or clues that frequently elude the untrained search responder. Even the most difficult terrain tends to produce clues that might eventually lead to a successful search. Experienced responders know that finding nothing (if done well) provides a major clue in itself.

Dimensions of Evidence

Evidence signifies something that makes plain or clear; it indicates the correctness or in fact truthfulness of something. As most people know, law depends heavily on evidence, especially when it comes to finding people guilty or not guilty of criminal acts. SAR finds evidence extremely important as well. Correct interpretation of evidence on-scene and in the process and context of a search makes a difference between life and death for some subjects.

Location and Elevation: Identifiable evidence shows specific location and elevation. The person was here. That means he/she gained or lost elevation. A starting point or last known position in a route of travel. It also indicates determination in the case of rough, hazardous terrain.

Time: How long ago someone left evidence *(track, broken vegetation, trampled grass, etc.)* or discarded it at the location. Things like lunch scraps (*banana peels, apple cores, orange peels, other food scraps*), all go through an aging process. TCA responders need to determine how long ago someone discarded the evidence in the environment. A well trained TCA responder will give a very good approximation.

Vector and Velocity: Determines the direction of travel and how fast the individual travels. Location with respect to Initial Planning Point for the search or the last known position. The nature of track and any change in length of stride compared to initial measurements also help give some indications for this question.

Corroboration and Ownership: The number of people and specific identifying characteristics of tracks or evidence. Objects or discarded items consistent with known possessions, equipment lists or rented gear all indicate ownership or corroborative evidence. Equipment often leaves specific types of sign or tends to corroborate ground sign.

Intent: The type of activity or intent the individual participated in. Lost and/or confused, goal directed, route focused, or right on track for intended activities or a given travel itinerary.

Character of Evidence: What was it? Hard evidence and indisputable clues such as items of clothing, possessions, etc? Corroborate evidence such as disturbances in vegetation, scuffs, loose impressions on the ground, but not identifiable tracks? First or second hand observations, etc.?

See What is There!

> . . . I saw the heavy foot-marks of the constables, but saw also the tracks of the two men who had passed through the garden. It was easy to tell that they had been before the others, because in places their marks had been entirely obliterated by the others coming upon the top of them.. . . . In this way my second link was formed, which told me that the nocturnal visitors were two in number, one remarkable for his height (as I calculated from the length of his stride), and the other fashionably dressed, to judge from the small and elegant impression left by his boots . . . .
>
> Arthur Conan Doyle
> Sherlock Holmes, *A Study in Scarlet*

Figure 9-7
Tracing foot print patterns or distinctive marks on clear vinyl, creates a composite print without complete tracks.

Sign Cutters, Trackers and TCA Responder Goals.

We need to look for the parts, not the whole. Looking for clues, marks, and various forms of evidence takes a shift in the mind set of the responder. Sometimes we discover the subtle pieces that string together the images of the whole.

Nature tends to use milder tones with uneven boundaries, rougher textures that tend to blend objects into each other, and weaker contrasts that make delineating one object from another more difficult. Unconscious, untrained or unfocused urban visual skills usually break down in identifying or recognizing target clues or evidence in a wilderness environment. In the natural environment, what we see is not always what we are looking for. Therefore, the SAR responder needs to adjust their viewing skills to clearly interpret what nature offers, and learn to see what is really there.

Well trained TCA responders look for the following:

Outline: A boundary, perimeter, or edge of an object. The outer limits of a shape. At time it looks complete, broken or even mostly obscure, but the visual perspective tends to give the illusion of the overall outline of the object.

Shape: The spatial form of an object, impression or mark. What it looks like. Is there a corresponding image in the memory banks? Is the perspective canonical or non-canonical? Recognition depends on shape (*see POD and vision chapter 19*). Shape includes the outline shape, and any non-natural features that contribute to building the overall picture.

Contrast: Consists of the relative lightness or darkness of an object compared to the surroundings. With little contrast, items, objects and evidence blend into the surroundings which forces responders to use other techniques to bring out or maximize the existing contrast.

Color: Tone or shade of color helps in determining the age or derivation of a clue. Very powerful colors stick out regardless of the surrounding environment's color. Colors completely outside the color spectrum of the surrounding terrain draw immediate attention. These items consist of discarded or transposed items such as candy wrappers, garments or articles of clothing with bright or florescent colors, vegetation, soil etc.

One of the most important color changes caused by human passage through the environment comes from exposed moisture in soil. The timing for these visual changes from the surrounding environment depends on ambient temperature, humidity and time of day or night.

Texture: Consists of the relative roughness or smoothness of a feature or impression compared to the surrounding terrain or surface. Someone stepping on the ground leaves an impression much smoother than the surrounding terrain and the impression remains *compressed* for some time. Eventually, that smoothness or compressed area goes back to normal and looks and feels like the surrounding surface area. The forces of nature like wind, water, melting or temperature change from day to night or vise versa and seasonal variations all impact the aging of sign. This makes the changing of textures over time an important part of the aging process of sign and visible evidence.

Movement: Not necessarily the movement of the sign, clue, track or impression. Although something discarded tends to move from wind, water or vegetation movement as a responder gets close, this presents only one circumstance among many possibilities. *Top Sign,* a term used by many involved in tracking or sign cutting, describes *sign* above ankle height. It means looking above the ground at the vegetation, the structure or elevated surrounding growth. This perspective provides very valuable insight into recent activities that occurred at that location.

Movement occurs in plant leaves, stems, tendrils, stalks and/or vines when someone or something passes through thick vegetation and undergrowth. Displacement of the growing parts of the plant from the position that they normally assumed in the growth process results in vegetation pushed or displaced into a position not normally assumed by the plant. In essence, the leaves and stalks become *cocked* and held in place by surrounding vegetation and undergrowth structures. Responders use tracking sticks to test the vegetation and see if it springs back to an original position (*movement*). This indicates that someone or something passed through the undergrowth. The direction the moving vegetation acts as a good indication of direction of travel. Try to corroborate top sign with ground sign as animals, game and even strong winds or storms sometimes create top sign.

The Tracking Stick *(Sign Cutting Stick)*

- A tracking stick ranges from 36 to 48 inches in length. It contains at least two rubber bands (*or rubber "O" rings*)which move along the stick, but fit tight enough to stay in place when desired. Commercially produced, sources for making your own inexpensive and expedient sign cutting stick exist everywhere. Even, long straight narrow tree branches work well for a one time use situations. Mark these expedient sign cutting sticks with a knife, pencil, or flagging tape. Other shafts such as the fiberglass poles used for electric fences, hardwood dowels, hiking (trekking poles) or ski poles or even an old yard stick, work exceptionally well for sign cutting as well.

Figure 9-8
Examples of a tracking stick. Top to bottom include a tree branch, a ski pole, a collapsible hiking or trekking pole and a fiberglass rod.

- To determine a persons stride length (or step length), responders need to find two consecutive foot prints. Position one of the markers on the sign cutting stick (*either rubber band, "O" ring, or other mark*) so that the distance from the tip of the stick to the marker represents the same distance as the stride or step length.

- Measure the length of one of the footprints. In between the tip of the stick and the stride or step length marker, place the second marker (*rubber band, or O'ring*) to indicate the length of the footprint. These markers form constant reminders of the approximate step length and footprint size.

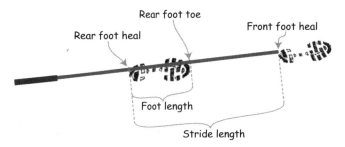

Figure 9-9
Using the sign cutting stick to measure stride.

- At the last print found, place the stick so that the stride mark is held just above the rear of the heel on the print. While keeping the marker above the heel location on the last print, move the tip of the stick through an approximate 60 degree arc in the area where the next print should logically be found. Concentrate the f*oveal field of view* (*see Chapter 19*) at the end of the stick as it is moved slowly across the arc, which leads to the next depression, scuff, anomaly or heel print.

- Considering straight ahead as 12 o'clock, slowly sweep the stick from the 11 o'clock to the 1 o'clock positions while taking visual snapshots of the area at the end of the stick. Stationary visual snapshots work more effectively than scanning. The ability to see some types of sign, depressions, anomalies or evidence ranges from very obvious, to very difficult, but it is there. If nothing shows up during the first sweep, make the next one even slower.

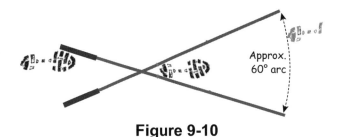

Figure 9-10
Using the sign cutting stick to locate the next sign.

Always keep in mind, the possibility of the tracked subject changing direction or altering their stride. The greatest effect on stride length remains terrain and stride length tends to shorten or lengthen by as much as 4-5 inches to avoid objects or to seek more secure footing. Any change in direction usually occurs over several steps, so look for changes in the individual foot orientation. Although uncommon, abrupt changes of direction tend to indicate evasive behavior or some other external influence on travel.

Note that an untrained person's eyes habitually dart indiscriminately, without any real awareness of the mechanics and physiology involved. Unless directed the eyes tend to wander. This makes the assistance of the sign cutting or tracking stick very important. The stick assists responders in training the eye to concentrate on the area of the *foveal field of view* (*see Chapter 19*) where the next indication, clue or print lies. As simple as this procedure seems, practice makes it perfect. It takes concentration, patience, attention to detail and what many call *dirt time*. That means getting down on the knees and sometimes on the stomach in varying conditions, different soil types and diverse ground cover to examine the evidence left by different people as they pass through the environment.

Strategies to Detect Clues

Currently, two effective strategies compete for detecting clues generated by the missing person. The first, <u>sign cutting,</u> designed by SAR professionals to save time and improve efficiency, and second involves <u>investigation,</u> which uncovers facts and information about the missing person to fill in the subject profile.

While track and clue aware searchers, skilled in tracking, methodically follow the line of sign in a step-by-step process, another tracking or sign cutting team simultaneously sweeps out ahead cutting the same trail further on, for sign. If they find tracks or sign which matches the characteristics of the missing person, tracking responders then jump to that sign, using a leap frog system to gain tremendous distance on the missing person.

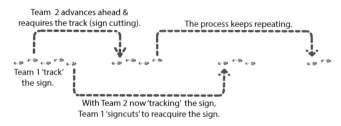

Figure 9-11
Leapfrog sign cutting with two tracking teams.

Sign Cutting

Sign cutting means looking for sign (tracks, clues, disturbances, discarded items, broken or damaged vegetation) or anything not normal to the baseline of that particular environment. The tracker intends to determine a starting point from which to either:

1. Follow the sign by tracking; or,
2. Process the surrounding terrain for any additional evidence, clues or information.

WHERE? The trackers first look for sign in areas associated with the subject and most likely where he/she went. The following key locations represent the most effective areas to look for initial sign:

- The IPP, LKP or PLS
- Around the missing persons parked vehicle
- Decision points along a travel route
- Toilet area near camps, etc

HOW? Sign cutting usually aims to intercept the missing person's trail perpendicular to the direction responders initially suspect the missing person travelled. In other words, they attempt to intersect the subjects path. Sign cutting involves more than just looking for footprints. Sign cutting individuals look for disturbances on the ground, top sign or vegetation impacts, out of place objects such as rocks or sticks, as well as things like crushed leaves. Experienced sign cutters use both available light and some artificial sources. They look in the direction of the light source for best results and in some cases they use a flashlight or reflected light from a mirror.

WHEN? Trackers prefer to seek track and sign in the morning and late afternoon when the sun sets low in the sky. Ideally, a trackers starts sign cutting in the morning, suspends any activity during midday, then resumes work late in the afternoon until sunset. Essentially, tracking occurs at anytime during the day, morning midday or at night, but in the morning and afternoon trackers use the sun to their advantage. Making these times the most opportune. Unfortunately, in SAR, responders never get to choose what time of day to search. When trackers work at night they totally control their light sources, which makes it easier than depending on the sun for your only source of light. They also adapt to tracking during mid day, by casting a shadow with a hat and using a flashlight for a low angle light source.

The Binary Search Technique uses the same principle as sign cutting described before. While team members stay at the last known point *(or clue)*, others make controlled sweeps through the probable search area trying to detect tracks or other evidence that someone passed through the area.

Success, when using these techniques, saves time and effort. The Binary Search Technique works most efficiently with limited resources and a time critical situation. It performs best due to the following:

- The easiest way to find someone is to know where they are not.
- With time constraints, **Selective sampling** of clues **works better** than looking at each and every one.
- **Searchers tend to find searching the area circumference easier** than the whole area.

> *"What you see depends mainly on what you look for."*
> - John Lubbock

Many search and rescue teams use sign cutting extensively, which helps eliminate vast portions of the search area from consideration *(or at least primary consideration)*. This also makes special training in sign cutting well worth the effort. However, like all things, sign cutting never works 100 percent of the time. Since humans perform it, we get imperfections; therefore repetition helps tremendously.

Trying to identify clues left by the missing person and constantly monitoring the search area for changes, remains the key to an effective clue oriented search. For example, use track traps as a tactic for confinement. Also, the complete absence of clues always presents a clue in and of itself.

Clues, like wisps of smoke, pop up one minute and then go away the next. Footprints tend to blow or wash away. Witnesses leave the search area. Summit logs get buried by snow, flashing lights go unnoticed etc. Always consider the constant volatility of a search area. Clues not generated by the missing person, but identified as such, also add to the confusion. A set of footprints or even a series of disturbances in the search area may contain several messages or signals, depending on who made them and where they went. If the missing person actually left these messages, then consider the following:

- I was in this location previously.

- My destination can possibly be derived from my direction of travel.

Tracking Team Configurations

SAR units use three-person teams as a common approach to the function of *following sign*. Two trackers and a team leader make up the three-person team for SAR and non-threat environments

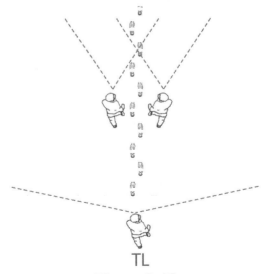

Figure 9-12
Standard 3 person team configuration - SAR

- This configuration allows the two trackers to consult in difficult situations and places a tracker each side of the sign making the best use of angles and light. The Team Leader (TL) performs the function of managing the team and situational awareness, as well as sign cutting any other exits.

- Training with this configuration builds confidence, reduces errors, and benefits students by allowing a verbal exchange of the details rather than just mutual observations of clues.

- Due to the visually demanding role of the tracking position, two trackers need to share the load up-front. Where required, the team leader rotates into one of these positions and allows one of the trackers to rest. With a limited amount of sign or clues, the tracker experiences even more fatigue in this position.

- This configuration allows the team to split up and probe potential exits if several trails diverge. The Team Leader, remains on the last good sign and manages the team. If a tracker then locates more correct sign the team then resets and continues to follow the subject.

Some situations, such as in the law enforcement context or when operating in suspected or known hostile environments, where one skilled tracker works on point and other team members operate as flankers. A three person team in this configuration helps provide cover and assistance to the tracker on point as well as sign cutting any potential exits or changes in direction.

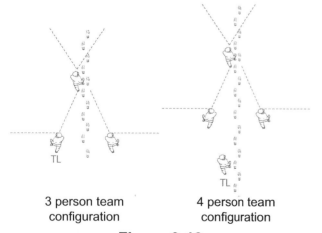

3 person team configuration   4 person team configuration

Figure 9-13

Tracking Team Responsibilities

Regardless of the formation chosen, the following responsibilities still apply for each team member:

Tracker/Point

- Concentrates on an arc of approximately 10-2 o'clock forward
- Stays on prime sign and the last track found
- Responsible for locating and confirming the next impression, print or piece of sign
- Marks the prints or sign as the team progresses
- Consults/seeks assistance where necessary

Sign Cutters/Flankers

- Watch to the side for incoming tracks or sign that might confuse or complicate the situation
- Watch for a sudden turn in the trackers trail he/she followed
- Look further ahead for changes in terrain, clues and/or dangers to the Tracker/Point
- Assist the Tracker/Point in finding the next sign from their vantage positions
- Provide armed cover of the Tracker/Point where necessary

Team Leader

- Maintains situational awareness, safety and liaison with search base
- Responsible for overall strategy and tactics
- Responsible for overall team welfare and safety

Restricted Environments

In restricted environments where vegetation or the terrain only allows a narrow avenue or approach to the prime sign area or tracks, adopting a linear formation works better. The roles remain essentially the same, however with a four person team, each Sign Cutter/Flanker needs to concentrate their efforts on one side of the line of travel. In this configuration, protocol still calls for rotating the Tracker/Point.

Conclusively Human or Corroborant

The two applicable types of sign traits divide into conclusively human or corroborant evidence.

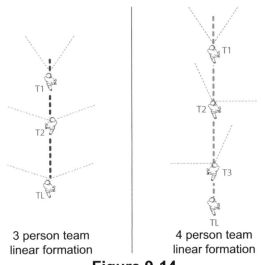

Figure 9-14

Conclusively human means that the sign or disturbance, when considered on its own with no other evidence, definitely shows that a human caused it and not an animal.

Corroborant sign, on the other hand, means that the disturbance inconclusively shows that either a human or possibly an animal caused it. This type of sign tends to corroborate other evidence, but when considered on its own, comes up inconclusive. It fails to show whether a person caused it or not, but possibly confirms or substantiates other evidence found with it.

Unskilled trackers usually discover conclusively human sign (*jump tracking*), but they often fail to discover corroborant sign. Frequently, corroborant sign sticks out to a skilled tracker, yet the novice never sees it at all; and, when a novice actually discovers the disturbance, they usually misinterpret it. Also, corroborant sign which by itself proves nothing, almost certainly gets left behind by the subject if it falls exactly between two other pieces of sign at approximately a stride's distance. This makes, corroborant sign just as important in the long run as conclusively human sign. Therefore never overlook or ignore corroborant sign.

Tracking teams need to continuously exchange ideas and information as an integral part of tracking. Never overlook this. Team members need to communicate constantly. Although a combination of opinion and observations, this simple interaction includes challenges to the observations or deductions that others make about any discovery. Team members usually achieve consensus with discussion and verbal exchange. Experience in this arena tells us that team communication aids in preventing overbearing individuals from pushing the team members in an undesirable direction. This also helps the team members stay involved at all times. If a track and clue aware responder takes the time to describe what they see and think relative to the missing person's actions, (*sign, clues or tracks*) then team members avoid jumping to a conclusion without just cause.

The TCA Essentials

Light: Light, as a requirement, never means that TCA only works during daylight hours. It simply means the importance of controlling the light source when visually searching the area ahead. During the day, the primary light source comes from the sun. Trackers need to answer the question, "*How do we effectively control that light source?*"

The answer: "*Place our eyes in a position, visually where the light source casts shadows into depressions, scuffs, and anomalies on the surface where searching.*" At certain times of the day, trackers find it easier to find sign, other than discarded items, on the ground.

Early in the morning and late in the afternoon when the sun sits at a low angle, tracks or other evidence of movement through the area tend to show up easier. These conditions create longer shadows that bring out the details of any depressions, scuffs, and anomalies on the surface which make them easier to see. Clouds, diffuse light (through pollution or clouds), and the sun high overhead all diminish the beneficial shadow effect. Essentially, trackers find it easier to look for sign, track and anomalies on the ground while facing the light source, and with that source at a low angle to the ground.

Mid-day conditions usually provide the most glare and tend to wash out shadow effects on the ground. Searchers compensate for this, by holding a hat or other object above to cast a shadow onto the ground while they examine it.

With the other hand, responders use a flashlight (*yes a flashlight in the middle of the day*) or even a mirror to focus light onto the shadowed area. In this way, the searcher controls the angle of light to the ground. By casting this bright beam of light from a low angle, the depressions, scuffs and other anomalies become very discernible. Therefore, at night, when looking for sign, a person controls the light source on their own, making tracking, sign cutting and looking for clues a lot easier.

Sign Cutting and Finding Clues at Night

At night, a tracker controls the light source 100% and with light playing such an important role in tracking and/or sign cutting, we tend to see why trackers prefer to perform this skill at night. Trackers possess the ability to completely rotate an artificial light source around any sign from a low angle to allow for the best view. Using the light in this way emphasizes otherwise unrecognizable sign. In addition, darkness hides many of the distractive nuances that show up during daylight, so the light source serves to focus attention and concentration where they need it.

Using more diffuse hand held lights seem to work best when sign cutting or looking for clues at night. Headlamps typically fail to work well for sign cutting when worn on the head. Instead, trackers attach the headlamp to the leg below the knee or even to the end of a walking stick for the best angle while walking.

Proper light for sign cutting depends on brightness. Bright lights tend to diminish night vision and bring out subtle sign during an otherwise dark night. Really bright lights over stimulate the eyes, which in turn makes a person's *eyes water* and experience visual fatigue more quickly. The ideal sign cutting light needs to maintain individual's night vision, yet remain diffuse enough to bring out the detail of subtle marks and depressions.

Inexperienced responders, at night, tend to incorrectly use their light source(s). These individuals tend to move the light too rapidly and not give the eyes enough time to really take in the surroundings. It takes time, or neural processing, to synthesize what the eye sees. For example, when responders go back and take a second glance or long look after the initial visual snapshot. Consider the second glance a follow up, where the brain processes what the tracker saw and compares it with their visual standard. In tracking, the visual expectation on each tracking assignment depends on properly moving the light slowly and allowing the brain to process what you observe.

The visual capabilities of each individual differ, therefore all SAR responders need to experiment with different lights and lenses to determine their optimum vision in differing conditions. Some responders prefer to use LED lights. Colored lenses, such as amber give greater depth perception. Some trackers report that using a blue lens filter when tracking on snow and ice helps as well.

Responders also attach different types of lights to the side of bumpers on a vehicle to spot for clues, sign or prints beside the road. Trackers on foot need to experiment with different lights under different conditions.

Shading of sign and the use of light to highlight detail works very effectively as a daytime technique. Sign that appeared washed out with too much overhead light tend to yield more clues when manipulated in this manner.

Labeling Tracks

When following the evidence of someone who passed through the environment, make sure to note and mark the recognition of right and left footfall. Both acknowledging and marking these distinctions makes the responder automatically aware of the nuances and subtleties that indicate direction of travel. In other words, it tunes the responder into the next clue or evidence of continued movement by the person they follow.

Mark tracks or sign in two ways:

1. Indicate whether the right or left foot made the print or sign.

2. If responders find a fully identifiable foot, put a circle around the print.

LEFT

RIGHT

Figure 9-15
Marking tracks and sign in the field

Mark a partial track, left or right, with a short hashmark at the right end of the arc to indicate right, and at the left end of the arc to indicate left. Remember to completely encircle a print with positively identifiable characteristics.

Figure 9-16
Clearly identified footfall impressions designated along a roadway using vegetation for left and right foot impressions.

Prints or Impressions: Track ID

Once trackers positively identify a print, they need to complete all three of the following:

1. Communicate the track to others
2. Differentiate the track from other similar tracks
3. Document the description for later use

Drawing a print, particularly a complete and identifiable one, always helps others to know what print to seek. Some find difficulty in drawing a print, but some trackers easily accomplish this by simply studying the print, measuring it, and then tracing it with a piece of pliable clear vinyl and a waterproof marker. Carefully lay the vinyl over the top of the print or partial print and trace around it. When responders lack complete tracks, using this process helps to develop a composite picture over a number of prints. Direct tracing aids in sorting through contamination and helps identify the correct partial prints.

Photographing the track works very well and the technology continues to improve every day. Ultimately though, drawing or tracing it offers the most detail. This aids the responder in not missing the tiniest of details and emphasizes subtle marks that photographs almost never pick up. Drawings offer SAR crews the capability to copy and hand out prints to searchers. Which, in turn, helps when looking for one specific print.

Key points when photographing prints or sign:

- Use a high mega pixel (MP) setting - ideally at least 8MP
- Avoid the use of zoom - move closer to the object
- When using zoom, optical zoom works better than digital zoom.
- Take the scene shots, then the close up shots
- Use an object or a ruler for scale
- Take the first shots of the prints/sign looking straight down - this helps minimise the oblique angle
- Use lighting and/or angles to highlight detail
- A dark image works better than a lighter washed out image *(photo editing programs help manipulate light levels)* Always take more photos, not less - if in doubt, photograph it. If anything, the photos show how well you searched.
- Never delete photos. A number of digital cameras fill the *empty* slot of a deleted photo with the next one taken, which puts your images out of sequence.
- Photographing detail at night takes practice.

Study and measure every aspect of a print and indicate the measurements on the drawing. Measure at least, the length of the track; the widest part of the sole and the heel; the length of the heel; the stride (*heel to heel*), if possible; widths of any lines or marks; distances between lines or marks; number and size of any geometric shapes; and the number of lugs or other sole characteristics.

Beware of suggesting a size for the print (*i.e., size 10 or 12*) from measurements made in the field. Manufacturers vary widely in their approach to sizing foot gear and no standards exist. Rather than convey an *estimated* size, relate the factual measurements.

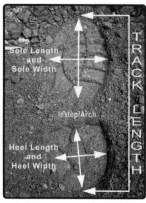

Figure 9-17

Occasionally trackers need to describe the print via radio. A person sees sign cutting and clue detection visually, and by contrast people communicate on the radio verbally. Therefore when verbally communicating a track, keep in mind to minimize confusion and maximize efficiency:

- Make sure to identify yourself and give your location, if necessary, as well as the direction of travel (*with a compass*) of the track
- Keep it simple. Paint a mental picture by using familiar words that everyone relates to.
- Always try to describe key characteristics including size and 2-3 readily identifiable features than describe an entire print

Further Considerations on Sign Cutting or Tracking Per Se

- The logical, analytical process of following sign, works because it deals only with facts, not conjecture, hearsay or emotions.
- Tracking, sign cutting or clue detection takes time; so when a responder rushes, effectiveness suffers. Following clues and sign involves a very *sense-intensive process*, so when a responder gets

- Use a standardized track report to record your finding

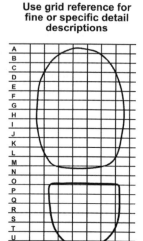

Figure 9-18

overwhelmed by sounds, sights, and unrelated thoughts, effectiveness also suffers.
- Track and clue awareness only offers one skill used to reach an objective, and although not a panacea, this powerful tool offers an effective option to piece together what happened.
- Consider the following thoughts when confronted with situations that cause you to discount, suspect or not trust a track and clue aware resource:
- Only trained track and clue aware responders know whether or not sign cutting or clue detection works effectively in any given situation.
- Only track and clue aware responders know how to decide when, and how thoroughly to search for subtle sign and track.
- Track and clue awareness works best when applied within an effective well organized management scheme.
- Think about track and clue awareness at all times. Always know that for every mile/kilometer a person travels, thousands of clues and readable sign indicates how someone traveled through that environment.
- TCA easily incorporates into most field tasks and enhances every searchers field search skills.
- Never concentrate on determining if and when sign cutting or clue detection fails to work. Rather, concentrate on how a skilled responder discovers evidence left behind when a person passes through the environment.

Processing Vehicles, Campsites and Other Locations

Search incidents very typically start at an abandoned vehicle, a campsite or in the parking area at a trail head or recreation site. As first on-scene responders, SAR team members know the basics of processing a vehicle or other sites for clues and signs of activity. Most often, the single most important objective remains in determining the direction of travel and in some cases, specific identifiable clues such as footprints or personal items left behind.

The acronym STOPPER aids in recalling the actions required to process any clue site. Remember, the process expands and shortens to suit each site.

Vehicle Processing

When starting at an abandoned vehicle, pay particular attention to the location of the prime sign or clues. (*The hot zone for clues and sign*) When a person exits

Figure 9-20
The paramount emphasis with any of these site processes is protection of the prime sign areas until all have been meticulously scanned, appropriately marked and documented if necessary. Here a team member identifies crushed vegetation and other recognizable top sign indicating movement away from the vehicle.

a vehicle, they often place their foot on the ground slightly under the side of the vehicle below the door. This area often produces a clear heel print protected from the elements by the vehicle itself.

The same holds true for other locations around the vehicle. If a person goes to the rear of the auto to

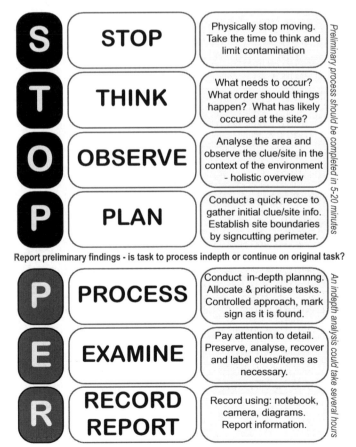

Figure 9-19

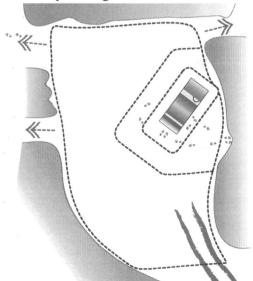

Figure 9-21
Parking a number of cars along a dirt road with the driver carrying out several activities at each site works as an excellent training exercise for SAR responders. After completing the proscribed activities, the driver then walks away from the site in any direction. Then, three to four person teams process each vehicle. Each team needs to determine direction of travel and find any discernible clues out to at least 10 meters. This exercise works during the daylight hours and after dark. Always process campsites, points last seen, last known position designations (in terms of discarded items, clothing or equipment) like an abandoned vehicle.

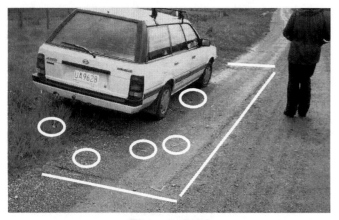

Figure 9-22
An abandoned vehicle with the prime sign location identified on the picture with white lines. In the picture, prime area is scribed on the ground. Circles are locations where foot imprints and other sign were found and marked with bright colored popsicle sticks. Crushed or deformed vegetation is marked with flagging tape or chalk powder.

Figure 9-23
The following flowchart shows the process for an unoccupied (empty) or occupied site.

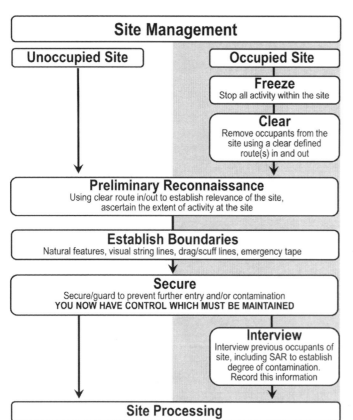

get possessions, a pack, or other gear, they often stand with a good portion of their feet extending under the back bumper which protects the prints also. Hikers often sort gear or organize clothing and other possessions on the hood of a vehicle which creates confusing sign around the vehicle. Establishing sign or evidence associated with those who exited the vehicle and matching this sign to any of the exit locations signifies the key to vehicle processing - thus determining the likely DoT.

The Nature of Other Clues

Just exactly what constitutes a clue and what is the nature of this very important *item* in the function of search? According to the dictionary, a clue represents a fact, an object, information, or some type of evidence that helps to solve a mystery or problem. In his seminal work *Mountain Search for the Lost Victim*, Dennis Kelly refers to clues as signals. Knowingly, or unknowingly the missing person generates various forms of signals about what happened, direction of travel, intentions, state of mind, and the list goes on. The searchers and the overhead team gets to interpret these signals into an organized, cohesive structure that tells a story.

The term *seek*, means to try to find, to trace or search for, to track down. Put the two terms together *(clue and seeking)* and you create the essence of what it takes to solve the classic mystery of finding the missing person. Clue seeking *(gathering all the facts and information possible)* assists responders in organizing and reasoning through the problem they need to solve. This makes devising a method by which to uncover clues relevant to a particular situation very important. Significant clues tend to provide the basis for major field tactics and strategies in specific locations.

Each of the four types of evidence constitute clues or potential *signals* generated by the missing person. The following list names the four types of evidence:

1. Physical Evidence
2. Testimonial Evidence

3. Written or Documentary Evidence
4. Statistical or Analytical Evidence

Often people think that only searchers trekking through the field find clues in the environment. Upon examination of the nature of what really constitutes a clue, one comes to the conclusion that

Figure 9-24
This candy bar wrapper is definitely a physical clue.

any bit of information or evidence that contributes to the reduction of uncertainty in the search effort consists of a clue. One fact or bit of information by itself sometimes means nothing, but when combined with another bit of information it creates a viable clue. Therefore SAR teams need to pay close attention to and repetitively scrutinize over clue logs, communication call logs, debriefing sheets, maps, and interview notes. The Command Post acts as the central repository of information, and crews need to analyze that data every OP period.

Detection and Recognition

We know that in general our capability to detect something in the area teams search gets determined by the size, shape and color of the object, the terrain and environment or conditions that exist there, and finally the capabilities of the sensor or searcher. Detection and recognition present a world of difference in how a searcher responds to what they see. Recognizing a clue for what it is focuses on a major problem about clue orientation. Crews find clues but consider them meaningless to the search and never act upon them. Recognition of clues comes from several important processes.

The question about searcher and/or overhead team member expectations needs major consideration. What is it that people expect to see or sense? Many researchers study *(and have studied)* visual attention to detail and the processes by which we recognize things. Capitalizing on these mechanisms in the briefing process by programming people to mentally detect and recognize things faster and more efficiently helps a search substantially. Vision basics and an understanding of the mechanisms of how the eye works also benefits a searchers capabilities.

The *canonical perspective* also drives expectations by something called the standard identifying view. Canonical perspective governs the discovery of physical evidence. A person's expectation tends to center on the clue presenting an image that matches or closely matches what already exists in our mind's eye. In many cases, this could not be further from the truth. In general most people underestimate the difficulty of detection in varying conditions and environments. People expect the clues to literally ***pop out*** but, research and practical field experience tell us differently *(see Chapter 19 on POD)*.

We improve clue or object detection through a process called ***priming***. The person that briefs both overhead team members and field searchers in essence *primes* the detection pump by effectively bridging the gap between distractions and meaningful clues on a specific search. This takes practice, but works very effectively.

Principles of Clue Orientation

- The clue seeking process starts with the pre-planning process, continues through a search and ends upon filing the critique and after action report. Sometimes it goes even further with more investigation.
- People learn the skill of recognizing clues, and need to practice in order to develop a sense of what minimum amount of information the search effort requires.
- Speculate about possibilities, but never form

hard and fast opinions without all the clues or information. Consider that undiscovered key pieces to the puzzle still exist.
- Never immediately form an opinion about the value or association of a clue. Finding another piece of information or evidence tends to change everything.
- Gather information, clues, or evidence from as many sources as possible. Finding one single source fails to provide all the facts.
- A complete subject profile provides a valuable source of clues. Continue gathering information for the profile throughout an operation and let it offer direction.
- Brief overhead team members and searchers about *personal expectations*, *canonical perspective*, and taking *snapshots* instead of scanning and the four main types of evidence.
- Always keep in mind the fragility and short life span of a clue and document, photograph and preserve it as quickly as possible.

Last Known Position (LKP)

- Exactly where was it?
- Recreate the scene
- Pinpoint the locations on a map
- Physically go to the spots and study them for signs of aging and/or environmental impact

As stated and emphasized several times before, responders never find clues in the same order as the subject generated them. The attempt in the search effort to discover clues and interpret them correctly, aids in the discovery of what happened and developing a time line. Any of the following reference LKP:

- The last clue found
- The most recent indication of the missing person's position
- A possible indicator of direction of travel
- A datum point that can move with every clue discovered

When responders discover a clue in the initial response period *(a foot track, a discarded item, a piece of gear on the trail, etc.)* and designate that position the Last Known Position, the responders need to base their actions on known information for that item. In this case, they make some assumptions with regard to timing. If they discover another clue and conclusively determine that the subject laid down the second clue before the previous clue, the LKP never changes. In the ensuing search effort as teams find more clues, they need to make every effort to ascertain a relationship in time to the first one discovered. At this point interpretation of clues becomes vital and at times involves other staff members not actually on-scene at the time a team discovered the clue.

Searchers Also Look For the Following

As mentioned previously, the job of the *Person conducting a Briefing* during SAR operations, centers on bridging the gap between previous targets and distractions compared to those present on this search (*See Chapter 22 - on Briefing and Debriefing*). Therefore they need to provide some description of objects, clues, sign or target types during the briefings. They need to at least mention these items in the briefing as a minimum.

Depending on the subject category, activity or unique circumstances, the following list of key items prove crucial as a clue during any search for a missing person.

Objects, Clues or Target Images

- Foot prints
- Scuffs & scrapes
- Broken vegetation
- Bones
- Clothing
- Shoes / boots
- Personal equipment
- Shells
- Firearms
- Arrows
- Indentations

- A body
- Food wrappers
- Smells / odors
- Displaced vegetation
- Distress signals
- Food
- Tracks
- Cigarettes
- Bottles/ bottle caps
- Disturbed water
- Food containers
- Knives
- Cell phones
- Toys
- Tools
- String /line
- Pop / beer cans
- Paper - *toilet or other*
- Pens / pencils
- Eye glasses - *sun*
- Gloves
- Hats
- Cameras
- Blood
- Dead animals
- What else?

In general, the following conditions make the detection of any clue, object, or even the missing person more difficult:

- When the target *(clue, object or person)* sits outside the central foveal vision *(taking visual snapshots greatly improves this)*.
- The target's background contains a poor contrast in color and texture.
- The target includes disguised or camouflaged contours, lines or shapes.
- The form or shape of the object remains outside of the usual searcher context.
- The object position falls differently than its ***ideal*** perspective *(canonical view)*.
- The searcher lacks a good idea of what the target looks like *(search image)*.

Sweep searching fails to detect form or shape as opposed to *taking visual snapshots* which tends to find them. Aircraft observers developed this technique a long time ago for searching and continue to use it today.

Barriers to Recognition

Searchers experience many distractions as they move through their field assignments. These search distractions consist of the influences that adversely affect the concentration, attention, comfort or safety of searchers as they move through the field on a search. The searcher experiences very minor distractions which only serve as irritants, while others constitute major influences to life, safety or physical injury. All of these adversely affect the probability of detection, and without fail, the searcher needs to report this during any debriefing process. Planners use the following information to plan further sorties in the coming operational periods to research specific areas.

- Precipitation
- Extreme cold
- Limbs or thick brush
- Obstacles like rocks or streams
- Wildlife / animals
- Wind / wind with debris
- Rough / steep terrain
- Hazardous footing
- Slick surfaces
- Deadfall
- Thick vegetation
- Noise
- Man made trash / junk
- Confusing / busy environment – people
- Traffic – foot, vehicle, etc
- Dogs & other pets
- Bright light & shadows
- Fog & occluded visibility
- Clothing/environmental mismatch
- Poor/incorrect briefing
- Confusion of task / assignment
- Fear - high risk terrain, safety issues
- Fatigue
- Conflict - within the team or with managers
- Radio traffic of clues being reported by other resources

Average Range of Detection - AROD or R_d

Previous research demonstrated that trained searchers usually fail to predict or accurately evaluate their Probability of Detection (POD)values. Recently Robert J. Koester completed new research that specified a field procedure for determining reasonably accurate effective sweep width (ESW) values and consequently develop meaningful POD values for any search effort expended in the field. The goal of Koester's research and paper (*Koester et al., Use of the Visual Range of Detection to Estimate Effective Sweep Width for Land Search and Rescue based upon Ten Detection Experiments in North America, 2013.*) developed a simple, objective procedure to obtain ESW values without conducting full-blown detection experiments.

R_d = The average range of linear distances that a search object is first detected when moving towards it from multiple angles.

Range of Detection Procedure for Field Resources

Immediately upon arriving at a designated search segment in the field, searchers need to perform this Range of Detection procedure. Designate and/or pick out a representative search object that will be used for the procedure. This should be an object or person that is determined to very close in color, size and description of that which is being searched for in the operation. Place the object or person on the ground in a random location that represents the vegetation and terrain within the designated search area.

With one or two searchers, the process takes about 15 minutes. With four or more searchers, it takes between 5 and 10 minutes. Keep in mind that the process requires 8 measurements. Since field personnel normally carry a compass, initially use cardinal directions from the object for the vectors – North, South, East and West. Use the inter-cardinal directions for the second set of vectors – Northeast, Northwest, Southeast, and Southwest.

(Each person will accomplish the same procedure) *See Figure 9-25 on the next page*: For one individual:

1. Pick an initial vector from one of the cardinal directions.

2. Walk away from the search object until it is well lost from sight. Turn around and walk back toward the search object. At the moment the search object is spotted, STOP.

3. Now count the number of paces that it takes to reach the search object and record the distance.

4. After the individual has reached the search object, continue in the same direction opposite the first vector until the search object is well lost from sight once again.

5. Turn around and walk back toward the search object again. At the moment the search object is spotted, STOP.

6. Once again record the number of paces that it takes to reach the search object and record that distance.

7. This process should be repeated on each of the cardinal and inter-cardinal directions.

8. All the distances between the searchers and the object would be expected to be different. This is due to the environmental conditions as well as vegetation or any ground cover in the immediate area or other obstacles that might be in the way such as rocks, logs or terrain variations.

9. Now average all of the measurements to determine the average range of detection (**Rd**).

In his 2013 paper by Robert Koester et al., Koester designates one of three correction factors when calculating an estimated effective sweep width. These correction factors tie to search objects categorized as high, medium and low visibility.

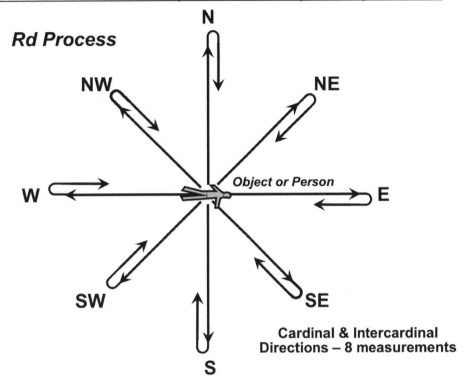

Figure 9-25 R_d Process

Search Visibility Class Correction Factors:

High Visibility = 1.8
Medium Visibility = 1.6
Low Visibility = 1.1

For example, using the process described below, for a high visibility object, use the correction factor of 1.8. Assume the R_d in the test area comes out to 20m. (20m X 1.8) = 36m. Effective Sweep Width (W) for the area being searched when looking for a high visibility object would be 36 m. If the object being searched for is a low visibility object and the Rd tested is 12m, then (12m X 1.1) = 13.2m. These figures can now be used to calculate a reasonably accurate Probability of Detection.

Sound and Light Lines For persons presumed to be alive and responsive.

Sound sweep, initially developed by Martin Colwell in British Columbia, states that by making noise in a disciplined, collective way search teams create the potential to attract the missing person. Several experiments show very impressive PODs with minimal resources.

The experiments took place in the coastal forests of British Columbia. In addition to normal search equipment each searcher carried a radio and a loud whistle. Colwell then spaced each searcher along a boundary of the search area at a predetermined length, also taking into consideration terrain and weather conditions. Colwell *(1992)* found coordinating a single start time unnecessary. The Searchers simply move into the search segment when they reach their starting locations.

A Base or Control Station broadcasts a count down call to all Searchers at regular intervals. The length of the intervals depends on the speed each searcher travels. Colwell *(1992)* suggested a time interval of one to two minutes. The BASE transmits:- "Whistle blast, 5 - 4 - 3 - 2 - 1 BLAST." When the searchers hear the whistle they stop, blow their own whistles, (ideally simultaneously) and listen for an audible response. When hearing no response continue with the sweep. This technique also minimized the problem of searchers mistaking response sounds from the missing person.

Ross Gordon, from the Search and Rescue Institute of New Zealand, capitalized on Colwell's work by adding a light component to maximize the attraction effect for night search operations. Studies using the sound, light lines produced huge success. By implementing the same sound part of the tactic as Colwell, we accomplish the light component in several ways. Each searcher, normally equipped with a powerful flashlight *(torch)* for navigation and safety, receives an additional flashlight, and swings it in a lazy figure eight pattern. This pattern maximizes light dispersal. Some searchers also used *light belts* or *light bandoliers* wrapped from the shoulders across the chest and flashing bicycle LEDs placed on the back of the head for added attraction.

Ross Gordon further modified the sweep in order to use it on linear features such as trails, routes and streams, hence the use of the term *lines*. This provided search teams with a search method to travel quickly, and at the same time maximized their attraction with both sound and light. They also utilize their tracking skills on the linear features with special emphasis on the decision points. For further information, see bibliography.

Search and Rescue Dogs

Original manuscript for this section submitted by: Jeff Doran and Marcia Koenig, 1989.

Some Comments and Perspective

Know Your Resource

The most effective use of any resource involves familiarizing yourself with it ahead of time. Although asking a dog handler for general information about capability, experience, and availability helps, a more productive and efficient use of time encompasses actually watching a dog and handler train.

Know How to Use It

When calling upon a dog unit, know the difference between a tracking/trailing dog versus a searching dog. Whether to use them early or late in the search, what type of weather, and other circumstances of the search need consideration when choosing the type of dog for the job (more on this to follow).

While a SAR dog unit possesses the ability to act alone and without external assistance, the groups need to prepare for some integration with established protocols such as navigation and communications.

Expect Competence

Nearly 100 organized dog units exist in the U.S. along with a very large number of individual handlers and dogs. The working quality of dogs varies considerably based on their experience and expertise and poses a problem for the agency deciding who or what to use.

It takes several years of exposure to evaluate dog teams. Units often lack the time necessary for this, and need to use other general criteria for assessing them. At the very least, an agency needs to expect the following from a person or persons professing competency in search and rescue dog work:

- The handler needs appropriate dress, foot gear and survival gear for the weather and terrain, demonstrating skill as an outdoor person and familiarity with elementary SAR procedures
- Dog units need to demonstrate an operational structure, adequate base camp support and a communications setup
- The dog*(s)* need an eagerness to work in addition to an agreeable temperament and a good manner around people

The next section clarifies the basic use and concepts of how dogs function in SAR work, their *application* to a particular mission, *Benefits* derived from the resource, and how to estimate *coverage*.

Scent Theory and How to Apply to Search

Traditionally search and rescue operations uses a tracking or trailing dog trained to follow the missing person by scenting on or near the footsteps of the victim. However, in the past several decades, the searching dog, trained to hunt the air currents for human scent, grew in popularity.

A basic understanding of how human bodies function links SAR dogs and their potential subjects. The human body gives off a constant stream of scent, much like campfire smoke. The average person's skin surface alone contains some 2 billion cells, of which 40,000 cells shed each minute. Shedding cells carry along bacteria and body secretions producing a vapor detectable odor of human scent. As the cells shed from the body and get carried by air currents, they lodge in vegetation or percolate through rubble, water or snow.

Several components make up the ground scent detected by a dog. Components include: crushed vegetation where the subject walked, a shedding of human cells, body odors, breath, as well as artificial scents coming from products used on a daily basis. The artificial components include things such as; hair gel, mousse or spray, gum, candy, cigarettes, body soap and laundry soap. All of these produce a host of differing and unique scents.

Tracking Dog:

The tracking dog follows the crushed vegetative scent of the subject's footsteps. The dog stays within one or two feet from these footsteps, despite the wind conditions. The dog keeps a head down posture, sniffing at the ground for evidence. The dogs basic orientation concentrates on the footsteps and not the human scent. Tracking dogs generally get sent to the IPP, PLS or LKP. In the Police role the tracking dog completes the chain of evidence between the scene of crime and the criminal.

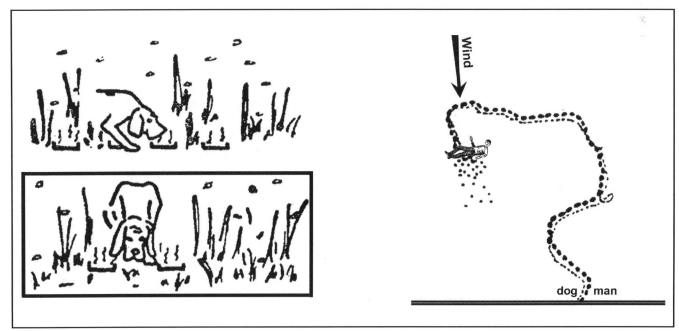

Figure 9-26 Tracking Dogs

from *Scent and the Scenting Dog,* by William G. Syrotuck

Trailing Dog:

Trailing Dogs orient themselves to the human cells falling to the ground along the person's route. The dog often works some distance from the actual footsteps. He tends to shortcut some corners and overshoot others. Some dogs even stop and sniff at leaves or vegetation two or three feet off the ground. Some dogs move from the actual steps to an outer boundary of cells and back again, a combination of tracking and trailing. Traditionally scent specific bloodhounds fit the picture of a trailing dog. Tracking dogs generally follow the most recent scent while the trailing dog identifies the specific track of a person.

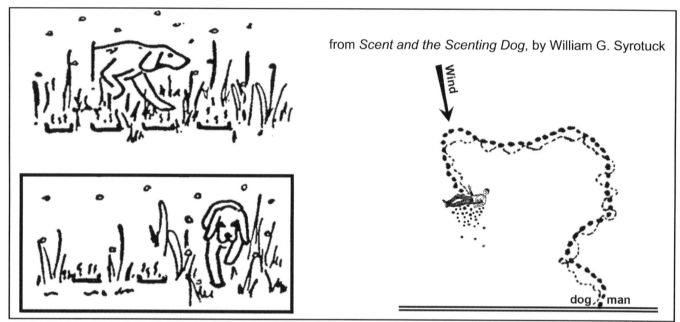

Figure 9-27 Trailing Dogs

Air Scent or Searching Dog:

Air scent or Searching dogs usually orient themselves to airborne cells. With his head held high, he searches air currents like a hunting dog finds game. If a trail exist he follows it or he may leave a trail and move in on the airborne scent. But he basically orients himself to the airborne scent of the human. Air scent dogs usually deploy down wind of the suspected location of the subject and home in on the scent particles while interpreting the air flow over the terrain. An experienced handler determines the possible direction of the source of the scent from where the dog makes a hit.

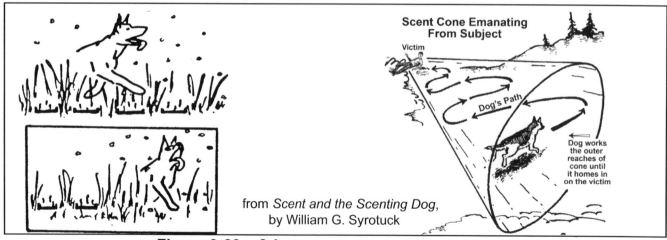

Figure 9-28 a & b Air Scenting Dogs (Searching Dogs)

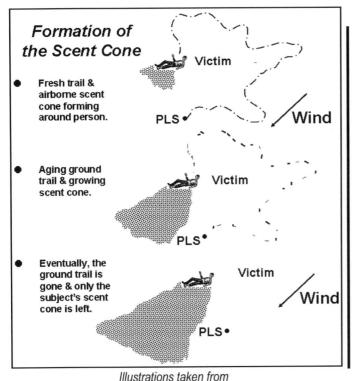

Illustrations taken from
"Wilderness Search Strategy for Dog Handlers"
by Marcia Koenig, 1987

Figure 9-29 Scent Cone

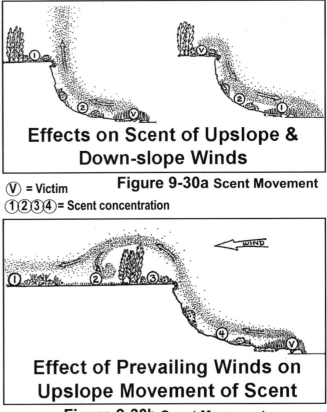

Figure 9-30a Scent Movement

Figure 9-30b Scent Movement

The illustrations *(above and previous page)* show what happens to scent over time and how different types of dogs key on different aspects of scent. Also, prevailing breezes or wind affects scent on a slope.

Dissipation of trail scent with time.

The illustration above shows the route taken by the subject to his present location and represents the pattern of mixed vegetative and human scent created by the subject passing along the way. In addition, the picture illustrates the *cone* of airborne scent developing downwind from the subject's location. The two most important factors for the tracking/trailing dog consist of the starting point and the ground scent. The dog begins at the Point Last Seen *(PLS)*, or Last Known Position *(LKP)* to work the ground scent. In order to discriminate the subject's odor from other conflicting odor, the trailing dog receives a scent article before beginning the search.

For effectiveness of the tracking/trailing dog, managers need to consider the conditions under which they these dogs achieve success. The ground picture of scent only remains for a finite period and how much time passes before a dog deploys as well as the prevailing weather *(extreme heat or rain are detrimental)*, correct identification and preservation of the PLS, LKP, and the availability of an unlaundered, carefully preserved scent articles, all influence the effectiveness of the dog.

The factors that govern the tracking or trailing dog affect the air scent dog to a much lesser degree. In illustration 9-29, note that the airborne scent around the subject increases with the passage of time while the ground scent diminishes. The illustration also shows how wind carries the scent out from the victim to ultimately form a cone shaped dispersal pattern.

A searching dog works across the air currents and into the wind in order to detect the scent cone even when the ground scent disappears. Sometimes extreme heat with no wind or a heavy downpour adversely affect them. Search managers need to use a searching dog to search an area of high probability as opposed to starting at the point last seen. Through coordination of search areas assigned to other SAR units, these dogs easily merge into an overall search plan.

Benefits of Dogs for Search

Units get the most value from dogs when used as an early response resource. A tracking/trailing dog gives a direction of travel, while a searching dog provides larger search coverage. Air support complements the use of dogs as well. Helicopters routinely transport dogs to search sites and work in combination with them. When the dog indicates a direction of travel, the helicopter then searches the area of highest probability, without disturbing the dog.

A searching unit of four dogs and handlers, with gear, fit easily aboard an H-60 helicopter for use in missions originating from remote base camps *(i.e. mountainside or wilderness areas)*.

You need to consider dogs as a primary night searching tool, when a human's impaired vision severely limits the ability to search and navigate. At night a dog possesses better mobility than that of a human. At night scenting conditions improve due to increased dissemination from the subject when temperature differences grow between a warm body and a cooler environment. Therefore, with their mobility unaffected, and because of enhanced scenting conditions, dogs tend to add a valuable capability to night searches.

An evasive or unresponsive subject needs consideration in terms of their detectability. Teams tend to fail at spotting a frightened child (hiding). Air scenting dogs, on the other hand, often find hiding subjects, or subjects covered with leaves or even light snow.

Dogs and handlers, as far as a hasty team resource, work as clue/victim finders. The search director expects ongoing information from the handler, important to the developing search plan. A dog handler provides different types of information useful to a search. The dog handler's skills consist of terrain evaluation, visual track awareness, and suspected victim behavior. Given an area to search, the dog handler needs an awareness of natural routes (drainages, old road grades, etc.) available to the subject. Frequently, a search lacks adequate trail system maps, so the dog handler needs to give information regarding confusion factors on trails. Track and clue awareness is important.

With SAR resources feeding information to the base camp, changes develop in the search plan and dogs and handlers help quite considerably with their ability to quickly and easily transport to a new area with minimal backup support.

Use of Dogs in Disaster, Avalanche, and Water

In addition to use in wilderness areas, dogs get used extensively to find victims covered by debris, snow, or water. They help find subjects buried in earthquakes, tornados, landslides, avalanches and for searching recent tsunami and flooding activity. The strength of the dog's alert, often clues the handler into whether or not subjects still live or died in the event. If alive, rescue efforts concentrate in that area. A number of years ago in Iceland, Icelandic rescue teams trained their avalanche dogs to seek human scent. However, during a catastrophic avalanche in the north, dogs homed in on clothing, bedding, and in fact anything with a human scent. Sadly, this resulted in a lot of wasted effort but, provided for new training. They trained dogs to only indicate a subject's body, alive or dead. Dogs also aid extremely well in identifying subjects recently covered by fallen snow and drowning victims in rivers and lakes. Although these searches involve recovery only, they save time and effort for divers and let the families find their loved ones as soon as possible.

The adaptation of a dog to another environment (debris, snow, water, etc.) requires distinct methods and experience, but still functions as an extension of basic search and rescue work.

Coverage

Tracking/Trailing Dogs. Unique feedback comes from the handler of a trailing dog, not covering a specific area per se. If the dog appeared on track and then lost the direction of travel, handlers need to make a decision and evaluate the direction the dog initially indicated, this direction determines possible deployment of more searchers, making the job very important (possibly according to the indications of that dog). Difficulties tend to arise when trying to accurately assess a trailing dog's work. Evaluating factors such as length of time, weather, and conflicting odor proves challenging, and search managers need to obtain these estimations from the handler. Trailing dogs who fail to complete an assignment, usually results in a low probability of indicating direction. In addition, the search manager needs to take into consideration factors of terrain evaluation, victim behavior, or visual track clues.

Air Scent Searching Dogs. Before explaining coverage in relation to air scent dogs, necessary information about this resource follows. Singly, they add a very limited resource to a search; therefore, the concepts presented in this text provide useful information for multiple dog/handler teams (a SAR dog unit).

Air scent dogs work an area after searchers get done working through it. After a length of time, about two hours, the level of scent left by other searchers decreases to a lower level compared to the airborne scent continuing to develop around the subject. This necessitates a recording of when searchers finished and area and the probability of detection for the area. This information aids in deciding and justifying whether a need exists for a repeated search by dogs or other resources.

These dogs work best by searching fast and efficiently in an area. Due to this, hasty search techniques combined with dogs produces a high yield of results proportionate to hours expended. On a large percentage of missions, by dispatching one dog and handler each to a number of possible routes or areas, high probability areas get searched quickly with a high possibility of detection. While this technique finds the subject only part of the time, other value lies in the type of information obtained from skilled handlers. Details on terrain barriers, escape routes, and other possible clues provide a valuable basis for solidifying the search plan.

When assigning an area to air scent dogs, the dog team's operational leader decides how to commit the resources within that area. When possible, the use of natural boundaries such as, paths, drainages, or ridge-tops subdivides the terrain for each dog and handler. To search the assigned area, the handler chooses an appropriate starting point, and then provides direction, encouragement and guidance to the dog who works off-lead ranging ahead and checking the scents in the area.

Preferably, each handler works independently, allowing them greater freedom and flexibility to adjust to wind direction and terrain features. Lacking any existing boundaries, handlers set up an arbitrary boundary between them and communicate via radio. They then meet occasionally to confirm the coverage given to this unnatural boundary.

Using dogs in a line search, seldom, if ever, benefits a search, regardless of the spacing between dogs, close or widespread. This tactic hinders both the ranging of the dog and the speed and mobility of the dog/handler team. Prior to working an area, the handler establishes the percentage of coverage he/she desires, taking into consideration the length of time allotted to work the area. This ranges from a high POD, a very thorough search in a smaller area, or a less thorough search (low POD) of a larger area.

Each Handler needs specific training in order to estimate their coverage after completing the area. Debriefing ascertains the appropriate coverage and ultimately POD (*see chapter 19 POD*). Debriefing tends to identify sections of the overall area less thoroughly searched (*or not at all*). Future planning needs to take these holes in coverage into consideration and plan accordingly.

The effectiveness of dogs as a SAR tool, directly relates to the degree of training the dog possesses and the knowledge and skill of the dog handler.

Dog Type Summary

Search dogs provide a highly successful resource for the search planner to use. The following summarizes the advantages and limitations of using different types of dogs, and the usefulness of the unit concept of several dogs and handlers:

Tracking/Trailing Dogs

Advantages:

- Possible local availability
- Able to find the subject in the early stages of the search
- Indicates a direction of travel so helicopters can search ahead of the dogs
- Useful in searching at night

Limitations:

- Use dogs early in the search, before the trail dissipate, or gets trampled out of existence
- Unsuccessful at working a trail in extreme heat or heavy downpour
- Need to correctly identify and preserve Point Last Seen (avoid scent left by searchers)
- Trailing dogs need un-laundered and carefully preserved scent articles available
- Difficulty in accurately assessing a partially completed trail

Searching (Air Scenting) Dogs

Advantages:

- No need to follow a trail, dogs search for point source of scent
- Useful in searching at night
- Hidden and buried subjects can be detected - evasive subject, disaster, avalanche, snow, volcano, water.
- Dogs work areas other searchers previously went through

Limitations:

- Weather - extreme heat with no wind, or heavy rains
- Extreme variations of terrain with scent voids and thermals
- Excessively deep or dense burial debris, limits escape of scent
- Technical climbing areas

Unit of Several Dogs and Handlers:

Advantages:

- Large coverage from a few dogs and handlers
- Transported easily
- Hasty team resource; handlers posses skills that provide ongoing information:
  - Terrain evaluation
  - Visual track awareness
  - Victim behavior
  - Mapping
- Utilize Probability of Detection both before and after searching an area

Using Horses in Search

Original manuscript for this section submitted by: Coleman P. Brown and Anne O. Bennof, Trail Riders of Today (TROT) SAR Team, Maryland; updates by Tomi Finkle, TROT SAR team Commander.

A search manager needs to look at the use of searchers mounted on horseback as a resource. Such units prove very effective in wilderness areas, urban areas, large parks, and farmlands. The search manager needs to remember the distinction between trained searchers on horseback, and local horseback riders volunteering to help.

Advantages

A mounted searcher usually carries food, water, first aid and survival equipment on the horse. The rider's energy tends to last longer than ground searcher's carrying the same equipment in a backpack. Carrying equipment on a horse gives the searcher the ability to search more effectively for a longer period, especially in rough or mountainous terrain, or even in extreme weather conditions.

Horses themselves provide value as searchers, and serve as good barometers for differences or something out of the ordinary in their environment. Experienced mounted responders know and understand their mounts well and take note of subtle changes in their animal's body language often leading to undiscovered clues. Like dogs, horses possess highly developed senses of hearing, smell, and eyesight. A search dog's training depends upon his ancestors' instinctive skills as a searcher of prey. Similarly, as a prey animal, the horse survives by its ability to detect and escape a predator.

One cannot expect a horse to consciously search in the same way a trained air scent or tracking dog does, however, horses instinctively maintain an awareness of their surrounding environment, and alert on anything out of the ordinary, especially the presence of another animal or person. A horse usually detects animals and humans in advance of the rider and a good search rider investigates anything attracting the horse's attention.

Applications in Search Operations

Searchers on horseback work cooperatively with other search resources, complementing their efforts. As a *hasty team*, a horse and rider covers large areas quickly: perimeter sweep; search known trails, ridges, drainages; locate unmapped trails; establish trail and road blocks; create and check *track traps*. Equines themselves naturally act as an attractant which then aids in drawing a subject to rescue. Trained mounted search teams also work exceptionally well to extract subjects from remote locations in appropriate situations.

Mounted searchers also engage in slow, thorough (or hasty search) off-trail searching of fields and open woods. In brush and tall grass, a team of three or four mounted searchers performs sweeps quicker than ground searchers, and more effectively due to their elevated perspectives.

Properly trained mounted searchers work as clue finders. Unless requested to hurry, horseback searching entails a walking pace. Clues as small as cigarette butts or gum wrappers, and larger items such as clothing and tracks, show easily to a horseback rider trained in clue detection and protection.

A mounted searcher, properly equipped, operates effectively in most weather conditions, though they succumb more easily to problems when searching in icy conditions. The search manager needs to rely on the rider's assessment of the situation. Mounted searchers usually operate best in teams of two skilled searchers and two equines (three during low light conditions) and work effectively without flankers.

Horses also search at night. However, riders tend to worry about riding cross-country or on ill-defined, steep trails in the dark, as the horse might step into a hole or other unseen hazards. The best night time applications include: broader trails or fire roads; open fields; dirt roads; country lanes. Trained mounted searchers practice in the dark with helmet lights, and will advise the search manager of safe areas to search.

Management Considerations

Many of the initial comments made in the SAR Dog section in this chapter apply to mounted search teams, as well. Know the capabilities of the available resources. If a SAR unit possess the capability to use trained mounted teams, they need to get to know the leaders, the members, their call-out procedures, training standards, equipment, and search skills.

Not all circumstances call for horse teams. Obvious exclusions include: some searches in the urban environment, water, cave as well as swamp operations, and any technical steep rock, ice or snow. And remember, the response time for volunteer searchers varies with location or distance, and logistics. In the case of mounted units, several additional factors affect response time. Mounted search teams need additional travel time to reach the horses, hitch the trailer, load the horses along with feed and water, etc. Calling these units early, or placing the mounted resources on standby improves response time.

What to Expect of a Mounted Search Team

- An organization, with defined leadership, a base support structure, and specific call-out procedures
- Radios, along with training in communications procedures
- Self-sufficient units, arriving with sufficient supplies for riders and horses, and overnight equipment
- Equipped with first aid and survival gear, and able to carry it on the horses while searching
- Riders trained in search theory and techniques, navigation, clue awareness, tracking, and basic SAR skills
- Calm and cooperative horses, trained to accept the sights and sounds of the search environment, including;
    - helicopters, search dogs, flashing lights, sounds associated with base camp and searching efforts
- Appropriately dressed riders, for the weather conditions and safety

What the Mounted Search Teams Need from Management

- Advance notice
- Space on firm ground to park vehicles and trailers
- Space to erect small, portable corrals, or establish picket lines (ropes strung between trees to tie horses)
- For extended searches access to water, shelter, and food resupply

A Guide to using Aircraft in Support of Land Search Operations

General Aircraft Capabilities

As mentioned earlier in this chapter, although very useful, aircraft usually fail to provide all the answers or solutions to search problems. If used properly, they greatly enhance a ground search effort. Aircraft arrive on-scene in minimum time for an initial search of the area, and route search or evaluate any surrounding terrain very quickly. The Search Manager obtains an overview of the area from the aircraft, as well as search tactic viability information, drop messages, supplies, para-rescue aid and even communication relays if necessary. They provide invaluable aerial photos, particularly in the urban environment (which virtually changes from day to day and never reflects on maps). Both helicopters and fixed wing aircraft serve any of these functions.

In addition, helicopters move both personnel and supplies to definite search areas, pick up victims, and because of their slower ground speed, sometimes search more effectively than fixed wing aircraft. Helicopters also track in some terrain with phenomenal success. While some fixed wing aircraft provide low, slow flight if equipped with Short Take Off and Landing (STOL) modifications, they never provide the same platform and capabilities as a helicopter. Keep in mind, that often weather, mechanical difficulties, fuel supply logistical problems and even pilot qualification difficulties preclude the use of aircraft resources. Always retain a backup plan for operational activities without the use and dependency on aircraft.

Air Management and The SAR Plan

- The authority and responsibility for conducting air search operations needs to be established and well known throughout local SAR organizations
- Collectively establish cooperative agreements between military, volunteers, federal agencies, state agencies and local law enforcement (Who's going do what?)
- Ensure proper communication between agencies, designate a liaison officer for each agency
- Know the air support request procedures and who makes them. Make note of specific channels required to request aircraft, and outline communication links in writing. Establish specific Standard Procedures for requesting and using military aircraft

- Plan for unavailable aircraft - i.e. develop a ground operations plan without air assets

Aircraft Capabilities and Limitations

Many factors affect an aircraft's capabilities and limitations. Dozens of aircraft suit specific functions and environmental factors based upon their specific design. Temperature, operational altitude, availability, high wing, low wing, payload capability and fuel consumption rate all impact decisions on whether to use a particular airborne resource. By the same token, someone will eventually ask about cost factors . . . . Who pays for the air time? How much is it going to cost and are free resources available (Military/Government)? When local military units, civilian organizations, individuals or specific organizations operate in your jurisdiction, set up some kind of working relationship. What about training and who sponsors such training? A little bit of investigation and effort answers all of these questions and more.

Pilots need special qualifications to fly search missions. Search and rescue demands an exceptionally well trained and qualified pilot. In many parts of the country, flying SAR missions requires extensive mountain experience coupled with collective search operations training and pilot to observer teamwork. No substitute exists for training and orienting probable air resources ahead of time in your area.

Trained and experienced spotter/observers for aircraft add an invaluable resource to the air operations already described. Thoroughly trained and experienced ground SAR team members make the best fit for this job. They possess a better overall aptitude for performing this function during air support of ground operations due to their familiarity with ground search. Any spotter/observer works very closely as a team with his/her assigned pilot, each with a valuable function separate and distinct but wholly dependent on the other.

Ground Crew and Air Operations Officer:

During a large search operation, one person often lacks the ability to handle all the necessary steps to keep track of all air operations. In most cases however, since only one or two aircraft work a search incident, one individual handles the functions alone. A trained pilot needs to fill this position due to their knowledge of aircraft capabilities, limitations, weather factors, servicing needs and other important safety factors.

In cases when helicopters and sometimes fixed wing operations work out of non-staffed airfields, a trained technician fills a ground crew position. He/she maintains safety practices for SAR personnel as well as the public, provides information regularly to the Operations Chief, coordinates flight patterns, flights, pilot needs and assignments, supervision of crews and loading and unloading of supplies.

Other ground crew support staff need specialized training and experience as well. They need an understanding of how to use smoke markers, signaling devices, parachute-cargo dropping procedures, one skid landings on rough terrain, heli-jumping as well as sling loading and ground crew safety rules.

Air Operations Base (airfield, air strip, heliport, helipad)

Establish air operations bases as close to the search area as possible while still maintaining needed support functions to minimize transit times and unnecessary fuel burn. Establish early and open communication with the staff at the Search Base. This insures less communication gaps in the overall air operation. Consider a location able to provide maximum air support time on-scene. In addition, as the size of an operation grows, personnel needs such as food facilities, sleeping quarters, phone, radio and other items for aircrew also need special consideration. Aircraft support and logistical supplies perform vitally important roles as well. If you cannot get the right fuel, or any fuel, then obviously consider other arrangements and/or another location.

Briefing the Pilots, Crews and Observers

Briefing checklist:

- Establish the entire operations chain of command. Discuss operational objectives. Give a run down

on the mission history up to this point, subject description, search area, pattern of proposed search and the track spacing used
- Designate the grid quad and distribute maps to everyone. Identify specific locations, making sure everyone knows the point location system in use (latitude / longitude, UTM, grid reference etc.)
- Establish communication call numbers, frequencies and compatibility with ground teams in the search area. The units on-scene and how to contact them if necessary
- Identify any potential hazards and safety rules in the area
- Describe terrain conditions, weather over the search area, expected turbulence, wind conditions and refresher information on mountain flying rules in mountainous areas
- Check in and check out procedures both at the air operations base and the search base while flying
- Establish who talks to the press and at what point. Usually specific agency policy dictates this function
- Identify the arrangements for food, rest facilities, fuel and special gear or available equipment

Air Search Procedures

Fixed Wing. Fixed wing aircraft generally provide the most effective missions in relatively open terrain (not necessarily flat, but open). Even at a low, slow flight speed, gear and flaps down the aircraft still travels somewhere between 60 and 100 knots. For safety purposes, fixed wing aircraft generally work from higher terrain to lower terrain. Therefore the Search Manager and Operations Chief need to understand the capabilities of the aircraft in use, and the primary missions they accomplish. Avoid using both fixed wing and helicopters in the same specific search area. If the situation calls for both, separate them with plenty of altitude.

Helicopters. Helicopters operate at lower altitudes, slower speeds and in tighter areas than fixed wing aircraft. Incident commanders often use helicopters to transport search personnel to summits quickly for energy and time savings, check out specific clues, transport supplies and crews to difficult areas and much more. While helicopters seem like the ideal search platform, they possess limitations, and even under ideal conditions or without special equipment, give only minimal probabilities of detection.

Assign each aircraft to its own area and never try to double up, or overlap areas. This frees pilots up to concentrate on altitude, speed and grid orientation.

For safety, aircraft working in adjacent areas need to communicate (establish common frequencies). When possible, communicate with ground teams and a location reference for air recon in that area.

Fly the roughest terrains early in the morning to avoid excessive turbulence and allow maximum use of aircraft capabilities. If conditions permit and the possibilities of a live subject exist, consider night flights to look for lights, fires or even signaling devices.

No hard and fast rules exist concerning search patterns on a given mission. Every situation and area dictates the most optimum use of the aircraft. Generally, each pilot flies missions to an area determined by grid lines or natural features. The Operations Officer and the pilot determine the altitude, speed and pattern to best accomplish the mission.

Typical Search Patterns *(Figure 9-31)*

Contour - Follows the elevation contours from higher to lower terrain.

Route search - If searchers discover a definite point of departure and destination, a route search merely follows the intended route of the victim. An expansion of this technique, flies parallel to the intended route off to one side and then again on the other side, with overlapping passes.

Expanding square - The pilot establishes a starting point and from there works outward in an ever expanding square pattern.

Creeping line grid - Using a projected sweep width and desired parallel track distance, the aircraft works

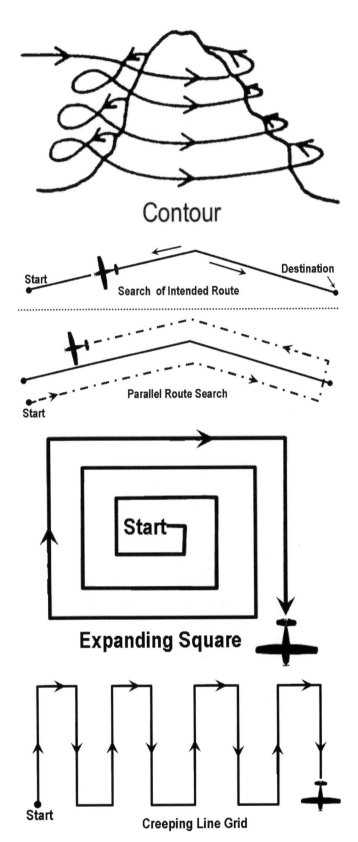

Figure 9-31 Air Search Patterns

back and forth moving further and further along a desired direction with each progressive parallel pass.

Debriefing

Maintain a checklist and routine procedure for extracting information from returning pilots and crews. Find out specifically what they saw, an evaluation of how well the flight went, and in particular, designation of areas not sufficiently checked. Try to solicit any suggestions from them about improving the search effort as well. Cross check the pilot's description of his/her flight path with actual data (e.g. GPS track etc.) before calculating POD or POS values.

Documentation

For future reference, retain all flight logs, plans and maps. Try to keep total man-hours, flight time, fuel used and other pertinent data not only logged but tallied for future records and potential budget recommendations.

Planning an Air Search for Missing Aircraft

The planning of an air search for an overdue or missing aircraft initially involves estimating the most probable position of a distress incident or survivors. First, determine a search area large enough to ensure the survivors fit somewhere within the area. Then choose the equipment or resources used in the search, and last, select search patterns to use in order to effectively cover the area.

Some air SAR operations present little or no difficulty in the search phase. A witness to the incident exists, or you know the aircraft's last known location close enough to preclude the need for an extensive search. Usually, in this case, coordinates from a beacon indicate a known position. In other cases, determining a search area assumes a very different character. Lack of sufficient information as to the position of the incident or survivors makes it difficult to determine what and where to search first.

The Possibility Area

The area of maximum possibility forms a rough circle with its center at the last known position, usually determined with transponders or radio transmissions. The radius of the circle equals the endurance of the aircraft at the time of its last position given the conditions at the time, expressed in terms of distance. It involves the assumption that the aircraft flew from its last known position until fuel exhausted, on any course, even at right angles to, or the reciprocal of, the intended flight plan.

Systematic search of large nebulous areas lacks efficiency, since that approach fails to concentrate initial search efforts in areas where the aircraft likely went down. Determination of the maximum possibility area, however, enables the Incident Commander to screen hearing and sighting reports coming in as leads.

The Probability Area

The SAR manager determines the most probable area, or the area in which the aircraft most likely landed within fairly narrow limits, based on the degree of accuracy attributed to the aircraft's last known position, and upon receiving the following information:

- Location where the aircraft disappeared off radar
- Bearing or fix provided by a ground station or emergency radio aid
- Dead reckoning (DR) aircraft position. A method based on time last known position, then applying estimated speed and course over a given time to plot a new position.
- Reports of sightings, ground or air

If one lacks the ability to obtain the information above, then try narrowing the probable position by gathering or assessing the following information or items below:

- A flight plan or route of aircraft
- Complete information on weather along intended track or route
- Proximity of airports along the track
- Aircraft performance
- Pilot's record, habits, experience
- Radar coverage along intended track *(as a limiting factor)*
- Nature of terrain along intended track
- Position and ground reports (leads)

When lacking vital information to determine the most probable position of the incident or survivors, more difficult search planning ensues. Unfortunately, impractical and time consuming barely begin to describe searching the potential areas in which aircraft incidents occur, even after applying the narrowing information above to the potential search area. For the operation, a Search Manager needs to reconstruct the incident with whatever information available to them. In cases like this, the planner bases their approach on an assumption that the aircraft encountered an accident, went off the intended course, or unpredictable actions forced the aircraft down near the intended course. The initial phase of an aircraft search focuses primarily on the intended course and surrounding areas. If searchers fail to obtain any results in the first phase, then search manager needs to extend the initial search area or determine other areas based on a hypothesis (scenario).

Unless information to the contrary exists, generally, the intended track from the last known position to the intended destination or within a reasonable distance either side of that track presents the most likely areas to search next. In this sense when talking about last known position, we refer to an enroute fix or the airport from which the aircraft last departed. However, Dead Reckoning estimates assume a 10 percent error for the distance from the last known position of the aircraft which creates a further variability.

What happens if you Fail to Locate The Aircraft?

"How long do we continue the search when nothing positive turns up?" - Probably the toughest question answered by a search coordinator.

In general, air searches run for approximately five

to seven good flying days. This number varies by a day, one way or another, but in most cases, limiting out at one full week. Why arbitrarily cut off a search after a period of time? The answer: the limit of credible leads, or the chances of finding survivors, and the number of resources spent in supporting such a mission.

No one likes to call off a search when a shred of evidence exists to substantiate the possibility of injured survivors somewhere waiting for rescue. But, searches cost money, and search managers need to address spending limits. In most cases, a combination of factors need consideration, such as previous statistics, evaluation of search effectiveness, fatigue of search pilots and observers, terrain, weather conditions, and known facts. These all contribute to the ultimate decision.

Historically, family members, friends and sympathetic fellow pilots usually carry on the search for a missing pilot another unspecified number of flying days. For the most part, these searches seldom result in anything positive. However, many times a local Civil Air Patrol unit, in addition to local pilots, conduct subsequent training missions in the area in hopes of finding something. Although nonproductive for the most part, they occasionally find an aircraft. In the fall when thousands take to the woods for hunting and camping, the chances of coming across a missing aircraft increases and in some cases turns out positive.

In looking back through past records, generally three reasons emerge as to why searches continued for an extended period of time. Political pressure holds an unbelievable amount of influence on the duration of search for any individual. Missing pilots with political importance or relatives of political figures, generally no limit to the length of time or the resources expended in the search exists. The search for John F. Kennedy Jr. in July of 1999, represents a good example of how this happens in the U.S.

Sometimes, clues and selected information shedding light on a crucial part of the search extends it. For example, someone remembers a statement, fact, or additional information throwing the entire search in a different direction or to an entirely new geographic location. Also, private pilots flying in the suspected downed aircraft area often call in reports turning into positive sightings.

The third reason, mentioned above, references the possibility of coming across a missing aircraft during routine training exercises in the suspected area. All of these potentially develop positive outcomes from time to time.

Emergency Locator Transmitters (ELTs) - An Evolution

In the early 1980s the U.S. mandated all aircraft carry ELTs. In the first year of mandatory use, upwards of 8000 false activations occurred. In the succeeding years that number eventually tapered off to around 5000 and stayed an extreme problem through 2009. Problems ranged from false triggering, and not functioning on impact, to battery and antenna problems. Unfortunately, while the system effectively saved hundreds of lives, the 97% false ELT activation rate presented a major investment of time and resources for Search and Rescue. Initial statistics showed 22 hours as the average time to locate a crash sight after an ELT activates. By contrast, when the ELT failed to function properly, the crash site took approximately four days plus 18 hours (114 hrs) to find. The odds of finding survivors in that extended time drop dramatically. In spite of all the headaches, false activations and shortcomings, ELTs and other beacons save lives, and represent the biggest single factor effectively leading searchers to aircraft crash sites at present.

406 MHZ digital ELT's

Today a new solution exists to help with problems associated with the original ELT concept. Current versions of the ELT utilize digital technology to transmit a more efficient burst signal to additional satellites. The digital data burst sent by each device includes a unique electronic serial number (ESN) for the individual unit and owners/operators register these devices with the National Oceanic and Atmospheric

Administration (NOAA). Since their introduction in the mid 1990's the prices for these units continue to drop considerably. Vendors sell 406 MHz ELTs for as little as $250.00 (US) up to around $1,250.00 at the time of this writing.

The old frequency band, 121.5 MHz, contains a high level of noise and interference and its use generated, as mentioned above, over 5000 false alerts worldwide in the COPAS/SARSAT system. Only around 200 real signals came from electronic distress beacons anually on 121.5 and its military analog 243.0 MHz. In addition, new designs for satellite systems now handle digital information instead of direct analog signals, so a crying need existed to improve the system. The new 406 MHz beacon systems offer a location accuracy of 2 nautical miles without a GPS interface and 100 meter accuracy with a GPS input within about 15 minutes of activation worldwide. Using the new system, operators crosscheck the registration data for each signal and call the owner/operator of the device before launching SAR resources. This process dramatically lowered the false activation deployments generated by the system.

Currently, each new GPS satellite added to the constellation and replacing those already in orbit carries a 406MHz receiver. With satellites traveling throughout the entire globe, at least four satellites possess a view of anywhere on the planet's surface, which in turn enables instantaneous reporting of any 406MHz signal received. These new 406 MHz beacons still contain the 121.5 sweep tone transmitter allowing SAR resources to track and locate the beacons once in the vicinity of the beacon using already available direction finding equipment in service. In February of 2009 the SARSAT/COSPAS satellite system stopped monitoring 121.5 and 243.0 MHz signals completely.

The Maritime community uses this same technology and frequency in devices called Emergency Position Indicating Radio Beacons (EPIRBs), The maritime beaconsall function in the same way at 406 MHz and use the same satellite system as ELTs to report someone in distress.

Personal Locator Beacons (PLBs)

These small portable units operate much the same as EPIRBs and ELTs. The design of PLBs call for handheld use by an individual instead of installation on a boat or aircraft. Unlike ELTs and some EPIRBs, PLBs only activate manually and operate exclusively on 406 MHz. And, like EPIRBs and ELTs all PLBs also utilize a built-in, low-power homing beacon which transmits on 121.5 MHz. This allows rescue forces to home in on the beacon once the 406 MHz satellite system puts rescue forces *in the ballpark* (about 2-3 miles away).

Most new model PLBs also integrate GPS circuitry into the distress signal. This GPS-encoded position dramatically improves the location accuracy (down to the 100-meter level or roughly the size of a football field).

Although the three types of devices look different, (ELTs, EPIRBs, and PLBs) because of the differing applications and users, they all work on the same principle and use the same satellite system to notify the authorities. When turned on (automatically or manually), each type transmits alert signals on 406 MHZ on the SARSAT-COSPAS infrastructure.

In the United States, PLBs saw limited use until July 1, 2003, after which they were fully authorized for nationwide distribution. The National Oceanic and Atmospheric Administration encourages all PLB users to learn about the responsibility that comes with owning one of these devices. PLBs work exceptionally well; but, users should only use one in an emergency. PLB users need to familiarize themselves with proper testing and operating procedures to prevent false activation and to avoid their use in non-emergency situations.

COSPAS/SARSAT SAR Satellite System

The acronyms COSPAS/SARSAT represent the search and rescue programs in Russia and in the United States respectively and the two systems operate jointly under treaty. Translated literally, the Russian acronym stands for Space System for Search of Distressed Vessels. The U.S. acronym stands for Search and Rescue Satellite Aided Tracking. See the NOAA website for more information at:

http://www.sarsat.noaa.gov/

An international program composed of Canada, France, Russia and the United States originally made up the COSPAS/SARSAT treaty effort and 35 countries participate in the program today. Go to http://www.cospas-sarsat.org/Management/listofParticipants.htm to see the current list.

Space Technology and Satellites Greatly Simplified SAR Notification

When a crash occurs or a user activates a device, a beacon sends a distress signal to one of the four visible satellites carrying an ELT receiver. A satellite in orbit 1200 miles above the crash or incident receives the distress signal almost instantaneously and the following takes place:

The beacon transmits an emergency signal to the SARSAT and/or COSPAS satellites

The satellite retransmits the emergency signal to the ground receiving station, which in turn processes the signal and computes the approximate location. (Typical accuracy is +/- 15 miles.)

The ground receiving station then transmits the distress location to the U.S. Mission Control Center (USMCC) at NOAA in Suitland, MD which forwards it to the proper land or sea rescue coordination center (RCC).

The United States Air Force or the United States Coast Guard alerts search and rescue forces depending whether the signal is on the ground or in the navigable waterways. This includes fixed wing aircraft, helicopter, ships, boats, and ground search parties.

Infrared - Omni-Directional

First used in law enforcement in 1984, this highly sophisticated resource utilizes thermal airborne imaging in a wide application of search environments. The technology involves registering temperature differences of houses, trees, cars and people (so slight as to be almost nonexistent) and projecting these minimum resolvable temperature differences onto a display screen. In law enforcement, this piece of technology offers many useful functions.

The units (a tough polymer/plastics cyclops-like ball) easily adapt to the mount on a normal helicopter's search or spot-light bracket. Installation takes minimal time and affixes to nearly any aircraft. The hand held detector moves up and down as well as from left to right and the (computer linked) joysticks consist of various buttons and toggles controlling field of view switching (wide or narrow), optimal signal presentation and travel sweep. 600 to 800 feet offers the best operating altitude (180-250 meters) and provides a 300-450 foot (100-150 meter) wide ground swath for observing.

Configuration involves positioning the monitor on the rear aircraft seat using standard helicopter power supply and making sure to connect the joystick and display monitor with shielded cables. The unit adds a total weight of 83 lbs. or 38 kg to any resource using it.

How it Works. Light splits into component colors via a prism, ultraviolet and infrared occupy opposite ends of the visible spectrum with all the colors in between. The ozone layer screens most ultraviolet rays from the sun. The earth's atmosphere warms from heat, or infrared rays, atmospherically absorbed. Every object on the earth's surface absorbs the sun's rays during the day and at night reradiates the stored heat in an eternal give and take of temperature. As well, atomic molecular motion occurs in every material object existing above absolute zero (-273C) and the more motion of the molecules, the more heat.

Therefore the greater the temperature of any body, the more intense the infrared frequency grows. The IR system collects and discriminates between these small temperature differences, assigning one particular shade of gray for each .2 degree of discrete temperature difference registered. The sensor discriminates over a wide frequency range, but the peak of energy levels registered depends on the body producing it.

On the imaging screen, an almost photonegative type image shows tree branches on a cold winter's night as almost white (warmer) and the tree trunks (that lose less heat) darker. Houses show up radiating white through glass windows, while car engines show a distinctive *glow*. The systems usually differentiate between temperatures as low as .2 degree Fahrenheit and as technology improves and cost increases, this number decreases.

Experiments and Actual Search results

Successful tests and actual searches occur at night, with uniform ambient temperatures and no localized heating by sunlight distorting findings. Penetration of forested areas works well, although dense leaf growth or evergreen coverage requires greater operator skill to detect visual differences. These units work under actual conditions of fog, rain, snow and extreme cold. They visibly detect images of people, dogs and various forms of wildlife as well as tracks in the snow (less than fifteen to twenty minutes old).

Any search requires good coordination between the operator and pilot, as well as a third team on the ground directing searchers to high interest points. An operator needs a thorough understanding of how to use this piece of equipment, particularly control/joystick manipulations, for instinctive movement in addition to recognizing initial disorienting negative/positive imagery and translating it (the picture) to actual coordinates on the ground. Routine use of the units builds confidence and a good experience base.

The monitor translates trees, roads, fields, shacks or buildings, all with marginally different temperatures, into a very clear picture, that gets digitally recorded and replayed later. With this device, even the smallest heat sources like tracks in the snow, a place where a vehicle stopped and started again and even where individuals stopped and then continued gets detected. When testing, experimenters ask ground team members to quickly identify themselves by showing a portion of their skin. Very difficult to detect individuals, wrapped in sleeping bags, showed their faces or put a hand or arm out making them immediately visible. High humidity, depending on how much rain and snow falls, affects the imager in varying degrees. However, even in high temperatures, operators still received good results.

Occasionally, a phenomenon known as *Radiometric Crossover* occurs, and an object disappears from the screen. This takes place when an object and its background share the same total of emitted and radiated IR. During ideal conditions, this occurs twice a day at differing times depending on the month. Therefore consulting with aircrews and equipment operators helps determine to the best times for deployment. Hand held versions of thermal imaging also exist and add value to searches under certain conditions like the urban environment or some wooded areas.

Night Vision Goggles (NVGs) and other observation equipment

Two categories of night observation equipment exist: Image-intensification devices and thermal-imagery devices (as described above). Image-intensification devices, or starlight scopes, fail to project detectable energy. They amplify the existing or ambient light at night to project an image on the scope or viewer. Ambient light consist of moonlight, starlight, or the glow from cities and towns. Light from flares, searchlights, and laser illumination improves the viewing capability, but try to keep from viewing directly by the device. Fog, smoke, heavy rain, and falling snow adversely affect Image-intensification devices.

Operators use thermal-imagery devices in daylight or darkness, and find them extremely useful due to their ability to see through smoke, dust, heavy rain, falling snow, fog, camouflage and light vegetation. The standard military models contain an infrared light source to aid in natural illumination and a positive control switch that permits close-in viewing from 10 inches to infinity. This allows a person wearing the device to perform everything from reading a map to driving a vehicle under night or low light conditions. The units weigh about 1.5 lbs. and continuously operate over a 15 hour period without battery replacement. When exposed to high levels of light for more than 30 seconds, the power shuts down to the goggles via a high light cutoff feature. (NOTE: In night helicopter operations, ground personnel need to not shine or flash lights directly into a pilot's or copilots eyes on approach or landing when wearing Night Vision Goggles. It can be FATAL!)

The price of NVG units varies depending upon the source. The Soviet Union and other producers around the world continue to flood both the U.S. and UK markets with new units. (Very affordable and in some cases high quality). Numerous police and government agencies apply this technology on a daily bases, and SAR units find it quite useful as well.

Global Positioning System (GPS)

In 1989 the U.S. Department of Defense launched the first production series of GPS satellites. Their efforts provided the initial step in revolutionizing how we find our location anywhere on earth.

The GPS technology consists of relatively simple components. A constellation of 29 satellites orbiting 12,000 miles above the earth emits signals to receivers on the earth's surface. The receiver calculates the distance from each satellite by measuring the travel time of the signal transmitted from that satellite. The receiver uses satellite positions as precise reference points to determine the location of the receiver. After receiving the signals from at least four satellites, a computer at the GPS receiver then determines latitude, longitude, altitude, and time.

A technique called *differential GPS* or *DGPS* further refines the accuracy of a GPS. DGPS makes use of a ground receiver at a known location to calculate any combined error in the satellite range data. Applying the correction to all other GPS receivers in the same locale eliminates most of the errors in their measurements.

The value and use of GPS technology soon became apparent to the civilian community. Even before becoming operational, surveyors used GPS signals to pinpoint sites within centimeters, mariners used them to place buoys and navigate across lakes and oceans, surface transportation vehicles found their way through busy cities with them, and railroads located and traced trains on remote tracks.

The accuracy of a GPS system stays within a range of inches, but for nonmilitary use falls within the range of 60 to 1000 feet *(18 to 305 meters)*. Current policy on the operation of the system states that 95 percent of fixes stay within 100 meters *(328 ft.)* of the true position. Most fall within about 50 meters *(164 ft.)*, but the possibility exists that one in a thousand reach a discrepancy of over 300 meters *(986 ft.)*. Users fail to know when the 5 percent error occurs due to the fact that most civilian receivers lack any warning.

Today's GPS receivers mostly fit within small, robust, inexpensive, weather resistant devices. More and more SAR teams use the units as they find their way into almost all of our mobile consumer technology. While GPS, in its current state, provides useful navigation information in the hands of an experienced user, the use of conventional map and compass for cross country navigation *(on foot)* continues as a vital skill for everyone involved in search and rescue.

Synthetic Aperture Radar

Synthetic Aperture Radar provides both the technology to locate missing persons or objects hidden by vegetation, weather or darkness and also in the creation of precision 3D terrain maps under the same visually obscured conditions.

The NASA *(Goddard Space Flight Center)* Search and Rescue Mission Office researched and developed a system that locates missing aircraft that crash under conditions that severely handicap normal visual search methods. The system works best in remote areas when vegetation and weather and/or darkness *(or combinations thereof)* hide the missing aircraft. NASA determined through this program, that currently synthetic aperture radar provides the best solution to meet these search requirements.

This program is referred to as the Search and Rescue Synthetic Aperture Radar *(SAR2)*.

Time critical search and rescue SAR operations often require the detection of small objects in a vast area. While an airborne search usually covers the area, no operational instruments currently exist to actually replace the human operator. By producing the spectral signature of each pixel in a spatial image, multi- and hyper-spectral imaging (HSI) sensors provide a powerful capability for automated detection of objects that are otherwise unresolved with conventional imagery (they're too small to see visually). This property of HSI naturally lends itself to SAR operations because the imaging sensors resolve so much smaller than the human eye. A lost hiker, skier, life raft adrift in the ocean, downed pilot or small aircraft wreckage can be detected from relatively high altitudes based on their unique spectral signatures when exposed to the radar energy of the system.

Concept of Operations:

A SAR2 system will consist of a side-looking radar unit carried onboard a search platform, such as a business jet flying at 25 to 30,000 feet above Mean Sea Level, a satellite or an unmanned aerial vehicle *(UAV)*. *(For SAR2 experimentation, NASA used a DC-8 jet equipped with a JPL experimental synthetic aperture radar system)*.

The radar platform images the ground as the crew flies a series of predetermined flight paths over the search area. The processed radar images reveal man-made objects present in the imaged area, making possible the selection of potential crash sites for closer investigation by search aircraft and/or ground teams.

SAR2 benefits include the capability to penetrate foliage and clouds and conduct wide-area searches of remote areas at all hours *(day or night)* and during periods of inclement weather. Designers anticipate the use of SAR2 when emergency beacons *(ELTs)* fail to operate or when other unusual circumstances prevail.

NASA conducted a number of SAR2 experiments beginning in the early 1990s. As a result, the system detects salvaged aircraft parts *(wings, tails, fuselage, etc.)* under trees and through clouds, using target discrimination and polarimetric-based automatic crash site detection techniques operating on the processed radar image alone *(without human intervention)*.

Summary

General principles of Applying SAR Resources.

- A local SAR Coordinator's need to encourage the development of new and diversified resources, as well as making sure they receive proper training and adhere to local, state or national standards.
- Local search managers need to know the location of outside resources and how to obtain their services as backup.
- A preplan includes all available resources and how they get used in the search *(Even the ones located a significant distance outside the local area)*.
- Match the resources and their capabilities to the needs of the jurisdiction and the search at hand.
- Resources need general initial tactical actions and require minimum direction and control by the search manager *(Initial resources, by the nature of what they do, are independent)*.
- The more diverse skills a resource possesses, the more they contribute to a search
- As a search progresses, all resources gradually advance from independent strategy to strategy dependent on the search manager.
- Use initial strategies that insure maximum chance of locating a responsive, conscious subject
- Clue finders can work independent under a general plan
- Clue/subject finders depend on the search manager for periodic reassignment and direction
- Subject finders need detailed plan and firm control
- Effective communications for control and monitoring directly affect a search manager's decision to use any resources.

Important Points to remember when trying to keep the search organization running smoothly with all resources:

- Efficient and effective team efforts achieve more than the same number of individual efforts
- Team efforts utilize the *buddy system* with a safety factor not available to individuals
- Use a Chain-of-Command when dealing with organizations and include their leadership in regular briefings as well as search strategy formulation
- Give each resource well defined and reasonable tasks to perform
- Never ask or allow an organization to attempt a function they lack training in or the equipment needed to perform the task.
- A Successful search missions depends on a quick response, adequate resources, efficient searching and good management.

Notes:

The Kim Family Search   10

Objectives:

- Discuss this search mission

- Identify the issues, functions, and problems associated with this mission

- Apply the lessons learned in home jurisdictions

Kim Family Search Mission

Josephine County, Oregon, December of 2006

NOTE: In the context of this Chapter and the referenced case study of the Kim Family Search, the views and conclusions here stem from multiple documents and accounts rather than simply expressing the view of one party or agency. Our analysis provides a synopsis of operational issues, and lessons learned from all sources. We identified best practices if appropriate, and tried to clarify situations or circumstances that ultimately led to the conditions that arose during this tragic mission. Hopefully, the entire SAR Community across the country and the world, will benefit in some way from this account and the lessons learned.

Search Synopsis

James Kim, a senior editor for CNET Networks in San Francisco, California, along with his wife Kati Kim and their two children, Penelope and Sabine, left their home on Friday, November 17, 2006 for a nine day road trip to Seattle, Washington and back. The family intended to return to San Francisco on Monday, November 27, 2006.

When both James and Kati Kim failed to show up for their commitments on Tuesday, November 28th, friends grew concerned for their safety. According to those friends and their family, the Kim's always kept in touch at least daily with friends and co-workers by phone or e-mail.

On November 29th, Charlene Wright, a friend and employee of the Kim family, reported James, his wife and two daughters as missing to the San Francisco Police Department. The San Francisco Police Department (*SFPD*) started an investigation and sought information regarding the missing family leading to the Portland Police Bureau issuing an All-Points Bulletin (*APB*) for the family on November 30th. That investigation continued through to the end of the search mission.

On Saturday, November 25th, the family left Portland headed toward Gold Beach, Oregon. They planned to spend several nights in Gold Beach and then continue back to San Francisco. Late that evening, the family missed the main turnoff for Highway 42 off of Interstate 5 leading to their coastal destination. While following an alternate route, they became lost in a maze of backcountry mountain roads.

The family finally stopped their car at a T intersection in a very remote and rugged location. They had passed through several stretches of snow covered road and did not want to go back through those sections again. Interviews with Kati Kim reflected that her husband had opened the driver's door of the vehicle and "carefully backed down the road to the intersection below a warning sign" on the road *(Figure 10-1, and 10-2)*. At this point, the couple tried to call 9-1-1 on all three cell phones they carried with them. None received a signal. They then took a right turn and continued for another 22 miles until they reached the T intersection.

Kati also indicated in interviews that she needed to get out of the car on numerous occasions to remove large rocks from the roadway simply to continue driving. They passed through several stretches of snow covered road and wanted to avoid going back through those sections again. When they finally stopped their car at the T intersection mentioned above, they decided to wait there for a passing snow plow or another local vehicle to pass by. The vehicle was never stuck in the snow.

The family stayed together at this intersection conserving food and trying to signal their distress by burning the tires from their car. On Saturday, December 2nd, early in the morning, James Kim left his family at the car and started an attempt to walk out for help. On Monday, the 4th of December, a helicopter spotted Kati and the girls at the vehicle. Another helicopter then accomplished their rescue.

Helicopter crews observed footprints leading away from the car and search staff redirected resources to search the surrounding area. After the rescue of Kati and the girls, additional helicopters tracked James' descent into the rugged terrain of the Big Windy Creek drainage *(an area with steep side walls of 60-70*

Figure 10-1 The Kims drove by all the signs shown above. Why? Night, rain, snow and unfamiliar roads all probably contributed. After they spotted the last sign on the lower right they backed up and took another road. The alternate road led to their survival situation with their stranded vehicle.

Figure 10-2 The intersection on Bear Camp Road where the Kim's made the first wrong turn (they took the lower road).

degree slopes on both sides). Ground searchers also followed the tracks left by James as he attempted to reach help for his stranded family.

Because of the extreme nature of the terrain in the Big Windy Creek drainage, the Mission Management Team requested specialty Mountain Rescue resources. Helicopters inserted some of the resources used at this point in the mission into the drainage via long line due to a lack of roads in the area *(the only road lay along the top of the drainage)*.

Once on the ground, team efforts in conjunction with air assets soon confined the search area to the bottom of the canyon and a much more definite search area. All of this ultimately lead to the discovery of James Kim's body in the water at the bottom of the Big Windy Creek drainage.

Chronology of Events Associated with the Search

Saturday, November 25th – Kim Family leaves Portland, Oregon headed home, via the Oregon Coast

Sunday, November 26th - Kim family becomes lost in a maze of backcountry roads while on the way to coastal Oregon.

Tuesday, November 28th – Friends and other family members notice that the family is overdue in California and efforts begin to communicate with and locate them.

Wednesday, November 29th – Employees and friends in California officially report family missing to the San Francisco Police Department.

Thursday, November 30th – Portland Police Bureau is notified and issues an "All-Points Bulletin" and investigative efforts as well as searches of probable driving routes begin.

Monday December 4th – Searchers locate Kati and the two daughters alive at their vehicle in the backcountry of Josephine County.

Wednesday December 6th – Searchers locate James Kim, deceased in the watery of Big Windy Creek drainage in Josephine County.

Reports of overdue vehicles traveling in and through the state of Oregon occur often and an overwhelming majority of them resolve very quickly. In the case of the Kim family, a number of hypothetical explanations surfaced during the search to explain their lack of contact with friends and family. These scenarios never came together in one location, but surfaced within the various management teams.

The four explanations follow:

1. The family unexpectedly changed their itinerary without notifying anyone. Although a distinct possibility, investigative reports revealed this type of behavior very much out of character for the Kim family and therefore unlikely.

2. The family fell victim to foul play. Although not out of the question, authorities felt this scenario also not very likely.

3. The family ended up stranded in a remote area where cell phone coverage kept them from reaching out for help. Although this happens occasionally, according to all of their verbal plans, the Kims never mentioned plans to go through or into any remote areas. Their itinerary called for a route *(Highway 42)* through small communities and over a more well-traveled road.

4. Their vehicle crashed into brush, a ravine or a body of water not easily seen by other motorists or searchers. Authorities felt inclined to think this scenario most likely.

The Oregon State Police *(OSP)*, and the Douglas, Coos, Curry, Jackson and Josephine County Sheriff's Offices all provided personnel to assist law enforcement investigators by searching primary and secondary routes from the Portland area to Gold Beach *(The next Kim family intended destination)*.

The majority of these efforts included primarily law enforcement, ***Be On the Look Out (BOLO)*** actions. This presented a very unique unclear line between the investigative efforts and specific search actions for the mission as a whole. Respective agencies conducted their independent functions as per normal within their jurisdictions.

As a result, no single official agency or person came forward to assume overall command of the search efforts at this point in the mission. After action reports suggested that an attempt to form a Unified Command earlier may have solved some of the coordination and communication issues that surfaced later.

Any joint command operation required more definitive information concerning the Kim's whereabouts, and no one possessed that information. All involved jurisdictions and agencies maintained separate, independent command of their respective resources up to this point in the mission.

NOTE: Oregon stands among eighteen states in the U.S. with an established position of State SAR Coordinator. The position provides better communication and coordination for missions involving multiple jurisdictions. The system design hopes to enhance the exchange of information about resources and to better communicate between jurisdictions operationally. A state coordination system also provides liaison between the state and Sheriffs who hold the responsibility for local SAR. For the SAR system to work effectively, several import locations need identification as early as possible to provide starting points for search operations.

The first location we call a Point Last Seen *(PLS)* or point where someone actually observed the subject; the next we call a Last Known Position *(LKP)* such

> as a vehicle driven by the subject or a discarded possession. Finally the last location we call an Initial Planning Point *(IPP)*. This location serves as a starting point for active clue seeking and also represents a baseline reference for taking measurements and comparisons with the International Search and Rescue Mission Database.

At this time in the Kim search no one had yet identified any of these locations. A simple report of a missing person or family usually fails to rise to the level of a statewide coordinated search effort.

Throughout the State of Oregon, search and rescue volunteers generally assist law enforcement during missions when standard agency resources need supplementation or extra manpower to meet the needs of the operation. In the case of the Kim search, law enforcement utilized SAR volunteers to check secondary routes to the coast. Some of these routes generated problems for travelers in the past, such as Bear Camp Road and the Glendale to Powers Road between Interstate 5 and the Pacific coast.

Backtracking from the family's known destination, (*Gold Beach*) some harbored concern about the Bear Camp Area in the southwestern part of the state. According to records, many winter travelers previously experienced disorientation in this area despite published warnings about hazardous winter conditions on the route. SAR resources actually searched Bear Camp Road both from the air (*a National Guard helicopter requested by Curry County*) and from the ground by vehicles and snow cats.

Bear Camp Road spans both Josephine and Curry counties in Oregon. It forms a major back county route, through forested land with 160 plus road spurs around and connected to it. The road connects to a vast network of hundreds of miles of County roads, Bureau of Land Management *(BLM)* and Forest Service *(FS)* roads, paved and unpaved, many of which often overlap, intersect, or the locals refer to them differently. To make matters worse, some of this complex of roads lay under ice and many inches of snow. Local references to road names in this region often confuse outsiders; indeed, even search experts, investigators and laypersons who worked on the Kim Search Review with the Sheriff's Association struggled to get a clear picture of which roads lead where. The Bear Camp Area definitely contains a very confusing and complex road system.

The Search - Day by Day

December 1st

On the morning of December 1st, the Curry County SAR Coordinator received a bulletin from the Portland Police Bureau concerning the missing Kim family. He immediately called the State Office of Emergency Management to get a mission number and to also request a National Guard Blackhawk helicopter to check the Bear Camp Road and other likely routes to Gold Beach. Curry County also notified the Josephine County SAR coordinator and they discussed searching the Bear Camp Road from their respective sides.

The route runs between Gold Beach in Curry County to the Merlin area in Josephine County. Curry County also notified the Coos County Sheriff's Office and requested they send people from their side to cover additional parts of the Bear Camp Area. At this time planners purely speculated about any potential search routes because no one possessed an appropriate Last Known Position. Because Curry County called the State for a mission number and ordered a Blackhawk, others assumed that Curry County then started coordinating the search effort from that jurisdiction.

Spencer Kim, *(James Kim's father and a resident of California)*, contacted a private helicopter company in Oregon during the morning of December 1st. He requested the company's assistance to search for his missing family members. He wanted them to cover (*search*) all of the main travel routes from Eugene to Gold Beach using aircraft on the known roads from Eugene to the California border and from the I-5 corridor to the coast. This included all the routes from Eugene south to Grants Pass, west from Eugene to Florence (*Highway 126*) and then the route south to Gold Beach (*on the coast*). The company committed

Managing the Inland Search Function - Operational Response

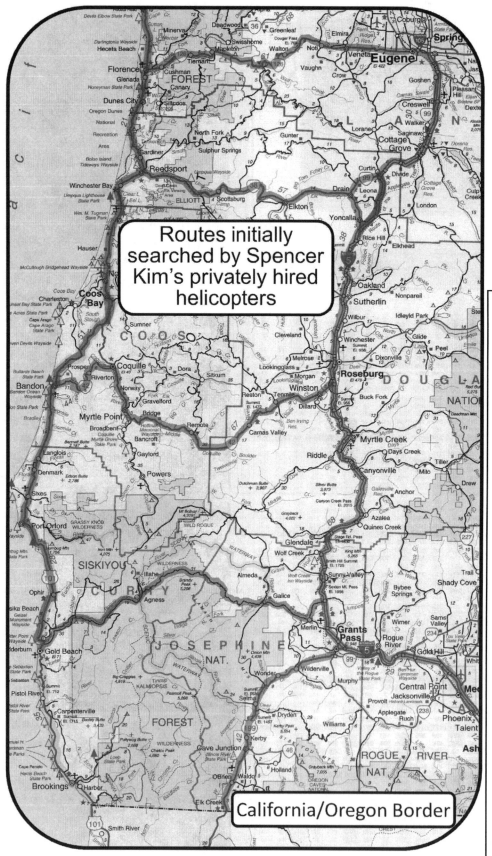

Figure 10-3 Private Helicopter search routes

eleven personnel and three aircraft to the search effort.

Their routes also covered Highway 38 and up Highway 101 north of Florence toward Lincoln City and included the route through the Bear Camp Area and the southern spur roads *(See Figure 10-3)*. The aircraft flew the rest of the day on different routes looking for a silver Saab station wagon, but discovered no leads.

> **NOTE:** Using private aviation assets to essentially carry out a personal family search effort carries certain risks in SAR operations; particularly when the private search effort unfolds without coordination with the official government search. While the intentions and humanitarian cause both feel good from the family's perspective, the potential ramifications sometimes end up catastrophic. Questions of qualifications, competencies, familiarization with local SAR units and their protocols, ground to air communications, insurance and also the fact that federal air assets from the Department of Defense (*DOD*) or National Guard use regulations that prohibit competition with private companies, all make this type of private search ripe for complications and

> unexpected calamities. Because Spencer Kim hired the private helicopter firm, the company's assets operated the way he wanted them tasked. They operated completely independent of any of the jurisdictional command points set up by both state and local officials.

Diligent effort by knowledgeable Sheriff's Office SAR personnel resolved the initial concern about conflicting mission assignments with regard to private and government *(National Guard)* resources. They coordinated different geographic assignments and specific search terrain for government and private helicopters to keep them apart. The end product eventually resulted in an efficient use of available resources. The National Guard H-60 helicopter searched the Bear Camp off-road areas and the private helicopter company concentrated on the roads and highways.

Near mid-day on December 1st, while trying to access their side of Bear Camp Road, Josephine County personnel, *(a Deputy and the County SAR Coordinator)* met two local citizens who owned property in the area *(The Black Bar Lodge)*. The individuals pulled a trailer with snowmobiles and indicated that they searched the road leading to the Black Bar Lodge access road, but because they rode snowmobiles, they only attained partial access to the road. Apparently, some of the road lay bare without snow, therefore preventing the snow machines access. In the after action process of the Search Review, both the Josephine County personnel and the two individuals perceived the conversation very differently.

According to the two individuals *(brothers)*, they informed the Deputy and the SAR Coordinator that a complete search of the road needed to occur. In addition, they commented, that in the past the road sometimes pulled in travelers attempting to drive the Bear Camp Road route. By contrast, the Josephine County personnel reflected that the brothers gave them the impression they already searched the road and intended to search it again. Speculation by some concluded that because of this misunderstanding, or misinterpretation, no one searched those roads from the ground. This simply was not true. This miscommunication leads to an important lesson, and emphasizes the need for clear communications. Searching a specific main route *(e.g. Bear Camp Road)* through this vast forested area, differs greatly from searching all of the spur roads, abandoned logging skid roads and short cuts that intersect and overlap the area. Hindsight always clarifies the correct interpretation when you know the eventual outcome. Even though searchers focused on this area of the road in later assignments, no vehicle road search ever located any trace of the Kim family.

The search effort covered the main Bear Camp Road route both from the air and ground, but not all the spur roads and off-shoots of it. At the time of the meeting on Bear Camp Road *(Dec. 1st)*, no appropriate Point Last Seen or Last Known Position yet existed and the search area still consisted of nearly all of western Oregon. None of the personnel from any of the counties *(Curry, Coos, Josephine, and Douglas)* had any idea if the Kim family location lay in their jurisdiction. At this point, only minimal personnel from each of these counties directly participated in the search.

The entire command and control situation ended up further complicated by a conversation that occurred between the Curry County SAR Coordinator and the Portland Police Bureau late in the morning on December 1st. The Portland Police Bureau Detective assumed that the Curry County SAR Coordinator from the Sheriff's Office was taking total control of the search for the Kim family. This apparently resulted from statements reflecting that the SAR Coordinator was talking *(communicating)* with all four counties *(Curry, Coos, Josephine and Douglas)* in regard to the search.

After the fact, in the Search Review process, the SAR Coordinator from Curry County felt that this was just a misinterpretation of the conversation. From Curry County's perspective, they never held command of the total search effort at any time.

Meanwhile, an Oregon cellular system field engineer *(from a wireless phone company)* heard the news about the missing Kim Family and called an Oregon State Police dispatcher in Salem. The busy dispatcher gave him the number for the Portland Police Bureau detective initially handling the case. When he called the number and heard a recording, the technician chose not to leave a message, but resorted to other avenues to find the Kim's cell phone numbers to work on a new theory. With James Kim's background in technology, the field engineer speculated that the family possessed wireless devices and probably used them until their coverage went out. The technician waited to call back again until the next afternoon *(the 2nd of December)*.

Later in the day on December 1st, authorities received a lead from the Oregon State Police tip line about a possible sighting of the Kim family at a Denny's Restaurant in Roseburg, Oregon. Though not confirmed initially, this put the family's last known location in Roseburg. Later in the evening on that day, the Detective from the Portland Police Bureau handling the case interviewed an employee at the Denny's in Roseburg on the phone who said she knew for a fact that she served the Kim family dinner on the evening of November 25th and even located their meal receipt. The time stamp on the receipt read 8:00 PM. Investigators confirmed the lead the following day. The search effort now included a specific Point Last Seen. Once substantiated, the Denny's Restaurant clue helped to narrow down the search area to about 5,046 sq. miles. *(Figure 10-4, The modified area was west of I-5 in the southwest corner of the state and from the California/Oregon border up approximately 85 miles north to State Hwy. 42).*

December 2nd

On the morning of December 2nd, the SAR Coordinator from Josephine County recalled that Josepine County requested USFS employees and County SAR volunteers to search the Bear Camp Road as part of the multi-county effort. At this point, Josephine County's involvement rose to a support role, but fell short of an official search mission. They performed road searches as a routine courtesy to the other jurisdictions involved. The SAR Coordinator possessed no indication at this point that gave evidence of the Kim family's location in Josephine County.

The Oregon cellular system field engineer ultimately made contact with an Oregon State Police Lieutenant in the afternoon and told him about information possibly narrowing down the Kim Family search area. With the news about the sighting of the Kim Family in Roseburg, Curry County advised the Oregon Emergency Response System of the curtailment of their efforts in that county for the Kim family. With the information obtained by the Oregon State Police from the cellular system engineer concerning the cell phone data, the primary investigator with OSP grew confident about the Kim Family's location lying somewhere in the Bear Camp area, which included parts of Coos, Curry,

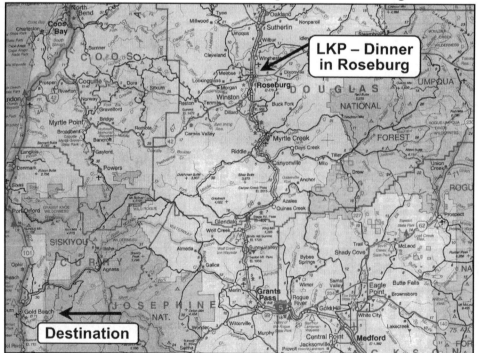

Figure 10-4 The Kim's Last Known Position relative to their final destination

Josephine and Douglas Counties. Those trying to coordinate the search faced tremendous difficulty understanding the cell phone data over the phone so they scheduled a meeting with search Overhead Team members and the cellular system field engineer for Sunday morning, December 3rd.

On this day *(the 2nd)* a handful of tips from the public required follow-up by personnel from multiple jurisdictions and other agencies *(phone calls and/or interviews etc.)* which taxed resources and further complicated the early efforts. The Josephine County SAR Coordinator received a tip concerning the Kim's vehicle possibly sited on the Bear Camp Road *(separate from the earlier report by the brothers who own the Black Bar Lodge)*. These were all followed up with interviews or physical visits. The helicopter company hired by the Kim family also used a liaison who received a tip about sighting the family on the coast at a gas station. Even though it turned out false, investigators spent precious time and effort following up and exhausting possibilities on these leads.

Another tip arrived from a Wilsonville *(Oregon)* Visitor Center employee. She contacted the Oregon State Police and advised that she provided the Kim Family with an Oregon map and also highlighted several scenic routes to take between Myrtle Creek and Grants Pass. According to the Visitor Center employee, the Kim family stopped at the Visitor Center between 12:00 PM to 1:30 PM on the 25th of November. Later on December 2nd, the employee from the Visitor Center duplicated that map with the routes highlighted for Oregon State Police detectives. *(According to Kati Kim in interviews after searchers located her, the Kim family never stopped at this Visitor Center)*.

Meanwhile, the private helicopter company hired by Spencer Kim continued searching additional routes for the missing family vehicle. Spencer Kim said that he believed his son drove down I-5, observed the quickest route to the coast and likely drove up over Bear Camp Road. Mr. Kim insisted that he personally fly in one of the helicopters and ultimately spent five and a half hours searching over Bear Camp Road to Highway 199. They tried to follow every spur road and logging road from Grants Pass to Brookings and then to Gold Beach. Another of the company helicopters took north from the Bear Camp area to the tri-cities and Highway 42 while the third aircraft took Highway 38 and the coastal route. Spencer Kim insisted that they heavily cover the Bear Camp area.

On the afternoon of December 2nd, personnel from Josephine County expressed a concern about not knowing who held operational command of the entire search. This stemmed from a need to report on a potential sighting of the family. The Oregon State Police controlled coordination of the information flow, but they lacked certainty on who coordinated overall search efforts. After the tip came in that the Kim family ate dinner at Denny's in Roseburg *(see Figure 9-4 page 148)*, the SAR Coordinator and other SAR personnel from Josephine County went back out to Bear Camp Road and covered additional spur roads until late in the evening on the 2nd.

Oregon State Police continued to designate areas in the state and specific roads for patrols and BOLOs for the Kim family silver Saab. A number of Oregon State Police personnel *(Four individuals – both Detective and Patrol Divisions)* now worked the mission on the investigation side. Clearly, a degree of ambiguity existed about who held responsibility for both the investigation and the operational search efforts. The perception about who filled the Mission Commander role in the management of the search varied among all the involved local and state resources. Local county SAR Coordinators from neighboring jurisdictions put resources on notice for potential call out, but the upper command and control structure remained ambiguous.

During the Kim Family search, the limited local SAR personnel experienced tremendous fatigue and an overwhelming situation. Other counties and private sector resources offered their assistance with communications equipment as well as management personnel but never received an actual request to deploy. State law outlines a system to provide support resources through the Oregon Emergency Management agency and all other Sheriff's Offices.

Managing the Inland Search Function - Operational Response

NOTE: At this point in the mission, investigators lacked any indication from any source about the Kim family's specific location in one of the respective counties *(Curry, Coos, Josephine, or Douglas)*. Because of this ambiguity, agencies *(state and local)* felt a reluctance to step forward and assume overall command of the entire operation; not by choice, but because of how Oregon State law allocates search and rescue responsibilities. This reluctance makes perfect sense given hindsight of the mission.

The State Office of Emergency Management in Oregon holds the responsibility of coordinating search and rescue operations State wide. While Counties maintain the duty to conduct search and rescue operations, the State fulfills the role of coordinating emergency workers, equipment, and other resources available for SAR Operations. The expectations spelled out in the statute grossly outstripped the staffing and funding of that office at the time. The post mission reviews recommended an evaluation of these responsibilities and proposed legislative changes if appropriate. Oregon Revised Statute – ORS Chapter 401 *(Now revised and renumbered under Chapter 404)* also specified the responsibilities for search and rescue at the local level. Chapter 401.560, at the time of the mission, outlined these functions pertaining to search and rescue:

ORS 401.560 Search and rescue activities; Responsibilities of sheriff; Delegation of Sheriff's duties.

(1) The sheriff of each county has the responsibility for search and rescue activities within the county. The duty of a sheriff under this subsection may be delegated to a qualified deputy or emergency service worker.

(2) If the sheriff does not accept the responsibility for search and rescue activities, the chief executive of the county shall designate the county emergency program manager to perform the duties and responsibilities required under ORS 401.015 to 401.105, 401.260 to 401.325 and 401.355 to 401.580.

(3) The sheriff or authorized person of each county shall notify the Office of Emergency Management of each search and rescue in the county and shall request the assignment of incident numbers therefor.

(4) The sheriff or authorized person of each county shall work with the county emergency program manager in coordinating search and rescue activities in the county of the sheriff and in registering emergency service workers.

At the time of this search, the State Statute neither identified nor clearly outlined responsibilities for multi-jurisdiction incidents of any kind. This provision only materialized in Oregon Statutes as a direct result of the Governor's Task Force assembled in the aftermath of this search.

Oregon law (*now **ORS 404.100**, formerly 401.550*) also establishes a State SAR Coordinator with these specific responsibilities:

(1) Coordinate the search and rescue function of the Office of Emergency Management;

(2) Coordinate the activities of state and federal agencies involved in search and rescue;

(3) Establish liaison with the Oregon State Sheriffs' Association and other public and private organizations and agencies involved in search and rescue;

(4) Provide on-scene search and rescue coordination when requested by an authorized person;

(5) Coordinate and process requests for the use of emergency service workers and equipment;

(6) Assist in developing training and outdoor education programs;

> (7) Gather statistics in search and rescue operations; and
>
> (8) Gather and disseminate resource information of personnel, equipment and materials available for search and rescue.
>
> As stated in the Review, it appears as though the system functioned differently than outlined by the statute. Testimony from the after action reviews indicate that only item number seven was ever carried out by the state agency personnel *(Gather statistics in search and rescue operations)*.
>
> In the official Search Review, Part I and II investigators explicitly noted that the State Office of Emergency Management, at the time of the Kim Search clearly received too little funding and staff resources to fulfill the responsibilities outlined in the statute.

December 3rd

On the morning of Sunday the 3rd of December, Josephine County personnel, (*the SAR Coordinator, a deputy and the Undersheriff*), met with two Oregon State Police personnel, and they contacted the cellular system field engineer who called the Oregon State Police Lieutenant the day before. The meeting occurred at the Josephine County Sheriff's Office. The day before, the field engineer searched the wireless coverage area data and found a "handshake" signal from one of the Kim's cell phones at 1:30 AM on the 26th of November. Only two pings from the phone showed, but they allowed for a general determination of distance and direction proximity for the phone in relation to the tower. The cell phone at the time of the signal lay within a 26 mile radius of the tower. *(The cellular technician also provided a map and a description of how to interpret the data)*.

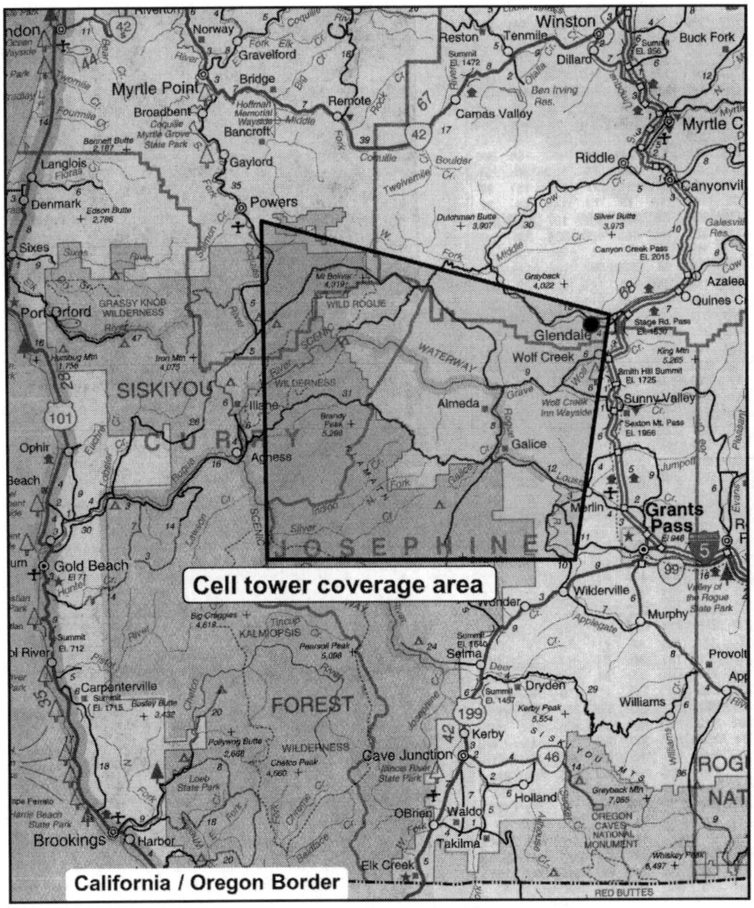

The cell phone data in no way placed a specific location for the family in Josephine County or Douglas County. The map actually showed possible areas of coverage through which the Kim family drove when the phone and tower generated a *handshake* signal *(Figure 10-5 at left)*. As it turned out, searchers found the car about 22 miles distant from the location on the map where the mobile phone made its connection. A considerable portion of the coverage area on the map lay in Douglas County and unfortunately that jurisdiction had a history of cell signals sending searchers to the wrong area.

Figure 10-5 An approximate cell tower coverage area (not the propagation map).

After the meeting, ground resources deployed to search roadways identified in the cell phone propagation map including a large portion of the Bear Camp road area *(See Figure 10-6 on the next page)*. As stated above, the data provided possible starting points for further searching, not an exact location. The cell tower map narrowed the search area to approximately 531 square miles.

Oregon State Police contacted the Kim Family wireless cell phone company and obtained cell phone records for all incoming and outgoing calls made on additional cell phones (2) belonging to the Kims. Those records confirmed three outgoing calls to the Tu Tu Tun Lodge in Gold Beach on the 25th of November. In addition, later that day OSP personnel met with Spencer Kim (*James Kim's father*) and the owner of the private helicopter firm that Spencer hired to help find his son's family. At that meeting OSP briefed Spencer Kim on everything uncovered to date about James and Kati Kim's travel. They also shared a copy of the cell tower map and the information obtained from the cell phone technician. The private helicopter company immediately redirected their search efforts to the area of coverage from the Glendale cell tower depicted on the map.

> **NOTE: The Importance of a Family Liaison**
>
> The Kim family conducted their own search efforts and investigation. The early assignment of a Liaison Officer from any involved agency or organization *(State or Local)* would have provided both the Kim Family and the search management coordinating body more timely information sharing. As an example, specifically reducing the duplication of air search efforts. In addition, minimizing the conflict of multiple aircraft in the same area, particularly the federal assets competing with private resources not allowed in the protocols established by the federal government.

In light of the cell phone company map and information, a Lieutenant from the Oregon State Police suggested activation of the Jackson County Search and Rescue SAR Team to assist in canvassing the Bear Camp area. They agreed to the suggestion but asked that the Lieutenant from the Oregon State Police personally coordinate the Jackson County

Figure 10-6 Search focus and the counties involved after analysis of the cell tower data

search efforts because of some difficulties in the past. The Lieutenant agreed, and on the morning of December 3rd OSP formally called the Jackson County Sheriff's Office to ask for assistance on the search.

Jackson and Josephine County enacted a major SAR callout for personnel and around thirty individuals responded for assignment that afternoon. When Jackson County SAR personnel arrived they assumed that OSP officially held Incident Command. Up to this point, an extremely nebulous and undefined structure for the management of the search developed because of the multiple jurisdictions involved *(Both state and local)*. And to make matters more confusing, as mentioned before, Oregon Statute at the time lacked guidance on responsibilities for multi-jurisdiction SAR Missions.

NOTE: The Director for the Oregon State Emergency Management Office, during the Search Review process conducted by the Governor's Task Force indicated awareness of a situation where Oregon State Police allegedly "took over" the search and that possibly the Oregon State Police Lieutenant took command. He was not aware of Oregon State Police ever taking over any type of search and rescue operation in the past. Also, the search review never interviewed the official Oregon State Search and Rescue Coordinator about the Kim Family Search mission during the Review.

Pilots and company personnel from the private helicopter firm hired by Spencer Kim made note of the organizational command structure for the search up through mid-day on Sunday, December 3rd. From their observations they found no established command for the search and who "ran the show." The search seemed "very loose and casual." On Sunday by mid-day when the State Patrol took the lead, the operation began to gel. They pooled resources and Spencer Kim advised everyone with the helicopter company to share all information with the local agencies.

From the helicopter company's perspective, the Lieutenant from the Oregon State Police served as the main contact and authority for the search. From their perspective, he filled the role of leader. As the stated IC for the operation, the OSP Lieutenant acted very receptive and wanted to hear from the helicopter company personnel. Although many concerns remained about unification between all the agencies and the private company, very open, communication began between the search operations staff and the helicopter company personnel. Barriers were broken down through the efforts of both the IC and the Logistics section of the search operation. Everyone understood the value and trained capability brought by the private helicopter company.

From the standpoint of both local and state law enforcement officials working on the search, decision to assume the function of Mission Commander by the regional Oregon State Police Lieutenant made good sense. The collective overhead team of State Troopers, and Sheriff's Office personnel made joint operational assignments to available SAR personnel.

Oregon State Police had no statutory guidance that provided any responsibility in the functions of search and rescue; and their training provides no basics in this discipline. That remains the case today.

The multi-jurisdiction nature of this mission contributed greatly to differing perceptions about the organizational structure and staff positions in the operation. After action investigations and interviews varied greatly about command and carrying out specific functional tasks at different times. The varying

> accounts stemmed from each individual's perspective at the time they communicated or coordinated with the Command and General Staff. Functionally searchers referred to the mission as a ***Unified Command*** even though nobody formally declared it.
>
> This highlights a technical issue in the National proscribed ICS training and operational protocols. It speaks to a general lack of understanding *(at state and local levels)* of how to manage more complex operations. A Lieutenant from OSP assumed the Mission Command position, Josephine County Sheriff's Office personnel took charge of operations and planning while the SAR Coordinator from Josephine County assumed the role of Logistics Chief. At first glance this structure appears different than standard ICS protocol, but the structure that eventually coalesced functionally served its purpose considering the circumstances.

During the evening of Sunday, December 3rd, the private helicopter company personnel and Spencer Kim received thorough briefings and then carried out a well-defined plan in a much more narrowed search area. Their plan centered on methodically working the Bear Camp Area in a radius from the Glendale cell tower out to a distance of approximately 30 miles. Since the estimated radius identified from the wireless company cell tower sat at approximately 26 miles, they wanted to make sure to conservatively cover that distance.

Once the Command and General Staff solidified in one location (*the Sheriff's Office in Josephine County*), planners needed to collectively determine what areas searchers already covered. Coordinators decided to move from the Josephine County Sheriff's Office in Grant's Pass, north to the SAR complex in Merlin. All Oregon State Police personnel involved, and county agency personnel involved converged for a major briefing and meeting on the morning of December 4th at 09:00am at the SAR complex in Merlin.

An unsolicited private pilot in the area read about the missing Kim Family and some of the speculation about potential locations. He possessed extensive knowledge of the area and its history. The pilot decided to take his personal helicopter and fly through the area to have a look. On the flight, he noticed tire tracks down a spur off of Bear Camp Road and saw no return tracks. Because of his low fuel state at the time, he flew into Medford where he contacted the Jackson County SAR helicopter pilot and told him about the tracks. After refueling, the private pilot flew back over the Bear Camp area and then went home.

> **NOTE:** A major concern in almost any search involves the spontaneous response by untrained, unskilled or improperly equipped volunteers. Well-meaning, but unsolicited resources entering the field without notification often hinder search efforts and leave false clues.

December 4th

All agencies involved in the search effort attended the briefing in Merlin and provided information on their respective search activities. The group identified searched and unsearched areas and gave resources assignments throughout the morning. Planners coordinated tasks in all four counties now involved *(Coos, Curry, Josephine, and Douglas)* including Oregon State Police personnel. Those with tasks shared information and coordinated between investigative and operational assignments.

Around mid-day on Monday, the same **unsolicited volunteer pilot** once again flew his helicopter into the area and spotted the same tracks as the day before. While flying, he also observed a group of SAR resources getting ready to go into the area. The pilot followed the tire tracks by air and also spotted footprints, later determined as those left by James Kim. From the air he saw that James Kim walked past a road leading to Black Bar Lodge, located about a mile down another side dirt road. "He was on dirt for a long time — for miles," the pilot said. "He was only on snow about 100 yards." The footprints led through the snow and over an embankment into the Big Windy Creek drainage.

The volunteer pilot continued flying up the road where he eventually spotted Kati Kim with her two daughters at the missing car. He immediately called on the radio to the helicopter company hired by Spencer Kim and told them about finding the car and an adult female trying to signal him. Because the pilot felt uncomfortable landing in the tight area, he requested the helicopter company aircraft to make the pickup. After ensuring the company sent another helicopter, the volunteer pilot continued to follow the tracks left by James Kim. Once again he found where they led over the embankment and into the Big Windy Creek drainage. The rescue helicopter arrived and transported Kati Kim and her two daughters to the Grants Pass hospital for evaluation and treatment.

> **NOTE:** While his efforts ultimately succeeded in finding Kati Kim and her daughters, unsolicited resources as well as media aircraft create the potential of very dangerous conditions for others flying in the region. When the volunteer pilot left the field to refuel and then tried to return to the search area, the hired helicopter company informed him that the FAA placed a flight restriction on the area. The FAA imposed a TFR *(Temporary Flight Restriction)* in the region immediately after the rescue of Kati and the children.

One of the aircraft flew up the road in the direction James Kim walked away from the vehicle. Both pilots observed and followed the tracks into the top end of Big Windy Creek drainage, but then the tracks appeared to stop. The aircraft then flew down into the drainage several more times looking for more sign or evidence of James Kim. They actually landed at Black Bar Lodge, knocked on doors and looked around thoroughly. From there the pilots next landed at the mouth of the Big Windy Creek drainage. They wanted to physically check on the ground for tracks just in case James walked out, but they found no sign/tracks there either. Eventually ground SAR team members also followed the tracks into the canyon. They described the tracks as made by tennis shoes.

Notification about the rescue of Kati Kim and her children quickly spread throughout the organizations involved; however, James Kim was still missing. Personnel already in the Bear Camp Road system, began concentrating their efforts on the roads in the area once again. Other resources redeployed from across the river in Douglas County. When resources arrived back at the Command Post their new tasks lay in or around the Bear Camp Area Road system as well.

Searchers speculated about a variety of reasons why James left a perfectly good road, particularly at that location. Firsthand accounts from SAR resources on the ground and helicopters in the air, stated descriptions of observed tracks clearly on the road in the snow and it appeared as though James potentially saw a bear ahead on the road, but still across the canyon. Just beyond the point where James left the road, trackers discovered an area that showed numerous and very obvious bear tracks. Given the excessive fear exhibited by both Kati and James of bears, searchers speculated that he saw the animal from a far, and headed for the brush and trees to avoid it. While searchers talked about this, nobody ever documented it officially in any records because no clear proof existed other than the tracks found on the road.

Once ground resources began tracking James Kim into the Big Windy Creek drainage they pushed as far as safely possible. The Big Windy Creek area in general exhibits extremely rugged and seemingly unpassable terrain in some areas, particularly at night. No access roads exist at the bottom with only very limited access at the top. As the search efforts continued that day, search team leaders decided that because of the terrain, further searching required technical resources. The Command Staff personnel specifically called Lane County to activate Mountain Rescue team to continue the search in the rough, steep terrain that night if possible. Mountain Rescue responded and immediately launched into the area late to try and track at night. However, ultimately the conditions forced them to stop and bivouac in place. The terrain simply became too treacherous for searching in the darkness. The plan called for starting from that location at first light.

The Douglas and Josephine County SAR Coordinators along with Oregon State Police Detectives interviewed Kati Kim at the hospital trying to hone in on the intentions of James Kim and perhaps what his tracks indicated. Because his trail led into the Big Windy Creek drainage, the Josephine Co. SAR Coordinator felt it appropriate to request a FLIR equipped aircraft to support the mission in that drainage. The SAR Coordinator made the request and an Oregon Army National Guard unit responded with an OH-58 helicopter equipped with FLIR on board.

The Josephine County SAR Coordinator *(who took on the Logistics Section Chief function for the Mission General Staff)* put an Army National Guard UH60 Blackhawk in Medford on alert to accomplish a hoist rescue for James Kim if needed. The National Guard OH-58 with FLIR assigned to search in the area that evening advised the Command Staff of several hot spots of interest to follow up on during search efforts for the next day. Oregon State Police provided updates and a complete briefing for Spencer Kim and the family that evening.

Kati Kim First Interview (*from the hospital*)

A very emotional Kati Kim provided Oregon State Police and the Josephine and Douglas County SAR Coordinators with detailed information regarding their trip and their eight day ordeal lost in the Bear Camp Road system. Kati provided the following investigative information to assist in the continued search for James Kim (*from the OSP report*):

- The Kims never stopped in Wilsonville to pick up a map or get directions.
- The Kims left Roseburg at approximately 9:00p.m.
- They missed the Highway 42 exit from Interstate 5 to Gold Beach.
- Using their Oregon road map, they decided to take Bear Camp Road to Gold Beach (*the family was not using a GPS*).
- The Kims realized they possibly took a wrong turn at approximately 2:00 a.m. on November 26th.
- The Kims stopped in an area where they thought motorists passed by regularly (*the vehicle was not stuck in the snow*).
- James left on Saturday, December 2nd at 7:45 a.m. in an attempt to locate help, only wearing jeans, a heavy jacket and tennis shoes.
- James walked away from the car toward the sound of the river. His plan called for leaving notes and strips of clothing along the route and returning back to the car by 1:00 p.m. if he failed to find help.
- Kati heard and saw a helicopter flying over her on Sunday the 3rd, however, her attempts to get the pilots attention failed.
- A private volunteer helicopter pilot looking on his own located Kati and her kids on December 4th.

December 5th

The search effort for Tuesday now concentrated in Josephine County and operated 24 hours a day. The effort involved hundreds of individuals combining both the management side and resources committed to the field. The search area centered about 30 miles from Grants Pass, Oregon, with an average elevation of about 3000 feet. It focused on a 5 mile long canyon *(Big Windy Creek)* which lay roughly 9.5 miles from the location of the car where Kati and her two daughters remained with the vehicle.

The search finally resolved to a specific geographic area. The helicopters all launched that day by 06:30 AM with one located in the Black Bar Lodge area, one in the middle of the Big Windy Creek drainage and the other flying at the very bottom near the creek. When they launched that morning they also carried 18 survival packets containing clothing, shelter, food, phones and signaling devices. The helicopters dropped them into both sides of the drainage with the hope that either James or other rescuers might find and use them.

At 10:00 am a news conference and media briefing on the details of the search led by the Oregon State Police Public Information Officer occurred. According to the briefing, the last reported signs and indications from the search efforts placed James Kim in the upper end of the Big Windy Creek drainage.

Isolation and only one direct access road into the Big Windy Creek drainage complicated the search efforts in this area, but aviation assets provided the key to the logistical transportation problems. With three helicopters committed to searching the drainage throughout the day and numerous search teams in the field, communications between teams and to the command post proved challenging. Oregon State Police activated their mobile communications unit with the intent to improve communications for ground teams. However, the resource required some time to get into position. As an interim, a number of agency personnel attempted to act as radio relay for operations in the field with hopes of improving communications in the remote area. But this also caused problems and confusion with field teams redirecting *(changing assignments)* through the radio relays. It proved a double edged sword as communications indeed improved, but with some negative impact on operations. Some thought the radio relays provided a huge help, but that view varied with many in the Incident Command Staff.

Two personnel from the Josephine County Sheriff's Office Marine Patrol, one individual from Jackson County and an American Medical Response *(AMR)* Reach and Treat *(RAT)* team paramedic took assignments to take rafts down the Rogue River and look for James Kim. During the drift they looked for tracks or other evidence and checked all the creeks on foot as far as the terrain allowed without climbing equipment. They even stopped at the then closed Black Bar Lodge, but the structure showed no signs of entry or attempted entry by anyone. The four left their rafts at a prearranged location and helicopters picked them up.

Because of the limited access to the terrain, many discussions occurred about the possibility of *short haul* maneuvers or *long line insertions* with some personnel to get searchers into the right areas as quickly as possible with the aircraft. Some of the Sheriff's Office personnel hesitated because of the implications created by using private company helicopters. Questions about training beforehand and competency with the pilots, using the right equipment, ropes and other inadequate technical equipment all formed the discussion. All of this occurred in the late afternoon as the hours of daylight slipped away. Some radio traffic surfaced earlier about ground resources finding a pair of pants while moving into the drainage from the top.

Ultimately team members solved the problems with the long line insertion by making some equipment modifications and a team member clipped in by carabiner for a drop near a tentatively identified blue backpack in the creek. From his observations when finally on-scene, the responder discovered evidence that someone bedded down or stayed in the area. He found ribbon, pieces of map and other items under a log, a wool sock, and a red shirt; all things included on the list of items that James Kim wore or carried in his pockets. The responder also discovered a child's blue dress in the creek, not a back pack, but still a very important clue. As darkness overtook the scene, the helicopter extracted the individual via long line.

The Army National Guard UH60 Blackhawk now located in Medford waited to accomplish a hoist rescue if needed. The assigned OH-58 searching Big Windy Creek with FLIR the evening before once again arrived on-scene in the canyon and also started searching along adjacent drainages. The Coast Guard also responded to evacuate an injured Deputy on this day – he suffered a collar bone fracture and other injuries due to an ATV accident. At approximately 9:45 PM on December 5th, all search helicopters returned to their temporary bases. Other than the tracks on the ground and the items found in or near Big Windy Creek, helicopters failed to find any more clues during the day's sorties.

December 6th

Thick fog grounded all aircraft on the morning of the 6th of December. All involved County SAR Units once again committed resources to the Big Windy Creek drainage, but only by foot (*Fog initially prevented any early insertions of resources by aircraft*). The schedule called for a media briefing at 10:00 AM by the Oregon State Police, Public Information Officer.

Managing the Inland Search Function - **Operational Response**

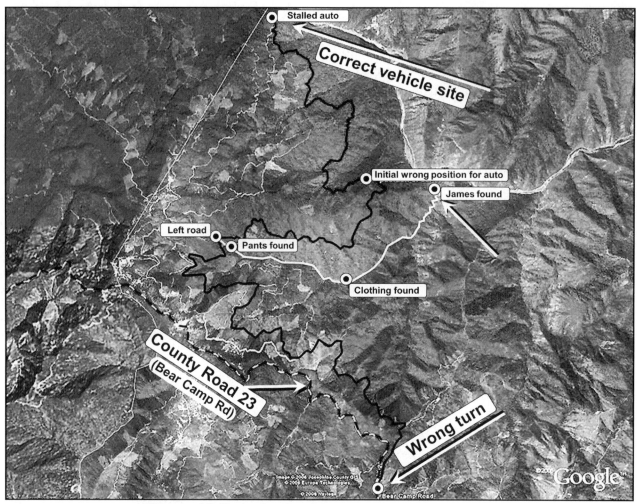

Figure 10-7 Kim Search After Action Search Overview.

As soon as the weather proved flyable, the private helicopter company hired by Spencer Kim started inserting resources again by long line. At noon that day, the company personnel, while inserting Jackson County SWAT into the canyon, spotted James Kim's body in the Big Windy Creek near the bottom of the drainage. Because they made the observation from approximately 300 feet above ground level, the pilots summoned medics just in case. Two SWAT medics descended from a helicopter to the body, located and marked his position and later they recovered the body. When this occurred, Coordinators released all aircraft committed to the search effort. The staff calculated that including the 9.5 miles from the vehicle to where he entered the Big Windy Creek drainage, then walking straight down the canyon to the find site, James Kim covered a total distance of about 14.5 miles *(See Figure 10-7 above)*.

December 8th

On Friday, the 8th of December, 2006 an all agency debriefing took place at the Josephine County SAR complex in Merlin, Oregon.

Although not all present for this debriefing, the following list of agencies and organizations provides a quick glimpse at the diversity and numbers of people directly involved in some way or another in the search and rescue effort that responded for James Kim. This impressive reminder illustrates the dedicated men and women that comprise our complex search and rescue response system all across this country today.

Oregon State Police
Oregon Emergency Management
Oregon State Governor's Office
Oregon Army National Guard Aviation Division

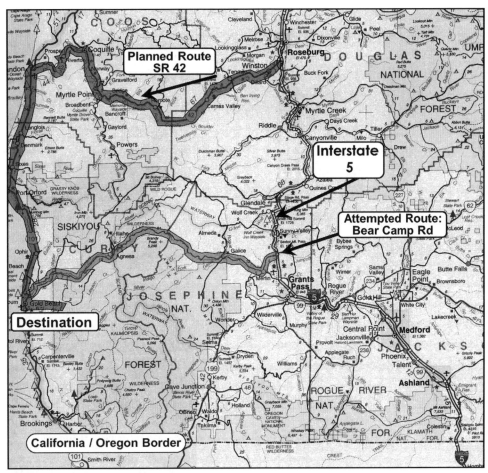

Figure 10-8 Planned and attempted routes for the Kim Family on November 25th, 2006.

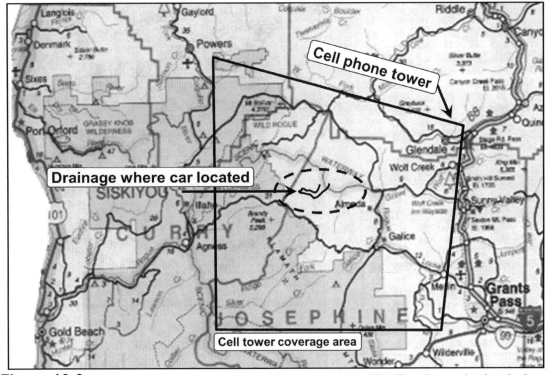

Figure 10-9 Cell tower coverage area and location of the Kim Family car in the drainage.

(*Oregon Military Department*)
Oregon Army National Guard Joint Emergency Operations Center (*Oregon Military Department*)
Josephine County Sheriff's Office
Josephine County Emergency Management
Jackson County Sheriff's Office
Curry County Sheriff's Office
Douglas County Sheriff's Office
Douglas County Emergency Management
Lane County Sheriff's Office
Siskiyou County Sheriff's Office
Klamath County Sheriff's Office
Coos County Sheriff's Office
Del Norte County Sheriff's Office
Lincoln County Sheriff's Office
Deschutes County SAR
San Francisco Police Department
Portland Police Bureau
U.S. Coast Guard
Bureau of Land Management
U.S. Forest Service - USFS
American Red Cross
Jackson County Special Weapons and Tactics Team
American Medical Response (*AMR*) **Reach and Treat** (RAT) **Team**
Three Private Helicopters Secured and Payed for by the Kim Family
The **Jackson County SAR Helicopter with Flight Crew Personnel**
Eugene Mountain Rescue unit
Multiple Volunteer SAR Unit Personnel from Multiple Counties – All supplying Vehicles - Specialty Gear and Equipment

Josephine County Request for Review

At the request of the Josephine County SAR Coordinator, the Oregon State Sheriff's Association *(OSSA)* initiated an unprecedented mission review. A team of eighteen investigators and search experts from Sheriff's Offices all across the State of Oregon interviewed private citizens, news agencies, investigators, volunteer search members and administrators involved in this search mission. Almost simultaneously, a review of statewide search and rescue policies and procedures occurred with a Task Force appointed by the Governor. This search and the resulting media coverage generated an incredible array of administrative efforts, commissions, reports and recommendations by diverse organizations involved in the effort. The Oregon State Sheriffs Association report addressed many of the things that worked, and at least some of the lessons learned. The investigation attempted to put the tragic pieces of the puzzle surrounding this case into a comprehensive set of practical and useful facts, and even provide lessons learned for future missions if possible.

The documented report findings and the analysis in this chapter stem from a variety of sources including personal interviews conducted by investigators, individual reports and phone conversations, as well as personal communications with some of the Incident Management Team members. During the context of the after-action investigation several conflicting accounts developed in the retelling of dates and events from one interview to the next. This often occurs where each person provides individual recollection or written records rather than any error in editing of the facts. The Agency Compilation Timeline formed as an appendix for the report for exactly this reason. The derivation of this chapter in the Textbook traces to multiple documents and statements both officially and unofficially created.

Executive Commentary from the Committee

The political situation in Josephine County, during the search, formed a remarkable backdrop. Every county operates within a unique political environment. When this mission materialized, the current Sheriff decided not to run for re-election and in fact announced his retirement before the election. The Sheriff spent no time on duty during the entire duration of this search.

The Undersheriff ran an office faced with a huge funding shortfall due to the potential loss of a federal funding stream. The entire office operated in the shadow of the recent political race and the looming threat of layoffs with the incoming administration. The Undersheriff actually ran for Sheriff and narrowly lost that race. The election occurred in November and named a new Sheriff-Elect. The Sheriff-Elect previously notified the Undersheriff that he was not going to keep him in the new administration. Understandably, the Undersheriff spent part of his time actively looking for employment during late November and his last scheduled work-week happened to fall in the middle of the search.

> **Sidebar of history about other SAR missions for Reference:** Numerous examples of high profile, well-covered in the media SAR missions provided the catalyst for positive change in local and state laws, policies, equipment and even overall management. The well-publicized search for Congressman Hale Boggs in Alaska, as an example, produced legislation to require emergency locator transmitters in aircraft.
>
> Another example responsible for important legislation took place just north of Oregon, in Washington State. Prior to 1967 in Washington, a variety of authorities carried out search and rescue such as police and sheriff's departments, state aeronautics, federal agencies and a host of volunteer groups. In 1965, little or no inter-jurisdictional coordination ever occurred.
>
> In May of 1965, a well-known City Councilman from Seattle disappeared with two other persons on a private aircraft flight from Okanogan County to Renton, Washington. A massive search ensued throughout the state. The media covered the effort extensively and described it in the Seattle Times headline: "SAR in Washington State is a travesty of bad administration and worse coordination." The search identified huge problems among county sheriffs, state officials, numerous volunteers *(unorganized and organized)* and with the federal agencies that also participated. Costs for the entire mission exceeded 4 million dollars (*in 1965!*).
>
> The governor of Washington State commissioned a series of Blue Ribbon Committee meetings and hearings concerning Search and Rescue throughout the state. The end result produced legislation that accomplished two very important benchmarks in Washington state law.
>
> The first levied a nominal fee on pilots to finance aviation Search and Rescue and pilot emergency preparedness education. The second established the position of State SAR Coordinator in the Emergency Services Department to coordinate and support local SAR efforts. The Emergency Services Department, *(now the Division of Emergency Management under the Military Department)* formed because of its capability and knowledge of state wide resources for use in Emergency Management *(then called Civil Defense emergency efforts).*
>
> The intent of the legislature provided a central point of contact to support local jurisdictions with resources, administration of volunteer indemnity coverage and to coordinate multi-jurisdiction missions if requested.
>
> The Wing Luke search taught a grim lesson in Washington State on the need for a statewide system of coordination for SAR. Unfortunately, this same type of situation *(intense media coverage, loss of life, politically sensitive situation)* often provides the catalyst for states to improve much needed statewide coordination systems. Legislators and subsequent SAR coordinators then refined and upgraded the network put into place in Washington several times.

Chronology of Official Reviews, Task Force Assignments, Reports and Recommendations resulting from the Kim family Search:

Friday December 8th, 2006 – After Action Review at the Josephine County Sheriff's Office Search and Rescue facility. What went right, what went wrong? Comprehensive review of mission with comments and synopsis of what worked and what didn't, and the needs for improvement and training.

Saturday December 23rd, 2006 – Josephine County makes a formal request with the Oregon State Sheriff's Association for an independent fact finding inquiry into the Kim family search and the decisions and procedures implemented during that mission. The Sheriff's Association requested an uninvolved Sheriff to lead an investigative review.

Tuesday December 26th, 2006 – The committee contacted more than a dozen investigators contacted from all across Oregon and tasked them to conduct interviews to determine the reasonable standard of care, the proper use of resources and to ask about lessons learned.

January 18th 2007 – Oregon State Sheriff's Association completes the Kim Family Search Review and releases the report to the public and the media.

January 19th 2007 – Governor's Executive Order 07-01 - Establishment of the Governor's Search and Rescue Task Force. The Task Force included 14 to 17 members appointed by the Governor to consider the necessity of changes to the laws, Oregon Administrative Rules and related policies concerning state and local authorities in search and rescue operations. The Governor directed the Task Force to make recommendations on changes where needed, particularly in the case of legislation.

March 2007 – The Governor's Search and Rescue Task Force makes 15 recommendations to the Governor concerning command and control, communications, training and resources for conducting search and rescue operations at state and local levels.

May 2007 – The legislature presented and passed Senate Bill 1002 providing more specific guidance for search and rescue missions involving multiple jurisdictions, the use of the Mission Command System and also affirming the responsibility for SAR resting with the local county Sheriff.

May 2007 – The legislature proposed, but failed to pass, Senate Bill 1003. The bill intended to provide funding and staffing for the Oregon Office of Emergency Management search and rescue function throughout the state to support local SAR operations.

November 2007 – Governor's Executive Order 07–23 – Establishment of the Search and Rescue Policy Commission, a non-legislative recommendation that originated from the Governor's Search and Rescue Task Force. The Search and Rescue Policy Commission would take up where the Task Force left off and work toward resolution on the issues they lacked time to resolve, particularly in the area of resource indemnification and insurance. The Commission also facilitated communication and coordination about SAR throughout all local and state entities.

February 2010 – Governor's Executive Order 10-02 - Amendment to Search and Rescue Policy Commission. The Commission consists of at least 14 members appointed by the Governor. The Commission continued to meet and consider statewide search and rescue issues and make recommendations to ensure proper coordination, and communications between federal, state and local authorities in search and rescue operations in Oregon. Annual reports summarized findings or recommendations.

Synopsis of the Kim Family Search Review Findings

Issues Identified by the Committee

On the 9th through the 11th of January, 2007, a SAR subcommittee of the larger OSSA review group mentioned earlier, met in Salem, Oregon to specifically assess the SAR component of the Kim search. The subcommittee, composed of six highly experienced SAR Coordinators, five from Sheriff's Offices and one from a private volunteer SAR group, identified the following issues with the search operation:

Command and Control

Originally developed as an integral part of the National Mission Management System (*NIMS*) in the United States, the Incident Command System *(ICS)*, arrived in the Department of Homeland Security in 2003 Presidential directive *(HSPD 5)*, and federal funds for local jurisdictions depend upon compliance. Compliance with this protocol forms a continuing effort, as individual skills perish and the personnel and volunteers turn over frequently. The OSSA Search Report reflected that Josephine County employed the Incident Command System *(ICS)*, but only in a very limited manner.

National, state and local protocols require the use of the Incident Command System *(ICS)* and the state of Oregon and its political subdivisions fall firmly within this protocol. That means staffing appropriate positions in accordance with the needs and the size of the mission, even if only using the simplest structures of the system and its principles. The National ICS Curriculum emphasizes, in all training, well-defined roles and responsibilities for specific positions in the system and identification of those positions in a visible manner. During the Kim search, managers never technically accomplished this in ICS textbook form. Large searches or any emergency response operations of appropriate size require both an adequate Command and General Staff established as soon as possible to meet the demand of information management. Another vital component centers on an assigned staff member in a functional position to record what happened in all phases of the mission.

> **NOTE:** Up until Saturday, December 2nd investigators never uncovered an appropriate Point Last Seen for the Mission. When investigators confirmed the sighting clue from Roseburg on the morning of December 3rd, no one possessed information, even generally, about where in the region to look for the family. Later that day, technical cell phone data narrowed the search more specifically to areas of Josephine and Douglas Counties. Uninformed individuals, as stated earlier, assumed because Curry County called the State for a mission number and ordered a Blackhawk, that Curry County coordinated the search effort from that jurisdiction. *(In hindsight, this scenario remains understandable given the situation up until mid-day on Sunday, December the 3rd because no one established a single official Command Post in an appropriate jurisdiction to manage the entire operation).*

At times, staff filled the primary functional areas, but the process lacked any formal posting of an organizational chart or the use of name, position tags or vests indicating staffing of the various positions.

The search lacked a clear designation of who held the position of Incident Commander. Periods of time went by in which Oregon State Police and local Sheriff's Office personnel both appeared to fill the role of Incident Commander. As mentioned earlier, this varied greatly depending on the perspective of the person or organization that communicated with the Command and General Staff and in which jurisdiction the coordination took place. Even though nobody formally declared it, many referred to the command structure as "a Unified Command." The multi-jurisdiction nature of this search contributed greatly to differing perceptions. The issue raised references the more technical aspects of the National ICS training and operational protocols. Consistently, state and local officials demonstrate a general lack of understanding of how to manage more complex operations. While not ideal or standard, the structure that formed grew into a workable organization and functioned due to the dedicated staff and their efforts trying to find James Kim and his family.

During the first three days of the search, the varied state and local agencies involved across Oregon and California created a great deal of ambiguity about who commanded the investigation side and the operational search efforts. The end result created questions about where State *(OSP)* and local Sheriff's Office personnel fit into the Incident Command structure. Not a question about their duties, but what role each needed to play in the overall management of the search.

- On Sunday, the 3rd of December, the Oregon State Police Lieutenant working on the Kim family search investigation, made a suggestion that formally organized the Command and General Staff structure for the search. Josephine county called for resources from adjoining counties to assist in the search efforts. Recall earlier that previous interactions with Jackson county led to some resistance from Josephine County

personnel. The solution put OSP directly in control of managing those resources.
- The decision by the Lieutenant to manage those resources started the solidification of a specific Incident Management Team in one location. In the eyes of many, verified through after action interviews, OSP assumed command in the IC position and maintained that function (*possibly alternating with the Undersheriff at times*) throughout the rest of the mission with the exception of late night shifts, etc.

Because of the early ambiguity about who actually managed the search, and from what location and in which jurisdiction, daily routines for specific staff never materialized until the 4th day of the mission. In an ideal scenario, briefings, specific operational assignments, debriefing, planning meetings and information liaison functions all flow from a single site. While all of these functions occurred in one county *(Josephine)* no consolidated central point of command and control existed. To facilitate additional information coordination, on Sunday the 3rd of December the operation moved from the Josephine County Sheriff's Office to the SAR complex located just outside of Grants Pass in Merlin. The overall operation needed a consolidated Incident Management Team. To this point, the scope of the mission, media attention and shear exhaustion slowly overwhelmed many of those that occupied management positions.

The OSSA Search Review stated that after defining a specific search area in Josephine County, *(the Kim's vehicle and James Kim's trail into the Big Windy Creek drainage)* that the Josephine County Sheriff's Office personnel then needed to assume operational control of the search. However, the consolidation of a Command and General Staff, due to unique circumstances already occurred and finally started to function efficiently. As mentioned earlier, the fact that OSP served in the IC function on this SAR mission marked a new situation in State history.

Communications

Lines of communication between the investigators and the Command and General Staff functions encountered many difficulties especially when viewed in the context of the timetables for the mission and when and where the information surfaced. The mission *(in general)* needed a single point in the management staff to evaluate and channel investigative information into the operational plan and assignments. No one set up or declared a Mission Command Post at any time before the operation moved to Merlin on December 4th.

Josephine County ensured that the search teams sent to the field were briefed and debriefed. As operational periods came to an end, everyone in the field who called in on the radio or came to the Command Post debriefed their search efforts appropriately.

Some of those working the investigation side of the mission were pressed into operational tasks within the search effort because of personnel shortages. Radio communications between field teams and the Command Post proved problematic because of the unique circumstances of the situation. Distance from the ICP, the terrain, the number of personnel on one frequency and inadequate human relays made communications difficult at times.

- The physical setup of the ICP required radio communications staff in a building adjacent to the ICP and then a transfer of the messages to the Command Post at the Merlin Complex. While most messages made it through accurately, a few felt that some of them changed slightly in the transfer process. Also, some reported information changing in the relay system as well but those reports lacked specific examples. Radio communication proved problematic and some things simply failed to get through to Incident Command staff. Unfortunately, this often occurs in a large emergency operation.

The Governor's Search and Rescue Task Force convened following this mission acknowledged the central role of communication to successful

SAR efforts. Some of the review investigators characterized the public safety radio network in Oregon as a dangerously out-of-date patchwork and that first responders frequently failed to communicate between agencies. However, all first responders in Oregon maintained access to the SAR simplex frequency on their radios. Air assets utilize their own frequency on a different band, requiring a different radio. Any of the air assets used regularly on SAR missions routinely programmed the SAR frequency into their radios to communicate with command, but not the private or hired air resources.

The OSSA Search Report revealed a number of statements concerning frustration experienced by civilians and law enforcement alike. As the investigation and search efforts hit full speed, some reported difficulty with contacting a live person at agencies and businesses to obtain or share information. Due to weekend schedules many agency personnel ended up out of contact on their days off, such as detectives in Portland, and the Denny's manager, etc.

Overhead Staff turned down an offer of assistance from an outside communication organization *(based approximately 5 hours away)* because of the availability of a van belonging to the Oregon State Police for communications. Logistics on the General Staff also called a wireless company's Sheriff Account Manager to inquire about how to address the poor cell phone service in the search area. The technicians worked on setting up a temporary cell phone site to dramatically improve communications in the remote area. A temporary tower would also give James Kim an opportunity to text or call out on his cell phone if he tried.

However, this type of tasking takes time, and the technicians failed to make these changes operational before the search ended. Despite the fact that the command post utilized numerous functional telephone lines *(it also functioned as the County Emergency Operations Center)* during the search, communication difficulties surfaced. The staff also made use of numerous cell phones.

- Innovation and professional expertise played a role in communications. The lead pilot and liaison for the private helicopter company hired by Spencer Kim took it upon himself to regularly provide jurisdictions with operational reports specifying aircraft, crew members and radio frequencies used at the time by the company. While these resources answered to the direction of Spencer Kim, at least they communicated with the local jurisdictions. The OSP Lieutenant that assumed command identified the communications deficiencies in the field at the Big Windy Creek drainage as soon as the effort identified it as the primary search area. He specified and appointed one individual to take Tactical Command primarily for communications (*Field Site Mobile IC*).

According to both national and international research, of the five most common operational problems encountered during emergency response operations across the country, the Lack of Interagency Communications stands prominently on that list. Rather than meaning the agencies never talk or communicate with each other before a mission, most of the problems stem from unique circumstances, such as multiple jurisdictions, distance, rugged terrain or other environmental conditions. The OSSA Search Review highlighting communication issues comes as no surprise.

Planning

Documentation of the Kim search and evaluation of the written records indicate that managers created a complete written Incident Action Plan (*IAP*) in advance for the following operational period on only one day during the course of the search. While this may seem like poor management on the surface, remember the conditions at the time and the multiple jurisdictions involved. Some searchers expressed concerns that the assignment planning process happened simultaneously with the daily briefing. Not that the staff failed to use Task Assignment Forms and Debriefing Forms *(ICS 204 and 204A)*, they completed these forms every day.

The events of Monday the 4th of December finally revealed the Kim family's location in Josephine County. Many involved up to that point lacked awareness of an official search designated by a specific jurisdiction. On Monday, December 4th, the organizational structure began to materialize with coordination, assignments and functional positions appropriate to standard ICS.

NOTE: The use and understanding of the Incident Command System *(ICS)* helps ensure effective coordination for management of a mission through the use of clear objectives. Management effectiveness occurs in this system through a repetitive cycle built into the system's structure. However, this differs from *search planning*. Mission management and search planning represent two separate functions, separate and distinct from one another. Sending resources into the field after the initial response period without real search planning eventually puts the search planner, when activated, in a continual position of trying to catch-up without getting ahead of the problem.

As the response to any potential search materializes, someone *(the Search IC or the Planning Section Chief)* usually assembles the components necessary for *search planning*. Planning for incident management *(this refers to overall field operations)* and planning for resource deployments on the search take very different paths. Very often, initial efforts, like Reflex Tasking produce results *(clues or leads)* that point to the location of the missing person. Using statistical guidance *(such as the International Search and Rescue Incident Database)* and the basics of search theory, managers need to activate the *search planning* function under the Planning Section Chief's responsibilities. Search planning involves specialized and technical expertise, in-depth knowledge of resources, understanding effort allocation and what strategies and tactics ensure maximum coverage of the search area.

Planners ask critical questions and then calculate solutions. How many people will it take to search a specific area? And, how long will the resources need to search that area adequately? Along with those questions planners also ask: what about probabilities of both detection and success? Based on the backgrounds and training of the Command Staff during the Kim search, no one ever established a formal search planning group.

Searching systematically through the *Fact Finding Detail* portion of the Kim Search Review points out several deficiencies in the organization that eventually consolidated to manage the mission (*in terms of both training and experience at the time*):

- The OSP Lieutenant that stepped forward into the IC position, held no statutory responsibility for managing a SAR mission and also lacked any formal training in search planning.
- The Josephine County Sheriff's Office lacked any formal written policy or procedure for the operation of SAR Coordinator *(also the County Emergency Manager),* as a civilian, answered to the Undersheriff as an employee of the Sheriff's Office. The self-stated job of the coordinator involved managing the nearly 100 SAR volunteers in Josephine County and to act as the Coordinator for those resources and at the time accomplished this with no formal training.
- On the second day of the search, Spencer Kim shared his investigative information and leads with Josephine County but no one in the local or state government Command or General Staff assigned anyone o follow up on those leads. The follow-up came from the private staff managed by Spencer Kim.

Despite these shortfalls and some conflict and confusion around properly completing ICS forms from all jurisdictions and organizations, Josephine County led the effort to track and collate the documentation.

Staff working on this search adapted to the conditions and circumstances at hand and overcame much adversity. Thanks to the leadership and management skills of several in the Command and General Staff, they prevented the situation spiralling completely out of control with many more complications. Particularly in light of a separate private company hired by one individual conducting search and investigation in parallel. The Command Staff managed the search overall, but with limited search planning at the Command Post.

The Media – Information Management and Public Information

The Kim search received an unusual amount of media attention from all over the country and the public information function tasked the Incident Management Staff heavily *(Figure 10-10)*. The number of media requests exceeded the capabilities of Public Information Officers *(PIO)* present. All forms of the media, *(newspapers, TV, radio)* came to the Mission Command Post for briefings and live shots, which distracted and interrupted mission activities in the command center. In some cases, it actually required all activity in the facility to stop for a period of time. Because of the extreme media demand, the Logistics Section Chief for the search actively sought another separate location to use as a Joint Information Center. They even considered the Interagency *(USFS/BLM)* Fire Center as an alternative. Unfortunately, this effort never located another facility.

- The Oregon State Police PIO officer *(requested as a resource by the Command staff)* contributed greatly to smoothing out the operation and demonstrated excellent interagency cooperation with up-date information and provided the same to the media where possible. They responded to on-camera interviews, and thus relieved other Command and General Staff team members of that duty.
- The information disseminated *(not only to the media, but to Command and General Staff positions and family members)* comes from a wide array of sources. The difficulty comes when trying to funnel that information to the correct recipient. Important or key investigation results, subject profile details, along with behavior information, clues, leads, weather impacts and tips from the public all need direction to the appropriate person. Most of the time the organizational system gets it right, but sometimes crucial data falls through the cracks. The multi-jurisdiction aspects of this mission added dramatically to this common operational problem.

During any mission regardless of the size or duration, personnel sometimes inadvertently release the source of information prematurely. As always, some in the media take particular information out of context. No matter how unfounded or contrary to the overall mission, inevitably some reports, quotes or media reporting contains completely inaccurate information. Unfortunately, this reality happens all the time in Search and Rescue and everyone needs to diligently make an effort to prevent or mitigate such scenarios.

The media role simply serves to educate and inform the public. This often involves disclosing how responsible officials handle a mission by providing a third-party perspective. Keep the media informed, if at all possible, rather than make them seek out information. After encountering a void or vacuum of information, the media will fill it with whatever they find. Sometimes, even after a mission concludes.

Figure 10-10 The overwhelming media presence, not only from the local and regional perspective but from national news organizations as well.

Coordinate Systems

During this search, the coordinate systems or map datum used by search units differed greatly. By agreement, SAR units in Oregon previously made a commitment to use Universal Transverse Mercator *(UTM)* as the standard coordinate system on ground searches. On the other hand, aviation assets almost exclusively use Latitude/Longitude as a standard, and the difference between these two systems created issues during the search effort. Some aviation assets lack familiarity with UTM coordinates *(i.e. DOD and State National Guard Military Aviation)*. For example, a helicopter pilot discovered that the radio operators involved in the search gave coordinates in latitude/longitude, minutes and seconds but failed to convert them correctly. This also created a spin-off impact on the private helicopter company under the direction of Spencer Kim. It appears all of the following coordinate systems and datums made an appearance during the Kim search:

Common Lat/Long coordinate systems:

Degrees – Decimal – Degrees
Degrees – Minutes – Decimal Minutes
Degrees – Minutes – Seconds

UTM Coordinates using common Map Datums:

NAD27
NAD83
WGS84

This operational problem resurfaces constantly between ground and air assets and between groups. Relative newcomers to map and compass or agencies/organizations that use different systems often overlook issues concerning map datums. However, SAR operations require accuracy, particularly when they involve multi-organizational agencies with both air and ground resources. Map datum mismatches often result in errors in accuracy up to 300 meters or more in the contiguous United States and much more in some regions of the world. Most current nautical and aeronautical charts use the WGS 84 map datum, not the NAD 27 datum common to most USGS topographical maps.

As a lesson learned, SAR units need to train, exercise and practice the conversion of the various coordinate systems or map datums, and those conducting coordinate conversions need to clearly understand the process.

- The pilot on the Jackson County helicopter attempted to go to the Kim vehicle and collect personal computers because they contained recent photos of James Kim and potentially what he wore when he left the car. Radio operators gave the pilot coordinates to locate the car, he found no vehicle at the designated spot.
- One of the private helicopter company aircraft transported an Oregon State Police officer who needed the location of the vehicle. He wanted to collect the Kim Family possessions and computer as discussed earlier. They failed to find the vehicle and only after a Jackson County pilot informed them of the coordinate mix-up in datum systems did they rendezvous and transfer the possessions *(computers, etc.)*.

During the official search review, some of the overhead team felt that this occurred because of a mix up with the map datum and inappropriate coordinate designations. Others pointed out that someone incorrectly placed the vehicle location on a paper map. While this mix up never affected the actual search efforts directly, it caused confusion and delay until staff resolved the problem.

Different or unfamiliar coordinates need reliable conversions by individuals with the right tools to accomplish the task. Most GPS and mapping software complete such transformations fairly easily with proper training.

Maps, Roads and Local Terminology

As mentioned earlier in this chapter, the network of routes in the Bear Camp area contain hundreds of miles of roads including Bureau of Land Management

(BLM) and Forest Service *(FS)* roads with many spurs, some paved and some unpaved. Everyone in and around this area calls the roads something different. This added to the confusion and complexity of the search operation. Since the Kim Search, many separate agencies worked to improve signage for the entire area.

Aviation Assets

The Kim search was unusual, in the number of private aircraft used, hired by, and paid for by James Kim's father in the search effort. The company that he hired committed three aircraft and a total of eleven personnel to the search. In addition, several other volunteer pilots searched on their own *(one of these helicopter pilots actually found Kati and the children)*. Jackson County also contributed to the search with a volunteer pilot and his helicopter. Counting the helicopter from Jackson County, the number of private aircraft totaled five. The National Guard and Coast Guard also sent several air assets.

During the first three days of the search very little coordination and information sharing occurred concerning aircraft and their assignments. The Curry County SAR Coordinator, using forethought and knowledge about how the SAR system works, requested National Guard assets to search in different areas than where the private helicopters flew. Some duplication of coverage occurred in the overall mission with some poor use of available air resources, but only when viewed from a retrospective point of view.

Federal laws prohibit competition by the National Guard, Department of Defense and other federal assets when private *(paid)* industries participate in the search effort. The real complication and safety issue about this situation stems from the lack of private aircraft coordination under the Command and General Staff. Spencer Kim directed the use of the private company aircraft and the Federal aircraft, according to regulation, only fly into areas with coordination between all aircraft. Any state or local agency, that requests federal assets must declare the mission as a "potential loss of life, limb or eye sight" situation.

The National Guard responded to the search and flew on several days with both an H-60 Blackhawk and an OH-58 Kiowa helicopter. When not flying, these aircraft maintained a standby status, prepared and ready to fly for a rescue in a moment's notice. The Search and Rescue aircraft logs portion of the Kim Search Review shows exceptional coverage of the mission using air assets. After the staff identified a firm location for the Command Post and identifying an IC, the information sharing and coordination reduced duplication of air coverage and took complete advantage of available air resources.

- Two factors contributed greatly to an improved coordination of air resources. First, the liaison from the helicopter company began giving local jurisdictions regular reports on aircraft, crewmembers, radio frequencies and assignments. While this proved invaluable, local County Sheriff's Office personnel reciprocated by complying with anti-competition protocols when using National Guard assets in their assignments. The private helicopter resources lacked Forward Looking Infrared *(FLIR)* or any other sensor enhancements for flying at night or in the daylight.

- Once James Kim's tracks led into the Big Windy Creek drainage, the staff requested an air asset with FLIR. The National Guard helicopters: an H-60 Blackhawk and Kiowa OH-58 with FLIR then launched. The H-60 provided hoist related rescue, and the OH-58 primarily provided FLIR enhanced search. The reason the OH-58 operated at night in the later operational periods of the search came from when they arrived on-scene in the Big Windy Creek drainage.

Some suggested a need for a Temporary Flight Restriction *(TFR)*, issued by the FAA, earlier in the search to reduce concerns of aviation safety in the search area. During the official OSSA Search Review process several also mentioned that federal air asset protocols require all non-government aircraft to remain clear of the search area before federal assets enter to work a mission. Jurisdictions running SAR missions with aviation in their local area understand these protocols well. Interestingly, placing the private pilot that found Kati and her children under a TFR, means he would not have been in the area searching.

Use of Resources

The State of Oregon provides support resources to jurisdictions through Oregon Emergency Management and it also provides coordination and liaison with all the Sheriff's Offices across the state. Based on the information uncovered in the official Search Review, it appears that this system failed to function as intended.

As part of the after action, the Governor's SAR Task Force convened with the explicit purpose of considering the necessity of changes to the laws, administrative rules and related policies of the State to ensure proper coordination and communications between federal, state and local authorities in SAR operations. The Task Force noted a lack of specific statutory guidance and practical implementation of command and control to efficiently utilize resources for large multi-jurisdiction search efforts. They also acknowledged that many SAR efforts span more than one county or jurisdiction, either because the missing party's probable location in one specific county, or because the circumstances of the mission drew from more than one jurisdiction, i.e. city police, county Sheriff, local fire district, Oregon State Police, etc.

- Some SAR personnel suffered from extreme fatigue and grew overwhelmed with the requirements for such a large operation. While several other counties and private sector resources offered assistance, they never received a request to deploy or assist with the response in Josephine County. Part of the complication of responding these resources across jurisdictional boundaries is that there is no state wide system or scheme to provide insurance coverage for SAR Responders.
- The Search and Rescue Task Force discovered a great disparity with insurance coverage by different counties. Some provide workers compensation, other counties provide no coverage at all. Some volunteers receive coverage through their regional SAR team, funded by their own dues. The Task Force left unanswered exactly what coverage exists for volunteers when responding to a mission outside of their own county or in another state.

At the time and date of the Kim Family search, a statewide resource coordination system existed and **Oregon Revised Statute Chapter 401.550** defined it *(see page 150)*.

The Task Force also concluded the multi-jurisdiction nature of the search compounded by a lack of funds in the Oregon Office of Emergency Management *(OEM)* prevented that office from performing its statutory duties, let alone filling in the gaps in county budget shortfalls. The Task Force recommendations provided two specific Senate Bills. The first one outlined guidelines for multi-jurisdiction situations along with specific requirements for use of the Incident Command System. The first bill also placed local SAR responsibility firmly in the county Sheriffs' Offices.

The second proposal outlined staffing and funding to adequately support the State Office of Emergency Management's statutory requirements for SAR coordination. Ultimately the second bill concerning funding and staffing, failed to pass the legislature. Oregon OEM provides logistical support to search and rescue efforts statewide, by obtaining state and military assets and assisting in other collaborative efforts. The State Office budget then and now falls far short of the statutory required resources or personnel to directly assist in search efforts in a local jurisdiction.

The Function of Family Liaison

At the direction of James Kim's father, the family conducted their own search efforts and an investigation independent of the official response from local and state government agencies.

- Because no one appointed an official Liaison Officer during the first several days of this search, neither the family or the Incident Management Team received timely updates from the other on the status of the search. This led to a lack of vital information sharing about resources, search assignments and investigative results. Although the private helicopter company and Josephine County personnel met a number of times and exchanged information, staff never established a specific Liaison Position.

The Search Review concluded that a Liaison Officer would have reduced the duplication of air search efforts and minimized the conflict of multiple aircraft in the same area.

- Finally, on Sunday the 3rd of December both factions, the family liaison from the private helicopter company and representatives from the newly formed Command and General Staff came together and consciously began to share information and investigative data. The communications barriers finally broke loose and started an open exchange of information. As a direct result, the groups formed a well-defined plan and a collectively narrowed search area for the next day's assignments.

Access to Wireless *(Cell Phone)* Device Information

Some complained that the Command or General Staff failed to act quickly when they obtained the information on cell phone *pings*. Official records show a different story, with one minor exception. Daylight serves as a precious commodity for any search and rescue operation. In retrospect, if the representatives from the Oregon State Police, Josephine County and the wireless company field engineer met the night of Saturday the 2nd of December instead of waiting until the next morning at 8:00AM, search teams might have started a few hours sooner. It meant that meeting during the morning realistically moved the beginning of the focused search to the afternoon, thus leaving only a few hours of search time that day. Keep in mind the ease of pointing out decisions like this in retrospect, after the mission wraps up and with all the known facts.

Interpretation of data generated from cell phone systems introduces a relatively new tool *(historically)* to the Search and Rescue community. At the time of this search, the cell phone service provider presented critical information previously unavailable to the public and first responders. At that time, under normal circumstances, access to this information without a written memorandum or pre-arranged procedures, required a court order to acquire. Technology rapidly changes. In late 2006, the capability to track, home in on, and locate a cell phone experienced a brisk expansion. Even today, cell-based phone location represents an emerging field. Handset capability and network based methods for locating or narrowing down the possible locations for a device improve all the time. Virtually all cell phones now contain at least limited GPS capability. The data steadily gets easier to obtain and to understand.

Current Federal Law *(18 U.S.C. 2702)* provides law enforcement with access to telecommunications records under exigent circumstances. However, never wait until right in the middle of a mission to determine the exact requirements for each service provider or to discover their available technology. Without an established relationship or prearranged process with communications providers, difficulties abound for obtaining location information. Sometimes providers only use one form of technology to determine locations, but they may possess many types. Early and proactive efforts to determine how the various forms of technology actually work always pay dividends on future missions.

Early access to wireless activity *(cell phone signals)* on a search creates the potential to reduce the size of a search area significantly. When switched on, the typical cell phone sends out a *handshake signal* approximately every thirty seconds. Each cell tower measures the signal strength emanating from the phone then the system electronically decides which cell tower acts to deliver the incoming calls. The system also determines when, because of motion, one of the cell towers needs to hand off a call to another cell tower. Records of these handshakes typically stay in the system for approximately 24 hours *(more or less, depending on the wireless carrier)*. When a customer makes a phone call, a text message or a device makes/receives a notification, the system creates a record for billing purposes. This record shows the cell tower, sector *(one of 3, 120 degree arcs from the tower)* and signal strength. Obviously, this information alone significantly reduces the search area.

A document called a coverage map forms an important tool in determining the source of signal locations from a cell phone. Virtually all cell phone providers develop coverage maps that display different colors in an area corresponding to different probabilities of receiving a signal. Each unique map's characteristics begin with the site elevation, height of the cell tower and the potential signal blocking terrain *(like mountains)*. These maps make up a part of the overall engineering scheme used to decide where to place additional cell towers. A coverage map produced by the wireless company field engineer during the Kim family search showed that the pings from the Kim phones likely occurred while the family drove through the Glendale cell tower's signal zone.

Even the reduced area coverage map, spread across the terrain, with hundreds of miles of roadway and varying snow conditions, presented a very sizable and challenging search area. While this map worked to narrow the search for the Kims, other documented searches ended up with misleading information which led the Management in those searches to assign resources into the wrong areas. Sometimes, cell signals simply travel beyond their assigned coverage areas; however, with each passing year, the technology improves. People with experience all agree these techniques provide very useful tools in SAR, but with limits. The Governor's Search and Rescue Task Force recommended increased and ongoing education and training of SAR leaders on how to use this technology in SAR.

Fitness and Qualification of Resources

An important issue in this search centered on some very dedicated resources in the field with assigned tasks. Leaders on-site then asked them to complete additional inappropriate assignments outside the resources' expertise or when they lacked necessary equipment. These resources accepted the assignments which placed them in a compromising situation (*Ironically, because of their willingness to try and help*). The situation ended well however these types of scenarios very quickly compromise safety with potentially tragic results.

- During the search, air assets requested individuals in a 4X4 unit to investigate tracks in the Big Windy Creek drainage. The air assets made a mistake in requesting the task and the ground teams made a mistake in accepting the request.

Aircrew members made several unconfirmed reports when searching in the bottom of the Big Windy Creek drainage about ground crews working independently and in an unfit manner for that environment. However, the official records and documentation leave this account unconfirmed. Their concern derived from the lack of roads or other access in the lower end of the drainage.

- Helicopter pilots and crews experienced difficulty seeing SWAT members dressed in camouflage while lowering them to the ground via long line. This issue presented a safety concern for the SWAT members easily remedied by clothing colors.

The state of Oregon contains trained and equipped resources for almost any type of environment. Reaching out to these resources ensures the safety of all the people involved and prevents the potential suspension or slow down of search efforts to rescue the rescuers.

History of Missing People in the Bear Camp Area

A Fatality *(Source Newspaper: The Missoulian)*
In 1994, Dewitt Finley, a 56 year old salesman for a camper company in Kalispell, Montana tried to take a scenic route from Gold Beach to Grants Pass, Oregon. Finley just completed a sales trip and intended to return to Montana. After sliding off of a single lane mountain road, he decided to stop for the night. A three day storm left the truck buried in deep snow. He kept a journal written on a legal pad with letters to his fiancée, children and other relatives. Mr. Finley

checked off nine weeks on his calendar and apparently succumbed to starvation. An attempt to walk back to the last town he passed on the road *(Agness, Oregon)* entailed an eighteen mile hike. He chose not to try. He made no apparent attempt at self-rescue or even to leave his truck. Since he failed to inform anyone of his intended route he apparently decided to wait for someone to come along.

Another Family

In March of the same year as the Kim search *(2006)*, six members of an Ashland, Oregon family ended up stranded in their motor home for two weeks. In addition to a couple named Stivers, the group included Mr. Stivers' parents, (*the Higginbothams*) and the Stivers' two children. The stranded RV sat near a spur road to Calvert Airstrip about 7 miles North-Northwest of the Kim family's location, but across the river in Douglas County.

Unlike the route of James Kim and his family who turned west up BLM 34-8-36 toward Bear Camp Road and Gold Beach, the Stivers-Higginbotham group took a different road. They actually missed the turnoff that the Kim's took toward Bear Camp at the start of BLM 34-8-36. They tried to head back down the road after turning around at the airstrip when their RV became stuck north of the Rogue River.

Confusion about the whereabouts and intentions of the group caused law enforcement officials to call off their search after five days. Police received conflicting information on the group's intended destination. Inside the motor home, the family watched television news reports of the search effort, and convinced themselves that rescuers would not find them. Two of the six person group hiked out to search for the searchers. Subsequently several Bureau of Land Management employees on routine patrol accidentally found them. Searchers rescued the other members of the group later that day, all of them in good condition.

Significant Changes in Oregon since the Kim search

Regional Coordination and Communication Organizations

As a direct result of the joint Mission Debriefing which ended the Kim search, a group of agencies and organizations coalesced into a functional networking organization called CORSAR. The acronym stands for **C**alifornia **O**regon **R**egional **S**earch **a**nd **R**escue. The objectives of the organization provided better regional communication and coordination for public assistance during major or extended search and rescue operations. The group includes Jackson, Douglas, Josephine, Klamath, Curry, Coos, Lake, Siskiyou, and Del Norte Counties, as well as the Bureau of Land Management, U.S. Forest Service, Brim Aviation, Crater Lake National Park and the Civil Air Patrol. The organization includes no paid staff per se, but many in the group donate their time to improve SAR at the regional and statewide level for the benefit of the volunteers and citizens.

Ironically, CORSAR fills the void created by the state's lack of funding and staffing in this region by using a team of individuals acting as a resource center and developing a database of mission ready personnel, specialty teams and equipment for deployment on a regional basis. The Governor's SAR Task Force encouraged the creation of other Regional Search and Rescue Councils in Oregon, modeled after CORSAR.

Sources of Information for this Chapter:

The Kim Family Search Review – Part I, II, and III – Oregon State Sheriff's Association – 18 January, 2007

The Governor's Executive Order No. 07-01 – Search and Rescue Task Force – 19 January, 2007.

The Governor's Search and Rescue Task Force Report – 31 March, 2007.

Governor's Timeline: Kim Family Search Chronological Listing of Events: Released 5 January, 2007.

"In Kati Kim's Own Words:" Transcript of Klamath County Sheriff Tim Evinger interview with Kati Kim.

The Lessons in My Son's Death: 6 January, 2007 by Spencer H. Kim.

Who's to Blame for James Kim's Death? It's not the federal government or law enforcement or the people who tried to rescue him from the Oregon wilderness – by Sarah Keech.

OSSA Kim Search Review List of Participants

Portland Police Bureau Report on Kim Search

Aircraft Flight Log Info for Kim Family Search

Kim Family Timeline Graphic for Mission

Search Mission Timeline Graphic – Search Review

Oregon Revised Statutes – Chapter 401 dated January of 2007

Oregon Revised Statutes – Chapter 404 dated January of 2016

Josephine County After Action Review – dated 8 December, 2006

Volunteer Pilot's Hunch Led to Family Missing in Oregon by Jeff Bernard, December 07th 2006. (Associated Press)

ABC Television Series 20/20 Program – "Wrong Turn" aired on February 11th 2011, by London Based Firecracker Films.

The First Notice & Determining Urgency

11

Objectives:

- Discuss the importance of training dispatch center personnel about First Notice Information in a potential search

- Relate the importance of the Initial Missing Person Report Form in establishing urgency and for preliminary data gathering about the incident

- Discuss the critical decision-making processes taking place during the First Notice phase

- Establish the importance of SAR incident investigation and gathering information in the First Notice phase

- Identify the factors involved in determining the urgency of a potential search

- Describe how these factors help determine the relative search priority and level of response

Regardless of how improbable or unfounded the report appears at the time, a compelling firehouse response is essential until SAR personnel have arrived on the scene and determined the accuracy of the information.
- Tim J. Setnicka,
Wilderness Search and Rescue,
1980

Receiving an initial report of a possible overdue, missing or lost person(s) triggers a sequence of actions consistent with and representative of a potential life threatening emergency.

- **Note:** For most people, reporting a missing person, investigation and planning never get considered as *actions*. **They only perceive** *deployment* **of searchers as an action.**

- Simultaneously, while collecting information for planning a specific incident, initiate initial response actions in the field. See Bike Wheel Model for Reflex Tasking, *(Chapter 14 - Lost Person Behavior)*. Possible actions include:

  - Application of passive methods such as limited confinement.
  - Application of active methods such as use of dogs, trackers or even aircraft.

Arrange a place for the reporting party to wait while a law enforcement official, SAR Coordinator, IC, or Team Leader responds to the incident.

Initial Contact

The impression given by the report-taker to the reporting party and any initial actions taken, set the tone for the rest of the mission. If the report comes into an agency, a sheriff or other police agency office, the degree of professionalism and responsiveness often affects public support for future missions as well. Efficiency needs to permeate every aspect of a search, or more specifically getting the job done thoroughly and in an organized manner without wasting time or resources. The report-taker needs to immediately consider the following:

- **PROPER ATTITUDE.** Initiate the right attitude regarding the mission from the very beginning. Contact the reporting party (*whether by phone, radio or in person*) calmly, professionally, inquisitively and with a definite tone of concern and willingness to help. The report-taker never lets personal feelings interfere with the obligations taking and accurate report.

NAME/CALLBACK NUMBER/LOCATION. Wherever the initial report originates *(Police or Sheriff's Office, Forest Service, Dispatch Center, etc.)*, the person taking the information and filling in a form needs to remember the top priority: getting the name, phone number *(where reachable now)* and location of the reporting party. Tell the party to stay at that location until contacted to do otherwise. When reported in person, keep the reporting party at hand until obtaining all necessary information.

Fact: **SEARCH IS AN EMERGENCY.** From the time of the call or notice, until finding the subject, avoid wasting precious time, without blasting full speed ahead without direction. Make every minute count through careful, efficient planning and organization: In short, good coordination.

Initial Information

Initially report takers tend to receive incomplete or very sketchy information on a situation. They need to obtain certain important facts immediately, but need to wait until after the initial information gathering before filling out the complete *Missing Person Report Form*. Quickly sort out pertinent information to make prompt decisions. The initial IC evaluates the following information:

- **MISSING HOW LONG:** The seriousness and urgency of the incident increases with the amount of time that passes from an individual's scheduled return or rendezvous time. Check for mistakes or misunderstandings between the subject and the reporting party *(or you and the reporting party)* regarding times or even dates and days of the week.

- **ACTIVITY:** Check to see what type of activity the missing person planned: hiking verses rock climbing or cross country skiing verses snowmobiling; i.e., it makes a difference if a an elderly gentleman left to collect a pension check as opposed to taking a walk in the park *(See Lost Person Behavior Chapter 14)*. This assists not only in judging the danger of the activity but also in considering the amount of distance travelled by the subject.

- **EQUIPMENT:** Equipment carried directly relates to the activity, e.g. a camping trip verses a day hike. At this point in the reporting process, the report taker looks for an itemization or general idea of the subjects ability to cope with the terrain and weather.

- **CLOTHING:** Ask what type of clothing the missing person wore or carried and how adequately protected it keeps the individual. Also consider the detectability the of clothing carried.

- **NUMBER OF PERSONS MISSING:** According to Koester's research on Lost Person Behavior, the larger the numbers of individuals the safer the group. The more people in a missing party the better the chances of searchers finding them in good condition, so long as they stay together. Obtain the following data on each missing individual.

- **AGE:** Generally speaking, the younger *(below 12)* or older *(above 50)*, the more serious the potential problem. Young children often lack the experience or presence of mind to take care of themselves. With older people complications arise from medical problems or aging.

- **PHYSICAL DESCRIPTION:** Height, weight, color of hair, wears glasses, color of clothing etc.

- **PHYSICAL CONDITION:** Often a very subjective opinion from the reporting party. However, any known medical problems or handicaps, physical or mental, including hearing or speaking problems add significance.

- **EXPERIENCE / ABILITY:** Even more subjective than physical condition, the general levels of capabilities provide more information, e.g. a beginner verses an experienced skier, aids searchers.

- **POINT LAST SEEN OR LAST KNOWN POSITION:** The more specific the better. If the reporting party states that the person left in a car, then enlist additional agencies such as neighboring police to find the car. Focus on establishing a starting point.

- **TERRAIN:** Preliminary identification of the potential search area gives an indication of the type and degree of difficulty of the terrain. Terrain directly affects the missing person's ability to travel, and protect themselves as well as SAR resource equipment, necessary skills, and tactics.

- **WEATHER:** Another factor to consider and include in evaluation for the subject and searchers. Mountain weather varies drastically from one area or elevation to another. When evaluating the problem, weather plays a critical role. Investigate the weather at the time the party went missing as well as the current conditions and the forecast for the specific area. As an example, trackers find it helpful to know when the weather changes and the corresponding changes in the appearance of sign.

The purpose of all this information:

Determines the nature of potential problems and the seriousness of the situation.

- Potential escalation of urgency
- Where the situation occurred and who it involved
- How and when it happened
- What steps searchers/staff need to take next
- Determine where and how to start looking
- Determine the need for special resources

Evaluation of the Problem

The information received from this *first notice* regarding a potential missing or lost person often comes from many sources and with varying degrees of reliability. The reporting parties tend to suggest their ideas about initiating action, but remember to evaluate all initial information in a calm, intelligent manner without jumping to conclusions.

Talk to the Reporting Party in Person? Some Search Managers prefer to talk in person with a reporting party. A Search Manager knows better than anyone what questions need answers and how to evaluate those answers.

Evaluate the Initial Information. The first reports on a missing or lost person usually consist of three general types of information. Each perfectly valid source possesses a reliability of its own. Never totally discard any information regardless of the initial evaluation.

- **CIRCUMSTANTIAL:** Information generally not substantiated *(at least not yet),* but reported by some person. Examples: a car left at a trail head but with no persons reported missing, or a sign-in sheet at the trail head with a signature but no sign-out signature.

- **SECOND HAND:** Information coming from a person who heard it from someone else *(hearsay).* Generally speaking for oral information, the more people communicating it, the less accurate or reliable. In any case, it usually trumps circumstantial information. This category also includes the person reporting an individual overdue from a distant town or another separate location.

- **EYE WITNESS:** Usually the best information comes from an individual on the scene and possibly a member of the missing person's party. The eye witness confirms someone definitely went missing and gives specific *last seen* information.

Evaluate the Source of Information: Consider any background knowledge and the state of mind of the people giving the information. When taking down information, make sure the reporting party understands the questions and possesses the background necessary to answer them accurately, without guessing. Determine if the individual shows signs of distraught or frantic behavior or if they display a calm attitude and a clear thinking process.

Managing the Inland Search Function - **Operational Response**

Case Name/Number _____

Missing Person – Initial Report
CONFIDENTIAL

Case Name/Number		Agency	
Date	Time	Information taken by	
Caller's Name		Call-back number	
Address			
Home Phone		Business Phone	
Cell Phone, Other Numbers			
Relationship to missing person			
Reason for reporting this person missing			

Missing Person

Full Name		Nickname(s)			
Subject's primary language					
Home address					
Home Phone		Business Phone			
Cell Phone, Other Numbers					

Description

Age	Race	Gender	Hgt	Wgt	DOB
General Description and Clothing Worn When Last Seen					

Missing Person – Initial Report Form 01/11   Page 1 of 2

Figure 11-1

Case Name/Number _____

Details of Loss	
Location missing from	
Point Last Seen (PLS)	
Day/Date Last Seen	Time Last Seen
Last seen by whom	
Vehicle description, if driving	
Destination(s), stated intentions	
Has this person been the object of a search in the past?	
If so, describe date(s), circumstances of loss, how long missing, when found, where found, condition when found and actions taken by subject while missing (if known)	

Additional Information and Comments

Call-out Information
Search base/command post location, directions, phone numbers, radio frequencies:
Resources notified:

Closing Report		
Subject Location:	Date	Time
Located By:		
Incident Summary:		

Missing Person – Initial Report Form 01/11   Page 2 of 2

Figure 11-2

CONSIDER THE FACTS: Look at the reasonably certain information. Including going back through information related to the weather along with an assessment of the terrain in the area. Take into consideration whether all the facts add up or not. Look closely at the subject's age, gender and known medical problems. Use deductive reasoning to form a foundation for building the evaluation process.

CONSIDER THE PROBABILITIES: Consider the highly likely items, such as the *probable* activity based on previous interests and the *presumed* experience level of the subject. Further on in the text, we discuss and refer to establishing zones of probability when establishing the search area. Planners attach probability to the zones by brainstorming possible scenarios and speculating about the missing person's intentions or activities. Make sure to obtain reliable information *(with questionable reliability of information)* without too much delay. If a possible issue or point arises, take the time to come back later and gather more information.

CONSIDER THE POSSIBILITIES: Now look at the usable information; i.e., reports on the general physical condition of the subject and equipment carried. Balance the time critical element with the need for further investigation

COMBINE THE INFORMATION OBJECTIVELY: Combine all of the information into a total evaluation of the problem while keeping in mind the reliability of sources and the relative accuracy of each item. From *facts* regarding the terrain and weather conditions in the general search area, assess potential hazards as they relate to the subject's *probable activity*. Then by taking into account the missing person's age, gender and *possible* physical condition, level of experience and subject type, as well as evaluating the adequacy of the person's *possible* equipment list, objectively evaluate the situation.

Determining Urgency

> "The relative urgency of a reported situation should be established - if it is not immediately apparent - during the First Notice and Interview phase. Despite the need for a constant firehouse response to all reports of any kind, some latitude for flexibility exists and should be exercised." - Tim J. Setnicka, *Wilderness Search And Rescue*, 1980.

Factors Affecting Urgency

- Subject profile *(unique factors)*
- Weather profile *(at the time, present, future)*
- Equipment available to the subject *(and the knowledge of how to use it)*
- Subject's experience (from *more than one* source)
- Terrain hazards *(local knowledge)*

Other Factors

The following factors directly influence the decision-making process concerning the urgency of the situation without usually influencing the behavior of the subject:

- **History of Incidents in Area:** The frequency of past incidents in the area and their outcome

- **Time:** The time elapsed from the moment the subject went missing and their reliability or punctuality

  - Is the person known as very punctual and on-time or notoriously late

- **Weather:** In inclement weather with inadequate clothing, individuals usually stay coherent for a specified period of time

  - Consider the effect of weather on clues and identifiable signs

- *Political* **Sensitivity** The combination of all external influences often affect decision-making. Among these influences:

- VIP involved
- Interest of politicians
- Pressure from relatives
- Pressure from media: publicity
- Pressure from higher up in your organization

Urgency Form

In Figure 11-3 on the following page, the Search Urgency Chart identifies factors affecting urgency of response when the call comes in and someone identifies circumstances reflecting a lost or missing person. On the form, note that the lower the numerical rating of the factor, the higher the *relative* urgency.

Use these factors as an evaluative checklist. This assures not overlooking an influencing factor possibly crucial to the welfare of the missing person. Viewed collectively, the factors provide an indication of the relative urgency for initiating a response.

Ask a critical question: Without a system like this, what drives the urgency of response in an objectively repeatable way?

Several axioms apply to scenarios with high risk to the subject.

> Whenever you set out to accomplish something urgent, almost invariably something else has to get done first!

> Overreaction is justifiable. Under-reaction is inexcusable!

As a rule, the more serious the previous incidents in the local area and the more time that elapses from the subject *going missing*, coupled with potential *political sensitivity* - the greater the urgency.

The combination of factors affecting urgency help determine not only how quickly to respond; but, the nature and level of response. Initiate some kind of response immediately - even if only an increase in planning for an anticipated or potentially serious problem.

Subject Condition Assumptions

After assessing all of the initial information available, the IC makes some assumptions as to the condition of the subject, relating to his/her MOBILITY *(ability to travel)* and RESPONSIVENESS *(ability and desire to respond to calls, etc.)*.

The Four possibilities:

- Mobile/responsive
- Immobile/responsive
- Mobile/unresponsive
- Immobile/unresponsive

Making these assumptions about the subject's condition helps dictate the type of immediate searching action *(tactics)* taken.

The IC Decides

Factors and considerations in this chapter facilitate Search Manager's in making the most appropriate decisions. In the end, the Search Manager's decision remains a subjective one, based on the total of collective information and assumptions, as well as the safety of the searchers.

Take an example of two elderly hunters reported eight (8) hours overdue from a days excursion to scout a favorite location for deer. The two went on a day hike, not hunting.

> **Age**: Fairly old *(early seventies)* = 1
> **Medical Condition:** Both, very healthy = 3
> **Number of Subjects:** Two = 2
> **Experience Profile:** Experienced, both know the area = 3
> **Weather Profile:** No hazardous weather predicted = 3
> **Equipment Profile:** Adequate for environment and weather = 3
> **Terrain/Hazards Profile:** Few or minimal hazards = 2

Even though all factors except *Age*, point to a low urgency, this one indicator changes the entire perspective of the situation. Certainly investigation calls for more information, but initially, age signal a high urgency

Managing the Inland Search Function - **Operational Response**

```
Date: _____                                                    ┌─────────────────────────┐
Time: _____         SEARCH URGENCY CHART                       │ Remember that the lower │
                                                                    │ the number the more     │
    A.  NUMBER OF SUBJECTS         B.  AGE                          │ urgent the response     │
        1 Person  ------------ 1       Very young ------------ 1    └─────────────────────────┘
        2 People  ------------ 2       Other      ------------ 2-4
        3 or more ------------ 3       Very old   ------------ 1
        (Unless separation suspected)
                                    ─→                              ─────→
    C.  MEDICAL CONDITION
        Known illness requiring medication ------------------------- 1
        Suspected illness or injury -------------------------------- 2
        Healthy ---------------------------------------------------- 3
        Known fatality --------------------------------------------- 4
        Potential vision impairment -------------------------------- 1

    D.  TIME
        Reliable, punctual, (being late is out of character) ------- 1
        Usually reliable, on time ---------------------------------- 2
        Reliability, punctuality questionable ---------------------- 3
        Completely unreliable -------------------------------------- 4

    E.  CIRCUMSTANCES
        At risk for any reason ------------------------------------- 1
        Adequate information, low risk ----------------------------- 2
        Questionable information ----------------------------------- 3
        High probability not in the area --------------------------- 4

    F.  EXPERIENCE PROFILE
        Not experienced, not familiar with the area ---------------- 1
        Not experienced, knows the area ---------------------------- 2
        Experienced, not familiar with area ------------------------ 3
        Experienced, knows the area -------------------------------- 4

    G.  PHYSICAL CONDITION         H.  CLOTHING PROFILE
        Unfit     ------------ 1       Inadequate or insufficient - 1
        Fit       ------------ 2       Adequate ------------------ 2
        Very fit  ------------ 3       Very good ----------------- 3
                                    ─→                              ─────→
    I.  WEATHER PROFILE
        Existing hazardous weather --------------------------------- 1
        Hazardous forecast (8 hours or less) ----------------------- 2
        Hazardous forecast (more than 8 hours) --------------------- 3
        No hazardous weather forecast ------------------------------ 4

    J.  TERRAIN & HAZARDOUS PROFILE
        Known hazards ---------------------------------------------- 1
        Difficult terrain ------------------------------------------ 2
        Few hazards ------------------------------------------------ 3
        Easy terrain, no known hazards ----------------------------- 4

    K.  EQUIPMENT PROFILE
        Inadequate for activity/environment ------------------------ 1
        Questionable ----------------------------------------------- 2
        Adequate --------------------------------------------------- 3
        Very well equipped ----------------------------------------- 4

          If any of the eleven categories are rated as (1), regardless of
          the total, the search may require an immediate response.
      ┌──────────────┐  ┌──────────────────┐  ┌──────────────────────┐
      │    10-15     │  │      16-27       │  │        28-41         │   TOTAL _____
      │URGENT RESPONSE│ │MEASURED RESPONSE │  │EVALUATE AND INVESTIGATE│
      └──────────────┘  └──────────────────┘  └──────────────────────┘
      *** The total should range between 11 and 41 with 11 indicating the greatest urgency. ***
```

Figure 11-3 Urgency Form

with an immediate priority response of some kind to the area *(The Subject profile information possibly gives additional indicators)*.

In contrast, using the same set of factors, consider a situation where two hunters, ages 22 and 23 get reported overdue. The rating in this case changes from a one to a two or even a three. Perhaps a cause for concern still exists, but if searchers continue their investigation, additional time gives the pair a chance to resolve the situation without a full scale response. If the two fail to return by morning, perhaps a response to the area indicated in the report, needs to occur. In this case, the urgency factors point away from a critical or high priority response. Remember, in some cases, just one factor dictates urgency. In others, a combination of factors provide direction. Re-evaluate all factors for urgency *every* operational period

Options After Determining Urgency

Urgent Response

Urgent response consists of immediately launching a search operation per the jurisdiction's PrePlan for a *seriously at risk* missing person from any of the urgency categories. Usually an indication like this presents a time critical situation.

Measured Response

Without sufficient information or when the overall circumstances fail to warrant an urgent response, a measured response follows. This level of response includes a mixture of minimal deployments of field resources for confinement or to check likely spots while aggressively gathering more information. Without exception, this level includes gathering more information through investigation, particularly in the urban environment. It also happens to provide legitimate response to very uncertain and relatively harmless circumstances.

Evaluate and Investigate

At this level of response no field resources deploy immediately, but information indicates circumstances requiring further investigation. Obtain and process information over a period of time, in case at some point the decision to respond with field resources arises. Additional information also helps in deciding whether to maintain an open investigative file, or conclude the entire operation. Strategy at this level also usually includes putting certain resources on standby.

Martin Colwell from *Lions Bay Search and Rescue, B.C.*, in his paper *An Urgent Response to SAR Emergencies*, strongly recommends establishing protocols relating to the buildup of any search operations where responsiveness and survivability of the subject appear at risk.

Search urgency also takes into consideration the effectiveness of search resources. Both traditional and new search technologies frequently demand rapid field deployment for effective utilization. Obviously, the effectiveness of various search resources often closely relates to the responsiveness and survivability of the missing person. Remember that different types of clues generated by a missing or lost individual deteriorate almost immediately. So, depending on the time frame, searchers begin looking for these types of clues first.

Urgency & Resource Application

In most cases, a risk assessment of a subject's responsiveness and survivability determines the urgency of a response. Effective use of search resources occurs when they receive adequate information on the responsiveness or mobility of the missing person.

In other words, the tactics used tie directly to the expected outcome. Early use of sound techniques such as whistles, shouts or horns coupled with light, indicate a live, responsive individual able to respond. This makes the use of Sound-light line sweeps unnecessary or perhaps inappropriate later on in the search.

In very inclement weather, the visibility of tracks and other environmental disturbances deteriorate as time goes on. Therefore immediate application of a track and clue aware resource increases the chances of finding those clues. By the same token, tracking and trailing dogs gradually lose the capability to follow a specific trail under some deteriorating conditions. Searchers also tend to use air scenting or search dogs later on in a search due to a growing cone of scent released by the missing person.

Urgent response and the use of specific search tactics tie inexorably together. Gather good information to support urgent decision making.

Getting More Information

At this point in a potential search, investigators regularly acquire sketchy and incomplete information. While making decisions and coordinating a search operation, information gatherers continue providing more information to the IC for use in planning and making strategic decisions.

- **APPOINT INVESTIGATOR***(S)* The investigator gathers, sorts and evaluates information on the missing person(s), the search area and the situation in general. Most of the time he/she never goes into the field during an operation as an active searcher. Instead, they operate completely by phone, computer or on scene, personally interviewing the reporting party.
- **PROTECT SCENT ARTICLES** Avoid washing, contaminating or misplacing usable scent articles needed later by trailing or tracking dogs. Clothing recently worn next to the skin of the subject, and not washed, worn or handled by others, provides the best scent articles. Searchers need to carefully pick up scent articles with a stick or tongs, place them in a clean paper bag and seal it up. Pillow cases work for storage of scent articles as well.
- **MAKE SURE NOT TO USE CHEMICALLY TREATED OR SCENTED BAGS OF ANY KIND**

> The effort required to correct a course of action increases geometrically with time.
> - Murphy's Law -

Summary - Major Points
Initial contact:

Keep in mind, the intent in gathering information focuses on providing enough information to make decisions and figuring out where to initiate a search.

- Attitude of the report-taker *(calm, professional, inquisitive, concern, willingness to help)*
- Name and call back information of reporting party
- Use the Missing Person Initial Report Form as a guide, to determine the following:

    - Does a real problem exist
    - Evaluate the seriousness of the situation
    - A possible escalation in the level of seriousness
    - Where the incident occurred and who searchers need to look for
    - How and when the situation occurred
    - Formulate a plan of action
    - Determine initial search areas
    - Determine the most effective way to look for the lost subject
    - Determine if searchers need special resources and what type

Initially, try to gather as much information as possible to keep from going back later and digging up more, thus saving valuable time in the long run.

Refer to the Missing Person Initial Report Form and Urgency Form:

- What type of information needs immediate gathering to determine whether or not a problem exists
- What type of information requires initial action
- What type of information to gather later in a follow up interview
- Make sure to clearly present and designate information on the Urgency Form

Some kind of response always needs to happen immediately. Search is an Emergency!

Planning Data/Searching Data 12

Objectives:

- Relate and discuss how all of the processes of pre-planning, the first notice phase, initial interviewing and investigation, produce needed data for both on-scene planning and searching

- Identify the minimum information needed to develop a search plan

- Describe the importance of the Missing Person Report Form to both documentation and subsequent operational period planning

The Essential Foundation for Planning

Planners develop strategy through a continuing investigative and clue seeking process. The IC in charge of the search effort, quickly establishes that a genuine situation *(a valid mission)* exists before making tactical decisions and committing resources to the field. After making the decision to start the formal planning process, management then provides searchers with additional relevant information *(searching data)*.

This chapter establishes the necessary categories of information to solve *a classic mystery* or more plainly to determine *where to look for the missing person*. Planning Data and Searching Data aid in matching facts about the missing person with clues discovered both in the field and in the command post.

Unfortunately, jurisdictions usually start a search effort with limited information. Initial calls often come in with incomplete information. Staff needs to quickly begin a subject profile with the initial Missing Person Report *(MPR)* form as a guide. *(See Chapter 11.)* The initial MPR form starts the process and the file. The full MPR report form at the end of this chapter provides the real substance of the subject profile for planning and documentation *(See page 192)*.

Collate the Planning Data and Searching Data using the MPR form as a source. Details in the MPR build as the investigation continues throughout the operation providing an easily accessible and reliable method of recording all the subject information gathered.

Planning Data

Category of the Subject

- Backpacker
- Hunter
- Dementia (Alzheimer's)
- 6 year old child
- Mentally Handicapped
- Despondent
- Gatherer / Picker
- Angler, etc.

The subject category usually provides clues and other behaviors to help determine the following:

- Detectability of the subject
  - Color of clothing
  - Expected to be conscious, upright etc.
- Potential travel aids used by the subject
- Potential actions and distances traveled *(see Chapter 14, Lost Person Behavior)*
- The potential survivability for the subject *(includes clothing, equipment and experience)*

Example, consider a hunter versus a hiker:

Detectability: Hunters usually wear bright clothing, while hikers tend to wear *earthy* colors blending in with the environment.

Travel aids: Hunters travel cross-country or follow game trails, while hikers normally travel on defined trail systems.

Distance traveled: Hikers on trail systems travel further than hunters chasing game.

Survivability: A hiker carrying a full backpack, all necessary equipment and clothing for extended back country living, usually possesses a higher potential for survival than hunters carrying a gun and the clothes on their backs.

The Initial and Other Planning Points for Search

Various points and their descriptions, plotted by search planners on maps during a search, represent the best estimate of the initial location of missing people and their activity. The plotted points also provide a chronology of discoveries and tactics applied during a search operation. Many opinions exist on how to determine reference points and their potential use. Unfortunately, the results of differing interpretations cause both ambiguity and misunderstanding among the ranks in the SAR community.

In his seminal work *Analysis of Lost Person Behavior (1976)* Bill Syrotuck used a straight line distance as a radius from the PLS *(Point Last Seen)* comparing distances traveled by different categories of lost persons. He used the term PLS even though in many cases, even without a relevant point where someone last saw the missing person. This blanket use of PLS led to scenarios like labeling a car in a parking area at a trailhead PLS when, in fact, no one ever saw the missing person there. PLS served as a catch all acronym that specified an initial location for planning and measurements in a search.

During the development of more sophisticated approaches to land search planning/training and practical field operations in the late 80's and early 90's, the term PLS gradually took on the real meaning of the original acronym *(a Point Last Seen by a witness)*. SAR Community individuals involved in operations and those more focused on training development realized the need for a distinction between labels of various reference points during a search. The issue boiled down to a relatively simple one: when comparing previous lost person incidents and comparing distances traveled in those cases, which point best serves as a reference for consistent comparisons?

Another question also surfaced repeatedly: *What to call the reference point where the search starts and how to compare distances traveled by people in the same category of subject with no PLS?*

An early suggestion from the land search community encompassed more than simply the point last seen. The term Point of Origin filled that role; however, the initial users discovered difficulty with the term when discussing its acronym *(specifically, POO)*. That term, thankfully, failed to fly and search professionals explored alternative points of designation. Those familiar with maritime search and the acronyms used in search theory suggested using the already tried and true term Initial Planning Point *(IPP)*. This term gradually gained acceptance, and prevailed in land search as the norm.

However, controversy still surrounded the use of IPP, where to designate the IPP and what it actually means. Never underestimate the importance of the IPP as a planning point and reference. By the same token, ICs and planners need to take care with placement, not using it as a catch all term with multiple meanings, like the original designation of PLS. Use multiple planning points in the context of a search for distance comparisons, reference for direction of travel, elevation or potential decision points for the missing person, but with only one Initial Planning Point for each search. As a general rule, the Initial Planning Point remains fixed.

This creates implications both for the search planner and the statisticians gathering data from search operations for future reference. The question remains though, where and actually how a planner locates this important reference point and what to use for determining its placement?

The following represent standard, generally accepted terms and define their use as reference points used in land search.

The Initial Planning Point *(IPP)*

Cartographers use the term Datum to describe any point on a map which conveys information to the person reading it.

The definition for Datum (Webster's) follows:

> Something known or assumed; a fact from which to infer conclusions.
>
> A real or assumed thing, used as a basis for calculations or measurements.

The **Initial Planning Point** *(IPP)* designates a datum on the search map where a planner indicates the start of the search. Even though the early stages of a search often lack credible information, for future reference recognize where planning began with the first point on the map.

Measurements taken in the International Search and Rescue Incident Database *(Koester, 2008)*, use distances traveled from the designated IPP in straight line miles or kilometers to where the searchers found the subject. In this way the IPP represents a good reference point to measure distance and to compare previous incidents involving missing persons from the same category.

Alternatively, in placing the IPP, imagine the location where the subject possibly tries to return *(a campsite, car, home, trail junction, etc.)*. From a tactical standpoint the IPP also starts the survey of the surrounding area for potential clues.

The IPP usually ends up some distance from the physical operations base. Sometimes, the place last seen *(PLS)* or the Last Known Position *(LKP)* quite possibly serve as the IPP, or some other point may serve based on the best available information.

When placing the IPP, it ultimately provides a valuable measurement reference. Examples like: a person suffering from dementia that goes missing from a care facility; or, a despondent driving to a remote parking area and leaving a car; both, lend themselves to a straightforward designation of the IPP. However, some situations call for more careful thought, investigation and clearly more indications of intent or circumstance. A reference point *(the IPP)* in the absence of a PLS or LKP used for distance calculations deserves careful placement.

Planners often find it difficult to designate the IPP when the missing person or persons intend to travel from one location to another, along a linear route or trail system. Usually, in these cases, the subjects set a destination with a clear point of embarkation and some form of transportation on both ends. The dilemma arises when trying to place planning points in general, not just the initial one.

Colwell *(1997)* suggested using decision points along a linear route *(trail)* to determine where the missing person conceivably made mistakes in navigation or possibly left the trail. Each one of these decision points constitutes a planning point for further consideration. Depending on circumstances and timing, designate either the destination point or embarkation point for a trail based search problem as the IPP with a number of additional planning points in between.

As mentioned above the IPP designation sits at the point last seen *(PLS)* or the Last Known Position *(LKP)*, or some other point based on the best available information. An example of this follows:

> Let's say that information reported about a person missing from home indicates that the individual intended to go backpacking alone. The individual stated he intended to do either Route A or Route B. The starting points for these two routes sit some 10 miles or 16 kilometers apart. In this case designate both hiking routes as start points.

- As the initial phase of a search and ensuing investigation continues, Points Last Seen *(PLS)* or Last Known Positions *(LKPs)* often change.

Chronologically number new planning points with the IPP remaining point #1. Let's look at another example pointing out some subtle differences for these reference points:

- Larry, vacationing in a campground with his wife, leaves their RV at 0900 saying he intends to go for a hike in the nearby hills and plans to return at 1600. At 2200 his wife contacts law enforcement to report him overdue. At this stage the IPP, and Datum point #1 is the RV, his most likely point of return, also the PLS and LKP at this time.

- A search and investigation begins and information comes to light that Larry probably rendezvoused with a hiker friend also staying in the campground. They traveled in another vehicle to hike in the next valley some 20 miles/32 kilometers away. Enquiries reveal the location of the car belonging to Larry's hiking friend unattended in the next valley at the trail-head. This new last known position *(LKP)* becomes another datum *(Datum point #2)*. Search history experience dictates using this location as a reference point (IPP in this case because of proximity to the area being searched) to comparatively measure lost/missing person distances. Extenuating circumstances in this situation call for re-establishing the IPP and as a return destination for the hikers.

- Continuing the previous scenario, new datums often unfold with further discoveries. During the process of a hasty search, searchers find an erected tent some 2 miles/3.2 kilometers from the car. Investigators confirm the tent belongs to Larry's companion and find a climbing diary inside saying the two set out to climb a nearby mountain. Though not actually seen at this location, this still represents another LKP *(deducing their presence)* and, in the absence of other information, now datum point #3. Once again the question arises: "To which location will the hikers return?" For this category of missing person, the campsite indicates a good place to locate a reference point for distance comparisons, but not the IPP *(It remains at the vehicle left at the trailhead as mentioned above)*.

Common situations involving despondent persons, dementia sufferers or children missing from suburban facilities or homes takes a little thought about the location for the IPP. The same straight forward approach applies to most hiker, hunter and gatherer settings. The unique situations like trail routes or multiple location options for differing scenarios complicate the planning process and placement of the initial planning point.

Guideline criteria for establishing the Initial Planning Point follow:

The Initial Planning Point Guidelines:

- The point from which the search begins
- The first planning point in the operation
- If possible, use a PLS or an LKP
- Make it relevant to the search area *(in terms of proximity)*
- A good location to start a survey of the area for clues

While establishing the Initial Planning Point seems at first glance rather mundane in the scheme of issues confronting planners and ICs on a search, a closer look reveals the importance of documenting search incidents for relevant comparison and future data retrieval. Gathering relevant data with consistent standards during a search maximizes its usefulness in the future. If comparing previous search incident cases and the distances traveled, then ask: *Where do we take the measurements?* Planners and statisticians measure from the Initial Planning Point. Their reason: to derive maximum benefit from lost and missing person behavior data in the future. For reliable conclusions from this data, apply the reference location measurements in a consistent way and clearly document a standard method for the placement of reference planning points, particularly the IPP.

Point Last Seen *(PLS)* Guidelines

Use the **Point Last Seen** to describe the point of the subject's last sighting by a witness *(i.e. the mother actually saw the child playing by a tree near the creek)*. Expect the PLS to lend credibility and reliability to the Initial Planning Point or another point for data comparison.

Last Known Position *(LKP)* Guidelines

Last Known Position *(LKP)* specifies the last substantiated *(by clues or evidence)* position of the missing subject. If subsequent clues or evidence point out another location, then that replaces the LKP. Expect the LKP to change with the discovery of more clues, physical evidence and direction of travel. The weight or strength of the evidence discovered governs the reliability of the LKP and often gives direction of travel with the discovery of more than one clue. *(See page 394 in Clue Orientation for more on LKP.)*

Sometimes the Initial Planning Point, Point Last Seen, and the Last Known Position all end up at the same geographic location initially, or sometimes all end up at separate locations. Usually, the first LKP or PLS discovered establishes the IPP, but not always. The discovery of clues almost never happens in the same order as the subject left them. Be as accurate as possible when identifying and using planning reference points.

Use the LKP as:

- A base point for plotting potential distances traveled by the missing person, depending upon the category *(i.e. an IPP if appropriate)*
- A starting point to begin surveying an area for clues

Circumstance of Loss

Pay attention to detail and make some notes. Good interviewing and investigative techniques always pay off. Determine exactly when and where the subject went missing, for example:

- Missing from a known location
- Missing en route
- Missing in wilderness or rural area *(off trail)*
  - Determine exactly where and when any initial responders *(parents, friends, companions)* looked
  - Any clues detected
  - What type of gear initial responders wore on their feet
  - Get a good description of the tracks they left behind
  - Time frame from when missing subject went overdue
  - A witness or reporting party verbally recreating the exact sequence of events helps immensely
  - Missing person's intent *(recent history?)*

Has This Person Been the Subject of a Search Before?

Subject's Trip Preparation

Reconstruct details. Did someone else aid in planning this outing? If the missing person(s) rented equipment, did someone in the rental shop hear important details. Perhaps parents and friends know the trip plans, including alternatives.

Equipment: Investigators need to find out exactly what kind(s) of equipment and clothing the subject possessed because:

- It presents clues to survivability
- The type of footwear *(description of sole pattern)* aids trackers
- Colors of clothing and equipment aid detectability
- The types, brand names of clothing and equipment help in determining clue relevance
- Possibly influences the potential route or direction of travel
- Determines the subject's signalling capabilities *(i.e., whistle, flares, fire, strobe light, firearms)*
- Influences the types of potential activities and potential whereabouts
- Inventorying equipment identifies the subject's capabilities and expertise

Experience: Determine the subject's experience *(or lack there of)* as accurately as possible, to assess survivability, total distance traveled, potential activities and destinations, etc. Remember, reporting parties tend to overstate already subjective descriptions of experience.

Obtain names, addresses, and phone numbers for all family, friends, or witnesses.

Physical Condition of the Subject

Prior to the time of loss: Get a feel for the normal day to day conditioning of the subject. Again, this information influences the assessment of survivability, distance traveled, activities, etc. At the time of loss: Was the subject fatigued, depressed, cold, hungry, or ill?

Medical and Mental Condition of the Subject

- Determine any known medical problems
- Family doctors offer the best information
- Families often distort physical or mental health problems

Personality Traits of the Subject

- Expressive, smart, assertive, realistic, confident, aggressive, independent, mature, composed, logical, or optimistic
- Basically, does the subject have a positive mental attitude and a good self-image?

   or

- Reserved, anxious, submissive, evasive, immature, unsure, pessimistic, neglectful, shy or depressed
- Does the subject have a bad mental attitude and/ or a poor self-image

A personality profile tells a lot about the potential behavior of the subject. What type of activities the subject may attempt and where they may go verses not go.

Weather

Analyze the weather. Look at the weather during the time frame consistent with the suspected time the person went missing. Look at present weather conditions and how that possibly impacts the missing person. Predicted weather, both for short term and long term, gives an indication for issues such as:

- Hypothermia
- Hyperthermia
- Restricted travel
- Stationary, seeking shelter
- Detectability
- Survivability
- Tracking

Terrain Analysis

The process of analyzing the terrain consists of a relatively simple set of steps centered on studying the applicable terrain on a topographical map. The later chapter on establishing the search area, refers to terrain analysis as one of many of subjective factors. In particular, how the surrounding terrain influences the missing person. Combining all of the factors discussed here in planning data, along with terrain analysis helps establish a probable search area. Consider studying a map to discover the following:

- Sloping or level terrain
- Existing terrain barriers for this individual
- Any escape routes by which the subject possibly left the area
- Possible confusion factors
- Sights or sounds of civilization
- Possible short cuts
- Paths of least resistance *(or travel aids)*

At this point the IC and his planning team **proceed to make marks on a map**. This process determines potential areas for initial search efforts. Terrain analysis assists in applying SAR resources properly in the field.

Searching Data

This includes all the information given to searchers. In order to commit resources to the field, staff needs to provide them with all the information gathered prior to deployment.

- Name to call
- Physical description
- Shoe/bootprint description *(to include tread, length, and width/ Provide a drawing if possible)*
- Clothing worn *(types, brands, colors, all layers)*
- Equipment description, especially items easily discarded
- Brands of cigarettes, gum, candy, other possible discardable clues

Search Manager's need to obtain planning and searching data in order to:

- Establish the priorities and urgency
- Determine the preliminary search area
- Apply initial search tactics and put searchers into the field
- Look for clues

MISSING PERSON REPORT FORM

The following form provides a format to collect information in an efficient and coherent manner and supports a missing person investigation. Use it as a guide for conducting an interview. If necessary, use multiple sources and interviews to complete the form. Use a separate form for each interview and collate the information in a master file. When a case contains more than one missing person use a separate form for each subject.

- The MPR accompanies the Missing Person – Initial Report. The vital information gathered aids in deciding the necessity of a physical search, and the initial data needed to initiate an operation
- The MPR form provides the detailed planning and searching data required to manage the search operation and to assist the on-going investigation
- Interview the most knowledgeable person available first
- Use as many forms as necessary to conduct multiple interviews
- When evidentiary issues exist, the investigating officer initiates and retains custody of each form
- Collate and compare information gathered in multiple interviews and on separate subjects
- Reference and detail additional information generated by the questions listed on the form and on the back of the page

Managing the Inland Search Function - **Operational Response**

Case Name/Number _____

Missing Person Report
CONFIDENTIAL

The MPR provides a format to collect information in an efficient and coherent manner and is used to support a missing person investigation. It may also be used as a guide for conducting an interview. Information used to complete the form may come from multiple sources and from multiple interviews. Use a separate form for each interview and collate the information in a master file. If there is more than one missing person associated with this case, use a separate form for each subject.

Case Name/Number			Agency	
Date		Time	Location	
Interviewer's Name			Title	Agency
Information given by				DOB
Address				
Home Phone			Business Phone	
Cell Phone, Other Numbers				
Occupation			Employer	
Relationship to missing person				
Other persons interviewed: Name, contact information, date, time & relationship.				

Missing Person				
Full Name			Nickname(s)	
Name to call			Aliases	
Safe word?	Y / N	Word	Who knows it?	
Subject's primary language				
Home address				
Business or local address				
Home Phone			Business Phone	
Cell Phone, Other Numbers				
E-mail address				

Missing Person Report Form 01/12

Figure 12-1

Case Name/Number ________________

Missing Person Report

Description									
Age	Race	Gender			Hgt		Wgt	DOB	
Build									
Hair Color			Length				Style		
If balding, describe									
Describe facial hair									
Eye color	Glasses	Y	N	Regular		Sun		Contacts	
Describe glasses									
Eyesight without glasses									
Facial features, shape									
Complexion									
Distinguishing marks, scars									
General appearance									
Clothing Worn When Last Seen: Note brand, style, pattern, colors, & size for each									
Hat/Cap/Scarf									
Shirt/Blouse									
Pants									
Dress									
Sweater									
Coat/Jacket/Raingear									
Footwear									
Hose/Socks									
Underwear									
Other									
Describe all accessories the subject may have been wearing, such as belt, rings, watch, pins, hair accessories, necktie, tie clip, etc.									
Describe all items the subject may have been carrying, such as pocketbook, wallet, backpack (describe contents of each), cell phone, keys, pocket knife, pager, camera, weapon, etc.									

Missing Person Report Form 01/12 Page 2 of 10

Figure 12-2

Case Name/Number _____

Missing Person Report

Details of Loss	
Location missing from	
Point Last Seen (PLS)	
Day/Date Last Seen	Time Last Seen
Last seen by whom	
Subject accompanied by animal(s)? Describe	
Vehicle description, if driving	
Destination(s), stated intentions	
Possible routes	
Weather at time of loss	
Events of last 24 hours leading up to time of loss	
Reported missing by:	Why?
Address	
Phones	
Relationship to missing person	
Where can this person be reached in the next 12 hours?	

Subject's Experience	
Resident of	How long?
Previous residence	How long?
Birthplace	
Has this person been the object of a search in the past?	
If so, describe date(s), circumstances of loss, how long missing, when found, where found, condition when found and actions taken by subject while missing (if known)	

Additional Information and Comments

Figure 12-3

Case Name/Number _____

Missing Person Report

Physical Health			
General physical condition			
Handicaps			
Known medical problems			
Pregnant?	How long?		Menstruating?
Physician			Phone
Address			
Mental/Emotional Health			
General mental health			
Known mental problems			
Suicidal?	Previous attempts (explain)		
Is this subject possibly dangerous to self or others? Explain:			
Does this subject have access to or is he/she possibly carrying a weapon?			
Are all weapons accounted for?			
Fears and phobias:			
Knowledgeable person			Phone
Address			

Medications: Prescription and Non-prescription	
Medication, strength and dosage	**Affect if not taken**

Figure 12-4

Case Name/Number _____

Missing Person Report

Identification

Drivers License:	State	No.	Date Issued

Other Identification

Is subject enrolled in Safe Return or similar program? Describe:

Electronic tracking device? Describe:

Finances

Credit cards: List card names and account numbers

Checking and savings accounts: List banks and account numbers

Does subject have credit cards or check book in possession?	Y	N	Cash carried:

Describe:

Detailed Subject History

Single		Married		Divorced		Widowed	

Spouse's Name	Phone

Address (if different)

Siblings (Name, age, residence) Use Back If Necessary

Fathers Name	Living?	Y	N

Contact Information

Occupation & Employer

Mothers Name	Living?	Y	N

Contact Information

Missing Person Report Form 01/12   Page 5 of 10

Figure 12-5

Case Name/Number _____

Missing Person Report

Detailed Subject History, continued				
Occupation & Employer				
Other relatives that may provide information				
Subject's primary occupation		Retired?	Y	N
Employer		How long?		
Contact person				
Previous employment history				
Education level				
Military service branch	Currently active or reserve?		Y	N
Contact person	Dates of service			
Religion or belief system		Active?	Y	N
Contact person				
Other persons who may provide information				
Hobbies, special interests				
Experience in outdoors, backcountry				
Favorite places to visit				
Athletic ability, mobility				
Active/outgoing or quiet/withdrawn?				
Attitude toward authority				
Recent, current or anticipated financial, legal or other problems				
Who does subject confide in and/or whom does he/she frequently talk to on the phone?				
Who last talked with subject at length?				

Figure 12-6

Case Name/Number ________________

Missing Person Report

Detailed Subject History, continued	
When and what was topic?	
Recent letters or writings?	
Does subject keep a diary?	
Does subject have access to a computer?	Describe locations, user name(s), password(s)
Does subject smoke, drink or use illegal drugs?	Describe in detail:
Additional Information and Comments	

Missing Person Report Form 01/12 Page 7 of 10

Figure 12-7

Case Name/Number _____

Missing Person Report

Children, Elderly, Special Needs				
Refer to mental/emotional health section				Mental age, if known
How old does the subject look?				
Fears and phobias:	Horses?	Dogs?	Dark?	Sirens, loud noises?
Other: (describe)				
Will subject answer, if called?				Preferred name to call
Any training on what to do if lost, such as Hug-A-Tree?				
How does subject normally travel? (Foot, bike, public transportation, family, friends, etc)				
Will subject talk to strangers, accept rides?				
Is there a "home place" or other special place?				
Does subject have a caretaker or a day care facility?				
Can the subject dress and/or feed him/herself?				
Does there appear to be any issues with family, school or care facility?				
Does the subject know how to call home or call 911?				
What would this subject most likely do if lost?				
Additional Information and Comments				

Missing Person Report Form 01/12

Figure 12-8

Case Name/Number ________________

Missing Person Report

Planning Information				
Local Responsible Agency				Phone
Address				
Name & Title of Responsible Agent				
Contact Information				
Other assisting agencies				
NCIC	Date	Time	Agency	
Amber Alert	Date	Time	Agency	
Other				
Obtain:	Identification	Photos	Scent Article	Records et al
Special precautions, instructions to search teams				
Search base/command post location, directions, phone numbers, radio frequencies				
Actions to date: (Date and time of this report)				
Person to be notified when subject located				
Additional Information and Comments				

Missing Person Report Form 01/12 Page 9 of 10

Figure 12-9

Case Name/Number _____

Dementia Supplement
(This section should be completed for all dementia sufferers)

Dementia Diagnosis (DAT, Vascular, Parkinson's etc):		
Pick the box below that best describes the missing person *(circle one)*		
Mild confusion and forgetfulness, short term memory affected	Difficulty distinguishing time, place and person. Some language difficulties	Nearly complete loss of judgment, reasoning and loss of physical control

	Yes	No
Does the missing person know their own name?		
Does the missing person know when they are at home?		
Does the missing person recognize the local neighborhood?		
Does the missing person recognize familiar faces?		
Does the missing person answer to his/her name being called?		
Does the missing person able to carry on a conversation?		
Does the missing person have the ability to tell time?		

Distance typically walked each day (during past week)	Miles
Greatest distance walked during the past 3 months	Miles
Greatest distance walked during the past ten years	Miles
Estimate the greatest distance believe the person would walk	Miles

Please rate the missing person's ability to walk *(Circle one)*

Confined to bed/unable to walk	Requires walker or cane to walk small distances	Walks unassisted for short distances by shuffles or limps	Walks with assistance	Walks effortlessly

Activity	No	Yes	N/A
Ability to choose appropriate clothing *(occasion, the weather, & color)*			
Dress himself/herself completely			
Decide what he/she needs to eat			
Attempt to telephone someone at a suitable time			
Find and dial a telephone number correctly			
Undertake to go out (walk, visit, shop) at an appropriate time			
Decide to use a mode of transportation (car, bus, taxi)?			
Reach a familiar or non-familiar destination without getting lost ?			
Safely take the adequate mode of transport (car, bus, taxi)?			
Can person take his/her medications at the correct time & dosage?			
Does the person show an interest in leisure activities?			

Figure 12-10

Notes:

Investigation, Interviewing and Callout

Objectives:

- Relate the importance of investigation

- Describe why the investigation process never ends until locating the subject, and in some cases even continues beyond that point

- Describe the fundamental elements of interviewing and the component triad

- Learn to identify key people with intimate knowledge of the missing person or the circumstances surrounding how the individual went missing

- Use of the Missing Person Report form to structure and guide interviews

- Describe and discuss the type of information resources need when assisting in a search

- Relate the guidelines for calling out paid or unpaid resources

Investigation

Chapter 3 of this text, in discussing the basic crucials of search management, stated that **Search Ties Inexorably to Law Enforcement Investigation**. The very nature of the investigative function links to standard police responsibilities, public expectations and everyday working protocols. Investigation in search focuses on gathering relevant facts to assist the IC in making decisions and to build a subject profile which gives the best indication of the missing person's whereabouts during an incident. The Missing Person Report *(MPR)* represents the physical record of the investigation concerning the subject and provides a guide and central repository for that information. It also becomes a permanent record for the incident.

What is the Goal of Investigation in Search?

Investigation involves gathering evidence, facts, information or inferences that provide a picture of what happened. Investigation relies on four essential processes to uncover evidence:

- **Conducting interviews** of friends, relatives, peers, eye witnesses, companions or any people with specific knowledge of the missing person relating to the circumstances surrounding the disappearance of the individual.
- **Observing and recording** the actions of people, the physical condition of individuals, appearances, continuity of events, or condition of things related to the missing person or circumstances surrounding the disappearance.
- **Examination of documents** containing information relevant to the missing person, such as records of chronology, log sheets or registration books. Also physical or informational clues left by the missing person such as notes, diaries, internet history or other computer records.
- **Analysis of statistical data** from either local or international databases possibly including computations or deductive reasoning that sheds light on the missing person's behavior, intent, or location.

In solving any mystery, determining right, wrong, true or false information depends upon evidence. The preponderance of evidence gives the search manager a factual basis for forming opinions, judgments, conclusions, or recommendations. In turn, the compilation of this evidence and the conclusions derived from it provide possible locations of the missing person and ultimately the methods needed to find the individual, and solve the puzzle of what happened to the subject.

Search mission reports often contain examples of critical information discovered by the operation or even information volunteered by someone, several days after the search begins. In retrospect, getting that information earlier will provide significant bearing on early decisions, and information that quite possibly saves time, effort, money and, potentially even the life of the missing subject.

Four Types of Evidence

> *Often, the most useful clues are comprised of several pieces of evidence of various types, from various sources, which, when considered together, form a coherent clue the way that pieces of a jigsaw puzzle can make a picture. Indeed, there is seldom one single bit of evidence that unravels the mystery and leads to the successful conclusion of the incident.*
>
> -Kenneth A. Hill,
> *Managing The Lost
> Person Incident*, 2007.

Testimonial Evidence: The most available form of information and evidence comes from the mouths of friends, relatives, peers, eye witnesses, companions or anyone with specific knowledge about the situation. However, sometimes this type of information gets called into question in terms of reliability or accuracy. Often issues of misinterpretation, misunderstanding, incompleteness, or hearsay require some form of interpretation *(See interviewing page 209)*. With that said, this type of evidence often provides the greatest source of information used on a search, therefore, make every effort to assure thoroughness and accuracy.

Physical Evidence: The type of evidence most immune to misinterpretation, usually the most useful and created directly by the missing person. Evidence in this category ranges from footprints, to discarded items in the field, a vehicle at a trail head or an article of clothing left at a camp site. Physical evidence often corroborates other types of evidence or information. A shell casing of the same caliber as the rifle carried by the person sought. Currently, digital photography or video gets used more and more to document physical evidence *(See documentation below)*.

Written or Documentary Evidence: National Parks and official wilderness areas provide good examples of areas requiring logs or registration systems posted to keep record of entry, exit or mountain summit climbs. Other types of written evidence include camping permits, credit card charges, rental charge slips, store receipts, fuel receipts, and letters or notes of intentions left in a car or on a computer. All of these help to pin point a location, time and the presence of the missing person. They also validate and further substantiate physical evidence in the field.

Statistical or Analytical Evidence: The International Search and Rescue Incident Database ultimately provides a broad spectrum of information about missing and lost person behavior. Local, state or regional databases do the same. Both inductive and scientific reasoning consist of making inferences, and speculation about scenarios and probable behavior. The process of deduction occurs when establishing alternatives by consensus and when substantiating physical evidence points specifically to one of the alternatives. This process arrives at analytical conclusions and essentially supplies evidence. Similar incidents, past training or real search operations also provide compelling analytical evidence.

The Importance of Investigation

Investigation provides the best function for solving a mystery, and generally proceeds through a process of elimination. Most missing person investigations follow a pattern similar to the following:

- Evaluation of the initial report and development of a subject profile
- Development of initial theories, and scenarios about what happened or at least events consistent with available information
- Active seeking of additional information
- Evaluation and ranking of information according to relevance and reliability

- Elimination of previous scenarios no longer consistent with the accumulated evidence or even the development of and modified scenarios consistent with the new evidence
- Continuation of the process until solving the mystery

In virtually all search cases, responders find available clues and reach a solution. It just takes someone, or a group of people working together, to uncover the facts and use them correctly.

Too often, responders fail to use good investigative techniques in missing person incidents, or they initiate them too late in the mission to take full advantage.

The Priority for Investigation

Begin investigation immediately with the *First Notice*. Typically, a law enforcement agency takes some type of report and the investigation process proceeds from there (*See initial Missing Person Report form in Chapter 11*). Some suggest that individuals in dispatch centers or official reception centers use the initial MPR Form as a guide. Thereafter, every formal planning meeting during the progress of a search mission includes a briefing from the investigator. Investigation begins at the first notice and continues throughout the incident and possibly continues well after the suspension of, or successful end to, the search.

The information determined through the investigation gets plugged directly into the planning process. An active part of the any management team consists of the investigative unit supporting the search operation. Include a briefing from the investigator per se or the Documentation Unit Leader in every formal planning meeting during the progress of a search. Update and analyze the subject profile almost on an hourly basis in order to properly act upon the clues and to modify the strategy and tactics accordingly. Include investigation in all planning meetings as well as a principle part of the interviewing process. Therefore investigative law enforcement personnel such as detectives or investigators need to constantly familiarize themselves with current search management protocols and concepts. Investigation, more often than not, holds the key to unlocking the mystery of what happened.

Criminal Possibilities

One of the overriding factors that place investigation squarely at law enforcement's doorstep relates to potential criminal activity. The number of criminal activities seems to rise directly with an increase in population. Therefore, evaluate every missing person incident with criminal lens until proven otherwise. As a daily functioning part of local government and authority, police routinely perform this function. Essentially, three possibilities stand out:

A Staged Incident - In this case an unknown person created a staged incident to make it appear as though the subject went missing, but in actuality, someone staged a disappearance. Actions such as leaving clothing or possessions on a bridge or beach, or leaving a note in a car parked at a remote site illustrate types of staged incidents. Good investigation pursues issues possibly social, economic or moral. Look for corroborating clues: very high debt, potential bankruptcy, extramarital affairs or starting a new life with another person all potentially lead to such incidents.

A Homicide - Remote or rural areas in general provide ample opportunity for those intent upon homicide. Though more rare than in urban areas, perpetrators assault or kill in rural areas too. In fact, where better to carry out a planned homicide *(make it look like an accident)* than in a remote or wilderness locations, and then report the victim as lost or missing?

A Kidnapping or Abduction - Both well planned or spur of the moment actions on the part of a person with criminal intent. Due to their vulnerability, these types of incidents sometimes involve children. If the incident occurs in an urban or urban/rural interface area, accomplish the reflex tasks (*see Reflex Tasking Chapter 14*) immediately. The more likely scenario involves parental custody issues or family related abduction, not overlooking sexual assault *(See reference to abductions in Chapter 23 - Searching in the Urban Environment).*

Criminal Runaways and/or suicide? Look for a record of this type of behavior occurring in the past. Investigate incentive for runaways further *(Runaways range in age, and socioeconomic class).* Whenever the investigation begins to show a possibility of criminal activity, activate specialized resources in the law enforcement community for criminal investigation. Look for anything missing *(clothing, medications, guns, weapons etc.).*

Despondence continues to grow as a major missing person category throughout the world. For some suicide presents a convenient departure from intolerable situations and begs further investigation for potential diagnosed and undiagnosed conditions. When a responder finds a missing person dead or badly injured, keep in mind the necessity to protect the crime scene without breaking any chain of evidence.

In a significant number of searches, after completing the initial missing person report, investigation tends to grow more low-key and haphazard. Often, this continues until something critical comes to light, even quite some time later in the incident.

Organizationally, separate the INVESTIGATION unit or function from the outset of any search. Immediately designate someone responsible for carrying out this function in detail and continuously throughout the incident.

The written PREPLAN needs to identify the importance of investigation and also identify specialized resources to accomplish it.

Some Considerations in Investigation

Figure 13-1 *(next page)* provides a checklist for personnel in the investigation unit. It provides a guide for investigation personnel to use for follow-up on data collected in the Missing Person Report.

SAR personnel find it easier to dismiss information not needed, than to find out too late they needed more clues. Frustration tends to develop when trying to go back after the fact and gather information or crucial evidence.

Where and How to Obtain Information

- **The reporting party:** Get location, call back numbers, reasons for reporting the subject missing
- **Reconnaissance:** Hasty teams, aerial survey, interview teams, lookouts
- **Vehicle:** Process as a crime scene, look for clues about possibly where the subject went (direction of travel)
- **Accommodations:** Interview, check room for notes or items left behind, check trash cans
- **Home:** Check for notes, any indication of intentions, missing clothing or equipment, leave a note to call the law enforcement agency if subject returns. *Always* check the answering machine
- **Place of Work:** Interview co-workers, check work space, check emails if possible
- **Friends and relatives:** Plans, physical & mental condition, habits, drugs, social media, personal email
- **Local businesses:** Interview, post flyers
- **Wilderness permits, registration cards:** Ask parties who resided in the same area as the subject if they saw him or talked to him, subject's plans, address, etc
- **On-scene:** Tracks, clothing, equipment, scent article
- **Trailheads:** Interview other hikers
- **Visitor Center:** Interview staff, post flyers
- **Summit Registers:** Check for subject, possible witnesses
- **Public transportation:** Interview employees, post flyers
- **Local Medical Facilities:** Interview staff, local record check
- **Campgrounds:** Check registers, fee receipts
- **Weather Records:** Local and regional records

Solving the Classic Mystery

The following six questions help focus any investigation. They reflect the same foundation questions asked by any newspaper, internet, radio or

LEAD OR CLUE	INFORMATION SOURCE
1. Subject Profile at point last seen	1. Family, companions, care givers
2. Equipment Possessed by Subject	2. Companions, relatives, friends
3. Intended Route, Trip Plans	3. Companions, relatives, friends
4. Actual Route - Subsequent	4. Witnesses from area sightings
5. Subject Experience	5. Relationship with wife, children, parents, friends, co-workers
6. Physical Condition	6. Companions, friends, relatives, doctor, clergyman, co-workers
7. Mental Condition	7. Companions, friends, relatives, doctor, clergyman, co-workers
8. Recent Changes in Behavior	8. Companions, friends, relatives, doctor, clergyman, co-workers
9. Habits, Drugs, Medicines, etc.	9. Companions, friends, relatives, doctor, clergyman, co-workers
10. Recent subject movements: fuel, food, snacks	10. Restaurants, grocery stores, stops in route, trailhead, or destination
11. Mental Attitude - How would subject react?	11. Companions, friends, relatives, doctor, clergyman, co-workers
12. Relationship with wife, children, parents, friends, co-workers	12. Companions, friends, relatives, doctor, clergyman, co-workers
13. Criminal history	13. Relatives, friends, co-workers, local law enforcement
14. Financial Situation, debts, withdrawals, pending action, bankruptcy	14. Relative, friends, financial institutions, creditors
15. Confirmation of equipment *(sole pattern, etc.)*	15. Relatives, friends, store where purchased
16. Photographs	16. Relatives, friends, school
17. Interests, hobbies, What might attract subject?	17. Relatives, companions, friends, co-workers
18. Profile of subject's companions	18. Relatives, co-workers, other companions, law enforcement

Figure 13-1 Checklist for follow-up

TV reporter making them familiar. They encapsulate the essence of inquiry and tell us what happened. It provides a good checklist of items to cover in a missing person investigation. Some information comes from interviews and some from other sources.

Who? What kind of a person are we looking for? Obtain a complete profile if possible.

What? What circumstances surround the disappearance? What specifically precipitated this incident? The investigator needs to dig a bit on this one.

Why? What made the person the object of a search? Reported missing by whom? Past history? Anything different here th an occurred in the past?

Where? PLS/LKP, possible destinations, incentives, attractions, ulterior motives. Recreate the incident.

When? Last night, yesterday, an hour ago or last week? How long before reported missing?

How? How the subject left or departed from the scene. Anyone else involved purposefully or inadvertently in the incident.

Environmental Information

The effects of the environment significantly impact the missing person, especially in remote areas. Check weather conditions at the time of the disappearance and up to the present time, then get predicted weather and update regularly as needed.

- **Weather forecast:** Possible effects of weather on the subject and searchers
- **Daylight:** Subjects move more in daylight, usually easier to search during the day, limited air search in the daylight hours except with night vision equipment
- **Moonlight:** Moonrise: The moons current cycle and the amount of light provided for walking or flying
- **Temperatures:** Possible effects on the missing person or even the searchers
- **Precipitation:** Potential effects on the missing person and searchers, snow cover influences travel

The Continuing Investigation

The investigator needs to think about all conceivable contacts with critical information. List the names from each of these:

- Family
- Caregivers
- Friends
- Neighbors
- Local businesses
- Recreational sites - pubs, bowling, games

Try not to forget to enter the missing person's name into NCIC *(National Crime Information Center)*, local/state systems as per protocol and then issue a BOLO *(Be On the Look Out)* for the individual to nearby jurisdictions. Notify community services, neighborhood watch members and community civic organizations. Then check relevant *non search* areas such as:

- Friends and relatives in the area
- Known hangouts
- Places of special interest to the missing person
- Hospitals for John/Jane Doe admissions
- Shelters

As an absolute minimum, the investigation needs to obtain the following facts:

- Basic information about the person *(Subject Profile)*
- The subject's ability to travel
- Survivability of the subject
- The intent of the subject
- The subject's ability to respond
- If the subject responds, what they respond to

> *"When you have eliminated the impossible, whatever remains, however improbable, must be the truth."*
> Arthur Conan Doyle

Interviewing

Good interviewing is an art. Not everyone interviews effectively. To conduct a successful interview in local situations, a pre-planning effort indicates how to contact people with good interviewing skills.

> *"The goal of an interview is to painlessly obtain information from a participant or witness to a trying incident in order to devise an effective course of action."*
> - Tim J. Setnicka, *Wilderness Search and Rescue*, 1980.

Interviewing Involves Face-to-Face Conversation with a Specific Purpose. Law enforcement agencies deal extensively with interviewing techniques and by far possess the best resources to fulfill this function. However, *Interviewing* differs from *Interrogation*, *Cross-Examination*, and *Testimony* and while some instances specifically call for each one of these, the Search Manager needs to know the proper use of each.

Terms and Definitions

These terms provided by Christopher Young, Contra Costa County Sheriff's Search and Rescue Team, Lafayette, California.

Interrogation: A structured accusatory process which confronts the suspect in a confident manner and convinces them to admit responsibility.

Interview: A structured non-accusatory process to obtain useful information. Use specific techniques to aid recall or elicit behavior useful in determining truth or involvement. Interviews also evoke lies and themes to use against the uncooperative.

SAR Interview: A structured, but yet informal process to obtain useful information from someone with firsthand knowledge of the missing person. Questioning in a non-accusatory, non-condoning and non-condemning manner. Structure questions to aid the interviewee in recalling specific details and events leading up to the disappearance of the missing person. Use the information gathered to develop a subject profile, collect lists of other persons to interview and aid in the planning of where to look for the missing person.

Due to past experience or negative encounters, some people tend to not respond well to interviews by uniformed law enforcement officers and respond better to non-uniformed or civilian personnel.

General Principles

- Interview the people with firsthand knowledge as quickly as possible, while fresh information still exists and before collusion with others takes place.

- Always interview witnesses separately.

Interviewing Techniques

Open-ended questions give the interviewed individual the latitude to structure or compose their own replies. **Example**: Can you describe her clothing when she left this morning?

Closed questions take less time, but maximize control. **Example**: Was he wearing a hat? Usually only used when seeking specific items of factual information.

Probes or follow-up questions provide clarification and direction. **Example**: I'm not sure I understood you. Could you explain what you mean by tired?

Active Listening means the interviewer provides both verbal and nonverbal active feedback to the speaker, giving the individual interviewed the impression that the listener is interested and in fact listening.

Reminders:

- Control your attitude and biases
- Stay in control of the interview

- Listen for off-the-cuff comments
- Make copious notes of the conversation
- Gather initial information as quickly as possible
- Respect the person's feelings, environment and viewpoint

Who Should Conduct Interviews?

Normally, reports of a missing person case go directly to a law enforcement agency and the first responding officer conducts a cursory interview. If the case possesses any merit, then a detective conducts additional interviews and gathers useful facts and personal data about the situation before the SAR team arrives. Unfortunately, most law enforcement officers lack an understanding of the type of information SAR needs to plan a search, which sometimes necessitates additional interviews.

Law enforcement officers often perceive information gathered in interviews as confidential, making them reluctant to share that information. The IC then needs to find an experienced SAR team interviewer to explain to the officer the specific information needed and to request any relevant data. If they express an interest, invite the officer to sit in on additional interviews to help improve SAR interviews for the future. A two person SAR interview team, one interviewer and one note taker, works very well. To avoid potential problems, when interviewing children or females of any age, a female team member needs to accompany the interviewer.

Keep in mind that if the incident turns out to involve a crime, then all of your written notes potentially become evidence and often get requested by both the prosecution and the defense. You also run the chance of getting subpoenaed to testify in court.

Where and Whom to Interview

Other individuals with information potentially critical to the outcome of the search include:

- Parents, spouse, children or other relatives
- Any companions - with the subject before going missing
- All members of the subject's household *(related or not)*
- Neighbors, friends and co-workers
- Schoolmates, school counselors
- Family doctors, health care professionals, or clergy
- Business associates
- Area businesses
- Public transportation services
- Persons from stores where the missing subject obtained equipment
- Other witnesses from the search area who potentially saw the subject
- Persons who transported subject to or from the search area
- People who know the search area well

With some sources of information, particularly from banks, medical practitioners, clergymen and attorneys, confidentiality problems exist with releasing information about the missing subject. Leave these interviews to law enforcement and if necessary, let them obtain a court order or other procedures to gather this information.

Setting Up The Interview

- Use a missing person report designed specifically for SAR, and use a separate form for each interview.
- Choose a private location free of noise, foot traffic and other distractions. Turn off any televisions and never allow others to listen to the interview.
- If possible, when interviewing, make sure same genders exist for the person interviewed and the interviewer.
- Always try to interview children without parents present, if possible, and always ask the parent's permission.
- Set up chairs so no heads need to turn in order to see one another. Tables tend to create the feeling of an interrogation so, if possible, eliminate the use of a table between the interviewers and the subject. Ensure sufficient lighting.
- Tell the subject you will be taking notes before the interview starts and, if possible, recording it. The use of a voice recorder helps to fill gaps in the note taking process. Be aware that a voice recorder usually intimidates people and often

stops them from speaking freely. Simply tell them that you use a recorder to avoid missing potentially vital pieces of information crucial in this search. Don't hide the recorder, but avoid asking for direct permission to use it, just place the recorder out of their direct line of sight.

The following proves helpful in avoiding the *traps* interviewers often fall into:

PITFALLS

Never assume that any individual tells the truth or cooperates to the fullest extent.

- Watch for potential crimes
- A person feels suspicious or afraid of the interviewer
- Beware of possible rivalry or jealousy between the lost subject and the witness
- Relatives, especially, usually exhibit embarrassment about the subject's condition or behavior
- The witness fails to understand the complexity or seriousness of the situation or the relevance of particular information requested
- Family and friends possess a natural tendency to make the subject or themselves look as good as possible by minimizing or ignoring faults, deficiencies, or exaggerating health or weather problems etc.
- Without malice, some people tend to *embellish the truth* while trying to help as much as possible (*A reason why some information gets held back from the press*).
- Always assume that **everyone will contribute information** if asked the right questions in the right way.
- Be aware, some people look for *publicity* or want all the *attention* on them.
- **Let the information guide the conclusions.** The greater the amount of information, the stronger the validity of the conclusion. Some people base conclusions on incomplete information. Good managers show flexibility and the ability to change conclusions and actions as information changes or improves.

PITFALL - Beware of the trap of forming your conclusion, then gathering or interpreting information to support it.

Be aware that different interests, conclusions, biases and past experiences of witnesses influence their answers.

EXAMPLE: One person may be much more tuned into geographical features than clothing.

PITFALL - Never assume that one person possesses all the information you need. Try not to concern yourself with conflicting information. Inconsistencies always exist. Evaluate differences and, when possible, *verify* the information.

- Interview in an **informal, relaxed, comfortable setting**, private and free from interruptions.
- Preferably, interviewers **work in pairs**, providing for two interpretations or evaluations, and reducing the chances of overlooking something. As mentioned previously, use a recorder if at all possible, particularly if working alone. Again, inform the witness of your intention to record.

PITFALL - Some people react negatively to recording; they *clam up*. Pay attention when writing down their responses or when you find yourself writing instead of listening. Writing often distracts from what the witness says.

- Interviewers need to introduce themselves, *explain in detail the purpose of the interview* and then try to set the person at ease, or in a relaxed mood. Start off with general conversation, and then try to establish a good interpersonal relationship.

PITFALL - A panicky person may have difficulty controlling their frame of mind. Statements such as "calm down" or "try to get control of yourself" rarely work. Start with general questions, or enlist their aid. As another solution or strategy, ask the individual to go to a designated place and write down statements and come back later, after calming down.

- **Convey a sense of controlled urgency and concern**, but not excitement, particularly in the presence of a relative or close friend of the missing person. If no urgent situation exists, at least try to convey a sense of action being taken.
- **Confirm identifying information about the witness** for the record, and for future contact.
- Try to **understand the person and his/her mental capacity** in order to ask appropriate questions. If interviewing a child, find someone who relates to children.

NOTE: WITH CHILDREN, COMPENSATE FOR HEIGHT DIFFERENCE -- GET AT EYE LEVEL WITH THEM.

PITFALL - Acknowledge biases. Recognize them when interviewing. If an interviewer tends to shy away from people who choose alternative life styles, he/she more than likely communicates that during an interview with someone in that category. It is easy to communicate disdain for the stupidity of a parent who let a small child wander away from a campsite. Try to control these biases or allow someone else to conduct these interviews. Be flexible and experiment. Sometimes a female interviewer gets more information from a male witness than a male, or vice versa.

- **Ask open-ended questions** rather than leading ones easily answered by yes or no.

   EXAMPLE: "What did Tom have with him?" instead of "Did Tom have a knife and canteen with him?"

   EXAMPLE: "Which trail did Mary take when she left camp?" This question much more likely gets a "trail" response than the more open ended, "Where did Mary go when she left camp?"

PITFALL - The presentation of questions programs people to give erroneous responses. The question possibly contains information reinforcing the witness's conclusions, biases or other hearsay information heard by the witness. Design questions to reinforce, not distort the *memory*. People want to appear knowledgeable and helpful. They often sense the direction of the interviewer and tend to go along, even if they really know very few facts.

- **Listen to your witness**. Ask the question, then *listen* to the answer. Try not interrupt or begin to think ahead to the next question. Wait until the individual completes the answer to the question, before clearing up confusing points or to deciding what to ask next.
- **Pause and listen after a witness gives an answer.** This gives the interviewer a chance to think, to digest the answer, and the *awkward silence* possibly prompts the witness to volunteer more information. Give no message to stop. Show acceptance, nod, "uh huh", "yes" . . . "please continue," etc.
- As necessary, **paraphrase or summarize the answer** to make sure you understood the intent. "Did I hear you say . . . ?"
- **Check validity by asking a question differently later**, or ask another question when you know the correct answer.

PITFALL - Try not to inadvertently put the person on the *defensive*.

- **Listen for key words or phrases, particularly when repeated.**
- **Make sure to explore each point fully** before going on to the next one.

PITFALL - Avoid jumping around. Go in the chronological order of the incident. Generally follow the continuum of events, even if the witness lacks knowledge of certain parts. One technique: let the witness tell his or her entire story first, even if this involves jumping around. Then by beginning to ask questions in the actual sequence of events, fill in voids to verify the story.

- **When you run out of questions, ask: "Is there anything else that you think might help?"** This may bring out something new or give the person a chance to add something important but unaddressed.

- **Ask what the witness thinks happened or what the subject did or will do.** Consider this an *opinion* and separate from facts.

How much do you play on the emotions of the witness? Make each witness understand that the information divulged (or withheld) possibly influences the well-being or survival of the subject.

- **Reduce the interview to a written statement.** Particularly if recording. If so, inform the witness of any further actions needed.
- **At the conclusion, thank the witness.** Reassure the witness of your concern and the helpfulness of the information. This leaves the person with a good feeling. If the person felt *on the hot seat* at all, this breaks down some reluctance and helps to generate helpful *off the cuff* remarks. Ask for contact information for follow ups, if necessary.
- **If using more than one interviewer, get together and compare information**, reactions, *gut feelings*, discrepancies, and missing information.

PITFALL - Without the information constantly forwarded, even if incomplete, to the command, planning and operations of the mission organization, it tends to hamper further functions.

Reminder of the Use for This Information

From Chapter 12, SAR members need two broad categories of data at the beginning of a search:

- **SEARCHING DATA** - Knowledge needed by the searchers going to the field. Looking for what and where?
- **PLANNING DATA** - The search manager or IC needs certain kinds of information to determine where to deploy resources and the best strategy and tactics to implement.

Special Considerations

- Hypnosis sometimes results in some success obtaining information from witnesses who otherwise cannot recall. In fact, many law enforcement agencies train staff in hypnotism for this specific purpose.
- Never overlook a polygraph or other technological advances in unusual situations.
- If, at any time, interviewers derive any information indicating the potential for criminal involvement, individual rights, and rules of evidence, consult proper authorities, before continuing the interview.

USE THE MISSING PERSON REPORT FORM TO STRUCTURE INTERVIEW QUESTIONS.

The Communication Triad

It helps to view the interview process through a concept called the communications triad. Three essential components make up this hierarchy *(See Figure 13-2)*. First, **the type of information sought**. For example, technical information dealing with something like climbing or a piece of gear for outdoor activity, or even information related to medications, drugs or medical conditions. Technical information also refers to information about personality and behavior characteristics of an individual. Often, specialized information of this nature involves unique terms or vocabulary making specific background necessary to understand or even converse.

The type of respondent makes up the second part of the communications triad. Factors influencing or adversely impacting the exchange of information in an interview include anything from peer pressure, socioeconomic class, color, race, technical specialty, special interest, or even someone unintentionally breaking the law. All of these influence the bias with which someone enters into an interview. E.g. someone with a mental age of 4 years old to speaking to a very emotionally distraught person present very tough challenges when trying to solicit good information from them.

The final leg of the triad centers on **the type of interviewer**. People often think that anyone in the police ranks conducts a good interview. However, some possess more skill than others, even in police organizations. If a situation calls for interviewing children of any age, perhaps because of the intimidation factor, find someone not in uniform to conduct the

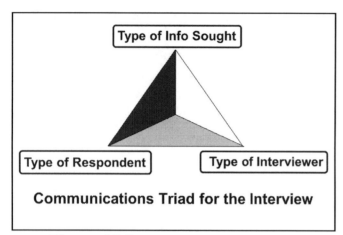

Figure 13-2 The Communication Triad

interview. A technically oriented respondent with very specialized skills, ideally requires someone with in-depth knowledge in that field to either conduct the interview or at least sit in.

The bottom line, maximize compatibility among all three components of the triad to maximize the information flow and to eliminate confusion or misinterpretation. Although not always possible in the real world, an awareness of these components helps an interviewer conduct a better exchange of information during a face to face conversation.

The following represent abbreviated example checklists used at Yosemite National Park when gathering information about a potential missing subject:

Information on the Subject - Where to Get It

- Direct from a Reporting Party: Detain, hold on phone, get phone number, identification, location, auto, photos, maps, return to scene, where staying
- Reconnaissance: Hasty Team, geographical viewpoints, loud hailer, hand signals, chopper, digital photos, back country *(trail crew)*
- Auto: Returned?, equipment, notes, maps, leave a note to call the Ranger
- **Accommodations:** Returned? Equipment, notes, maps, leave note to "call Ranger"
- **Home:** Returned? Equipment, notes, maps, leave note to "call Ranger"
- **Place of Work:** Returned? Equipment, notes, maps, leave note to "call Ranger"
- **Friends:** Returned? Plans, physical & mental condition, habits, drugs
- **Relatives:** Returned? Plans, physical & mental condition, habits, drugs
- **Co-Workers:** Returned? Plans, physical & mental condition, habits, drugs
- **Registration Cards:** Returned? Plans, experience, equipment, who to contact, etc
- **Registration Cards:** Of other parties who possibly saw subject
- **Wilderness Permits:** Of other parties who possibly saw subject, subject's plans, address, etc
- **On-scene:** Track, equipment
- **Clues:** Candy wrapper, dog scent articles
- **Fliers or Posters:** Mailed to wilderness permit holders in same area, at trail heads
- **Fliers or Posters:** In stores
- **Trail heads:** Interview hikers.
- **Visitor Center:** Interview staff, put up *wanted* poster
- **Summit Registers:** For subject, possible witnesses
- **Tour Bus or Van Drivers:** Let subject out where? Make announcement on bus
- **Local Medical Facilities:** Interview staff, local record check
- **Local Law Enforcement:** Separate the overdue from the emergency
- **Campgrounds:** Check registers, fee receipts.
- **Weather Records:** Local and regional records

Information about the Incident - Where to Get It

Some categories and specifics to look for when talking to witnesses *(not all necessary for the initial response)*:

What happened? Overdue, cries for help, crime, slipping, stuck, cold, thirsty, fallen, injured, dead, symptoms, walking wounded, equipment/personnel on scene, instructions by/to the subjects, reason for overdue.

Where? Very important *(show maps, photos to witness)*. On the ground, how far up/down, what climb, what pitch, in water, on bank, what trail, where last seen, headed which direction, landmarks, mileage, type of terrain, route taken before accident, afterwards, washed downstream, how long did witness take to get out, car parked, was he/she staying in the area?

When? Last seen, supposed to return, injured, ran out of water, symptoms appeared, fresh tracks or old, did storm hit *(match itinerary to the weather)*

Who? Name, age, sex, weight, address, phone, parents, friends, condition *(mental/physical)*, vehicle, skills, experience, personnel with subject, back country personnel in area, kind and size of shoes *(sole)*, clothing types and equivalent and colors, complete list of equipment.

Why? Family problems, drugs, avalanche, rockfall, illness *(hypothermia)*.

Callout

If the call comes in to the dispatch center, take initial information to determine urgency and make arrangements to meet with the reporting party in person. Make follow-up contact and gather initial investigative information on the Missing Person Report form. Staff then compiles and collates further in-depth information for both planning and searching. In urgent situations a callout of resources needs to take place.

Callout involves a myriad of available resources, not just people required to carry out an effective search. These resources include searchers and aircraft, logistics support such as food service, medical, communications, overhead team members and even technical rescue specialists. Every jurisdiction's SAR Pre-Plan needs to include an organized section on resources that takes into consideration availability, capabilities, specialized skills, strategic and tactical uses and ideally some indication of response time *(see Chapter 7 on the Preplan)*.

The first question: What resources will make this effort successful?

Most jurisdictions just call available resources. Unfortunately, most search coordinators at the local level lack in diversity of resources from which to pick and choose. Thus, making it acceptable to call in specialized resources from outside the jurisdiction or ask for special assistance from regional or national sources. This makes the preplanning function absolutely essential in describing sources of specialized skills and the protocols needed to procure them.

The next question: Is the resource paid or volunteer?

The answer makes a difference on length of use and specific strategies and even tactics. If using a paid resource, access all the right channels for authority to release money to pay for the expenditures incurred ahead of time. Examples include a helicopter from a neighboring jurisdiction or a contract aircraft operating for a land management agency in the area. As technology becomes more and more sophisticated, specialized capabilities for search from the private sector increase in availability. File and document all agreements and memorandums of understanding necessary to use these resources on a search.

Calling volunteers early inspires urgency and motivation in those team members. Even though they come willingly on any call, pay attention to a volunteer's availability and time spent with the least disruption to their jobs and professional lives *(i.e. nights, weekends, days off, etc.)*.

Information provided to resources expected on-scene:

- Mission number or incident designation *(if applicable)*
- When do you want resource to report? Approximate travel time, day, hour
- A brief description of the situation *(who, what, when, where, how)*
- Special skills needed
- Which other units are responding
- Number of persons *(and/or teams)* required Request a call back and confirmation numbers actually responding before departure
- Current and forecast weather in the search area:

- Road conditions *(in area and en route)*
- Flying conditions *(in area and en route)*
- Terrain description
- Elevation range
- Personal equipment needed by searchers
- Group or specialized equipment needed
- Communications procedures; frequencies, and call signs
- Map identification and quadrants or coordinates being used
- Meeting place:
  - Signs
  - Markers
  - Route suggested
  - Rendezvous point en route
- Whom to report to upon arrival at the search area base
- Exactly when to report
  - An indication for length of time needed
  - Callback number
- Stand down procedures *(in case subject is found while responders travel)*:
  - License numbers, vehicle descriptions
  - Check-in periodically while en route
    - Toll free number for responders to call
    - Successful use of public radio
    - Responders own communication system *(cell phone number or radio frequencies)*

Provide resources called out with organized and operationally significant, current information. People appreciate up-to-date information as it reduces difficulties, unpreparedness and misunderstanding. This results in a much more efficient operation.

Seriously consider the use of staggered reporting times to avoid swamping the Base or Command Post with the simultaneous arrival of large numbers of people needing briefings before heading to the field.

Call early! Do not delay! A search with resources on hand beats waiting around for them to arrive. Virtually any resource working in SAR never minds turning around while en route to a potential search.

Volunteers willingly come when called, but out of common courtesy try to call them early and keep them informed. A big hit early signifies a high level of urgency to volunteers and that they have a chance to save someone's life. Importantly, remember that volunteers cost time and money, they just don't charge for their services. Take this into account when calling them to respond. Volunteers form an essential contribution to the search effort, so use them accordingly.

Missing and Lost Person Behavior

Objectives:

- Discuss the importance of Search Manager familiarity with Lost Person Behavior

- Discuss the value of collecting local behavior data for future searches and to add to the ISRID database project

- Integrate behavior data with the particular influences of the geography and history of the search area

- Apply lost person behavior data to the strategy and tactics in search operations

NOTE: The context of this chapter includes facts, information and data from:

Lost Person Behavior - A Search and Rescue Guide on Where to Look - for Land, Air and Water by Robert J. Koester, dbS Productions, 2008.

For the most part, Koester incorporated previous research efforts on lost person behavior conducted by Kelley, Syrotuck, Mitchell, Hill, Cornell, Heth, Perkins, Roberts and Twardy in the International Search and Rescue Incident Database (ISRID).

> *ISRID data serves as a guide (and search planning tool). The data collection and study of Missing & Lost Person Behavior deals with generalities, not absolutes.*

The Subject Profile

Any effective search requires a profile of the sought individual *(both a physical and mental subject profile)*. The profile continually develops physical and mental descriptions focused and refined on the missing person. Ultimately the goal consists of acquiring as much information as possible about that person. The Missing Person Report (*or Lost Person Questionnaire*) forms the foundation for this compilation of data. This type of information aids on any search and on establishing a local data base helping in the future to predict the actions and possible locations of missing or lost people.

A preliminary subject profile contains the following as a minimum:

- **Physical and mental description**
- **Names,** nick names or aliases
- **Physical resources** carried by the subject
- **Known activity** at the time of the loss
- **Point last seen or last known position** *(PLS/LKP)*
- **Personality traits** - aggressive, despondent, confident, low self esteem, happy-go-lucky, stable, etc.
- **Interests and activities,** i.e. hobbies, alternate vocation, outdoor pursuits, etc.
- **Experience** - novice versus seasoned veteran etc.
- **Subject lost** before?
- **Predetermined** emergency **strategies** or options discussed with other party members - *e.g. bad weather routes or options, estimated time and location of destination, alternative goals, turn-back policy, etc.*
- **Personal tragedies, family crisis, work environment or relationship problems** - possible influences to behavior
- **Known friends, family and associates** for contact and assistance in compiling the subject profile

Use the Missing Person Report Form for guidance on gathering subject profile info about the missing or lost person.

Missing and Lost Person Behavior Data

Early studies by Dennis Kelley and Bill Syrotuck concerning lost person behavior primarily involved rural/wilderness incidents based on emphasizing behavior of subjects truly *lost* in the traditional sense within those environments. Later studies expanded the subject category types and also addressed people missing for other reasons. Initially Robert Koester's research into Dementia (*Alzheimer's type*) patients in Virginia, provided the springboard into data specifically focused on the urban environment. While pure urban data remains in short supply, Koester's latest ISRID database publication contains the most comprehensive of those works.

Behavior studies related to SAR, to date, really give us two important things:

Number 1: Distances traveled by category of subject. Not exact distances, but generalities reducing the potential area searched for planning purposes.

Number 2: Statistics providing more and less likely places to look.

The purpose of studying lost person behavior facilitates prediction of a missing person's location with some reasonable degree of accuracy. Not an exact science, it therefore only deals with generalities. Not all missing people fall into any of the categories represented in the collected data, requiring investigation to uncover factors and combine them from several different categories.

General Guidelines

NASAR's earlier publication *Managing the Lost Person Incident*, contains a list of general traits initially compiled by Ken Hill. Though not absolutes, they provide some generalized possibilities for two broad based categories - Children and Adults. Comparative example of general traits for children compared to adults:

Lost Children

- Posses a relatively poor *mental maps* of their environment
- Usually search for familiar places rather than for routes
- Rarely judge direction or distance well
- Often become lost when taking a *short cut*
- Often try *trail running* or *direction sampling*
- May climb a tree to improve their view
- Sometimes move randomly
- Show signs of extreme panic

Lost Adults

- Usually search for paths and routes not places
- Bushwhack *(go cross country)* when **positive** they know the right direction
- Commonly stay on a trail if not absolutely certain of the correct direction
- Sometimes climb a hill to improve their view
- Rarely move around randomly
- Seldom attempt to travel in an arbitrary straight line
- Rarely reverse direction on a trail unless absolutely convinced they went the wrong way
- They attempt to apply *woods wisdom*, such as traveling downstream
- May *regress* to less effective methods when panicky
- Rarely find their own way out of the woods
- Seldom answer searchers calling their name

General reactions to becoming lost include:

- Astonishment and disbelief
- Initial emotions run anywhere between fearfulness and dread of embarrassment to peers
- Initially subjects try to *hurry up* and find a familiar place, soon replaced by some type of strategy to resolve the problem *(See Common Lost Person Strategies next)*.

Common Lost Person Strategies

By Kenneth Hill, Ph.D. Professor of Psychology, St. Mary's University, Nova Scotia.

- **Random Traveling:** Random movement, path or least resistance looking for something familiar

- **Route Traveling:** Trying to find familiar ground by following a trail, path or other travel aid
- **Direction Traveling:** Moving in one direction across everything in pursuit of conviction that safety lies in that direction
- **Route Sampling:** Using a trail intersection or other junction as a base and trying various routes to look for something familiar
- **Direction Sampling:** No trails or routes involved but use a wagon wheel configuration to move out from a set location and then back
- **View Enhancement:** Climbing a hill, tree or other feature to get a view of the area *(also consider cell phone reception)*
- **Backtracking:** This involves trying to retrace steps or routes to find a known location
- **Employing Folk Wisdom:** Using advice like following a stream out to civilization
- **Staying Put:** Unusual but used by more experienced or older outdoor users and children trained in *Hug a Tree* or similar programs
- **Doing Nothing**
- **Contouring:** Analysis by Koester noticed an additional strategy in lost person behavior, the subject chooses to maintain the same elevation while traversing the terrain

Notable Behaviors of Lost People Include:

Failure to Make a Shelter or a Fire

The ability to build or seek shelter and get a fire started dramatically changes the survival equation. Does the subject have the knowledge, skills, and/or resources to do these things? Campsites or fire circles provide clues as the search progresses. Fires also signal distress extremely well, while shelters in general, provide good camouflage. As noted in Syrotuck's *Analysis of Lost Person Behavior*, remarkably few individuals take the time or effort to build a shelter or fire to protect themselves when lost. Of those that do, they commonly forget the difficulty of seeing someone in a natural material shelter and even more surprising, very seldom with a realization of fire as a good signal!

Weather & Visibility

Weather and visibility play an important role in determining the potential activities of lost subjects. Impending bad weather obviously threatens life, but perhaps a more immediate concern to the Search Manager centers on how it forces the subject to stop and seek shelter, resulting in both positive and negative effects. An immobile subject, increases the chance for confinement but as stated above makes an unconscious victim difficult to spot. Visibility plays a similar role; darkness or extremely foggy conditions often immobilize the subject. However, subject movement under these conditions generally becomes random wandering, which further complicates the search effort. Additionally, attractions such as roads or lights at night also lose their effectiveness in foggy conditions.

Discarding Equipment

While a significant number of lost persons begin poorly equipped, many leave or discard equipment during the process of their ordeal. The rifle, the knapsack, the walking stick, or even gloves and other clothing articles tend to get laid down or dropped while traveling. Attribute some of this to exhaustion, just plain forgetfulness, or in some cases a result of later stages of hyperthermia or hypothermia.

Disrobing

Many shed all or a significant portion of their clothing. Persons often become quite irrational in behavior and appear to lack a sense of feeling (*hot or cold*) in the advanced stages of both cold and heat exposure.

Going it Alone

Lost subjects actually feel surprised to know that people come out and look for them. Cases exist where individuals ignored search aircraft because the concept that someone came out to search for them never entered their minds.

Detectability

Lost people who endured a cold, wet miserable night usually find a sunny, warm spot to sleep during the warmest part of midday. With continued cold, wet or windy weather, individuals tend to find a location that protects them such as under a log, under leaves or boughs or in next to the protected trunk of a tree.

Travel Aids

Open ridges, old roads, game trails, paths, clear-cuts, and drainages all constitute travel aids. Essentially the paths of least resistance for the lost person. Interestingly, not all people choose to use these travel aids. Where noted, those that used them are identified in the data.

Generalized factors to Consider

Gender Differences:

Very few significant gender differences manifest in behavior. Survival rates tend to favor women who travel just as far as their male counterparts in the respective category.

Multiple Subject Searches:

According to Koester, few behavioral differences show up in the data between single subject searches and multiple subject searches, probably because of the lack of data specifically on multiple subject searches. However, children over five usually respond with more maturity when accompanied by another child. Children under five frequently separate during their ordeal while older children and youths *(teens)* seem motivated to stay together. In the case of multiple subject searches, consideration as to whom, if anyone, exacts the greatest influence on the decision making process. Assess this factor of interactive personalities where two or more persons comprise the focus of the search.

> **NOTE:** With all reports of missing children, carry out a thorough investigation with the realization that parents tend to hold back some of the most important facts. Children often worry about the consequences if they come home late. Quite possibly when a child acted naughty, or felt threatened in the past with a parent sending them away or punishing them in another way. These factors probably cause a child to hide initially, but as time progresses or darkness falls, the fears of the unknown overcome their worries of the consequences of going back home. This presents another significant reason for searching at night.

Factors specific to lost person behavior that tend to affect search strategy:

General State of Health: Recent illness, poor physical condition, chronic disease, poor nutrition or lack of sleep, impair a subject's ability to cope with unusual situations, especially physical stress. In a group scenario this might even result in a change of leadership. Therefore making it imperative to establish a subject profile for each member of a group since any of them potentially serves as the group leader (*or decision maker*).

Past Experiences: Previous experiences with challenging situations, strange environments or isolation improves anyone's ability to deal with the problems brought about by injury, disorientation, being lost or coping with the environment.

Physiological Effects of the Environment: Heat, cold, altitude, wind and precipitation likely produce adverse effects on the body and brain causing reduction in problem-solving capability.

Mental Impact on the Lost Person

- Those who dwell in population centers or adjacent areas usually rely upon technology and modern conveniences for the necessities of life
- Unpredictable usually describes how a person reacts under stress when isolated and alone
- The mental impact of lost or disoriented individuals varies, but generally a shock-like behavior and disbelief overcomes them
- When subjects feel fearful, the fear potentially overrides normal behavior and directly impacts the outcome of the situation
- Thoughts fluctuate from a sense of abandonment to a fear about the reaction of others when the situation ends
- A common outcome of high anxiety incidents manifests as a loss of short term memory, a lack of ability to concentrate, an inability to solve

complex problems or pick up environmental hazard cues normally recognized
- After a period of time, varying with each individual, all subjects seem to control their emotions

All of the above factors potentially lead to poor judgment and irrational behavior

Implications for Preventive Search and Rescue (PSAR)

The study of lost person behavior also shows that lack of knowledge and practical skills in the outdoors creates anxiety and fear leading to irrational behavior. Knowledge about the characteristics of lost or disoriented people in the environment, provides educational opportunities for SAR responders and teams alike. Design these initiatives to offer guidance in specific outdoor situations or even prevent incidents from occurring in the first place. Fear diminishes when a person knows or understands about a particular skill or subject area.

A good example: The long advocated PSAR program called *Hug a Tree* for kids by the National Association for Search and Rescue. Research and common sense shows that with the right educational programs, children learn to stay in one place and protect themselves from the cold. Snowmobile, hiking, and mountaineering clubs along with outdoor groups of all kinds regularly give preventive search and rescue education. Many SAR responders and teams also provide educational opportunities to high-risk groups in their jurisdictions as a preventive measure.

The Most Successful SAR Mission:
One That Never Needed to Happen!

Missing Children - Additional Information

(Yvonne Antoft, Stockholm, Sweden)

The left and right side of a child's brain develop separately and completion of the bridge between the two sides occurs at about 12 years of age. Consider this developmental process and the relevant consequences of it when developing both strategy and tactics.

Children (1 to 3 years)

The left side of the brain, which deals with logic and reasoning, develops slower than the right, which establishes feelings, emotion and imagination.

The Child fails to understand the concept of being lost. From their perspective, the child is not lost; it is Mommy or Daddy who is lost. As a consequence of this logic, if Police or other searchers call out the child's name he or she tends not to respond and in some cases they even hide. A child's bone flexibility also allows them to hide in the most unlikely small spaces. Younger children often sleep at sometime during the day; the investigation process needs to make an attempt at establishing the child's normal sleep pattern and any recent variations caused by illness, toothache etc. A sleeping child most likely never responds to parents and if they crawled into a small space to sleep, they go undetected without a very thorough search.

Children (4 to 6 years)

At 4 to 6 years of age, the left side of the brain begins to develop and the child potentially grows aware of being lost. However, the side or the brain that deals with feelings and imagination dominates. When the child is aware of being lost it sometimes causes the reasoning side to collapse, leading the child to attempt to solve their problems with fantasies. A young boy in the United Kingdom related that he spent his time, while lost, fighting dinosaurs. Seeing them, he frightened them off with his stick. Consequently, while in this fantasy world, the child possibly hides from his searchers believing them to be monsters, or some similar fantasy threat to avoid. Consider even the use of a helicopter in a search for a child a potential negative influence. Children get used to seeing helicopters flying high in the sky and accept them in that position. However, the noise and down draft from one flying near the ground in search mode possibly conjures up the most horrendous images to a small child in their fantasy world, perhaps driving the child to hide even more thoroughly.

Establish the current interests of a missing child. If lost or afraid, these children tend to retreat into his or her fantasy world. A police dog becomes a dinosaur, the uniformed police officer, *Darth-Vader*, or a helicopter becomes a dragon from *Harry Potter*. The very resource you deployed potentially creates a negative reaction from the child and ultimately the success of the search.

In this age group *(sometimes earlier)*, parents teach their children to recite telephone numbers and/or addresses by heart, allowing the child a little more freedom of travel *(example: walking from home to a nearby playground)*. If the child becomes lost and fearful, the logic side of the brain collapses, and the youngster goes entirely into fantasy mode and loses the ability to remember names, addresses, numbers, etc.

Place Preferences of Children

A research paper written in 1979, by R. Hart, first presented a systematic description of children's paths, shortcuts, ritual routes, and activity centers. Through interviews and observations Hart identified four general categories of place preferences of children.

Land uses - places valued for play attributes:

- Playgrounds
- Rivers and lakes
- Forts & houses
- Woods, fields & hills with views
- Lawns *(large)*
- Brooks or frog ponds
- Climbing trees
- Places for:
  - Sliding
  - Swinging & jumping
  - Hiding
  - Sand piles & dirt play

Social places - where an individual lives, works or where social events occur:

- Friends houses
- Where relatives or parent lives or works
- Public recreation facilities
- Locations for social events
- Pools
- Gymnasiums
- Schools
- Ball fields
- Fairs or festivals

Commercial - places to obtain or purchase favorite things:

- Sweets or candies
- Ice cream
- Favorite foods
- Toys and/or Pets
- Variety stores
- Balloons
- Models
- Dolls
- Games, etc.

Aesthetic - places valued because of their atmosphere, preferred because of their beauty or effect on the child:

- Quiet
- Isolated
- Near water
- A good view or perspective of people
- Previous good time with someone

The Difference -- Lost or Not?

Virtually all people possess the ability to maintain a cognitive map in their minds regarding their location in relation to familiar places and the routes to and from specific locations. To find a route, most everyone uses landmarks, estimation of both distance and time, and a sense of direction tied back to known landmarks *(See figure 14-1 on the next page)*.

Example: Five minutes after leaving the city center on Benton Street, a church sits off to the right. To get home, take an immediate right up the hill on West Park Street to the crest of the hill and then take the first left. The house sits to right four houses down.

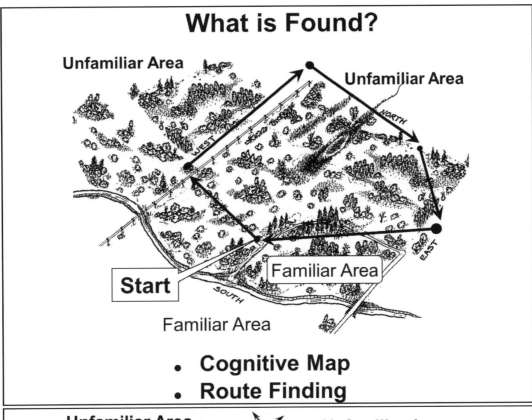
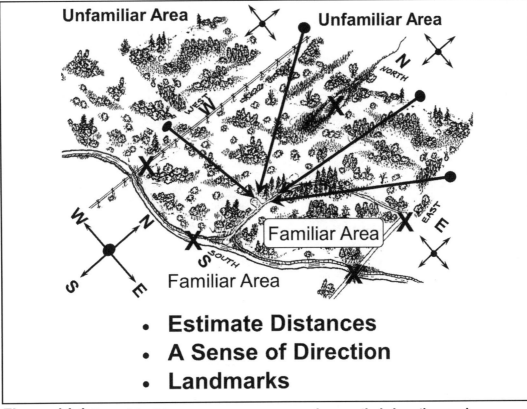

Figure 14-1 Found in this case means a person knows their location and orientation, and knows which way to get to a specific destination. It requires five factors: Ability to maintain a cognitive map to find a route, an ability to estimate distance, a sense of direction and the ability to establish and recognize landmarks.

A person suffering from dementia (*Alzheimer's type*), with virtually no recent or short-term memory, lacks the ability to judge time and thus distance, possibly losing all visual-spatial cognitive skills. They lack the ability to judge distance, create a cognitive map, and judge the nature of things such as thick vegetation, water or other obstacles. In other words, they lack the capabilities that normal people use for maintaining a cognitive map in their minds. Essentially they stay lost all the time. Couple this with the fact that many remain oriented to environments and landmarks *as they existed in the past*. The past orientation stems from their minds using data about the information on the environment stored in long-term memory instead of short-term. To compensate for this short-term loss in the home or in a care facility, care givers sometimes label commonly used objects, entrances, clothing and other daily use items.

Subjects falling into one or more of the categories listed as dementia, intellectually disabled or mentally ill often exhibit diminished capability in the cognitive map skills area. Intellectually disabled *(mentally handicapped)* people learn some degree of cognitive map skills through repetitive behavior over longer periods of time depending on their mental age. However, if their routine changes, most lack the skills to immediately rebuild another map about locations, distances or landmarks. They will be *lost*.

In the case of very young children, they simply may not have developed these cognitive skills yet. Research supports the conclusion that most children under the age of eight or nine find constructing useful cognitive maps difficult. Although at this age children remember images of the surrounding terrain, they bear little resemblance to the real world.

Past emphasis in search operations appropriately focused on the lost person.

However, remember: All lost persons are also missing, but not all missing persons are lost.

Eco Regions as the Basis for Combining National & International Data

For decades, search managers and SAR responders complained about using non-local or international data that neglected to reflect local conditions concerning lost or missing persons in a set geographic region. In many cases a very small amount of data sat within specific regions and included significant differences in terrain, visibility, ease of travel, etc. In 2004, Robert Koester established an innovative way to categorize and group behavior data into fairly consistent zones or regions throughout the world. He suggested using the well defined concept of Eco regions to group behavior data.

In response to increased involvement by land management agencies for long range planning in ecosystem management, Robert G. Bailey developed the Eco region system of mapping for the U.S. Forest Service during the 1970's. Focusing on North America initially, and now dividing the world into a hierarchy of domains, divisions, and provinces based on climate, vegetation and topography, Eco regions represent land areas with internally similar ecological characteristics.

For example, North America breaks down into four domains representing climatic zones with altitudinal variations: the Polar, the Humid Temperate, the Dry, and the Humid Tropical Domains *(Figure 14-2 on the next page)*. As a further example, the Humid Temperate Domain then breaks down into six Divisions which in turn break down into specific Provinces addressing altitudinal similarities that affect land forms, climate, vegetation, soils and animals.

Koester postulated that these factors dramatically influence the makeup and density of ground cover, the visibility and incentives or disincentives for people traveling across the ground and the kinds of environmental conditions that people confront during any kind of outdoor ordeal. Within any specific defined region, similar conditions facilitate

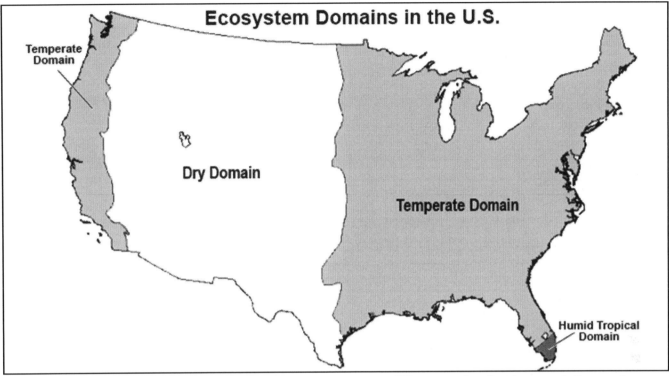

Figure 14-2 Eco Regions in the U.S. These domains key to differences in climate, vegetation and topography. The temperate domain receives enough rainfall to generate forests and four seasons. The dry domain experiences a greater loss of water from evaporation than it gains from precipitation. Since vegetation has a major impact on lost person behavior, domains provide a very good basis for separation of data on behavior.

the combining of international or national data concerning lost or missing people based on similar Eco regions. The example on the next page shows some preliminary data differences in two categories of missing persons, with comparisons in Temperate and Dry Eco regions.

Subject Categories of Lost/Missing Persons

In the *ISRID* Database, Koester identifies forty-one different categories of lost persons by varying characteristics, age groups, activities, etc. Although each of the groups exhibit specific traits, exceptions exist. Thorough search operations concentrate on the most likely. Keep in mind that different researchers use different classifications in their research. Koester very clearly classified both previously identified groupings and new categories not fitting the mold from the previous databases. Choosing the subject category for each type of incident depends on interpolation, judgment and available information.

ISRID Categories of Missing/Lost Persons:

- Abduction
- Aircraft
- Angler
- ATV
- Autistic
- Camper
- Caver
- Children (*in 4 groups*)
  - Children 1-3
  - Children 4-6
  - Children 7-12
- Adolescent Youth 13-15
- Climber
- Dementia
- Despondent
- Gatherer
- Car Campers
- Hiker
- Horseback Rider
- Hunter
- Intellectually Disabled

- Mental Illness
- Mountain Biker
- Other *(Base Jumper, Extreme Sports, Motorcycle)*
- Runner
- Skier- Alpine
- Skier- Nordic
- Snowboarder
- Snowmobiler
- Snowshoer
- Substance Abuse
- Urban Entrapment
- Vehicle Related *(Vehicle, 4wd, Abandoned)*
- Water Related *(Powered Boats, Non-powered boats, Person in the Water)*
- Worker

Figure 14-3 Ecoregions in Europe showing area classification worldwide. Although smaller distinctions exist in the classification scheme, ISRID only distinguishes between the dry and temperate domains

(ISRID Data - 2008) Hunters & Hikers -Mtn. *(1,282 cases)*				
	Temperate Mtn.		Dry Mtn.	
	Hiker	Hunter	Hiker	Hunter
Count	568	355	221	138
25%	0.7 mi	0.6 mi	1.0 mi	1.3 mi
Median	1.9 mi	1.3 mi	2.0 mi	3.0 mi
75%	3.6 mi	3.0 mi	4.0 mi	5.0 mi
95%	11.3mi	10.7mi	11.9mi	13.8mi

Figure 14-4 The ISRID Data above shows the difference in recorded find distance for the hunter and hiker categories when comparing temperate and dry domains

How to determine Subject Category

From a response perspective, determine the general categories of missing persons as soon as possible Similar to an urgency assessment about subject-type and priority response, this sets the stage for general strategy planning and call-out protocols. The general categories follow:

General

- **Voluntarily Missing:** People intending to be missing or specifically start out that way. These include runaway children, adults, suicide potentials, fugitives from justice or even those people that just don't want others to find them. These individuals often change their mind when things change from the way they intended.

- **Not Lost:** Overdue, temporarily detained, someplace else, altered plans, unexpected delays, or circumstances beyond the control of the missing person. Generally these people fall in the category of innocent victim from miscommunication or misunderstanding between the reporting party and the person overdue, or something just happened to interrupt plans or activities.

- **Lost:** Someone disoriented and confused about their surroundings and unable to solve their location predicament through normal reasoning processes. For one reason or another, establishing or maintaining a cognitive map, distance or time relationships or a correct sense of direction escapes them. Dementia patients, mentally retarded, or young children sometimes find themselves lost in the urban environment. Confusion about directions because of terrain, lack of signs, distraction from other influences like weather, or focus on specific activities like mushroom picking or hunting, contributes to disorientation in a wilderness environment.

- **At Risk:** Missing persons deemed *At Risk* pose an immediate urgency factor requiring quick and definitive action by virtue of their characteristics. The category includes the elderly unable to take care of themselves, children of a younger age *(less than 12)*, persons with dementia, mental impairments, or special medical conditions such as diabetes, or even those individuals caught in severe environmental conditions.

Specific Subject Category Determination

Three basic queries determined subject category hierarchy in the ISRID Database.

1. **Mental status of the subject**: Mental status trumps all other subject characteristics (*Autistic, Dementia, Despondent, Substance Abuse, etc.*).
2. **Subject's age *(if age is 15 or younger)*:** Category groups more refined than Syrotuck's initial work. (1-3), (4-6), (7-9), etc.
3. **Subject's primary activity:** (*Gatherer, Hunter, Angler, Runner, etc.*)

Lost or missing persons seldom fit into nice neat categories. As a result, Koester developed an algorithm to refine the process of category determination. See definition below:

Definition: Algorithm

Any special method of solving a certain kind of problem.

In mathematics and computer science, an algorithm is an effective method expressed as a finite list of well-defined step-by-step instructions for calculating a solution *(In the case of Lost Person Behavior, determining a category of subject)*.

Specific Category of Subject Determination For ISRID

Algorithm by Robert J. Koester for determining category of subject in the ISRID database:

Subject Category Algorithm

- Do any of the following external forces apply?
  - Abduction
  - Aircraft incident
  - Urban entrapment
  - Water
  - NO *(go to the next level)*

- Is the subject involved in an activity using wheels?
  - ATV *(Quad)*
  - Mountain Bike
  - Motorcycle
  - Vehicle - (if abandoned then apply cognitive rule)
  - NO *(go to the next level)*

- Does the subject have any cognitive disorders?
  - Autism
  - Dementia *(Alzheimer's)*
  - Despondent
  - Intellectual disability (mental retardation)
  - Mental illness
  - NO *(go to the next level)*

- Is the subject a child? (If a group use age of oldest child)
  - Age 1-3
  - Age 4-6
  - Age 7-9
  - Age 10-12
  - Age 13-15
  - NO *(go to the next level)*

- Does the subject have special equipment to move in the snow?
  - Skier
  - Snowboarder
  - Snowmobiler
  - Snowshoer
  - NO *(go to the next level)*

- Choose the activity that best matches the subject.
  - Angler
  - Car camper
  - Caver
  - Climber
  - Gatherer
  - Hiker *(default category for those on foot)*
  - Hunter
  - BASE Jumper
  - Extreme Sports

- Runner
- Substance Abuse
- Worker
- ...etc.

What happens when the categories fail to match up with the missing person?

Some missing/overdue or lost people fail to fall into any of the categories represented in the collected data. Never fall into the trap of thinking every lost subject falls into some nice neat category with all the appropriate distances and characteristics recorded. Continue to investigate and try to uncover factors to use from several categories. Combine several different scenarios or more of the category descriptions and the existing data to come up with the best fit.

Examples with No Match

As an example: consider looking for someone who went into the forest or woods to pray, to quietly think and commune with God. The list of categories fail to meet this description but the subject exist. Perhaps a primary match falls under the category **gatherer** and a secondary match might be either **hiker** or some factors under **despondent** *(i.e. scenic or significant locations, viewpoint of beautiful scene, pastoral setting, etc.)*. In other words, not lost.

Another example: a soldier or someone in the military undergoing field training. For instance, aircrew members undergoing SERE (*Survival, Evasion, Resistance, Escape*) training at the Air Force Survival School. For a primary match of this missing person combine **worker** and **hiker** with a secondary match of **extreme sport**. Much of this depends on circumstance, personality, weather and other unique conditions that exist.

Creating New Categories

Creating new categories of lost or missing people, while not impossible, consists of a long and arduous process involving a lot of research, data compilation, statistical analysis and most of all perceptive interpretation of raw data like Koester accomplished. The possibility of new categories exist but, insufficient data to identify those specifically, stands in the way at this time. Some categories contain significant numbers of cases, but involved either rescues or no distances recorded. The study of lost and missing persons continues with additional categories emerging. Turning this raw data into easily understood simple statements defines the whole study of Lost Person Behavior, ISRID and 40 years of statistical analysis

Using the LPB Book

Lost Person Behavior: A Search and Rescue Guide on Where to Look - Land, Air and Water, Robert J. Koester, 2008.

Koester's book begins with a history of lost person behavior research and identifies both key terms and personalities that marked the progress of the collection and study of lost/missing persons. The publication emphasizes the role and importance of statistics, while at the same time describing the attributes and limitations of the ISRID database. In addition to the behavior data the author clearly lays out the recent history of lost person behavior. Koester thoroughly explains the use of Eco regions as a mechanism to combine both regional and international domain data from around the world. A synopsis of ISRID findings examines the data in several key ways relating to population density, group behavior, special groups and scenarios. The examination of these factors clearly provides insight into the utility of this data during search operations.

In the chapter on Lost Person Strategies, Ken Hill, Ph.D., Professor of Psychology at St. Mary's University in Nova Scotia outlines different strategies for getting *unlost*. Basing this information on structured interviews with rescued lost persons soon after their recovery. In Koester's LPB book, Hill elaborates on these strategies with good clear examples. Now with some initial investigative efforts, search planners use some substantive behavioral information upon which to apply their field strategies and tactics.

Myths and Legends

Another important piece in the lost and missing person behavior puzzle revolves around myths and legends about the activity of individuals when lost. For instance, what influences the direction a person might go if either right or left handed? Do lost subjects travel at night? By using the database and what statistics tell us, answering and examining these questions and many more just got easier.

As a final entry into the all important Chapter 8 *(which details all the subject categories and the real meat of the database)*, Koester gives an exemplary description of what the tables and charts mean in Chapter 7 with the actual tables and profiles themselves in Chapter 8. If a search planner or IC thoroughly reads the first seven chapters in Koester's publication, the solid gold value of the data included in Chapter 8 emerges very quickly.

Using ISRID and the LPB Book During Search Operations

Each section within *LPB* Chapter 8 *(Subject Categories)* deals with a separate and specific Category for a total of 41 different subject types in alphabetical order. At the beginning of every Subject Category, a provided profile contains background on how to define the category, overall traits and helpful descriptive information. Koester created these subject profiles from search mission statistics, incident comments and researched background. Interestingly, many of the profiles remain consistent with Syrotuck's original behavioral descriptions.

The Missing Person Call Comes In: How do we use ISRID and the Manual?

Let's assume that a call comes in for a potential missing person suffering from Dementia *(Alzheimer's)*. How do searchers put the database and Koester's LPB publication to work from the 1,051 documented cases related to Dementia?

> Chapter 8 - Dementia (*Alzheimer's*) - *Lost Person Behavior,* Robert J. Koester, 2008. Copyrighted material **used with permission** and under license from dbS Productions LLC.

Profile Information for Dementia (Alzheimer's)(1,051 cases):

Dementia includes Alzheimer's disease and several other related disorders *(vascular dementia, Parkinson's disease, and dementia with Lewy bodies among others)*. From a search and rescue perspective no appreciable difference between the different dementias emerge. Alzheimer's disease, the most common form of the irreversible dementia, often represents all dementia. Regardless of activity, search subjects with dementia get placed into this category.

Dementia results in a wide range of changes in behavior and cognitive *(thinking)* skills. It ranges from mild, with the person still able to perform all activities of daily living, to severe. With severe dementia, the subject tends to wander more and sometimes experiences symptoms such as hallucinations and psychosis. Dementia subjects lose memory, reason, judgment, and language to such an extent that it interferes with daily living. Some of the earliest symptoms involve problems with short-term memory. The following terms describe disturbances of one or more cognitive area:

- Aphasia *(problems with language, e.g., finding the right word)*
- Apraxia *(cannot move body correctly)*
- Agnosia *(cannot recognize common objects, especially faces)*
- Decreased executive functions *(planning, organizing, abstracting)*

Dementia often results in severe disturbances affecting how a person perceives and interprets events, sights, and sounds around him.

Furthermore, the visual field *(peripheral vision)* narrows, creating *tunnel vision*. A reduction in peripheral vision results in poor navigators using only what the individual sees in front of them versus excellent navigators who combine active scanning for remembered landmarks.

This accounts for dementia wanderers' trademark behavior of essentially moving straight ahead: *They go until they get stuck.* Direction of travel predicts a dementia subject's final location better than in most other subject categories.

Every subject differs, and determining the severity of the individual's dementia provides additional important insight. Associate mild to moderate severity with more goal-directed wandering. Initially, the subject knows in their mind where they want to go, the distances traveled possibly greater. The subject often uses public transportation. In a short conversation with the subject nothing detectable stands out. However, inappropriate dress, unsafe or inappropriate behavior, asking for assistance, or an inappropriate response generates recognition. Repetitive questions, phrases or words raises suspicion. Subjects with severe dementia tend to show random *(i.e., no discernible goal)* wandering, travel shorter distances, and potentially profound sensory disturbances. Both mild and severe dementia exhibit exit-seeking behavior. This demeanor manifests when in a new location or taken out of a familiar environment.

Hallmark behaviors:

- Going until they get stuck
- Appear to lack the ability to turn around and tend to ping-pong off some barriers
- Direction of travel predicts ultimate location. Look for sign and attempt to determine exit door
- Oriented to the past. The more severe the dementia, the further in the past they exist

Figure out what time period in the past the subject currently *lives* in order to determine possible destinations (*e.g. a former residence, a work place*). Investigative questions assist to better understand the subject's past (*which, for them, may be the present*).

The person possibly attempts to travel to a former residence, favorite place or what appears to be former place, or workplace. In an urban environment, the subjects typically end up in structures or walking along roads. In both urban and wilderness environments, the subject tends to cross or depart from a road most of the time *(66%)*. If the subject leaves the road or travel feature, he rarely travels far, often going unnoticed unless dressed unusually. Track offset statistics for dementia provide the shortest of all subject categories. In the wilderness, the subject typically walks or gets stuck in brush/briars or drainages. Searchers typically find them in structures if any exist in the area. Water features attract subjects who walk into the water *(perhaps without even realizing it is water)*. Generally mobile for only a short period of time, in temperate domains half of the subjects move about for less than an hour.

In dry domains, subjects remain mobile longer, not leaving many verifiable clues. They seldom cry out for help or respond to shouts - only 1% of subjects respond. *Passive-evasive describes* some dementia subjects. These subjects fail to perceive themselves as lost, therefore they rarely attempt to signal or even respond to shouts. *If searchers fail to find the Dementia subject within the first 24 hours 25% of the incidents end in a fatality.* Fatality rates increase in very hot and cold rainy climates.

Currently, many states develop highly effective *Senior* or *Silver* alerts similar to AMBER alerts, efficient in alerting the general public.

Upon locating the subject, approach from the front, make eye-contact and use nonverbal body language every time. After assessing safety, slowly move to the subject's side. Speak calmly and in simple, concrete terms. Break down commands, questions or directions into simple, easy-to-follow components. If appropriate touching the subject helps. Arguing with a dementia subject proves pointless and even leads to catastrophic reactions. Instead, redirect the person with a new line of reasoning. Telling the person that a favorite person or thing awaits him back at base sufficiently works. Keep in mind the possibility of other impairments associated with age, such as decreased vision, hearing, and walking ability.

To reiterate the importance of category profile information:

In virtually all cases the profile information at the start of each category of subject section contains important clues, background defining the category, plus significant traits, and helpful descriptive information. In the category profile described above for Dementia, the shaded areas in the book denote the particularly significant data. This kind of pre-read and notation designation proves helpful for all search planners and ICs on virtually all of the categories listed in Koester's manual. Timely rapid response and the appropriate preparation pays big and rapid dividends on real search incidents.

Initial Actions

Virtually without exception, every search incident begins with inadequate facts and information. As an initial first step, gather some required data about the incident and most importantly, about the suspected missing or lost person. Investigation and interviewing clearly plays an important role in any incident.

Standard protocol for search management long advocated the gathering of both planning data and searching data from a wide array of sources. For planning purposes, determine where to begin looking *(Initial Planning Point)*, subject category, mental condition, destination and/or probable route(s), etc. For searching purposes, get a name, a description with clothing and possessions as well as the activity or pursuit at the time of the loss. Gather all of this type of information as a precursor for Reflex Tasking described below.

Reflex Tasking

Reflex Tasking depends on a subject category and remains the same on every search for a specific category of subject. As the term implies, very little planning or thought process occurs before assigning and carrying out these tasks, yet they rest on firm statistical data to justify their use. This never requires the first person on-scene to carry out the tasks but creates standard protocols for tasks to help start the process and assign resources appropriately as they arrive. Using Reflex Tasking as mentioned above, also means coordinating and executing a search in a way that worked well in the past.

The process gives the IC and any other potential overhead staff an opportunity to get set up and organized, develop the appropriate map work and collate information. It also ensures initial rapid deployment of resources on-scene to *likely spots*. With only limited information available, initial action tactics prove their worth repeatedly. As the example mentioned in the dementia *(Alzheimer's)* profile, some documented characteristics in the database provide solid clues about where to look. One of the most visible attributes of Reflex Tasking, shows the resources immediately *working on something* in the field. This comforts the family, and satisfies the media, peers or companions at the scene. Reflex Tasking shows immediate purpose and solidly gives the impression of someone running the incident based on facts. People get an overall impression that someone knows how to initially react and perform during the first critical stages of a search.

Initial Planning Point *(IPP)*, **Point Last Seen** *(PLS)*, **Last Known Position** *(LKP)*

Initial Planning Point *(IPP)* represents the base datum point for the search *(not the physical operations base!)*. Plot the distances from the IPP when comparing the search subject category with previous missing person behavior data. The place last seen *(PLS)* or the last known position *(LKP)* both represent possible IPPs. Based on the best information available at the time, locate it at some separate point if necessary. An example of this follows: A person missing from home. The information received points out that the individual went backpacking alone. The person stated he wanted to hike along either Route A or Route B. A distance of 10 miles or 16 kilometers measures between each departure point. In this case, we contemplate two scenarios and both route departure points represent an IPP, one for each scenario until further investigation eliminates one of them.

Point Last Seen *(PLS)* describes a point where a witness actually saw the subject. The PLS lends credibility and reliability to the Initial Planning Point for data comparison and thus helps define the search area. Sometimes the PLS changes as a search progresses, such as when an eyewitness reports seeing the person at another location. However, if the witness saw the subject driving away from his home in Eastern Washington State, on his way to hike 200 miles away, in Mount Rainier National Park, the PLS provides very little relevant information.

During the early years of Syrotuck's data collection and collation of lost subject behavior, he only used one point designation for all the measurements. He designated that point the PLS. In the absence of other terms Syrotuck's use of PLS led others to use the term PLS even when it failed to describe a location where anyone actually observed the missing person. At the time, the search community lacked additional terms for land search planning.

Last Known Position *(LKP)* describes the last location of the missing subject substantiated by clues or evidence. If subsequent clues or evidence point out another location, then that becomes the LKP. The LKP changes with the discovery of more clues, direction of travel and physical evidence. The weight and strength of evidence governs the reliability of the LKP and often illuminates direction of travel after the discovery of multiple LKPs. LKP indications rarely establish the exact time and date, they only show the missing person's location at one time in the past.

The Relevance of the Last Known Position *(LKP)*. The last known position helps to establish the search area and consists of any of the following:

- **The Point Last Seen** *(PLS)*: A point that some other person last physically saw the lost subject.
- **A departure point**: The assumed departure location *(corroborated by evidence)* to some *(usually predetermined)* destination. Examples:
  - A trailhead
  - A campsite
  - The top of a ski lift
- **A clue**: The location of a discovered clue linked to the subject gives direction of travel, intent or other important information.

Due to investigation and the discovery of clues, always expect the LKP to change during a search! Only the first in a series of Last Known Positions usually fit as the Initial Planning Point, because the LKP changes when clues surface during the search. With each new LKP, a chronology of events begins to unfold in the mystery of what happened *(See Page 394 in the Chapter on Clue Orientation for more on LKP timing)*. In fact, sometimes the search area shrinks as the search effort closes in on the subject.

Sometimes the Point Last Seen, the Initial Planning Point and the Last Known Position consist of the same location and sometimes each point ends up in an entirely separate area.

As the investigation and preliminary search continues, new PLSs and LKPs emerge, and often necessitate the introduction of new planning points. Keep track of these new points chronologically starting with the IPP as reference point #1.

Keep in mind the possibility of the Initial Planning Point, Point Last Seen, and the Last Known Position to all end up at the same geographic location initially, or equally all may locate separately. Usually, the first LKP or PLS discovered remains the IPP, but not always. Remember that clues turn up in a different order than the subject laid them down. Stay as accurate as possible when identifying and using planning reference points, particularly the IPP.

REMEMBER, plot the IPP, the PLS and all of the LKPs on a map with time and date indicating when searchers established each point. This helps to create the best picture of the events leading up to the incident.

To review the characteristics established in Chapter 12 for the IPP *(See page 187)*. The **IPP** stands outside of, and away from, the physical operations base. The operations base usually ends up some distance from the search starting point. Sometimes the IPP falls on the place last seen (**PLS**) or the Last Known Position (**LKP**), or even some other point based on the best available information. Follow the Guideline criteria below for establishing the Initial Planning Point.

The **IPP** should:

- Be the point from which the search begins
- Be the first planning point in the operation
- If possible, mark as PLS or an LKP
- Be relevant to the search area (in terms of proximity)
- Be a good location to start a survey of the area for clues

Functional Groups for Reflex Tasking

Koester established six (6) functional groups of tasks for each of the subject categories. The functional groups of tasks remain constant throughout each category of subject. The functional groups of tasks follow:

- Investigation
- Initial Planning Point
- Containment
- Hub/Immediate Area
- Travel Corridors
- High Probability Tasks

While the functional groups remain constant throughout all categories, specific tasks in those functional groups depends on the subject category. As an example with the subject category of **Dementia** under the functional group Travel Corridors, Reflex Tasks include:

Travel Corridors

- Hasty search of trails, roads, drainages, and other routes leading away from the IPP, patrol roads
- Look for decision points and cut for sign at turn off points
- Dogs into drainages
- Corridor search parallel to roads and routes

By comparison look at the same functional task group *(Travel Corridors)* and the Reflex Tasks for **Children 7-9:**

Travel Corridors

- Hasty search of trails, roads, drainages, and other routes leading away from the IPP
- Cut for sign along routes and at shortcuts
- Look for various routes to familiar places

Going back to the example database for Dementia in Koester's manual learn more by filling in the other Reflex Tasks under the other five functional groups.

Investigation

- Determine planning data
- Determine searching data
- Start MPQ *(Missing Person Questionnaire/Lost Person Questionnaire)* Ask specific questions
- Previous wandering
- Potential destinations
- Severity of dementia
- Check taxis, mass transit *(all shifts)*, hospitals, EMS, jails, shelters, etc
- Alert municipal workers
- Issue a *Silver* alert

Initial Planning Point

- Preserve IPP
- Local search around the IPP *(300 M)*
- Highly systematic grounds and structure search
- Repeat search of grounds and structure
- Task sign cutters/trackers

- Tracking/Trailing dogs; ideal if having practiced with persons with dementia

Containment

- Establish containment
- Use statistical max zone or theoretical zone
- Containment provided by road patrols/air
- In urban environment, use road, bike, air patrols
- Contain entrances to gated developments

Hub/Immediate Area

- Canvass campground
- Canvass neighborhood
- Thorough search of 25% zone
- Sweep/area dogs
- Notify community by media, flyer, door to door, and/or telephone system

High Probability Tasks

- Check historical finds
- Previous lost locations
- High hazard areas
- Previous homes
- Ensure to search heavy brush

It often involves a number of operational periods to complete all the Reflex Tasks listed under the functional groups, particularly in an urban area. Enhance the Reflex Tasking process by using a very simple analogy called the Bike Wheel Model.

The Bike Wheel Model for Reflex Tasking *(Koester & Gordon - 2004)*

The bike wheel model consists of a wheel shaped guide describing a template for the rapid planning processes using both response activity and purpose. It provides rapid deployment of initially available resources along with consistent management functions. Simultaneously, the Overhead Team develops specific strategies and an Incident Action Plan for the search. Robert Koester in Virginia and Ross Gordon in New Zealand, originally devised and refined this concept, offering a very valuable tool to the SAR community and proving its worth on searches around the world.

The model provides consistent, high probabilities of success while more detailed plans develop for later operational periods. Plus, it is easy to remember. When you think about a bike wheel, characteristic parts and functions come to mind. Everything spins on the *axle* and depends on the integrity of that piece. The *hub* encases the axle with grease and bearings and connects the rest of the wheel together. The *spokes* connect the hub to the *rim* where the tire attaches and somewhere between the length of the spokes set the *reflectors* for safety and visibility.

Let the Model Provide Guidance

Rapid Planning using the Wheel Model in the Early Stages

- The best minds available usually form a quick consensus. The consensus represents an initial best guess at the subject's location using all the initial information. A quick consensus requires no segmentation, math or detailed forms and gets completed with a minimum of time and effort. The process encourages the staff to initially point out areas of higher probability based on immediately available information.
- The Overhead team marks the planning map with several appropriate initial tasks, *(beginning to build the wheel model)*. It only takes about 10 minutes to quickly draw eight to ten tasks on the map for immediate action.
- Reflex Tasking and using the Bike Wheel model normally gets the Incident Commander through the first 2 to 3 operational periods, and sometimes even more. After that, search or possibly re-search the gaps between the spokes or larger areas. This takes more in-depth planning, resources, detailed briefings and the use of search theory.

Acquire as much information about the person and the incident as possible.

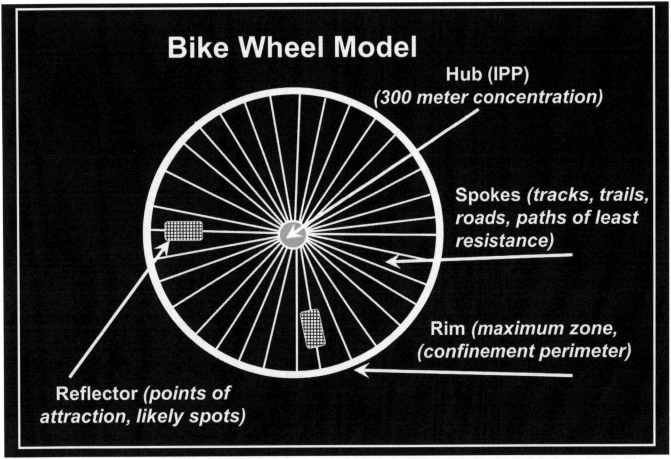

Figure 14-5 Bike Wheel Model analogy by Robert Koester, Virginia and Ross Gordon, New Zealand

Use and Parts of the Wheel Model

- Mark the planning map with several appropriate initial tasks to begin Building the Wheel
- The axle, hub and bearings of a wheel carry the weight so keep it greased and in good operating order. In the wheel analogy, the IC and the overhead team lubricate the axle, hub and bearings with good communications, good briefings and clear objectives.

  - Axel
  - The IPP serves as the **Axle** of the wheel.

- Preserve it well on the ground and on the map
- Structures involved in an incident need to be searched and researched repeatedly
- Immediate locale search around the IPP
- Sign cutters/trackers
- Tracking and trailing dogs

Hub functions:

- Thorough building and structure search as standard protocol
- Canvass campground if appropriate
- Assign tracking & clue detection functions with both humans & dogs if available
- Very thorough 300 meter search for clues and subject or 25% zone if less than 0.2 miles/ 0.3 kilometers

Spoke functions

Describes linear functions leading away from the hub and to connect the hub to the rim.

Linear tasks involve Type I searches that hold the search area together.

- Check the roads, highways and transportation routes

Reflex Tasking Worksheet

Wheel Elements	Steps	Tasks
Axle	① Plot the IPP.	✓ Preserve IPP ✓ Immediate locale search ✓ If a structure, search and re-search repeatedly ✓ Signcutters/trackers ✓ Tracking/trailing dogs
Rim	② Determine subject category. ③ Determine statistical ring. ④ Draw 50% and 95% rings. ⑤ Reduce search area using subjective and deductive reasoning. ⑥ Mark boundary on map.	✓ Establish containment ✓ Consider camp-ins, road/trail blocks, track traps, patrols, attraction and string lines.
Hub	⑦ Mark 25% ring if appropriate.	✓ Canvass campgrounds if appropriate ✓ Thoroughly search from IPP to 25% when less than 0.2 miles/0.3 km.
Spokes	⑧ Draw travel routes: • Blue lines (water features, drainages) • Dashed lines (trails) • Black/red lines (roads, man-made features) • Travel corridors (ridges, contours) • Corridor tasks, if appropriate	✓ Conduct hasty search of trails, roads, drainages, and other travel routes leading away from IPP. **Emphasis at likely decision points.**
Reflectors	⑨ Mark high probability/hazard areas	✓ Send hasty teams to areas of high probability, high hazard, historic locations of finds.
	⑩ Prioritize and deploy tasks using quick consensus method.	

Form by Robert J. Koester, dbS Productions. Adapted from Lost Person Behavior by Robert J. Koester
The short form above can be used in a field operations kit as a quick reference and easy to follow checklist that gives a priority listing of the steps and tasks using the Bike Wheel analogy to cover all of the functions.

Gaps between Spokes	✓ Generally not searched in the first operational period ✓ Searched once the areas have been more refined ✓ More resource intensive

Figure 14-6

- Check established paths, trails or tracks
- Run ridges, clearings or lines of little resistance
- Check streams, rivers or creeks
- Run power line access routes and other utility corridors

Reflector functions:

- Check likely spots
- Identify attraction areas for this category of subject
- Assign tracking & clue detection functions to all decision point locations

Rim functions:

- Based upon the statistical maximum zone or theoretical travel distances
- Establishes containment/confinement - i.e. *shut the doors*

Gaps between Spokes:

- Often not searched in the first operational period(s)
- Searched only after completing all other reflex tasks
- Very resource intensive

By using the functional Reflex Tasking groups, the sub-tasks in those groups and the Bike Wheel Model, even a moderately trained planner or IC easily assembles an initial task map in a few minutes *(See one page overview of the Reflex Tasking process using the bike wheel model, Figure 14-6 opposite page).*

The combination of sign cutting and clue detection with the initial planning point, travel corridors, containment, likely spots, decision points and high probability locations, identified on the map, puts the number of initial tasks into the upper teens. Often these tasks exceed the numbers of teams or resources immediately available. Try not to get discouraged or dissuaded by your overall plan and strategy if not completed for at least to 2 to 3 operational periods depending on availability of resources.

ISRID Tables on Distance and Behavior
(Koester- 2008).

Distance from the IPP

The *ISRID* database gives distance from the IPP which measures the crow's flight distance between the IPP and a find location. Distances in the tables come in both miles and kilometers. The letter **n** in the table signifies the numbers of cases in the database that fit the Eco Region description.

Dementia *(ISRID Data - 2008)*				
Distance (horizontal) from the IPP (miles)				
Temperate		Dry		Urban
Mtn	Flat	Mtn	Flat	
n	95	175	14	15	336
25%	0.2	0.2	0.6	0.3	0.2
50%	0.5	0.6	1.2	1.0	0.7
75%	1.2	1.5	1.9	2.3	2.0
95%	5.1	7.9	3.8	7.3	7.8

Figure 13-7 Horizontal Distance

Distance (horizontal) from the IPP (kilometers)				
Temperate		Dry		Urban
Mtn	Flat	Mtn	Flat	
n	95	175	14	15	336
25%	0.3	0.3	1.0	0.5	0.3
50%	0.8	1.0	1.9	1.6	1.1
75%	1.9	2.4	3.1	3.6	3.2
95%	8.3	12.8	6.1	11.8	12.6

Figure 14-7 Horizontal Distance (Km)

Elevation Change from the IPP

The ISRID database contains significant numbers of incidents where elevation change occurred. With more reviews since the release of Koester's book, additional data yields reliability in this factor for future editions of the manual. The amount of Urban data in the ISRID database still remains low due to significant human alterations in the landscape. At this juncture, Koester continues to use only the median and quartile percentages based on the measurement's accuracy *(it uses the entire data set to derive the median).*

Dementia *(Alzheimer's)*

	Elevation (vertical) Change from the IPP (feet)					
	Temperate			Dry		
	Uphill	Down	Same	Uphill	Down	Same
%	19%	42%	39%	50%	38%	13%
25%						
50%	75	60		317	187	
75%						
95%						

Figure 14-8 Elevation Change

Mobility Hours

This chart designation represents the amount of time the missing subject spends on the move. The ISRID database documented roughly 2000 incidents where the subject moved. Virtually no urban data exists on this factor.

Mobility (hours)		
	Temperate	Dry
n	42	6
25%	0	
50%	0.25	4.5
75%	3.8	
95%	18.0	

Figure 14-9 Mobility

Dispersion Angle

The original ISRID data contained 607 case numbers involving dispersion angles and offers a useful method to define probability within a search area. A dispersion angle records how far off *(right or left)* responders found the subject, measured against a straight line between the IPP and the subject's intended destination. Research requires the recording of three points of data: The IPP, the find location and the intended destination *(or direction of travel)*. 180 degrees defines the maximum dispersion angel value to the right or left of a line to the intended destination from an IPP.

It seems that temperate domain data reflects smaller dispersion angles than those recorded in the dry domain. Koester speculates that in the more open terrain of the dry domain, greater lines of sight make it easier to travel in a given direction. The data explores other speculation about correlation of dispersion angle and distance traveled; it also references theoretical dispersion angles in urban environments for children with a study completed in Alberta, Canada by Heth and Cornell as well.

Dispersion Angle (degrees)	
	Temperate
n	11
25%	11
50%	23
75%	66
95%	70

Figure 14-10 Dispersion

Find Location

The find location tables identify the actual location of the missing persons in each category. Koester broke the data into three domains for analysis: Temperate, Dry and Urban. The database identifies 3,189 incident locations. However, because of cultural and other variations collation of the information proved daunting at best. 124 categories of locations were consolidated into 22 and then into 18. Even this proved overwhelming for simple description, ultimately boiling it all down to the ten categories of locations listed in the table.

In Chapter 7 of his LPB Manual, Koester explains these locations with clarification on some of the nuances encountered when compiling this portion of ISRID.

Find Location (%)			
	Temp	Dry	Urban
n	207	7	223
Structure	20%	29%	35%
Road	18%	14%	36%
Linear	9%		9%
Drainage	9%	14%	4%
Water	7%	14%	6%
Brush	6%		1%
Scrub			
Woods	17%		3%
Field	14%	29%	6%
Rock			

Figure 14-11 Find Location

Scenario

The Scenario table lists the documented reason causing the individual to be missing or lost. Determining this factor after the incident and roughly half of the cases in ISRID, *(16, 207 cases)* the documentation and comments identified the type of scenario. Initially using eight scenario definitions and those eventually evolved into eleven (11) as listed in the table. Once again within the LPB manual, Koester explained in detail what these scenario descriptions consist of, their definitions and some of the nuances per category.

Scenario (%)	
n	1,050
Avalanche	
Criminal	
Despondent	
Evading	
Investigative	2%
Lost	96%
Medical	
Drowning	
Overdue	1%
Stranded	
Trauma	

Figure 14-12 Scenario

Track Offset

Track offset comes from a term used in searches for downed or missing aircraft. Essentially it designates the perpendicular distance from an intended track or route to the location of the lost or missing person. In aircraft search, track offset describes the distance off of an intended flight path. Koester's uses the term in the manual as an adaptation for ground SAR referring to a distance off of a linear feature such as a road, trail or drainage. No measurement exists if searchers find the missing person on a linear feature. The closest linear feature not always correlates to the feature from which the missing person departed. The figure in the chart gives the probability of finding the subject near a linear feature. Currently ISRID contains 351 track offset points for all categories. Due to insufficient data Koester combined all the domains.

Track Offset (meters)	
n	110
25%	4
50%	15
75%	71
95%	307

Figure 14-13 Offset

Survivability

The last table portrays the factor of survivability but doesn't take into account factors such as domain, weather or other important considerations. At present, the survivability data only considers time. The chart contains information pulled from broad-base groupings in wilderness/rural and urban areas. Koester very wisely states, never use survivability as a criteria for deciding to suspend a search. Conversely, when applicable, he says, some searches use survival statistics as the sole reason to prolong a search. Realize that while ISRID supports the conclusion that 99% of subjects found alive are found within approximately 50 hours, it also shows that a significant number of individuals survive past 50 hours. For instance, in the past, searchers found 55% of dementia subjects alive, even out to 72 hours.

Survivability		
	Wilderness	Urban
Well	73%	80%
Injured	17%	14%
Fatality	8%	6%
No Trace	2%	5%
Survivability	Alive	n
< 24 hours	95%	736
> 24 hours	77%	79
> 48 hours	60%	30
> 72 hours	60%	20
> 96 hours	46%	13

Figure 14-14 Survivability

The End Product

In Chapter 8 of Koester's LPB Manual, he presents the capability to combine investigative on-scene planning data with the ISRID database findings to identify very quickly, on the map, the locations needed to carry out Reflex Tasking. In addition, Reflex Tasking enables an IC or Planner to identify and pinpoint high probability locations, finite limits and boundaries of a potential search area based on the ISRID findings, all part of initial on-scene search planning.

Additional Investigative Questions

Koester emphasizes a specific point in his book about the importance of investigation during search incidents. Questions about whether or not the missing subject actually exists within the current search area or in the *rest of the world* constantly haunt search operation IC's. Factually, almost all searches include a second *search* component, and that consists of an investigative effort nearly always carried out by law enforcement. One of the compelling reasons why the new search management ***crucials*** identified in this textbook states clearly that "Search Inexorably Ties to Law Enforcement Investigation."

Each of the subject categories in Chapter 8 of Koester's LPB book contains a separate section on Additional Investigative Questions. Experience tells us that far too many searches terminate after a few days due to opinions that the missing person departed the area. The shortfall, little or no effort exist in the area of investigation to back up that thought.

The additional investigative questions compiled from incident documentation, forms, outdoor activity protocols, research and search incident experience, remind searchers about facts and information vital to the subject category. Going back to our example data for Dementia in Koester's book, the additional investigative questions for that subject category follow. As you look through these questions, remember back to the Subject Profile information on the Dementia category and remember the importance of severity of the disease. Therefore questions related to that determination become paramount. Notice the emphasis on that line of questions.

Dementia *(Alzheimer's)*
Additional Investigative Questions
(ISRID - 2008)

- What is the exact diagnosis of the type of dementia?
- Name and contact number of neurologist/ gerontologist
- Last Mini-Mental Status Exam *(MMSE)*, if known
- Describe subject as mild, moderate, or severe dementia
- Determine which description most appropriately fits the subject:
  - Mild confusion and forgetfulness, short-term memory affected
  - Difficulty distinguishing time, place and person. Some language difficulties
  - Nearly complete loss of judgment, reasoning, and loss of some physical control
- Does the subject know his own name?
- Does the subject know his location when at home?
- Does the subject recognize the local neighborhood?
- Does the subject recognize familiar faces?
- Will the subject answer to his name being called?
- Is the subject able to conduct a conversation?
- How long can the subject do or discuss something before forgetting?
- How long does a conversation last until an average person suspects something is wrong or not quite right?
- Describe the subject's ability to tell time
- Has the subject experienced personality or emotional changes? Describe
- Does the subject have delusions? Describe
- Does the subject have paranoia? Describe
- Does the subject have hallucinations? Describe
- Does the subject have depression? Describe
- Has the subject experienced an emotional breakdown? Describe
- Has the subject shown violence towards others? Describe
- Is the subject registered in the Alzheimer's Association's Medic Alert or ***Safe Return*** program or any other similar registry? Describe any identification or marking jewelry or labels the subject might be wearing
- List all of the subject's addresses, dwelling types, and how long he has lived at each address going back to childhood. List locations even if they no longer exist
- What jobs and occupations did the subject have at each location?
- Did the subject recently move or change locations? If so, when? What was the previous location? How has he adjusted to being in a nursing home/new location?
- How have caregivers adjusted their routines?
- List of all immediate relatives and distant relatives the subject communicated with during their lifetime?

- Is the subject familiar with the area where last seen?
- What is the subject's favorite place?
- Has the subject been involved with outdoor classes, scouting, military, overnight experiences, or outdoor recreation? Describe
- Is the subject afraid of noises, crowds, dogs, traffic, water, horses, the dark, or other items? Describe how he reacts
- How does the subject respond to strangers? Does he approach strangers?
- Is the subject dangerous to himself? Dangerous to others?
- Has the subject ever wandered away before, and you (*the interviewee*) did not know his location for 5 minutes or more? If so, for each incident describe the following:
  - Where was the subject last seen?
  - What was the subject doing when last seen?
  - Events that might have caused the subject to have wandered?
  - What actions were taken?
  - Where was the subject found?
  - What was the distance *as the crow flies* from the point the subject was last seen and where found?
  - How was the subject found? List any medical problems that resulted from being lost
- What jobs and occupations has the subject held throughout his life?
- Subject's hobbies and interests? Able to still engage in hobby?
- What are subject's daily habits? Did they occur on the day last seen?
- Distance subject typically walks each day (*e.g., during the past week*)
- Number of walks during the past week
- Greatest distance subject has walked during the past three months? During the past ten years?

NOTE: Clues may be on old maps

Gain access to old maps of the area to help to decide what points of reference the missing person possibly uses. *(e.g. footpaths, roads, residences, workplaces, etc. even those that no longer exist.)* An example of this strategy occurred when searchers found a 78 year old man alive in the middle of a field of corn five days into the search. The search management team, only a few hours into the search, located an old map showing a footpath leading from the village to the victim's previous home long since demolished. They rescued the victim within a few meters of the old path despite the fact that it too no longer existed.

Never Underestimate The Capabilities
Of An Elderly dementia Subject!

They Commonly Surprise Everyone
When All The Facts Are In.

General Information Relevant to the Prediction of Lost Subject Behavior

Category and circumstances of the loss:

- Children differ from hikers, etc
- The elements of the loss contribute greatly to prediction of likely actions

Terrain:

- Flat terrain generally yields different travel distances from hilly or mountainous terrain
- Examine the area for barriers, escape routes, confusing drainages or ridges

Weather:

- Restricts a subject's movements
- Contributes to hypothermia
- Imminent adverse weather possibly calls for increased efforts

Personality:

- Consider the aggressive person versus the ponderer or pessimist
- Substantially effects a person's ability to survive

Physical Condition:

- Any handicaps that encumber the missing or lost person
- Poor physical condition means an increased susceptibility to environmental injury/illness, *e.g. hypothermia*
- Directly effects the distance a subject travels

Medical Problems:

- Anything that possibly precipitates abnormal behavior
- Sometimes effects the distance a subject travels
- Indicates an increased urgency with significant time constraints

Circumstances of loss:

- When establishing a search plan, responders need to understand the circumstances in which an individual became lost and thoroughly evaluate the surrounding terrain.
    - Known location
    - Enroute
    - No specific location

Map interpretation and terrain analysis:

- Terrain influences peoples' movement

The Subject Profile:

- New information and updates can prove very useful

Interactive Subject Profiles:

- Behavior (*movement*) of the missing person may be influenced or completely controlled by another
    - One person may influence the other dramatically
    - They may each decide to separate if both are strong willed
    - There may be criminal implications - *e.g. abduction*

Reminder:

Studying lost/missing person behavior facilitates prediction of a missing person's location with some reasonable degree of accuracy. Not an exact science, it therefore only deals with generalities. Some missing people tend to end up outside of the categories represented in the collected data. Try not to fall into the trap of thinking every person missing or lost person fits into some nice neat category with all the appropriate distances and characteristics recorded. Sometimes it takes some investigation to uncover factors that define subject categories.

Organization: Incident Command & Functional Mgmt. 15

Objectives:

- Discuss the functions, structure and importance of an effective search organization.

- List and Discuss the critical components of an effective search management system

- Effectively organize a search and delegate appropriate functional responsibilities

The complexity of SAR management, coupled with a growing need for multi-agency and multifunctional involvement on searches, increases the need for a standard incident management system used by all emergency response disciplines. Without it, people make unnecessary mistakes and agencies often duplicate efforts, expending time and resources without results.

Successful search operations depend on the efficient and effective utilization of available and potential resources applied to the problem at hand: finding the missing person. Good organization and management structure helps channel, apply, regroup, and evaluate resources to concentrate efforts, avoid redundancy, and promote search success.

The Importance of Good Organization and Management

Although most successful searches involve small search areas and very few searchers, they also resolve in a short period of time. Occasionally, the magnitude and complexity of an operation exceeds routine search capabilities *(see Chapter 10 on the Kim Search)*. Search Incident Commanders (*ICs*) use their day-to-day response in managing the smaller searches comfortably; but, when an initial response hasty team fails to find the missing person or even good clues, the IC must immediately begin to plan and organize for a potentially difficult and complex operation. At this point, the situation rapidly develops, but without specific information. This defines the critical need for preplanning coupled with a dynamic response. Management actions during the first few hours of an incident often mean the difference between success and failure in the long term.

By definition, the term emergency implies some degree of unpredictability in the situation, along with a high probability of threat(s) to human safety. In the majority of emergency incident cases, time plays a critical role. Managers must organize the efforts of responders in such a manner that both the subject (missing person) and responders stay clear of additional or undue hazards. Therefore, any management system that deals with emergency always keeps human safety as a very high priority.

The nature of emergencies in natural environments also emphasizes high degrees of uncertainty. Ask the question: *How do we minimize uncertainty?* The answer lies in the degree to which information flows freely throughout the organization. In the real world, this includes an open flow, both on the management side and the operational side. Research into emergency response situations definitively shows that communications link directly to effective operational response. Bertrund Russel (*Nobel Laureate, 1950*) said it best in the quote:

> *"Frustration is inversely proportional to the amount of information that is available."*

Emergency situations typically create interactions between groups, agencies or specific personnel who never work together on a daily basis. Try not to wait for an emergency situation to sift out responsibilities or job descriptions from ambiguous documentation. Any management system at the local level needs to sort through the myriad of issues with clearly defined job descriptions, responsibilities, tasks, obligations and accompanying authority with a minimum level of redundancy.

Management By Objectives

Management by objectives *(MBO)* requires the specification of time referenced *attainable* and *measurable* goals. This accountability factor simply asks: Did responders accomplish what they set out to do in a specific time period?

The three key elements listed below define how every successful operation unfolds. Each element falling under the control of the Incident Commander (IC).

- **Resources.** The operation needs specific equipment, people, and other resources available to respond. The leadership knows their capabilities and how to get them on scene.
- **Strategy.** The person in charge needs to know the fundamentals of search theory to develop sound objectives for each SAR operation.
- **Tactics.** The development of adequate plans to apply specific resources in the most appropriate locations at the right time and in the right order to efficiently and effectively meet the given objectives.

Operational Objectives. All searches ultimately strive to locate the missing person in the best possible condition and in the shortest amount of time. According to *best practice* management philosophy good managers use objectives in organizing, responding to, and managing search incidents. Remember the acronym **SMARTER**: The Incident Commander needs to develop the following objectives for the search effort:

- **S**pecific for each operational period
- **M**easurable and verifiable
- **A**chievable in a practical sense
- **R**elevant and/or realistic
- **T**ime related
- **E**valuated by the overhead team
- **R**eviewed/Recorded for documentation

Good search objectives allow managers to direct their efforts toward actions that result in a successful mission. They provide direction for the resources to operate most effectively along with a means for evaluating mission progress while allowing for adjustments, if necessary, to ensure a smooth running mission.

Because emergencies generally tie in with time and urgency, successful operations rely on high levels of delegation onto many subordinates, as opposed to only a few. Therefore, giving subordinates in the chain of command the latitude and capability to make decisions within their areas of responsibility without the need to constantly consult someone back up the chain. For this to happen in real operations, the size of the management staff grows in relation to the requirements of the situation. Or, more broadly, the management system grows according to the span of control and delegation of authority to subordinates in the operation.

SAR Success Requires Interagency Coordination

More than ever before, the level of care expected by the public constantly rises due to the speed and accessibility of mass media. Individual emergency agencies, such as police or sheriffs departments lack *(and normally do not)* provision of all the resources required for every type of emergency situation *(Particularly concerning specialized search or rescue capabilities)*.

Specialization in the SAR responder community uses information on strategy and tactics from as many sources as possible to solve problems both unique or environmentally specific. Therefore, peer networks, conferences, professional organizations and even social networking gain importance in adequately providing the specialty information to meet expected levels of care.

Throughout the world, search and rescue now stands as an emergency management specialty in its own right. A specialty with unique disciplines within the broader spectrum of public safety. The trends in search planning and management now favor interagency *mutual aid agreements*, central resource coordination points *(i.e. the Rescue Coordination Centers or RCCs located throughout the world)* and greater utilization of highly trained and specialized resources. A flexible management system allows maximum use of available resources and state of the art technology. Flexibility becomes key to integrating resources with technology, while at the same time promoting coordination and cooperation. This flexibility provides for optimum control and efficient flow of information during on-scene incident management.

On-Scene Functional Management

Any good management system builds around major functional units, not personalities or rank in the organization. Thus maximizing the responsibility of delegated supervisors to carry out their tasks and duties within those functional areas.

Many factors affect the management of emergencies and bring up the need for efficiency and cost effectiveness. Although not applicable to every incident, some of the most common factors include:

- Population growth and spreading urban areas
- Language and cultural differences
- More multi-jurisdictional incidents
- Legal changes mandating standard incident management systems and multi-agency involvement at certain incidents
- Shortage of resources at all levels, requiring greater use of mutual aid
- Increases in the number, diversity and use of radio frequencies
- More complex and interrelated incident situations
- Greater life and property loss risk from natural and human caused disasters
- Sophisticated media coverage demanding immediate answers and emphasizing response effectiveness
- More frequent cost sharing decisions on incidents

These factors all accelerate the trend toward more complex incidents, considering the fiscal and resource constraints of local, state and federal responders in the last few years. The Incident Command System (ICS) represents the primary organizational management tool for the delivery of coordinated emergency services to the public on-scene.

ICS resulted from the obvious need for a new approach to managing rapidly moving wildfires in the early 1970s. At that time, emergency responders faced a number of challenging problems.

- Too many people reporting to one supervisor
- Different emergency response organizational structures
- Lack of reliable incident information
- Inadequate and incompatible communications
- Lack of a structure for coordinated planning between agencies
- Unclear lines of authority
- Terminology differences between agencies
- Unclear or unspecified incident objectives

The need to solve recurring problems for multi-agency response units, resulted in the development of the Incident Command System. That development took several years and extensive field testing, but through an interagency task force made up of local, state and federal agencies called FIRESCOPE *(Firefighting Resources of California Organized for Potential Emergencies)* ICS emerged. ICS represents a functional management system with an appropriate hierarchy of positions that address all of the issues mentioned above.

Currently, Homeland Security Presidential Directives 5 and 8 both require the adoption of the National Incident Management System *(NIMS)* by all jurisdictions throughout the U.S. as a prerequisite for any Federal emergency funding. And, the Incident Command System *(ICS)* provides the standard management scheme of functional management for NIMS.

The United Kingdom, Canada, New Zealand and other countries around the world widely use ICS *(or variants)*, and the United Nations recommends using it as an international standard.

As a system, ICS flexes and adapts to a variety of emergency situations. It also functions well on small searches where just one person, the Search Manager *(or Incident Commander)*, performs all of the major functions. He or she directly supervises all of the searchers, develops and implements an action plan, provides logistical support and also manages the planning aspects of the operation.

ICS allows the Search Manager (Incident Commander) to integrate all available resources into an effective response organization without the problems of *defending turf,* inadequate communications or conflicting objectives. It also allows all responding personnel to focus on the main objective: locating the lost or missing person.

As mentioned before, most successful searches involve small areas, only a few searchers and end in a fairly short time frame. Occasionally though, a search exceeds these routine operational capabilities. If the situation escalates and the structure grows faster than the overhead team's ability to control it, or the management structure fails to grow fast enough or large enough to handle increased demands, the entire effort gets compromised. Remember, even a routine search requires good management.

Think Functions, Not People

To organize any search effort effectively, the IC needs to think of all the jobs performed in terms of functions or categories of tasks. The leadership fulfills certain functions, regardless of the number of searchers involved or the size of the search area. Management orchestrates the response into a dynamic, emerging organization; one that changes to meet the increases or decreases in complexity of the situation. The team of managers that make up the primary functional positions of management tasks in any organizational structure consist of the *Overhead Team.* In the ICS structure, both the *Command Staff* and the *General Staff* form the *Overhead Team.*

Command Staff Functional Positions

- Incident Manager - *(Incident Commander)*
- Information Officer
- Safety Officer
- Intelligence/Investigations Officer
- Liaison Officer

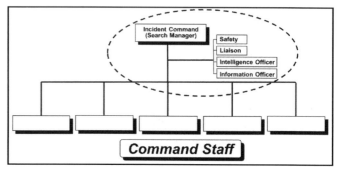

Figure 15-1 Command Staff

General Staff Functional and Unit Positions

- Operations
- Planning
- Logistics
- Finance/Administration
- Intelligence/Investigation

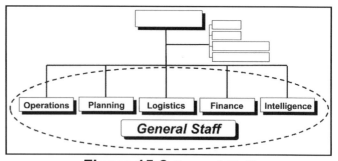

Figure 15-2 General Staff

Focusing on functions not people means using the most qualified person, regardless of rank or organizational status, to responsibly manage particular functions as necessary. Although impossible for some organizations due to structure, precedent or procedures, this approach represents a highly desirable goal. Management of search operations centers on *finding missing persons,* not status, politics or building a career. The most capable people always carry out the required functions.

*Throughout this publication, **Search Manager** refers to the specific title given to the functional position. Incident Commander, SAR Mission Coordinator, Search Master, or Search Controller, refer to other titles used to describe this position.*

Manageable Span of Control

Before looking into specific players within the ICS structure we need to discuss one of the foundation principles making it so effective. In the early stages of an incident, if established by the unit, one or two people posses the ability to carry out all of the functions of the emerging organization. As the incident grows in size and complexity, the functioning of the organization grows more complex with it. At some point, as the search increases in size, the Search Manager needs to delegate authority *(and some measure of direct control)* to individuals trained and qualified for those tasks. Consider this delegation necessary sooner, rather than later.

The nature of the task, hazards, safety factors, experience and ability all influence span of control and considerations made. As a general rule, managers function well with between three *(3)* and seven *(7)* direct reporting individuals, with five *(5)* as the optimum span. When the organization grows to the point where one manager controls more than 7, bring in an additional manager; conversely, when a functional manager controls less than 3 individuals consider eliminating a management position and absorbing the subordinates into the next higher level of management.

Consider span of control issues as part of the natural growth of an incident. Anticipate the changes to the organization caused by increased or decreased numbers of elements and prepare appropriately. The rapid build up of an organization always presents a management challenge due to so many reporting elements in need of direction and information. Effective organizations use span of control to dictate the need for an expansion of operations, or to spool it down appropriately.

Functional Management Positions

Whether an organization uses ICS or some other management system, *best practice* search management dictates the assignment of certain functional positions as the incident escalates. According to current ICS management doctrine, *specific functional categories or tasks* tend to show up at some level during a search. In the application of standard ICS to search management, consider the functional positions listed below as essential to an efficient structure. Each one falls under the five functional areas identified in ICS.

- Agency Authority
- Liaison
  - Agency
  - Investigations
  - Family
  - Volunteers
- Media
- Logistics
- Evaluations & Critiques
- Agency SAR Plan
- Team Standards & Compliance
- Reimbursement
- Funding
- Training

Agency Executive or Agency Administrator (AA):

In most state jurisdictions, statutes identify a responsible person *(appointed or even elected, like a county sheriff)*. The chief executive officer *(or designee)* of the agency or jurisdiction holds ultimate responsibility for SAR incidents within that jurisdiction *(The AA is sometimes called the legally "Responsible Agent" or RA), h*owever, not necessarily the Incident Commander!

Agency Representative:

Similar to the Agency Executive, most jurisdictions designate a person to be responsible for the day to day operational requirements of SAR *(e.g. a county SAR coordinator)*. This individual retains delegated authority to make decisions on most SAR matters affecting that jurisdiction including plans, training, coordination with volunteers and deployment locally *(and in other jurisdictions)*. Agency Representatives generally report to the Agency Executive Officer. Keep in mind though, the Agency Representative never plays the role of Incident Commander by default!

Roles and Responsibilities
Command Staff Positions

Incident Command - The Incident Commander wields the authority and responsibility for all functions at a given incident, and needs qualifications for this role. As incidents grow in size or grow in complexity, they require a more highly qualified Incident Commander. Even without the need for other functions, every incident requires the designation of an Incident Commander.

The Incident Command function unfolds in two ways:

Single Command
or
Unified Command

Unified Command generally comes into play for multi-jurisdictional and/or multi-agency events, and embodies a major feature of ICS. However Single Command, *(one Incident Commander)* most commonly refers to management applications.

Initially, the Incident Commander *(IC)* directly supervises the assignment of tactical resources and oversees operations. However, as incidents get bigger or grow in complexity, the IC delegates authority for performance of certain activities to others as required.

Usually, the person in charge of the first arriving units at the scene of an incident assumes the Incident Commander role. That person remains in charge until formally relieved, or until accomplishing a formal transfer of command. Such a transfer of command at an incident always requires a full briefing for the incoming Incident Commander, and notification on the change of command for the rest of the staff.

(IC) - The Search Manager accounts for the overall management of the incident to include:

- All on-scene activities and minute to minute decisions
- Establishing the *Command Post* and Base site
- Initially, he/she fulfills all staff responsibilities and delegates functions as they emerge
- Develops and implements the initial strategic plan with objectives for all operational periods
- Develops, approves and oversees the Incident Action Plan (Search Action Plan)
- Establishes communications with the local responsible agency and its representative(s)
- Carries out the policies, rules and regulations of the jurisdiction

Sometimes one or more deputies from the same agency or even from other agencies or jurisdictions arrive on scene and fulfill the position of Incident Commander. The only ICS requirement regarding the use of a deputy, whether at the Incident Command, Section, or Branch level, depends on full qualification to assume the position. The following encompasses the primary reasons for designating a deputy Incident Commander:

- To perform specific tasks as requested by the Incident Commander
- To perform the incident command function in a relief capacity, e.g., to take over the next operational period *(In this case the deputy eventually assumes the primary role)*
- To represent an assisting agency that shares jurisdiction or assumes jurisdiction in the future

Transfer of Incident Command

The proper use of ICS allows the transfer of command with minimum disruption. Transfer of Command at an incident generally takes place for any of the following reasons:

- A more qualified person assumes command
- The incident situation changes over time which legally requires a jurisdictional or agency change in command *(or it makes good management sense to make a transfer of command)*
- Normal turnover of personnel on long or extended incidents

The decision to transfer command also stems from complexity of the incident, personnel qualifications, and experience.

When an outgoing IC transfers command to a new IC, a good briefing includes the following:

- Situation status
- Objectives and priorities
- Current organization
- Resource assignments
- Resources en route and/or ordered
- Facilities established
- The communications plan
- Prognosis, concerns, and related issues

Liaison Officer - This position handles interactions with various groups as the SAR incident unfolds:

- The point of contact for assisting and cooperating agency representatives and monitors inter organizational problems
- Assists with other agency resources and information about the management of those resources:
  - Inventory
  - Maintenance, deployment, recall and use
- Fulfills family liaison duties if necessary and acts as point of contact for the family members for information regarding the status of the search

Safety Officer or Risk Analysis - Monitors and assesses any stressful, hazardous or unsafe situations. While usually starting as a management position, the Safety Officer also deploys to monitor specific tactics or special rescue operations in the field. Additional responsibilities include:

- Identification of any potentially dangerous or unsafe practices or conditions during the search
- Safety briefings about field operations for the Incident Action Plan *(IAP)*
- Monitoring planning meetings that involve application of resources into the field
- Reviewing medical, rescue or evacuation plans
- Identifying the need for and scheduling of any critical incident debriefing or counseling
- Investigating all accidents

- Assessment of all searcher and overhead personnel fatigue factors before individual release to return to normal duty stations/home

Intelligence / Investigations Officer - This function handles both security and the ongoing investigation concerning the missing person and the circumstances of their disappearance. Virtually every search and rescue incident eventually implements some type of Investigation function. As mentioned earlier, in 2003, the U.S. President issued Homeland Security Presidential Directive-5 *(HSPD-5)*, Management of Domestic Incidents, which directed the Secretary of Homeland Security to develop and administer a National Incident Management System *(NIMS)*. One of the base elements of NIMS centers on the Intelligence/Investigations Function within the Incident Command System *(ICS)*.

Intelligence, within the ICS structure, provides a flexible and scalable framework to allow for the integration of intelligence and investigations activities and information. The public often views these activities and information gathering as primarily the responsibility of traditional law enforcement. And in many cases, law enforcement departments fulfill intelligence/investigations duties; but, this function contains aspects that cross many disciplines. In fact, one of the foundation *crucials* for managing land search operations states that *Search Inexorably Ties to Law Enforcement Investigation.*

Current ICS doctrine allows a great deal of organizational flexibility in placing the Intelligence/Investigation function. Placement occurs at an equal level with Command, Operations, and Planning, or alone in an entirely new section; all suffice. Regardless of where it ends up, direct communication *(information flow)* about the Investigation freely takes place between Command, Operations, and Planning *(see Figure 15-4 on page 255)*.

Law enforcement people generally fill the Investigations position but not in all cases. Additionally, this person collects and collates the following:

- Investigation
  - Filling out the lost person questionnaire
  - Assembling a subject profile
  - Interviewing
  - Analysis of missing/lost person data
  - Historical comparative analysis
  - Scenario analysis
  - Following up on leads or clues
  - All information collected and documented through interviews about the missing person situation
  - Probable scenarios determined by those initially arriving on-scene
  - Copy of the Missing Person Report form *(MPR)*
  - Photographs or video of the missing person
  - Meets and interviews as appropriate any members of the family or friends, peers, colleagues about the missing person
  - Maintains a log of all contacts and interviews
  - Reviews clue map and log on a regular basis
  - Attends all planning meetings and relates current status of investigation
  - Meets with the IC, Operations and Plans Chief on a regular basis for briefings and direction on further leads

Information Officer *(I.O.)* - This position controls the formulation and release of information about the search to news media and other appropriate organizations *(and to search personnel)*. The IO executes the following activities:

- Develops a media policy which includes protocols for communicating when searchers find the missing person *(dead or alive)* and include it in the Search Action Plan
- Determine constraints on any release of information about the operation from the IC or local jurisdiction
- Establish a central point of information contact with the media if possible. That means a site, facility, room, cleared area, or convenient location with access to all of the appropriate support amenities such as power, rest rooms, lighting, telephone service, as well as flip charts or dry erase boards, multimedia, social media, etc.
- Arrange media conferences at appropriate times
- Respond to special requests for information
- Keep searchers informed about developments and/or key discoveries in the search
- Ensure that a missing person status never gets released before notifying next of kin
- When appropriate and approved, set up escort for media into the command post and specified areas of the field

General Staff Positions

The Operations Section dictates the direction and coordination of all incident tactical operations. The Operations Section Chief directs this process when the Incident Commander determines the need for a separate Operations Section at a search. Until establishing Operations as a separate section, the IC retains direct control of responding SAR resources.

Only one Operations Section Chief serves for each operational period *(usually encompasses an 8 to 12 hour portion of an incident)*. The Ops Section Chief normally hails from the jurisdiction or agency with the greatest involvement either in terms of resources assigned or search area covered.

The Operations Section expands or contracts based upon the existing and projected needs of the incident. Initially, the Operations Section usually consists of those few resources first assigned to an incident *(and these resources initially report directly to the Incident Commander)*.

As additional resources commit to the search and the incident grows in complexity, the IC establishes a separate Operations Section. Within the Operations Section, again as the incident grows, additional levels of organization evolve as necessary. The Operations Section develops from the bottom. First by establishing Divisions, Groups, and if necessary, Branches. Also, the Operations Section often uses staging areas and, in some cases, an air organization.

Operations Sections encompass all actions necessary to carry out the Incident/Search Action Plan. Operations

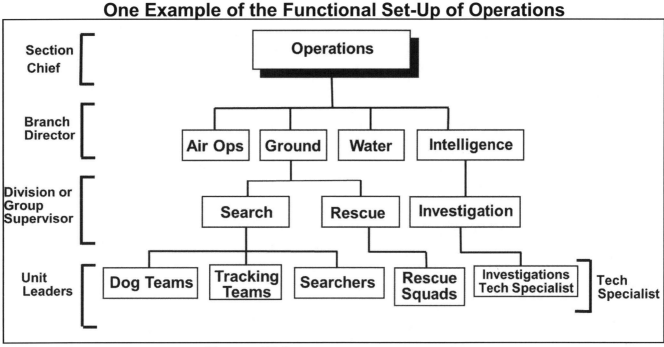

Figure 15-3 Example Operations Section

carries out the transformation of search objectives and strategies into on-scene actions in addition to:

- Coordinating and carrying out all tactical activities
- Determining needs and ordering resources
- Keeping track of and overseeing activities in the air, water and ground environments
- Giving, briefing, and debriefing tactical assignments
- Implementing the tactical aspects of the Incident Action
- Planning *(IAP)* and allocating operational work assignments
- Acting as the IC's Executive Officer

Branches

Some incidents require another level of organization within the Operations Section called a Branch. Branches generally either fall under geographic divisions or alternatively functional areas. Geographic branches emerge due to span of control considerations, e.g. after establishing more than five divisions; or, functional branches also emerge to manage special operations constraints such as those associated with air, ground and water resources.

Geographic and functional branches occasionally work together on an incident.

Branches in turn take direction from a Branch Director, who subsequently uses deputy positions as required. In multi-agency incidents, the use of deputy branch directors from assisting agencies greatly enhances interagency coordination.

Generally three reasons surface to use Branches on a SAR incident.

1. **Span of Control** - When the number of Divisions and groups exceeds the recommended Span of Control, another level of management emerges.

2. **Agency Coordination** – Some incidents involve multiple disciplines, e.g. law enforcement, fire, medical, and volunteer SAR units, which at times require integration into incident operations using a functional branch structure.

3. **Multi-jurisdictional Incidents** - In some SAR incidents, jurisdictional lines make better organizational dividing lines. In these situations, Branches reflect the differences in the agencies involved. For example, searches that involve

federal, county, and city jurisdictions. One organizing option for these kinds of incidents simply designates a separate branch for each of the agencies involved.

In addition to the Operations Section positions discussed so far, two other important organizational elements commonly occur in connection with Search and Rescue: Air Operations and Staging.

Air Operations

Some incidents invariably make use of aviation resources to provide tactical or logistical support. On smaller incidents, aviation resources often report directly to the Incident Commander *(or to the Operations Section Chief if appropriate)*. Within larger incidents, a separate Air Operations organization coordinates the use of aviation assets. The Air Operations organization then operates at the branch level, reporting directly to the Operations Section Chief.

The Air Operations Branch Director generally establishes two functional groups. First, the Air Tactical Group, which coordinates all airborne activity. And Second, the Air Support Group, which provides all incident ground based support to aviation resources.

Staging Areas

Staging occurs wherever necessary to temporarily organize and locate field ready resources awaiting assignments. Once the management team creates a Staging Area, they also assign a Staging Area Manager. The Staging Area Manager reports to the Operations Section Chief or to the Incident Commander based on the size of the incident. But, Staging Areas and the resources within them, fall under the functional control of the Operations Section Chief.

- Staging Areas allow temporary location of resources available on very short notice *(3 to 5 minutes)*. Anywhere in which mobile resources temporarily park awaiting assignment may serve as a staging area. Staging Areas often include temporary sanitation services and fueling. Mobile kitchens provide for the feeding of personnel or even sack lunches. Staging Areas also need a high degree of mobility. The Operations Chief also assigns a Staging Area Manager for *each* Staging Area.

All resources move to the Staging Area specifically for assignments and subsequent deployment. Avoid using Staging Areas to locate out-of-service resources or for other permanent logistics functions.

In some *(rare)* applications, branches set up separate staging areas for specific resources. For example, a medical branch with an assigned ambulance staging area.

The Planning Section collects and evaluates incident situation information, prepares situation status reports, displays situation information, maintains status of resources, develops an Incident Action Plan, and prepares any required incident related documentation. This function falls under the direction of the Planning Section Chief, possibly with a deputy.

The Planning Section takes care of these important functions:

- Maintaining resource status *(RESTAT)*
- Inventory of all resources
- Resource information management
- Status, maintenance, deployment, recall and use
- Maintaining and displaying situation status *(SITSTAT)* What has happened?
- What is happening?
- What will likely happen?
- Preparing the Incident Action Plan *(Search Action Plan)*
- Developing strategy - *(Think Tank)*
- Providing documentation services
- Maps, records, photographs, meteorolgy
- Preparing the Demobilization Plan
- Providing a primary location for Technical Specialists assigned to an incident

The primary *(and most important)* functions of the Planning Section look beyond the current and next operational period, to anticipate potential problems or events. They ask: "What will likely happen?" The Planning Section generally divides into four unit-level positions: Resources, Situation, Documentation, and Demobilization Units.

The Resources Unit covers all check-in activity, and maintains the status on all personnel and equipment resources assigned to the incident.

The Situation Unit collects and processes information on the current incident as it unfolds, they prepare situation displays and situation summaries, then develop maps and projections appropriately.

The Documentation Unit prepares the Incident Action Plan, maintains all incident-related documentation, and provides copy services.

During large, complex incidents, the Demobilization Unit ensures an orderly, safe, and cost-effective movement of personnel at the conclusion of the operation.

The Planning Section is also the initial place of check-in for any Technical Specialists assigned to the incident. Technical specialists serve as advisors with special skills required at the incident. They come from any discipline required, e.g., aviation, environment, hazardous materials, etc. depending on their assignment, Technical Specialists work within the Planning Section, or reassign to other incident areas.

The Logistics Section. Logistics service and support to an incident provides all the critical materials and facilities needed for everyone else to perform their duties. Early recognition of the need for a separate logistics function and section usually reduces time and money spent on a SAR incident. The Logistics section provides:

- Whatever support Operations requires
- Supplies and equipment to carry out the mission
- Transport, medical services, food, sleep facilities, personal hygiene facilities, etc
- Installation, maintenance and operation of necessary communications networks
- Interface between communications systems
- Messengers, operators, message logs and improvisation *(setting up and running the search base)*

The Incident Commander determines the need to establish a Logistics Section for the incident. As mentioned in other sections, the size of the incident, complexity of support, and how long the incident lasts all contribute to that decision. Once the IC determines a need to establish a separate Logistics function, he/she assigns an individual to the duties of Logistics Section Chief.

The Logistics Section Chief often establishes separate units for one or more of the logistics support or service activities. On large incidents, after activating all six Logistics Section units, or with many facilities and large amounts of equipment, a two branch structure reduces the span of control for the Logistics Section Chief. The two branches operate as the Service Branch and the Support Branch to manage the following responsibilities:

Service Branch

A Communications Unit - Develops the Communications Plan, distributes and maintains all forms of communications equipment, and manages the Incident Communications Center.

A Medical Unit - Develops the incident Medical Plan, and provides first-aid and light medical treatment for personnel assigned to the incident. This unit also develops the emergency medical transportation plan *(ground and/or air)* and prepares medical reports.

A Food Unit - Determines and supplies the feeding and potable water requirements for all incident facilities, and for active resources within the Operations Section. The unit prepares menus and food, provides them through catering services, or uses some combination of both methods.

Support Branch

A Supply Unit - Orders personnel, equipment, and supplies. The unit stores and maintains supplies, and cares for non-expendable equipment. In ICS, all requests for resources travel through the Logistics Section's Supply Unit. Without a designated Supply Unit, the Responsibility for ordering rests with the Logistics Section.

As the incident grows, the need for additional logistics functions often require even more specialized functions. For example, a possibility exists where the following units report to the Logistics Section Chief.

A Facilities Unit - Sets up and maintains whatever facilities the incident requires. Provides managers for the Incident Base and camps. Provides security support for the facilities and incident as required.

A Ground Support Unit - Provides transportation, in addition to maintaining and fueling vehicles assigned to the incident. Importantly, remember that the functions of the logistics unit, except for the Supply Unit, focus on supporting personnel and resources directly assigned to the incident. For example, the Logistics Section Food Unit never provides food for people sent to shelters during a flood. Under ICS, the Operations Section handles food for shelters and orders food supplies through the Logistics Section Supply Unit.

Finance/Administration Section Monitors incident-related costs, and administers any necessary procurement contracts. The IC determines the need for a Finance/Administration Section, and designates an individual to perform that role. Without a Finance Section, the IC performs all finance functions.

The Finance/Administration Section functions primarily for any incident requiring on-site financial management. More and more, large incidents use a Finance/Administration Section to monitor the following costs:

- Damage surveys *(lost or damaged property)*
- Resource costs *(actually used)*
- Injury claims/compensation
- Man/hours/days
- Documentation and logs
- Cost accounting figures for future decisions

Smaller incidents often require certain Finance/Administration functions. For example, the Incident Commander establishes one or more units of the Finance/Administration Section for such things as procuring special equipment, contracting with a vendor, or for making cost estimates of alternative strategies.

The Finance Section may establish four units as necessary. Not all of the units activate, instead they grow based upon need.

A Time Unit - Ensures the recording of all personnel time on an incident or event.

A Procurement Unit - Processes administrative paperwork associated with equipment rental and supply contracts. They tally equipment running time and document how and when of equipment use.

A Compensation/Claims Unit - Combines two important functions. Compensation keeps track of all documentation related to workers compensation and ensures adherence to appropriate regulations, forms etc. Also, Compensation maintains files of injuries and/or illnesses associated with the incident. Claims also handles investigation of all issues involving damaged property associated with or involved in the incident.

A Cost Unit - Collects all cost information, then provides analysis, cost estimates and cost savings recommendations.

When agencies communicate with each other and work together to support one another, they usually find ways to grow more efficient and effective. Eliminating *turf* problems also gives way to a climate of understanding and support.

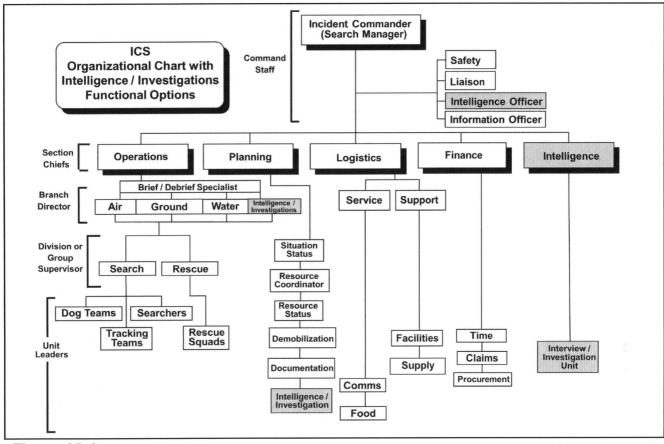

Figure 15-4 A Model Organizational Chart (With Optional Placement of Investigations/ Intel Function)

> *Good organizational structure never just happens, it requires dedicated effort.*

Intelligence / Investigations Section

The Intelligence/Investigations function forms the section/unit in the management structure responsible for information gathering and collation of that data for decision making. During a search incident, this function also provides the foundation for the subject category and profile. It also establishes the Initial Planning Point, helps with basic scenarios and even where in the search area to look for a missing person. Depending on the subject, this section provides many clues or critical information which eventually result in a find. Intelligence/Investigations starts with the First Notice and often carries on well beyond the termination of the mission after searchers locate the subject*(s)*.

This function traditionally falls within in the Planning Section, but now NIMS/ICS allows for movement to other parts of the ICS organizational structure based on Command needs. These needs vary from national security, classified information or other operational requirements for incidents like missing person searches, terrorist attacks or even major disasters. The organizational chart *(Figure 15-4 above)* shows five different options for placement of this function depending on the requirements of the Command Staff.

1st Option: Intelligence / Investigations Officer – Command Staff. Under this option the Intelligence/Investigations Officer serves as part of the Command Staff and reports directly to the Incident Commander *(IC)*. Consider this option with limited sensitive information, only released on a need to know basis.

2nd Option: Intelligence / Investigations Section Chief – General Staff. Under this option the Intelligence/Investigations Section Chief serves as its own section equal to Operations, Plans and Logistics. As with the others, this Section Chief reports directly to the IC. Use this option on any incident where intelligence factors drive the operation. Examples include an urban search, probability of criminal activity, dealing with classified or law enforcement restricted information, etc. Think about the size of the support staff. With a larger Intelligence/Investigations staff required, the Section Chief option grows more appropriate.

3rd Option: Intelligence / Investigations Officer – Unit Leader. Under this option, the Intelligence/Investigations Unit Leader serves as part of the Planning Section. This falls under the traditional ICS placement, reporting to the Plans Section Chief. This option functions well during incidents with little or no investigative or specialized information requirements. Usually not a good option for protracted searches.

4th Option: Intelligence / Investigations Branch Director or Group Supervisor. Under this option, the Intelligence/Investigations Branch Director or Group Supervisor serves as part of the Operations Section and reports directly to the Operations Section Chief. Choosing this option works well when the situation requires a high degree of coordination between investigative efforts and tactical response. The Branch, in and of itself provides one of the main objectives. Some incidents in the urban environment call for this option. Groups under this Branch sometimes include Intelligence, Investigation, Canine Lab/Forensics, and Support Functions.

5th Option: Intelligence / Investigations Specialist. Under this option, the Intelligence/Investigations Specialist operates in any situation as a technical specialist assigned as needed within the ICS organizational structure.

Essential Components of the ICS

Management By Objectives. Good objectives allow the IC *(or Search Manager)* to focus efforts on actions that work toward a successful search. These objectives provide direction for the resources, benchmarks for mission progress and adjustment for new information that comes to light for succeeding operational periods. Planners develop objectives through a formal process, and then integrate them into the Incident Action Plan *(IAP)*.

Incident Action Plan (IAP) or Search Action Plan (SAP). The IAP describes the actions associated with a search and how specifically those actions occur. Initially the IAP exists only in the IC's head, but needs documentation after the first operational period.

The Search Action Plan brings together a variety of resources dedicated to finding the missing person. Every search needs some form of an action plan. For small situations of short duration, the plan never grows into a formal document. However, the following list shows several examples of appropriate scenarios for written action plans:

- When using resources from several agencies
- When involving several jurisdictions
- When the search requires changes in shifts of personnel and/or equipment

The Search Manager *(IC)* initially establishes objectives and makes strategy determinations for the search based on urgency, extenuating circumstances, the time critical nature of the situation and lastly, the established protocols of the jurisdiction. In the case of a unified management structure *(see below)*, the search objectives need to adequately reflect the policy and requirements of all the jurisdictions involved. The Action Plan functions dynamically and updates for each operational period. It consists of the objectives and strategy along with an organizational chart, assignments, and maps.

Continuity and Chain of Command. In ICS, continuity of command, every individual reports to a designated supervisor. With *Chain of Command,* an orderly line of authority flows through the ranks of the organization with lower levels subordinate to, and connected to, higher levels.

In a very high percentage of SAR incidents, the

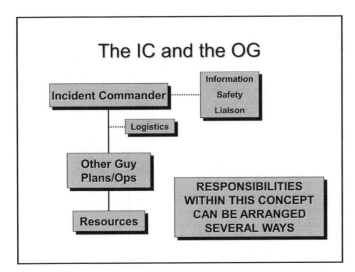

Figure 15-5 A Two Person ICS Structure is sometimes referred to as the Incident Commander and the Other Guy. (The Other Guy handles Planning and Operations- initial planning, determines tactics and deploys resources.) The IC handles initial contact, information gathering, liaison, and establishes objectives.

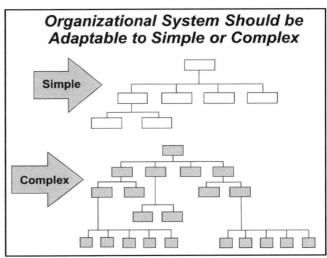

Figure 15-6 ICS Adaptability

organizational structure for operations consist of only Command and single resources *(See Figure 15-5 above)*. As SAR situations expand, the Chain of Command extends through an organizational structure and consists of several layers as needed, i.e.:

Command
Sections
Branches
Divisions/Groups
Units
Resources

Organizational Flexibility. The ICS organization adheres to a *form follows function* philosophy. In other words, the organization's size at any given time reflects only those functional components required to meet planned tactical objectives *(Figure 15-6)*.

The size of the organization during any time frame and that of the next operational period takes guidance from the incident action planning process. In fact, organizational elements tend to get activated in some sections without activating the sectional chiefs or other positions.

Each activated element contains a person in charge. In some cases a single supervisor initially controls more than one unit. Deactivation of elements no longer serving a continuing purpose, insures the flexibility of the organization to reduce size when necessary.

Unified Command/Management Structure. The concept of unified management simply means that all agencies with a jurisdictional responsibility at a multi-jurisdictional search contribute to the process of:

- Determining overall search objectives
- Selection of strategies
- Ensuring that joint planning for tactical activities occurs
- Ensuring the conduct of integrated tactical operations
- Making maximum use of all assigned resources

A unified management structure usually consists of a key responsible official from each jurisdiction involved, or it consists of several functional groups within a single political jurisdiction. It usually invites the advice of individuals or agencies with applicable expertise or capability.

Write out common objectives and strategies on major multi-jurisdictional searches. The objectives and strategies then guide development of the search action plan.

Under a unified management structure the implementation of the search action plan occurs under the direction of a single individual - the Operations Chief. As mentioned before, the Ops Chief normally comes from the agency with the greatest jurisdictional involvement.

Modular Organization. The organizational structure develops in a modular fashion based upon the size of the operation. The staff expands logically with responsibility and performance placed initially with the Incident Commander.

For ease of reference and understanding, personnel assigned to manage at each level of the organization carry distinctive organizational titles as shown in Figure 15-7.

The use of position titles in ICS serves three important purposes:

1. Titles provide a common standard for multi-agency use at an incident. For example on a multi-agency search, if one agency uses the title *Branch Chief*, another *Branch Manager*, another *Branch Officer*, etc., all for the same position, this generally causes confusion and reflects the lack of standardization on the scene.

2. The use of distinctive titles for ICS positions allows for filling ICS positions with the most qualified individuals independent of their rank within their own organizations.

3. The lack of standardization of position titles often confuses the ordering process when requesting qualified personnel. For example, in ordering additional personnel to fill unit positions, proper communications between the incident and the agency dispatch facilities need to know their assignments as Unit Leaders, Unit Officers, Supervisors, etc.

Common Terminology. Whether discussing search team assignments or ordering resources, SAR Responders need to communicate clearly with each other. ICS establishes *common terminology*

Terminology for Each Level in ICS

Functional Position	ICS Title	Backup Position
Search Manager	(IC) Incident Commander	Deputy
Command Staff	Officer	Assistant
Section	Chief	Deputy
Branch	Director	Deputy
Division / Group	Supervisor	None
Unit	Leader	Manager
Single Resource	Leader	None

Figure 15-7 Common ICS Titles for SAR

for functions, resources, and facilities. ICS uses common terminology for:

- Organizational elements
- Position titles
- Resources, and
- Facilities

Organizational Elements - Designating each level of the organization creates a consistent pattern *(e.g. sections, branches, etc.)*.

Position Titles - Position titles in ICS refer to those charged with management or leadership responsibility such as Officer, Chief, Director, Supervisor. etc. This provides a way to place the most qualified personnel in organizational positions, on multi-agency incidents without confusion caused by various multi-agency rank designations. It also provides a standardized method for ordering personnel to fill positions.

Resources - Common designations also identify various kinds of resources.

Many kinds of resources also fall out by type, which indicates their capabilities *(e.g. types of helicopters, patrol units, sweep teams, etc.)*.

Integrated Communications - A simple understanding of all communications among organizational elements at a search needs to exist. Stay away from codes and confine all communications to essential messages. The Communications Unit provides all communications planning for field operations at the search. This includes established radio networks, on-site telephone, public address, and off-site telephone/microwave/radio systems.

Comprehensive Resource Management involves the overall supervision, tracking and direction of incident resources. Established check-in procedures, status tracking and adequate staff help ensure accountability. Managers generally arrange resources in the following ways:

- **Single Resource** - The smallest unit which operates independently; perhaps, a helicopter, a search dog with handler, or an ambulance and each represents a primary Tactical Unit. Additionally, a single resource includes all the appropriate equipment plus the individuals required to properly use it.

- **Task Force** - A Task Force combines any number of resources temporarily for a specific task or objective. All resource elements within a Task Force need common communications, and each Task Force also requires a Leader. Task Forces form to meet a specific tactical need and subsequently demobilize or reorganize into another Task Force configuration as single resources fall out or change.

- **Strike Team** - A Strike Team utilizes a set number of resources of the same type, and contains an established minimum number of personnel. A Strike Team always includes a Leader with common communications. Example Strike Teams usually contain search crews, search dogs, or any other kind of resource where the combination of single resources of the same kind becomes a useful tactical unit.

The use of Strike Teams and Task Forces helps to maximize the use of resources, increase the management control of a large number of single resources, and reduce the overall communications load.

Maintaining an up-to-date and accurate picture of resource use requires:

- All resources use a current status condition
- All changes in resource locations and status conditions occurs promptly through the appropriate Functional Unit

Status Conditions for Resources. Search Operations usually use four status conditions to describe tactical resources during any incident:

1. Responding/En-route
2. Available
3. Assigned
4. Out-of-Service

Several status keeping methods or systems prove useful in keeping track of resources at a search:

- Manual record-keeping on standard ICS forms
- T-Cards with different colors for each type of resource. The cards record different information about the resource and reside in racks or status board slots according to current location or status
- Magnetic symbols on maps or status boards in different sizes, shapes and colors, with spaces to write in the resource designator. Subsequently managers place these markers on the map or status board by locations prescribed by the incident
- Any Computer software for resource tracking and management. A variety of software applications exist including simple spread sheets in Microsoft Excel™

T-Cards and computer software represent the most commonly used methods.

Changes in Status. Any individual who changes a resource's status provides that same information to the central resource status keeping function.

Designated Functional Facilities. Several kinds of facilities spring up around the average search incident. The determination of kinds of facilities and their locations depend upon the requirements of the incident and the direction of the management team. The following facilities define a few average search facilities *(See Figure 15-8a and b right for Common ICS Map Symbols).*

Search Base - The Search Base houses primary management and support activities. Also, the base contains all management equipment and personnel support for operations. *The Search Logistics Section,* which orders all personnel, equipment, and supplies also resides at the Base. Only one Base serves each search, and normally, once established the Base stays in one spot. If possible, the written preplan lists potential Search Base locations. The Command Post and the camp area for personnel normally fall within the search base as well.

- Normally SAR personnel designate the name of the Base by incident *(e.g. Marshal Base).* In locations with frequent major incidents, pre-designated possible Base locations with pre-planned layouts pay large dividends.

- The management of the Base falls under the Logistics Section. Along with an established Incident Base comes a Base Manager who, in a fully activated ICS organization, falls under the Facilities Unit of the Logistics Section.

Incident Command Post. Designated as the **ICP**, the Incident Command Post serves as the control center for all search operations. Only one Command Post exists for each search *(including multi-agency and multi-jurisdiction searches).* Normally the planning function takes place at the Command Post,

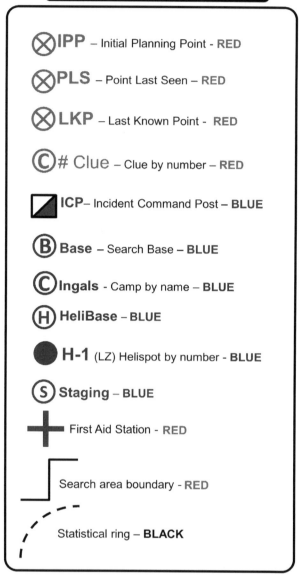

Figure 15-8a ICS Map Symbols
Reference *ASTM F1846-98*

along with the Communications Center functions. Most Command Posts co-locate with the Search Base, assuming an adequate communications capability.

- The initial location for the ICP considers the nature of the incident, its growth or movement, and whether the ICP location provides safety for the expected duration of the incident.

- A vehicle, trailer, tent or even a building all serve adequately as an ICP. On long-term incidents, an ICP facility which provides adequate lighting

First coverage of segment
Diagonal lines — Bottom to Top — L to R
Color relates to type of resource
Density of lines can relate to POD

Second coverage of segment
Diagonal lines — Bottom to Top — R to L
Color relates to type of resource
Density of lines can relate to POD

Third coverage of segment
Vertical lines. Color relates to type of resource.
Density of lines can relate to POD

Fourth coverage of segment
Horizontal lines. Color relates to type of resource.
Density of lines can relate to POD

Resource Specific Color Examples
Green: Ground Field Teams
Brown: Dog Teams
Blue: Helicopter
Orange: Fixed Wing

Figure 15-8b ICS Map Symbols
Reference *ASTM F1846-98*

and/or protection from the weather grows in importance.

- Larger and more complex incidents often require larger ICP facilities. Examples of incidents that usually require an expanded ICP facility include:

  - Multi-agency incidents run under a Unified Command
  - Long-term incidents
  - Incidents requiring an on-scene communications center
  - Incidents requiring a separate planning function
  - Incidents requiring the use of Command Staff and Agency Representative positions

- Some incidents grow large enough for an on-site communications center to dispatch assigned resources. For obvious reasons, the communications center often ends up with or adjacent to the ICP. Also, some incidents require space at the ICP to allow for various Command Staff and Planning Section functions.

Camps - Within the general search area, Camps provide staff, equipment, and facilities for sleep, food, water, and sanitary services to incident personnel. Camps differ from Staging Areas in that support operations occur at Camps, and resources located there generally lack the availability for immediate use. Not all incidents include camps.

- Camp facilities spring up separately from the Incident Base. They tend to stay in one place for several days, and then move depending upon situational needs.

- Initially, the staffing requirements for Logistics Section units located at Camps originate from the Incident General Staff, based on the incident and expected duration of Camp operations. After establishment of a Camp, additional personnel and support needs to flow via the Camp Manager. Common practice designates Camps by a geographic name or by a number. For example the Swauk Camp, or Camp #3.

Helibases - Helibases serve as locations in and around the search area where helicopters usually park, take repairs, fuel, and load up with personnel or equipment. On a very large incident the requirements dictate more than one Helibase. Once established, a Helibase usually stays in the same place.

Helispots - Helispots consist of temporary and less used locations where helicopters land and take off to load or unload personnel and/or equipment.

Field Operations

A list of proven priority elements for on-scene direction and control in SAR follow:

- Orient all activities to the subject
- Identify all hazards *(maintain safety)*
- Efficient reconnaissance, including terrain analysis
- Protect the access to the search base site

SUCCESS OFTEN OCCURS IN PRIVATE, FAILURE IN FULL PUBLIC VIEW!

- Monitor and control communications flow and volume;
- Always keeping a backup
- Brief and debrief as a matter of routine
- Establish victim care as soon as possible
- Establish and log subject's destination and ETA at a medical facility

Potential Problem Areas:

Mission logs and case studies of searches continue to reveal some consistent problems that generally crop up if someone fails to pay attention.

Include solutions to these problems within the context of checklists or procedures to routinely take care of them before they emerge as a problem.

- Identifying all responders on-scene
- Responder units or individuals staying with their assigned tasks *(accountability)*
- Relief of overhead/command staff and support people *(backup resources)*
- Ability to shift gears into expanded operations *(making the organization bigger)*
- Use of resources within their abilities and expertise *(assign qualified people)*

When a major search operation launches, specific management and structure functions must be addressed. **Five common operational problems** often arise during emergency response of any kind. Attention to these problem areas in the preplanning process helps to avoid the same difficulties in future operations:

1. Ambiguity of authority
2. Inability to communicate between agencies
3. Poor use *(or no use)* of specialized resources
4. Unplanned, negative relationships with the media
5. Inability to deal with unplanned *(emergent)* volunteer response

Summary

The Incident Command System, *(or an equivalent organizational structure)* brings together many autonomous agencies and organizations, each with its own jurisdictions, policies, funding, and other capabilities and constraints. Emergency responses in past decades functioned without cooperative agreements and associations using this structure. The concepts are not new. They now come together in a workable system giving benefit to all emergency response organizations. The ICS and variations of its basic concepts have been successfully used to improve many aspects of emergency response throughout the U.S.

Remember: When in charge, take charge!

From past experiences specific to both search management and emergency response in general, we know that some specific organizational pitfalls deserve special emphasis. The six step process *(See Figure 15-9 below)* continues to provide the redundancy that serves to remind everyone that some things need continuing review in our thought process. This cyclic approach helps to ensure the continued successful use of relatively mundane items.

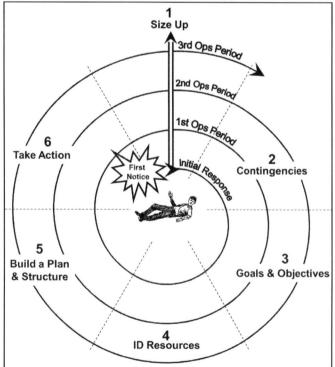

Figure 15-9 The six step management process represents a simple repetitive cycle for almost any emergency incident. Remember, you work for the missing person! Organize and Manage!

On-Scene Planning   16

Objectives:

- Describe the specific functional planning tasks carried out while search members complete the on-scene initial response Reflex Tasks

- List the components of the Incident Action Plan and how to use the IAP in the assessing operational period objectives

- Describe the difference between *Action Planning* on-scene *Preplanning* for SAR operations and *Search Planning* for a specific operational period

- Discuss the importance of specific, time related, measurable, and documented operational period objectives

Inexperienced SAR members often want to deploy search teams quickly in the field. SAR personnel feel an overwhelming amount of pressure from family, relatives, friends, media or a combination of all of these to immediately resolve the situation. Everyone commends SAR personnel with the ambition to find the missing person as fast as possible, but this often results in inadequate planning and a host of wrong decisions. Over the years, SAR professionals created several initial response actions which proved very productive in the beginning phases of a search, and when initiated quickly, they produce excellent results.

This chapter covers on-scene planning and the critical steps every team needs to take in the initial phases of a search, regardless of the circumstances. But remember, that using unproductive initial response methods over and over again accomplishes very little in an extended search. No one wants to get caught in this pitfall. Sending resources into the field after the initial response period without any real planning, puts search planners in a continual position of trying to catch-up and never getting ahead of the problem.

The use and understanding of the Incident Command System *(ICS)* and the Six Step Process helps ensure effective coordination for the management function on an incident. Management effectiveness occurs with these systems through a repetitive cycle built into each of the system's design structure. However, this initial search task fails to replace search planning. *Incident management and search planning differ*, therefore in this chapter we present a clear distinction between the two.

As the response to the incident begins to materialize, someone *(the Search IC or perhaps the Plans Chief)* assembles the components necessary for *search planning*. Planning for incident management and planning for the search happen simultaneously.

Very often, initial efforts produce results and lead to the location of the missing person. If not, then the IC activates the search planning function and puts into high gear.

Even during the initial phases of a search, the IC needs to use basic search theory concepts to provide the foundation, justification and documentation required for sound decision making and later apply more formal strategies and tactics if the need arises.

Initial Response On-scene

Standard protocol for search planning advocates gathering both planning data and searching data from a wide array of sources. For planning purposes, we need to determine where to begin looking *(Initial Planning Point)*, subject category, mental condition, destination and/or probable route(s), etc. For search purposes, investigators need a name, a description with clothing and possessions, as well as the activity or pursuit at the time of the loss. *Reflex Tasking* requires the gathering of this type of information as a precursor.

Reflex Tasking

As explained in Chapter 14, *Reflex Tasking* depends on subject categories, using the same elements and strategies on every search for a specific type of subject. As the term *reflex* implies, very little planning or thought process needs to occur before search managers assign tasks and carry them out. SAR units use a standard protocol for tasking, which helps to start the process with defensible decisions based on an accumulation of prior successful searches, which in turn leads to the assignment of appropriate resources as they arrive.

Thanks to the diligent efforts of Robert Koester in his publication *Lost Person Behavior (dbS Publications - 2008)* each category of subject in the ISRID Database coincide with detailed reflex tasks outlined under six functional groups *(Investigation, Initial Planning Point, Hub/Immediate Area, Containment, Travel Corridors and High Probability Tasks)*. Reflex Tasking also means working a search in the same manner as the vast majority of successful cases in the past. This gives the IC and any other potential overhead staff an opportunity to get set up, organize, do the appropriate map work and collate information from the beginning.

Differences in the Planning Function

- Planning for the management of an emergency incident *(a search)* falls directly on the ICS Plans Section Chief and consists of organizing and managing the emergency response
- Search planning differs from pre-planning in that it takes into account all of the unique circumstances of the present situation and depends on specific subject category behavioral data
- Search planning requires a technical specialist for the position and involves the details of search theory including effort allocation and deriving success with available resources in the least amount of time.
- Search Planning consists of:

- Correctly identifying high probability segments in the search area
- Assessment of the available resources and expected probability of detection
- Applying resources correctly, in the right order, and ensuring backup for ensuing operational periods
- Setting priorities in the allocation of effort to maximize success

Levels of Search Planning

Two levels of search planning occur at the operational level.

Informal Search Planning: The first level, and undoubtedly the most common and widely used throughout local response organizations with several exceptions. These exceptions include the knowledge and capability to shift gears and move into the next level of planning. Continual application (without results) of informal planning and automatic tasking with little documentation or justification, usually fails to bring any good to the situation, least of all the missing person.

Informal search planning includes using hasty searches to cover routes such as trails, tracks, roads, and *likely spots* including decision points and terrain attractions. This level uses an informal management structure and applies search theory based upon local statistics of prior similar searches to maximize efficiency of effort and quick action.

The Search IC sets the strategy for the initial response and it often takes place *on the hood of a vehicle*. Initial strategy gets the operation moving into the field, primarily focusing on *containment*, and getting good reconnaissance and intelligence about the incident *(Refer to Reflex Tasking - Chapter 14)*.

Upon completing the informal search process and focus on reflex tasking, lacking results, a transition into more formal planning needs to occur. To succeed, planners need to put foundation elements into place during the initial informal phase which provide the anchor of both documentation and retrospective evaluation.

Reflex tasking tends to encompass two or even more operational periods. However, before completing these tasks, decisions about area searches and applying resources with specific assignments in the next operational period needs to take place. Additionally tracking time spent and documentation of selected details along with recommendations for assignments using R_d *(Average Range of Detection)*.

Complete a retrospective evaluation of search effectiveness using debriefing notes and coverage estimates from searcher speed and R_d measurements. Note and document consensus values along with continued and expanded investigation efforts. Note times for key functions and establish detail logs to post for constant reference. All of this occurs with the anticipation of potentially not finding the missing person using only reflex tasks.

Formal Search Planning: This Provides the most detailed level of search planning. The formal planning phase results from a protracted search that outwardly appears unsuccessful in its early stages *(the initial response phase or even the 1st or 2nd Operational period)*. Successful formal search planning needs to accomplish a number of basic tenets early in the operation and to clearly document them. These include a detailed log of assignments, coverage estimates and a proportional consensus for probability distribution, together with the values for POA and POS *(see Chapters 18 and 20 respectively)*.

Formal search planning involves the sharing of information by all of the management team with discussions of tactical alternatives, objectives and the formulation of a detailed action plan. Dealing with policies and protocols for handling information at all levels requires information management. Teams conduct thorough searches of trails, tracks, roads and likely spots, with segment searches continuing and expanding according to a formal appraisal of areas based on effort allocation and a consensus including lost subject behavior. Formal search planning also applies *search theory* with a POS value calculated for each segment based on intensive debriefing and coverage estimates from field resources. As the investigation continues and expands, planning members postulate scenarios and apply values through consensus. Every operational period convenes with a formal planning meeting.

Words of Caution For Initial Tasks

- If all initial tasks occur at night, repeat them again in the daylight
- If team members believe a lost person continues to move around or evade searchers, repeat tasks

The Incident Action Plan - *(Search Action Plan)*

- Start in-depth planning with specific objectives, defined strategies and a preliminary Incident Action Plan
- Reflex Tasking and the use of the Bike Wheel model, accomplishes planning through the first 6 to 12 hours for the Search IC and staff (*and in some cases even longer*). After that the search expands into area searching and requires a portion of formal search theory and planning
- Every search involves an action plan. While no requirements exist for a written plan in small searches, a large search needs a written form for documentation and constant reference

Search Action Plan Development

The development of a Search Action Plan initially takes place with the Plans Section or the Incident Commander.

- The IC establishes information requirements and reporting schedules for all organizational elements.
- The IC provides general control objectives and alternatives which define legal, policy, resource, and fiscal constraints for the search in accordance with the preplans and policies of the involved jurisdiction(s).
- General staff discusses Strategies/tactics and objectives relative to:

- Resource status and availability (*RESTAT*)
- Situation status including hazards, risks, work required (*SITSTAT*)
- Situation predictions *(Guessing likely outcomes)*
- Communications capabilities
- Weather

- The Plans Section then takes this information and develops the Search Action Plan *(SAP)*
- Plans coordinates strategies with the Operations Chief and resource support and service needs with the Logistics Chief
- Plans develops the SAP in written form with alternatives
- Plans presents the search plan to the Search Manager for approval

Plans Section conducts briefing of general staff, makes necessary adjustments to the plan and duplicates and prepares for distribution at field team leader briefing.

Important Considerations for Overall Search Incident Management

Proper management of information avoids irritations and distractions, and allows all aspects of the search to focus on finding the lost person not specific problems as they crop up and threaten to overwhelm the unprepared.

Suggested Sequence of Actions for any Search Operation (See Figure 16-1 on Page 268)

NOTIFICATION and INITIAL RESPONSE: Consists of a relatively simple but important phase getting operations rolling. In general, it:

- Functions as gathering pertinent information and good reconnaissance on-scene, creating initially important paperwork
- Contacts the reporting party and determines whether or not a genuine missing person incident exists

Establish Category of subject using *ISRID* LPB algorithm (*see Chapter 14, page 227*).

Start Search planning by marking the **IPP, LKP and/or PLS** on the map - **and** the **median distance and maximum zone** for the category. Also crosscheck a theoretical travel distance for the subject, if appropriate, for the time frame and scale of map.

Overlay the map with distances and behavioral characteristics. As an example, if you measure the distance on the map for the median in a particular category of subject, then we know that 50% of the cases in the database were found inside that distance. Therefore, with no other factors considered, allocate 50% of the probability inside this distance. Using the missing/lost person database as an initial indicator of probability distribution, helps staff to allocate probability to the segments in each of the scenario based regions.

Interview and gather information for planning and searching, *(Missing Person Report Form)* use the Initial MPR Form or the local equivalent, even a longer version, as a guide.

Develop a subject profile and begin investigative efforts collecting additional data from the community, and continue this process throughout the remainder of the search.

Use this profile to:

- Define what searchers need to look for
- Estimate the numbers and types of resources needed
- Determine an overall strategy of either passive or active techniques or a combination of the two
- Provide initial and subsequent guidance in mapping the search area according to barriers, attractions, incentives or avenues of least resistance
- Provide a comprehensive briefing for each team on how and where to look for clues, sign, an absence of clues, disturbances, colors, evidence, unknowing witnesses, and even typical behaviors

(Consult *Lost Person Behavior* see Chapter 14 and the *Search Urgency* factors in Chapter 11.)

Shut the Doors by establishing **confinement** if possible.

Urgency determination. Fill out the urgency form and keep it updated every operational period as an *incomplete*, but living document.

Begin Reflex Tasks in all 6 functional groups using the Bike Wheel Model:

- Travel Corridors
- Investigation
- Initial Planning Point
- Containment
- Hub/ Immediate Area
- High Probability Tasks

- The initial priority of the reflex tasking concentrates on *shutting the doors* around the **Initial Planning Point,** therefore minimizing the possibility of the missing subject leaving the area without anyone discovering them

- Reflex Tasking requires a subject category for assignments and responding resources receive their initial tasks accordingly

- Reflex Tasks take anywhere from one to several operational periods depending on the terrain, geographic location and subject category

- The ultimate goal focuses on creating a plan for execution if reflex tasking fails to retrieve the missing subject

    - Synthesize all information gathered concerning the missing person

Develop plausible scenarios explaining the missing person's absence - which direction the missing person possibly traveled, any alternate routes leading to a suspected destination *(See Scenario Analysis in Chapter 18)*.

Construct at least three plausible scenarios that fit the circumstances of this missing person incident.

- Encourage Input! Try not to plan in a vacuum. Consider any ideas searchers, family, and the locals offer. Organize a brainstorming session if necessary
- Invite key people to participate, including the IC, Operations Section Chief, investigators, selected family members, representatives of participating organizations, individuals with special knowledge of the search area, persons well skilled in strategy and tactics, as well as free-lance locals
- Provide a briefing, allowing each person two to five minutes to make and justify recommendations, listing them on a flip chart or dry-erase board
- Once everyone provides input, allow a certain amount of time for discussion
- Use subjective analysis to determine the influences of terrain, weather, and personality on subject movement or preferences *(Terrain analysis)*
- Evaluate specific subject capabilities based on objective opinions and update scenarios

These techniques allow everyone the opportunity to provide input. They also draw the appropriate locals into the operation, provide for the family to participate, and identify original ideas while still making decisions in a timely manner.

Establish regions of probability consistent with developed scenarios. This consists of drawing the area on the map consistent with each scenario.

- The IC weighs each scenario using the proportional consensus process if a specialized search planning section exists. Although not necessary, the numerical weighting process adds refinement and an opportunity for more detailed information in the analysis of specific scenarios
- Consensus considers subjective, statistical, investigative and deductive factors along with information from the subject profile, local history, and lost person behavior data from ISRID or other databases. Regions of probability need a clear definition with boundaries easy to identify on the map and in the field

Weights assigned to each region, used in conjunction with lost person behavior data, distribute probability

Sequence of Actions for a Search Operation

1. Phone call and notification *(A person is potentially lost or missing)*
2. Category of subject using LPB algorithm by Koester
3. Locate the IPP, the median distance and maximum zone for the category from ISRID/LPB by Koester
4. Interview – Gather information – Planning & Searching Data –*(Missing Person Report Form)*
5. Shut the doors – Establish confinement if possible
6. Fill out Urgency Form with available information
7. Begin Reflex Tasks in all 6 functional groups using the Bike Wheel Template:

   - Travel Corridors
   - Investigation
   - Initial Planning Point
   - Containment
   - Hub/ Immediate Area
   - High Probability Tasks

The overall objective for this initial response phase of the incident focuses on accomplishing these tasks as quickly & efficiently as possible.

Depending on the terrain, geographic location and subject category, Reflex Tasks take anywhere from one to several operational periods. If it takes more than one operational shift to accomplish these required tasks, briefing/debriefing, urgency updates and planning meetings need to occur accordingly. In case of unsuccessful Reflex Tasks, overhead team members, if any, and the IC continue with the remainder of this checklist and the required search planning functions.

8. Construct at least three plausible scenarios
9. Surround the terrain on the map consistent with each scenario – *(Regions of Probability)*
10. Subdivide *(segment)* regions into searchable areas *(accomplishable in 1 operational period)*
11. Use Consensus Worksheet #1, #2 and #3 *(Scenario, individual and collective consensus)*

---

12. Develop objectives for the next operational period – ICS Form 202
13. Assess available resources on-scene and needed – RESTAT
14. Develop IAP *(Incident Action Plan)* for coming operational period
15. Assign staff member to track info about the status of the situation in total - SITSTAT
16. Prepare task assignments to meet the objectives
17. Brief
18. Commit resources to the field
19. SEARCH
20. Debrief, document details and send info to Plans Section with amended recommendations for next Operational Period objectives
21. Brief incoming IC and Overhead Team
22. Update Urgency Form for incoming shift
23. Amend, update, eliminate or add new scenario information for Regions of Probability
24. Repeat process starting at item #12 above for every subsequent Operational Period
25. Document everything relentlessly!

Figure 16-1
Recommended sequence of actions for on-scene formal search planning

through out the designated search area. Remember the search area remains the *smallest* area consistent with known facts and speculation of the missing persons actions.

Subdivide the scenario based regions of probability into searchable segments. Determine the size of these segments by operational period capabilities. Make sure to provide one resource type with a segment size small enough to cover the entire terrain in an operational period.

- Segments need clear, well defined and easily identifiable boundaries, both on the map and in the field *(for most of the forested or moderately vegetated terrain across the U.S. 80 to 100 acres fits this requirement of searchability in 4 to 6 hours)*. 4 to 6 hours excludes access, egress, briefing and debriefing. Always consider ground cover, barriers, and topography when designating segments.

Establish Consensus about the priority and plausibility of both scenarios and locations most likely containing the missing person.

- The proportional consensus method calls for using a reference value of 100 *(although 10 works equally as well)* to indicate the segment or region of probability most likely containing the missing person. The reference value of 100 is not a percentage or a probability but a comparison reference value and everyone needs to use the same reference value *(See Page 310 in Chapter 18)*.

Prepare Objectives in writing *(ICS202)* and remember to base Search Objectives on the acronym:

SMARTER

- **S**pecific for each operational period or sortie committed
- **M**easurable and verifiable within a specific time period
- **A**chievable in a practical sense within the time frame identified
- **R**elevant and/or realistic to the actual goal stated
- **T**ime related - accomplished in what time frame
- **E**valuated and assessed by the overhead team
- **R**eviewed and recorded for documentation

Objectives usually proscribe a level of coverage and effort allocation that maximizes POS values for searching both the entire area and the individual segments.

Estimate numbers of resources and the effort allocation options needed to maximize POS in the shortest amount of time.

Consider:

- The type of resources needed and those available
- The length of time resources offer
- Time available versus coverage area
- Estimated coverage for each resource *(POD values for terrain type)*
- Effort allocation to maximize the product of POA × POD = POS

Develop Search *(Incident)* Action Plan

- The Search Action Plan initially gets developed by the Plans Section Chief or by the Incident Commander *(Search Manager)*.
- The Search IC establishes information requirements and reporting schedules for all organizational elements.
- The IC provides general control objectives and alternatives which define legal, policy, resource, and fiscal constraints for the search in accordance with the pre-plans and policies of the involved jurisdiction(s).

The Search - Incident Action Plan provides the following:

- Defines operational periods
- Provides written objectives reflecting the policy and needs of all jurisdictions

- Incorporates subject profile data and missing/lost person behavior
- Provides an organizational chart (*ICS 207*) and assignment lists *(tactical assignments)*
- Establishes search maps delineating assignment areas
- Lists operational objectives for defined periods
- Outlines a communications plan (*ICS 205*)
- Gives resource status and availability (*RESTAT ICS 210*)
- Provides regular situation/status reports (*SITSTAT*)
- Documents weather information
- Provides situation predictions
- Outlines medical, rescue and recovery plans (*ICS 206*)
- Provides a transportation plan
- Identifies safety considerations for weather, hazards, etc. (*ICS 208*)

A search for a missing person is where the rubber meets the road, and the planning effort gets it's report card.

Discuss strategies/tactics and objectives with general staff relative to:

- Resource status and availability
- Situation status including hazards, risks, work accomplishment
- Situation predictions *(The best guess at a likely scenario)*
- Communications capabilities
- Weather

The Plans Section then takes this information and develops the Search Action Plan *(SAP)*.

- Coordinates strategies with the Operations Chief
- Coordinates resource support and service needs with the Logistics Chief
- Develops the SAP in written form with alternatives
- Presents plan to Incident Command for approval

The Plans Section conducts briefing of general staff, makes necessary adjustments to the plan and duplicates and prepares for distribution at field team leader briefing.

Assign staff to track status of the situation. This includes Information Management. Assign a specific person to monitor maps and resource status, *(e.g. en route or responding, on call, standing by, in staging, out of service, crew rest, disabled, committed or in service, and even checked out, or en route home).* It also includes assignment summaries, logs, and other tools as well as follow-up actions for correlation and incorporation into subsequent operational period objectives and strategies. Delays in establishing this function result in loss of data caused by poor documentation and poor information management.

A good deal of managing the incident as a whole involves the management of information. Properly managed information reveals guideposts to logical actions *(ie. a plan)*. People in charge of Plans need to consider the following when developing strategies for handling information:

- Routing the investigation results to the search planner
- Collate subject profile details such as personalities, influences, and background
- Research lost subject behavior from local, regional or international databases and bring it together in a coherent fashion
- List available search resources by types, numbers, when available and for how long, and any specialized training
- Reports and descriptions of terrain and vegetation analysis for visual obstruction and avenues of least resistance
- Clue leads, log entries, personal interview details, unknowing witnesses, follow up and synopsis for planning meetings *(Especially important in urban areas)*
- Weather - past, present and predicted along with a projection of the time critical nature of the situation
- Outside political pressure or inquiries for information, assistance or status

This seems like an overwhelming amount of information, especially in an urban search, but really only a portion of it needs consideration. If organized and filtered correctly it provides clear direction and ensures effective use of resources. Some ideas on how to collect and manage this information follows:

Prepare Assignments in writing to meet objectives (*ICS 204 Task Assignment Form*).

A copy of the map and instructions, together with information such as subject profile details, operational period objectives, communications plan, and debriefing questionnaire serve as the briefing packet given to each team leader by Operations:

- Sketch/create all assignments for individual handouts *(computer/printer, copier etc.)*
- Combine all overheads assignments in one operational period over a map and photocopy
- Write additional instructions on a separate piece of paper
- Date and time stamp each map and instructions
- Prepare both the photocopied map and the instructions as decisions get made
- A copy of the map and instructions, together with other information such as subject profile, operational period objectives, communications plan, and debriefing questionnaire serve as the briefing packet given to each team leader by Operations (*A suitable computer program accomplishes many of these functions*).

This method minimizes preparation time, provides for fast briefings, serves as documentation, allows searchers to carry into the field, minimizes confusion, and lets everyone know the plan.

Also, list team assignments in large letters on flip chart paper or blackboard and post for quick reference at Plans. Include columns for status, and accomplishments. These charts allow for quick reference, and comparisons.

Brief/Commit resources to the field for searching and Plan for Operational Periods: Always plan for at least 24 hours. Outline a general plan for the next shift, and update as further information filters in.

First Operational Period after completing Reflex Tasking: (*Realize that it often takes a number of operational periods to complete all the Reflex Tasks listed under the functional groups, particularly in an urban area.*)

This phase of the incident begins by continuing investigative fact finding along with refinement of the designated search area on a map. To this point resources arrive on-scene and receive Reflex Tasks in all of the functional groups identified for the category of subject. The IC and/or the overhead team now need to focus on more definitive planning and the development of a comprehensive probability map. Even though the proportional consensus process provides subjective information, it uses all the available information and a consistent repeatable process to establish the probability distribution among regions and segments. The process identifies more and less likely locations in the search area for the missing person. It prioritizes identified geographic areas, specific locations and assigned search functions.

> **NOTE:** At the first opportunity, schedule operational periods to begin and end at either 6 pm or 6 am, depending when the initial response and first operational period took place. Experience generally suggests 12 hours for an operational period with 4 to 6 hours of actual search time in the field.

Subsequent Operational Periods: Briefing, debriefing and analysis of reconnaissance information from previously deployed field searchers incorporates into a 12 hour time frame for operational periods.
- Focus on the numbers as a guide to high probability areas and secondary search areas already identified with continued investigation.
- Criteria for planning now consists of efficiently maximizing success per searcher hour of effort.
- Review, and if necessary, revise the search objectives, resource needs, subject profile data, and versions of plausible scenarios, etc.

In this phase of the search, tasks usually involve expanding the organization and increased searcher effort. At this point, lack of clues often causes an expanded effort into a new area, or alternatively, specific clues sometimes require more focus on specific areas with specialized resources.

- Task resources in terms of effort allocation and desired probability of success
- Diversify resources with respect to location, tactics, and resource type
- Plan the necessary resources for the next operational period

Debrief. Debrief returning team leaders *(or teams)*. Document debriefing information on transparencies overlaid on a master map.

Crunch Numbers. Prepare a summary of Probability of Success sheets for each segment and the overall search area *(See Chapter 20)*.

The new cumulative POS's for each segment, and the search area overall, indicate priority areas needing searched; The updating strategy requires these new cumulative POS's. Although not very difficult the calculations continuously repeat themselves.

Plan for and Brief next shift's general staff. In most searches the search planning section need to think ahead at least 12 to 15 hours. This creates greater continuity and avoids time consuming research and figuring while other people wait. It also gives staff in logistics an opportunity to stay ahead of the game as well.

Update Urgency Form for incoming shift. Every operational period needs to keep this document updated and current.

Repeat process starting at item #12 of Fig 16-1 page 268 for every subsequent operational period.

Document everything relentlessly!

Suggestions

- Maintain an attitude of positive urgency, and try not to make the situation worse
- Make sure to adequately brief the overhead team and orient them to possible clues and information crucial to the operation
- Remain focused at all times and encourage everyone to keep sight of the action plan objectives
- Good managers delegate as much work as possible in order to handle any additional problems
- Indecision, the only thing worse than a *bad* decision. When using all the information available to you, as well as good judgment, *bad* decisions usually cease
- Assign inexperienced team members to various overhead operations so they learn from *shadowing* a mentor
- Secondary and alternative assignments during the initial briefing ensure a fallback position for field teams if any problems arise. Particularly in the urban environment

A Planning Checklist

Initially developed by Ken Hill

- Make sure enough lost person data exists to plan the search
- Determine the urgency of the incident
- Compute the theoretical search distance for this subject
- Compute the statistical search distance for this subject
- Establish the subject's direction of travel from the IPP
- Identify all natural boundaries *(roads, blue lines, etc.)*
- Identify possible confinement points
- Identified all travel aids or linear features *(roads, trails, drainages, clearings etc.)*?
- Make sure the plans follow a logical sequence from the Incident Objectives
- Identify at least three logical scenarios and their respective regions of probability
- Divide the regions of probability into manageable segments
- Assign a Probability Of Area to each of the segments
- Task resources in terms of effort allocation and desired probability of success

AN EXAMPLE SEARCH PLANNING TIME TABLE
Using a 12 hour (24hr clock designations) time table.

18:00	- Shift change *(field personnel)*.
18:00-19:00	- Debrief personnel coming in from field.
19:30	- Brief new overhead shift.
20:00	- Overhead shift change.
20:00-23:00	- Collect and evaluate data, document action, resource status, situation status, develop predictions for next shift.
23:00	- Planning section meeting: Develop alternatives, make section assignments for overhead briefing meeting preparation.
24:00-02:00	- Prepare overhead briefing/strategy meeting.
02:00-03:00	- Conduct management and general staff briefing *(planning meeting)*.
03:00-05:00	- Prepare Search Action Plan: Develop, assemble, duplicate, update. *(could be as much as three hours in some cases)*
05:00-06:00	- Present briefing to field personnel.
06:00	- Shift change *(field personnel)*.

Remember that 4 to 6 hours is appropriate for field personnel to maintain "searching" status. Management operational periods will be longer as a general rule, but should rotate in shifts as well.

Figure 16-2 Search Planning Time-line

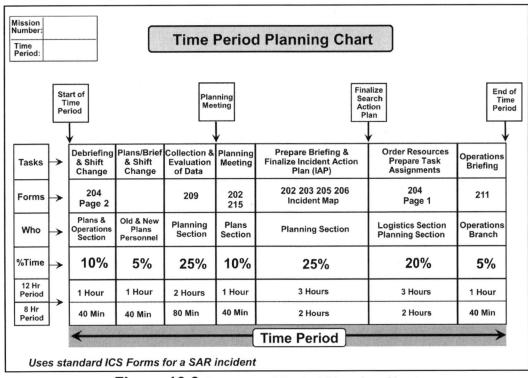

Figure 16-3 Operational Period Planning Chart

- Diversify resources with respect to location, tactics, and resource type
- Plan the necessary resources for the next operational period

operations with any degree of competence, they need a basic working knowledge of necessary resources, tactics and skills.

Strong Fundamentals create a Successful Search

This text presupposes readers and course participants posses a strong academic or practical knowledge base, upon which to apply the principles forming the foundation of modern search management. So, in order for a prospective search manager to adequately direct search

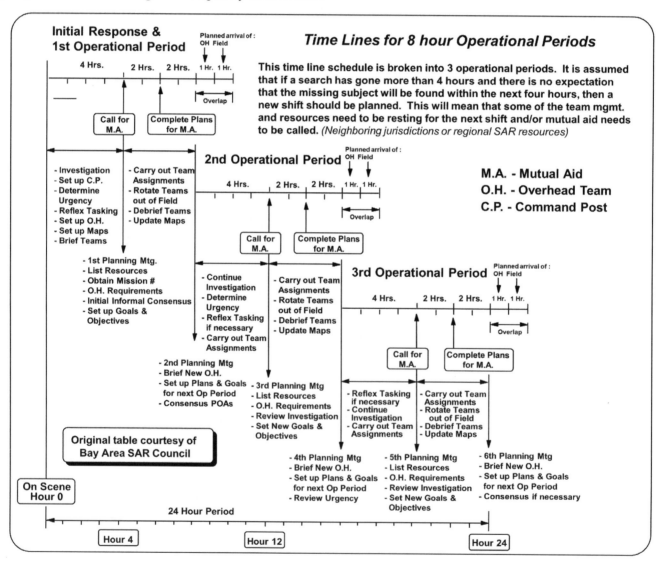

Figure 16-4 Operational Period Time-line

Introduction to Search Theory and Applied Probability

Objectives:

- Discuss *Probability of Success (POS)* as it relates to search

- Understand importance of quantifying or measuring search efforts

- Explain the value of *numbers, probabilities,* and *equations* (mathematics) as search management tools

- Use basic unit analysis to break down and understand mathematical equations, their usefulness, and how they describe the relationships between numbers and practical reality

- Relate the common definitions used in search theory and the utility of these terms for search planning

The Short History and Split Path of Land Search Theory

A wartime environment with a critical need often leads to very innovative and crucial discoveries. The derivation of **search theory** for our purposes in search traces back to World War II and something called *Operations Research (Koopman, B.O. 1946)*. The theme of Operations Research centered on the war at sea, and finding enemy submarines in the North Atlantic. Allied success in Europe depended on accurate predictions about the locations of Axis submarines to protect transatlantic supply convoys. Attempting to locate these elusive submarines, in a large area with limited resources, provided the foundation for modern search theory. The U.S. Navy also conducted searches to locate and recover lost or missing personnel. The work done during this period constituted the first formal scientific research on the general problem of search. This investigative work applied the established principles of statistics and science to a wide variety of search problems in the maritime environment.

After WW II the U.S. Navy and Coast Guard continued maritime research into the present, spending millions of dollars applying Operations Research to a multitude of search problems. Their research dealt with signaling, specific characteristics that make objects easier to find, as well as improving search platforms, methods, and sensors. Prior to the mid 1960's the unique problems associated with the arena of land search, received virtually no research or funding. Correspondingly, virtually nothing in terms of the formal scientific discipline, initiated in the 1940's by the Navy, transferred over to similar efforts on land and the then developing ground search methods.

Over the next 30 years numerous individuals attempted to put land search planning on a more scientific footing. Unfortunately, these efforts usually dealt with very specific topics without taking a true *systems approach* that treated "*...the operation of search as an organic whole having a structure of its own—more than the sum of its parts*" *(Koopman, 1980)*. Fractured approaches stemmed from volunteers doing separate research on topics of individual interest. A few even attempted to conduct field experiments, but lacked training in the intricacies of how to design and conduct those experiments or interpret their findings. As a result, the experiments fell short in many important respects. Although a few professional mathematicians tried to lend a hand, they failed to realize the considerable body of published research already accomplished by Koopman and others in the 40s. In defense of those trying to improve land search, finding the already established scientific data on search theory and the practical application of it, involved many difficulties, especially since the United States government only declassified it around 1958 without any fanfare or public announcement. In retrospect, these piecemeal attempts at improving land search failed to provide a comprehensive approach, and even contained a number of misconceptions and conceptual errors.

On the other hand, many volunteers made outstanding contributions. Dennis Kelly, circa 1973, first referenced Koopman's work in his SAR Management book *Mountain Search for the Lost Victim*. Bill Syrotuck, for the first time, showed the importance of establishing and using lost person behavior profiles. He also showed the need for a more formal approach to the use of probabilities in land search, but unfortunately never fully developed such a system. Jon Wartes discovered the importance of effort allocation when attempting to find subjects sooner rather than later. He correctly concluded that a method where searchers marched through an area shoulder-to-shoulder, while very thorough, slowed the search so much, that often others *(relatives searching randomly)* found the subjects before the searchers got to them. However, he failed to correctly formulate his findings for effective, repeatable use in search planning.

Later, land search in the 1980's and 1990's revolved around very dedicated, and at times innovative, efforts from volunteers building on the early works of Wartes and Syrotuck.

Although correct in many respects, others often misinterpreted conclusions by these two individuals, which led to a compounding of errors and misconceptions. In short, volunteers tried unsuccessfully to reinvent search theory often without a scientific background, or the necessary education, equipment, and funding.

In 1998, primarily through the efforts of J.R. Frost and D.C. Cooper, *Search Theory and Its Inland Application*, the method of Land Search as an organized approach to finding missing people changed, realigning itself with the recognized science of *search theory*. This realignment process created a great deal of controversy among practitioners and resulted in the choice between two basic approaches to search. To use numerical assessments *(the numbers)* or to rely on repetitive management systems which performed the same functions over and over again as originally developed on land decades before. In addition, a collective awakening to the real components and benefits of search theory and it's underlying principles began to take place. Incident management and search planning consist of two separate functions. They diverge dramatically in practice and we need a clear distinction between the two.

Approaches to Search Planning, Management of a Search and Training

A Unified Strategy —

A unified, all discipline, approach appears the most credible for managing searches in today's liability prone, government assisted environments *(A combination of proven initial tactics for specific subject categories combined with scientifically based protocols and numerical assessments to provide the proper balance and foundation for careful and deliberate planning)*. The application of selected definitions, notations, mathematically provable and successful methods all combine to form a winning paradigm.

Using the Incident Command System *(ICS)* and the Six Step Process developed by the International Association of Chiefs of Police, helps to ensure effective coordination in the management function for the incident. This effectiveness occurs through a repetitive cycle built into the management structure. As mentioned earlier, this is not search planning.

As the response to the incident begins to materialize, someone *(the Incident Commander or perhaps the Search Planner in the Plans section)* assembles the components necessary for *search planning*, referencing missing/lost person behavior data, results from interviewing, investigation, and preliminary hasty searching in *likely spots* as well as assessment of resources available and terrain analysis. Very often, these initial efforts produce results and lead to the location of the missing person very quickly. If not, then the *search planning* function activates, documentation formalizes and potential scenarios *(theories about what happened)* get recorded.

The different approaches to handling missing person incidents should never compete with one another. Initial responses *(Reflex Tasking based on Lost Person Behavior)* evolved due to certain functional tasks consistently producing results if used early on in a search (*i.e. Looking in Likely Spots*). However, when initial tasking fails, the components of formal search theory apply in preparation for a tougher search. A simple approach then develops into a more formal and scientifically based approach to cope with a more difficult problem.

Some very innovative and educated members of the land SAR community continue to actively guide land search efforts toward more scientifically valid approaches to solving the problem of finding missing people. Identifying new areas of research and defining sound parameters for land search occurs by applying the underlying principles initially learned in Operations Research.

The Compromise of Both Science and Common Sense
from
An Introduction to Land Search Probabilities & Calculations
by William D. Syrotuck

> *Search probability theory (probabilities and statistics) introduce formulas and calculations that use the language of science, which is mathematics. These numerical assessments measure optimum planning choices, change, compromise or progress at any time during a search. The use of these numbers opens up an array of very powerful science based tools that are available to the search planner.*

Quantification

Numbers permeate modern society, mostly because numerical comparisons present the simplest description of alternatives, actions, or results. Evaluation of the effort expended on a search gives the search manager a reason to make choices. Investigative facts and information about the missing person, the area, and the circumstances of the situation serve to give a Search Manager some limited, tangible indications about where to search, and with what resources. Speculation and intuition, though sometimes powerful, fail to give real meaning when compared one to another with descriptive terms. On the other hand, using numbers to compare evaluations leads to accurate tracking of those numbers and to solid results about one factor over another. *Consistent mathematical comparisons better justify team action.*

The use of *numbers* to express *relative* indications of probabilities, and manipulating combinations of variables, results in *calculating alternative* strategies.

Instead of interpreting the use of numbers as the application of precision analysis, use math to justify systematic search management decisions over other alternatives.

- Abstract words fail to express results accurately enough.

- Using probabilities resembles *playing the odds* or *trade-offs*. Numbers express relative values not absolutes. In probability calculations, 70% by itself means very little. In context though, 70% is relatively better than 60%, but not as good as 80%.

Analysis of Results Using Math

Many view mathematical equations with a certain apprehension, or even complete disinterest. However, equations and computations allow us to see and understand the relationships among various important quantities. They also bring a level of objectivity to the decision-making process not obtained any other way. Study and practice turn the concepts presented in the next few chapters into powerful tools for land search. Although difficult at first, once grasped they seem quite logical and straightforward, even obvious at times. Working with each concept or idea from its introduction and understanding it thoroughly before moving on, develops an intuition for later application. The application of probability and mathematics not only helps the search effort directly but leads to a defensible foundation for the decision making process.

Physical scientists routinely use the basics of math to describe nearly everything in the world. In fact, mathematics is the language of science. For example, when figuring the size of an area, the product of the length multiplied by the width expresses an area *(i.e., square feet or ft^2)*. The numbers in the measurement behave as expected, but the units behave like the numbers too.

$$8 \text{ ft.} \times 6 \text{ ft.} = 6 \times 8 \times \text{ft.} \times \text{ft.} = 48 \text{ (ft.} \times \text{ft.)} = 48 \text{ (ft)}^2$$

Though obvious on its face, without this concept some of the equations expressed in Chapters 18 through 20 potentially generate confusion rapidly. Expressing the numbers in terms of their basic units helps make the most complex equations and concepts much easier to understand and manipulate.

Continuing with the mathematical discussion; all the basic math functions applied to numbers apply to the units of measure as well.

An object traveling steadily that moves 32 miles in 2 hours can be expressed as:

$$\frac{32 \text{ miles}}{2 \text{ hours}} = \frac{16 \text{ miles}}{1 \text{ hour}} = 16 \text{ miles per hour}$$

The process breaks into two steps; first divide 32 by 2 which equals 16;

$$\frac{32}{2} = 16$$

Next, express the units, in this case *(miles/hr)*, saying miles per hour, but it really means the unit of distance *(miles)* divided by the unit of time *(hours)*.

$$\frac{\text{miles}}{\text{hour}} = \text{miles per hour}$$

Next, just like with numbers, multiplying by one unit and then dividing by that same unit cancels it out.

As before: $8 \text{ ft.} \times 6 \text{ ft.} = 48 \text{ ft}^2$

Now, for example, lets divide by 12ft

Expanded for simplicity, this is

$$\frac{48 \text{ ft.} \times \text{ft.}}{12 \text{ ft.}}$$

The first step is to divide 48 by 12 which equals 4.

$$\frac{48}{12} = 4$$

Next for the units, we multiply feet times feet and then divide by feet.

$$\frac{\cancel{\text{ft.}} \times \text{ft.}}{\cancel{\text{ft.}}} = \text{feet}$$

The end product comes out to 4 feet.

The more numbers and units involved the more important this analysis. Account for all units multiplied, divided, canceled, and carried through to the end product. In this way each piece of the equation *(numbers and units)* shows how it affects the outcome of the mathematical operation. In addition, this type of analysis often shows possible errors or combinations of inappropriate quantities. The following examples use a few of the concepts introduced more explicitly later. Not intended to be difficult, they illustrate the basic concepts of unit analysis which eases later understanding of POA and POD.

On a search we ask the question "Resources effectively search how much area in the field during a given period of time, to achieve a specific level of coverage?" *(Coverage defined later in Chapter 19)*. A search planner needs to know information like this. For example: one resource searches at one square mile every 6 hours to achieve a coverage of 1.0 in contrast to another type of asset capable of searching at a rate of one square mile per 3 hour period to achieve that same coverage. Comparisons like this potentially make significant differences to the allocation of search effort.

In another example, we place a piece of string between two people 10 feet apart and move them at a steady speed of 3 feet per second for 10 seconds. How much ground did the string pass over as it moved during those 10 seconds?

$$10 \text{ ft.} \times \left(\frac{3 \text{ ft.}}{\text{sec}}\right) \times 10 \text{ sec} = ?$$

First multiply the numbers...
$$10 \times 3 \times 10 = 300$$

Next multiply out the units...
$$\text{ft.} \times \left(\frac{\text{ft.}}{\text{sec}}\right) \times \text{sec} = \text{ft.}^2 \times \left(\frac{\text{sec}}{\text{sec}}\right) = \text{ft.}^2$$

The answer, combining the two results in 300 ft^2, or 300 square feet passed over in our 10 second example. Additionally, changing each piece of the equation changes the overall end product. Simply working through a few math problems on a piece of paper helps develop and verify *intuition*.

For example, it might be possible to achieve a *coverage* of 1.0 in eight hours using six searchers moving at an average search speed of one mile per hour. However, searching the same segment yields the same *coverage* in only four hours with 12 searchers moving at the same speed. Three searchers assigned for eight hours, reduces the coverage from 1.0 to 0.5, assuming the search speed remains at one mile per hour. Changing the number of searchers, walking speeds and spacing to achieve *coverage* all becomes clear in due course and thinking in these terms eventually becomes second-nature or even *intuitive*.

Extrapolating these basic concepts a little, the search manager sees the applicability to land search in terms of area covered, and the amount of time it takes to accomplish the desired *coverage* for a given search segment. In the next three chapters these concepts and many more relating to basic statistics, searcher effectiveness, and target detection will unfold.

Note: Increasing *coverage* requires increasing the level of effort, either by adding resources or increasing time spent searching or some combination of the two. Chapter 19 - Probability of Detection, presents methods for computing coverage and obtaining the corresponding POD.

Statistical Concepts

Statistical analysis rationally groups and summarizes information to illuminate:

- Consistencies, patterns and trends
- Inconsistencies or things out of place
- Significance of information or conclusions, i.e. the level of confidence in the information or conclusions

Lost person behavior and search planning provide perfect arenas for the practical application of statistics. Statistics make sense of individual and corporate experiences and relates them meaningfully to similar situations in the past.

Databases

DATABASES consistently provide valuable and often critical information. A data base consists of many individual results, organized for easy accessibility. Normally a single database considers one category related to the information inside, for example in Lost Person Behavior, *Dementia* or *Hikers*. As a general rule the larger the data base the more reliable the conclusions drawn from it. As an example: 100 cases provide a greater reliability in statistical data than 50, which is better than 20, or in turn 12.

The *distribution* of similar variables in a database describes the relative numbers of times each possible outcome occurs in a given number of trials. It represents or arranges the statistical information to help interpret it.

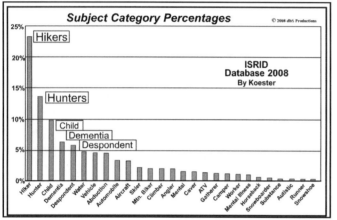

Figure 17-1 This bar graph shows the relative percentages by subject category found in *ISRID*

Statistical methods provide recognizable terms to describe the groupings that occur in the historical record, which then helps to develop strategies and tactics in combination with other relevant information.

Common Terms Used in Statistics

MODE - The value occurring most often.

MEDIAN - The middle value. Within a set of data 50 percent of the values fall below the median and 50 percent above it. *(see Fig. 17-2)*

Example: When analyzing Missing Person Behavior data, the Median remains a constant reminder of the middle distance in a category set of values *(Half of the values fall below the Median and half of the values above the Median).*

MEAN - The average value for the entire distribution. *(see Fig.17-2 and 3).*

STANDARD DEVIATION - Standard Deviation indicates how spread out the numerical values in a distribution lie from their average.

SKEWNESS - Skewness measures symmetry or lack of symmetry *(non-symmetry)* to one or the other end of the distribution; either positive or negative. A symmetrical distribution looks the same to the left and to the right of the center point.

STATISTICALLY SIGNIFICANT - In plain English, *significant* means important, while in Statistics *significant* means probably true *(not due to chance)*. Data points that occur but give no importance to the analysis. When statisticians describe a result as "significant" they mean very probably true. They do not *(necessarily)* mean it is highly important.

NOTE: In lost subject behavior the maximum zone uses only statistically significant data points. In layman's terms, those analyzing and compiling subject data usually choose not to use data at the extreme ends of the spectrum, treating them as anomalies instead *(see Figure 17-6)*.

NORMAL DISTRIBUTION - A normal distribution portrays a group of data with very specific characteristics. In this distribution the median, mode, and mean all fall at exactly the same point, and the other data points fall off symmetrically around this middle value at an equal rate both ways based on the standard deviation. A charted normal distribution creates the familiar *Bell Curve* data set, familiar in almost all forms of statistics. Often, the higher

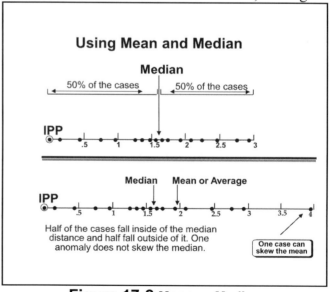

Figure 17-2 Mean vs Median

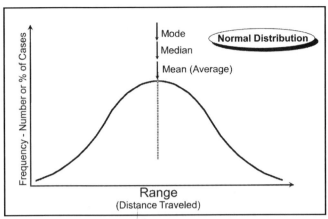

Figure 17-3 Normal Distribution

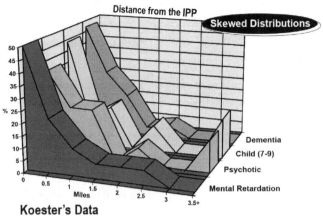

Figure 17-5 ISRID Distributions

the number of real-world data points, the closer the total distribution matches a theoretical *normal* curve *(figure 17-3 above)*.

SKEWED DISTRIBUTION - A data set not fitting the norm. Sometimes unusual factors influence data sets so that the expected outcomes fail to materialize, pulling the data *(skewing it)* to one side or the other. In the case of search, searchers find subjects either further or closer than expected with a significant bias toward the Initial Planning Point *(See Figure 17-4 below)*.

Theoretically, the more cases used and the more specific that data, the more reliable and useful the data for prediction purposes. Additionally, using data gathered in the local area maximizes the benefit to later searches in that same area.

The concept of probability represents a fundamental piece of search management. Very few events occur with absolute certainty, rather statistics represent the *chances* of an event occurring or of some expected behavior relative to the other possible outcomes.

Utilizing a distribution in search requires known values for the Mean, Median, Standard Deviation, and Skewness. However, with regard to Lost Person Behavior, searchers most commonly use the median together with a value for the spread of results. The reliability of distributions and the conclusions drawn from them depends on the quantity and quality of the information gathered in the first place *(i.e. The*

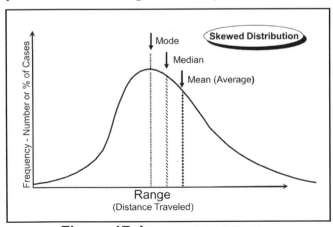

Figure 17-4 Skewed Distribution

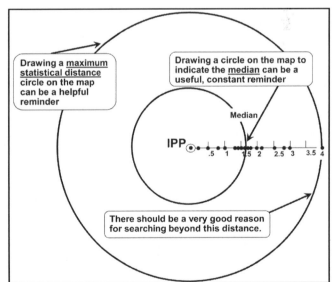

Figure 17-6 The Statistical Max Zone or maximum statistical distance in this case means the same as statistically significant. In other words, what distance, based on the database, needs consideration when a search planner tries to estimate the maximum distance travelled by a missing person in a specific category.

more information or cases used and the more specific the detail established in gathering that information, the more reliable and useful the distribution). In a search for a 5 year old, if only a dozen cases exist from which to draw conclusions, the reliability or usefulness of the statistics leave some doubt. In this example, the small number of results may represent unique circumstances. However, when several hundred cases exist, the reliability and usefulness of that distribution increases significantly.

For example, within the ISRID database, we track *(among other factors)*:

- Distance from the Initial Planning Point *(straight line distance)*

- The likelihood of a subjects presence in a particular type of area, feature or structure

Quantifying this information requires converting these descriptions into values *(numbers)* that relate to a scale for comparison. Even though most find descriptions with words more comprehensible, difficulty comes up when trying to compare verbal descriptions to other verbal descriptions accurately on any scale. Numerically, probabilities present as either percentages or a scale of 0 to 1. For example:

```
75%  =   .75
50%  =   .50
12%  =   .12
```

Probability Theory

Probability theory systematically deals with uncertain events. A search manager needs a correct understanding of that theory to appropriately manage a search and planners need understanding to appropriately evaluate options for resource deployments in prior and upcoming operational periods.

Specifically, the approach most useful to Search Managers involves Bayesian Probabilities. Very simply this means using past probabilities to predict future results with an almost infinite number of *possible* outcomes. Using these methods, search planners attempt to make predictions about sets of facts concerning subject behavior in the field, and then test the validity of those predictions in the search environment, while constantly making adjustments for current conditions and new information.

Applying Bayesian methods to search planning means that a Search planner considers many possible outcomes to an action or decision, then selects the outcome with the highest probability of generating success or predicting behavior.

Example: In a defined portion *(segment)* of a search area, the lost subject either presides in that segment *(probability = 1)*, or not in that segment *(probability = 0)*. But, when the probability that the subject presides in one segment compared with any other segment, this comparative value lies somewhere between 0 and 1 *(or expressed as a percentage, somewhere between 0% and 100%)*. As each segment gets searched the relative probabilities for all other segments change, and planners reallocate resources appropriately.

Why Do Searchers Need Probabilities?

Answer: To know how effective the search went, or could go, in a repeatable way, to:

- Distribute or redistribute resources
- Search or research a search area segment; increase or decrease the size of a search area segment; or expand the search area
- Decide whether or not to suspend or when to suspend an unsuccessful search
- Rationalize your actions to the family, media, or higher authority
- Use as potential justification in litigation

The Area

Basic investigation concerning the facts of the incident coupled with a thorough subjective assessment of terrain factors determines the smallest search area consistent with available information.

The Management or Plans Section determines several plausible scenarios explaining why and where the missing person disappeared. Through a consensus process the overhead team determines the likelihood that each of the scenarios happened and based on this consensus, which areas posses the highest chance of containing the missing person. Planners then establish a probability map *(concerning the likely location of the subject, Figure 17-7 below)*. Planners then segment the area into manageable *(or searchable)* segments. Based on the probability distribution *(chances the missing person occupies any given location)* and the capabilities of available resources, the search planner decides which areas present the greatest chance of success in the shortest possible time *(Chapter 18 - Establishing the Search Area describes this process in greater detail)*. These values change and get modified as a search progresses and the searchers uncover more information and clues.

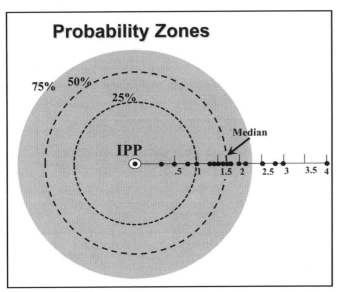

Figure 17-7 Probability Zones from a Distribution

Detection

While searching a segment *(considering type of resource doing the searching, the <u>way</u> they search, how many times they search the segment, etc.)* some probability exists *(between 0% and 100%)* that the searchers will find the missing person or at least a clue. However, a number of factors affect whether responders find the subject or miss them, even assuming the subject is definitely in the area *(In Chapter 19 - Probability of Detection, readers find a detailed description of considerations involving effort in a segment and how to determine the probability of detecting something).*

This analysis and prioritized hierarchy applies to searching for virtually anything including:

- Finding lost car keys *(everyday life)*
- Finding lost cities *(Archeology)*
- Finding oil and minerals *(mining)*
- Finding old shipwrecks *(treasure hunting)*
- Finding lost persons *(SAR, sea and land)*

> *"Only with the advance of modern technology have we learned to examine search in the light of science as an operation having various structural patterns and obeying laws of its own."*
> – B.O. Koopman, 1946

Success

During a search, many of the segments in the area will get searched one or more times without finding the missing person. *Search Theory* advocates maximizing success in the shortest amount of time. Using the standard notation of the search theory formula *(POA × POD = POS)* a Search Manager makes very simple calculations to provide optimum planning options, optimum effort allocation, and to evaluate and debrief ongoing efforts. These same calculations also help justify expanding the search area, researching some segments, searching somewhere else, or completely suspending further search efforts in the area.

Primary Elements of a Successful Search

- Look in the right place
- Be able to detect what it is you are looking for

***Search Theory* represents a scientific discipline unto itself regardless of its application.**

While the formal discipline of Search Theory traces its history to the maritime environment, its transition into land applications is now occurring at a very rapid rate. Presently the application of Search Theory principles occurs in the following ways:

- **Scientific Methods:** *Use of Formal Search Methods*
- **Mathematics:** *Use of Statistics and Probability*
- **Computers** - *Software - Calculations for Coverage - Documentation*
- **Common Sense and Intuition** - *The Human Experience Factor*
- **Field Experiments and Hard Data**

Conventional mathematics state that if multiplying the chance that the subject resides in an a specific area *(POA = a numerical value in percentage)* by the chance of detecting that subject in the area *(POD = a numerical value in percentage)*, the result expresses the chance of success *(POS = a numerical value in percentage)*. These components form the conventional notation and application for Search Theory. POA X POD = POS.

POA represents the Probability of Area, or chance the subject *(or clue)* occupies a specific search area/segment.

POD represents the Probability of Detection, or chance of detecting an object or the missing person if present. POD measures sensor effectiveness for an individual sortie in a given segment.

Cumulative POD. When searching the same segment multiple times, either by different resources or by the same resource, the chance of detecting an object or the missing person increases compared with searching only once. Cumulative segment POD or POD_{cum} refers to an increased probability of detection after multiple searches in the same segment.

Predictive POD. The estimated POD values determined prior to searching a segment. Based on predicted values for sweep width, effort required to get the area effectively swept, and *coverage*.

Retrospective POD. Computed after the search of a segment by using information obtained from debriefing searchers. It encompasses effective sweep width *(or R_d)*, effort to get the area effectively swept and computing the ratio of area effectively swept to the size of the assigned segment *(coverage)*.

POS represents the Probability of Successfully finding the person or object sought. Like POD, POS accumulates over multiple searches and we refer to that as *cumulative POS (or POS_{cum})*. The POS simply accumulates from operational period to operational period by adding the values together. The sum of all Segment POS values at any time, equals the Overall Probability of Success at that time. So, the sum of all Cumulative Segment values *(one for each segment)* equals the *Overall POS_{cum} (Cumulative Overall Probability of Success)* for the entire search area.

Conventional Notation of Search Probability Theory

POA x POD = POS

The goal [*of search planning*] is to maximize the **o**verall **p**robability **o**f **s**uccess (OPOS) in the least amount of time.

NOTE: Wasting time trying to predict hyper-accurate values at the start of a search, while laudable, misses the utility of search theory. Establish values quickly, and monitor the *critical changes* in the data during the progress of the search.

If there's a 20% probability of the subject's location in Segment A and searchers use a 50% probability of detection method to search, one assumes a 10% probability of success. On the other hand, if a 40% probability exists that the subject resides in Segment B and searchers use a 60% probability of detection method to search, then the probability of success changes to 24%.

We use these calculations to allocate our resources in such a way that maximizes the increase in Overall POS. In other words, as a predictive tool, if one combination of resources and segments and effort results in an increase in $OPOS_{cum}$ of 32% and another combination results in an increase of 60%, the greater increase in $OPOS_{cum}$ *(60%)* consists of a better application of resources, with all other variables equal.

If the Cumulative Overall Probability of Success increases after multiple searches, the chance that the missing person or search object actually occupies the area searched, reduces proportionally. In plain English, since responders searched the area *(one or more times)* and failed to find the subject, the chances of finding the subject elsewhere increase.

The Retrospective POD value determined after the search of a segment represents a relatively accurate perspective of the effectiveness of the effort within that segment. Debriefing, terrain, weather, sweep width values, and speed of the searchers all deserve consideration in establishing Retrospective POD values for that segment.

Concepts and Terms

To fully comprehend the concepts and examples used here in this chapter it is essential to define a series of consistent terms from within Search Theory. These terms, while initially appearing rather complicated, provide the basis for the vocabulary and concept analysis used in successful search. Many of these definitions stem from a paper entitled *"Selected Inland Search Definitions"* by D.C. Cooper and J.R. Frost *(1999)*.

Initial Planning Point

The Initial Planning Point (IPP) refers to a reference point designated on the search map where the planner or IC indicates the start of the search. The early stages of a search always lack credible information and for future reference we need to recognize the location of the first planning point on the map. Distances plot to this point when comparing the category of subject with previous lost person behavior data.

Point Last Seen

The Point Last Seen (PLS) exclusively describes a point where a witness saw the subject or a camera recorded their image (*i.e. the mother physically saw the child playing by a tree near the creek*). The PLS adds credibility and reliability to the Initial Planning Point or to another point for data comparison.

Last Known Position

The Last Known Position *(LKP)* falls at the last substantiated *(by clues or evidence)* location of the missing subject. If subsequent clues or evidence point out another location, *(later in time)* then the new point becomes the LKP. The LKP changes with the discovery of more clues, direction of travel and physical evidence. The weight or strength of the evidence discovered governs the reliability of the LKP and then gives direction of travel with the discovery of subsequent LKPs. Date and time-stamp each discovery. Previous LKPs turn to clues with the discovery of a new LKP.

Sweep Width

Sweep Width *(W)* or **Effective Sweep Width** *(ESW)* refers to a measure of Detectability or a *Detectability Index*. Factors that affect sweep width include, among others, the size of the item sought, the sensor involved, and environmental conditions at the time and place of the search. Accurate sweep width values on land derive from relatively simple field experiments derived from the formally published results of rigorous experiments *(Sweep Width Estimation for Ground Search and Rescue by R. Koester, D.C. Cooper, J.R. Frost, R.Q. Robe - 2004)* and *(Use of the Visual Range of Detection to Estimate Effective Sweep Width for Land Search and Rescue Based on 10 Detection Experiments in North America by R. J. Koester et al - 2014)*. These researchers completed an analysis of the results and they developed relatively simple procedures for establishing an Effective Sweep Width *(ESW)* for ground search teams in the field.

The sweep width concept usually defies intuition *(at least at first)* and many find it difficult to grasp. Once understood, however, it provides great insight into both the science and art of searching. Sweep width will be explained in more detail later *(See Chapter 19 on Probability of Detection)*. For now, regard it as an experimentally determined statistic with a useful geometric interpretation for search planning.

> **NOTE:** *Practically speaking, a single, comprehensive, set of sweep width tables for land like the ones developed for maritime search simply does not exist. The sheer number of different combinations of terrain, vegetation, seasonal variation, search object types, etc. defy creating truly comprehensive tables. On the other hand, teams operating within their normal area of responsibility, require only a few variations for effectiveness. Therefore we recommended that teams or groups of teams in the same geographic area develop benchmarks for their own sweep width values using the simple experiments mentioned above.*

Average Range of Detection (*Rd*)- Previous research into Sweep Width on land demonstrated that trained searchers experience trouble when asked to evaluate their own Probability of Detection *(POD)* values in the field. Robert J. Koester completed research that specified field procedures to determine reasonably accurate effective sweep width values and consequently develop meaningful POD values for any search effort expended in the field. The goal of Koester's research and paper centered on developing a simple, objective procedure to obtain effective sweep width values without conducting full-blown and time intensive detection experiments.

Rd = The average range of linear distances where searchers first detect a search object when moving towards it from multiple angles.

Range of Detection Procedure for Field Resources - Immediately upon arriving at a designated search segment in the field, searchers perform the Range of Detection procedure *(See Chapter 18 Probability of Detection)*.

Track Line - The track or route that searchers or a search resource follows as they pass through a search segment.

Track Line Length - (TLL) The length of the path taken by a resource while searching in a designated segment. Compute Track Line Length by multiplying the speed of the resource by the time spent searching in the segment *(e.g. One mile per hour X 4 hours = A four mile Track Line Length)*. The value measures in units of length.

Total Track Line Length represents the total length of all the paths of people or resources searching in a segment combined. Simply measure each resource's track line or alternatively, multiply the length of one searcher's path by the number of similar searchers.

Effort Allocation. The IC always asks a fundamental question: *"How long is it going to take to search that area?"* The effort *(searcher hours)* required to search a portion of the search area derives from the total track line of the resource searching; or, more specifically how long it takes to make that track line in the given segment.

> With *effort allocation,* planners manipulate a number of variables to accomplish different potential tasks in a rapid, but efficient manner, all focused on bringing about success in the shortest possible time.

Area Effectively Swept (Z). This value helps to compute coverage. it also represents a geographic area expressed as area. Sweep Width designates a range or distance on either side of a resource and Total Track Line Length represents how far the resource traveled. Multiplying those two values together, the product comes out as an area. This result expresses how much terrain the resource actually looked at. Planners calculate it by multiplying the *Effective Sweep Width* (**ESW**) by the *Track Line Length* (**TLL**). It describes an area of ground that has length travelled *(Track Line Length)* and width searched *(Effective Sweep Width)* therefore giving *area effectively swept*.

$$Z = W \times TLL$$

Coverage (C) This value is the ratio of the area effectively swept (**Z**) to the total area being searched.

A search segment contains a specific area. Expressed normally as an area derived by multiplying a length times a width. If a Search Planner compares this area to the size of the area effectively swept *(as calculated above)* this ratio describes how much of the search segment was covered by the resource.

Essentially coverage describes a ratio comparison between the size of the segment and the area effectively swept by a resource. With this coverage factor, probability of detection flows from a theoretical curve developed through long years of research in Search Theory *(See Figure 17-8 below)*.

Example:

If a particular search segment contains an area of 40,000 square meters and the area effectively swept by the searchers was 20,000 square meters, then the coverage ratio boils down to the area covered by the searcher divided by the total area of the segment (*20,000 divided by 40,000 which reduces to ½ or 0.5*).

The 0.5 coverage leads to the POD for that search by using the curve below *(Figure 17-8)*. The graph shows that coverage of 0.5 equates to a POD of 39%.

Optimal Resource Allocation – Describes a process where planners assign available resources in such a way as to maximize probability of success *(POS)* in the least amount of time.

Probability Density – This value also represents a ratio. The ratio of a segment's Probability of Area

$$P_{Density} = \frac{POA}{Area}$$

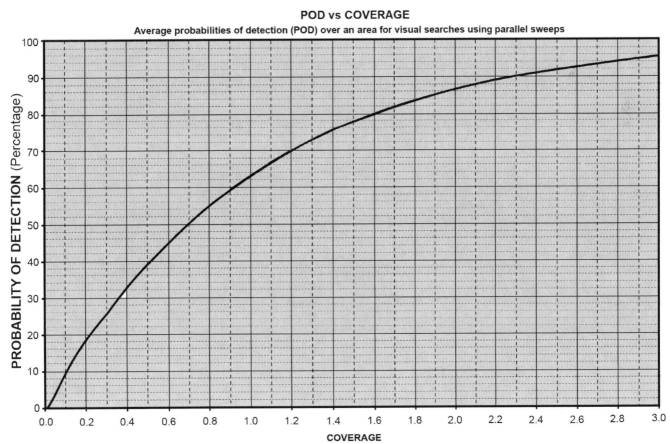

Figure 17-8 Koopman's POD vs Coverage Curve:
POD = $1-e^{-c}$ where c=coverage and e = the exponential constant

(POA) to its physical size or geographic area. Both Koopman *(1946)* and Wartes *(1983)* used the concept of Probability Density. With larger Probability of Area and a comparatively small search area the Probability Density increases.

Proportion Based Consensus – A process where probability allocates to search segments or regions by consensus. The scheme provides simple, proportional and a consistent mathematically defensible process. It involves the use of a reference value *(usually 100)* that represents the baseline for comparisons with other segments or regions *(not percentages)*. This process works out much like *scoring* or *rating* a product's quality or an athlete's performance on a 100-point scale. The process then *normalizes* these scores *(they all add up to 100%)* to produce initial proportional POA values *(See Chapter 18 - POA)*.

Planners sometimes distinguish between *Segment Probability of Success* values and *Overall Probability of Success* values for the entire search effort.

Segment Probability of Success (SPOS). Probability of Success for each of the search segments individually. In conventional notation this expresses as:

$$SPOS = SPOA \times SPOD$$

This simply indicates that the product of multiplying the segment POA times the segment POD equals the Segment POS.

Overall Probability of Success (OPOS). To arrive at OPOS simply add the Probability of Success values from each separate segment together for the entire search area. Conventional notation for the Overall Probability of Success expresses as:

$$OPOS = SPOS_{1st} + SPOS_{2nd} + \ldots SPOS_{nth}$$
Where "n" refers to the last segment.

This simply indicates that all of the Segment Probability of Success values add together to comprise the Overall Probability of Success for the entire search area.

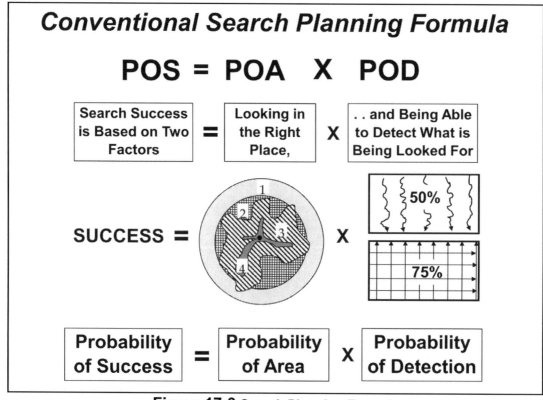

Figure 17-9 Search Planning Formula

Establishing the Search Area   18

Objectives:

- Describe the primary methods of establishing a search area in any lost or missing person incident

- Designate a search area in a map exercise and relate how scenarios influence the size and configuration of specific terrain

- List the reasons for segmenting a search area

- Describe the influences and processes to segment a search area

- Outline the process and components for assigning probabilities to search area segments using the proportional consensus approach

The Call Comes In

After gathering preliminary information, the situation looks serious and justifies a search effort. Now, where to search?

The standard search theory equation starts with POA:

$$POA \times POD = POS$$

POA represents the Probability of Area or chances that the subject *(or a clue)* lies in the search area or in a particular segment.

Establish the Search Area

The first and most crucial step in search planning requires a decision on the limits of where to look.

- **Initially, someone draws a line on the map** around a piece(s) of terrain. Sometimes search areas integrate or connect together, but not always. Usually, an Urban or rural/urban environment provides a good example of this, where neighborhoods lie apart from each other or apart from other likely locations.

- During future operational periods, as additional information surfaces, **this preliminary search area expands or contracts** becoming even more sharply defined

Remember that the Search Area includes all the areas teams need to search. The factors defining the boundaries of this area include:

- How far the missing person possibly traveled? *(Based on physical condition)*

- Any probable routes?

- Previous lost person behaviors in the same category?

- Influences of the weather?

- Influence of terrain & ground on travel?

Also, a chance exists that the subject never spent any time in the search area. Expand the area if new information or clues warrant it.

Four Standard Methods of Establishing the Search Area

1. **Theoretical.** The distance the subject traveled in a given time period. How far, how fast?

2. **Statistical.** Information reflecting the distances other subjects traveled given similar conditions, i.e. data from the research on Missing/Lost Person Behavior.

3. **Subjective**. The Management team evaluates any limiting factors for the specific incident and local geography. The information gathered about the site influences decisions about the subject's behavior, e.g. barriers, attractions, routes with the least resistance.

4. **Deductive Reasoning**. The methodical step by step analysis of circumstances and evidence surrounding the loss of the subject. Each step starts with general information and gets more specific. This method calls for developing potential scenarios with available facts.

For the purposes of this text and the discussion that follows, the authors list the four methods of establishing the search area and their uses separately. Under field conditions and a real search, all of these methods combine to develop a plan. Near the end of this chapter, an example brings all of these methods together and shows how they contribute to search planning and prioritization.

Theoretical Search Area

The Theoretical Search Area represents the distance the subject possibly traveled from the last known position *(LKP)*, point last seen *(PLS)*, or from a suspected point of departure during a given time.

When considering the probable actions of a lost subject, **remember that an individual may travel in any direction from the IPP, PLS or LKP**. Initially a Search Planner considers the total area *(that of a circle)* as a possible subject location. For example:

- A subject capable of walking 1 mile in any direction from the last known position, creates a total search area encompassing 3.1 square miles.

Theoretical Search Area = πr^2 *($\pi = 3.14$)*
(r = the radius of the circle)

Example: subject walks 1 mile:

The area of a circle with a radius of 1 mile =
Theoretical Search Area = $3.14 \times 1^2 = 3.14$ sq. miles.

- A subject capable of traveling 2 or more miles from the point last seen, etc.:

2 miles: 3.14×2^2; or $3.14 \times 4 = 12.6$ sq. miles.
3 miles: 3.14×3^2; or $3.14 \times 9 = 28.3$ sq. miles.

Calculate the theoretical search area for the following distances potentially walked by a missing person.

*4 miles   6 miles   8 miles
10 miles   20 miles
The search area grows exponentially!*

Factors influencing these theoretical distances relate directly to the missing subject's capabilities, the terrain and the time periods involved. *Remember, relatives and next-of-kin tend to give poor estimates of the subject's physical condition and stamina. Trust but verify if possible.*

Make a note that, in some instances, the theoretical search area designation never gets used. For example, when a large number of hours pass between a missing person report and when the search actually starts. Theoretically, enough time went by for the missing person to travel beyond the borders of any usable map. Another example of this occurs when a subject possibly used public transportation. In this case as well, the theoretical distance easily exceeds the area covered by most search maps. On the other hand,

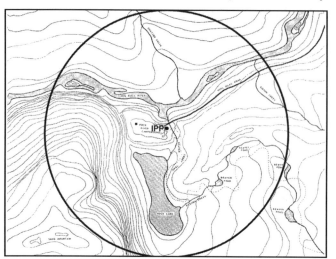

Figure 18-1 Theoretical Search Area

SAR crews use the theoretical search area to their advantage when the missing person only covers a short distance due to age, terrain, or weather conditions. In these cases the theoretical distance often comes up much less than the Maximum Zone for that category of subject, and consequently search planners need to mark it on the map.

Statistical Search Area

Statistical data derived from previous search incidents involving similar missing persons works as an extremely valuable resource in establishing a search area. Although they provide assistance, statistics never represent absolutes and always come with exceptions. Some counties possess case studies on the behavior of missing individuals stretching back as far as 30 years and provide the basis for useful search information. These statistical distributions give us the median and maximum distances by category of subject.

Using Statistical Data to Establish the Search Area.

An example use of case study data on the relevance of median distance *(See Figure 18-2)*.

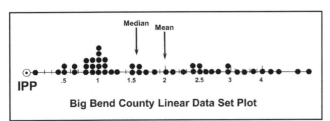

Figure 18-2

- Big Bend County begins keeping records on their lost hiker incidents over a multi- year period. After ten years, a simple linear plot of distances develops representing how far certain categories of subject traveled from the IPP. When used properly, search planners quickly establish search areas for local missing person incidents involving that category of subject.

- A simple analysis of this data also reveals that searchers found a large number of hikers in and around one mile from the IPP. In other words, the data collected portrays a clustering of data points around a specific distance. A Search Manager looking for increased efficiency, uses this information in determining search areas in the future.

- In applying statistical data gathered and collated from missing/lost person incidents, always remember the following three distinct distances:

1. **The Initial Planning Point to where search efforts actually found lost subjects** - expressed in terms of straight line distance not the true path of the subject. i.e. Perhaps the missing person walks *(or wanders)* a total of 5 miles during the search, but turned up only 2.1 miles from the IPP.

2. **Median distance** - the median distance within the entire range of case histories consisting of that *middle point* where an equal number of cases lie at further distances and at shorter distances *(See Figure 18-2 and 18-3)*. Half the cases fall above the median in distance and half fall below the median in distance.

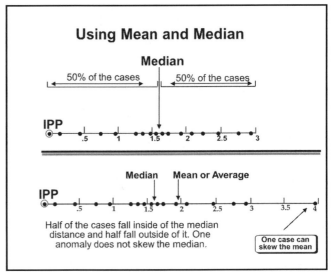

Figure 18-3

3. **Maximum Distance** – in missing and lost person behavior data, this measurement shows the maximum statistically significant distance traveled by a category of subject. In other words, the search manager needs a very good reason to conduct search efforts outside this distance *(Figure 18-4)*.

NOTE: Use the median distance as a constant reminder in plotting a search area. The statistics show that an equal number of cases lie in an area further than the median, and closer than the median, to the IPP.

Probability Zones Based on Distances Traveled.

In 1976, Syrotuck first introduced the concept of probability zones for land search with his Analysis of Lost Person Behavior study. The publication introduced the advantages of recording the *straight line distances* between the PLS and the point where searchers found the missing person. He hypothesized that the compilation of lost subject data by category aids in establishing the probability zones in a search area. He felt it unimportant to know exactly how far the lost person walked, but important to know the percentage of missing people found in each category at various distances from the PLS. These distances defined a radius of concentric circles centered on

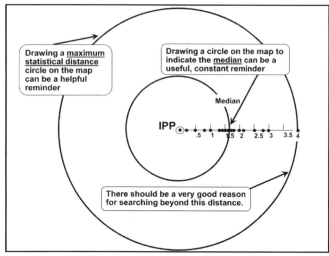

Figure 18-4 Maximum Distance

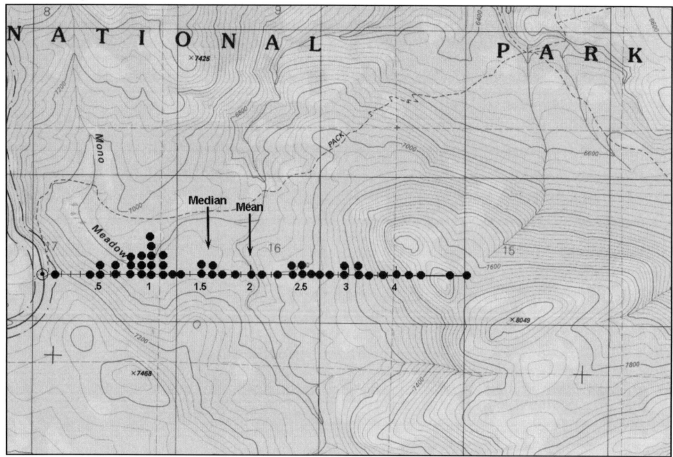

Figure 18-5 Linear scale of case histories - Example from Big Bend County

the PLS *(NOTE: At the time of Syrotuck's studies, the terms IPP and LKP did not yet exist in land search)*. He determined the Search Manager needed to visualize various zones in the projected search area and determine some rough odds of finding the subject in each zone using the missing/lost person data.

- Initially, planners assume the subject traveled in any direction from the point last seen or last known position lacking information to the contrary. By overlaying the previous linear scale of case histories from Big Bend County onto a map, the following representation developed. See Map Illustration on the previous page *(Figure 18-5)*.

- The distribution of finds gives some useful measure of clustering or grouping tendency. It also points out that Lost/Missing Behavior data generally produces abnormal or skewed distributions *(Reference Chapter 17, page 281)*. In the example below, the clustering shows up around the one mile distance. The most significant point of grouping for this set of cases lies at this location. Some data sets lack this type of clustering or even any grouping at all, particularly with a very small set of cases. In general, try not to use small data sets. The larger the number of cases, the more potential for usable lost subject behavior.

NOTE: Probability zones based on lost/missing subject research data consist of statistical predictions that tend to fit or not fit the current search situation. They represent guidelines that vary with every individual and circumstances of the incident. However, experience shows that using these zones correctly helps in making faster and more effective decisions.

- Recall the Big Bend County data set *(Figure 18-2)* with many subjects clustered around the one mile distance. This sample illustrates the importance of local data to the Search Manager. Consider whether a sufficient number of cases in the data base near some point warrant committing manpower around that distance. As mentioned in the Lost/Missing Subject Behavior chapter,

the credence of national or international data in differing Eco-regions gives added emphasis to many cases, but local experience always proves more useful.

If a Search Manager wants to identify a 25% zone *(Figure 18-6)* of probability, *(this means he or she expects to find the subject there 25 times out of 100 cases with identical information, or 12 times out of 48 for this example)* they draw a circle encompassing the 12 cases with distances closest to the Initial Planning Point. The Initial Planning Point represents the reference point for comparison and the center of the probability circle. Remember, searchers sometimes lack the ability to determine the direction of travel so, always consider a 360 degree circle. The zone between the initial planning point and the distance up to the 12th case in the data set represents a 25% zone of probability *(also the 25% zone with the smallest area)*. Also note that in the example data set above, the next distance above the 25% zone on the linear scale consist of five cases total at that distance. In expanding the zone to include those five cases, the probability value raises up to 35%. This example shows how local data influences search area boundaries and eventually the allocation of resources.

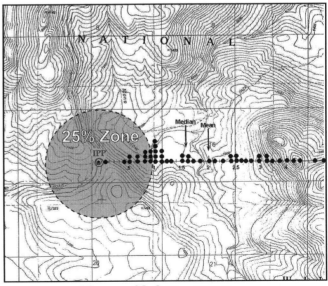

Figure 18-6 The 25% Zone

> **NOTE:** At this point, no consideration goes into factors that change these zones from a 360-degree circle.

When examining statistical data, note that any other group of 12 cases in the Big Bend County data set also represent a 25% zone of probability. However, if a non uniform distribution exists *(a more likely occurrence)* and shows a clustering at any distance, then consider that clustering in local search planning.

Notice the difference in search area sizes at different distances!

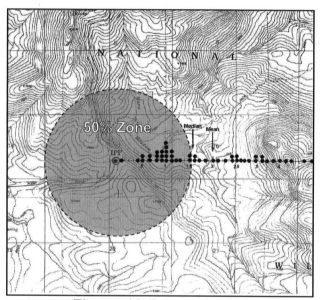

Figure 18-7 The 50% Zone

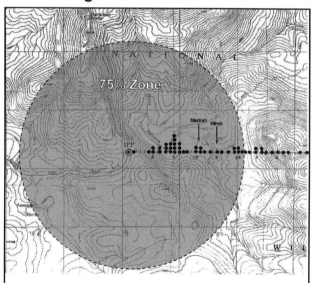

Figure 18-8 The 75% Zone

- What parameters exist for using various probability zones from the statistical data? Shall searchers use the 25% zone, the 50% zone or the 75% zone? Available time, manpower, number and diversity of resources, terrain, and the time critical nature of the incident, all help define which zone to use.

Example: After thorough analysis of on-scene conditions at the start of a missing person situation, the Search Planner correctly assesses the value of time *(Time critical)* after recognizing the approach of darkness and impending storm. Terrain naturally limits the missing person to very specific corridors of travel, and logistics hamper initial responders for the first few hours of a search. Initially, limited resources and time constraints lead the IC to determine the 50% zone the most appropriate *(Figure 18-7)*. The local data also indicates a high number of finds around the one mile distance *(The Search Manager expects to find the subject, in the zone, in 24 cases out of 48, based on the example data set)*. Correspondingly, with the manpower available and little time the IC might choose to use the 75% zone initially *(Figure 18-8) (The Search Manager expects to find the subject, in the zone, in 36 cases out of 48 according to the example data set)*.

- Remember that with relatively uniform case histories across a linear scale of distances, the chance of finding the subject inside the circle bounded by the median distance equals the chance of finding the subject outside that distance. However, the current lost subject data reflects skewed distributions toward the IPP for the various subject categories *(See Figure 18-9)*. What does this mean in terms of where to search? Almost universally, searching close to the IPP

- In Syrotuck's database *(1976)*, the median distance represented the center of his probability zones because he expected more case histories to show a normal bell curve distribution. What this meant was that for years the 25, 50 and 75% zones in Syrotuck's methods expanded from either side of the median and not the IPP. After

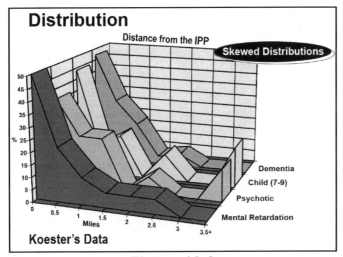

Figure 18-9

gathering even more data, researchers found many more faults in Syrotuck's original assumptions.

- Analyzing case history distance data, allows the Search Manager to better define acceptable zones of probability (*The Search Manager and the Search Management team will define acceptable*). Clustering in a local database provides helpful information in addition to indicating local conditions, activities, and geography.

- When defining behavior zones from statistical data, consider the expanding nature of the search area which encompasses the new zone. *(i.e. the 75% zone or the Maximum Zone.)* Next we consider factors which limit these zones into much more manageable places to search.

- Search and rescue teams also use statistical data such as the number of missions in a given time period, and types of missions to justify budgets, i.e. increasing numbers of specific missions might justify additional training and/or personnel and equipment.

- In recent years, the compilation of data from previous searches regularly proves useful in establishing search areas. The only major drawback in the use of this method lies in the reluctance to keep accurate, meaningful SAR records in many jurisdictions.

Subjective Considerations Influencing the Search Area

The following list represents a broad spectrum of subjective factors affecting the size and shape of any search area:

- Likely spots
- Natural barriers and terrain features
- Physical clues left by the subject
- Historical data of the area from case histories
- Gut feeling or intuition based on experience and special circumstances
- Physical and mental limitations of the subject

Understandably, a number of intangible considerations weigh into these factors. For the most part, intangibles allow one authority or personality to strongly influence the perception of probable search areas. However, without the last known position directly linked to the search area, these factors prove invaluable.

Likely Spots *(Jones, 1983)*

The following features or areas, for one reason or another, take on a greater significance and the locations usually offer some attraction to the missing person:

- Ease of movement
- Shelter
- Food or water
- Curiosity or companionship

Additionally, several locations consistent with common strategies followed by lost subjects fit into this category. These locations offer better clue finding opportunities. Some examples of *likely spots* include:

- An unmarked path or trail
- A possible *short cut*
- Abandoned or unused buildings
- Adits *(horizontal mine entrances)*, mine workings or shafts
- Natural caves, cisterns, abandoned wells
- Berry patches and other natural sources of food
- Stream banks and other lines of travel that offer little resistance

- Any potential man-made or geologically natural shelter from the elements
- Open high ground *(for view and cell reception enhancement)*
- Alternate destinations from an unclear trail fork

NOTE: Seasonal changes and weather changes alter the significance of particular likely spots or generate a different set of attractions.

Searcher awareness, resulting from a proper subject behavior briefing considerably influences the identification of possible likely spots. The significance of any particular feature depends on the attraction of the feature and the behavioral profile of the missing person.

Likely spots only add value to the search if searchers recognize and act upon them. Opinions in a field search party often vary as to the significance or even existence of a particular likely spot. The more individuals in the search party agree on a particular likely spot, the stronger that feature justifies a field decision on the time required for investigation.

The entire overhead team needs to understand the concept and importance of likely spots. **During team briefings, include a short discussion on likely spots.** Remind the members of a search team about the likely spot concept and tell them to:

- Look for them

- Mark them on their maps

- Investigate them whenever possible

- Discuss them at the debriefing session

Developing a better understanding for identifying likely spots occurs in the field and needs inclusion in the basic training for all field search personnel. The concept, if properly applied, helps develop the essential inquisitiveness necessary for any search party.

In every search look for, note, and report likely spots as they surface. Never use departures from predetermined search tactics as an excuse to bypass, ignore or forget an attraction feature. Searchers need to at least note and report any likely spots they see because sometimes those features fail to show up on the materials used by the overhead staff. Although impossible to investigate every single likely spot immediately, appoint someone for follow-up and give some closer scrutiny. This follow-up action assumes even greater importance in the urban environment. Look at the stronger likely spots immediately, with less compelling spots recorded for possible future investigation. Sound judgment represents one essential ingredient for high quality search work. More than anything, the successful use of likely spots depends upon good field judgment.

Natural Barriers and Terrain Features

Natural terrain features influence the subject's chosen direction of travel, both positively and negatively. A fairly large stream presents a barrier, while providing an avenue of low resistance along the bank in a forested valley. All of the following influence lost or missing subjects:

- Cliffs
- Rivers
- Dense vegetation
- Clear-cuts or open power line trails
- Switchbacks - zig zag paths uphill or down
- Shortcuts
- Steep terrain
- Confluence of drainages
- Visual/Electronics incentives – view/signal enhancement
- Old roads or railroad beds and other avenues of minimal resistance
- Areas of confusion during limited visibility *(fog, snow, rain)*
- Indistinct or grown-over stretches of trail
- Game trails

Additional features might influence decisions when exiting the high country after a subject walked off an established trail.

Physical Clues Left by the Subject

Searchers look for clues or evidence proving conclusively that the subject spent some time in a specific location.

> **NOTE:** After discovering evidence or physical clues, *(i.e., the subject's footprints, articles of clothing or equipment, eyewitness accounts)*, redesignate the last *LKP*, when appropriate. Clues often turn up in a different order than the subject laid them down. Therefore, reassess the essential chronological order of events based on newly uncovered information *(e.g. before or after the last rain/snow, tire tracks on top of footprints, etc)*. Clues regularly change the entire strategy used by a Search Planner.

Clue examples:

- Footprints *(known to be subject's)*
- Disturbances in vegetation or terrain
- Remnants of game birds or animals *(gut piles, feathers, etc.)*
- Articles of clothing
- Equipment
- Wrappers - cigarettes, chewing tobacco, candy, food
- Soda, water, beer or juice containers
- Eyewitness reports
- Campsite disturbances or discarded items, etc.
- Vehicle contents
- Shell types *(gauge of shotgun or caliber of rifle)*
- Weather conditions *(foggy in confusing terrain, etc.)*
- Trail, summit or visitor registration logs
- Campfire pits or coal beds
- Disturbances in abandoned buildings
- Missing subject's intentions
- Subject's special interests, orientation or experience
- Backcountry hut use or disturbances
- Previous residences, routes, neighborhoods, friends, workplaces, etc.

Historical Data

Information from past local missing person cases often indicates that subjects lost or overdue in a specific area tend to take the same actions again and again. The way drainages funnel lost subjects into definite locations illustrates this concept well *(i.e., roads, river bottoms, or canyons)*.

> **Example from Pierce County, Washington:**
>
> After looking at searches in this area for the last six years, researchers discovered the PLS always turned up on or near State Route-165 between milepost #6 or #7 *(**Note:** A well known DOT gravel pit sits at milepost 6.8)*. To the west of this portion of the SR-165 a steep hill drops down into the Voight's Creek drainage. If a lost subject followed the hill down into this drainage, they more than likely run into the Voights Creek Road, paralleling Voights Creek. . . In the searches conducted by the Sheriff's Department in this area over the last six years, the lost person turned up on or near the Voights Creek Road over half of the time.

Intuition or Gut Feelings *(Visceral Override)*

Experienced Search Managers develop a sense of *intuition* or a *sixth sense* about the circumstances leading up to a missing person incident. Intuition encompasses a mental summation of past experience. It helps to resolve important search issues. Sometimes a search manager's intuition leads them in the wrong direction, but experience also provides great insight into some situations. Analyses of many subjective factors combine to create this effect.

Examples and Caution: An experienced search planner on an overhead team running a search looks at a map, reviews all of the gathered information and intuitively feels that certain areas require immediate attention. In many cases, the planner's lack any explanation on why or how they feel that way. More often than not, through experience, comparison with similar incidents and knowledge of the local terrain, their efforts end up focused in a particular area. This visceral override presents a double-edged sword in the world of liability and instant communication. Never simply ignore information or discount it based on a gut feeling; however, pay attention to and balance past experiences with developed instincts as well.

Ken Hill, a researcher and experienced search planner from Nova Scotia gives the example of planners immediately searching nearby game trails because they suspect a missing child followed a deer *(a common occurrence in that region)*. No physical evidence points toward the child taking off in this direction, but personal experience and networking with other Search Managers makes this scenario a reasonable inference.

Intuition sometimes fails, but experience usually provides insight into many situations.

Physical and Mental Limitations of the Subject

Examples:

- Adults in general travel further than young children
- Rough terrain restricts handicapped individuals
- Physiological effects of medication or lack of medication restricts a subject's movement
- Mentally handicapped individuals often exhibit no clear-cut objective in their movements *(i.e., wandering aimlessly)*
- Slick-soled, low quarter shoes or *flip-flops* in rough terrain limit travel
- Children up to the age of 7 or 8 usually lack good cognitive map skills for orienting themselves in respect to their environment

> **NOTE:** As mentioned before, friends and relatives characteristically overestimate or underestimate the capabilities of a missing person. Third party subjective evaluations often provide much more valuable information when available.

Examples:

- A **camp counselor's** evaluation of a child's capabilities
- A **nurse's** evaluation of a senior citizen from a convalescent home
- A **teacher's** evaluation of a child's personality and social interaction

Each of these usually provides a better picture than that given by family members.

Deductive Reasoning

The Search Planners looks at general facts and circumstantial evidence and logically deduce probable non-obvious conclusions. In search management, we call it scientific reasoning, or going from specific observations to general conclusions. Sir Arthur Conan Doyle's well known character Sherlock Holmes, possessed extreme deductive reasoning powers.

SEARCH IS THE CLASSIC MYSTERY

Deductive reasoning assumes conclusions and follows a series of logical and valid premises. A premise asserts a basis for argument. The important aspect of deductive reasoning stems from a true premise or series of true premises that result in true conclusion. In fact, the search planner essentially runs an experiment, and develops an *If - Then* process. Based on the facts at hand, he or she makes a hypothesis about what happened to the missing person. He or she then commits resources to the field in an attempt to prove the hypothesis *(or scenario)*.

After conducting the search *(or experiment)* without finding the missing person or any clues, try to analyze the initial premises and identify the incorrect one. More thorough investigation now enters the equation. Keep in mind that our experiment *(conducting the search)* tries to validate the most likely explanation of the observed phenomenon and initially gathered facts and clues. By validate we mean see if the facts and clues match the scenario, rather than only looking for facts and clues to match a pre-conceived idea of what happened. Let the facts and clues tell the story.

Evaluate this real situation which illustrated the value of using deductive reasoning from Bill Syrotuck.

> Some individuals find a parked car on a small turnout of a secondary road in Mt. Rainier National Park. It looks like someone parked it there several days ago. Known facts:
>
> - No trailhead exists at that location

- No possible mountain views at that location
- Registration check of auto: registered to an Airman at McChord, A.F.B
- McChord A.F.B. reports the Airman overdue from a 3-day pass
- Preliminary search of the surrounding area reveals no clues or additional information
- Turnout located at the base of a small canyon with timbered terrain
- The searched car reveals the following articles:
  - One *(l)* pair of low quarter shoes
  - Empty container for a Micro SD Card *(for a digital SLR Camera)*

More extensive searching in the area revealed no leads or clues. Someone deduced the Airman probably changed shoes *(more than likely into boots for climbing)*. The empty memory box indicated he carried a camera with him. Since no view of the mountain readily presented itself from that point, searchers thought he might look for a unique or unusual view of the Mountain to photograph. Bill Syrotuck took this line of reasoning and tried to project himself into the missing subject's place. "Where would I go if I wanted a unique, unusual or strikingly beautiful photograph, if I started from this turnout?" Subsequent searching of the canyon revealed that the subject climbed to such a location and fell from a high cliff.

Deductive reasoning works as a retrospective tool when concluding a search by improving deductive skills in future operations. At the end of a search, a search manager knows the conclusion. Searchers either found the person or not. However, an instructive and very informative process results from going back and looking at all evidence to see if it pointed toward the known conclusion. In hindsight, check to see if any possible clues or pieces of information got overlooked

Brains Trust

As part of the deductive process Mitchell *(1990)* suggested that a small group of experienced people devote themselves to the *heavy thinking* essential to the planning process. Such a *Brains Trust* doubles as part of the ICS Staff and operates with no administrative distractions. Further, he suggested a variety of tasks for the Brains Trust. One of the most important involved constructing a series of hypothetical scenarios and then attempting to confirm or disprove those scenarios. Much of this activity falls under the above definition for deductive reasoning.

Hill *(1992)* posed the question: "At what point in a prolonged search do you abandon a preferred scenario and begin searching segments having a higher priority according to some alternative scenario?" He proposed a method for the consideration of this question. *(See "Scenario Analysis," later in this chapter.)*

> "Imagination is sometimes more important than intelligence."
> - Albert Einstein

Summary of Establishing and Marking the Search Area on a Map

By using combinations of the methods described above, the *IC* decides on and planners designate the boundaries of a defined search area consistent with all facts and information at their disposal. This area usually ends up on a map with a line drawn around a piece, or pieces of terrain. In urban environments often planners designate multiple noncontiguous small areas. Consider reducing the size of the search area*(s)* to the smallest possible that still fit the facts and information gathered. Searchers also call this *confinement* as described in Reflex Tasking (*see Chapter 14*).

Putting it all Together to Establish the Search Area

An Example:

- At 4:30 p.m. on Sunday afternoon, parents report a six-year old boy named Ben missing from the **Rock River Campground**. Consider yourself the responding police officer. In early fall the weather just turned cold with increasing rains *(this immediately points to a time critical situation)*.

The parents stated that they last saw their son over an hour ago and that their initial search efforts failed to turn up any clues or possible leads. At this point, the parents helped establish a last known position: searchers identify it, and mark it on the map. The following tasks need to occur in parallel to the Reflex Tasking process described in Chapters 14 and 16. The formal planning process starts immediately in case the bike wheel model and Reflex Tasking fail to turn up the subject.

- Interviewing the parents while waiting for SAR resources to arrive reveals the following:

  - Mature 6 year old boy
  - Adventuresome with many experiences in the outdoors
  - The boy loves animals and wildlife fascinates him
  - He dressed lightly expecting a warm day
  - His parents instructed him not to play near the large Rock River without an adult
  - Ben spent a great deal of time at the campground playing in the small tributary stream that flows through the area and into the river.

- At 5:30, six hasty team members show up announcing the arrival of twelve more volunteers at approximately 9:00 p.m. With one hour of daylight left a light rain begins to fall.

- Although not entirely out of the question, the river forms a very substantial barrier on one side of the campground. The cliffs form another barrier to easy travel, since six-year-olds tend to not climb them without compelling incentive. The road borders the river and defines a fairly open and flat area around the lake. This cuts the size of the *search area pie* down substantially. After checking the Point Last Seen, searchers discover a direction of travel *(through footprints)* indicating the terrain up the small stream represents a highly probable search area.

  - Whether by past experience or local visual clues, this process of dividing up the probable search area starts to feel like second nature.

- Remember, identify areas where the missing subject might go, and conversely, potential areas where the missing child likely never went.

- The use of deductive reasoning further narrows the possibilities. Specific activities commonly pursued by children around creeks give leads to pursue. A fascination with animals, coupled with the heavy presence of beavers in the stream *(Beaver Creek)* defines another set of activities. Locations or trails where beaver live and play further highlights some potential possibilities. If the family took a hike and noticed beaver dams, this also provides a further clue. Ask the parents if he ever wandered off before? All of these possibilities provide the basis for multiple scenarios which help in identifying regions of probability.

- Initially, with minimal clues or leads, a Search Planner needs to assume the subject might travel in any direction from the Point Last Seen. Estimating how far the subject traveled in any direction gives the first potential area to deal with in terms of distance.

$$(Distance\ Traveled)^2 \times \pi = \textbf{Search Area}$$

If the subject covered 2 miles in the given time since the parents last saw him, this translates to a theoretical area of 12.6 square miles.

$$(2)^2 \times 3.14 = \textbf{12.6 Square Miles}$$

- After consulting the lost/missing person data base for children from Koester, you discover the median distance for children *(Ages 4 to 6)* seems more representative. Upon further comparison of a later research data base from Koester, one notices a .4 of a mile median distance in a set of 90 cases.

> **NOTE:** If local data exists and it differs from Koester's figures, then use that information. Some cases fail to clearly indicate which data fits the scenario and at times require interpolation. Any analysis of previous mission activities helps; especially, distances from the Initial Planning Point by category of subject.

- With time constraints and limited available resources, consideration of the whole statistically probable area rapidly proves impossible. The 50% or even the 75% zones of probability represent more manageable search areas. Additionally, further subjective evaluation of the area quickly reduces the search area to a more realistic and manageable size (*See Figures 18-10, 18-11, 18-12 and 18-13*).

- This map represents those areas identified as high probability based on interviews, subject profile, last known activities, and terrain evaluation. This information coupled with data base distances from lost/missing person behavior studies, or local historical data aid in identifying initial locations for the deployment of limited first response resources to the field.

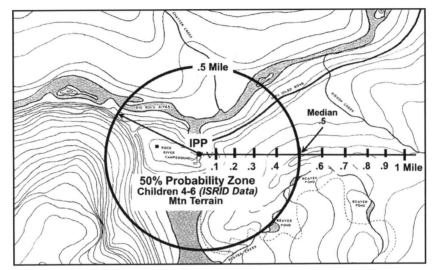

Figure 18-10 Rock River Campground

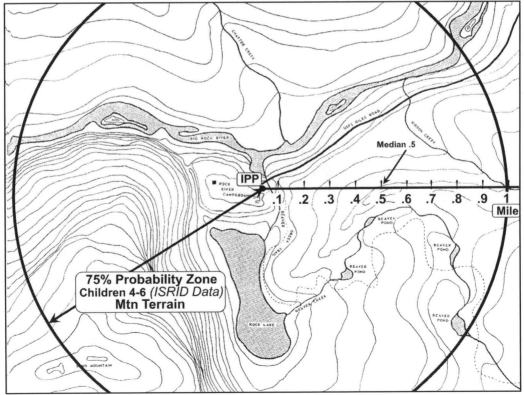

Figure 18-11 75% Zone Children 4-6

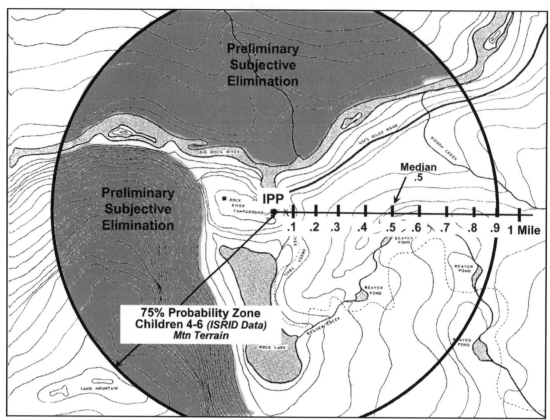

Figure 18-12 Subjective Elimination

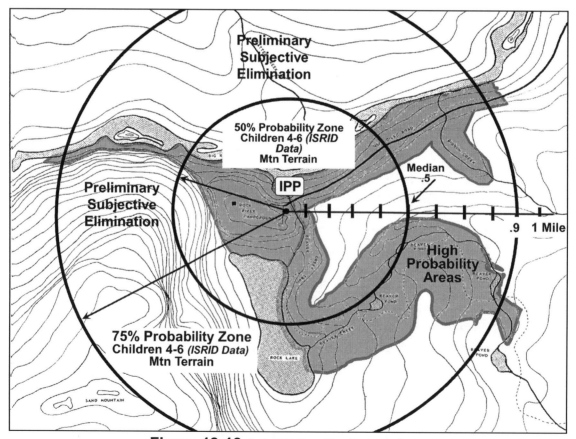

Figure 18-13 Subdividing the Search Area

Strategy - Subdividing the Search Area

Overview of the Process for Distributing Probability

Basic investigation concerning the facts of the incident coupled with a thorough assessment of subjective terrain factors determines the smallest search area consistent with available information. Searching, by definition, occurs when inconsistent or even contradictory but insufficient information exists. However, the availability of reasonably self-consistent clues, evidence, investigative reports, and other information gives light to possibly finding consistent subsets within the clues *(Note that individual pieces of data quite possibly belong to multiple possible scenarios)*. These subsets, along with carefully considered assumptions, help form the alternative scenarios. Thus creating a foundation for effective search planning.

The Search Manager or Plans Chief determines several plausible scenarios explaining why and where the missing person disappeared. Through a consensus process *(described later)* the overhead team determines the chances that each of the scenarios is correct and which areas have the highest chance of containing the missing person. By surrounding the geographic area on a map that is consistent with each scenario and then consulting Lost/Missing Person Behavior statistical distances, planners then establish a probability map *(Where is the missing person most likely to be?)*. Planners then segment the area into manageable *(or searchable)* segments. Based on how the probability distributes over the regions and segments and the capabilities of available resources, the search manager decides which areas present the greatest chance of success in the shortest possible time. Remember that the search area and probability distributions might change. They will change and shift as a search progresses and more relevant information comes to light.

The Concept of Probability Density

The problem of search centers not only on determining where to look in general, but also about deploying resources in the most efficient manner available. In his original research from the 40s, Koopman discovered that one essential element for effective search planning centered on an estimate of the search object's Probability Density Distribution. Probability density *(PDEN)* defines, in this context, as the ratio of an area's probability of area *(POA)* to its physical size. Consider the concept when dealing with the need to search significant amounts of area with limited resources.

For the purposes of calculating PDEN, search planners assume the chances of the missing person being in a specific segment as equally distributed

$$\text{PDEN} = \frac{\text{POA of a segment}}{\text{Area of that segment}}$$

throughout that segment *(a specific geographic area. Example: An Overhead Team determines that there is a 10% chance that the missing person is in that segment)*. This assumption rests on the notion that if something causes a significant difference in probability density in various portions of that *segment*, the planner simply subdivides the segment accordingly to make the density uniform. If that particular segment contains a small area and a fairly high POA in relation to other segment POAs, then using the formula below gives a relatively high PDEN *(See Figure 18-14 below)*. The formula means that with all other factors equal, searching produces a higher probability of success factor if you start in the geographic area with the highest probability density value. However, all other factors always

Probability Density

Segment	POA	Size	P_{DEN}
#1	60% (.60)	.75 sq. mile	.80
#2	40% (.40)	.35	1.14
#3	50% (.50)	.46	1.09
Or if POA values are similar			
#1	65% (.65)	.75	.87
#2	62% (.62)	.46	1.35
#3	60% (.60)	.35	1.71

Figure 18-14

come into account for land search! In most cases, complications such as variations in terrain, vegetation, environmental conditions and hazards make areas more or less searchable. This variability influences sweep width, and effort allocation and driving the maximization of Probability of Success *(discussed later)* in the shortest amount of time. While usually a major influence, PDEN represents only one criterion for deciding which segment to search first.

Searching for a 100 dollar bill in an office building illustrates the concept and its unique challenges quite well. With an equal chance of locating the note in a specified room or, as an alternative, in *all* the rooms within the building, where would you look first? Given only this information, most assume the building divides into some number of similar rooms with similar size and content. Based on this assumption, most choose to search the room first because it contains a much smaller volume than the building as a whole plus the capability of searching it much more quickly. Searching the room first also presents fewer logistical problems for searching thoroughly and efficiently.

However, if we find the room crammed full of machinery, junk, convoluted partitions and boxes of scrap paper, and find the rest of the building mostly clean and empty changes the evaluation to potentially searching the rest of the building first. This analogy presents the same dilemma that real life searching gives us in search areas that contain widely varying environments such as flat, open regions as well as rough or very irregular terrain, dense brush, etc. Probability Density describes a ratio of probability to the size of the area summarized by using this guideline: Search the area with the higher probability density first with all other factors the same. To repeat, the best search plan usually depends on many more factors than PDEN!

Regions of Probability

Once officially underway, a search quickly evolves and someone always defines the search area by drawing lines on a map. They accomplish this because of limited resources and to search everywhere simply wastes time and effort. This preliminary search area often gets reduced or expanded and more sharply defined during future operational periods and as additional information surfaces.

Basic investigation coupled with a thorough assessment of subjective terrain factors usually determines the smallest search area consistent with available information. Unfortunately though, searching often occurs without complete information. In fact, sometimes the only available information points to two inconsistent or even contradictory scenarios at first. Meticulous investigation usually uncovers reasonably consistent subsets of available clues, evidence, investigative reports, and other pieces of information to further subdivide the search area.

Usually two separate, distinct, and largely independent reasons drive subdividing the search area. The first reason revolves around speculating where to locate the missing subject and the second centers more on logistics and physical resources. The first process *(figuring out possible locations for the subject)* involves scenarios and identifying the locales associated with suspected activities, travel routes, hazards and incentives. We assign probabilities to these areas in a manner that prioritizes and identifies what we think likely occurred.

The probability values come from careful assessment of all the known facts including: behavior statistics, cautious assumptions to fill voids, and a history of the area. All of this assessment gives weight to different scenarios. The final probabilities then emerge in distinct subdivisions of the search area through a consensus process. We will call these subdivisions *regions of probability* or just *regions* for short.

The second reason for subdividing the search area, as mentioned above, centers on physically searching the environment and managing that effort. Proper search planning requires a specifically assigned area for each search resource within a specific operational period. We call these pieces of terrain *search segments* or just *segments* for short.

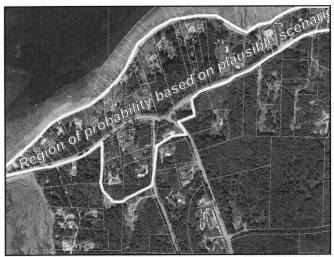

Figure 18-15 Regions of Probability

The size, shape, boundaries and location of regions of probability may coincide with or diverge completely from the logistical or management problems associated with searching a given area. Similarly, segment size, shape, boundaries and location usually relate to regions of probability only in the sense that both segments and regions partition the same search area— no requirement forces planners to subdivide the search area in the same way since regions of probability and segments solve different problems. Another way to state the difference between *regions* and *segments* follows:

- Regions of Probability answer the question, "Where in the search area is the subject more likely and less likely to be?"

- Segments answer the question, "How can we subdivide the search area into manageable pieces for searching by the available resources?"

Regions of Probability and their associated POA values provide weight factors to help determine how to allocate available resources. Segments then provide a specific search assignment for each individual resource.

A region of probability really represents the first subdivision of a potential search area. Essentially, a planner creates this subdivision by determining where significant changes in probability occur. Ask the question: What do we think happened? Initially, two general ways guide the determination of where to make distinctions between probabilities. The first relies on subjective evaluations and suspected decision points based on information gathered at the start of the search. The other relies on distances collated from Lost/Missing Person Behavior data. One invariably leads to the other and their combination usually ends with the construction of hypothetical scenarios.

Experienced planners usually advocate constructing scenarios based on speculation about what happened. Each hypothetical scenario coincides with a specific area of terrain. As an example, imagine two scenarios. In one scenario the missing person took the right fork in the trail leading them to make their way to Little Creek Campground at the lake. If the missing person took the left fork, it leads them to Ptarmigan or Pica Lakes. In either case, a very specific geographic area provides the options for searching. In fact, different scenarios sometimes contain consistent, diverging or separately defined geographic areas each with distinct regions of probability.

More specifically, continuing a hypothetical search within each scenario, if the subject encounters a river or stream it requires a decision—to cross or not to cross. The probability of the subject crossing the stream substantially affects the POA values for another region of probability on the opposite side. With a bridge or recognized ford at a suspected crossing, then perhaps the other side of the stream provides consistency with the suspected scenario. Or in a different example, walking off of a well-marked hiking trail also involves a decision for a hypothetical missing subject—left or right—that will in turn depend on a host of factors related to the subject's probable behavior. Deductive reasoning now influences the distribution of initial probability.

Remember that not all of subject's decisions rise to the level of a conscious choice. For example, a game trail that intersects a hiking trail at a bend might cause an inattentive hiker to mistakenly follow the game trail and not realize his or her mistake, until sometime later. These kinds of considerations may lead to an assessment that the probability of leaving the trail to one side gives higher probability than leaving the trail on the other. This hypothetical gives rise to two regions of probability with a trail as the boundary between them.

The second step, which refines the regions of probability within each scenario, involves overlaying Lost/Missing Person Behavior data on top of the initial regions of probability. A major benefit of lost and missing person behavior statistics comes from not only clues about behavior, but distances from the IPP where specific numbers and categories of similar subjects were found. For instance, if we look at a median distance for a given category of subject, then we know that 50% of the subjects in that category turn up between the IPP and the median and 50% turn up beyond the median. These statistics also provide distances for the 25 and 75 percent zones as well as the statistically significant maximum zone. Within each of the initial regions of probability, established based on suspected scenarios, we then estimate similar probability distributions for the current missing person.

Regions center on probabilities (*that often largely depend on subject behavior*). Regions generally end up too large for consideration as candidates for search segments, and most often it makes sense to further subdivide regions of probability into searchable segments. As a practical matter, geographic features that make good region boundaries usually make good segment boundaries as well.

When evaluating the definitions of regions and segments remember that the explanations attempt to convey the way a theory works. Analogies sometimes give powerful insights but at the same time limit how we think about a problem. Similarly, when we say a region covers any size and shape, larger or smaller than a segment, we mean region size is independent of segment size. Segment size (*as traditionally constructed in land SAR*) depends on specific parameters unrelated to the subject's suspected location within the search area.
Traditional segmentation rules include:

- Segments have a size such that the assigned resource should be able to search the segment to the desired coverage within the time allotted *(4-6 hours)*.
- The segments contain no internal barriers to searcher movements, if possible.
- The segment's boundaries correspond to obvious natural or man-made features whenever possible, especially those found on maps of the area.
- Searchers need to locate their assigned segments easily, both on the ground and on the maps provided.

The time required to search a segment varies with: the size of that geographic area, terrain type, vegetation density and other environmental factors, and also the level of coverage desired *(Can we search that whole segment in the next operational period with that resource?)*. Regions of Probability, on the other hand, depend on entirely different criteria. Planners determine region values based on likelihoods of the subject's activities in one particular area versus another particular area. The boundaries between these different geographical areas really result from subjective analysis. Remember, these boundaries help us divide the map based on where we think the subject traveled, or did not travel.

To illustrate how a region sometimes turns up smaller than the typical segment, refer to the Rock River example incident discussed on Pages 301-302. Each small beaver pond in the area may only encompass the area of a few thousand square feet or less, but the probability of finding the subject in or under the surface of one of those ponds clearly separates from the surrounding forest. Additionally, to search one of those ponds requires a different resource and time frame *(i.e. divers, underwater scenting dogs etc)*. In this case we say each pond represents a separate region of probability *(they all present large enough areas to represent small segments)* for searching and allocating POA separately. In a different scenario, if those beaver ponds now represent caves, wells, cisterns or other underground features, the same analysis applies.

Regions of Probability Construction and Segmentation

Throughout the world, searchers give subdivisions

of search areas different names: segments, sectors, zones etc... All provide acceptable descriptions. Dividing a search area into regions of probability, and then those regions into segments *(or sectors etc.)* helps to prioritize resource application at any one time. Subdividing probability regions allows resources to cover assigned search segments in a specific time period. Remember, designation of segments in the search area falls as a management function about time and effort only and provides a snapshot of searchable areas contained in a region of probability for one operational period.

Segmentation as a management tool accomplishes the following in developing search strategy:

- Segmentation using geographic features that influence behavior helps define boundaries, these obstacles and barriers provide consistency with established scenarios and regions of probability.
- Segmentation helps to assure manageable resource deployment.
- Correctly sized segments insure the accomplishment of stated objectives in the specified time of an operational period.
- Good segmentation inside high regions of probability focuses the effort of searchers per operational period.
- Segmentation also provides accurate tracking of search tasks within the overall search area.

Defining Region and Segment Boundaries

The drawing of boundaries requires careful thought, good map reading and, ideally, knowledge of the geographic area. Segment and region of probability boundaries center on what searchers readily see and identify in the field.

The following features provide suitable boundaries:

- **Man-made:** Fences, roads, ditches, power lines, trails, firebreaks, survey/boundary lines, cut lines, railroad tracks, and even walls.
- **Natural:** Ridge lines, canyon bottoms, rivers, streams, creeks, topographic breaks, vegetation breaks, geomorphologic features (boulder fields, scree slopes, and cliffed areas).
- **Improvised:** Compass lines (stringed or flagged), point-to-point (line of sight), GPS or computer generated boundaries transferred to a handheld device.

NOTE: Once placed, keep strings or flags in place for the entire search.

The use of imaginary or illustrative lines on the map such as latitude and longitude, National Grid, Universal Transverse Mercator *(UTM)* or Uniform Map System *(UMS)* lines present little practical value to searchers without the tools or knowledge to recognize them. The searchers in the field seldom have the time, skill or inclination to use these lines as identifiable boundaries.

To minimize confusion and insure complete coverage of each segment, ensure that:

- Segment size relates appropriately to the resource, environment, and level of coverage desired.
- Convenient and clearly defined boundaries.
- Searchers easily find segments on the map.
- Searchers easily locate boundaries in the field.

For decades segments or *sectors* represented the only subdivisions of a search area. We now know that this sometimes conflicts with the principles of search theory established in operations research from the 1940s. Regions of probability make sense because they address our best idea about what happened. Regions set the parameters for an experiment: "This is what we think happened; this is the geographic terrain that we think is involved; and now we will send resources to the field to either prove us right or wrong." The concept of assigning probability to given geographic regions provides a sound methodology to meld the subjective information gathered at the beginning of a search with objective statistics as the operation unfolds. Regions of probability set the stage and help answer the question "Where do we search?"

In flat areas with few discernible features searchers need to make and mark their own boundaries. They often accomplish this using flagging *(e.g., biodegradable strands of paper or ribbon, marking tape, etc.)* or string lines along compass bearings. Where possible put these in ahead of the search teams. However, in some cases boundaries end up unavoidably vague. In these cases strive for duplication of coverage rather than gaps or strips left un-searched.

Segments Sizes

Segment size depends in large part on terrain-cover and weather. Complete *(or desired)* coverage in 4-6 hours defines reasonably sized areas for search. Remember an operational period must include: the time necessary to brief searchers; transport them to the field; search the designated area; egress via some mode of transport; and finally, the time required to debrief them before going off shift.

- Too large segments:

  - Cause a bad influence on searcher morale.
  - Make it almost impossible to manage leftover un-searched areas carried from one operational period to another.
  - Too difficult to cover in the allotted time.
  - Create unnecessary delays while a team finishes the segment.

Guidelines to reduce effort by searchers:

- Avoid interior barriers. Instruct units not to cross and recross fences, creeks, rivers, roads, highways, hedges, etc.
- Assign resources most appropriate to each segment *(e.g., mountain rescue for cliffs; helicopters for open areas; dogs for heavy cover)*.
- Consider starting searchers at higher points *(transport them)*. It is easier to search diagonally downhill.
- Save energy and time with prearranged rides back to base or to another segment.
- Make segments appropriately sized for an operational period: approximately 80 - 100 acres *(see Figure 18-16 opposite page)*

> **NOTE:** Consider the problems of coverage along segment boundaries. Gaps in coverage easily occur on rounded ridges, canyon bottoms, along creeks, and on streets or alleys in the urban environment. Searchers often assume that the adjacent crew searched it *(See also Chapter 23 - Searching in the Urban Environment)*. Consider trails that mark boundaries between segments as separate search segments unto themselves and search them accordingly.

After identifying and drawing boundaries, letter the regions and number the segments.

Numbering and lettering the segments ensures conformity, and makes identification and communications easier *(See Figure 18-17 page 311)*. If all teams have copies of the segment map, redirection or re-tasking becomes a relatively simple matter. The letters also help to eliminate confusion when later representing other numbers such as Regions of Probability, POA or POS values on the map.

Assigning Probability Values to Regions of Probability and Segments Using Consensus

A successful initial planning process depends on reasonably determined POA assignments and more importantly how those numbers change as the search unfolds. A search manager should never plan alone. Several members of an Overhead Team usually help in the assignment of POA values to the regions of probability and subsequently to the segments.

Consensus for Probability Distribution

To reduce argument, fights and arbitrary personality differences, Bob Mattson *(Col. U.S.A.F. Ret.)* proposed a consensus method *(The Mattson Consensus System)* for reaching an unbiased average POA value for each segment in a search area. He developed this system while instructing at the USCG/USAF staffed National Search and Rescue School, at the USCG base on Governors Island in New York City. Mattson proposed that the consensus involve a voting process to identify numerical values for the

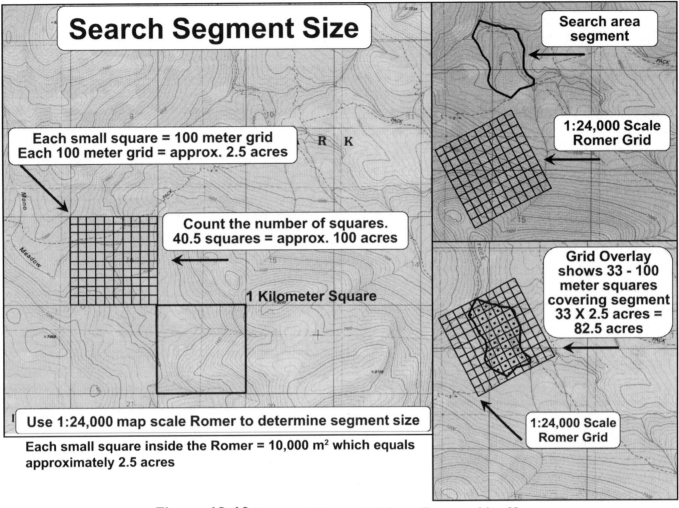

Figure 18-16 Segment Size and Using a Romer with a Map

chances of a missing person or aircraft etc. located in any given segment of a proposed search area.

The process served two purposes. First it lightened relations between adverse personalities and second it assigned numerical values to segments that allow better allocation of resources. We now know that the original Mattson Consensus System and even a later version *(Modified Mattson)* for assigning probabilities to segments contained a number of serious flaws. A new, redesigned and refined process includes both proportionality and consistency.

In 1999 Cooper and Frost also pointed out that consensus required much more attention to proportional assessment. The basis for this focus stems from long standing Operations Research in search theory mentioned previously in Chapter 17.

- The proportion of one region of probability assessment, or one segment probability assessment to another is vital. The proportion between regions of probability or segments in a region is more important than the specific assessment values assigned to each.

To provide the most accurate probability distribution, we add a few additional pieces of information to the POA puzzle. Providing accurate assessments requires search planners to put forth a common frame of reference to describe the probabilities involved. The probability for one scenario over another must be in relative proportion to the other scenarios that make up the regions of probability for the search area, or the information misleads at best, and at worst sends us down the completely wrong path.

Proportion Based Consensus

DC Cooper and JR Frost developed the *Proportion-Based Consensus* method modeled after Mattson's *(1975)* consensus and methods derived from the U.S. Coast Guard's use of probability maps in maritime search. Probability allocation to pieces of terrain through the use of a simple proportion-based consensus scheme ensures a consistent simple process and proportionality. This system calls for the use of a reference value of 100 *(or 10 works equally well)* to indicate the segment or region of probability most likely to contain the missing person. If the evaluator believes that more than one segment or region equally likely to contain the missing person above all the others, then the evaluator gives each the value of 100. This is *not* a percentage or a probability value, we use it as a reference value. However, evaluators need to use the same reference value when comparing probability between segments.

When an evaluator assigns a specific geographic area with a reference value of 100, the remaining regions of probability then all receive values *(assigned by the evaluator)* proportionally related to that reference value. This process resembles the scoring system used at the Olympic Games. Just as several independent judges rate individual athletes, all using a standard scale, individual regions or segments in the search area get rated by independent evaluators all using a standard scale.

For example, if the evaluator believes a certain scenario or segment is half as likely to contain the subject as the reference area, they assign a value of 50; a scenario or segment three fourths as likely equals 75; and a scenario or segment one quarter as likely gets 25 etc. It follows that a scenario or segment given the value of 75 represents three times the likelihood of one that is rated at 25. The method demands similar relationships between all the regions of probability *(scenarios)* or segments. The values used by each evaluator need not add up to any number, and a consensus member may assign the same value to multiple scenarios for weighting or to multiple segments within a region.

All evaluators need to use the same reference value *(they do not need to assign the reference value to the same place, everyone just needs to use the same value as a reference)*. Consensus assigns values to each geographic area, additional computations in the process *(covered later in the chapter)* normalize these values and convert them to POAs expressed as percentages.

Levels of distinction between regions of probability represent practical changes in probability only. Planners ignore the very small differences in favor of practical expression. Fractions and/or decimals such as 12.5 work because they represent a proportional relationship such as 1/8, but evaluators should avoid using extremely high levels of precision. Proportion based consensus represents a subjective process where high levels of precision remain unjustified and only complicates computations.

Providing accurate assessments requires consensus team members to put forth a common frame of reference to describe the values. All evaluators need all available information about the search. Without accurate information, these evaluations could delay the search or even cause it to fail.

If planners come up with more than one highly likely scenario, then each scenario requires separate consideration. This means the consensus only considers a region of probability appropriate to one scenario at a time *(See Scenario Analysis on the next page)*.

Never search plan by yourself if possible. Use the best minds and ideas available. Any or all of the consensus team member assessments might point in the right direction. Given real world constraints on available personnel, implement the overhead team concept and consensus methods as soon as possible.

In the Reflex Tasking phase of the search the effort always gathers information through interviews with companions, family, peers, or other witnesses. As these tasks complete, the planner consults Lost/Missing Person Behavior statistical data from international, regional or local databases for the category of subject distances and other clues. This process helps a search planner to establish a probability map and refine likely locations. When overlaying Lost/Missing Person Behavior data on the map, quickly identify generalized locations and distances where previous missing persons in the same category turned up.

Scenario Analysis

The first phase of the consensus process centers on the search planners discussing and coming to consensus on a number of possible scenarios. Ken Hill *(1992)* stated that "Any scenario that has a nontrivial possibility of being valid, as estimated by the Search Planners, should be included in the analysis." He suggested including any scenario with a 10% chance of validity in the initial analysis. He felt it reasonable for any search to include at least two or three scenarios.

Consider in the following examples: three different scenarios which potentially describe a missing person incident and we perform consensus for all the segments because they all fit within all three scenarios. For this example reference *Figure 18-18* on the next page.

The three scenarios have all segments in common for a circuitous route involving several possible climbs, *(segments 6, 4 and 2),* a visit to a special lake *(segment 6),* and an area particularly known for it's photographic beauty *(segment 4).* Scenario A is consistent with the missing person having gone through segment 7 to the lake in segment 6, then intending to continue on around the circuit after spending time at the lake. Scenario B is consistent with the person having gone through segment 1 to take pictures in segment 2 and continuing around the circuit in that direction. Scenario C is consistent with the missing person having proceeded through segment 1, 2, and 3 up to the mountain in segment 4 for a climb and proceeding on through 5, 6 and 7 back to the trailhead. Consensus by the overhead team picks scenario C as the most plausible which is the climb in segment 4 *(See Consensus worksheet #1 Figure 18-19).*

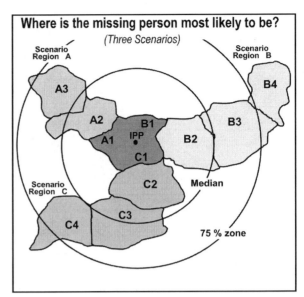

Figure 18-17 Using Scenario Analysis as a Tool to evaluate different pieces of the Search Area

Consensus Worksheet # 1

With Worksheet # 1 we establish a probability distribution through a consensus process that addresses the likelihood that each scenario occurred, and using the reference value of 100 *(See Worksheet 1 Page 313).* Also refer to the Scenario Analysis Identification and Development Form on pages 319-320.

NOTE: If more than one scenario/segment is considered to be equally likely, then each should be given the value of 100.

The Overhead Team uses all of the available information gathered on-scene about the incident at this time. Each evaluator estimates and assigns relative scores to the scenarios based on Proportional Consensus. These scores then *normalize* to give consensus POA values in percent for each of the regions of probability as per Worksheet #1 on page 313. The search planner then surrounds the geographic terrain on the map consistent with each scenario. In this case the three scenarios and thus three regions of probability drawn on the map. During this process, subjective factors and terrain analysis refine and designate these regions. The initial consensus gave probability values for each scenario and these values then attach to each region of probability designated on the map. The regions of probability label accordingly *(e.g. A, B, C, etc.).*

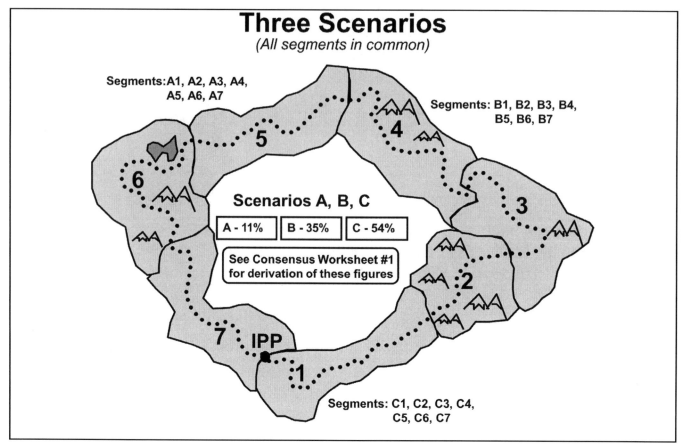

Figure 18-18

These scenario values or regions of probability give us two important things. First, the process gives a designation of where the planners rank the highest region of probability with respect to the ranking of other regions. Second it gives us the capability to use weight factors that emphasize certain segments consistent with high probability scenarios. Remember that once planners designate the probability values for the regions of probability, these figures weight the subsequent segments within the regions. This describes part of the scenario analysis process.

By surrounding consistent geographic areas on a map with each scenario we identify regions of consistent probability. This process also identifies the smallest search area consistent with known facts and suspected occurrences. The next step involves subdividing the regions of probability into manageable segments for searching in a single operational period as described earlier in this chapter.

When planners subdivide the regions of probability into searchable segments, each of these segments ends up respectively designated with a letter and number *(A1, B1, C1, etc.)*. As mentioned before, separate regions of probability *(scenarios)* sometimes contain common, diverging or separate defined geographic areas. With a category of subject designated, we then overlay the 25, 50, 75 percent and maximum zones onto each of the regions of probability (*see Figure 18-20 on page 314*).

These delineated zones form a constant reminder that 50 percent of the probability allocates to the segments inside the median and 50 percent to those segments outside the median. This applies to the 25% and 75% zones as well. The consensus process subjectively takes this into consideration clustering or skewed distributions toward the IPP with available data. Segments consistent with that information then receive appropriately more probability. If the area between the IPP and the 25% zone remains consistent with all scenarios, then the terrain inside that distance subjectively receives approximately 25 percent of the probability and so on. In the case where all regions of probability derived from the different scenarios form completely separate areas, then each

Consensus Worksheet 1 — *Weighting for Scenario Options*

1. Evaluator names go in left column.
2. After a complete and thorough description of all scenarios, each evaluator assigns the value of 100 to the scenario that he or she believes is the most likely to be true. Then each evaluator must estimate the likelihood of each scenario as a proportion of the reference value 100. There is room on this sheet for 6 Scenarios (A-F).
3. Add each Scenario column and put this sum in the "Subtotal Down" space at the bottom of each column.
4. Add the "Subtotals Down" row across and put the sum in "Total Across" for all of the rows. This value now becomes the denominator for the fraction that will be used to determine the scenario weight.
5. Calculate Scenario Weights by dividing each "Subtotal Down" figure under each scenario column by the total of all scenario weights. *(Subtotal Down ÷ Total of all evaluator weights = % Weight for Each Scenario)*.

Scenario Designation	Option A	Option B	Option C	Option D	Option E	Option F	
Smith	25	30	100				
Andrew	10	50	100				
Price	25	75	100				
Evans	10	50	100				
Green	30	100	75				Subtotal Across
Subtotal Down	100	305	475				880
Consensus Weights ③ ÷ ④ = Weight	$\frac{100}{880}$ 11%	$\frac{305}{880}$ 35%	$\frac{475}{880}$ 54%	=.11	.35	.54	100 %

Date: 05/26/16   Mission #: 22   Op. Period: 2nd   Time: 06:55am

Figure 18-19

region of probability gets evaluated separately and the respective segments within those regions receive weights according to the initial consensus determined about the scenarios. Consensus POA values for the individual segments come from multiplying them by the probability of the scenario to which the segment belongs.

Managing the Inland Search Function - **Operational Response**

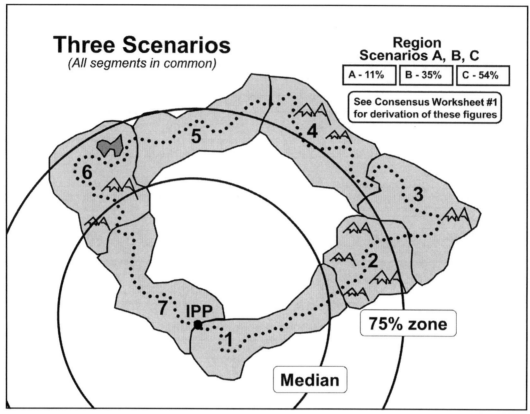

Figure 18-20

Consensus Worksheet # 2

Consider that the overhead team now takes a consensus of seven segments where the combination of all three scenarios contain at least one segment in common.

Place each evaluator's segment likelihood designations on a single worksheet with no totals calculated. Reference all number values for segments to the number 100 as a benchmark for determining values *(See Worksheet 2 on page 315)*. Remember that the numerical values used on this sheet represent *personal subjective values considering how each segment relates to all the others, not percentages.*

Consensus Worksheet # 3

Transfer the individual segment designations to the third worksheet and compile totals for each segment. Total the sums from all of the segments. Use that total as the denominator for a ratio designation in each segment. Convert that fraction to a percentage for the POA of that segment *(See Worksheet 3, on the next page)*. This process averages the value designations of those contributing as per Proportional Consensus.

Remember that in the example consensus forms on the next page, we considered a search area that contains seven *(7)* segments. Everyone used a reference value of 100 for most likely, with a total of five evaluators. A consensus probability then applies for each scenario based region on Worksheet #1 *(Page 313)*.

Consensus Worksheet 2
One for each Evaluator

→ Evaluators should be in possession of all available information regarding this search. *(Construct at least three possible scenarios - See Consensus Worksheet 1)*
→ Evaluators should consider only one scenario at a time when assigning values. Use one worksheet per scenario.
1. Evaluators can decide and use the value 100 or 10 as their reference value when assessing segment values. The values assigned each segment must be proportional to this reference value.
2. Assign an appropriate value to each segment.
   - The proportionality of the assigned values is extremely important and must be thoroughly considered.
   - All segments with the same assigned value have the same likelihood of containing the subject.
   - There is no upper or lower limit to the proportional assessment values that can be assigned to a segment, and they need not add up to any value. Whole numbers are sufficient and should be used.
3. When filled out, consensus worksheet goes to Plans Function staff member who will tabulate evaluator values on Worksheet #3.

Evaluator Name: __Andrew__   Scenario: __A__   Reference Value: 100 or 10

Segment Designation →	A_1	A_2	A_3	A_4	A_5	A_6	A_7	A_8	A_9	A_{10}
Likelihood Number	33	50	100	25	10	100	75			

Date: __05/26/16__   Mission #: __22__   Op. Period: __2nd__   Time: __06:30am__

Figure 18-21a

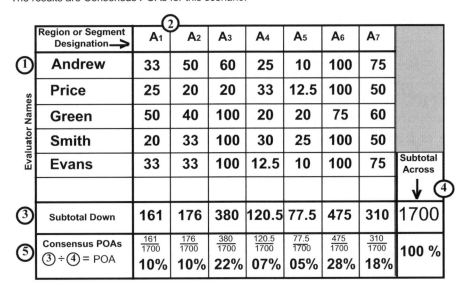

Figure 18-21b

Scenario Analysis Overview and Example Computation

- Apply lost/missing person behavior data along with information gathered on-scene to the map to identify potential distances, previous incident clustering, clues and likely spots *(IPP secured, marked and documented)*.

- The search planning team discusses and comes to consensus on a number of scenarios *(Possible events explaining what happened to the missing person using the Scenario Analysis Identification and Development Form Figure 18-24 page 319 and 320)*.

- The search planner then surrounds the geographic terrain on the map, consistent with each scenario.

- Evaluators estimate and assign relative probability scores to the regions for each scenario based on Proportional Consensus. The process then *normalizes* these scores to give consensus probability values in percent *(See Worksheet #1 Figure 18-19)*.

- Next, subdivide the regions of probability into manageable segments searchable within one operational period.

- Then, distribute probability to each searchable segment within each of the regions of probability. The segments within that region receive probability by consensus as well using all the data available. Weigh each consensus segment POA value by multiplying it times the probability of the scenario to which it applies. When a segment or segments lie within more than one scenario then add the weighted values together.

- Planners want to use a single weighting factor on each of the segments to more precisely *load* probability onto the map for analysis and resource deployment. Sum the weighted probability of area *(POA)* values for each scenario *(region of probability)* assessment to produce a single set of POA values for each Segment.

- Average the planning POA values as described *(See Worksheet # 3, Figure 18-21b)*. Remember that while these values initially come from a subjective process, these values then shift and change as the search proceeds and operations commit resources to each search segment.

Planning POAs for all Scenarios

In summary for the example here, the search planner*(s)* come up with several different scenarios and assign a probability for each scenario based on their perception of the most likely events. The assigned values in this process give the percentage chance for each scenario *(In this case, those values are 11%, 35%, and 54% for scenarios A, B, and C respectively)*. Next we multiply the POA values for each segment in a region by the weighting factor of each possible scenario *(Region of Probability - .11, .35, and .54)* and then add those values to give the total POA *(in each segment)* for all three scenarios. This method allows a search manager to consider the influences of all three scenarios at the same time.

Determining Collective Weights for the Segments from all of the Scenarios

Segment weighting for **Scenario A**		
A1	.10 X .11 =	.01
A2	.10 X .11 =	.01
A3	.22 X .11 =	.02
A4	.07 X .11 =	.01
A5	.05 X .11 =	.01
A6	.28 X .11 =	.03
A7	.18 X .11 =	.02

Scenario Weights: A - 11% | B - 35% | C - 54%

Segment weighting for **Scenario B**		
B1	.08 X .35 =	.03
B2	.40 X .35 =	.14
B3	.05 X .35 =	.02
B4	.10 X .35 =	.04
B5	.18 X .35 =	.06
B6	.15 X .35 =	.05
B7	.05 X .35 =	.02

Scenario Weights: A - 11% | B - 35% | C - 54%

Segment weighting for **Scenario C**		
C1	.12 X .54 =	.06
C2	.30 X .54 =	.16
C3	.09 X .54 =	.05
C4	.10 X .54 =	.05
C5	.20 X .54 =	.11
C6	.15 X .54 =	.08
C7	.04 X .54 =	.02

Scenario Weights: A - 11% | B - 35% | C - 54%

Adding Scenario Weights Together For Planning POAs

Segment	Weighted POAs Scenario A	Weighted POAs Scenario B	Weighted POAs Scenario C	Planning POAs all Scenarios
1	.01	.03	.06	.10
2	.01	.14	.16	.31
3	.02	.02	.05	.09
4	.01	.04	.05	.10
5	.01	.06	.11	.18
6	.03	.05	.08	.16
7	.02	.02	.02	.06
				Total 100%

An example adapted from Hill *(1992)* provides the data for this calculation. *Figure 18-22a* below forms a composite for all segments. The example considers a search with seven segments *(1 through 7)* with three scenarios that have all segments in common.

These figures started on Consensus Worksheet #1 *(as shown on page 313)*.

Scenario A probability = 0.11
Scenario B probability = 0.35
Scenario C probability = 0.54

Composite of Process to Determine Planning POAs

This multiple scenario analysis rates POA from one region of probability to another, depending on the values assigned to each scenario. In this example, we have three scenarios with seven segments in common and figured all the planning POAs for the segments with the scenario weights.

Seg	Initial POA Scenarios			Weighted POAs			Planning POAs Includes all Scenarios
	A	B	C	Scenario A (Weight = .11)	Scenario B (Weight = .35)	Scenario C (Weight = .54)	
1	.10	.08	.12	.10 x .11 = .01	.08 x .35 = .03	.12 x .54 = .06	.01 + .03 + .06 = .10 = 10%
2	.10	.40	.30	.10 = .01	.40 = .14	.30 = .15	= .31 = 31%
3	.22	.04	.09	.22 = .02	.04 = .02	.09 = .05	= .09 = 9%
4	.07	.10	.10	.07 = .01	.10 = .04	.10 = .05	= .10 = 10%
5	.05	.18	.20	.05 = .01	.18 = .06	.20 = .11	= .18 = 18%
6	.28	.15	.15	.28 = .03	.15 = .05	.15 = .08	= .16 = 16%
7	.18	.05	.04	.18 = .02	.05 = .02	.04 = .02	= .06 = 6%
	100%	100%	100%	100%	100%	100%	Total 1.00 = 100%

Figure 18-22a

Another Example:

This example adapted from Hill *(1992)* is tabulated below in *Figure 18-22b* and in *Figure 18-23* on the next page. This example considers a search with nine segments *(1 through 9 as shown below)* with one common segment in the three scenarios. Consensus among the overhead team designates the following probabilities:

Scenario A probability = 0.50
Scenario B probability = 0.30
Scenario C probability = 0.20.

Segment weighting for **Scenario A**		
1	.50 X .50 =	.25
2	.30 X .50 =	.15
3	.20 X .50 =	.10
4	0 X 0 =	0
5	0 X 0 =	0
6	0 X 0 =	0
7	0 X 0 =	0
8	0 X 0 =	0
9	0 X 0 =	0
Scenario Weights		
A - 50%	B - 30%	C - 20%

Segment weighting for **Scenario B**		
1	.10 X .30 =	.03
2	0 X 0 =	0
3	0 X 0 =	0
4	.40 X .30 =	.12
5	.30 X .30 =	.09
6	.20 X .30 =	.06
7	0 X 0 =	0
8	0 X 0 =	0
9	0 X 0 =	0
Scenario Weights		
A - 50%	B - 30%	C - 20%

Segment weighting for **Scenario C**		
1	.10 X .20 =	.02
2	0 X 0 =	0
3	0 X 0 =	0
4	0 X 0 =	0
5	0 X 0 =	0
6	0 X 0 =	0
7	.40 X .20 =	.08
8	.30 X .20 =	.06
9	.20 X .20 =	.04
Scenario Weights		
A - 50%	B - 30%	C - 20%

Adding Scenario Weights Together For Planning POAs

Segment	Weighted POAs Scenario A	Weighted POAs Scenario B	Weighted POAs Scenario C	Planning POAs all Scenarios
1	.25	.03	.02	.30
2	.15	0	0	.15
3	.10	0	0	.10
4	0	.12	0	.12
5	0	.09	0	.09
6	0	.06	0	.06
7	0	0	.08	.08
8	0	0	.06	.06
9	0	0	.04	.04
				Total 100%

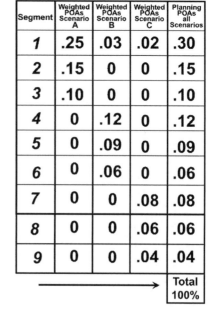

Three Scenarios
(1 common segment - 1)

Figure 18-22b

Seg	Initial POA Scenarios			Weighted POAs			Planning POAs Includes all Scenarios
	A	B	C	Scenario A (Weight = .50)	Scenario B (Weight = .30)	Scenario C (Weight = .20)	
1	.50	0	0	.50 x .50 = .25	.10 x .30 = .03	.10 x .20 = .02	.25 + .03 + .02 = .25 = 30%
2	.30	0	0	.30 = .15	0 = 0	0 = 0	= .15 = 15%
3	.20	.10	.10	.20 = .10	0 = 0	0 = 0	= .10 = 10%
4	0	.40	0	0 = 0	.40 = .12	0 = 0	= .12 = 12%
5	0	.30	0	0 = 0	.30 = .09	0 = 0	= .09 = 9%
6	0	.20	0	0 = 0	.20 = .06	0 = 0	= .06 = 6%
7	0	0	.40	0 = 0	0 = 0	.40 = .08	= .08 = 8%
8	0	0	.30	0 = 0	0 = 0	.30 = .06	= .06 = 6%
9	0	0	.20	0 = 0	0 = 0	.20 = .04	0 + 0 + .04 = .04 = 4%
	100%	100%	100%	100%	100%	100%	Total 1.00 = 100%

Figure 18-23

Composite Process to Determine Planning POAs for This Example

Figure 18-23 above shows how multiple scenario analysis *loads* probability into segments based on credible scenarios. While the basis for this process starts subjectively, it forms the only way to include the host of unique factors into the search planning process. Once planners incorporate these influences into the POA values, the process takes over and provides options for resource allocation and success factors based on those influences.

The Scenario Analysis Identification & Development Form

Use the form *(Figure 18-24 below and on the next page)* as a template for Scenario Analysis. The filled in spaces below show reminders of example statements, facts, clues, factors and/or speculation that the Search Planner uses to build credible scenarios for the incident. Fill out the blank form in the Appendix as a planning document using the filled-in form as a guide. The weighted values for the Segment POAs also

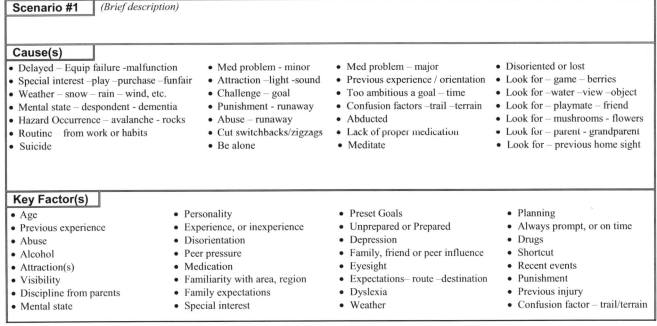

Figure 18-24 Scenario Analysis Form

Figure 18-24 Scenario Analysis Form continued

Likely Subject Actions
- Seek shelter or hole up
- Keep moving - try to get oriented
- Set up a signal - leave sign or a mark
- Walk toward light / sound / civilization
- Take line of least resistance - go down
- Climb up to get oriented
- Find a secluded beautiful/prominent spot
- Cut switchbacks or zigzags
- Keep going until stuck or hit barrier
- Try to find a way out
- Go in a straight line
- Go for help
- Hide and/or evade
- Stay put - wait
- Backtrack
- Hitchhike
- Try to find friend / mate
- Try to find water
- Try to find old residence
- Push on to try and make goal
- Find better picking / gathering
- Direction sample from one spot
- Wait for daylight and then move
- Take a nap
- Play in stream while moving
- Follow the flowers / berries, etc.
- Get confused and wander
- Follow an old path
- Look in a specific spot
- Board mass transit
- Return to old worksite
- Build a shelter - boughs - snow
- Look for another play spot
- Follow a stream / ridge / gulley
- Try to start a fire
- Go to a friend's house

Unlikely Actions
- Stop
- Build a shelter - natural
- Climb a steep hill -(rough terrain)
- Stop if subject crosses road or trail
- Abandon skies, snowmobile, etc.
- Allow weather to influence them
- Go without being prepared
- Call for help
- Get on any mass transit
- Start a fire
- Respond to attraction modes
- Turn back
- Not be prompt
- Talk or visit with strangers
- Respond to searchers
- Try to cross a river or stream
- Take a shortcut
- Walk out on their own
- Give up
- Disobey rules of behavior
- Travel at night without light
- Be late, or not follow through
- Leave the trail with a bike
- Leave trail
- Come back on his/her own
- Do something without asking

Appropriate Search Action/Methods
- Gather more information
- Interview family and friends
- Search residence
- Door to door canvassing
- Type II search of high POD areas
- Send Type I hasty team search
- Sound / light line
- Search residence again
- Level I door to door search
- Interview peers at work place
- Wait until daylight
- Helicopter over flights
- Use attraction methods
- Level II door to door search
- Send dog & handler to PLS
- Sound line
- Search "Likely Spots"
- Conduct evidence search
- Level III door to door search

Speculate Condition of Subject
- Mobile: Speculate yes
- Immobile: Within several hours after dark
- Responsive: High probability
- Unresponsive: Low probability

Implications / Deductions
- Most likely down because of hypothermia
- Combination of subject likely down along with color of clothing means more effort to achieve acceptable POD
- Terrain and vegetation dictate that we must use more thorough methods
- Research some areas again regularly
- Door to door canvassing will be essential in these neighborhoods
- High probability that subject took mass transit out of the immediate search area
- Subject most likely attracted to lower elevations by lights and/or sounds
- Subject most likely attracted off of the trail by attractions visible at key locations along the route

provide guidance for incorporating the scenarios into the overall management strategy.

Some Pitfalls of the Initial Response

The initial hours of a search incident define the response phase. During this time resources receive alerts, mobilize, make phone calls, determine urgency, and move to the incident site. Preliminary investigation and interviewing of witnesses also takes place as part of this phase. In addition, the IC and eventually planners, study maps and access data for a more complete assessment. All of this potential activity takes time and often the general public perceives nothing happening in the field and develops a perception of a stalled search process.

New search managers sometimes fall into the trap of not committing resources to the field until establishing and accurately subdividing the entire search area. Prevailing experience tells us not to think that way. Reflex Tasking gives plenty of optional field activities independent of the comprehensive planning effort. These statistically powerful tools often prove very successful at finding the subject.

Thoughts About Assigning Probabilities and On-Scene Planning

As mentioned previously, Reflex Tasking such as checking all the likely spots, the IPP, terrain analysis, containment and completing initial interviews always occurs as a precursor or even in parallel to planning for area searches. The area search phase entails subdividing the search area into regions and then segments for potential detailed searching and effort management.

Regions of probability stand as the first subdivision of a potential search area and use broad based factors to assign probability to scenario options. Lost and Missing person behavior data helps define regions and further *loads* the probabilities according to past incidents. For example a high percentage of Alzheimer's patients turn up less than one-half mile from the IPP.

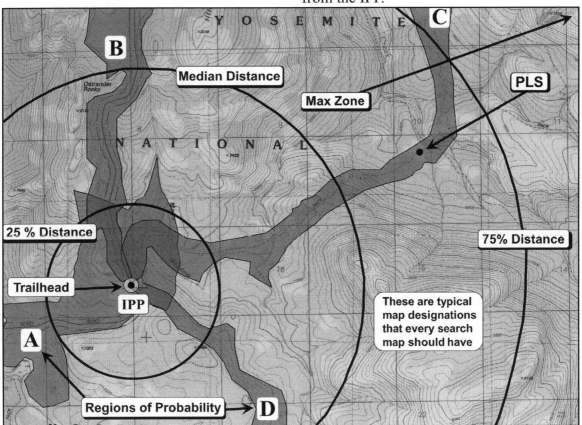

Figure 18-25 Mapping Regions and Database Distances

Figure 18-26 Report of a Missing Hiker/Climber

Putting it All Together to Assign Probability

At 12:00 PM on Monday afternoon, a distraught wife reports a 43 yr. old man named John failed to come home from a hiking trip to the Snow Lakes Wilderness Recreation Area. Consider yourself the responding Law Enforcement Officer.

In late fall the weather stays warm in the afternoon but drops well below freezing at night. No Snowfall yet, however it often falls at this time of year. The woman reports her husband left on Friday afternoon with plans to hike into the Snow Lake Wilderness, stay a couple days and hike back out late Sunday afternoon. John never arrived Sunday night, and initial efforts to contact him by cell phone or through close friends turned up nothing. After dispatch, you travel to the Snow Creek Campground and trail head. A car in the parking lot matches the description given by the reporting spouse. You mark the LKP on the map, and while waiting for SAR resources to arrive conduct a phone interview with John's wife. The interview reveals the following:

- John often hikes alone
- He loves photography
- He hikes often with over twenty years experience in the high-country
- He climbs, but not technical climbing. He will scramble and free climb steep and rugged terrain to get on the top of a peak or vantage point to take dramatic or spectacular photos.
- John carries a medium pack, light clothing, a small amount of food, a sleeping bag, and a small tent.
- His wife describes him as a loner both in his work and in recreational or social settings.
- He often talks to friends and family of his wilderness navigation, survival skills and preparedness.
- Not always, but he often likes to go cross country his own way as opposed to the established trails; i.e. he likes to explore new country.
- He sometimes changes plans mid-trip to climb a peak *(or more than one)* in the area.

At 2:00 PM four hasty team members arrive on scene, and relate that twelve more team members, and their portable command center, will arrive by 5:00 PM. Dispatch contacts the local mountain rescue team and starts their response. The fifteen members of the local team should arrive by 5:00 PM. The weather forecast calls for temperatures to drop into the mid twenties overnight with the possibility of snow on Wednesday. Two 2 person hasty teams start up the main trails to the first of the lakes, and to search likely spots in those areas. You establish, mark and secure the initial planning point (IPP). After consulting the county records and referencing the international database (ISRID) on subject behavior, you find the median distance for the Hiker Category is 2 miles, and the 75% zone lies at 4 miles from the IPP.

The data for climbers suggests a slightly larger median value of 3 miles and then 4.8 miles for the 75% zone. Playing a situation like this on the conservative side follows standard practice. Therefore use the values of 3 miles and 4.8 miles since the subject category could be in either the Hiker or Climber category and those figures cover both categories.

An experienced Incident Commander arrives on scene at 3:00 PM and staff gives a briefing on accomplishments so far. The new IC agrees with the analysis of the behavior data and begins providing additional suggestions to develop scenarios for defining regions of probability on the map. Planners keep working while waiting for the initial hasty team reports from the field.

Through a quick consensus process, discussion, his wife's statements and the history of the area, you and the IC come up with four credible scenarios that possibly explain John's whereabouts.

The search area lies in very steep and mountainous wilderness terrain. There are three trails leaving two campgrounds that are within a short walking distance of one another *(See Figure 18-26 on the previous page)*. The Snow Creek Trail and the Shield Lake

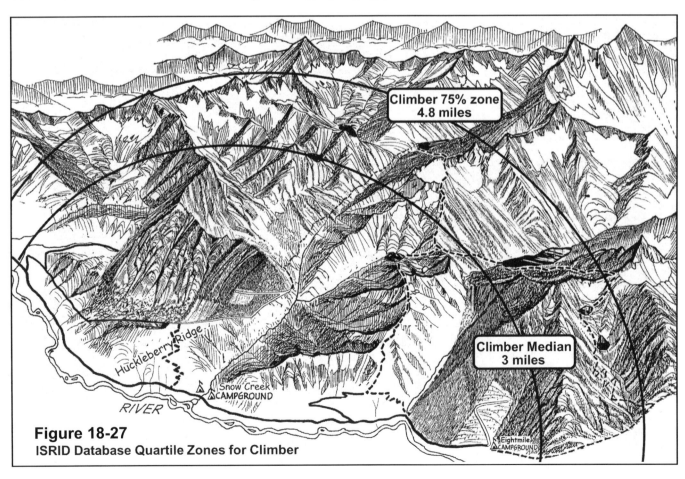

Figure 18-27
ISRID Database Quartile Zones for Climber

Figure 18-28a Potential Scenarios

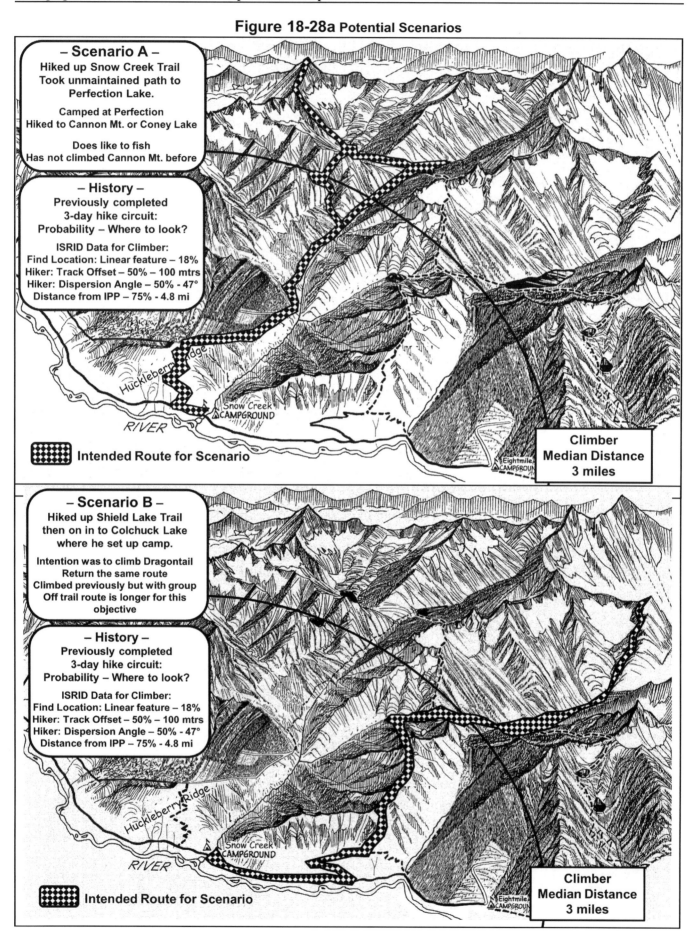

Figure 18-28b Potential Scenario

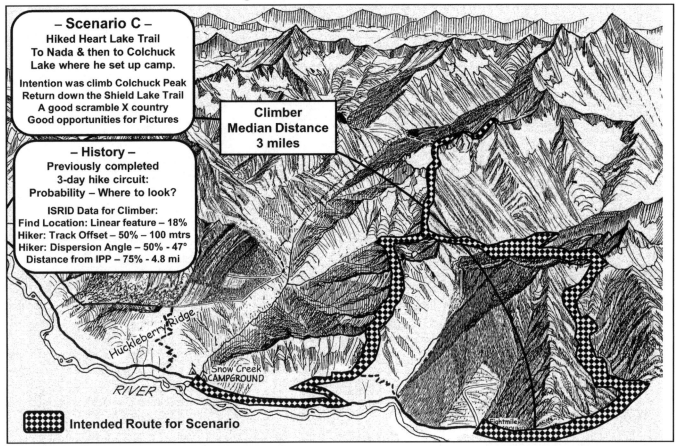

Trail both provide easy access to the area from the Snow Creek Campground. The Heart Lake Trail departs from the Eightmile Campground and starts several circular routes that hikers often take into the wilderness area.

After conversing with the IC about scenarios, routes and travel times, planners plot the ISRID median distance and the 75% distance on the map of the area. *(see Figure 18-27 on page 323)*. Each of the three trails from the two Campgrounds out to the 75% zone represent a distinct scenario and also a different region of probability. Using appropriate terrain features *(such as cliffs, vegetation, drainages, elevation etc.)* the planners define their boundaries on either side of the trails. To make sure they reasonably include as much ground within the scenarios as practical, planners use the Hiker Track Offset of 100 meters as well.

While the route for scenario A goes beyond the 75% zone from the IPP, the trail forms a standard route to Cannon Mountain and other remote alpine lakes. The eastern lakes and peaks *(Heart, Nada, Colchuck and Shield lake along with Dragontail Peak and Colchuck Peak)* represent separate regions of probability, because hikers regularly use them as objectives for circuit routes through the area. Rangers also maintain the trails in that region between and around the lakes.

Four Scenarios Proposed

Scenario A *(Figure 18-28a)*: John hiked up the main Snow Creek Trail to an un-maintained path and then hiked to Perfection Lake. Both the Perfection and Cony Lakes trails receive little to no maintenance. John set up camp at Perfection with the intent of getting up early and climbing Cannon Mountain or alternately hiking up to Cony Lake to catch some cutthroat trout. John likes to fish, but his wife cannot confirm whether he took a fishing rod and kit *(John never climbed Cannon Mountain on a previous trip even though he hiked here many times. Cannon Mtn stands as one of the few unclimbed (by him) peaks in the area)*.

Figure 18-28c Potential Scenario

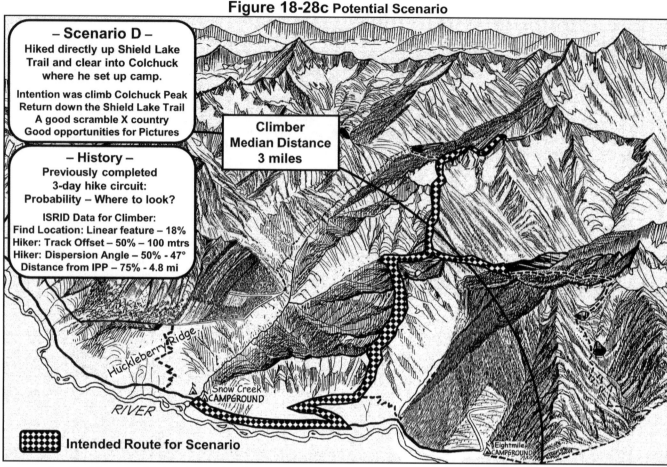

Scenario B *(Figure 18-28a)*: John hiked up the Shield Lake trail to Shield Lake, then up to Colchuck Lake where he set up camp. This camp served as a base for climbing Dragontail Peak. He intended to hike back out the same route. The peak summit of Dragontail offers unusual and unique perspectives of the Snow Lake Wilderness and the entire Cascade Range *(He climbed this Peak years ago, but with a group)*.

Scenario C *(Figure 18-28b)*: John walked up to Eightmile Campground or caught a ride with other hikers, then hiked up Heart Lake trail to Heart and Nada Lakes, continued to Colchuck Lake; set up camp, spent the night and then climbed Colchuck Peak. On the return hike, he would come back down the Shield Lake trail to Snow Creek Campground. John climbed this Peak before as well, but a long time ago. The circular route up through Heart, Nada, Colchuck and Shield Lakes sees a lot of traffic during the summer season but not much traffic this time of year. John travelled this route previously in the summer.

Scenario D *(Figure 18-28c)*: John hiked up the Shield Lake trail and camped at either Shield Lake or Colchuck Lake. He spent the night and was going to climb Colchuck Peak and return by the same trail. Like Dragontail, Colchuck Peak offers unique views of the Wilderness area, Snow Lake and the high Cascades.

Using the proportional consensus process, the planners place the following values for each scenario respectively:

These probabilities represent the chance that each scenario is correct given all the factors and when compared to the other scenarios. They also represent relative weight factors for scenario analysis.

> A. Scenario A - Region A = 40%
> B. Scenario B - Region B = 20%
> C. Scenario C - Region C = 25%
> D. Scenario D - Region D = 15%

Rational for Ranking

Planners assign the value of **40%** for **Scenario A** because it most fits with his habits and the attraction of an uncompleted climb. The non-maintained paths between lakes, the possibility of fishing and the challenging climb all point to this as a possibility.

Planners assign the value of **20%** for **Scenario B** because of the longer cross-country section discouraging John from such a route in the time span allowed. Also the intended route and return follow the same path.

Planners assign the value of **25%** for **Scenario C** because of its unique trail segments leading to four different lakes. The cross country to make the climb on Colchuck Peak covers only a little ground and still provides good possibilities for photos. All of the lakes contain abundant fish.

Planners assign the value of **15%** for **Scenario D** because of only a short span of no-trail terrain and returning on a familiar trail probably carries little appeal for John based on his past hiking behavior.

In previous examples, ISRID subject behavior data not only helps to define regions of probability, but also gives us a rough way to allocate probability inside and outside the specified quartile (i.e. 25%, 50%, 75%, 100%) statistical zones. For example the 75% zone means 75% of the probability lies inside that zone and 25% outside. In other words, the probability for the regions inside the 75% distance contains three times as much probability as outside, all other factors equal. As in the previous examples, the proportional consensus process transforms these relative reference values to appropriate probability percentages. Remember that local database statistics such as clustering or skewed distributions make the most useful predictions as opposed to international subject category data.

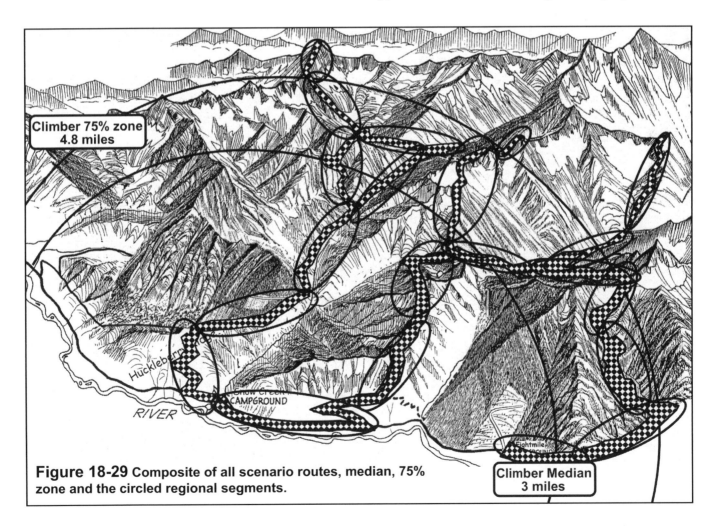

Figure 18-29 Composite of all scenario routes, median, 75% zone and the circled regional segments.

The pictorial map *(Figure 18-29 previous page)* identifies all the discussed scenarios along with the 50% and 75% zones, the probability distribution for this example follows fairly simply. Consider the circled areas on the suspected routes as segments in the respective regions of probability. The segments inside the median distance contain roughly 50% of the overall probability. Between the 50% and 75% zone, contains roughly 25% of the probability and outside the 75% zone lies roughly 25% probability.

The initial allocation concentrates probability in the established trails, routes and mountain peaks. With the discovery of clues or other information, the search area then expands to include other peaks or destinations and the approaches to them. This expansion of course requires one or more new regions of probability, a new consensus, and a redistribution of overall probability.

Putting it All Together to Assign Probability - Example # 2

At 8:00 PM Mrs. Bentley reports her 78 year old husband Richard missing when she returns home from a church function and discovers his absence. Consider yourself the county SAR Coordinator.

In late summer the days reach fairly high temperatures but at night the temperatures fall into the mid fifties. Mrs. Bentley last saw her husband at the kitchen table finishing a meal before she left for her weekly church bowling night. Mrs. Bentley admits Richard sometimes gets disoriented, but in every previous case, he caught a ride home with friends or neighbors. You mark the LKP on the map and call dispatch to start a missing person search. While waiting for the IC to arrive you conduct a more thorough interview with Mrs. Bentley and determine the following:

- Richard maintains a fairly active lifestyle and level of physical fitness.
- He often walks or hikes in the local area.
- In the past he enjoyed outdoor sports like hunting and fishing, and though now retired, spent twenty years as a commercial pilot.
- He used to serve as an officer in the local shooting club and spent several days per week at the gun range northeast of the community.

Figure 18-30 Alzheimer's Behavior Data Overlayed on a map with the IPP

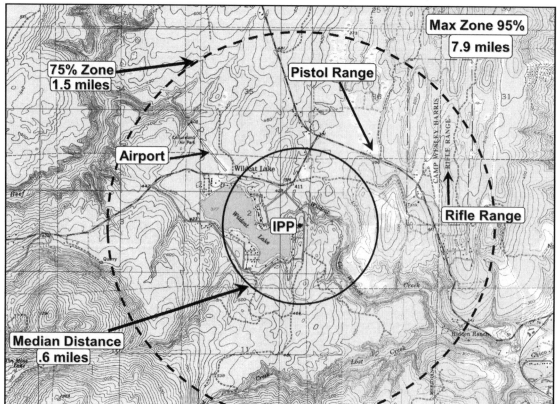

- During his tenure as an officer in the gun club Richard coached a local pistol team, and helped sponsor several youth shooting groups.
- Richard shot skeet and trap at the state and national level.
- He previously owned his own aircraft which he parked at the local airport west of town.
- Richard flew for the Forest Service, 12 years ago.
- He prided himself on making repairs to and maintaining his own aircraft with an A&E certificate for aircraft maintenance along with his private pilot's license.
- He spent many years as a senior advisor for explorer scouts and provided flying lessons to any scouts interested in flying.
- In recent months he frequently walked the area hitching rides with anyone who stops to talk.
- Lately one of his favorite activities centers on taking his 6 and 9 year old grandsons out on Wildcat Lake fishing.
- Richard often rents a boat from a local dock facility.
- The family admits to Richard's Alzheimer's dementia condition, "…but it isn't that bad."

Another Deputy Sheriff and an experienced SAR Team Leader arrive on scene within a short time, and other volunteer searchers also mobilize for a full scale search starting within three hours of notification.

Consulting the lost subject database for Alzheimer's Dementia you quickly realize that half the cases in this category of subject were found within 0.6 mile of the IPP, and the 75% zone falls only 1.5 mile from the IPP.

You plot these distances on the map, then mentally begin thinking about where the behavior data places the probability on the map. You also make note of the area inside both the median and 75% zones, as well as outside these distances *(Figure 18-30 previous page)*.

Using the information obtained during interviews with the family you determine the lake, the airport the gun range, and Wildcat Creek represent likely destinations, and subjectively eliminate terrain not part of a route to one of those spots. This involves surrounding terrain on the map that is consistent with each scenario. This process is defining regions of probability.

The three of you discuss four plausible scenarios to account for Richard's disappearance:

A. In his mind Richard headed for the airpark to check on his aircraft and to accomplish some maintenance, or to meet someone for flight lessons, got confused along the way and ended up lost.

B. In his mind he traveled toward the gun range to get ready for a shoot or to open the facility for a weekly meeting. He misjudged the distance or route and got confused. He is probably on one of the side roads along the route to the gun range.

C. Richard tried to find a boat rental facility to go fishing with his grandsons. After trying to find a facility he either failed to find the dock, or worse, ended up in the water.

D. Richard wanted to explore Wildcat Creek for a location to take his grandsons fishing along the stream. He spoke about teaching them how to stream fish in Wildcat Creek. He went into the woods along the creek and ended up confused/stuck.

After identifying the regions of probability using subjective factors from the interview with the family and terrain analysis, accomplish a quick consensus to derive the weights respectively for each scenario *(See Consensus Worksheet Figure 18-31 on the next page)*.

As before, divide these regions of probability into manageable segments searchable within one operational period. The segments within each region receive probability by consensus using any data available. Remember that when working with diverging scenarios, each consensus segment POA value receives weight by multiplying it times the probability of the scenario to which it applies.

Managing the Inland Search Function - **Operational Response**

Figure 18-31 Consensus Worksheet

Option A: Airport
Option B: Gun Range
Option C: Lake Fishing
Option D: Stream Fishing.

Scenario Designation →	Scenario Option A	Scenario Option B	Scenario Option C	Scenario Option D			Ref. Value **100**
Smith	100	30	25	50			
Andrew	75	100	10	75			
Price	100	50	25	25			
Evans	100	75	10	12			
Green	75	100	50	25			Subtotal Across ↓
Subtotal Down →	450	355	120	187		→	1112
Consensus Weights	450/1112 .40	355/1112 .32	120/1112 .11	187/1112 .17			100% or 1.00

Date: **10/26/16** Mission #: **046** Op Period: **2nd** Time: **06:55 am**

NOTE: Reemphasis on the Need for Quantification

Remember that numbers allow people to make sense of complicated events, and to apply some sort of predictability to something too large for common sense and intuition. The point in all of these calculations lies in providing useful information for predicting similar future events. Mathematics applied to data without a distinct purpose often gives confusing results. For example, lost or missing subject behavior describes a set of distances traveled by missing subjects of the same category. The data usually shows some sort of pattern and skewed distributions toward the IPP *(see right)*, or around given distances. These distributions show the aggregate result of a large number of cases, each separate and distinct in its own way. This data provides value when used to help with effort allocation inside or outside specified distances. By the same token, however, when manipulated in different ways, e.g. a linear drop in probability per foot from the IPP, though mathematically interesting, presents no useful application in the field.

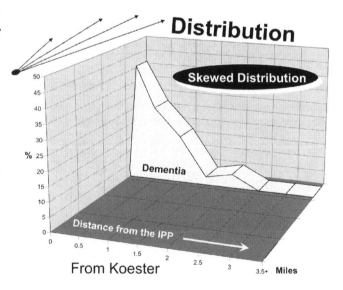

From Koester

Back to the Wildcat Creek Example

Remember, while planners develop scenarios and assign probability other responders complete the Reflex Tasks for the applicable subject category.

The region of probability for Scenario A *(Figure 18-32)* lies below and encompasses an area of approximately 321 acres. If we use the benchmark of 80 to 100 acres then the area of this region of probability could realistically be broken into 4 searchable segments, each with approximately 80 acres apiece. This forms realistic sized segments in this terrain for planning purposes.

The region of probability for Scenario Option B *(Figure 18-33)* encompasses an area approximately 229 acres. The area of this region can logically be broken into three segments with approximately 65, 100 and 65 acres respectively. The terrain, boundaries and shape of this region lend themselves very well to this planning division.

The region of probability for Scenario Option C *(Figure 18-34)* and encompasses an area of approximately 108 acres. This region represents Wildcat Lake and the shoreline surrounding it. Searching a body of water not only encompasses the reality of the shoreline obstacles, but also includes below the surface of the water itself. This obviously includes specialized resources and the extra time for subsurface search.

The region of probability for Scenario Option D *(Figure 18-35)* encompasses an area of approximately 86 acres. The area of this region, while relatively small contains fairly thick forest and the heavy brush along Wildcat Creek. The effort allocation to search this area may well preclude this terrain during the Reflex Tasking phase.

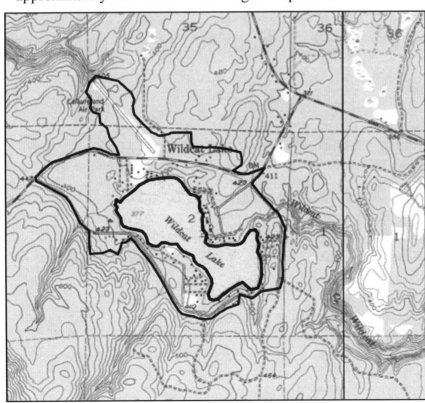

Figure 18-32 Airport Scenario Region of Probability based on Scenario Option A

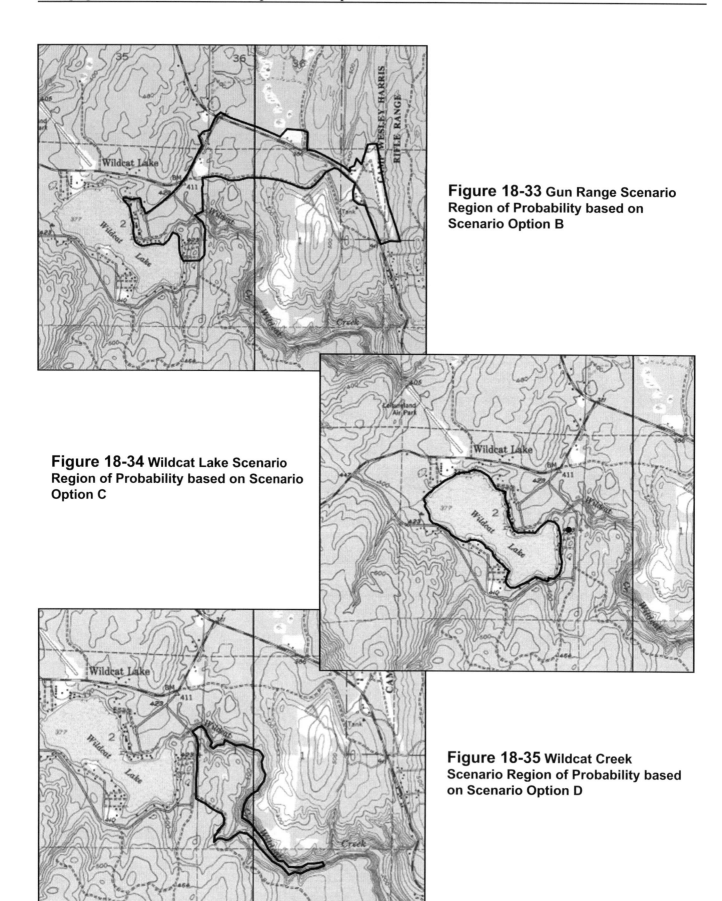

Figure 18-33 Gun Range Scenario Region of Probability based on Scenario Option B

Figure 18-34 Wildcat Lake Scenario Region of Probability based on Scenario Option C

Figure 18-35 Wildcat Creek Scenario Region of Probability based on Scenario Option D

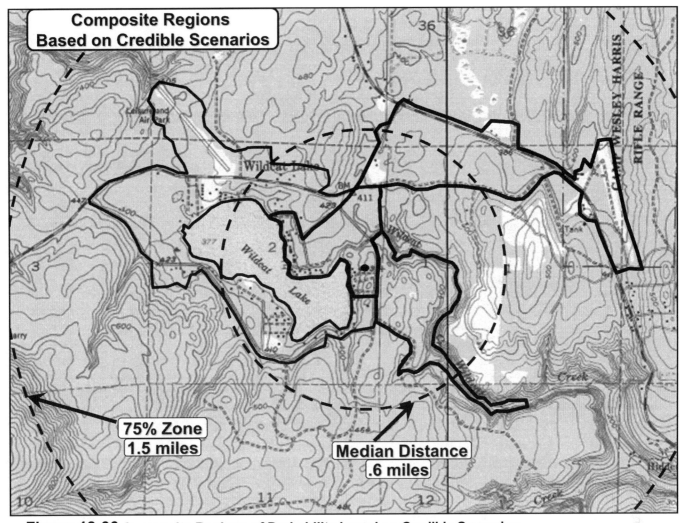

Figure 18-36 Composite Regions of Probability based on Credible Scenarios.

Once we annotate the regions of probability and in turn, subdivide those into searchable segments, we use both subjective factors gathered through interviewing at the scene and lost/missing person behavior data to initially distribute probability onto the potential search area map. The map on the next page *(Figure 18-37)* shows segmentation based on the criteria already discussed about size and boundary designations plus an initial consensus of probability distribution from overhead team members using ISRID statistics from this category of subject *(Dementia of Alzheimer's type)* as a guide.

Notice that approximately 50% of the probability lies inside the median distance scribed on the map. Approximately 25% of the probability lies in the zone between the median and 75% distance and the last 25% of probability rests from the 75% distance out to the statistical maximum zone. In the absence of any other information or subjective factors gleaned from the family or other witnesses, this presents enough data to start the formal planning process.

However, we find some additional information from the family and neighborhood witnesses. Based on the interviews and other subjective information gathered near the IPP, we establish a few scenarios. Based on those scenarios and the initial consensus, we now proceed through the formal Scenario Analysis Process.

To use a formal weighting process for the segments, every scenario and the segments that each covers must get addressed separately treating the scenario as true and that one of the segments involved actually

Managing the Inland Search Function - **Operational Response**

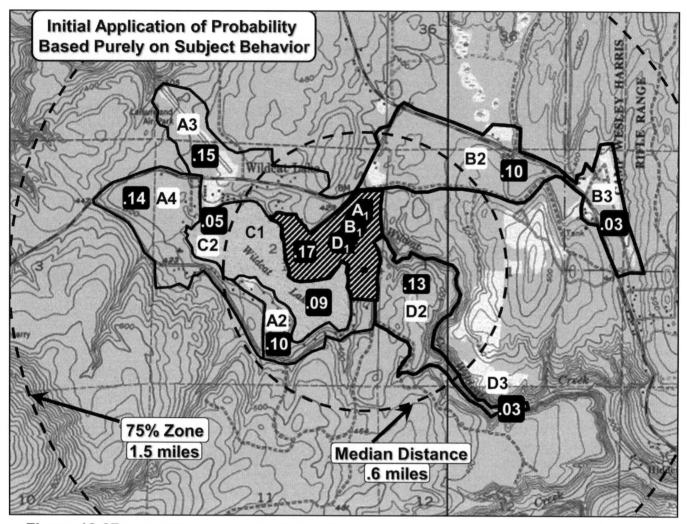

Figure 18-37 **Probability based on the Subject Behavior Database.** Note the overlap of terrain on two of the scenarios. After subdividing these regions of probability into searchable segments, this overlap will be addressed through the Scenario Analysis Process and the respective segments weighted accordingly.

contains the missing subject. With that in mind, lets assume that the following ratings come out of the consensus process. Refer to the worksheets on page 315 and the scenario weights on page 318.

As before the tables displayed on the next page show the Scenario Analysis Process. The tables contain the computations for determining one set of POA values for the segments in all of the regions of probability for this example. *Figure 18-40* at the bottom of page 336 gives a good comparison between those derived through Scenario Analysis and the values initially provided on the area map *(see Figure 18-37 above)* based only on statistical behavior data. Also see *Figure 18-41* on Page 337 for a direct comparison.

Figure 18-38 Determining Initial POA for Each Segment in Each of the Potential Scenarios

Scenario Option A

Segment	Segment Consensus POA Based on Scenario Option A
A1	.30
A2	.15
A3	.25
A4	.30
	Total 100%

Scenario Consensus Weight

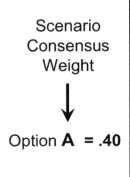

Option **A** = .40

Scenario Option B

Segment	Segment Consensus POA Based on Scenario Option B
B1	.50
B2	.40
B3	.10
	Total 100%

Scenario Consensus Weight

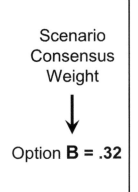

Option **B** = .32

Scenario Option C

Segment	Segment Consensus POA Based on Scenario Option C
C1	.60
C2	.40
	Total 100%

Scenario Consensus Weight

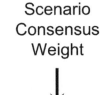

Option **C** = .11

Scenario Option D

Segment	Segment Consensus POA Based on Scenario Option D
D1	.30
D2	.60
D3	.10
	Total 100%

Scenario Consensus Weight

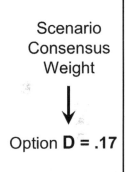

Option **D** = .17

Segment weighting for Scenario A		
A1	.30 X .40 =	.12
A2	.15 X .40 =	.10
A3	.25 X .40 =	.06
A4	.30 X .40 =	.12
Scenario Weights		
A- 40% B- 32% C- 11% D- 17%		

Segment weighting for Scenario B		
B1	.50 X .32 =	.16
B2	.40 X .32 =	.13
B3	.10 X .32 =	.03
Scenario Weights		
A- 40% B- 32% C- 11% D- 17%		

Segment weighting for Scenario C		
C1	.60 X .11 =	.07
C2	.40 X .11 =	.04
Scenario Weights		
A- 40% B- 32% C- 11% D- 17%		

Segment weighting for Scenario D		
D1	.30 X .17 =	.05
D2	.60 X .17 =	.10
D3	.10 X .17 =	.02
Scenario Weights		
A- 40% B- 32% C- 11% D- 17%		

Figure 18-39 Adding Scenario Weights Together For Planning POAs

Same Segment	Segment	Weighted POAs Scenario A	Weighted POAs Scenario B	Weighted POAs Scenario C	Weighted POAs Scenario D	Planning POAs all Scenarios
A1 B1	D1	.12	.16	0	.05	**.33**
	A2	.12	0	0	0	.12
Scenario Consensus Weights	A3	.10	0	0	0	.10
	A4	.06	0	0	0	.06
↓	B2	0	.13	0	0	.13
Option A: 40%	B3	0	.03	0	0	.03
Option B: 32%	C1	0	0	.07	0	.07
Option C: 11%	C2	0	0	.04	0	.04
Option D: 17%	D2	0	0	0	.10	.10
	D3	0	0	0	.02	.02
		Add across →				Total 100%

> While this process seems a little awkward at first, it provides a clear and repeatable protocol with the capability to include factors not otherwise possible to consider in the search planning process. The most uncomfortable part of this scheme usually involves learning to use, and rely upon, the numbers involved.
>
> With correct application of the Scenario Analysis process, terrain that overlaps between scenarios or that fits with more than one scenario will *load* with additional value for computation in the process. While some advocate this occur only on a subjective basis through experience or intuition, we strive to accomplish a repeatable process that works the same way every time. Quantification and the use of numbers provides this for search planning processes *(Excel spreadsheets built ahead of time work well for these calculations)..*

Figure 18-40 Composite Scenario Weights For Planning POAs

Same Segment from overlapping scenarios

Seg	Initial POA Scenarios				Weighted POAs				Planning POAs Includes all Scenarios
	A	B	C	D	Scenario A (Weight = .40)	Scenario B (Weight = .32)	Scenario C (Weight = .11)	Scenario D (Weight = .17)	
A1	.30	0	0	0	.30 x .40 = .12	0 = 0	0 = 0	0 = 0	.12 + 0 =.12 = 12%
A2	.30	0	0	0	.30 x .40 = .12	0 = 0	0 = 0	0 = 0	.12 + 0 =.12 = 12%
A3	.15	0	0	0	.15 x .40 = .06	0 = 0	0 = 0	0 = 0	.06 + 0 =.06 = 06%
A4	.25	0	0	0	.25 x .40 = .10	0 = 0	0 = 0	0 = 0	.10 + 0 =.10 = 10%
B1	0	.50	0	0	0 = 0	.50 x .32 =.16	0 = 0	0 = 0	.16 + 0 =.16 = 16%
B2	0	.40	0	0	0 = 0	.40 x .32 =.13	0 = 0	0 = 0	.13 + 0 =.13 = 13%
B3	0	.10	0	0	0 = 0	.10 x .32 =.03	0 = 0	0 = 0	.04 + 0 =.04 = 4%
C1	0	0	.60	0	0 = 0	0 = 0	.60 x .11 = .07	0 = 0	.07 + 0 =.07 = 7%
C2	0	0	.40	0	0 = 0	0 = 0	.40 x .11 = .04	0 = 0	.04 + 0 =.04 = 4%
D1	0	0	0	.30	0 = 0	0 = 0	0 = 0	.30 x .17 = .05	.05 + 0 =.05 = 5%
D2	0	0	0	.60	0 = 0	0 = 0	0 = 0	.60 x .17 = .10	.10 + 0 =.10 = 10%
D3	0	0	0	.10	0 = 0	0 = 0	0 = 0	.10 x .17 = .02	.02 + 0 =.02 = 2%
	100%	100%	100%	100%	100%	100%	100%	100%	Total 1.00 = 100%

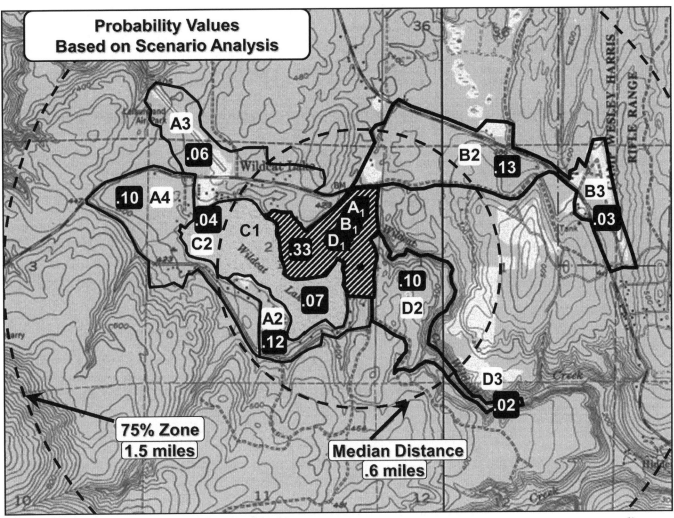

Figure 18-41 Scenario Analysis POA Values

A Reminder About Priority and Changing Values

The initial values of POA assigned to the segments *(i.e. what are the chances that the missing subject is in a specific segment)* sometimes vary throughout the search. The values of POA change after searching segments, adding or deleting segments and or finding clues.

One might think that once planners assign probability values to the segments that this automatically ranks the order of priority for searching and with what resource. However, this sometimes defies simple intuition. Consider the first stated goal of search planning *(and Search Theory)* which maximizes Probability of Success *(POS)* in the shortest amount of time. This brings up the subject of effort allocation.

Where and how can we apply our limited resources in the search area and to what segments to maximize our probability of success? *(Chapter 20 will address this issue after we discuss the concepts of POD and effort allocation in detail).*

Rest Of The World *(ROW)* and other *Open* Systems

Typically, the search area encompasses more than a closed system from the IC's perspective. We want to express a chance that the subject lies outside the designated boundaries of the search area or, even after the search started, left the area entirely. In this context, the *Rest of the World (ROW)* represents the segment and some associated probability that encompasses everything else, outside of the general area of the search.

By definition, an open system implies a significant chance the missing person lies outside the search area. We call this the Probability of Area for the ROW and adjust it mathematically by using Bayes' Rule. However, in true Bayesian mathematics all possible outcomes must be considered to make the math work. If one acknowledges the possibility that the subject lies outside of the search area, then one must also acknowledge the possibility of finding the missing person there through investigative and other techniques, and one must acknowledge some probability that such a find will occur – i.e. a POD for ROW. **No technique for assessing probability and coverage of the whole planet works well in a practical sense!** Specifically, if we speak in terms of segmentation (*ROW as a segment*); then, how do we search ROW in terms of coverage, thoroughness, and effort. The rest of the world generally represents a really big place!

The analysis of ROW, therefore, moves into the subjective, because we never intend to actually search it as a segment. The overhead team evaluates the information gathered in the closed system *(i.e. within their jurisdiction or designated search area)*, and makes effort allocation appropriately using search theory *(POA, POD and POS)*. The ROW concept in this application, represents the growing possibility that the subject lies outside the jurisdiction or the designated search area. In essence it represents another scenario to explain the events leading up to the search. A scenario that grows in relevance, the longer the search progresses without turning up any evidence or if new evidence comes to light.

Finally, from the perspective of the search planner, the mathematical evaluation of ROW becomes irrelevant because the planner simply lacks the resources to effectively search the entire planet. Search plans mathematically assume the subject lies somewhere in the search area and needs assistance (*See chapter 20 on applied search theory for a further discussion of ROW*).

Therefore, the ROW will be addressed through investigation and scenario analysis plus as a reason to expand the search or encompass new areas outside of the original designated search area.

Adding or Subtracting Segments

New information often requires the addition or deletion of segments. When a modification like this occurs, revisit the consensus process and calculate new appropriate POAs which consider the new information. Chapter 20 details an explanation of reallocating POA without throwing out the old figures.

Relevance of Clues on POA

Successful adaptive search planning depends on properly accounting for clues found during the search. Indeed, field teams need *to search for clues and for the subject*. However, considerable debate revolves around on how to handle clues while still consistently using the numbers. Any clues found influence planning and ultimately affect POA values for the next operational period. Experience tells us that after finding a viable clue in a segment, planners reassess region POAs through consensus. This recalculation, in effect, takes into account the planners' perceptions about the validity *(reliability)* of the clue. Not to carry out such a reassessment and recalculation means essentially ignoring the clue.

The Search Manager or members of the overhead team decide about the clue's value subjectively. Use as much information as possible about the circumstances surrounding the find to decide on its validity. Consider the age of the clue, the chances the subject left it versus someone else, confidence in the resource that discovered the clue and the proximity to other clues.

John Bownds et al. *(1992)* published an extended methodology for the quantitative handling of clues and/or information data. They defined a clue as "any information, in any form, which, in the judgment of the search management overhead team, reasonably relates to the whereabouts of the subject." They suggested evaluating clues in a two step process:

1. First, evaluate the effect the clue will have on the search.

2. Second, evaluate the authenticity of the clue together with some type of rating system.

> **NOTE:** Remember to devise some method of placing value on a clue! This represents a way of incorporating the influence of a clue into the process of determining where to look with available resources.

Some Guidelines for Managing Maps and Paperwork

These suggestions and tips regularly help veteran search managers and overhead team members in keeping track of maps, paperwork, messages and resource status during field search operations.

- After drawing segments on the master map at Base Camp, prepare copies for hand outs to the Team Leaders when briefing them for field work.

  - Give Team Leaders a copy or copies of the segment map but also, as much as possible, describe the area and boundaries during the briefing. Emphasize the assignment in the adjacent segment and their radio call-signs. It works very well to provide the Team Leaders with a transparent overlay of the segment so they can lay it over their own maps. This eliminates confusing details on poorly reproduced maps.

- Everyone involved in the search needs the same scale map or a set of equally scaled maps.

- Use proper topographical maps. The scale of the map depends on the size of the search area, the amount of detail required and, of course, available quantities for the scale of the operation. Wilderness guides, outline maps and other such *cartoons* cause more harm than good. Many contain no consistent system of gridding and, therefore provide inaccurate position fixes or any relevant descriptions of location.

- At Base Camp cover the segment map with a transparent overlay to record all pertinent information for each shift. Tough pliable and clear vinyl overlay material works well for this function. Many teams now also have computer programs that automatically record search areas and size on the digital maps within the software.

- Debrief all teams returning from the field thoroughly; summarize their information and add it to the overlay on the master map. This map now provides a concise record of completed assignments, along with estimates of coverage and identification of weak coverage or gaps in search effort on a shift by shift basis.

- Generally, determine search segments after defining regions as required for each search.

  - In some areas predetermine regions and search segments for commonly occurring scenarios and subject profiles. Print and store these transparent overlays ready for use.

> **NOTE:** A helpful addition to a Search Management Kit. Try making yourself some search segment sized templates. With the maps that you normally use during a search, identify how much area constitutes an 80 to 100 acre plot or *(less than 1/4 square mile)*, or what ever size you choose. Establish several different sizes and shapes and transfer them to transparent vinyl templates for use during searches.

Some Useful Data Considerations as Guidelines:

Terrain, Ground Cover and Weather substantially influence segment size. Use the following figures gathered in the moderately dense vegetation of the western part of the United States as guidelines for setting up search segments.

- 80 to 100 acres is usual size for 1/2 day.
- 80 to 100 acres with non-thorough sweep searching takes 3 - 4 searchers about 4 hours.
- 100 acres takes a dog team 2 to 6 hours.

> **NOTE:** These can easily be converted to square miles or any other area system as appropriate *(100 acres = 0.156 sq. mi. = 40.468 hectares = 404,686 sq meters, See Figure 18-16 on page 309).*

Log Areas Where Searching May Be Difficult or Require Higher Effort

Deep snow in the area or harsh weather conditions substantially reduce segment sizes by simply curtailing searcher ability to move effectively in an allotted period of time.

Search resources need to conduct timed exercises in the typical terrain for the local area. In some cases this entails several exercises in varying terrain and vegetation to determine *benchmarks* representing the time necessary to search given areas. Recording average searcher speed over the ground while searching also provides an important input for estimating coverage in actual searches *(See Chapter 19 POD)*. Create segment template overlays for maps of varying scales for use during searches, even in representative urban neighborhoods.

Identify search areas *(segments)* based on responder debriefings which need increased resources because of the terrain or vegetation. In other words, specified terrain will need extra effort to accomplish success in the same allotted time?

Review Notes and Synopsis Report

Consistently during any protracted search outside influences such as the media, agency representatives, family, VIPs, peers or friends will either formally inquire or want answers about status or events on the search. We recommend the establishment of formal press and family liaisons to speak for the overall organization. However, both the Search Manager *(IC)* and members of the Overhead Team need a current synopsis of notable events and any other extenuating facts or circumstances that currently guide the operation.

A set of bulleted notes or what could be called a Synopsis Report forms a helpful tool for review and quick status reporting. The IC may access these at a moments notice but needs to update them every operational period. In the long run this also forms an excellent tool for reconstruction of the operation if any legal questions arise or a formal inquiry develops.

The information in this synopsis includes:

- Analysis of each of the four methods of establishing the search area
- Details of the subject profile and missing/lost person behavior
- Time elapsed since the person was reported missing
- Regions of probability that fit with one or more of the suspected scenarios
- Potential survivability of the missing person in hazardous or difficult to search segments
- Reconnaissance information from the field, e.g. influence of the terrain
- Analysis of clues reported and the reliability of the clues
- Detailed terrain analysis of the search area
  - Complexity of the ground
  - Density of vegetation
  - Weather & conditions unique to some segments
  - Avenues of little or minimal resistance to the missing person
  - Natural or man-made barriers/obstacles
  - Access to search areas and available transportation
  - Predicted weather and environmental conditions

Summary - POA

In 1992, John Bownds indicated that some aspects of search will inevitably remain an art. Insight gained by real world experience in the ICs chair will also make a big difference as to how a person manages a search. Often good judgment comes from making mistakes. Unfortunately, mistakes in this arena sometimes result in extremely negative consequences. While establishing the search area forms only one part of the process of planning a search, it plays a crucial role for success in looking for a missing person when other, quicker methods fail. Which area to search first, second and so on.

Search as an organized approach to finding missing people like other processes continually evolves, changes and now aligns itself with the recognized science of *search theory*. New techniques, protocols and methods will continue to improve the conduct of land searches; especially, those that advocate the use of science based repeatable processes. Always remember that what computer search software and mathematical protocols suggest also needs consistency with our own experience and wisdom. As John Bownds stated, "search theory is a science that we must artfully apply".

Summary of Establishing the Search Area

(Accomplished while simultaneously completing Reflex Tasking)

1. Mark the IPP, LKP, and/or the PLS on the map; also, Mark the theoretical travel distance if possible or appropriate
2. Overlay map with historical subject behavior data from a local database or ISRID
    - Mark median and maximum zones
3. Synthesize information from interviews – Planning & Searching Data – Missing Person Report Form
4. Shut the doors – Establish confinement if possible
5. Develop scenarios – at least three – and encircle geographic terrain to delineate search area regions and prioritize scenarios by consensus
6. Subjective analysis – Terrain evaluation
7. Subdivide regions of probability into searchable segments for single operational periods
8. Allocate POA values to searchable segments based on subject behavior and consensus
    - Statistical probability loading first and then consensus
9. **Optional:** Weight segments based on scenario probabilities
10. Determine Effort Allocation to maximize Probability of Success based on:
    - Number of searchers
    - Number of hours to spend
    - Speed of searchers
    - Multiple searches – same resource
    - Multiple searches – different resources
11. Document specifics of operational period objectives and map legend details
12. SEARCH

Figure 18-42 Establishing the Search Area Checklist

Notes:

Probability of Detection (POD)   19

Objectives:

- Define POD and factors influencing POD
- Discuss the importance of quantifying the Probability of Detection
- Relate the importance of briefing to detection capability
- Demonstrate the ability to compute search PODs and the POD of multiple resource coverage

The call comes in; Managers gather information and establish the search area.

What chance exists of finding a missing person, after applying diverse resources to different segments in the search area?

Remember the standard search theory notation:

POA × POD = POS

In the previous chapter we discussed the first component of this formula, POA.

POD represents the second component in the formula. The Probability of Detection means the chance of detecting a clue or the missing person *(in retrospect)* by a search action. A caveat to this involves basing the chance of detection on a clue's, or the missing person's, actual presence in the search area or segment. This develops an *if then* relationship for later debriefing and evaluation.

Introduction

From an objective perspective, an accurate value of POD only comes from a careful determination of how well a particular resource operates in a given environment under specific conditions. In 1999, DC Cooper and JR Frost proposed a merger of well established and proven methods from Operations Research and the proven building blocks of probability and math with land search methods.

According to Frost (1998), Four groups of variables affect POD.

1. The **SENSOR** used in the search, e.g. people, electronics, infrared, etc.;

2. The **SEARCH OBJECT** or what searchers try to find;

3. The **ENVIRONMENT**, where and what conditions exist at the time plus the size of the area searched; and

4. The **METHOD of SEARCHING** or tactics used by searchers. Tactics also dictate the level of effort searchers expend.

All of these affect each other, and the ultimate search results when used in conjunction with one another.

THE SENSOR *(Factors that Affect POD)*

Searchers utilize the human eye more than any other sense. While this sensor appears straight forward in its application and utility, human vision includes several shortfalls requiring compensation. Enhancements to vision such as infrared, binoculars and Night Vision Goggles (*NVGs*) provide added capabilities, and hearing, smell and touch also add dimensions to increase searcher POD capability. Under normal conditions, dogs and a wide variety of other *(including electronic)* sensors also increase POD. POD values for any search resource depend on:

- Training *(experience)* of the field teams
- Motivation of the searchers *(particularly untrained volunteers)*
- Size of the segments
- Terrain complexity, vegetation cover, etc.
- Quality: Confidence in individual capabilities, Motivation, Fatigue
- Searcher boredom *(i.e. second or third searches of the same terrain)*
- Programming: Briefing techniques, Quality of training, Up to date technology and protocols used
- Limitations: Technology includes inherent shortfalls and resource training, as well as experience for specific conditions, which often falls short of acceptable standards

Variables Open to Manipulation:

- Time on-scene or number of hours to search a given segment
- Use of conservative detection values or average range of detection (R_d) in high probability segments
- The speed of searchers assigned to a segment
- Number of searchers or other resources *(multiple sweeps)*
- Briefings to prime searchers on visual expectations

John Bownds *(1984)*, suggested a variability in the detection capability for specific teams in different situations. Although many factors influence POD as a search progresses, searcher fatigue obviously plays a big role as evidenced by Koester's North American Sweep Width experiments between 2010 and 2014.

Searcher Fatigue

Over the past half-century, the U.S. Coast Guard and the U.S. Air Force conducted numerous experiments concerning fatigue impact on search effectiveness *(POD)*. Unfortunately, these studies failed to address data on fatigue and the effectiveness of ground searchers on land, but after looking at their *maritime* and *air* SAR fatigue studies several relevant hints emerge. In fact nothing suggests these studies apply any differently on land than in the air or in maritime search.

According to the study, the first four hours encompass peak searcher effectiveness. Maximum efficiency occurs within the first hour, levels off and then sharply declines after four hours, bottoming out at around eight hours. Searchers need adequate rest after each shift. Longer times in the field require longer subsequent rest periods and restricting field searchers to shifts *(actually searching in the field)* for no longer than 4 to 6 hours fits this eight hour window of effectiveness.

NOTE: In recent sweep width experiments conducted in four states across the U.S., fatigue negatively influenced all the participant's detection capabilities.

Dog handlers also reflect that unless given some type of reward, their animals lose interest or alertness after approximately 30 minutes *(plus or minus)*. Rewards help dogs refocus their attention.

Target Orientation, Human Vision and the Detection Process

The questions of how or if searchers see clues, or even the missing subject, defy simple explanation. Perceptual judgment combines the complex processes of sensation *(vision)* and decision making.

In its simplest and most elementary form, the process starts with stimulation of the eye by visible light. The searcher sees the environment, patterns, and the objects in it. As these objects come into view *(briefly or not)*, neural activity or mental processing occurs. Unconsciously, the searcher makes a comparison between the environment and a personal preconceived standard image. Based on this comparison, the brain makes an instantaneous decision to take action, *(declare a find)* or to take no action.

Vision and Perception

The concepts in the following section originated in a presentation given at the Washington State SAR Conference by researcher, Dr. Kenneth Hill, of Halifax, Nova Scotia in 2004.

Hill and other SAR professionals believed search

managers and planners improve a searcher's POD in the field, by *priming* them during pre-search briefings.

Detection Versus Recognition

In most cases, detection and recognition present vastly different results in search! As an example, a missing person always leaves clues. The question remains: did the searchers see those clues? Tracking experts estimate a person leaves approximately 2000 pieces of evidence or sign in the environment for every mile walked through that environment. Unless searchers train to detect **and** recognize those subtle signs, they potentially *see* the signs but fail to *recognize* the meaning or importance of them.

Without recognition, detection gives little value. Try to ask search planners and managers *if the searchers sent into the field recognize what they see as relevant and/or potentially critical to search success?* Are they Clue Aware? Recognition by searchers really involves a relevant interpretation of sensory inputs *(sights, sounds, smells, etc.)* to determine a meaningful source and association. This means that the searcher recognizes a clue as search related or directly related to the subject. This aspect of POD relates to both training before the search and briefings during the search. To comprehend how all of this fits together in POD try to understand how perception changes with vision and mental preconceptions.

Memory and Search

Research *(Schneider and Shiffrin - 1977)* shows a division in how human memory operates. Working Memory consists of a transient, limited capacity, only holding new data or recently refreshed information. Searchers place the Search Manager's briefing information in their brain or short term *Working Memory* during the briefing. The more long term Reference Memory contains a vast amount of relatively permanent acquired knowledge gained through education and experience *(With experienced searchers, this includes a great deal of good and bad experience from previous searches)*. People address the new Working Memory through a slow and time consuming, serial process *(one piece of information at a time, like serial numbers in a list)*. However, people access the more permanent Reference Memory through a parallel process *(multiple pieces at the same time)*, which consists of a much faster and more efficient use of information. In every search effort the searchers learn the distinction between targets and distractors for the new environment.

The briefer bridges the gap between previous targets and distractions and those present for this search. The previously mentioned memory research indicates that practice brings changes in the way the brain transfers multiple memory items from Working *(short term)* to Reference *(long term)* Memory. Reference memory accesses *multiple pieces of information at the same time*. In other words, practice looking for specific items in differing environments pre-loads the more rapidly accessible and efficient Reference Memory for searches!

Attention

Attention refers to our allocation of mental processing resources. It describes an ability to focus on a task or to concentrate on a specific item. Searcher's possess limits in their ability to pay attention just like with any other mental process. When the brain pays attention, some stimuli get more processing than others, in turn, opening the door to conscious perception and memory. Relating to search, the question is, **What grabs and keeps searcher attention while they search?**

Visual Attention

Humans pay attention visually in three different ways: Selective, divided, and automatic. Most people find difficulty in paying attention to more than one thing at a time with any degree of efficiency. Attending to one task over another requires selective attention. Humans automatically define some attention processes, such as reading, while others occur unconsciously, such as attention driven by fear. In divided attention, only one cognitive process occurs efficiently at a time. Something gets full processing and something else gets only limited attention. As an example, think about a searcher in a dangerous environment, *(rough, steep, rocky terrain)* preservation or safety attention naturally takes precedence over clue awareness.

In another example, think about faces in the last class you attended. At first everyone essentially looks like everyone else. Then someone talks to you or asks a question *(Now we paid attention to detail and differentiate that particular face from the others)*. We remember that to which we paid attention.

Automatic visual attention requires no focus at all. A good example occurs while driving a car and reading road signs with a glance. As a driver, we glance then process what we saw after passing the sign. Even walking casually up a forest path and noticing a profusion of wild flowers occurs automatically. Attention uses absolutely no focus, we perceive broadly, but not in detail.

Reading the following presents a great example of the automatic attention function:

Amzanig ?

cdnuolt blveiee taht I cluod aulacrty uesdnatnrd waht I was rdgnieg

THE PAOMNNEHAL PWEOR OF
THE HMUAN MNID

Aoccrdnig to a rscheearch at Cmabrigde Uinervtisy, it deosn't mttaer in waht oredr the ltteers in a wrod are, the olny iprmoatnt tihng is taht the frist and lsat ltteer be in the rghit pclae. The rset can be a taotl mses and you can sitll raed it wouthit porbelm. Tihs is bcuseae the huamn mnid deos not raed ervey ltteer by istlefi, but the wrod as a wlohe.

Prtety Amzanig huh?

Bottom Line

Individuals focus their attention on complex visual stimuli to synthesize it into a meaningful pattern or a recognizable feature.

Feature Integration Theory

The brain codes different visual features, in parallel, to mental templates described as *feature maps*. People *(searchers)* easily distinguish single features visually. The brain recognizes the feature

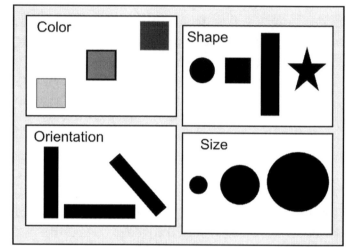

Figure 19-1

almost instantaneously requiring no attention *(See figure 19-1 above)*. Finding a blue circle among red circles presents a parallel process. However, when multiple features enter the problem *(this is processing combinations of features)* with a confusing background, the process reverts to serial and slows down dramatically.

Figure 19-2

Example: Find the arrow on the side of Figure 19-2 above.

The arrow shape results from the white space between the capital E and the x in the logo

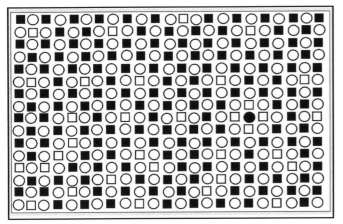

Figure 19-3

Another good example: Is there a black circle in figure 19-3?

Searching the figure for multiple features forces the brain into a serial processing mode.

Form, Organization & Grouping

Organizing features and grouping them into some recognizable form involves a number of simple but vitally important processes. These perceptions materialize out of the information present. First the brain differentiates between some type of figure or form and a background for recognition. Winter landscapes make this process more difficult than it sounds.

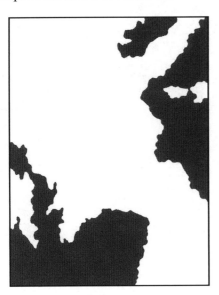

Figure 19-4

Example: In the illustration below *(Figure 19-4)*, which portion needs recognition, the black portion or the white? Which section identifies the figure and which section designates the background? Mentally turn the image 90 degrees clockwise to make recognition easier. Orientation defines recognition here *(hint, think Mediterranean)*.

In some cases, form recognition occurs when mentally grouping elements of the image. *Good continuation*, a principle uncovered in 1923, refers to our tendency to group together in a single structure things appearing aligned in smooth directional continuation of form. If a searcher sees a foot sticking out from behind a tree, even though no other body parts show, the searchers eyes automatically shift to the other side of the tree to look for continuation or some indication to find the rest of the person's body. Remember that natural and man-made camouflage makes use of these principles of image organization to make the perception of objects different from the object's natural state, by obscuring the form of the objects or creating a misperception concerning objects not actually present.

Proximity and similarity also play into our perception of form. With all other things equal, humans tend to organize objects close together as parts of an overall whole, or to group similar objects, using similarities in color, lightness, size, or even texture. Intervening objects, vegetation or substances like snow occlude form but also fills in the gaps for seemingly disconnected parts. The following example demonstrates how this works. Try to visually combine the disconnected pieces in the illustration at the top of the following page *(Figure 19-5)*.

Managing The Inland Search Function - **Operational Response**

Figure 19-5

Answer: Superimpose an object over the top of the pieces. Now the brain sees Bs *(figure 19-6 below)*.

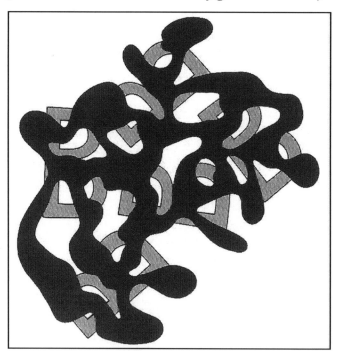

Figure 19-6

When searchers go to the field, they create a mental picture of the target*(s) (missing person or clues)* that they seek. That target or search image develops through perceptual experience *(participation in previous searches)* or occurs based on how a briefer tells them to look. This image guides the visual search conducted by these people and directly affects POD.

The length of time a searcher takes to look at a specific spot defines *dwell time*. The searchers expectation directly affects the dwell time for any specific spot or object and terminates with a decision that the target lies in the area for detection. However, visual scanning techniques and the way a person's vision works also affect these phenomena.

Vision Basics: Each eye's normal field of vision consists of 135 degrees vertically *(60 degrees up and 75 degrees down)* and about 160 degrees horizontally *(that means about 100 degrees toward the temples, and 60 degrees toward the nose)*, only the Fovea *(see Figure 19-7 below)* possesses the ability to perceive and send clear, sharply focused visual images to the brain. This foveal field of vision represents a small conical area of only about 1 to 2 degrees. Use a U.S. quarter *($.25)* on a window 4.5 ft. away to illustrate

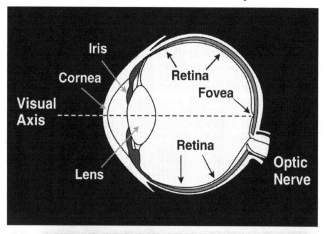

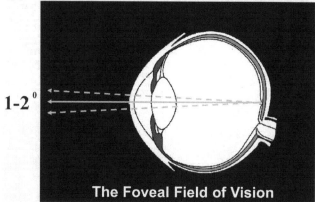

Figure 19-7 Components of the eye and the Foveal field of vision

the size of this area. Outside of a ten degree cone concentric to the foveal field, you only see a tenth of what you see inside the cone. This means that any part of the image transmitted to the back of the eye that falls outside of the fovea goes unrecognized due to edge detection and form recognition only occurring within the foveal vision cone. To summarize, visual scanning with constant movement of the eye and head results in blurred images and a low chance for recognition. The searcher needs to take mental snapshots, not moving scans *(Figure 19-8 below)*.

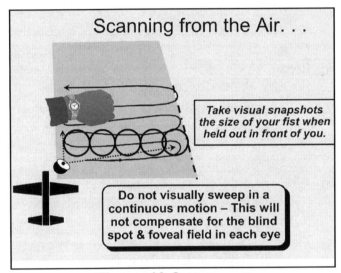

Figure 19-8 Air Search

Searcher expectations impact a searcher's probability of detecting a clue or the missing person as well. This directly affects the scanning rate and how often a person returns visually for *follow-up* inspections. In other words, expectations affect how long we look and the tendency to *take a second look*.

Easy to see clues present a relatively large image when viewed in nature *(such as a shirt or other article of clothing)*, they contain high contrast when compared with their background and provide the searcher with something familiar to look at. Expect greater difficulty in detecting more subtle clues like *top sign (broken or displaced vegetation)* and foot impressions on the ground. Searcher expectation leads directly to success or failure in this kind of detection. Will searchers build an expectation image of what a person of a particular description looks like, on the ground, wet and in various prone positions, after a briefing about the subject's normal clothing and physical characteristics *(height, weight/build, hair, eyes, etc.)*?

Searching for multiple clues or targets, due to processing more than one image during any visual scan, presents a more difficult task than searching for a single target. However, searchers usually improve with practice, in a process called *priming*. For lack of a better analogy, a person needs to *prime* the visual pump. We define the brain's ability to recognize things through a mental process called *canonical perspective*.

Canonical Perspective

Canonical Perspective concerns the authoritative or accepted view of any object from an individual's viewpoint. With no additional input or description *(hat, key, cup, glove, etc.)*, a person tends to accept and expect the canonical perspective or *standard identifying view* of what an object looks like. Unfortunately, this perspective often gives a view different from what searchers eventually see in the environment *(See Figure 19-9 below)*. For example,

Figure 19-9 Canonical and Non-Canonical Perspective of Keys

a *baseball hat* or Teddy bear turned upside down and smashed into the surrounding vegetation, *(See Figure 19-10 on the next page)* falls outside of the average canonical perspective. The searcher sees an undisturbed baseball hat in the mind's eye, not one lying upside down in the grass or even smashed and slightly covered by the surrounding vegetation. Even though he or she sees the object, it fails to register as recognizable and results in *no find*. In many cases, this explains why searchers sometimes fail to find the

Figure 19-10 A Canonical and Non-Canonical Teddy Bear

crucial, yet glaringly apparent *(in hind-sight)*, clue until later in the search. Objects, clues and missing persons in search usually fall outside the canonical perspective and therefore require a lot more dwell time. Several distinct barriers to searcher clue or target detection exist, including:

- Searchers underestimate the difficulty of the task in varying conditions
- Although different, they confuse seeing and detecting
- They expect clues to visually pop out, or be apparent

In general, the following conditions make the detection of any clue, object, or even the missing person more difficult:

- The target *(clue, object or person)* remains outside of the central foveal vision
- A target's background contains poor contrast in color and texture
- The target includes disguised or camouflaged contours, lines or shapes
- The form or shape of the object falls outside of the usual searcher context with other objects
- The object orientation falls differently than its *ideal* perspective *(canonical view)*
- The searcher lacks a good idea of what the target looks like *(search image)*

Taking visual snapshots detects form or shape as opposed to *Sweep searching* which fails to take this into account. As mentioned before, aerial observers often use this technique to search for missing aircraft.

Conclusions About Target Orientation and POD

- Detecting clues and/or the missing subject often involves more difficulty than just *seeing them (Searchers need recognition)*
- When searchers believe in a low probability of detection, they tend to *miss* more clues *(The Search Manager may control this component. i.e. Sending searchers to clear a low probability area and telling them all about the low probability)*
- Form and edge recognition occur in the central foveal vision *(Solve this with comprehensive instruction for searchers in visual techniques)*
- In a complex visual field, the eye rarely detects form on the first *visual pass (Searcher technique needs to emphasize detection opportunities. Search the segments more than once)*
- While searching, the searcher usually needs to return his/her gaze back to the object to perceive it *(Regularly take a second look)*
- The threshold for form recognition depends on the match between the real retinal image and what the searcher expects to see *(Include a component that addresses visual expectations in all briefings)*
- How to *Visually **Prime*** Searchers to enhance POD
- Face searchers away from the briefer
- Place assorted clues on the ground; hat, shirt, rucksack, glove, jacket, etc.
- Make searchers detect clues by walking around a small area. Ensure they view them from different perspectives
- When placing objects on the ground, alter them from the canonical perspective.

Search Objects

When searching, the characteristics of things or objects definitely affect POD and include:

- Size
- Color
- Contrast with the background or environment
- Degree of movement
- Ability to make noise

- Mental perspective in the searcher's mind *(What the searcher expects to see)*

A difficult object to see *(i.e., dark color and small size Figure 19-11)* requires more effort to search the segment at a high *Coverage*.

Figure 19-11

Environment

An extensive list of environmental conditions affects POD. They vary from those affecting lighting and visual clues, to those that affect movement, footing and safety of the searcher. Shadows, precipitation, time of day or night, distractions such as people in the urban environment, steep, hazardous terrain and hosts of other influences all factor into the assessment for segment POD. Obstructions, low visibility and difficult terrain mean reduced sweep width, so require extra effort allocation to search a segment to a higher POD.

Search Methods

Search managers make comparisons and decisions about purposeful wandering vs organized grid searching and then determine the necessary level of effort to accomplish an operational period coverage goal for a particular segment. For years search managers worked at providing everything possible to aid or assist searchers in the field. Managers transport teams to higher ground in order to travel down hill while searching, avoiding obstacles in assigned search segments such as creeks, rivers, fences, and natural barriers, and they assign proper segment sizes with conveniently positioned follow-on assignments.

While random searching assumes some uniformity in their *coverage*, experience tells us something different. While searchers aspire to cover a segment as completely as possible, left to their own devices and completely random schemes, the results often achieve less than desirable results. In considering the options at each end of the spectrum: random searching versus organized searching with locked in parallel tracks. A given level of effort usually produces higher PODs using a slightly organized approach without focusing on exact spacing as teams move through an area.

Significant Probability of Detection Calculations and Experiments

Washington State ESAR Experiments *(Wartes, 1974)*

One of the first efforts in the land search arena to try and quantify Probability of Detection took place in 1974 by Jon Wartes. He conducted his experiments in moderate to dense underbrush in Washington State with Explorer Search and Rescue Units. Wartes titled his paper, *An Experimental Analysis of Grid Searching*. Although these pioneering studies in land search experimentation drove search management for decades, the experiments used only searcher spacing for determining POD. Now, search experts use sensor capability rather than spacing in the determination of Detection. This early study also explored other important concepts in search. The experiments finally established the amount of effort, *(manpower)* needed to grid search for one geographic area and provided a spring board for innovation, by redirecting the thinking of others working in the land search management field around the world.

Critical Separation *(Perkins and Roberts, 1989)*

During the latter part of the 1980s Dave Perkins and Pete Roberts from the United Kingdom followed up the work of Jon Wartes and others. They called the fundamental concept they developed *CRITICAL SEPARATION*. This field tactic placed searchers at a determined Critical Separation when the visual horizon for each searcher falls at roughly the middle of the measured distance between any two searchers *(In other words, an individual searcher's visual horizon neither overlaps nor falls short of the visual horizon of the team member on the left or right of any individual as in Figure 19-12 below. While Critical Separation defines this ideal distance, searchers find it is difficult if not impossible to maintain in many environments and only well trained searchers attained it consistently). Additionally the extra effort involved in keeping exact spacing leads to distraction for searchers from the job of searching*

The impetus behind the development of this tactic revolved around increasing searcher efficiency, not necessarily determining POD. However, the impressive results and positive values for finds pointed toward desired detection levels. Critical Separation combined both increasing efficiency and establishing a reasonable POD estimation. The hypothesis postulated that searching with spacing equal to Critical Separation represented the most efficient use of search manpower. The researchers

Figure 19-12 Searchers spaced at critical separation

felt that overlapping visual horizons on individual searchers made efforts more inefficient, especially in crucial manpower situations. Searchers use a procedure called the *Rain Dance* to determine the visual horizon and then Critical Spacing between searchers. The procedure presented a reasonably good start for establishing POD values, in fact the published experimental procedures developed and published in 2014 uses an even simpler process than that used for Critical Separation.

Average Maximum Detection Range (AMDR)

Average Maximum Detection Range *(AMDR)* built on, or followed from the tactics developed in Critical Separation. The process for determining AMDR integrated three major variables that influence detection in the land environment, horizontal obstructions vertical obstructions and variations in terrain. The team places an object, on the ground in terrain and vegetation like the search environment.

Next, members situate eight searchers or eight points around the object, each representing one of the cardinal directions at a range where the team member fails to see the object. Searchers then move toward the object until detection occurs *(Detection Range)*. They record the distance to the object. The searcher then moves away until unable to see any part of the object *(Extinguishment)*. Team members measure the distance for DETECTION on each leg and averages it with the average ranges for EXTINGUISHMENT. The average of those two values represents the AMDR for that object in that environment.

These procedures provide utility for determining a conservative sweep width value in the field; however, Robert Koester published research in 2014 which indicates that only half of the AMDR procedure produces an effective sweep width value just as accurately as both values *(see Average Range of detection later in this chapter)*.

Sound Sweeps and Sound/Light Lines
(Colwell, 1992) (Gordon, 2002) (Koester, 2009)

Initially developed by Colwell in British Columbia, these tactics involve spacing searchers along a boundary of a search segment or along a trail. Spacing varies between 500 to 600 feet *(or approx. 150-200 meters)*. Searchers move into the segment when all reach their pre-designated positions. All carry radios. Search base provides count downs at regular intervals via radio. On reception of the radio command to whistle, searchers stop, blow their whistles and listen for audible responses. Searchers need to wait two to three minutes between whistle blasts. A sound sweep and sound/light line sweeps *(described below)* presume a living and responsive missing or lost person.

Ross Gordon, Search and Rescue Institute of New Zealand *(SARINZ), along with Robert Koester*, capitalized on Colwell's work with sound and added the light component for night search operations and published a paper in September of 2009 entitled *Sound-Light Line Detection Index Experimental Methodology for Search and Rescue*. New Zealand searchers use Sound-Light lines with good success. Teams implement the sound part of the tactic the same as Colwell's in B.C. however, the light component occurs in several ways. The searcher normally carries a powerful flashlight for navigation and safety. In addition, searchers use another powerful flashlight swinging in a lazy figure eight pattern to maximize light dispersal. Some searchers also use *light belts* or *light bandoliers* wrapped from the shoulders across the chest and flashing bicycle LEDs placed on the back of the head for added attraction.

NASARC Sweep Width Experiments

(R. Koester, D.C. Cooper, J.R. Frost, R.Q. Robe - 2004) As described in Chapter 17, the National Search and Rescue Committee and the Coast Guard sponsored a series of field experiments to find a procedure to verify on land, the procedures developed through Operations Research in the maritime environment. Their research and results paved the way for the relatively simple and effective techniques described by Koester in his later research on the Average Range of Detection.

Some Definitions and Explanations for Determining POD

Effective Sweep Width *(ESW)* more commonly known as ***Sweep Width*** measures detectability. Factors affecting sweep width include, the size of the item, the sensor *(the one searching)*, and environmental conditions at the time and place of the search. Initially, using research pioneered in the 1940s, only rigorous experimentation established sweep width values for any given location. Those experiments defined a reasonably accurate *detection index* for specific conditions in that local area. Researchers published their methods for conducting similar experiments *and* developed computational aids for setting up similar experiments and analyzing the results.

Once searchers understand the Sweep Width concept, it provides great insight into both the science and art of searching. Although this chapter explains Sweep Width in more detail later, for now, regard it as an experimentally determined value providing an area effectively swept *(searched)* by resources in the field. Planners then use that value for computations and comparisons in search planning.

A useful analogy illustrating sweep width involves a searcher's visual horizon represented by an extended long pole. The length of the pole defines the searcher's visual horizon or maximum detection capability for a specific item in a specific type of environment. Sweep width values differ in varying environments or terrain conditions. This represents a detection range for an object lying within the range *(See Figure 19-13 on the top of the next page)*.

If the searcher brings that pole to a position where half the length of it extends to the right and half to the left, the visual distance represented by the ends of the pole equates to one half the maximum detection range for that environment. This presents a starting point to describe a conservative effective sweep width value.

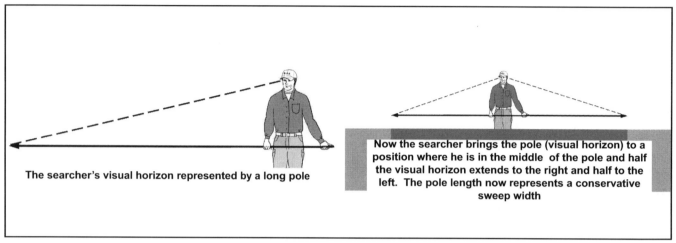

Figure 19-13 Sweep Width

To further refine this description *(and make it more accurate)*, consider the chances of seeing something outside of this range as equal to the chance of missing something inside of this range. The lateral range curve from search theory shows this distance graphically *(See Figure 19-14 below)*.

Searcher speed through the environment affects sweep width as well. Intuitively speaking, the faster searchers go, the less effectively they find things. However, if they go too slow, they fail to complete the search assignment in the allotted time. Rough, steep and dangerous terrain affects speed and also degrades a searcher's attention to detail in the environment. All of these negatively affect detection and the sweep width value.

NOTE: *Given the numerous combinations of terrain, vegetation, seasonal variation, search object types, and the like, makes it impractical to create a single, comprehensive, set of sweep width tables for land like the ones developed for maritime search. On the other hand, teams operating within their normal geographic area of response possess the ability to develop their own sweep width benchmarks to work with.*

Average Range of Detection (R_d) - The Sweep Width Experiments described earlier demonstrated an inability for trained searchers to predict or accurately evaluate their own Probability of Detection values. In 2013 and 2014, Robert Koester completed research that specifies a field procedure to determine reasonably accurate effective sweep width values. That research led to meaningful POD values for any search effort

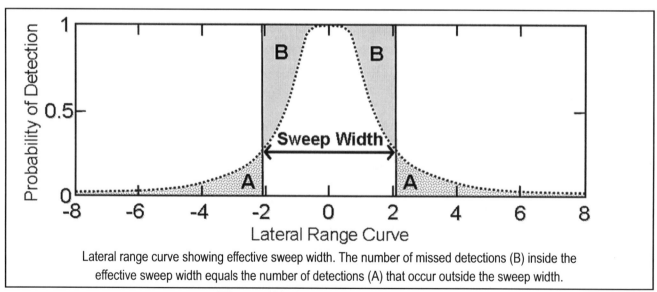

Lateral range curve showing effective sweep width. The number of missed detections (B) inside the effective sweep width equals the number of detections (A) that occur outside the sweep width.

Figure 19-14 Lateral Range Curve

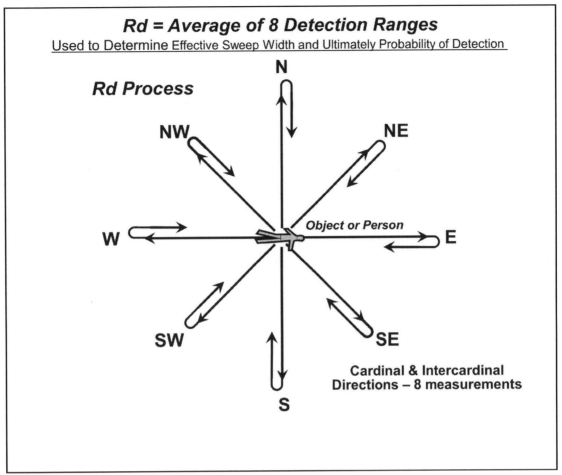

Figure 19-15 Average Range of Detection Procedure carried out on-scene by searchers when they arrive at a search segment.

expended in the field (see *Use of the Visual Range of Detection to Estimate Effective Sweep Width for Land Search and Rescue based upon Ten Detection Experiments in North America* by Robert Koester et al.). Koester's research and paper strived to develop a simple, objective procedure for obtaining effective sweep width (ESW) values without conducting full-blown detection experiments as outlined by Operations Research from the 1940s and the Land Sweep Width experiments in the early 2000s.

R_d = The average range of linear distances first detecting a search object when moving towards it from multiple angles *(Figure 19-15 Above)*.

Range of Detection Procedure for Field Resources

Immediately upon arriving at a designated search segment in the field, searchers need to perform this Range of Detection procedure and either record the value or pass it immediately to the search planners. Designate and/or pick out a representative search object to use in the procedure. Try to choose an object or person close in color, size and description to the missing person or evidence searchers need to look for in the operation. Place the object or person on the ground in a random location representing the vegetation and terrain within the actual search area.

With one or two searchers, the process takes about 10 minutes. Four or more searchers, it takes between 5 and 10 minutes. Keep in mind, searchers need to take 8 measurements. Everyone carries a compass, and uses the standard cardinal vectors – North, South, East and West which indicate the initial directions from the object. The second vectors consist of the inter-cardinal directions – Northeast, Northwest, Southeast, and Southwest.

(Each person carries out the same procedure with different vectors): For one individual:

1. Pick an initial vector from one of the cardinal directions.

2. Walk away from the search object until you lose sight of it. Turn around and walk back toward the search object. STOP the moment you spot the search object.

3. Now count the number of paces it takes to reach the search object and record the distance.

4. Repeat this process on each of the cardinal and inter-cardinal directions.

5. One expects the distances between the searchers and the object to differ due to environmental conditions, vegetation or any ground cover in the immediate area, or obstacles in the way such as rocks, logs or terrain variations.

6. Now average all of the eight measurements to determine the average range of detection (**Rd**).

In his 2014 paper, Koester designates one of three correction factors used by planners when calculating an estimated effective sweep width. These correction factors represent high, medium and low visibility search objects.

Search Visibility Class Correction Factors:

High Visibility = 1.8
Medium Visibility = 1.6
Low Visibility = 1.1

If the process illustrated below consisted of a high visibility object, it contains a 1.8 correction factor. Assume the Rd in the testing area comes out to 20m. (20m × 1.8) = 36m. This determines an Effective Sweep Width (W) of 36m for the search area when looking for a high visibility object. If searching for a low visibility object and the Rd tested comes out to 12m, (12m × 1.1) = 13.2m. Then the Effective Sweep Width (W) comes out 13.2m for the search area when looking for a low visibility object. Calculations using these figures, allows for a reasonably accurate Probability of Detection using the relationship between coverage and POD established by Koopman in Operations Research. How to make the connection between Sweep width and POD follows after a review of some definitions:

Track Line - The track or route that searchers or a search resource follows as they pass through a search segment.

Track Line Length - The total distance covered by a resource. To determine the *Track Line Length* (*with units expressed in meters, yards, miles, or kilometers*) multiply the speed of the searcher by the total time spent searching in the segment *(Figure 19-16)*, or simply measure the track line from a GPS track line etc. Varying speeds in a set time period directly affects track line length. Track Line Length stems directly from the allocation of effort *(searcher hours)* on the search of any segment in the search.

Total Track Line Length - Refers to the length of all the paths of resources or people searching in a segment. Simply multiply the length of one searcher's path by the number of searchers for a quick estimate or measure each track specifically for more accuracy. Every search IC and overhead team member usually asks: "How much of the segment did the searchers really search or actually lay eyes on?" The answer to this questions represents *effort*.

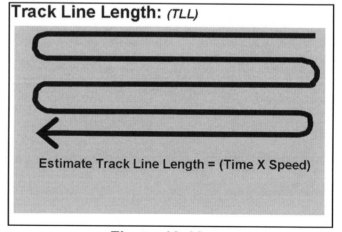

Figure 19-16 TLL

Search Effort - Measures man-hours and represents the amount of work accomplished by the searcher(s) in a segment while searching. Remind searchers to maintain **optimal speed for the environment through the entire Track Line Length**.

When a team searches a specific segment, a search planner needs a recording of the total distance traveled by all members of the team. Summing all the individual team members distances searched provides a value equal to the total distance covered by all the searchers. Alternatively, if all members moved at about the same speed for the same amounts of time while searching, then the distance covered by one searcher multiplied by the number of people in the team equals the total distance covered in the segment. The planner multiplies the track line length times the measured *Sweep Width* (from the R_d procedure) thus producing an *Area Effectively Swept* (*Z*) either for an individual searcher or for the whole search team *(Figure 19-17 below)*.

To review calculating **Area Effectively Swept**: multiply the sweep width value *(Detection range in feet, yards or meters)* by the Track Line Length *(How far each search resource travelled in meters, yards, miles or kilometers)*. Express the resulting value in terms of area *(Make sure to calculate W and TTL in the same units -miles, kilometers, yards, meters, feet, etc.)*.

Area Effectively Swept (Z) = Sweep Width(W) X Track Line Length(TLL)

$$Z = W \times TLL$$

Coverage

Coverage *(sometimes called coverage factor)* measures how thoroughly team members searched an area. *Coverage* takes the area effectively swept and compares it to the physical area of the entire segment searched. The process produces a unit-less value described as a ratio between the two.

Searching an area and achieving a *coverage* of 1.0 therefore means that the *area effectively swept* equals the area searched exactly.

Figure 19-17 Track Line Length multiplied by the Sweep Width gives us the Area Effectively Swept (How much area did we eyeball?)

NOTE: that does not necessarily mean that every piece of ground was scanned nor does it mean that the POD of a coverage 1.0 produces 100% POD. Coverage measures how *thoroughly* crews search the segment. The higher the coverage, the higher the POD. However, a linear relationship fails to accurately describe the relationship and doubling the coverage <u>will not</u> double the POD. Figure 19-19 *(POD versus Coverage)* shows the relationship between coverage and POD as derived by Koopman *(1946, 1980).*

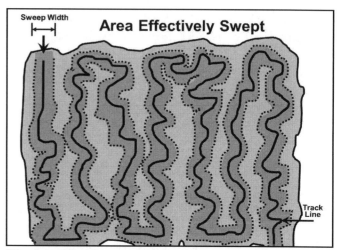

Figure 19-18 Comparing area effectively swept to total segment area for coverage

$$\frac{\text{Area Effectively Swept}}{\text{Area of Search Segment}} = \text{Coverage}$$

If the searchers effectively covered 20,000 sq. meters of a 40,000 sq. meter segment then the coverage calculation entails 20,000 sq. meters divided by 40,000 sq. meters which equals a coverage of one-half or 0.5.

The graph tells us that coverage of .5 gives a POD of 40%. If searcher sweep width passes over every part of the segment, *(the product of the TLL and Sweep Width is the same as the total area of the segment)* then searchers reached a coverage of 1.0. The graph tells us that a coverage of 1.0 gives us a POD of 63%.

Initially, SAR individuals think of this as a fairly elaborate and technical process, but upon practice, usually find it simple and only involving elementary math. The process and the Coverage Curve both provide objective POD values, repeatable, and

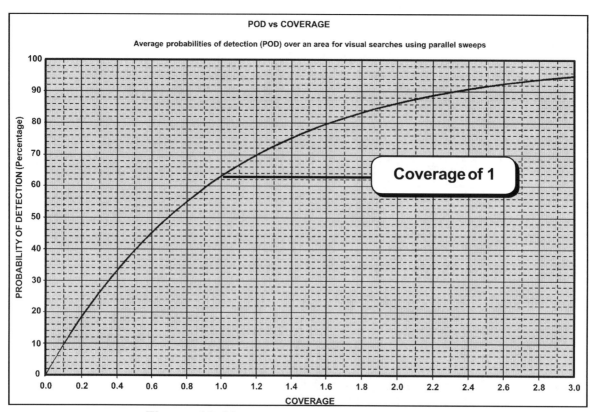

Figure 19-19 Koopman's POD vs Coverage Curve
POD = $1-e^{-c}$ where c=coverage and e = the exponential constant

defensible data from a process scrutinized and tested by professionals for over fifty years.

Types of POD

For years, in land search, instructors advocated the following to establish or improve POD:

- **Field Research** and the proper use of the Average Range of Detection (R_d) determines *Sweep Width* values for varying terrain and vegetation. Determining POD requires the use of a range of detection values.

- **Training** improves, but never establishes POD, unless used in conjunction with field research based procedures.

- **Historical:** Shows effective search techniques, but fails to assign POD values.

POD measures sensor effectiveness, thoroughness, and quality for an individual sortie in a given segment. Historically, managers often set POD goals, such as an 85% POD in the four highest probability segments, given immediately available resources. This means hypothetically 85 times out of a hundred, the searchers succeed in those areas; however, what level of manpower will generate an 85% POD? Koopman's curve says an 85% POD stems from a coverage of approximately 1.9. That means an equivalent of effectively sweeping every bit of the segment almost twice...perhaps 85% represents a lofty or unrealistic goal in most cases.

Objective POD presents **cumulative** information, the ability to make predictions and also creates a potential for **retrospective evaluation**.

- **Cumulative POD** for a segment. After searching the same segment multiple times, with different resources or with the same resource more than once, the chances of detecting an object or the missing person increase when compared with searching the segment only once. This increased probability of detection in one segment with increasing coverage describes cumulative segment POD.

- **Predictive POD** projects values for planning purposes prior to searching a segment. The predicted values stem from expected coverage, numbers and types of available resources, expected performance of the resources, the detectability of the object in the environment and the time allotted for searching.

- **Retrospective or Calculated POD** presents an opportunity to apply real data as experienced by the searchers to search planning after the search of a segment. Information obtained from debriefing searchers, average range of detection (R_d), coverage based on time, speed, difficulty of terrain, vegetation and other variables all factor in.

Probability Density, Effort Allocation, and Sweep Width

Search planning attempts to allocate the available search effort *(resource hours)* and to maximize the probability of finding the search object in the minimum amount of time. In other words, search managers want to maximize POS *(Probability of Success)*, the third and final part of the equation POA × POD = POS.

The Variables:

Probability Distributions in the Search Area *(These identify regions of high probability within the search area based on suspected scenarios, databases, hazards or occurrences)*. Traditional methods of probability allocation to segments within a search area often lead to deploying resources in segments with the highest POAs. However, this fails to address the issue of search effort and often produces suboptimal results. The true indicator for deployment of resources lies with POS *(see chapter 20)*.

The following illustrates an example search planning solution using POD: After deploying to the field in the initially high POA segments, the teams quickly compute their *Average Range of Detection* using a similar object or similarly dressed person *(See Average Range of Detection Procedure on Page 354)*. From this calculation, the overhead team assesses the effort required to produce an acceptable level of success quickly. With a small R_d the Search Manager (IC) or Search Planner faces four possibilities to increase *Coverage*:

1. Decrease the size of the segment
2. Increase the number of searchers
3. Decrease coverage with the consequences of lowered POD/POS
4. Research the segment later with another resource

For reasons already discussed in Chapter 18 concerning the math and what lost/missing person behavior tells us, a planner needs to assume that probability density distribution remains constant throughout any given segment. That assumption gives us the practical leverage to work with the numbers in the search theory formula.

Realistic, Reliable Resource PODs: To determine realistic PODs never use subjective descriptions of effectiveness, try to base them on objective processes consistent with research established sweep widths. Establish R_d for each environmental type within the search area. When using a measured R_d for conservative *Sweep Width*; the *Track Line Length*, *Area Effectively Swept*, and *Coverage* all provide meaningful information to *get effective and reasonably accurate PODs*.

Allocation of Search Effort:

As already mentioned, search effort consists of more than just the number of searchers multiplied times the number of hours of availability. Search effort also depends on the effective sweep width, the total length of all the tracks covered by the searchers and how long it takes to accomplish that length. The total length of the tracks depends on the number of searchers available and the searcher average speed of advance in the given terrain. The area effectively searched *(swept)* presents a reasonably accurate measure of how much searching personnel accomplished using the distance traveled in an operational period. To summarize: the number of searchers, and the speed of advance, produces the search effort expended.

Remember: More searchers committed to a segment usually means less time spent obtaining the desired coverage at a given sweep width. On the other hand, reducing the number of searchers increases the time required to accomplish the same amount of coverage.

The third variable represents *Searcher Speed*. Searchers tend to slow down when rough field conditions such as, steep, timbered terrain or foul weather dictate their actions. On flat easily traversable terrain the search manager modulates speed with an order about searcher speed. During the NASARC experiments in 2004 the researchers found no appreciable difference in sweep width when the experimental searchers maintained between 1.8 and 3.0 mph. (*More research needs to occur concerning the exact relationship between sweep width and searcher speed*). Remind searchers to maintain **optimal speed for the environment through the entire Track Line Length**. (*Where possible, eliminate barriers, and internal diversions; place resources where they maintain optimal speed easily; and finally move them to other high probability segments in the search area quickly.*) **This also emphasizes the need to establish benchmarks for speed and time during training exercises.**

Obviously, searcher speed through the environment affects sweep width. If searchers vary the speed of search in the field, for whatever reason, then they need to relate this information in the post search debriefing on calculating effective sweep widths. For example, if following the R_d procedure, planners calculate an effective sweep width at 50 feet, but further into the search segment, conditions dictate a slower speed based on the increased density of ground cover, then a reduction in sweep width also occurs and Searchers need to accomplish another R_d procedure. Communication and familiarity with concepts between planners and searchers facilitates this process.

Area Effectively Swept Calculation

As mentioned before, POD calculations depend on an estimate or measurement of the distance covered by a resource or resources in the search segment. Therefore, establishing *Benchmarks* during training exercises aids in calculating the POD during real search operations. Ask searchers to estimate how fast they searched and then use the amount of time the resource spent in the segment. As a rough guideline use the speeds mentioned on page 360. Now multiply this speed by the time spent in the field to calculate the distance traveled by the individual. With more than one searcher, *(all traveling at about the same speed)* multiply the first calculation by the number of searchers to get the total **TLL** distance.

Computing Multiple Coverage Values

Both in planning and in actual operations, a search planner often re-searches a segment utilizing different resources or different sorties using the same resource. If the Planner calculates a POD from the coverage determined in a specific segment then he/she simply adds the coverage factor for another sortie to the already accomplished coverage factor. The combination *(adding the two together)* of these two coverage factors gives a cumulative coverage and through Koopman's curve, a cumulative POD for the segment. Example: First sortie in the segment gave a coverage of 1.0 for the effort. Second sortie gave a coverage of 0.2 for the effort. A combination of the two searches produces a coverage for that segment of 1.2. That equates to a cumulative POD of 70%. *(See Figure 19-20 on Page 364)*

Effectiveness of Specific Resources

Estimating PODs for Search Dogs

In 2014 Dr Kenneth Chiacchia published a first of its kind paper entitled *Deriving Effective Sweep Width for Air-Scent Dog Teams*. The results of these first experiments show a distinct difference between Sweep Width values obtained by human searchers vs humans combined with air scent dog teams. Chiacchia also set the parameters for further research in this area by validating a repeatable method to conduct further experiments using dogs to establish *Effective Sweep Widths* for dogs.

Determining POD with Untrained or Minimally Trained Volunteers

What happens when using untrained personnel to search? We suggest using the same R_d procedure *(Average Range of Detection)* for *Sweep Width* calculations. This method works equally as well for trained and untrained personnel. According to Koester's research, using this technique determines an effective sweep width for searcher POD under the real field conditions at that time.

Factors Essential to POD Calculation in a Local Area.

- How long trained search teams take to search over set distances in local terrain
- Searcher *Average Range of Detection (R_d)* values in varying terrain
- A searcher's speed when traveling in different conditions

Remember, Comparing POD calculations only works with the same *parameters (R_d Procedures conducted under the same conditions for the same category of object)* If different; make adjustments or conduct additional R_d Procedures.

Calculate POD and Coverage
Example 1 Using Kilometers and Meters:

Four searchers spend 4 hours in a segment searching at normal speed = 2.0 Kilometers per hour.

Estimate Track Line Length
= *(Time Spent × Speed × Number of searchers)*
(4 hours × 2.0 kilometers per hour × 4 searchers) = TLL = 3200 meters = 32 kilometers

Area Effectively Swept: *(Track Line Length × Sweep Width)*

Example:

Sweep Width = 15 meters

Track Line Length = 3200 meters or 32 kilometers

(32 kilometers × 15 meters = 32 kilometers × .015 kilometers) =

Area Effectively Swept = 0.48 Sq. kilometers

Coverage: *(C)* The ratio of area effectively swept to the total area of the segment.

The search segment is 600 × 600 meters = *(0.6 km. × 0.6 km.)* = 0.36 Sq. Kilometers

Area Effectively Swept from above = 0.48 Sq. Kilometers
0.48 km^2 ÷ 0.36 km^2 = Coverage of 1.3

Coverage of 1.33 *(see Figure 19-20 on page 364)* equates to a **POD of 74%**

Calculate POD and Coverage
Example 2 Using Miles and Feet:

Four searchers spend 4 hours in segment searching at normal speed = 1.0 m.p.h.

Estimate Track Line Length
(Time spent × Speed × Number of searchers)
(4 hours × 1 m.p.h. × 4 searchers) = TLL = 4 miles × 21,120 feet × 4 searchers = 84,480 ft. = 16 miles

Area Effectively Swept: *(Track Line Length × Sweep Width)*

Example:

Sweep Width = 45 feet = .0085 mile

Track Line Length = 84,480 feet or 16 miles

.0085 mile × 16 miles = .136 sq miles =

Area Effectively Swept = *0.136 sq. miles* = 3,791,462 sq. ft.

Coverage: *(C)* The ratio of area effectively swept to the total area of the segment.

The search segment is 100 acres or 0.156 of a square mile. *(An area normally searchable in 4-6 hours.)*

Area Effectively Swept from above = 0.136 Sq miles
0.136 ÷ 0.156 = **Coverage** of .87

Coverage of .87 *(see Figure 19-20 on the next page)* equates to a **POD of 58%**

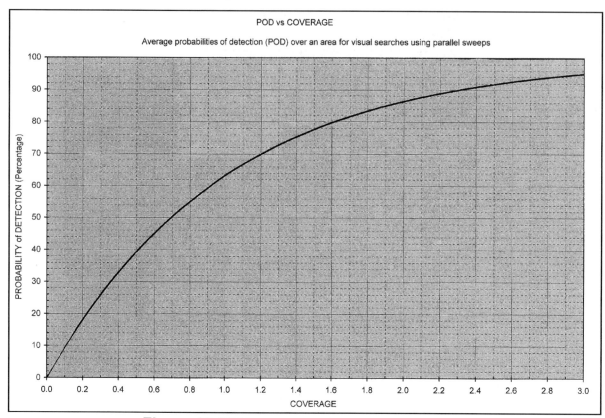

Figure 19-20 Koopman's POD vs Coverage Curve
POD = $1-e^{-c}$ where c=coverage and e = the exponential constant

Guidelines for Researching a Segment

- Rotate teams from one area to another, never searching the same area
- Clearly define the search area boundaries
- Some lost subject categories require researching areas several times
- Teach the concepts of *Sweep Width, Track Line Length* and *Coverage* to team members & leaders to familiarize them with otherwise counter intuitive strategies

Spread the Word.

Team members and experienced search managers often feel uncomfortable with new concepts.
- Educate team members about all of the variables that influence POD and how the values change under differing conditions.

- Encourage Search Team members to practice Average Range of Detection experiments

When to use thorough search methods

- With abundant effort available
- Where circumstances make wide spacing impractical, such as:
  - Dangerous, rough terrain
  - Searching for small objects – evidence
  - Non homogenous areas such as mixed residential and buildings

When not to use thorough methods

- When presented with a large search area in relation to the available effort
- When time plays a major factor in the search
- When using skilled clue detection resources – i.e. trackers, and they expect numerous objects or clues *(thorough searching destroys the remaining evidence)*
- Before additional excess manpower arrives

Applied Search Theory and Planning - POA × POD = POS

Objectives: A Student will be able to:

- Discuss reasons for effort assessment and quantification for every operational period in a search.

- Relate the numerical assessments made by Search Managers or search planners during any search operation.

- Express the implications and uses for Probability of Success in both field strategy and tactics in search operations.

- Use the standard notation formula *(POS = POA × POD)* to make specific choices about effort allocation and alternatives available for searching specific segments in the search area.

> *"We have never lost a game, but once in a while, time ran out on us."* - Vince Lombardi

Probability of Success ...the product of searching in the right place with the right resource

So far this text discussed two main ingredients in the formula for search theory:

1. Chapter 18 outlined the process of determining the location of the search subject in the search area *(POA)*. That chapter also discussed the process for establishing the search area and distributing probability, with suggested protocols and methods for using statistical data, subjective analysis and deductive reasoning to determine where to search.

2. Chapter 19 outlined the way to determine whether a resource will detect the subject or clues, if present, and the effort required for coverage of a designated segment. That chapter pointed out the many factors that make up POD values for different environments. Reasonably accurate values come from simple Average Range of Detection procedures.

The final piece of the Search Theory puzzle centers on Probability of Success *(POS)*. Remember, search managers cannot simply pick up the finer points of Search theory in an afternoon while planning a real search. These concepts take practice, homework, and dedication to preplanning. Future search planners need to understand the capabilities of each available resource, and the particulars of the local environment. This knowledge stems from working with search teams, continual training, and even pre-segmenting maps based on search demographics. The following explanations and examples provide a small sample of the possibilities available through the full use of search theory *(and search planning)* concepts.

In this chapter, we examine the implications of *POS* values derived from POA and POD figures. For decades, in land search training and in actual field application managers only used the value of POS as an after-the-fact indictor of success *(Either the missing subject was found – 100% or the person was not found - 0%)*. With no firm foundation in search theory, land search planners and managers ignored the implications and utility of POS values. The infusion of methods and the application of search theory principles, planning concepts and definitions introduced into land search starting in 1999 entirely refocused and changed the philosophy for land search practice. The computed values for POS reveal significant implications for planners and managers in strategic and tactical applications.

Initial Actions on a Search Incident

During the initial response phase of the search the IC makes an early assessment of the incident and assigns available resources to complete Reflex Tasks *(see Chapter 14)*. These originate with the subject category and functional tasks like Investigation, Initial Planning Point, Containment, the Hub and its immediate area, Travel corridors and High Probability tasks. While these initial efforts play out, the search base command center takes shape, the overhead team arrives and begins developing scenarios based on investigative findings, consensus occurs and planners define regions of probability on a map based on suspected subject activities.

Unfortunately effort allocation for the first operational period usually begins with limited information. Where to search first? ISRID *(The International Search and Rescue Incident Database)* chronicles successful search incident tasks from 50,000 cases initially and currently tops 150,000 cases. Using the Bike Wheel Model as a guide, these tasks statistically provide the answers over 90% of the time.

After completing the Reflex Tasks without finding the missing person, the formal search planning function takes over to drive the search effort.

The Formula as a Planning Tool

Properly using numerical values from the Search Theory formula ($POA \times POD = POS$), truly represent the combined information about potential subject location with the best data available about resource performance and capabilities. In an ideal search planning process, the probability of success factor *(POS)* for each segment prior to resource deployment integrates all available information about behavior, prior searches, resource capability, and terrain to evaluate the environment before the search even begins. Obviously, planners seldom combine all of these parameters before deploying resources in the majority of searches; however, the idea sets a worthy goal for effective search planning.

By applying the techniques described in Chapter 18 for establishing the search area, each region of probability, and the segments within them respectively, contain probability based on consensus and behavior data. Applying the techniques described in Chapter 19, a search planner uses reasonably accurate sweep width values for available search resources on scene. By quickly multiplying these two values together we see which combinations provide the highest POS, and then get a rough idea of what the search effort will produce in any segment.

It follows then, that lacking other contrary information, planners commit resources s to segments that produce the highest POS values first. Of course on-scene evaluation of the terrain, history of the area, or emerging weather conditions color these predictions and their application.

How Search Planning Works

Lets look at a simple illustration relating to one segment on a search where family members reported a dementia sufferer missing. Planners identify four scenarios that make up the regions of probability with a total of nine segments in the entire search area. The maps you see on the next page originate from a 7.5 minute *(scale)* USGS orthographic projection. Most county planning departments create this type map with a simple request, markedly improving both visual and practical effectiveness for search operations and planning. The highlighted segment contains easily observable boundaries on all edges of the segment, both in the field and on the map.

The segment, stemming from one of the scenarios *(See page 332 in Chapter 18, Fig 18-35)* covers approximately 100 acres in size. As a search planner, let's determine how long a reasonable search will take, and how many searchers form an optimal group to do the job in this segment. This relates directly to operational period length and manpower available. Also, we calculate Probability of Detection for the effort and then expected Probability of Success in the segment. These calculations form the basis for analysis of the search by a search planner before committing additional resources.

Meanwhile, as described in Chapters 14 and 16 initial efforts on-scene strive to complete the reflex

Figure 20-1

tasks identified for the Dementia subject category. All six of the Reflex Task functional groupings need assignments and tracking. Realistically this takes a number of operational periods to complete. At the end of these functional taskings, without finding the missing subject or clues, then the search planner and the IC make assignments to search the segmented areas. In the meantime, the search planners work to complete an analysis.

In Figure 20-1 above, the scale from the topographical map allows planners to calculate the segment's length and width which then leads to calculating the segment's total area.

Reflex tasking turns up nothing. Search teams from the segment call in to the Search Base when they arrive on-scene and complete the R_d Procedure in the segment terrain. The determined R_d value measures at 23 feet and they describe the object they used in the procedure as a low visibility target *(An individual laying on the ground with low visibility colored clothing)*. Multiplying this value times 1.1 *(Koester's low visibility correction factor)* we calculate a sweep width of 25 feet.

Let's assume a total of 6 persons available for initial deployment into this segment. In this case the team

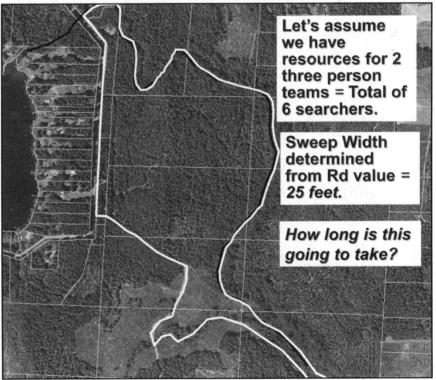

Figure 20-2

367

leader elects to use 2 three person teams making sweeps across the segment while searching. How long will the search teams take to search the area *(Figure 20-2)* and next, will 6 searchers realistically accomplish the job in one operational period?

Because of the relatively heavy vegetation *(Figure 20-1)* the planner runs the numbers using 0.5 mile an hour for the speed of the searchers. Keep in mind that the planner does not have to be spot accurate with these calculations, rather he/she needs a relative understanding of how long these search teams take to search in specific types of terrain. The goal centers on giving the IC an estimate for planning and manpower requirements.

Track line length for each of the six searchers in 6 hours covers approximately 15,840 feet or 3 miles. Each searcher covers a measured sweep width of 25 feet giving each searcher an area effectively swept of 396,000 sq. ft. Multiplying this by 6 searchers gives a total of 2,376,000 sq ft effectively swept in 6 hours by this team in this area *(see Figure 20-3 below)*. A normal operational period usually lasts from 4 to 6 hours. This time accommodates briefings, debriefings, transportation, breaks, etc.

Next compare how much of the real-estate covered by the searchers compares to the size of the segment: 100 acres = 4,356,000 sq. ft. Create a fraction and divide using a calculator.

$$\frac{2,376,000}{4,356,000} = 0.54$$

If we reference Chapter 19, Figure 19-20 on Page 364, a Coverage of .54 equates to a 42% Probability of Detection.

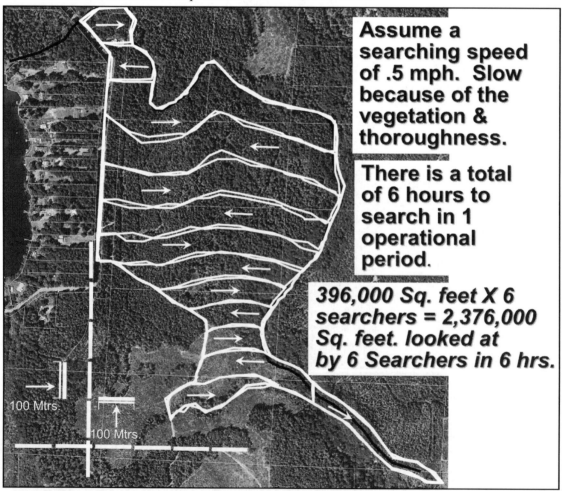

Figure 20-3 100 acre segment with projected sweeps using the six searchers

Now let's run the numbers at 1 mile an hour and see if this fits into the operational period. Benchmarking the speed of searching *(discussed in Chapter 9)* now shows its value for SAR teams. One searcher walking at 1 mph for 6 hours gives a track line length of 31,680 feet. Remember the sweep width measured from the R_d Procedure at 25 ft. This calculates how much actual ground one searcher covered in the time allotted. 31,680 ft. × 25 ft. = 792,000 square feet total for one searcher *(Figure 20-4 below)*.

Remember, there are six searchers. 792,000 square feet for one searcher multiplied by 6 yields 4,752,000 square feet total scanned on the ground by the 6 search team members.

Next compare how much real-estate covered by the searchers compares to the size of the segment. Again, create a fraction and divide using a calculator. The amount of ground scanned amounts to 4,752,000 square feet which we use as the numerator in the fraction. The total amount of ground in the segment amounts to 4,356,000 sq. feet. This is used as the denominator in the fraction *(Figure 20-5 next page)*.

$$\frac{4,752,000 \text{ sq. ft.}}{4,356,000 \text{ sq. ft.}} = 1.09$$

The result 1.09 gives us the coverage for the search in the segment and using Koopman's curve results in a POD of 66%.

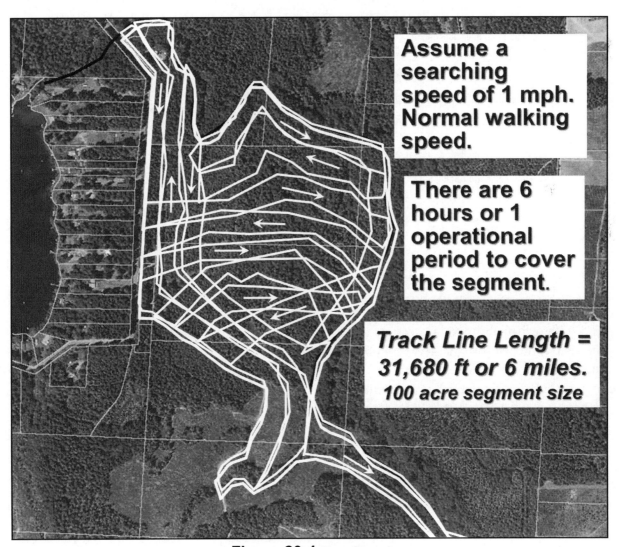

Figure 20-4 New Speed

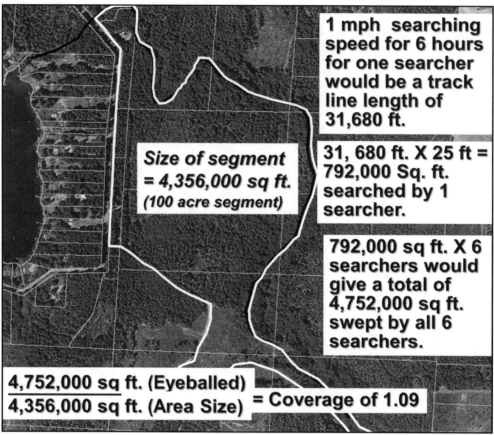

Figure 20-5

The Planner now possesses something tangible to work with. If we go back to this example in Chapter 18, pg. 334, the Probability of Area for this whole segment sits at 13% with no consensus or weighting due to scenario analysis.

Try the computations for POA × POD = POS.

The Probability of Area value for this segment equals 13%, and with a Probability of Detection value of 66%, the search theory formula gives a Probability of Success factor of a little less than 10%. When you compare these figures with other segment values, we now have a consistent, verifiable and repeatable method of comparison between segments and options within segments.

Without unlimited budgets, unlimited resources and unlimited time to search planners must make choices between various search options.

Past search planning methods emphasized the different components of the search equation. Some emphasized high POA or on the other hand some reflected that maximizing POD led to the best approach. These methods, while well intentioned, eliminated one or the other elements critical to determining success. The combination of detection and location provide a complete picture not always visible without calculation. Particularly when including the allocation of effort required to attain that success factor.

Specifically, in the previous example we considered a specific segment, the effort required to achieve that level of success factors heavily in evaluating how to deploy resources. A segment with a high POA might remain un-searched until appropriate resources arrive and until then the calculated POS for that segment rests at zero.

The POS calculation allows planners to predict the performance of one resource compared to another, coupled with a critical *time* element. In most environments, a sweep width for a resource at a set speed of advance covers a specific area in a given time. SAR team benchmarks give this extremely important information to planners. Tactical knowledge about how to attain the fastest coverage in an area generates a desired POD more quickly, and thus drives the POS higher, earlier in the search.

Chapter 19 on POD, mentioned the benefits of field detection exercises in local areas and running them at various times of the year. These exercises greatly enhance searcher confidence and planner confidence in each other, not to mention the familiarity with the area for future missions. The following examples show some quick calculations to compare variables in a potential search operation. While certainly not infallible, these calculations point out some otherwise unknown options.

Example of Search Planning Analysis:

A search team arrives in the field and reports that when they perform an Rd Procedure in their assigned segment, the average range of detection is 45.5 feet for a low visibility target *(an individual prone on the ground with low visibility colored clothing)*. Calculation of the effective sweep width multiplies this value times 1.1 *(Koester's correction factor for low visibility targets)* Effective sweep width would be 50 ft. in this terrain under current conditions. If search team members were traveling at 1 mile per hour in a 0.25 square mile segment *(6.9 million square feet)* they would cover an area of 264,000 square feet in one hour and 1.584 million square feet in six hours. A three person team covers an area of 4.752 million square feet in six hours.

Another search team completes the Rd Procedure and it is determined that they have an effective sweep width of 20 ft. for a low visibility target. Traveling at 1 mile per hour, a searcher would cover 105,600 square feet in an hour, and 633,600 square feet in six hours. A three person team in this case covers 1,900,800 square feet in 6 hours.

    50 ft sweep width × 5,280 feet per hour = 264,000 square feet per hour.
    264,000 square feet per hour × 6 hours = 1.584 million square feet.
    1.584 million square feet × 3 searchers = 4.752 million square feet.
    4.752 million square feet ÷ 6.9 million square feet = 0.69 coverage
    0.69 Coverage = 50% POD
    Segment Probability of Area has been determined to be 20%
    .20 POA × .50 POD = 0.10 or 10% POS

---

    20 ft sweep width × 5,280 feet per hour = 105,600 square feet per hour
    105,600 square feet per hour × 6 hours = 633,600 square feet
    633,600 square feet × 3 searchers = 1.9 million square feet
    1.9 million square feet ÷ 6.9 million square feet = 0.28 coverage
    0.28 Coverage = 24% POD
    Segment Probability of Area as above is 20%
    .20 POA × .24 POD = 0.05 or 5% POS

> The search planner compares the predictive result for different resources in the same 6.9 million square foot segment that has a 20% POA, to determine which resource *(and how many)* to send prior to the operational period. The separate resources yield a POD of 50% and 24% respectively and a POS of 10% versus 05% for that operational period of the search.
>
> Change the parameters for the second resource, increase it to a 10 person team, each individual with a 20 ft sweep width, and the POS jumps to 12%.
>
> > 20 ft sweep width × 5,280 feet per hour = 105, 600 square feet per hour
> > 105, 600 square feet per hour × 6 hours = 633, 600 square feet
> > 633, 600 square feet × 10 searchers = 6.3 million square feet
> > 6.3 million square feet ÷ 6.9 million square feet = 0.91 coverage
> > 0.91 Coverage = 60% POD
> > **0.20 POA × 0.60 POD = 0.12 or 12% POS**

From a practical perspective adding extra resources (*specifically 6 extra searchers in this segment*) theoretically changed the POS from 05% to 12%. These calculations show how an IC with knowledge of available resources and the basics of search planning manipulates available resources between segments in a planning mode before the next search of that segment begins, and potentially maximizes POS for that operational period.

As mentioned in Chapter 17 - Introduction to Search Theory, sometimes during a search many segments get searched one or more times without locating the missing person or even a clue. Any number of outside entities may demand a quantification of the ongoing search effort *(media, elected officials, family and relatives, etc.)*.

Search Theory advocates maximizing success in the shortest amount of time. By using the standard notation search theory formula *(POA × POD = POS)* properly, fairly simple calculations provide a means of measuring the most beneficial planning options, alternative outcomes, effort allocation, and chances of success in both individual segments and the entire search area. These same calculations also justify expanding the search area, researching some segments, searching somewhere else, or completely suspending further search efforts in the area. Planning and the use of this conventional formula help the following:

- Initial resource application.
- Evaluation of search effectiveness.
- Redistribution of resources.
- Re-searching segments.
- Increasing the size of the search area, or looking elsewhere.
- Suspending an unsuccessful search.
- Rationalizing actions to higher authorities; relatives, and the media.

Review of Search Effort

Allocation of Search Effort: At its simplest, the distance a search resource *(searcher)* travels within the search segment during an operational period defines search effort for that period. Total search effort depends the total track line length *(TLL)* of all of the tracks covered by all the searchers up to that point. The total length of the tracks depends on the number of searchers available and the searcher average speed of advance within their respective segments. The area effectively searched *(swept)* reasonably measures how much searching was done in an operational period. So search effort for a given coverage is a product of number of searchers, *(# searchers)*, speed of advance, *(meters or feet per hour)*, and sweep width, *(meters or feet)*.

Local Average Range of Detection (R_d) procedures with the associated corrections *(See Chapter 19)* represent conservative Effective Sweep Width values for teams in varying terrain and conditions.

Remember, search theory attempts to maximize POS in the least amount of time. More searchers in an area means it takes less time to cover that area. On the other hand, reduce the number of searchers and the time to cover the area increases.

NOTE: Search always draws on many resources from a variety of outside sources. Unfortunately, these resources have finite limits. Search teams come from families, jobs, and need rest to function. Each resource comes with a timeline of availability including delays in application and possible conflicts pulling them off the search early. Plan ahead for early and late arrivals, early departures, and sustaining resources during the search *(things like food and sleep)*.

Where to Search?

Several examples of potential search planner analysis during the context of a difficult operation follow.

Example 1: *(Figure 20-6)*

Consider that all searchers search at the same speed. The planner has two segments in the search area with an equal POA of 25% *(each derived by overhead team consensus)*. In one of the segments, the effort required to achieve a POD of 50% takes an estimated TLL of 24 miles, and a coverage of 0.7 *(Based on terrain analysis, available resources and conservative sweep width values determined with Rd measurements)*. In the other segment, the effort required to achieve a POD of 50% takes an estimated TLL of 48 miles to get the same 0.7 coverage value. Which segment would you search first and why? What causes the change in TLL?

With everything else equal, it takes twice the number of searchers to achieve the same POS in segment A2 in the same amount of time. *(POS = POA × POD)* .25 × .50 = .125

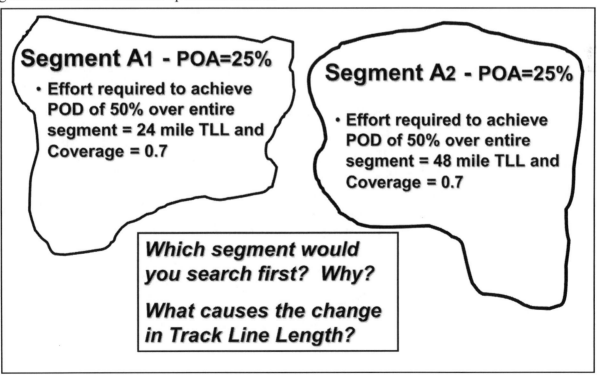

Figure 20-6 Example 1

Example 2: *(Figure 20-7)*

In one of the segments, the effort required to achieve a POD of 50% in the segment takes an estimated 24 mile TLL and a coverage of 0.7. In the other segment, the effort required to achieve a POD of 25% in the segment also takes an estimated 24 mile TLL and a coverage of 0.35. The question follows "Which segment to search first and why? Why a lower coverage in Segment A2?

Can you see that the search operation would have to search segment 2 twice with the indicated effort to achieve the same POD?

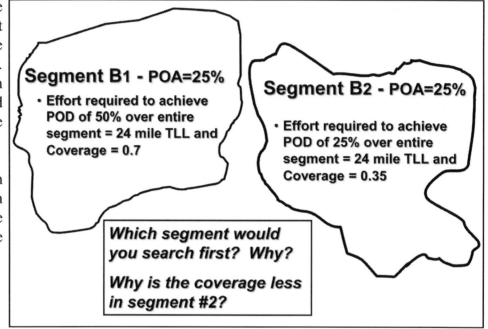

Figure 20-7 Example 2

Example 3: *(Figure 20-8)*

Segment A1 has a POA of 25%. Segment A2 has a POA of 50%. In segment A1, the effort required to achieve a POD of 50% takes an estimated 24 mile TLL and coverage 0.7. In segment A2, the effort required to achieve a POD of 50% also takes an estimated 24 mile TLL and coverage 0.7. The question follows: Which to search first and why?

With everything else the same, searching in segment A2 results in a higher POS because of the higher POA. Remember, try to achieve the greatest increase in POS with the least effort *(searcher hours)*.

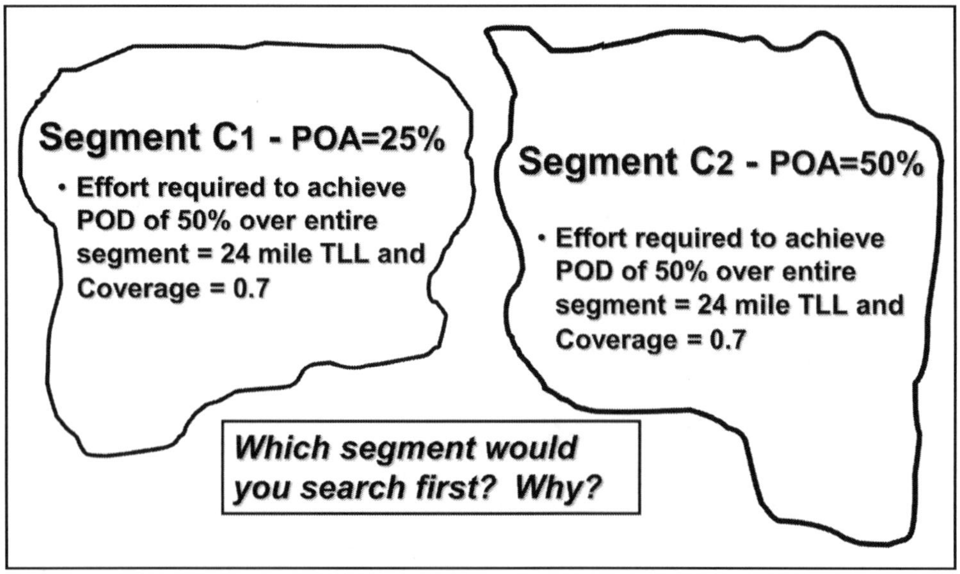

Figure 20-8 Example 3

Example 4: *(Figure 20-9)*

Segment A1 has a POA of 25%. Segment A2 has a POA of 25%. In segment A1, the effort required to achieve a POD of 50% takes an estimated 24 mile TLL and a coverage of 0.7. In segment A2, the effort required to achieve a POD of 50% also takes an estimated 24 mile TLL. The question follows "Which segment would you search first and why?

Even though segment A2 contains a higher Probability Density value, they both take 24 mile TLLs to search to a 50% Probability of Detection. That means even though the resulting POS value for 24 mile TLLs come out the same, planners need to consider the factor of time. With extremely difficult terrain in segment A2 and requires significantly more time to search, then perhaps focus on segment one first.

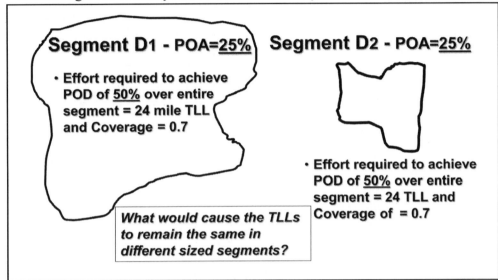

Figure 20-9 Example 4

These decisions use numbers and assessments made by search planners armed with search theory. As mentioned in Chapter 17, evaluation of the effort expended on a search gives the search manager a reason to make choices. Investigative facts and information about the missing person, the area, and the circumstances of the situation serve to give a search planner some limited, intangible indications about where to search, and with what resources. Speculation and intuition, though sometimes powerful, fail to give comparative value with descriptive terms alone. Using numbers for comparison leads to accurate tracking of those numbers and to solid results about one factor over another.

An Example, Putting it all Together.

The examples given in the POD chapter show how searcher effort influences POD and enables us to maximize the POS in the shortest time possible *(This example uses only the metric system)*.

Six searchers spend 6 hours in segment searching at normal speed = 1.6 Kph

Example calculation:
  R_d including correction = 15 meters
  Track Line Length = 57.6 km
  (6 hours × 1.6 km = 9.6 km × 6 searchers)
  Area Effectively Swept = 0.86 Sq km
  (15 meters × 57.6 km = 0.86 Sq. km)

Coverage: *(C)* The ratio of area effectively swept to the total area of the segment.

Lets say that the segment in question measures 800 × 800 meters = 0.64 Sq. kilometers.
  Area Effectively Swept = 0.86 Sq km
  0.86 ÷ 0.64 = a **Coverage** of 1.3
  A **Coverage** of 1.3 equates to a **POD of 74%** *(Using the curve on page 364)*

> To increase searcher effort and consequently POD and POS, only one variable needs to change: Track line length. The sweep width value remains constant at our measured R_d. Three methods alter the track line length.
>
> 1. Increase the amount of time the searchers spend in the segment. This conflicts with our goal to maximize POS in the least amount of time.
>
> 2. Increase the number of searchers. This increases the total track line length with a resulting increase in the area effectively swept.
>
> 3. Increase the speed of the searchers; however, too fast and searcher sweep width decreases, objects get missed and, with difficult terrain, searchers pay more attention to ensuring foot placement than on searching.

Now Double the Number of Searchers

12 searchers spend 6 hours in the same segment searching at normal speed = 1.6 kilometers per hour

Estimate Track Line Length = *(Speed × Time)*
(6 hours × 1.6 kilometers per hour × 12 searchers
TLL = 115.2 kilometers
Area Effectively Swept: *(Track Line Length × Sweep Width)*

Example Calculation:
  R_d including correction = 15 meters
  Track Line Length = 115.2 km
  (6 hours × 1.6 km = 9.6 km × 12 searchers)
  Area Effectively Swept = 1.72 Sq km
  (15 meters or .015 Km × 9.6 km × 12 searchers = 1.72 Sq. Kilometers).

Coverage: *(C)* The ratio of area effectively swept to the total area of the segment.

Again, the search segment measures 800 × 800 meters = 0.64 Sq. Kilometers.

  Area Effectively Swept = 1.72 Sq km
  1.72 ÷ 0.64 = a Coverage of 2.7
  A **Coverage** of 2.7 equates to a **POD of 95%** *(Using the curve on page 364)*

Example Summary

By increasing searcher effort *(in fact doubling the number of searchers)* we substantially increased our POD and consequently our POS. Common sense dictates that by increasing the number of searchers the POD will go up. However, this illustrates the non linearity *(its not a straight line)* of the POD/coverage curve. By doubling the number of searchers, the POD increases only 50%. Looking at the Coverage chart devised by Koopman *(Figure 19-20)* on Page 364, we find a non-linear graph. It shows that as planners apply more effort and get more coverage, the POD rises by smaller and smaller amounts.

Shifting Probability of Area after a Search

During the search, assigned probability values within the area change constantly. Or more specifically, POA values change as searchers cover segments. A shifted, updated or adjusted POA value for a segment represents a modified value after an unsuccessful search, i.e. searchers covered a segment, but the missing person or any clues failed to turn up. Planners use the Shifted or Adjusted POA to measure the decrease in probability in a segment after unsuccessfully searching it but still needing to compare it to the other segments. After searching a segment, its POA decreases in relationship to the Probability of Detection of the resource applied to the segment. Additionally, after a segment gets searched without success, the other POA values now potentially rise in priority since another segment now carries a higher POA compared to the one just searched.

For example, consider the composite Figure 20-10 and 20-11. The four segments, *(A1, A2, A3, and A4)* each of about the same size and taking the same amount of time to search, for the following example they hold initial POA values respectively at 30%, 30%, 20% and 20%. If segment A1 gets searched without success, its POA decreases while the POA values for the remaining segments stay the same *(but they increase relative to the segment we just searched)*. In other words, after searching a

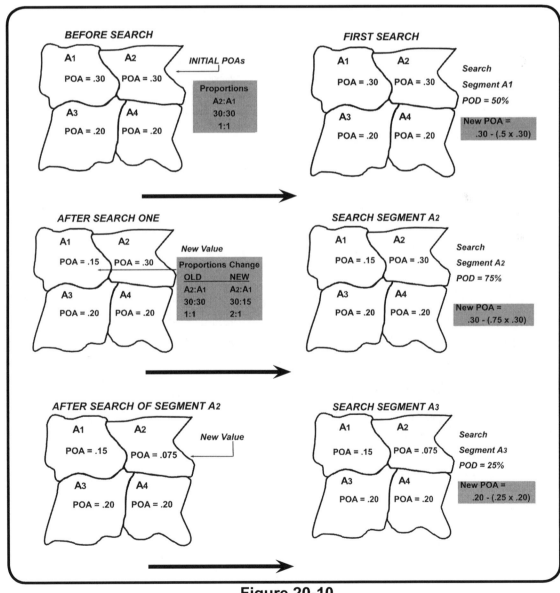

Figure 20-10

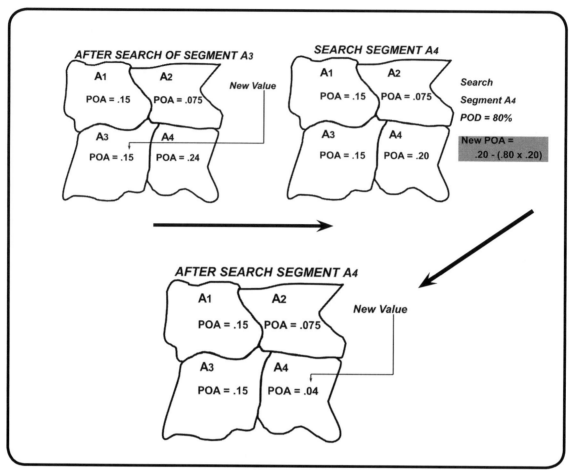

Figure 20-11

segment without success, the chances of the subject or a clue lying in the segment decrease, while the relative chances of the subject or a clue lying in one of the unsearched segments now has a higher value than the first segment.

Looking at the respective figures after search one, the POA for Segment A went down and *proportionally* the values for the three remaining segments went up.

The exact increase or decrease for each POA value, depends on two things: the original POA for each segment (POA_{old}); and the cumulative POD for the resource(s) that searched the segment (POD_{cum}). The figures also show subsequent searches of the other segments.

The third sequence in Figure 20-10 and then Figure 20-11 *(above)* shows how the POA values change or *shift* after searching segments A3 and A4 with PODs of 25% and 80% respectively.

NOTE: In the example above, notice that the values no longer add up to 100%. This is not necessary in the computation for shifting POA and subsequently for Probability of Success. The numbers simply represent proportional values left in the segment. Think of the missing POA value as converted to POS.

Segment and Overall Probability of Success

POS values exist in two forms. First; the Probability of Success for each search segment.

In conventional notation:

Segment POS = Segment POA × Segment POD

The product of multiplying the segment POA times the segment POD equals the Segment Probability of Success. After multiple searches of the same segment planners need a designation called Segment POS_{cum} or Cumulative Segment Probability of Success.

Remember the stated goal of search planning:

Maximize Probability Of Success in the least amount of time.

Adding Cumulative Probability of Success values from each segment together establishes an Overall Probability of Success for the search area. Formal notation for the establishment of the Segment POS follows:

Segment POS_{cum} = Segment POS_{1st} + Segment POS_{2nd} + . . . Segment POS_{nth}

Where *n* refers to the nth *(however many occur)* search of the segment.

Notation for the **Overall Probability of Success** for the entire search area follows:

Overall POS = Segment POS_{1st} + Segment POS_{2nd} + . . . Segment POS_{nth}

In this formula *n* refers to the last segment in the search area.

As the search continues, establish cumulative figures for each segment, and sum those values to determine the **Cumulative Probability of Success** for the whole search. Notation for Cumulative POS follows:

Overall POS_{cum} = Segment 1 POS_{cum} + Segment 2 POS_{cum} + . . . Segment n POS_{cum}

In this formula *n* refers to the last segment in the search area.

Figure 20-12 Adding Probability of Success

Visualize the POA, POD and POS values while searching a segment. A good analogy for this involves the use of a bucket, sponge and a barrel. The analogy of the sponge and the bucket for POS follows *(Figure 20-13 below)*:

A bucket only holds so much water - *(By the same token, a segment only holds so much POA – Think of the water in the bucket as POA and the bucket as the segment)*. Each time you put the sponge *(Resource with a given POD)* in the bucket, it only takes so much of the POA out to place into the *(Probability of Success)* barrel for the segment. Taking the POA from the segment *(bucket)* with the resource *(sponge)* transforms it into POS. Therefore, the POS for any given segment never exceeds the initial POA value established for that segment- *(starting water level in the segment bucket)*.

When searchers complete a segment, calculate a cumulative POS value for that segment *(A POA bucket holds only so much water and the sponge or resource takes an amount of water based on it's capacity and how much was in the bucket to start)*.

Measure all the POS buckets by dumping them into the **Overall POS Barrel**. That amount indicates the Overall POS for the search.

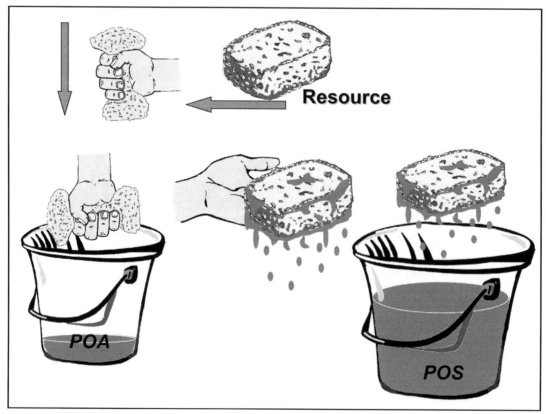

Figure 20-13

The POS Tracking Sheet

The worksheet below provides an easy to use tool for tracking POS calculations and the Shifting POA values in each segment. Add the individual segment POS calculations to determine Overall POS for the search. Use one worksheet per search, per segment *(This provides an easy system to track multiple resources)*. Don't worry about the figures adding up to 100% *(not necessary)*, but remember the Segment POS_{cum} for any segment never exceeds the initial POA established for that segment.

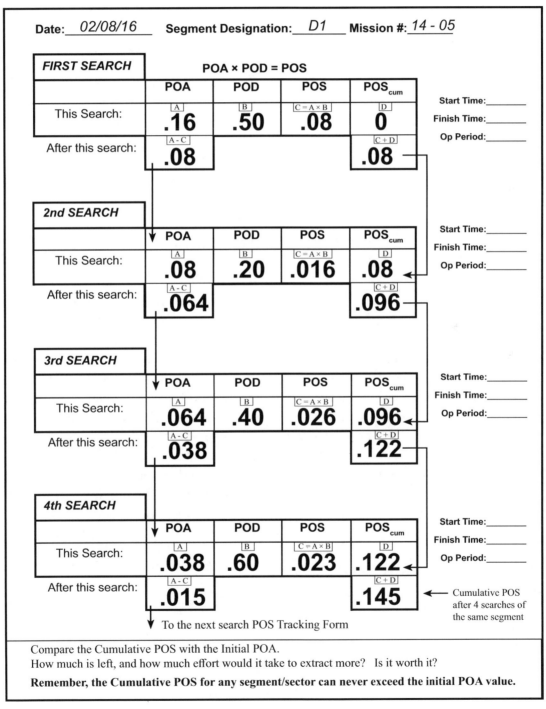

Figure 20-14

Coverage and Search Effectiveness

Verbal Descriptions of Search Effectiveness or *Coverage* occur all the time throughout the history of land search operations. Descriptions like:

- Great!
- Pretty thorough.
- Very thorough.
- Very nearly complete.
- Complete.
- Intense.
- All most all of it.
- Ain't no way he's out there!
- That area's done.
- It's cleared.

All of these describe how well searchers felt they searched or *covered* a segment. Ask yourself this question: How do you evaluate these verbal descriptions, one over another? Answer: You can't! Search requires some type of quantification, or standard numerical system for an assessment.

Benefits of the POS Tracking Form

The POS Tracking Form describes in detail, the operational period for what occurred in one segment for each search sortie. In the example given *(Figure 20-14 on the previous page)*, the initial POA value of 0.16 changed after 4 searches to a reduced value of 0.015. The overall POS value at the end of four searches ended up at 0.145. This follows the law of diminishing returns. Only 0.015 POA (1.5%) remains in the segment...no matter how many resources search the segment again. This question follows: *How else can you measure the amount of effort expended in searching a segment?*

The form, if used properly, provides justification for searching elsewhere or re-searching the same segments again. In addition it provides the basis for not searching some segments. It also provides a rationale for expanding the search or bringing in specialized/more capable resources.

But, the POS Tracking Form also comes with provisos.

Using it requires a familiarity with *Search Theory* and keeping track accurately. This means the use of, and an understanding of the *Proportional Consensus* methods for establishing POA values plus R_d and coverage in the search segments for determining POD.

It also means that planners and managers both need a reasonable knowledge of resource PODs and the factors that influence or change those values. This stems from a thorough understanding of the relationship between *searcher effort* and the Probability of Success goal of maximizing success in the least amount of time.

Remember, no silver bullet exists in Search Management. However these analysis techniques help planners and ICs make informed and justifiable decisions.

Adjusting Probabilities after a New Consensus

If new information arises or teams find a clue that forces a new consensus, it makes no sense to zero the cumulative POS calculations done so far. The cumulative POD *(in each segment)* stays the same after a new consensus, the effort expended, Rd values and coverage all remain the same. The POA values after a new consensus often change, which leads to a decrease in Overall Probability of Success, but sometimes it will increase or stay the same, depending on how and where Operations conducted their original searches. Cumulative Overall Probability of Success should not return to zero unless discarding all previously searched segments.

Adjustment Steps with new information
Step #1

Prior to performing a new consensus take note of or make sure to compute the following:

- Cumulative Overall Probability of Success *(Overall POS_{cum})* and each Segment's Cumulative Probability of Success *(Segment POS_{cum})*.

- Initial POA for each segment.
- Cumulative Segment Probability of Detection *(Segment POD_{cum})*.

As a quick example of how this works, assume that each of the four segments in the search area all start with a POA of 25%. Before searching, the segment and overall probability of success values rest at zero.

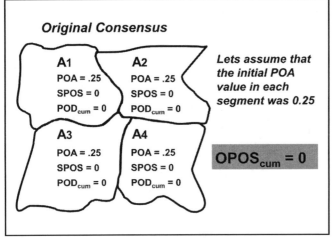

Figure 20-15

The cumulative POD values for each segment also sit at zero *(Figure 20-15 above)*.

After a number of search sorties with different resources, planners document the following figures.

POA for segment A1 now equals 0.125.
POA for segment A2 equals 0.063.
POA for segment A3 equals 0.023 and finally
POA for segment A4 equals 0.05.

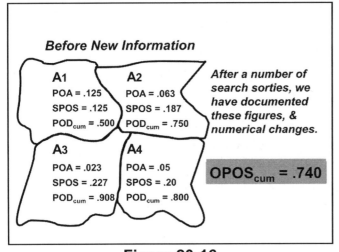

Figure 20-16

Segment POS factors for each of the segments sit at 0.125, .0187, 0.227, and 0.200 respectively.

The figures sum to an Overall Probability of Success of .740 *(Figure 20-16)*.

Notice the respective Cumulative Probability of Detection values for the segments now stand at .50, .750, .908, and .800.

Investigators discover new information or searchers find an important clue.

The situation requires a new consensus, but without re-segmenting or throwing out the cumulative probability of detection values calculated for the sorties up to this point.

Step #2

Assign new segment Probability of Area *(Segment POA)* values to segments using Proportional Consensus. For our example, the new consensus

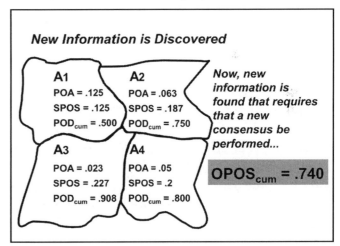

Figure 20-17

New POA values follow:

POA for segment A1 equals 0.30.
POA for segment A2 equals 0.40.
POA for segment A3 equals 0.15, and
POA for segment A4 equals 0.15.

NOTE: The Cumulative Probability of Detection values for each of the segments stay the same *(Figure 20-17 above)*.

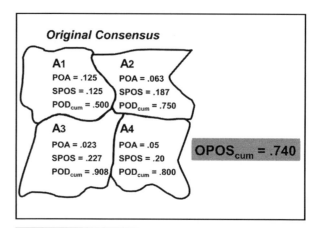

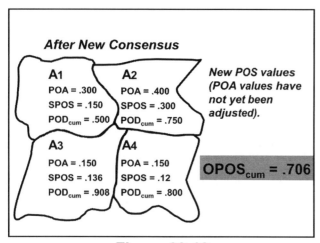

Figure 20-18

Step #3

Compute the Cumulative Probability of Success values for each of the segments by using the standard formula *(POA × POD = POS)* and add those values together to determine the Overall Probability of Success for all 4 segments. This process involves multiplying the new POAs times the Cumulative POD values for each segment. Remember, never throw out probability of detection factors from the previous sorties.

The respective POS values have been calculated in figure 20-18 above. Notice however, that the POA values after the calculation have not yet been adjusted. *(In other words, when you search a segment with a resource and nothing is found, the probability that the subject is in that segment goes down.)* After the new consensus, apply the Cumulative POD values from previous sorties to the new probability of area values to update the Cumulative POS values.

Step #4

Adjust or compute the respective POA values to reflect searching those areas during previous sorties.

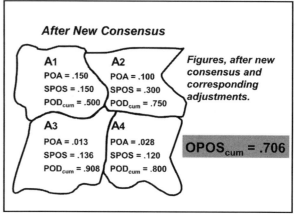

Figure 20-19

Step # 5

Compare the figures from before the consensus to the adjusted calculations *(Figure 20-19 above)*, note the Overall Probability of Success for the entire search area (all four segments) reduced slightly. However, the adjustment accommodated previous values with the new consensus and the effort expended. The effort expended still applies to the updated POA values! Continue adjusting Segment POA and POS values as before with subsequent searching.

Reminder on the Use of *Rest of The World* (ROW)

As mentioned in Chapter 18 on POA, technically, the search area is not a closed system, simply because the subject might travel outside the boundaries of the search area. If the search subject leaves the confines of the search area, planners sometimes consider the missing person as located in the *Rest of the World (or ROW), and some attempt to label it as an additional segment.*

By definition, an open system implies a significant chance that the missing person lies outside the search area. Bayes' Rule from Bayesian mathematics requires consideration of all possible outcomes in such a system. In acknowledging the possibility of finding the missing person outside the search area, then some probability exists for them to be in that additional segment. Unfortunately, the rest of the world rapidly loses focus as a searchable segment when viewed through search theory terms like coverage, effort and POD. How do we determine *Coverage* for ROW and from there *POD* for ROW? Think of the closed system as the part of the designated search area within the appropriate jurisdiction and apply the search theory math within that closed system.

We suggest addressing the POA of the Rest of the World through investigation and scenario analysis, not mathematical computation. On its face, the concept of ROW provides an immediately intuitive answer to searching for someone outside the search area. "If the POA for ROW rises to a certain level then we expand the search..." Search Theory as described in this text assumes a closed system *(i.e. the subject lies somewhere in the search area)*. However, remember the lack of any clues becomes a clue in its own right.

Using the Search Theory Solution to a given level of effort or POS value without finding a clue, *then* expanding the Search to ROW for a re-evaluation serves the same function as the growing ROW value described above, without violating the baseline for Search Theory mathematics in a closed system. Use it as a scenario in a proportioned based consensus when evaluating new evidence, or the lack of evidence after a given expenditure of effort.

Guidance for these evaluations needs to take place at the policy level before a major search effort.

Remember, a Successful Search Depends on Strong Fundamentals

Success components include the Crucials - both old and new:

- Search is an Emergency
- Search is Tied Inexorably to Law Enforcement Investigation.
- Search for Clues and the Missing Person.
- Concentrate on factors that are:
  - Important to search success.
  - Controlled by the Search Manager.
- Confine the Search Area and Gather Good Information.
- Apply Trained Appropriate Resources in a Definite Order.
- Use Thorough Grid Search *(close spacing)* only as a Last Resort.
- Document Decisions and Assignments Early with Numerical Assessments for Justification.
- Detection Capability Variables Must be included in Effective Search Planning.
- Allocation of Effort Combined with Detection Capability can Maximize Probability of Success.
- Success in the Shortest Time Possible is the Ultimate Goal in Search.

Search Theory and planning fundamentals provide the redundancy that assures success when Reflex Tasking and other short cuts fail to find the subject! As a successful Search Manager, always remember and include the crucials of search theory and management in your thinking and planning strategy.

REVISIT: The Importance of Using the Numbers

Quantify the ongoing search effort. Conventional Search Theory and the use of the standard formula POA × POD = POS helps:

- Initial resource application.
- Evaluation of search effectiveness.
- Redistribution of resources.

- Re-searching segments.
- Increasing the size of the search area, or looking elsewhere.
- Suspending an unsuccessful search.
- Rationalizing actions to higher authorities, relatives, and the media.

Necessary Values assigned by the Search Manager include:

- A value that gives a priority to the search urgency.
- Values that help give priority to segments in the search area.
- Values on the likelihood of resources detecting the subject or clues.
- A product of POA × POD that measure expected success.
- Search effort to effectively search a segment or number of segments.

The Search (IC) Makes A Difference

- Organize quickly and put the infrastructure for good management in place.
- Control and delegate functional responsibility.
- Use qualified trained resources *(if possible)* and know their capabilities.
- Create a team effort environment.
- Keep current on innovative tactics, new research and trends in search management.
- Maintain victim orientation and remember that *search is an emergency*.

Continuing Operational Problems in Search

- No assessment of the real scope of local SAR incidents in the planning process.
- Failure to use the right resources in the right order.
- Gross under estimation of manpower or resources needed to adequately search the established search area or specified segments in an operational period.
- No visible leadership.
- No proper immediate action after the first notice.
- Failure to delegate key functions.
- Poor interagency communication.
- Failure to properly document search activities.
- No plan for the use of unexpected high numbers of volunteers.
- Adversarial, or negative relationships with the media.
- No backup relief for overhead management team.
- Poor management of specialized resources.
- Lack of education and training about new search management concepts and tactics.

Clue Orientation 21

Objectives:

- Describe clue detection and what an important part it plays in the function of search

- Identify the four broad based categories of clues

- Discuss the relationship of clues to searcher expectancy and vision basics

- Relate why clue orientation depends on key training

- Discuss why important clues surface both in the field and in the command post

The Nature of Clues

What constitutes a clue and what important role do clues play in the function of search? According to *Webster's* dictionary, a clue consists of a fact, an object, information, or some type of evidence that helps in solving a mystery or problem. In his seminal work *Mountain Search for the Lost Victim,* Dennis Kelly refers to clues as signals. Knowingly, or unknowingly the missing person generates various forms of signals indicating what happened, direction of travel, intentions, state of mind, and the list goes on. Searchers and overhead teams work to interpret these signals an organize them in a cohesive structure in order to tell a story.

The definition of *seek,* means to find, trace, search for, or track down. Putting the two terms together, *clue and seeking,* in essence, describes what it takes to solve the classic mystery of finding the missing person. Clue seeking, gathering as many facts and information as possible, assists searchers in organizing and reasoning through problems, in hopes to solve the missing person case. Devising a method which uncovers significant clues relevant to a particular situation provides a basis for major field tactics and strategies in specific locations.

> *"Clues evaluated through hindsight can be thrown in the wait till next time department, but this isn't enough. Search is a special task with life or death consequences. We must be able to account for our actions."*
> — Jeff Doran - SARDA

In Chapter 13 we discussed in detail, four basic types of evidence. Each of the four types of evidence constitute clues or potential signals generated by the missing person. The four basic types of evidence include:

- Physical Evidence
- Testimonial Evidence
- Written or Documentary Evidence
- Statistical or Analytical Evidence

Searchers tend to think clues only exist in the environment and finding them only happens in the field. However, upon careful examination of what really constitutes a clue, professionals came to the conclusion that any bit of information or evidence contributing to the reduction of uncertainty in the search effort produces a clue. One fact or bit of information by itself holds very little value or meaning, but when combined with another bit of information it offers a viable clue. Investigators need to keep close and repetitive scrutiny of clue logs, communication call logs, debriefing sheets, maps, and interview notes to build a case. All information and data gets deposited at the Command Post, where personnel analyzes it every Operational period and correlate facts into clues.

Detection and Recognition

In Chapter 19 we discussed target orientation, human vision and the detection process. In general, a human possesses the capability to detect something in the search area based on the size, shape and color of the object, or by the terrain and existing environment conditions, and by the capabilities of the sensor or searcher. The chapter also pointed out the difference between detection and recognition. Not recognizing the real meaning or value of a clue always presents a major problem in clue orientation. Often searchers fail to recognize a clue as meaningful to the search effort so, although they detect the clues, they neglect to act upon them. Recognition of clues comes from several important processes.

Always consider searcher and/or overhead team member expectations, such as what they expect to see or sense? Studies (See *Chapter 19*) clearly identify a humans visual attention to detail and the processes by which we recognize things, making it easier to capitalize on those mechanisms in the briefing process. Knowing this, allows search professionals to program people in ways to mentally detect and recognize things faster and more efficiently. Vision basics and an understanding of how the eye works benefit a searchers capabilities while scanning to detect these clues.

The *canonical perspective* or standard identifying view, drive expectations and govern the discovery of physical evidence. Searchers develop an image of the clue in their minds and expect that clue to match or closely match what they find in the environment. This mind set contains many untruths. In general most people underestimate the difficulty of detection in varying conditions and environments. Searchers expect clues to literally *pop out*. On the contrary, research and practical field experience tell us differently.

That said, the possibility to improve clue or object detection exists through a process called *priming*. The person briefing both overhead team members and field searchers *prime* the detection pump by effectively bridging the gap between a distraction and a meaningful clue on a specific search. And, although very effective, the above mentioned process takes lots of practice.

Principles of Clue Orientation

- Clue seeking starts with the pre planning process, continues through a search and ends upon filing the critique and after action report. In some cases, it goes even further with more investigation.
- One considers the recognition of clues a learned skill, and when practiced, people develop a sense of just how much information the search effort needs.
- Speculate about possibilities, but shy away from forming hard and fast opinions without all the clues or information. The potential of finding key pieces to the puzzle always remains.
- Try not to immediately form an opinion about the value or association of a clue. Another piece of information or evidence quite possibly changes everything.
- Gather information, clues, or evidence from as many sources as possible. A single source usually fails to provide all the facts.
- A complete subject profile provides a valuable source of clues. Continue gathering information for the profile throughout an operation and let it offer direction.
- Brief overhead team members and searchers about *personal expectations*, *canonical perspective*, taking *snapshots* instead of scanning and the four main types of evidence.
- Do to the fragility, transitory or short lived aspects of a clue, make sure to document, photograph, or preserve it as quickly as possible.

Six Elements of Clue Orientation

Untrained searchers tend to focus their attention on looking for and detecting the missing person. Therefore new searchers tend to miss many of the small signals generated by the lost person. Decades ago, search efforts concentrated entirely on the missing person and as a result, overlooked multiple clues pointing towards the missing subject. Today, search depends on clue orientation and the detection of those clues. Clue orientation involves **six basic elements**:

1. The **Missing Person** - clue or signal generator
2. The **Clues** or signals sent by the missing person
3. The **Area or Sources Personnel Search**
4. The **Searchers/Overhead Staff** or signal receivers
5. **Time of Events** or the sequence of events
6. **Signcutting/Investigation** as methods to detect clues

The Missing Person as a Signal Generator

Experience tells us that only very skilled trackers or persons trained specifically to evade possesses the ability to pass through an environment without leaving a trace or human generated signal. A common problem among searchers and managers relates to the multiple signals generated in the form of witnesses, the public and even other searchers. Problems arise when trying to identify which sign or clues belong to which individual? Remember the importance of identifying personal characteristics of the missing person and anything they carried on them at the time. Descriptions of the missing person, his or her clothes, and any gear for making identification of footprints and discarded articles all contribute to gathering information. Bottom line, searchers need to recognize a clue if they see it.

- More clues exist than lost subjects
- The ultimate clue includes the lost person

The Clues or Signals Sent from the Missing Person

In general, anyone involved in a search effort needs to try and detect four, simple *(but very important)* lost or missing person messages:

- The **present location** of the of the missing person is _____.*(Person found)*
- The **previous location** of the missing person was _____.*(Clue found)*
- The **destination** or intent of the missing person was _____.*(Clue found)*
- The **missing person was not here** _____. *(No clues found)*

Although obvious on the surface, theses messages sometimes come across as very subtle and difficult to interpret. In Chapter 18 we discussed the importance of establishing scenarios. Advocating, based on experience from previous searches, that a management team always come up with at least three likely scenarios and expecting one to come close to the actual case, given the available information. Make sure to construct all the scenarios with specific destinations, intent and routes in mind.

These scenarios, make it possible to define scenario specific regions of probability. By definition, this also creates the smallest search area consistent with known facts, analytical analysis and missing person behavior. Then send clue conscious resources into specific locations to confirm or discount any speculation about the missing person's behavior or activities. Of course, the question about reliability of the resource detecting any clues in those areas always surfaces but objective track and clue awareness training covers that area well.

As stated several times previously, the four categories of clues *(evidence)* searchers need to look for include:

Physical or Events

- Footprints, sign, disturbances
- Discarded candy wrappers or other trash
- Articles of clothing, equipment, gear, etc.
- Flashing lights, shouts, smoke, cell phone call or radio transmission
- Whistle, mirror flash, flare, noise or loud sound

Recorded or Documented

- Summit logs, receipts, notes, letters
- Trail registers, permits, maps, guide books

People or Testimony

- Witnesses, relatives, friends, vendors
- Bystanders, companions, sales persons

Analytical

- Previous behavior, previous searches, deductive reasoning
- Distances from local or international data

Clues and/or Sign Offers:

- **Location and Elevation**
  - Coordinates/up or down
- **Time**
  - How long ago
- **Vector and Velocity**
  - Direction and how fast
- **Corroboration and Ownership**
  - Conclusively human or specific identity
- **Intent**
  - Activity, intentions or purpose
- **Character**
  - What is it

The key to an effective clue oriented search consists of trying to identify clues left by the missing person and constantly monitor the search area for changes. For instance, track traps as a tactic for confinement. Keep in mind, the complete absence of clues presents a clue as well.

Clues, like wisps of smoke, appear one moment and disappear the next: footprints blowing or washing away; witnesses leaving the search area; occasionally summit logs end up buried in the snow; searchers miss flashing lights. Search areas constantly changing create a volatile clue discovery environment. Some clues not generated by the missing person, but identified as such, add to the confusion. A set of footprints or even a series of disturbances in the search area offer several messages or signals, depending on who made them and their current location. If the missing person left them, then the evidence sends a message that:

- The missing person spent time in that location previously
- We possibly identify the missing person's intended destination derived from his/her direction of travel

Searching the Area and other Clue Sources

Dennis Kelly said it best in his book *Mountain Search for the Lost Victim*. "A search without the subject *(the ultimate clue)* is nonsense."

Normally, the Searchers and the overhead staff qualify as the best people to recognize and act upon clues. This begins by properly briefing and orienting experienced searchers and overhead staff to the differences between distractors and clues pertaining to the search.

Clues emerge in many places other than the field. Remember, the Command Post acts as the central repository of information for the entire search, where data gets analyzed on a regular basis, meaning close scrutiny of clue logs, communication call logs, debriefing sheets, maps, and interview notes.

In every search, staff needs to take positive steps to assure the subject never leaves the search area without detection. This also extends out to include any location where the availability of evidence or information reduce the certainty of the search effort. To clearly identify a clue, the staff needs a considerable amount of understanding and expertise to interpret its message. Sometimes in the urban environment this function creates a real nightmare due to the easy availability of transportation.

The IC needs to agree to an integrated attack on the problem, to properly act upon a clue and follow it to a logical end. Occasionally, prominent non-search area clues surface in the person's home, a friend's house, or even the local drinking establishment. Search efforts need to include these areas. Other noncontiguous search areas include the location of witnesses or other clues, such as an abandoned vehicle or one recently impounded. While unusual, once in a while crime causes a person to go missing or become lost. In this case, the missing person generates clues before someone reports them as missing, and consequently staff needs to backtrack if possible to a point where activities no longer pertain to the situation.

The Searchers and/or Overhead Staff

This particular element finds it necessary to depart from what transpired during search operations in the past. All staff members in the search effort including field resources and overhead staff require briefings oriented to clue detection and what to watch for in their respective jobs.

Develop **an overall strategy** to assure that staff take the appropriate action regarding clues wherever they turn up.

That last statement, *taking the appropriate action,* holds considerable significance. Search teams need to revise their training programs to teach searchers how to follow up on the detection of various common clues and to reach a logical conclusion. In the urban environment, due to the shear number of clues identified, managers need some logical protocol for reporting the specifics. The urban environment *(urban and suburban environments)* overflows with ambient trash, making sifting for the real clues very difficult. Therefore, a searcher needs to interpret the message before *acting upon* a detected clue, and although not easy or intuitive, try to address it in some sort of pre-planned protocol. The following functions help enhance a searchers interpretation:

- Immediately notify the CP of a suspected clue or signal received.
- Through group action, try to evaluate the clue or message in the field *(work together with other team members)*.
- Take action in consultation with the Team Leader, the Search Manager and the search planning section.

Fatigued searchers and overhead team members tend to miss relevant clues. Human nature will cause a searcher to lose concentration and miss the obvious when fatigued. Redundancy helps to combat the lack of concentration and improves detection by searchers and staff. However, long before reaching exhaustion, these people lose most of their effectiveness as clue detectors.

Experienced, well trained searchers recognize and act upon clues due to their extensive training.

- Know what clues to look for
- Strain out distractions from useful clues
- Define expectations in the field by briefing personnel on what the command staff expects them to see and not what searchers envision seeing

Timing and the Sequence of Events

To help reconstruct the scenario leading to the missing person incident, searchers need to time tag all clues and messages. Sometimes searcher's find clues in an order different from when the missing person laid them down. This procedure takes time but helps keep everything in perspective. Always document key times in a search, such as:

- What time the subject got lost or went missing
- Projected time frame for survival
- Time frame for the existence of clues (*Specific types of weather change the life expectancy of a clue*)
- What time resources deployed
- What time searchers found the clue or when the missing person left the clue
- The time frame in which searchers found clues

Ideally, a searcher needs to log their activities. Some Explorer Search and Rescue groups create information units who constantly keep track of logs, documentation, clues found and follow-up action for the IC.

Clue Seeking Using Timeline Analysis

The Search and Rescue Institute of New Zealand developed an interesting process in clue seeking. Drawing from law enforcement experience, this investigative process transforms information into intelligence using something called Analysis of Timelines. It systematically studies events, common times and correlations to come up with otherwise non-obvious clues.

Information versus Intelligence

Often raw information from any source comes in fragmentary, contradictory, unreliable, ambiguous, deceptive, or just plain wrong. Intelligence on the other hand usually gets collected, collated, evaluated/analyzed, interpreted and integrated into operational planning guidance. Actionable or usable intelligence emerges as the final product in an information gathering cycle, ready for delivery to the decision makers.

Timelines

Establishing and using timelines serves as an investigative tool and as a planning tool. It visually represents and compares events as they occur over a designated period. The goal centers on finding clues about event relationships, correlation of factors or influences that otherwise fade away.

Planners use two main types of timeline analysis:

- Linear – depicting one subject area over a known time frame and location

- Comparative – depicts two or more subject areas *(entities, events, weather, etc.)* which ostensibly occurred at the same time in that same location.

We study the timelines from a linear and calibrated perspective both independently and together to see how events, locations, terrain, weather, or any other factor impacts or influences the situation. Look at the weather in the area at the time. Potential storms with excessive rain (and corresponding rise in water levels), high winds and blowing snow, unplanned and unexpected route or travel plans, or even medical or accident difficulties that caused delays or deviations from a plan. These events or factors all help us paint a scenario *(The plausible story of what we think happened)*.

We first determine the initial intent as the situation started to unfold. Always use the same time scale throughout the comparison and evaluation process. Reference some details to logs, registers or other documents to keep it uncluttered. Denote periods of inactivity with bracketed gaps or spaces. When looking at the information, mentally interrogate the timeline: *"What does this sequence of events suggest?" "Do we know all the influences that may have been present and influencing this person?" "Did earlier events have any influence on what happened here?"*

Start the timelines analysis well before the incident began. Try to use separate lines to represent separate entities in the context of the situation and co-joined lines to represent commonality. Separating co-joined lines serves to emphasize a point or specific personality. Use graphics, maps, photos or diagrams, as well as colors to highlight entities or events

Signcutting/Investigation

Essentially two effective strategies exist for detecting clues generated by the missing person. The first, sign-cutting follows each and every step *(as much as possible)* made by the lost subject, while the second, called *Binary Search Technique* saves time and helps trackers function more efficiently. In the first case, a tracker, or track and clue aware searcher, stays with the line of sign, methodically following a step-by-step trail of clues, in the second, several other track and clue aware team members make a sweep out ahead to cut the projected track for sign. If the roving searchers find tracks or signs they think belong to the missing person, they then use a leap frog system which gains distance on the lost or missing person. While team members stay at the last known position *(or clue)*, others make sweeps through the probable search area trying to detect tracks or other evidence that someone passed through the area. The Binary Search Technique proves efficient with limited resources or in time critical situations. The Binary Search Technique:

- Rules out unlikely places. Making it easier to find someone.

- With time as a major factor, a **selective sampling** of clues **works better** than looking at each and every one.
- Searching the area's circumference takes less time/effort than searching the entire area itself.

> *"What you see depends mainly on what you look for."*
> -John Lubbock

Many search and rescue teams use sign-cutting extensively. Thus, eliminating vast portions of the search area from consideration *(at least primary consideration)*. This makes special training in sign-cutting well worth the effort. However, like all things, circumstances preclude the use of sign-cutting at times. In addition, since humans perform the sign-cutting redundancy avoids placing all chances for success in one resource.

Selective sampling usually benefits the search more than sampling every single clue. A famous bread crumb example illustrates this: A reports states that people last saw a subject eating sourdough french bread topped with sunflower seeds. At a strategic fork in the trail we check for crumbs. Surprisingly, searchers find both sunflower seeds and pretzel crumbs. Sign-cutting each fork separately they also find that the seeds went one way, and the pretzels went the other. Note that a trail of footprints or tracks act as a continuous signal from the subject in many cases, making the use of selective sampling appropriate.

The effectiveness and efficiency of sign-cutting makes it a better choice than grid searching. Close order grid searching an area requires numerous man-hours while sign-cutting only needs significantly fewer man-hours to produce the same results. However, some conditions necessitate using grid searching, such as: a search area covered with a foot of snow since the subject went missing.

Always search for clues <u>and</u> the subject, because:

- More clues exist than subjects
- Clue detection reduces uncertainty in the search effort

The worth and level of information some clues possesses approach the level of finding the subject. In other words, the clue represents the next best thing to actually finding the missing person.

Guidelines for Gathering Clue Information

Make sure to gather and collate information relating to the following items:

- Category of Subject
- Point Last Seen *(PLS)*, and/or Last Known Position *(LKP)*
- Circumstance of Loss
- Physical Condition, Health and Personality
- Equipment
- Track identification
- Terrain Analysis

Did you ever run out the door or leave on a trip and notice you forgot something? What made you remember you left something behind? In general, to discover the missing item, a person needs to mentally go backward through his/her activities or down a list in a step-by-step fashion. Applying this to search makes organization very important, and as things begin to unfold staff needs to write everything down to help keep track. Small notes or even single words about the accuracy or potential of a clue helps if the operation continues for an extended period of time.

As the first sketchy information comes in, the process starts. Eventually, everything gets organized in chronological order. Since first reports contain limited information, a search begins with clues from limited topics. Calls reporting someone missing generally end quickly and produce one or two pieces of evidence such as the sex and activity of the subject (*male hiker, or a elderly mushroom picker etc.*). Clues from a local or international database often provide the responsible organization a start.

Information Categories

The following list of information provides many hidden clues. Each category presents a series of questions or points helpful in the search manager's quest for pertinent facts:

Category of Subject (*ISRID database*)

- Examples: Child, Dementia, Hunter etc.
- Reflex tasks for the category drive the initial search actions.

Detectability

Examples:

The male hunter - likely wearing bright colored clothes, and dressed moderately well for weather. Elderly female mushroom picker - statistically harder to detect, and dressed for a fair weather activity, which means less prepared for a change in the weather.

Survivability

In any type of weather, the susceptibility of an elderly berry picker out weighs the male hunter.

Initial clues like this help determine the priority of the situation, and the appropriate type of first response from one incident to another.

Initial Planning Point, Point Last Seen (PLS), and/or Last Known Position (LKP)

- Determine the exact location for each
- Recreate the scene
- Keep the Initial Planning Point constant, but update the Points Last Seen and Last Known Positions as witnesses and clues give evidence of the subject's movement
- Pinpoint the locations on a map
- Physically go to the spots and study them for signs of aging and/or environmental impact

Note the importance of **Last Known Position** *(LKP)*. As stated and emphasized several times earlier, searchers find clues, but not always in the same order as the subject laid them down. Search efforts depend on the discovery of clues and interpreting them correctly to then recreate what happened. Traditionally, searchers reference the LKP as any of the following:

- The last clue found
- The most recent indication of the missing person's position
- A possible indicator for direction of travel
- A datum which moves every time searchers discover another clue

In the initial response period when teams find a clue *(a track, a discarded item, a piece of gear on the trail, etc.)* and designate the Last Known Position, they base it on known information for that item, at that time in the search effort. But, some assumptions exist here with regard to timing. Upon discovering another clue, teams conclusively determine that the subject laid down the second clue before the first one, and the LKP never changes. As the search effort ensues and teams find other clues, they need to make every effort to ascertain a relationship in time to the first one discovered. At this point, the interpretation of clues plays a vital role. In fact, sometimes it involves other staff members not actually on-scene at the time teams discovered the clue.

Make sure to accurately nail down the *Point Last Seen* or *Last Known Position* in *the field* in order to establish an *Initial Planning Point* for data analysis. The Initial planning Point:

- Provides the base point for determining distances traveled.
- It provides a Starting point for surveying an area for clues such as tracks, confusion factors on trail, shortcuts, of other likely spots.
- It also indicates a possible return location for the missing person. Which in turn establishes a logical location for the IPP.

Circumstance of Loss. Recreate the circumstances and the location to the best of your ability by placing the missing person:

- At a known location
- En route to a particular destination
- In a rural, wilderness or inaccessible location

Investigate the IPP with detail in mind. The witnesses and others in the area add accuracy to <u>when</u> and <u>where</u> the subject went missing *(or was never there, as this is just as valuable)*. In the preliminary stages of a search, the reported missing person falls within one of the following categories:

Missing from a known location

A known location such as a picnic area, home, car, etc. This information frequently involves children and elderly people. Many times, the subject wandered off, unnoticed, in some direction, making it difficult to limit the search area. Under this classification, try to keep the scene secured to allow visual trackers or tracking dogs to work on direction of travel.

En route

En route refers to a grouping where the subject traveled *(a trail, ridge, logging road, etc.)* to a known destination. Subjects who get lost enroute to the destination tend to experience confusion due to poor maps, poorly marked or maintained trails, intersections, etc. When returning from these locations a fatigued subject chooses shortcuts or pursues straight line routes or wanders off marked trails. Information of this nature leads staff to send people into the field with training on how to look for these types of clues.

Wilderness or Rural

Generally composed of hunters and pickers involved in activities that take them off main trails or paths. This subject frequently becomes preoccupied with their activities and fails to pay attention to changing terrain, weather or the location of rest of their party. Once again, staff needs searchers trained to seek these clues by *placing themselves in the subject's shoes* and filling in the grey areas concerning circumstances of the incident.

For complete documentation of the search, always get the timing of the events up to and after the incident, including all aspects of the weather then and now. Pay special attention to key points such as:

- **How involved was subject in preparing for the trip?** Questions of this type equip staff with insight into the subjects personality or underlying factors. *(Such as anxiousness, or ready to go, go go!)*.
- **Ask witnesses to replay the events where they happened.** This helps in pin pointing the time and location they last saw the subject. Also work with other people in the area to *balance* the accuracy of information. For example, if possible, talk with everyone on the trail or in the area, at the time.
- **Try to identify as accurately as possible, exactly when and where the witnesses and initial responders went to look for the subject.** This helps in assessing the subjects actions when they went missing and shortly thereafter.

Example: The entire family shouted for Grandpa in the vicinity where he picked mushrooms. Judging from his doctors report, no health conditions existed. So, conceivably grandpa stayed in the immediate area and never responded to the family shouting for him, but more likely, he wandered farther away. When searchers found him 1.5 miles away, resting under a shady tree, it proved responders reacted appropriately to a subtle clue.

- **Ask about the weather as it occurred that day.** Basic knowledge of the weather conditions helps determine whether it affected the missing person or not. Effects of climate change include: Impaired vision from fog or low clouds *(nighttime)*, impaired judgment - hypo/hyperthermia, exertion from deep snow or slippery side hills.

Physical Condition and Health

- General capabilities *(from two or more sources)*
- Based on relatives or friend's assessment or third subject party

- State of health and condition at time of loss
- Diabetic
- Alcoholic
- Drug user
- Medications - effects and how often taken
- Heart problems

Gather this information in two parts. One, make sure to find out how the subject felt on this particular trip. A detailed description goes a lot further when looking for clues than just a brief answer like *she/he felt pretty good*. Test it by asking exactly what the missing subject ate, or look for other clues that possibly indicate whether the subject functioned above or below their norm that day. Secondly, get a feel for the usual day to day conditioning of the subject.

For example: when an elderly subject went missing, searchers thought for sure the terrain stopped her from traveling out of the immediate area. However, opinions changed when the family mentioned she recently purchased a new bicycle for herself!

Get answers from at least two sources to compare accuracy. Preferably, one person outside the family such as a friend or fellow coworker. More often than not, this requires bringing someone to the search area for an interview. If possible, try to remember some of the following when questioning people:

- Many witnesses fail to recognize signs of fatigue, hypothermia or inadequate calories.
- Family tends to unintentionally withhold information about physical or mental problems.
  - Reluctant to mention dementia
  - Reluctant to mention mental illness *(depression or even mental disability)*

Interview family members separately. Watch for uneasiness as they try to avoid referring to a *problem*. Reassure them that answering their questions to the best of their ability helps find their loved one. Family doctors also offer a lot of insight into the subject's health. In any case, remember that desperate family members constantly under or over emphasize a missing person's mental or health problems.

- Over emphasis: heart attack, stroke, arthritis
- Under emphasis: dementia or mental health

Personality
- Aggressive
- Ponderer
- Loner
- Self-sufficient
- Upset easily or irritable
- Despondent

Once again, make sure to gather information from several sources, such as hunting partners, co-workers, initial witnesses or family members. Keep in mind, not all the sources reside at the search site. Never wait to seek these individuals out after plans fail.

1	2	3
Independent	Aggressive	Dependent
Persevering	Anxious	Reserved
Realistic	Neglectful	Composed

From these three simple groupings, which type most likely over exerts or takes chances? Which one possesses the best chance of surviving in poor conditions? Which type seeks shelter? Which one most likely keeps moving? Choose the most high risk? High priority?

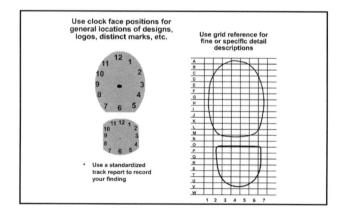

Figure 21-1 Track ID Form

Equipment

- Size
- Color
- Brand names
- Extra gear
- Shoe size and description
- Candy, cigarettes, etc. with labels and variety

When getting descriptions of the subject's equipment and clothing try to assess their capability or expertise at their activity. Think about predicting the risk level between two hunters, one wearing rubber boots and blue jeans while the other wears a pack, boots with felt liners and wool pants. Obviously the hunter with pack, boots and felt liners knows more about prepping for the conditions. An accurate list of the missing persons equipment, clothes and colors helps searchers tune their eyes for finding a particular article and frequently becomes an important clue. Thus, creating a major shift in search planning. Failing to compile a detailed list costs searchers valuable clues and prolongs the search efforts even more.

Track Identification

Again, the cost of ignoring a possible track, or identifying the wrong track effects the overall search tremendously.

- If available **use a catalog of prints**. *(Available through Foster and Freeman, USA Sales Office telephone: 888-445-5048 or email to usoffice@ fosterfreeman.com).*

- **Go to town and pick out an identical pair of boots or shoes.** The time used in acquiring this pales in comparison to the time spent on the wrong track.
- **Accept no ball park figures on the size of a track found in the field.** Carry a small tape measure or if necessary, break a small stick to the size of the track you found.
- **Preserve the initial track(s)**.

Terrain Analysis

Always look for terrain clues in two parts. First, take into consideration how the terrain affects the subject into becoming lost. Never accept that the person went missing from the last known point, and randomly start looking some distance away for distinguishing features. Place yourself in the subject's shoes, visualize the subject's situation and visualize where they ended up as a result. Consider some of the following:

- Maze-areas, riddled with so many intersections the subject most likely made a wrong turn. Make sure to accurately map the area.
- Confusion factors such as multiple routes, forks in trails, dead ends, terrain features the subject failed to recognize that divert them a short distance their plan. Look for any sights or sounds that attracted the subject. Potential shortcuts or switch backs. Also, any hard to find trails or trail parts due to of lack of use.
- Cut off the escape routes *(confinement)*.
- Look for routes of least resistance.
- Plan for all possibilities, not just your favorite.
- Consider the shortest distance for them to disappear.

Second, look at how the terrain affected the subjects route of travel. Certainly some searches present difficulty in determining the likely routes of travel but, assuming the subject went in a particular direction makes assessing the terrain possible. This also applies to any likely routes from the last known position. If you suspect a particular direction of travel, look for terrain lures that affect continuation along that route.

The following factors limit Search areas:

- **Major barriers such as rivers, highways, cliffs, some trails, slippery banks, lava fields, railroads.** All of these features tend to stop the subject's direction of travel and quite frequently lead to a new direction *(i.e., walking along a powerline)*.
- **Minor barriers include small streams, dense**

brush, downfall. These types of barriers make passing them easy if a subject really wants to cross them for some reason.
- **Natural routes offer less resistance to movement and sometimes confine a victim** *(e.g. large steep drainage)*. These include old road grades, game trails, and drainages, or clearings.

> **NOTE:** Establish definitions in your unit for words similar in nature, i.e., borders, boundaries, and barriers.

- **Look for areas that allow the missing person to continuously move forward without main roads or barriers cutting them off.**

SAR units wishing to practice on terrain analysis need to work with maps of varying topography for the sake of identifying, labeling, and discussing how terrain features possibly effect the missing subjects route of travel.

Critique of the Mission

Critiquing the Mission provides rich information as well as any overlooked clues.

- How well the overall search went
- Anything initially overlooked
- Functions the searchers performed correctly and functions that went totally wrong

If catalogued and noted appropriately, this information helps on nearly every future mission. If not for strategy or tactics, then for planning or visa versa. Include everyone if possible, even the subject.

Summary

- Search depends on clue detection so search for clues and the subject(s).
- Four categories of clues: physical and events, recorded, people, analytical.
- Everybody involved in a search effort needs to focus on clue detection. This includes both the searchers in the field and the overhead staff.

- Assemble a complete profile on the missing person.
  - Investigators continuously seek clues, even beyond finding the missing person.
  - Although sign-cutting provides searchers with an effective field search tactic. Everybody needs to interpret clues.
  - If searchers know where the subject never went, then finding them just got a whole lot easier.
  - Always place time frames with clues when trying to discover what actually happened.

SEARCH BASE ALWAYS NEEDS A TEAM READY TO RESPOND or FOLLOW-UP ON A *HOT* CLUE.

Briefing and Debriefing 22

Objectives:

- List the important elements and process of a good briefing.

- Construct and present a comprehensive briefing.

- Relate and discuss the importance of *priming* to searcher effectiveness in the field.

- List and discuss the types of information and data needed in the debrief.

- List the important elements and overall strategy for conducting debriefings.

- Relate how to incorporate debriefing details into the next operational period strategies, tactics and objectives.

The Purpose of Briefings and Debriefings

Taking the time to brief personnel provides them with a short, concise summary of the most important points about some event, effort or activity that brings together all of the pertinent instructions or information about that endeavor. On a search, briefings also provide oncoming shift personnel a summary of all efforts expended from the outset to the present. This helps to orient the new staff members to the environmental, safety, strategic, and tactical factors of the search.

In every search effort the searchers need to learn the distinction between targets and distractions for the new environment *(see Chapter 19)*. A briefing conducted to search resources leaving for the field always contains several key components. The briefer acts as the catalyst to bridge the gap between previous targets and distractions and those present for this search. The briefing sets the stage for searcher expectations and clear target images.

Staff briefings implement objectives for the upcoming operational period and the overall strategy used to accomplish those objectives. In the context of the stated strategies, briefings outline tactical assignments necessary to get the job done. SAR units need this as a standard for any basic search briefing and debriefing. This chapter provides detailed information on each of these subjects.

Debriefing creates a conduit through which members review accomplishments, observations, tasks and shortfalls and compare them to operational period objectives and the overall Search Action Plan. Data and information collected through the debriefing process directly affects the strategy and tactics used in the next operational period. In essence, debriefings consist of both interviews and interrogation of field search units, with the intent of gaining a thorough understanding of everything search crews encountered.

Briefing and debriefing takes place either verbally, in writing or a combination of the two. Unfortunately this depends on the size and complexity of the search, and not from the standpoint that written briefing and debriefing statements, task assignments and other written documents reduce confusion and improve communication. Written briefing statements help ensure that personnel record important items.

Part I - Briefing

The Importance of Briefing

Briefings give us the direction, instructions, and orientation to performing any action in the search effort. Poor or incomplete briefings tend to result in poor implementation of assignments, terrain not searched, loss or destruction of clues, and ultimately, missed opportunities to locate the missing person.

Functional Areas that Briefings need to Cover During a Search:

- Search situation status to date
- Subject Profile detail related to searching such as medications, and intentions
- Objectives - By Operational Period
- Strategy - Effort Emphasis and Alternatives
- Tactical assignments - Specific to Terrain and resource
- Safety - Hazards in the Area and Injured Searcher Protocols
- Media, family, friends, or medical authority protocols
- Clothing, possessions, or other incidentals the missing person carried
- Expected terrain, vegetation and weather related visual impacts to searching
- Examples of visual cues to look for, and techniques of visual searching
- Debriefing instructions with information guidelines, locations for check in and what to expect

Who Needs a Briefing in Person?

Difficulty in briefing and debriefing personnel arises when staff changes or moves into another aspect of the search effort. Especially in cases involving hundreds or even thousands of searchers. ICS advocates a ratio of supervisor to working staff of 5 to 1 *(five staff for every one supervisor)*. The collection and dissemination of information at the field searcher level needs to come from a designated staff member(s) in the system. Making sure a system like this works depends on collecting information at specific levels then collating and distributing it based on specific protocols.

Who Coordinates Briefings?

Just prior to shift change each general and command staff position briefs their own replacement. The ICS doctrine states that Operations brief/debrief field teams. In larger searches, a specific individual in the Operations Section performs this function. That person obtains information from the Task Assignment Form and briefs all Field Team Leaders with a complete list of expectations along with all other relevant information. As field teams return from the operational period assignment, the Briefer/Debriefer interviews Team Leaders and gathers any pertinent information from their search efforts.

Who Briefs and Who Gets Briefed?

Someone in the organization needs to brief all personnel involved in the search. An effective search operation requires that every authorized responder remains in the communication network. Information provided to responders ranges from general knowledge to *need-to-know*.

Operations:

- Primarily briefs and debriefs field tasks
- Debriefing information tends to immediately effect tactical decisions

Plans:

- Plans prepares Incident Status briefings for staff, Responsible Agent *(sheriff, police chief, etc.)*, and the media

Information Flow Looks Roughly Like This

- The outgoing IC briefs the incoming IC at shift change
- The IC briefs the Responsible Agent during every shift
- Operations briefs Team Leaders on every assignment and debriefs at the conclusion of every Operational Period
- The media gets briefed at scheduled conference times by either the IC or the Responsible Agent
- Family members usually get briefed on a regular or scheduled basis by the IC or the Family Liaison Officer
- Field Team Leaders brief team members every shift assignment and debrief with them at the conclusion of every operations period

> *"The degree of one's emotion varies inversely with one's knowledge of the facts... THE LESS YOU KNOW, THE HOTTER YOU GET!"*
> — Bertrand Russell

Where Briefings Take Place

Conduct briefings in a designated area, with plenty of space, shelter, quietness, and no interruptions. Necessity dictates using the Command Post *(or in front of it)* for both convenience and timing. Separate, controllable and pre-scheduled locations make it easier to closely monitor attendance *(In urban or suburban areas, this helps to screen the media, and provide isolation from general public onlookers or family members).*

When Briefings Take Place

Team leaders need to conduct, briefings just prior to the team leaving for their search area.

Try to brief non field searchers and overhead staff, after teams move out to the search area and activity dies down a little, or when the overhead teams change shifts.

Briefing Time-Limits:

- Maintain or improve morale of personnel
- Maintain management credibility in the eyes of subordinates
- Ensure timely response to the field and maximum time for task accomplishments
- Keep briefings to a maximum of 30 minutes

KEEP IT SHORT, FACT FILLED, AND TO THE POINT!

The Search Action Plan, *(SAP or IAP)* if properly prepared, serves as a ready-made briefing statement *(see Chapter 16)*.

Field Team Leaders Briefings Need to Contain:

- Situation status, objectives, strategies and predictions
- Mission organization chart *(Who's in charge of what)*.
- Subject information - Includes any information about the subject that aids the searcher in recognizing the subject, finding clues, or determining the subject's behavior, such as:

  - Complete physical description
  - Clothing and equipment *(clothing carried, worn, clothing underneath, R_d procedure)*
  - Physical condition
  - Mental condition
  - Behavioral traits
  - Circumstances causing the search

- Vital Concerns - Medical/Health Problems?
- Medicine or treatment the subject may be in need of, or is incapable or providing to themselves.

Keep Briefings Simple and Uncomplicated

Clue Considerations:

- Sole pattern of footwear
- Items the subject carried on them at the time of disappearance, that they dropped left behind
- How to report clues
- Instructions on logging clue locations and times found
- How to protect clue locations for follow-up

Priming Searchers

- Face searchers away from the briefer
- Place assorted clues on the ground - hat, shirt, rucksack, glove, jacket, etc.
- Make searchers detect them by walking around a small area. Ensure they view them from different perspectives
- When placing objects on the ground, alter them from the canonical perspective

Remind searchers that the characteristics of objects sought affects POD. These include:

- Size
- Color

- Contrast with the background or environment
- Degree of movement
- Ability to make noise
- Mental perspective in the searcher's mind *(What the searcher expects to see? The briefer needs to program or plant mental images in the searcher's mind)*.

Tactical assignments with explicit searching instructions for Teams and Team Leaders:

- Specific area, where to start, and how to get there
- Configurations and instructions on when to report
- **NEVER** imply an expected POD, brief R_d procedures
- Marking procedures
- Adjacent teams *(who will work next to specific teams)*
- Have other teams searched the area, and if so, when *(Implications for trackers and dog teams)*
- When to start, when to stop, and any extenuating circumstances
- Make sure to note speeds for specific areas with assigned segment terrain
- What steps to take if searchers find the subject - alive, injured, or dead and instructions on protecting the scene
- Emphasize medical plan, rescue/evacuation plan

Remember to always tell Team Leaders the specific objectives, exactly where and when. To avoid deficiencies and gaps in the search plan implementation.

- Subject's trip plans *(including Likely Spots)* Likely spots hold of conceptual significance to Search Managers, and of practical importance to every member of the field search teams. Therefore Search Managers need to understand the concept and importance of likely spots and decision points when briefing teams, try to include a short discussion on likely spots and decision points. Always remind search team leaders of the likely spots and decision points concepts and tell them to:
- Look for them
- Mark them on their maps
- Investigate them whenever possible
- Discuss them at the debriefing session
- Terrain, hazards, safety considerations and risk mitigation in assigned search areas. E.g. helicopters, terrain hazards, snakes, coyote traps, other hazards for dogs, or other pertinent local safety considerations.
- Current *(and predicted)* weather in assigned areas
- Equipment searchers need including:
  - Clothing
  - Safety equipment
  - Food and water
  - Recording equipment
  - Specialized equipment
  - Others...
- Communication details - designators, use of codes, frequencies, etc.
- Reporting details: When to report in and where
- Transportation details
- How long teams spend out in the field
- The names of the subject's relatives or close associates and their location
- Media procedures - their location, the media liaison, and any instructions if searchers come into contact with them
- Debriefing instructions - where the debriefing takes place and when, who to report to, what type of information the debriefer needs and in what format
- If possible, try to give an estimated time of shift changes
- Procedures if team member get injured, need evacuation or any other assistance

Briefings for Overhead Team Members Contain:

- Specific information needed by each to perform his/her functions
- Mission organization chart *(who's in charge of what)*
- Situation status, predictions, and R_d findings for Effective Sweep Width calculations
- Subject information - Any information that helps Overhead Team members discover clues, missing person behavior correlations, or data indicating

the subject's whereabouts such as:
- Complete physical description
- Clothing and equipment *(clothing carried, worn, all layers)*
- Physical condition
- Normal activity routine
- Special activity preferences
- Mental condition
- Personality traits
- Circumstances causing or leading up to the search

- Overall strategy, and potential scenarios driving them.
- Operational period objectives.
- Media procedures - their location, the media liaison, and any instructions if the Overhead Team comes into contact with them.
- The names of the subject's relatives or close associates and their location *(Possible designation of liaison for family & friends)*.
- Communication details - call designators, codes, frequencies.
- Clue Documentation:

  - Items carried by subject that they dropped or left behind
  - Instructions on logging clue locations, times found and follow-up actions *(Map and log designation)*
  - Operational period time lines - shift changes, planning meetings, debriefings

Briefing Techniques to Improve Personnel Communications

- Distribute written briefing statements if possible.
- Outline task assignments with diagrams, maps, photos, or sketches.
- Provide a recent photo of the missing person if possible.
- Provide a sketch of the individual's sole pattern if available with a grid for identification.
- Provide a reproduced map showing assigned areas and searching details.

The search base requires photocopying or printing capability. Reliable information for all personnel to constantly refer to, drastically reduces mistakes and omissions.

Part II, Debriefing

The Purpose of Debriefing

The overall design of the debriefing process, preserves the observations and impressions of field units for both documentation and future strategy justification. Debriefing also works as a mechanism for consolidating and verifying information in the overhead team management structure and the scenario analysis process.

SAR units depend on thorough and complete information, to avoid unrealistic, misdirected, and inadequate planning in the future.

Who Coordinates the Debriefing?

The Operations Section conducts and coordinates debriefing. Normally the same person who conducted the briefings for assignments coordinates or literally conducts the debriefing.

Who Receives a Debriefing?

All personnel need an opportunity for debriefing.

- Overhead personnel debrief at the oncoming shift briefing.
- Field personnel receive debriefs in several ways:

  - In small incidents, debrief all personnel as they return to the search base.
  - In larger operations, debrief only team leaders after they debrief their team members.
  - In large, complex operations, division supervisors/branch directors tend to debrief the plans officer after debriefing their own personnel.

Smaller search operations, require individual debriefs if possible to reduce *joint opinion*, and instead focus on *individual beliefs and impressions to avoid one searcher who sees something the others miss.*

Timing the Debriefing

Due to the fact that people talk to each other about observation, opinions, and difficulties in the field, the debriefing of field teams needs to take place as soon as they come out of the field. Like it or not, casual conversations influence a searchers feedback, and thus changes the quality of information coming back from the field. Therefore, gather facts immediately while searchers still posses fresh information from the field, and before searchers or crew members talk with other search resources.

What Type of Information a Debriefer Needs to Obtain

As a minimum, debriefers need to collect the following information from the search teams:

- Explicit routes and/or coverage that the team ACTUALLY carried out.
- Specific information about efforts expended in the segment terrain. Including a detailed description of the Average Range of Detection testing by the crews when they arrived or carried out after the initial measurements.
- Approximate speed of the search effort.
- Consistency of the search effort speed.
- Confidence in segment boundaries and coverage
- Any extenuating circumstance while searching, that affected the probability of detection:
    - Steep, slick, heavily vegetated, uneven terrain, obstacles.
    - Bad weather conditions - fog, sleet, snow, rain.
- The location of any clues found, regardless of how insignificant.
- Search difficulties or gaps in coverage encountered. (*i.e. What parts of the assigned segment the searchers never properly searched and why?*)
- Hazards in the area.
- Problems encountered with communications.
- Suggestions, ideas, recommendations for future searching efforts.

Most importantly, a debriefer needs to gather exact information from the area covered, speed, spacing, gaps and how effectively personnel canvased the segment. The use of sketches, diagrams and maps in plotting this information adds even more value to the overall report.

Record the Debriefing Process in Writing or on Tape

- Written information reduces misinformation, misinterpretation, and confusion.
- Written information documents activities and becomes part of the incident record.
- See Example Debriefing Checklist at the end of this chapter.
- Consider using individual maps if appropriate.
- Taping debriefing interviews and transcribing them later, insures access to what searchers actually said and provides a good method of documentation.

Effective Debriefing:

- Leaves no stone un-turned
- Occurs in a timely manner
- Focuses on individual belief
- Involves getting everything in writing
- Includes recommendations

EXAMPLE DEBRIEFING REPORTS

Note: Use this "checklist" to develop a Debriefing Report Form or debriefing process after assignments have been completed and searchers return from the field. *(Develop a similar form and process for the overhead team.)*

☐ Unit Name: _____ ☐ Date Prepared: _____ ☐ Time Prepared: _____

☐ Field Team Leader Name: _____

☐ Member(s), *(Names - provide all team member names):* _____
_____
_____

☐ Operational Period: _____ Time Shift Began: _____ Ended: _____

☐ Debriefer's Name: _____

☐ Segment, track or trail searched *(or other assignment)*: _____
_____

☐ Explain what you did during your assignment and estimate Track Line Length and R_d for Coverage:
_____
_____
_____

☐ Describe extent to which objectives were, or were not met: _____
_____

                                                                 Consistency of Speed

☐ Speed of searching effort: Slow - *(.5 mph.)* _____   _____
                                        Normal *(1 mph.)* _____   _____
                                          Fast - *(1.5 mph.)* _____   _____

☐ Total time spent searching in segment: _____ Number of Team Members ___

☐ Calculated sweep width for team members based on R_d Procedure in segment: _____

☐ Area effectively swept during search effort: *(Combined Track Line Length × Corrected R_d)* _____

☐ Calculated coverage factor for segment: _____

☐ POD computed from coverage factor: _____

☐ Factors affecting POD *(e.g. terrain that is slick, steep, uneven, fatigue, weather, hazards, precipitation, re-searching same segment, etc.):* _____

Figure 22-1a

Managing The Inland Search Function - **Operational Response**

- ☐ Adjusted POD factor if necessary: _____

- ☐ Clues, indications, sign, alerts *(Specify Locations and Times)*: _____
_____
_____

- ☐ Areas of difficulty, hazards, voids, other intelligence: _____
_____

- ☐ Gaps or breaks in coverage where objectives were not met: _____
_____

- ☐ Condition of team members, morale, injuries, problems with equipment or gear: _____
_____

- ☐ What do the team leader/members think happened? Ideas on where subject is: _____
_____

- ☐ Communications problems or suggestions: *(areas of bad reception or no communication)* ____
_____

- ☐ Ideas, suggestions, recommendations: _____
_____

Attach This Report To:
- → Team Assignment Sheet.
- → Segment map with Coverage.
- → Clues logs or maps.
- → Footprint transparencies.
- → Accident form if appropriate.

Figure 22-1b

Figure 22-1c
TASK ASSIGNMENT

Team Number / Call Sign	Mission Number	Operational Period	Date
Team # 6 - Charlie Zee,ro, Six	WA - 14 - 128	3rd Op Period	04/04/2016

Type of Team		Name (Team Leader First)	Resource Name (TL, Comm, Navigator)	Skill / Equipment
☐ Area ☐ ATV ☐ Communications ☒ Confinement ☐ Dog ☐ Fixed Wing ☐ Grid/Line ☒ Hasty ☐ Helicopter ☐ Horse ☐ Litter ☐ Snowmobile ☐ Technical Rope ☒ Tracking ☐ Vehicle	1	Paul Beckley	Team Leader	Track/Clue Aware - Med Kit - Pyrotechnics
	2	Skip Barlow	Communications	Track & Clue Aware - Radio - GPS
	3	Tim Andrew	Team Searcher	Track/Clue Aware - EMT - Emerg. Shelter
	4	Roger Jones	Team Searcher	Track/Clue Aware - EMT Med Kit - GPS
	5			
	6			
	7			
	8			

Assignment Date	Estimated Departure Time	Actual Departure Time	Estimated Time in Segment
04/04/2016	07:00	07:20	6 hours
Radio Frequency	**Briefed by**		**Reviewed by**
VHF - 155.160	Scott Bradley		Ops - Green

Sketch Map of Assignment

Track traps & confinement, for lake basin area including access & departure routes
Lakes
Lake
Main Trail Access
Maintained trails
Cross country shortcut
Cross country lake access route, not maintained trail
IPP
Trailhead Parking Lot
Single lake access trail
Access Road

Briefing Summary
☒ Overview
☒ Org. Chart
☒ Time Frame
☒ Communication
☒ Check-in Plan
☒ Maps / Datum
☒ Safety
☒ Terrain
☒ Weather
☒ Pickup Time
☒ Tactics
☒ Subject Info
☒ Lost Person Stats
☒ Condition Code
☒ Clues /Search Images
☒ Rescue Plan
☒ Family / Media
☒ R_d Procedure

Assignment and /or Location in the Field:

Team 06 assigned to the high lake basin for hasty search, confinement and to establish track traps. This basin is on the extreme eastern edge of the search area. There are no recognized, maintained trails in the basin so make sure that all avenues of least resistance are checked, appropriately marked and track traps designated.

ICS 204 — Template from New Mexico State SAR Program — Page 1 of 2

Managing The Inland Search Function - **Operational Response**

Figure 22-1d
DEBRIEFING

Team Number / Call Sign	Mission Number	Operational Period	Debriefed by
Team # 6 - Charlie Zee,ro, Six	WA - 14 - 128	Op Period - 3	Green - Operations
	Date Returned	**Time Returned**	**Actual Time in Segment**
	04/04/2016	14:00	4 hrs - 15 min

Explain What the Team Actually Did

All four team members of Team #6 (Charlie 06) accessed the lake basin via the main trail. Two team members took the south basin and agreed to cover the three lakes located in the south portion of the basin. That included going all the way down to Single Lake from the basin. The other two members covered the northwest corner of the basin and swept through the three lakes situated there. All camp sites and shorelines checked. Track traps were established at all main access points and marked for follow-on inspection. Sound signals with voice and whistles were made at key points with a minimum of 3 minute listening periods for each site.

Assignment Was: [X] Completed   [ ] Not Completed   Percentage of Completion: 100 %

Rd value established at start 45 ft.
High (Medium) Low visibility target
Trackline length covered 22,440 ft
Area Effectively Swept 1,615,680 sq ft
Coverage .37   Correction: 1.6
POD from this sortie in segment 28 %

Describe the Location of Any Clues Discovered
Entrance to the basin - there are a number of good camp sites. Not searched very thoroughly. Several composite prints were collected from several sites and are now being combined to compare with subjects known boot prints.

Current Status of These Clues
Composite print patterns now being combined and compared with subjects known boot prints.

Describe Difficulties or Gaps in Coverage
The trails between lakes in the basin are make-shift, and are not established and maintained. It is evident that there were numerous routes with easy lines of least resistance between some lakes which means that hikers could go a number of routes from one lake to another.

Describe Any Hazards in Search Area
Lots of very steep terrain, cliffs and large granite boulders where a slip or misstep could result in a fall with injury. Climbing shoes or good grip soles on boots are essential.

Suggestions, Ideas, Recommendations for Future Searches in Same Area
Suggest that another team go back in and spend more time between the lakes as there are numerous hazardous locations and multiple routes to choose from.

ICS 204   Template from New Mexico State SAR Program

Searching in the Urban Environment   23

Objectives:

- List the primary differences between managing a search in an urban setting as opposed to one in a rural or wilderness setting.

- Describe detailed strategies and tactics particularly successful in urban or mixed urban/rural interface areas.

- List the most important initial actions and identify key search locations identified in a suspected case of abduction.

Many thanks to Chris Young of the Contra Costa County Sheriff's SAR Team *(California)* for his contributions to this chapter and tireless dedication to Search and Rescue. For more information on Urban Search refer to Chris's book on the Subject titled *Urban Search: Managing Missing Person Searches in the Urban Environment*, dbS productions, 2007.

The Urban Environment Defined

Most people lack a clear understanding of the term urban, especially in the context of a missing or lost person incident. On one end of the spectrum, picture a pure urban environment, such as the high rise buildings which create man-made canyons in New York City or San Francisco for instance and, on the other hand, a pure wilderness area in Alaska or the Rocky Mountains. The term suburban means anything from densely populated areas adjacent to an inner city, to the urban/rural interface or transition zone, to the transient populations of public campgrounds in our National Parks. For the purposes of this chapter the term urban describes urban/suburban areas set apart from rural/wilderness areas.

Most urban/suburban areas contain a mix of rural/wilderness type terrain, such as heavy trees or forest, steep hills, rocky terrain near fast moving water, and even some open grassland. Consequently, even the most obvious urban areas need searchers with wilderness management and field skills. Searchers without the skills necessary to transition between these environment types comfortably or safely cause more harm than good.

As law enforcement communities discover the usefulness of SAR resources in urban environments, search and rescue teams find themselves conducting an increasing number of searches in these areas. SAR teams around the US continue to increase urban search training and advertise their capabilities in response to an increased need for trained resources operating in this type of environment.

SAR teams encounter major problems when adapting typical wilderness strategy and tactics to urban search incidents, which in turn, lead to a less than effective effort. These issues include things such as: SAR personnel and dogs working in heavy traffic; searching in and around residences; searching through homeless encampments; and the necessity for a police presence in some areas.

Defining the search area also presents unique issues in the urban environment. The wilderness model of drawing a statistical circle around a chunk of real estate and then dividing it up into manageable sectors never works. The complex mix of terrain features found in urban areas gives rise to a new standard. For example, a child wanders away from a suburban housing development. Search teams need to develop a list of the most logical places to look first. The immediate neighborhood? Consider what borders the neighborhood: a park, an industrial complex, major thoroughfares, an airport or other urban features.

Searching an entire city or even a significant portion of it presents challenges too. Information produced by the investigation and the subsequent profile and scenarios determines the search area almost entirely. Perhaps resulting in writing search assignments made up of small focused areas widely scattered around the city or narrow corridors, and seldom in one contiguous area. This often complicates the planning and documentation of the operation, and creates an even bigger challenge for the Planning Section.

With a multitude of established paths of travel and landmarks, most people never consider that someone got lost. Certainly, an adult suffering from Alzheimer's (*dementia*) or the young child without developed cognitive mapping skills may think they are lost. However, always manage the urban search effort as if the subject went missing and focus the investigation on why the person went missing.

Many searchers find it tough to understand that an elderly person with Alzheimer's tends to wander for miles, going TOTALLY unnoticed by the local populace. A person walking around with only socks on never even raises an eyebrow in an environment where people work hard at tuning OUT their surroundings. Consequently, the notion that "If he went in there, someone for sure noticed him" just doesn't hold water. Searchers need to learn new tactics and new ways of gathering information for success in this environment.

Problems of Concern

Searchers need to learn how to navigate through the complexities of a clue rich urban environment. In the wilderness, searching usually involves looking for one subject in a large open environment. In the forest, a team finds a child with very little information. In the middle of the city though, teams need a lot more information to successfully search for a missing child. Searchers need very specific and detailed information to pick the subject out of the crowd.

In addition to the natural places to conceal a person, SAR units also need to consider the massiveness of man-made hiding places. Searching these areas includes: checking out every crawl space, thoroughly investigating every pipe or culvert, opening every door and searching every room. All of which takes an enormous amount of time and effort.

The urban environment includes a lot of unsafe areas, especially at night. In missing person cases, responsibility lies on the law enforcement agencies with the jurisdiction to act. Involve them from the beginning in all search operations and provide escort when required (*see Searcher Safety*). Unfortunately, one negative effect of mixing SAR team members with law enforcement involves *mistaking* SAR team members for law enforcement and search dogs as drug dogs. This tends to make interviewing more difficult, even if the missing person comes from the neighborhood. Currently, the inherent mistrust of police officers in many inner city areas presents even more obstacles for SAR teams to overcome.

The Preplan

In addition to a better understanding of the urban environment, SAR preplans need more information in the urban environment, in particular, the *vulnerability assessment*. Units need to make the following additions to these documents for urban searches:

Included in the Preplan

- Lists and locations of city open spaces and parks
- Lists and locations of city, town and adjacent walking and cycle trails
- Location and detail of retirement communities, assisted living, skilled nursing homes and other health care facilities
- Location and detail of boarding and care facilities, including shelters and halfway houses
- Location and detail of day care centers *(both child and adult)*
- Lists of local transit terminals and routes
- Mapping of high crime areas
- Hazardous and high risk areas such as industrial complexes or manufacturing facilities
- Attraction areas for subjects of all ages *(e.g. kiddy rides, community centers, skateboard parks, sports areas, lakes and parks)*

Map Management

Search teams use topographical maps for search operations every day. However, topo maps in the urban setting often prove less than adequate and lack accuracy. With most of the details blocked out by the housing commission and the rapid changes due to construction and development, units need to turn to other types of maps to augment the topo maps. Other useful maps include plat (*assessor*) maps, standard roads/streets maps from various published sources, utility/infrastructure service area plans, police and fire districts, aerial photographs and internet maps like Google ™. Utilizing Air Support, particularly during the initial response phase, provides aerial photographs and gives a current update on topography of the search area. Aircraft provide a vital role in urban search even when not used more extensively as an observation platform.

Rapid improvement of computer map programs utilizing the latest in Graphic Interface Programs (*GIS*) easily update at the most municipality's data servers. Good city street map programs tend to show street and feature names, block numbers, grid references for correlating GPS's and topo maps and a host of other features. Some include a draw program used as an overlay for maps during the task planning and task documentation phases. Always try to tag locations of interest with date, time, item of interest and other information. Print everything and make it part of the permanent case file. Computer generated maps still need a ground check though.

As a first step, units getting ready to deploy, need to obtain an area survey and update all available maps. In an area where locations get referenced by street addresses, information such as address ranges and block numbers become more important rather than latitude and longitude or UTM Grid references.

Managing the Urban Incident

Urban SAR requires as much, if not more, discipline than searching in wilderness areas. Searchers tend to experience a large of amount sensory overload during these types of operations. Normally, teams look for clues in areas just off a country lane, but an urban team deals with literally tons of ambient trash. Clue management in an urban search quickly becomes a nightmare without an accurate subject profile as a means of culling through everything found. As always, the law enforcement agency in charge deals with investigation and the investigative section of SAR management teams assists in this effort combing through an overwhelming number of clues needing research.

Searchers tend to find difficulty in adapting rural search thinking to the urban environment. Every possible hiding place, hazard and cubbyhole needs a search, all of which untrained personnel cannot perform. Units struggle at getting the trained searcher to pick through a homeless encampment, and find it even harder, if not impossible to get the average citizen to search through one. Sometimes homeowners tend to not comply with a request for them to check their own property. If necessary, request permission for trained searchers to thoroughly check a home owner's property, including unlocking storage buildings, opening crawl spaces, garages or even vehicles.

Building the Subject Profile

For many years, teams used *The Lost Person Questionnaire* or the *Missing Person Report* in various forms as a primary tool in developing the subject profile. As the search community puts more emphasis on missing instead of lost, the types of information needed to build a usable profile changes. A searcher considers the brand of ice axe useful when looking for the missing climber, but the Alzheimer patient in suburbia more than likely never carries anything this exact with them.

Searchers need to thoroughly develop the following types of information:

Intent – The missing person's intent? What's on their mind? What are they trying to get to? What are they trying to get away from? Did they leave a note? Do they have a journal or diary? Are they on Facebook?

Mobility - Can they walk? Do they have access to a vehicle, bicycle or do they know how to use public transportation *(Alzheimer's Type Dementia – Older Children)*?

Survivability – Do they have money, or a cell phone? – Do they know how to use them? Are they familiar with their surroundings? Can they call 911?

Ability to Respond – What is their ability to respond? Will they avoid responding because they are afraid of punishment? Do they have the mental capacity to respond? Do they have a nickname?

Password – Is there a password established? If so, what is it and who knows it?

Language – Is there a physical or language problem? What is the primary language?

Risk – Is the person a risk to themselves or to others?

Tracking Devices – Is the person enrolled in a safe return program or equipped with an electronic tracking device?

Computer – Does the person have access to a computer? With whom do they regularly communicate?

A complete profile needs a lot more information to predict the missing persons' behavior. Urban search focuses on why the person went missing, just as much as possible behaviors they exhibit while missing.

Strong Investigation

In general, investigation units usually fall within the Planning Section. However, the urban environment needs an increased number of personnel to accomplish all of the tasks required to perform a thorough job, which in turn, necessitates moving investigation into a single unit. Sifting through the flood of potential clues requires numerous trained personnel. Ideally, police investigators cooperate with the SAR management teams and share information. Always share information gathered by SAR teams with the police investigators, even if not reciprocated.

The agency in charge needs to issue a BOLO *(Be On the Lookout)*. Send it throughout the immediate area, especially neighboring jurisdictions. BOLOs typically go statewide and sometimes regional or national, depending on the nature of the case.

When the media covers the search and broadcasts subject information, sighting reports come from all over the city. To avoid every helpful citizen calling 911, establish a toll free number that comes into an adequately staffed call center, then brief the operators on how to document and route information.

From a tactical standpoint, door-to-door interviewing plays an important role in urban search (*See House to House Inquiries under Urban Tactics*). Brief teams on proper interview techniques and safety. Plan interview tasks for reasonable hours unless the urgency of the search dictates different hours. If it becomes necessary to carry out door to door interviewing late at night, delegate the task to police, or at least require an officer to accompany each SAR team member. Get an okay to physically search the property during the initial interview if possible.

Check all modes of public transportation, including those serving the area but not based there. Ask if the subject uses, or knows how to use, public transportation?

Information and Clue Management is Crucial to Urban Search

For effective search operations, try to include every authorized responder in the communications network *(information flow)*. Information on a search ranges from general knowledge, to absolutely need to know; so, without a serious preplanning effort in urban areas, this part of the operation quickly overwhelms most standard search staffing. Include or consider the following sources in information management:

• Investigation results and the report facts generated

- Dispatch reports and status of available normal and special resources
- Hot lines or Crime line information from the general public
- Personal data on the missing person from those with firsthand knowledge of the missing subject such as family, peers or friends
- Team debriefings about conditions and factors in the field
- Interview data, especially from unknowing witnesses *(those people who saw something but never realized the importance of it)*
- Clues and leads found within specific geographic locations
- Media reports, observations, film footage or interview information
- Technical manuals with lost or missing person data
- SAR Hazard Vulnerability Assessment terrain and ground cover analysis
- National Weather Service weather predictions
- Political pressure or inquiries

Often, individuals and/or agencies with little or no search training coordinate searches in urban areas. As a result, these endeavors marked by enthusiastic effort and good intentions, often result with a deceased missing person. More often than not, this results from jumping to conclusions, without good investigative information about the circumstances of the event, or assuming that individuals ultimately show up on their own.

Withholding crucial information and data never helps. Therefore, map out exactly where to route different types of information and/or communication. A complimentary diagram or map identifies exactly who gets briefed and by whom at what time during the operational period. Always ask yourself, "Am I accessing all the information needed about this situation?" Designate a specific person, sometimes referred to as the Clue Meister, as the advocate for clues. The Clue Meister reviews every clue from physical to investigative, to team debriefings, and catalogues them all, assuring their relevancy. Most importantly, the Clue Meister exploits the clues that need follow up, making sure not to lose opportunities to resolve the incident.

Using the Media

Expect the media to arrive in force with at least one representative for each station or paper. If not controlled, the search base quickly evolves into a forest of satellite and antenna towers. In high profile cases, the media interest creates a frenzy, especially when the incident involves a child. The media almost always asks SAR team members to give on-camera interviews, especially team leaders and overhead staff. Establish media protocols early on with the responsible agency and brief teams accordingly.

Sometimes, using press releases to get the word out to the public results in a double edged sword. It gets the information about the subject on the street, but it also creates a flood of citizen clue reports ranging from "I think I found his sock?" to "I just saw him get on a bus heading towards the city center!" Always keep essential personnel handy to react on these reports. Note that one research study shows that media intervention, assisted in 31% of all cases, hindered 6%, despite contrary belief, and never even effected 63% of the cases.

Note: Remember, as an effective strategy, to hold back certain information for test/lie verification *(withholding something crucial in the description to sort out the genuine clues from extraneous information).*

Institution Check

Check area hospitals or medical facilities. A John Doe admitted with injuries or a mental problem provides a meaningful clue. Also contact local jails, shelters, alcohol or drug detoxification and rehab centers. Sometimes crisis phone lines or emergency migrant worker housing sites produce results.

Multiple Tasks Still Required

With an area as complex as the urban environment, multiple tasks through a given area become even more important. Searchers easily miss things in a rural environment but, the distractions in the city make missing a clue inevitable. An alert operations section notices these gaps and holes in areas searched, and takes the necessary precautions to plug them as soon as possible. Very detailed debriefings also become more important.

Searcher Safety

As mentioned before, teams face very hazardous searching conditions in the urban setting, and with all incidents, safety always ranks as a number one priority. Local police know which areas to search only in daylight. Never hesitate to request a police escort for any task. Common sense things like never sending people alone on tasks, and always providing radio contact with your teams lessens the possibility falling prey to one of the city's hazards. Thoroughly brief teams on both the assigned task and the possible dangers. Manpower requirements for police escort functions influences the number of teams called out as well as the number deployed. Base the number of callouts and on the number of police personnel available for escort.

Detailed Documentation

To identify *(and plug)* shortfalls or holes in a search effort, management in any response effort needs to use chronological documentation. Organized documentation, insures that teams adequately searched an area. Often, even the smallest geographical areas require numerous complex tasks. The potential flood of information generated by the searches and the media requires immediate processing. All of which eventually gets processed by the Documentation Unit in the Planning Section. Always view every bit of information as potential evidence. Sometimes, urban missing person cases turn into criminal cases, requiring all of the units mission data in court. To create case files necessary to back up testimony in court months or even years after a search, managers appoint personnel to the Documentation Unit.

Containment...In the City?

Yes, the possibility of containment in the city exists. Stakeouts (*park-ins*) at intersections and non-police road patrols provide good containment. While still possible for an evasive subject to slip through the net, it requires conscious effort and intent. Driving containment assignments offers an ideal function for family members and untrained volunteers who undoubtedly want to assist. Watch out, they tend to lack discipline and attention to detail.

Strategically placing a minimum of two people at opposite diagonal corners of a building, conceivably contains an entire building. Two additional people on the roof at the adjacent corners, completely contains a building or possibly a whole city block.

Additional checking of public businesses as well as private residential security cameras provides a

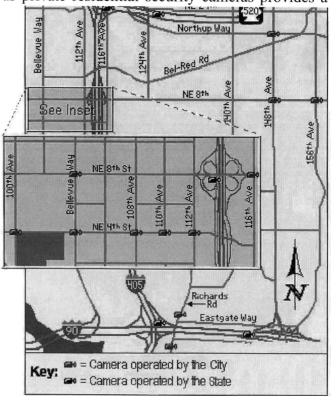

Figure 23-1 Hundreds of cities throughout the world have now installed video cameras to monitor streets, malls, train and bus stations, airports, parks, office buildings and schools. They are an excellent source that can be used for surveillance, documentation and evidence.

form of containment, and even more importantly, a direction of travel if the video camera captured the missing person *(See Figure 23-1 previous page)*.

Mandate Thoroughness

Thoroughly saturating a ¼ mile *(300 meters)* area around the Initial Planning Point *(IPP)* represents a good rule of thumb in managing an urban missing person incident. Make this mandatory, and always brief teams on your expectations. Rapid sweep tasks tend to overlook things such as; locating a child sleeping under the bed. Therefore, search EVERYWHERE! Literally leave no stone unturned (*see Reflex Tasking Chapter 14*).

Urban search stresses the need for a thorough search more than using anything that relates to a number. Urban teams find POD values based on sweep widths for a complex urban area not very user friendly, and almost impossible to evaluate numerically. For example, how do you assign a POD to posting flyers and conducting random interviews in a neighborhood? In addition, if the search potentially consists of a mobile dementia patient, then teams find it necessary to search and re-search the same area frequently. Bottom Line: Applied Search Theory in the urban environment needs further study!

Complex Areas Require Smaller Tasks

In a rural environment teams conduct sweep tasks on 80 to 100 acres *(40 hectares)* and take about 4-6 hours to complete, but adequately searching a similar sized area in the urban environment with the same number of resources takes several days. Therefore, the urban environment calls for smaller tasks due to more complex areas. Small search/interview teams searching block by block prove more efficient.

Welfare and Safety of Searchers and Resources

Useful Equipment

Urban searchers often face a variety of search challenges. Some requiring the use of work gloves and even facemasks with some sort of deodorant. Looking through trash whether in a home, out on the street or in a homeless encampment rates as one of the most distasteful search problems of all. Especially searching one of these on a hot summer day; but, someone needs to get the job done. Very high risks come with this type of task. Coming up with your hand impaled by a needle recently discarded by the local junkie produces disastrous consequences. Some police departments search suspects with puncture resistant gloves for this very reason. **Check on their availability!**

Team Briefings and Debriefings

Brief teams and resources thoroughly, giving them enough information about the missing subject in order to identify the missing subject or to determine ways in which to act when particular situations arise. Provide personnel with the autonomy to make decisions in the field, but make sure to give them enough information to effectively make these decisions.

Team leaders debrief their teams before reporting to base debriefing. Always double check and make sure teams documented all tasks as well as possible, noting any discrepancies or holes in the assigned tasks.

Urban Search Tactics

Both police and fire service Special Operations tactics provide many of the techniques outlined in this chapter. In most cases, the only real difference in tactics surfaces when searchers try to find someone unfamiliar with that particular location and the subject possibly needs assistance to stay alive in it.

Neighborhood Canvassing or Door to Door Interviews

Neighborhood canvass means checking by police or trained volunteers, around the area of the missing person's last known location and/or the person's known intended destination. It also means conducting interviews in the vicinity of any site deemed important to the incident investigation. The purpose of this effort encompasses locating facts or observations about the circumstances of the incident and typically involves door to door interviews.

Typical assignments include:

Level I: Household interview along with a property & yard *(garden)* search by SAR and a request for an interior search by residents. Searchers believe the subject not only resides on the property, but perhaps in the house or outbuildings

Level II: Household interview with a request of the resident to search their own property and yard. There is little reason to believe the subject would be inside a structure and the subject most likely could be sighted if in the confines of a back yard or garden.

Level III: Resident not home. Searchers put a flyer on each door with a description of the missing person and a request that the resident search their property and back yard.

Essential for follow-up:

NOTE: Each search takes as much as 15-20 minutes per house depending on whether searchers conduct a Level I, II, or III assignment. If each team uses 2 to 3 searchers and they spend 15 to 20 minutes per residence property, a small cul-de-sac with 16 separate homes takes approximately 5 hours and 20 minutes to effectively cover. This makes theses tasks very labor intensive, time consuming and more importantly, **require lots of resources.**

Additional Planning and Management Considerations:

- Action is time limited – For the most part, perform during daylight hours
- Action requires interpersonal skills by those searching and interviewing
- Give very specific briefing information to those conducting this action
- Responders *(searchers)* in 2 to 3 person teams *(Safety man, interviewer and note takers)*.
- Rehearse questions before starting the process. If possible, prepare statements and information in writing to ensure consistency.
- Alert search team members to look for anything out of the ordinary when approaching a house.
- Always make an escape plan, e.g. dogs wait behind doors or some criminals conduct business at the residence.
- Listen carefully before knocking.
- Knock hard *(no doorbell and no knocking with a flashlight)*.
- Stand far enough away to encourage the resident to come out.
- Never enter a house, even if invited.
- Always give minimum amounts of information about the incident or missing person.
- Watch for people who eagerly help or provide loads of information and note them for further investigation. If they provide good information, find out how to re-contact them later.
- Always consider: What was normal about the encounter and what was not?
- Remember searchers look for that unknowing witness who possibly saw something but never realized the importance of it.
- Ask about any normal routines in the neighborhood. Like the guy across the street getting package deliveries all day. Talk to the delivery person as a potential unknown witness.
- Look for people in the neighborhood with a recorded security camera system.
- Always act polite and thank people for their time.

Respect Property

Due to the exigent circumstance (*some circumstance requiring immediate action and extreme urgency by law enforcement*) of a search for a missing person, some searches need to take place in and around private property. Never come across as cavalier about private property. Homeowners get very sensitive about people intruding on their property.

As discussed in Chapter 4, always obtain permission to enter a property. If possible, try asking law enforcement officers in uniform, particularly at night, to accomplish this task. If SAR volunteers need to search the property alone, make sure each one carries proper identification and again obtains permission. If denied access to property, document the homeowner's name, the address, the time and report this to search base.

A better solution: try to provide each interview/search team with a uniformed officer. This lends credibility to these strange folks poking around the neighborhood and asking lots of questions. Sometimes, just the presence of a police car visible in the area helps. Note also that trespassing laws vary from state to state within the U.S. and other countries. Each searcher needs to know and understand applicable laws in the jurisdiction. Folks who live in some parts of the country sometimes shoot first and ask questions later (*See Chapter 4 on Legal Issues for trespass discussions*).

Single Story Building Search

Searching a single story building occurs the same as a multistory building except, after containing the building externally, teams start at one end and search systematically toward the other. Move containment to hall intersections as the teams go through, this helps in keeping the subject from slipping through your line. Once completed, the building remains secured or external containment stays in place.

Search each room twice in opposite directions to avoid missing anything and to maximize detection opportunities. Things look different in one direction then in the opposite direction.

Open and check every locked area, then re-lock them. Ask the building superintendent with a master key to accompany the team. Never assume that a currently locked door was also locked earlier, and never ask the building staff to search their own building with available SAR teams on site.

Multi-Story Building Search

Tactics learned from police and firemen involve a floor-by-floor detailed search with moving containment. Start by containing the outside of the building. Ideally, keep people within sight of every exit, but two individuals at opposite corners works adequately for most buildings. Place one person at every elevator, remaining there to prevent the missing person from using the elevator to move about from floor to floor. Finally, position one searcher at the top of every stairwell to cut that route of travel off. Starting from the top down, search each floor thoroughly and completely (*remember to look in attic or roof access entry ways and/or utility accesses*). Upon completion of each floor, the containment moves down one floor and repeats the process until they get to the basement floor.

After thoroughly searching the entire building, lock it down or leave the external containment in place, before moving to the next building. This type of search requires a systematic approach. Open and search every door, locker, ceiling space and utility access. If possible, ask for a building floor plan, and then make sure searchers systematically go through each room checking it off the list. However, in the absence of floor plans, another systematic approach involves using nonpermanent marking devices, such as flagging tape on door knobs or chalk marks on doors. To insure no one entered or departed a room after searchers checked it, place a strip of masking tape across the edge of the door and door frame. Write the date, time and searcher's initials on the tape.

Attractive Nuisances

In certain subject categories, one asks the question: "What things tend to attract this individual?" Some of these likely attractions include: malls, stores of one kind or another, churches, community centers, amusement parks, bright lights for autistics etc. Each of these attractions creates a special draw. The local grocery or convenience store offers things such as video games or products of particular interest. For children, think about culverts, ditches, canals, creeks, construction sites or avenues of little resistance like utility easements. On private property, focus on fenced backyards (*gardens*), abandoned cars, old refrigerators, out-buildings, sheds or woodpiles.

Resources:

SAR Dogs in the City

Scent discriminating trailing dogs work very effectively in the city. One primary factor, as in all other environments, includes proper training of the dogs! A good dog trails on almost any surface. The scent trail becomes disturbed much more quickly in heavily traveled areas so, application of this resource needs to occur as early as possible. Air contamination, especially vehicle exhaust adversely affects any dog. The dogs work most effectively at night when the temperature usually drops. Also, when a trailing dog follows a trail, and loses interest at a bus stop, the dog and handler easily leap frog to the next bus stop to attempt to reestablish the trail.

Search units find a lot of success in using air scent dogs as well. However, the air scent dogs work most effectively in areas with very few people. This includes parks, overgrown areas, vacant lots and warehouse buildings, back alleys and other places where the dog may detect a single person. Air scent dogs normally run off lead; so, urban areas present many risks for this type of dog. Handlers train their dogs and themselves to work on a long lead similar to that used by bloodhounds or trailing dogs.

Another technique involves using both types of dogs. A trailing dog leads to a garage or other large building and an air scent dog clears the inside.

Air Support (Primarily Helicopters)

Aircraft only provide marginal assistance in urban areas, but never overlook them. Helicopters help by looking into backyards to locate potential search sites like abandoned vehicles and outbuildings limited only by the amount of trees and foliage. Thermal image devices (*i.e. Forward Looking Infra Red, or FLIR*) work in parks, open spaces, yards or the actual location of the downed subject. However, when the subject moves around a lot, like in a large crowd, the FLIR loses effectiveness. Helicopters also act as an attraction device for potential witnesses.

Mantracking in the City

Usually, SAR units think of Mantrackers last when it comes to urban searching, but they offer a viable resource. Although concrete sidewalks never yield sign very easily; but, under certain conditions and knowing where to look, trackers sometimes find evidence that someone walked across the area. The biggest problem consists of tying nondescript sign to the subject rather than someone else just passing by.

In infrequently occupied buildings, if given the right lighting conditions, mantrackers detect the disturbance of the thin accumulated layer of dust by a passing foot. They also pick up on any transfer of dirt from the outside to the inside of a building. Due to the fragility of these clues, contamination and destruction occurs very easily. Therefore pay close attention to protecting the areas around the IPP to maintain an effective tracking capability.

Urban Logistics - SAR Base Considerations

Search operations often lack many basic amenities on their own, especially in the city. A relatively simple task, such as parking a car develops into a major headache for searchers, especially when only side street parking exists. Police usually assist with parking, but sometimes the lot they provide ends up blocks or even miles away. When this happens, the Logistics Section needs to allow for a shuttle bus and a secure place at the base for searchers to store their gear. Sleep and rest for searchers also creates additional problems. Staying in a vehicle or pitching a tent on the minuscule front lawn of a nursing home or convalescent center, present undesirable or even illegal alternatives depending on local laws. Local fire stations usually make some room and many police departments even spring for motel rooms *(using maximum occupancy)*.

The availability of restrooms also raises concerns. Often the city maintenance department brings out portable toilets *(maintaining them as well)*. Feeding everyone on a long protracted search requires bringing in food and drink in urban environments as much as in rural operations. Make arrangements through a local franchise, or through prior arrangements with mobile disaster food kitchens, like the Red Cross or Salvation Army.

Permanent municipal buildings or parks work for most search bases. Although schools and churches work, scheduled activities tend to cause conflicts. Elevated multistory parking centers or lots provide another functional and secure environment for base operations. Readily controlled access to the upper floors makes these structures ideal SAR bases. Most of the time these structures come with toilet facilities close by or within. The top floor makes an ideal helicopter pad, and an excellent sight to secure team gear, vehicles or specialized equipment in otherwise non-accessible locations. In addition, these structures provide covered areas for sleeping, crew rest or even setting up a chow hall *(See Figure 23-2 below)*.

Communication problems also crop up in the urban environment. If using civilian SAR personnel, check that their radios operate within the inner city canyons. If not, check to see if protocol allows the local law enforcement agency to issue SAR members police radios. Sometimes the situation makes cell phones an absolute necessity. As always, brief team members that the media likely listens to everything, including, in some cases, cell phones.

Abduction

According to national statistics in the U.S. 85% of all missing persons reported involve children and 0.01% of all children who go missing, end up in an abduction-murder by strangers. This also equates to less than ½ of 1% of all homicides and less than 5% of all children homicides. The rarity of occurrence contributes to the limited experience and lack of realistic preparation. Unfortunately, when a child goes missing the parents and law enforcement think abduction, but before law enforcement implements abduction protocols they need to rule out the following possible scenarios:

- Child just late or distracted *(not in danger)*
- Miscommunication among adult guardians
- Lost child *(unaware they are lost)*
- Lost child *(attempting to self-rescue)*
- Child injured *(unable to self-rescue)*
- Runaway
- Family abduction *(witnessed or not witnessed)*
- Staged abduction to conceal emotional family homicide
- Stranger abduction *(witnesses or not witnessed)*

Once investigation and clues start pointing toward stranger abduction, then the incident shifts gears into criminal and abduction protocols without delay.

Published studies in the United States (*Missing Children Homicide Reports, State of Washington, Office of the Attorney General*) and the United Kingdom (*The CATCHEM Database*) tell a grim story:

In the great majority of child abduction murders, the victim knows the abductor *(family friends, neighbors, people that frequent the neighborhood)*.

40% to 68% of missing children are reported within 3 hours

Figure 23-2 Elevated parking structures make good choices for a search base in the Urban Environment

Of children murdered, from the time of abduction:

- 44% in first hour
- 74% within 3 hours
- 91% within 24 hours
- 99% within 7 days

The data reflects the need to react quickly and decisively. **SEARCH IS AN EMERGENCY.**

Although the law enforcement investigative function deals with the potential abduction of children, law enforcement often calls in other resources to aid in the search for a missing child. These circumstances usually involve a host of SAR resources from the local area. Searcher tasks involve searching the four sites involved in the incident:

- Initial Contact Site
- Abduction Site
- Murder Site
- Dump site
- Plus the Home/Room

Initial Contact Site

The initial contact site describes where the missing child and the abductor first made contact. Sometimes the abductor makes physical contact, but more likely they make visual contact, like watching the child playing in the local park. Contact usually occurs days or even weeks prior to the abduction. Studies show that in 80% of all cases, the Initial Contact Site occurs within ¼ mile of the victim's LKP *(Last Known Position)*. Additionally:

When searchers never find or document an initial contact site, the number of solved (*cleared*) cases drop 40% below the average rate of other solved cases.

58% of the time the solved cases fall within ¼ mile of the victim's residence.

The contact site also represents the site at which the greatest chance for a witness to observe the killer and victim together, and where the killer most likely exposes himself to observation by others.

Conclusion: Always try to find the initial contact site through interviews, use the media to generate leads, and search for clues within at least a ¼ mile of LKP.

Abduction Site

The abduction site consists of the point where the abductor actually took the child. Possibly witnessed by others or not. In 62% of all cases, abductor's use a blitz assault to subdue the victim. When the abduction happens so quickly the site lacks forensic cleanliness; the suspect possibly left some clues. The suspect sometimes uses ploys such as; "your mom sent me to get you" or lures "Want to see some puppies?" to get the victim close enough to grab and subdue, or to get the victim into a vehicle.

Conclusion: Always try to find the abduction site through interviews, use of the media to generate leads, and to search for physical evidence or that unknown witness.

Murder Site

In 72% of all cases, the murder site lies within 200 ft. of the final location of the body. Statistically a murderer only occupies the site for a short period of time; and, in only 15% of all cases the killer kept the body longer than necessary to dispose of it.

Conclusion: Searchers often find the dumpsite first, therefore try to conduct a thorough evidence search for at least 200 to 250 feet in every direction from the body location or any point where evidence turned up.

Body Dump Site

As noted, the killer not wanting to keep the body any longer than necessary, leads them to dispose of it quickly. Perpetrators normally select the dump site by ease of access (*porous area*) and concerns over someone detecting them during the act of hiding the body. 72% of all cases, locate the victims outside urban areas. Sometimes the perpetrator uses a pull off on a road seldom traveled during certain times of the day. They seldom base the site on the ability to conceal the body, they just use the site available at the time. In fact, in only 52% of the cases suspects made some effort to conceal the body. The suspect rarely takes time to dig a hole in which to bury a body.

Conclusion: Focus search planning on areas with easy access, not areas requiring effort to access. Consider the probable time of the concealment *(night or day)*. Start with roadways leading out of town.

Home/Room Site

Searchers only need to consider the home/room site as crucial if the suspect took the child from their residence in the course of the incident, but no matter, searchers still need to secure the location for possible evidence. Protocols include:

- Attempt to obtain samples of the victim's hair *(hairbrush, hooded clothing, hats, pillowcases)*.
- Attempt to obtain unwashed clothing for the victim for possible forensic evidence.
- If no known fingerprints of the victim exist, attempt to develop latent fingerprints *(prints not visible to the naked eye)* from items the victim handled.
- Obtain elimination fingerprints *(prints of people with legitimate access in order to eliminate the fingerprints that belong to those people)* from anyone known to have access to that area. This decreases the number of prints to search in the computer.
- Obtain an item containing odor of victim to serve as a canine scent article *(collected in the prescribed method to prevent contamination)*.

Conclusion: Seal the room off from access by everyone including the parents/guardian as soon as possible. Forbid any laundering of clothes or bedding to prevent loss of evidence.

Missing Child or Possible Abduction?

Aside from a witnessed abduction, first consider the standard list of missing child scenarios such as a distraction, miscommunication, runaway, etc. Then before committing resources and efforts on an abduction scenario review the following questions:

- Does the child know the area, or could they just be lost?
- Thorough and deliberate search of the area with no clues, leads or evidence.
- Clues, leads or evidence that suggest an abduction possibility.
- Thorough investigation yields no clues or rules out other scenarios.

DO NOT SWITCH TO ABDUCTION SEARCH STRATEGIES UNTIL TOTALLY RULING OUT THAT THE CHILD COULD BE LOST

Abduction Search Strategy

Once staff makes a decision and shifts search strategies, consider the following:

Initial procedures for possible abduction search Include:

- If not already done, set up and use an Incident Command System
- Video tape neighborhood
- Secure PLS and/or house as crime scene
- Coordination with law enforcement
- Conduct a more thorough missing person search
- The search area for an abduction search grows much larger in size than that of a lost person search; therefore, order sufficient resources (*mutual aid*)
- Use an abduction search profile to define the search area
- Use local law officers to assist in defining areas that meet the profile (*it's their beat – they know it best*)
- Search Profile *(to build strategy)*
- Map out locations of possible body disposal sites and crime scenes near a road. Focus on searching pullouts and parking areas in remote areas (*never park searchers in pullouts!*)
- **Note:** Few incidents occurred in professionally landscaped areas, parking lots, or fenced in land
- In 72% of all cases, searchers located the victims

outside urban areas, however, the suspect took them from urban areas
- Look for areas that offer concealment during time of abduction *(day vs. night)* think about what it looked like during the abduction

Abduction Search Tactics

Deploy ground and K-9 teams 100 to 300 feet from roadway pullouts adjacent to fields and vacant lots with the potential to conceal a body or crime scene Allocate as little effort as possible to searching trails, fields, or other areas away from drivable roads.

Give teams specific assignment such as:
- Search 300 foot perimeter around all pullouts along a country road *(again, never park in pullouts!)*.
- Use appropriate spacing for clues and victim based on vegetation, terrain, and the R_d procedure
- Use ground searchers to follow up dog teams

Pullout Search Tactic:

1st – Secure pull out
2nd – Cut for sign around perimeter
3rd – Send in the Cadaver dog *(protect dog from traffic)*
4th – Determine Average Range of Detection
5th – Grid search *(from back to front)*
6th – Document actions

Urban Search Guidelines:

Successful searching in the urban environment depends on a number of key factors:

When it comes to conducting searches for missing persons, the urban environment differs from rural terrain. Success, depends on a well-developed preplanning that addresses key issues like a good vulnerability assessment of the area, overwhelming numbers of clues and the difficulty of searching in and around private property.

- All SAR units need training in urban operations.
- When used appropriately, traditional SAR resources benefit operations greatly in the urban environment, but only with proper training and informed local law enforcement officials. Two very effective resources to use in the urban environment include, trailing dogs and mantrackers.
- All operations consider the Safety of searchers above anything else.
- Develop an accurate profile of the missing subject as quickly as possible.
- Meticulously investigate, interview, brief and debrief.
- Use investigative results and scenario analysis to prevent wasted effort.
- Increase overhead staff to appropriately handle clues and the follow up function in an urban search.
- Take advantage of all media outlets to gather useful information.
- Issue BOLOs early, especially to adjacent jurisdictions.
- Notify all public transportation systems, including those who serve the area, but base there operations elsewhere.
- Encourage the adoption of protocols that request trained resources early *(MOU for mutual aid)*.
- Train staff and usable resources to implement intensive investigation and door-to-door interviewing.

Suspending the Search   24

Objectives:

- List and discuss the key factors involved in deciding to suspend a search mission where searchers never found the missing person.

- Discuss the importance of family and friends involvement in the process of making a decision to suspend search operations.

- Describe the importance and interrelationships of these factors to the suspension decision process.

- Describe a limited, continuous search and the benefits this type of operation offer to the family, the public and the media.

The Decision

Immediately upon locating a missing person, search managers always suspend the search and initiate demobilization.

But, what happens when search teams never locate the missing person and the Search Manager *(IC)*, encounters serious pressure *(perhaps even self-generated)* to suspend the search?

> "The act of suspension is simple - a short message is broadcast over the radio net. But the process of arriving at that verdict is one of the hardest and most important decisions that the search manager will ever make."
> - Tim J. Setnicka
> *Wilderness Search and Rescue,* 1980.

At some time or another, a search manager faces the responsibility of suspending a mission without locating the subject *(see Mission Suspension Decision Process in Chapter 27 - Managing External Influences)!*

Try to answer the following questions before deciding to suspend a search:

- At this point are crews searching for a deceased or living person *(which is most likely)*?
- Did personnel search and research all the search segments and trails /roads.
- What are the chances the subject lived?
- What is your assessment of search area coverage, effort expended and success?
- Is searcher safety a paramount concern?
- What is the overall family political climate? Are there pressures from outside the operation and if so, what influence does this have on the operation?

Additional Factors to Evaluate in Considering Suspension of a Search

- Consider whether the evidence points to a conclusion that the subject left the search area
- Whether a thorough and effective execution of the search plan occurred
- The staff thoroughly researched and studied the survivability of the missing person
- Any unresolved or unanswered clues
- The depletion of search resources, which increase counter pressure to release searchers and their equipment, plus the availability of replacement resources
- Political and/or family counter pressure to continue or maintain the search
- Other SAR incidents occur *(simultaneously with the current efforts on the search)* and the other incident demands a higher priority *(response)*
- Current and forecasted weather
- Any serious equipment malfunctions, i.e., a radio repeater?
- The cost of a continued search effort.

Other factors to consider:

- Perhaps in analyzing the search data, relative to suspending or continuing the search, staff finds

poorly defined search areas in terms of planning data.
- Perhaps an assessment to continue or suspend combines these or other like factors *(Nothing significant in and of itself, but, when viewed collectively. . .).*

The Decision to Suspend a Search Usually Involves a Combination of Factors

Not all searches mirror one another. Therefore when staff makes the decision to suspend a search, they base it on the facts and efforts of that particular search effort.

A Consensus Technique

Use a group consensus technique as a vehicle in helping to *(as Search Manager)* make the final decision to, or not to, suspend the mission.

This technique requires each person on the overhead team to review all of the significant factors, assign his percentage of probability or value ranking *(scale 1 = low; 10 = high)* or, simply list for or against. As in the example outline in Chapter 18 on *Proportional Consensus*, make sure to maintain proportional relationships with the values *(e.g. a reference value of 10 and others proportionally valued at half, a third, a quarter, or some fraction of that reference value).*

Mission Suspension Decision Process

One of the most difficult and potentially controversial decisions made on a search, concerns suspension of the operation. Although the search manager ultimately makes this decision, successful implementation depends on the consensus of relatives, media, and interested political entities. Family holds the key to gaining this consensus and then the media and political entities generally follow their lead.

Use the penultimate meeting *(next to last)* as a collective forum and decision-making process to bring about a culmination to a search. Present all available information and facts along with a detailed list of any additional tasks not yet completed. Relatives begin to realize the reality of what happens when staff completes the list of tasks. If the IC makes the statement, "that in the absence of any significant new information, the search terminates at the conclusion of the next operational period", it involves the relatives in the process and adds a positive spin to this phase of an operation. The search continues for another operational period *(there's still hope)* while family eases into the realization that the search will eventually end.

Meeting to Suspend

The Plans Section Chief follows the IC by summarizing all information gathered to date. This

Example Suspension Factors:				
Factors	**For**	**Against**	**Rank**	**Decide**
1. No leads or clues	___	___	___	___
2. Weather	___	___	___	___
3. Unresolved Clues	___	___	___	___
4. Cost/expenditures	___	___	___	___
Make a decision <u>yes</u> or <u>no</u>. Then, before finalizing, consider one additional technique: *A limited continuous search*				

Figure 24-1 Suspension Worksheet

includes subject profile(s) investigative results, search efforts completed, areas searched, quantitative analysis *(cumulative PODs, shifting POAs, etc.).* In addition, clues found and how each received resolution, possible scenarios that caused the missing person(s) to get lost, safety concerns including exhaustion of searchers, predicted weather and hazards, and any other relevant information. The Plans Section Chief then opens the meeting for the presentation and discussion of possible future tasks. After identifying all tasks, an evaluation of each one takes place, and those considered reasonable and realistic by consensus get selected for future action. The IC then adjourns the meeting by thanking all the participants and assuring them that execution of the final tasks occur in a timely manner.

The Plans Section incorporates these select tasks into the incident action plan at the next scheduled planning meeting. Based on these plans, staff establishes time objectives, selects specific tactics, identifies resources needed, and develops a demobilization plan. Participation in this meeting mimics similar planning meetings held during the incident. Normally, attendance consists of the command, general staff, and other key personnel.

Limited Continuous Search - What/How?

Overflights: Scheduled over the search area on an intermittent or infrequent basis.

- **Detection of clues.** A modest search effort for any *new clues, (e.g. snow covered the ground during the initial search; i.e. personnel searches again when the snow melts).*
- **Signs.** Post signs at campgrounds, trail-heads or in urban neighborhoods to inform the public that a person went missing in the area.
- **Inform public and media.** Particularly people going into the search area *(during an impending hunting or camping season).*
- **Use the search area/segment(s) for training exercises.** Conduct further ground search technique training programs in the search area such as sweep width experiments or aircraft spotter training.

If you elect to use the limited continuous search technique versus suspending all efforts or terminating. Then the following occurs:

- A suspended *mission* -- but not the search
- Continue the search -- on a limited basis
- An *open* case still exists *(missing person)*

This concept helps because:

- When searchers find additional clues or new information, make staff available and ready to take additional action.
- Communicates to survivors/media that at the time, crews continue to search and not give up.
- Reminds the Search Manager, that his/her suspending of the mission necessitates gathering the additional information during demobilization. It provides a knowledge base, in case teams decide to reactivate the search in the future.

Point out the difference between mission suspension and termination.

Ideas and Techniques for a Final or Closeout Debriefing Session

Chapter 22 Briefing/Debriefing, identifies general debriefing techniques.

> The final closeout or debriefing sessions that the search manager *(IC)*, holds with each team leader and overhead team member constitutes the final opportunity to gather facts and suggestions needed to prepare for the search critique session.

Objective of the Debrief: Collect, record and exchange information on what happened during the search and assess effectiveness.

> REMEMBER: A Staff members limited time and fatigue, makes organization imperative.

Consider these criteria:

- Interview team leaders one at a time. Consider

using a tape recorder, secretary, or other note taking aids.
- Review the exact terrain covered, refer to maps, worksheets, logs.
- Review the percent of coverage and configurations. Number of sweeps?
- Identify any clues found during the search. By whom? Where?
- Discuss any hazards *(searcher)* observed. Safety?
- Give instructions on what needs doing now, including any assistance needed for the search critique. Give options such as appearing in person, perhaps writing up comments and submitting report on team's actions
- Discuss: Each leaders performance. Including the Search Manager and each team
- Discuss: Feedback. Too little, too late? Just right?
- Other operational concerns or events relative to the team
- Identify what personnel need to improve? Minimum standards? Physical fitness? Practice?

SUGGESTION: Either the Action Plan, or an annex to the Action Plan, needs to include the criteria for suspending a search. Formalize the process for arriving at a decision to suspend the mission *(see Mission Suspension Decisions Chapter 27 - Managing External Influences)*.

Summarize information obtained from debriefings. Evaluate new things you tried, trends, common problems. This information helps form an important base for the search critique.

Remember to keep records on all the information pertaining to your decision to, *(or not to)* suspend the mission.

Survivors

Just about the time a Search Manager and overhead team decide to suspend a search operation for a missing person, reflect on these incidents. In a previous iteration of this textbook, written by Ken Hill, these incidents represent extraordinary circumstances taken from the annals of search and rescue. While it would be ludicrous to expect things of a similar nature to occur on a regular basis, they do occur on occasion, and help maintain perspective when trying to make the decision to suspend search operations for a missing person.

Case #1:

In Nova Scotia, Canada, a young boy four years of age went missing after following a deer into the woods. Despite three days of intense searching by massive numbers of people, they failed to find any clues in the search effort. At the start of the fourth day the young boy wandered out of the woods and stopped a passing vehicle.

Case #2:

In the incredible hostile environment of a Florida swamp teeming with poisonous snakes and other dangerous creatures, an autistic ten year old boy went missing. Searchers found him on the fourth day of the search in good health and apparently none the worse for the experience.

Case #3:

While on camping trip in Plumas County, California, a ten year old boy went missing. For over a week searchers combed the area in cool weather. SAR units found him approximately one and an eighth miles from the campground. He survived the whole ordeal by burrowing into leaves for insulation and protection.

Case #4:

Two girls, aged thirteen and nine found themselves separated from their leader in the Amazon jungle when the adult died from malaria. Over a month later, the two wandered out of the jungle to safety.

Case #5:

After five days of searching for a forty eight year old hiker near Bishop, California, a rescue unit suspended the search effort. Two weeks later, the man made it to safety on his own accord.

Case #6:

In New Brunswick, Canada, a SAR unit found a sixty five year old man approximately 10 kilometers from his point last seen. Search crews worked this particular incident for five grueling days.

Case #7:

In the State of Virginia, after four days, search crews called off a search for an eighty year old mushroom picker. Searchers thought he went into some nearby water and drowned. Eventually, the older gentleman walked to safety after 39 days.

And finally, if someone still needs convincing that strange circumstances sometimes occur. . . .

Case #8:

In the mountains of Argentina, two children, ages six and four *(a brother and his younger sister)* got lost on an outing. Ultimately, searchers found them 95 kilometers away, where the two took shelter in an abandoned hut. The children's ordeal lasted three weeks.

Never underestimate a missing person! even after extraordinary circumstances, a search effort always includes looking for a survivor!

Why Searchers Never Found the Missing Subject

In the process of assessing an operation, that after days or even weeks turned up unsuccessful *(never located the missing person)*, searchers need to discuss and/or investigate possible reasons why the search efforts failed. Despite massive or extended search operations, searchers still sometimes fail to find the missing person. In the following list, by Ken Hill, he explains a few reasons why searchers fail to sometimes find the subject.

- Searchers neglect to look just outside of the designated search area. In other words, the person went just a little further than anticipated and the search effort stopped short of their position. A good example of this happened in Oregon to an elderly elk hunter. Search crews eventually found him deceased about 100 yards outside the search area on a ridge. Not looking beyond the designated area, commonly causes searchers to come up empty handed during initial search efforts.

- The missing person traveled into a segment or part of the search area previously searched by personnel and designated as thoroughly searched. Searchers often make the mistake of thinking that re-searching an area already searched once, or even twice, wastes time. Some subject categories such as *Alzheimer's Dementia* calls for going back and re-searching areas again and again in case the person remained in a mobile state.

- The missing person actively evades or hides from searchers. In the past, cases such as this, involved mentally retarded, suicidal adolescents or teens in conflict with their families or peers. For some reason, the Yosemite National Park area, reports a lot of cases like this.

- Searchers never found the missing person due to an inadvertent gap in the coverage. A central median *(or reservation)* of a four lane expressway concealed the body of a women for 3 years despite extensive searching less than 400 meters from where she went missing. Crews searched the roadway on both sides, but no one thought to assign a group to search the median.

- The missing person never went into the search area. In other words, someone filed a bogus or concocted report for a missing person. They set up the entire search to cover up an ulterior motive *(Start a new life, get away with a girl friend for the weekend, etc.)*. Keep in mind, hundreds of reasons exist as to why someone might want to create a situation like this.

- The missing person engaged in some type of criminal activity (*Drugs, abduction, abuse, custody, etc.*). This type of situation prevails mostly in urban and suburban areas. Although extremely rare, abductions happen to people of all ages. Custody battles over children, as well as *abuse* cases involving the elderly, precipitate some extraordinary circumstances.
- The area where searchers located the missing person never received a thorough search, or never got searched with the right resources. This happens when the subject ends up in extremely dense or impenetrable brush, some type of opening like a cave, cistern, or well, under water, inside a building, a car or other structure. Searchers ultimately found a young boy in Clovis New Mexico in the back of a station wagon parked in his parents driveway after two weeks of intensive searching in the community. The subject climbed into the spare tire compartment of the car and searchers only detected him by the foul odor coming from the station wagon.

These represent a few reasons for unsuccessful searches after a concerted effort. It is worth going back *(without pointing fingers)* and asking some additional questions when unusual circumstances prevail.

Documentation 25

Objectives:

- List and discuss the reasons for documenting the entire search effort.

- Describe the advantages and possible applications of good documentation and how teams find this information from one search useful in future operations.

- List and discuss the best methods for documenting a search.

To paraphrase Tim Setnicka in his classic work, *Wilderness Search and Rescue*:

> *There is no substitute for proper, accurate, and complete documentation. There is no question that accurate records which are in some kind of retrievable form will prove essential and to some "a Godsend" if legal complications materialize. A jurisdiction responsible for search can never collect too much information about a particular operation. Suffice to say that it is impossible to generate accurate records after the fact!*

Reasons for Documenting a Search Effort

- Assists with the ongoing planning efforts
- Allows for personnel shift changes without losing continuity
- Documentation makes disseminating accurate information to searchers possible
- Enables teams to reconstruct the entire search effort at a later time
- Critique purposes: What went right, OK, or wrong, and why?
- Aids in improving SAR Functions: Aspects that need work to update the pre-plan and increase effectiveness on future missions.
- Helps protect individuals and government agencies from litigation and liability.
- Documenting the search effort helps provide evidence in court.
- Aids in gathering data on subject behavior for future searches.

Proper record keeping proves what the teams accomplished.

Important Things to Document

Documentation begins with the initial reports and ends with the revision of the pre-plan and follow-up on problems identified.

Documentation happens continually, creating an unending process.

- Keep a chronological log of all significant events, decisions, communications, etc.
  - A unit's dispatchers and maps/records person needs to keep records current.
  - Consider using specialized information units or assigning several people just to keep records.

Other information units need to record:

- Team briefing and debriefing reports
- Maps
- Weather progress
- Details about clues
- All major strategy and tactics planning sessions
- Any injuries incurred by searchers
- Expenses
  - Any lost or damaged equipment
  - Rosters of personnel involved

- Mission Suspension:
  - Interview and keep record of subjects found alive *(videotape, or written transcription)*.
  - Document the rationale and process used to suspend a mission where searches never found the subject
  - Document the demobilization plan.

How to Document

The following techniques aid in producing detailed documents.

- Digital voice recorders
  - At meetings, briefings, debriefings, etc.
  - Voice activated recorders connected to radios or phones
- Stenographers
- Note takers and/or log keepers
- Key personnel carry small dictation units or apps on cell phones to record decisions, events, observations, thoughts that are otherwise often forgotten
- Portable electronics lap-top, tablets, cell phones etc.
- Digital photographs
- Contour map overlays
- GPS Coordinates
- Social media (*screen shots etc.*)
- Video Recordings

Recent initiatives to fight crime and potential criminal behavior gave rise to the installation of literally thousands of video cameras in urban areas around the world. Years ago, British police officials pioneered the approach against the IRA. Since then, hundreds of cities installed cameras to monitor streets, malls, train and bus stations, airports, parks, office buildings and schools. The cameras not only perform a surveillance function, but also give access to information for documentation purposes and evidence of activities in search areas.

> **Gathering too much information and discarding portions of it later works better than frantically trying to find accurate information in the future.**

Search Base Operations   26

Objectives:

- Identify the various types of search base facilities and explain their function.

- Discuss the importance of predetermined Command Post and search base sites.

- Relate important factors teams need to consider in selecting a search base site in both rural and urban locations.

Preplanning represents the single most important aspect of Search Base Management. Determining the location and layout of a search base and or Command Post ahead of time considerably improves efficiency.

The search base provides a central location which collectively coordinates all initial administration, decisions, support, staging, communications, planning and directions for a search effort. Although conceptually simple, a search base's structure, composition and location make it more complicated. Small operations normally run off the hood of a vehicle, or in the back of a recognized and well designed mobile command post. Local units respond and with everyone knowing their particular roles, the operation unfolds according to plan.

However, when the wheel comes off and a search grows into a major operation, simple and easy management goes away and complications set in. Many major search operations involve upwards of a thousand individuals, and efforts of this size need practiced management skills to successfully handle the load with any degree of efficiency. This type of search emphasizes the worst case scenario. If a unit needs to build a major search base operation, what physically defines the base and how it operates?

Types of Management Facilities and Coordination Points Normally Established on a Search

Search Base

This location provides the primary support and management activities. All management, equipment and personnel support operations take place at the search base. The base also houses the logistics section, which coordinates resources and supplies for the mission. Each search incident develops one and only one search base; and normally, it stays in one spot. If possible, include potential search base locations in the preplan. While a staging area provides a temporary support location, and sometimes ends up adjacent to or near the base, in the long run, staging works as a separate location and function (*see below*). Normally search base operations include the following designations:

- **Command Post:** Designated as the CP, the command post directs all incident operations. Only one command post functions for each search. In a unified command structure involving several agencies or jurisdictions, all responsible individuals co-locate at the command post. The command post also performs the planning function and typically includes the communications center.
- **Camps:** Camps provide a location for resources to offer better support to the search operations. Camps maintain certain essential support operations such as feeding, sleeping, and sanitation. Camps also perform minor maintenance and servicing of equipment.
- **Helibases:** Helibases provide locations in and around the search base to park, maintain and fuel the aircraft, load them with supplies, personnel, or equipment. Once established on a search, helibases rarely relocate.

Staging Areas

Staging areas provide a location which accommodates resources for short periods of time. The Operations Chief establishes the staging area to locate resources not immediately assigned to a task, but assuming a tasking will arrive shortly. A staging area consists of anywhere in which mobile equipment/resources temporarily park awaiting those assignments. Staging areas sometimes include temporary sanitation and fueling services as well as mobile kitchens or sack lunches for feeding personnel. Staging areas need the capability to move at a moments notice. The Operations Chief assigns a staging manager for each staging area. The Manager checks-in all incoming resources; dispatches resources at the request of the Operations Chief, and requests logistics section support necessary for resources located in the staging area.

Helispots

Helispots provide very temporary locations for helicopters to land, and operations tend to use them less than helibases; which helicopters land, take off, and in some cases deliver search resources or supplies.

Spike Camp

Spike Camps consist of small, temporary camps established in the search area, which services a specific segment or division of a search. Spike camps usually serve as a *mini-staging area* away from the base, or provide a specific tactical function, ie, A Wilderness Trail Block.

Guidelines for Establishing Search Bases

Proximity to Search Area: Always consider safety, sanitation, and travel time for search personnel.

Aesthetic Values: Consider the temporary and permanent effects on the area used.

Public Interference: Consider the proximity to concentrations of people, job seekers, curiosity seekers, etc.

Existing Facilities: Facilities in the area that either add value to the search effort or hinder the overall needs of personnel. e.g. Communications - Any other CB radio operators in the area? Sanitation - condemned outhouses? Shelter - an unsafe barn?

Use an Aerial Photo to Plan a Search Base Layout. Instead of letting things grow randomly.

Ownership of the Land: If the search takes place on private property; immediately secure permission to use the land by obtaining a written agreement and written release.

Communication: Consider any communications the dispatch office needs, within base operations (radio, telephone service), and in the actual search areas.

Ready Access: Consider how far personnel need to transport supplies, and transportation routes to the search area, supply sources, etc. Again, make sure to obtain permission to travel over private property.

Terrain: Take into account safety, and environmental limitations such as slope and vegetation.

Size and Character of the Search.

Expected Duration: Always project an initial forecast of total search time, but plan for additional expansion space, if necessary.

Dispersion of Searchers: Consider the use of spike camps.

Expected Manpower and Equipment Requirements.

Components of a Search Base:

- Command Post
- Staging Area for Personnel and Equipment
- Communication Center
- Transportation Depot
- Media/Medical/Family Areas
- Plans/Operations/Logistic Centers
- Heliport/Helibase Locations

Guidelines for Establishing Search Camps

Environmental Constraints: Look into any environmental constraints concerning the selected site and search area. Consult the multiple use plan, land use plan, or any other similar survey currently in use for the area.

Safety and Sanitation: Keep the welfare of search personnel in mind.

Adequate Space: Avoid congestion and disturbances to camp activities. Estimate the duration of the search, and allow for expansion.

Water Supply: Check to see if the site contains potable water any possible contaminants. If unsure, ask public health officials to check the water supply or make other water arrangements.

Shelter: Allow for shelter from the elements. Wind, sun, rain, snow, sleet, hail.

Security: Make sure to provide security for government and personal property.

Parking: Provide adequate parking for vehicles and heavy equipment. Keep them separate from supply depot areas to enhance security.

Fuel Storage and Vehicle Maintenance Area: Always post *no smoking* signs in these areas.

Supplies: Equip search camps with a facility for storage, and a supply depot. Provide for access and security.

Crew Assembly and Briefing Areas: Consider including a bulletin board and warming fires.

Sleeping Areas: Allow for a day and night search personnel and overhead team sleeping area.

Latrines: Consider separate facilities for women and men. Keep them at least 150 feet or more from a water source, 300 feet downwind from the kitchen area, and accessible to sleeping areas.

Washup and Showers

First-aid Stations

Kitchen: The kitchen location depends on how the kitchen plans to prepare and serve food.

Guidelines for Establishing the Command Post (CP)

Location: Always consider access, noise and security.

Accessibility: Sites need accessibility to searchers *(e.g., bulletin boards, resource status flyers)* but security from the media representatives and the general public.

Identification: Make sure to adequately identify the Command Post for all personnel with signs, colored tape, etc.

Facilities: Provide protection from the weather, lights for night missions and *Creature Comforts* for the Search Management Staff. Also consider the needs/space for the communications and planning staffs.

Guidelines for Establishing Helibases

Accessibility: Consider arrival and departure of both aircraft <u>and</u> fuel vehicles. Never allow aircraft to fly over the search base.

Security: Due to the hazardous conditions of Helibases; make sure and block off the area to searchers, the general public or media representatives unless approved by the Search Manager.

Location: Consider aircraft flight paths, engine noise control, proximity to food and sleep facilities and control of dust and debris when locating a Helibase. Make sure and provide accessibility by ground vehicle, and never place them near the Command Post, feeding and sleeping areas or communication center aerials.

Guidelines for Establishing Staging Areas

Location: Locate staging areas according to response time. Keep in mind resources need to respond for assignment within a very short time period.

Facilities: Although temporary in nature, consider placing facilities with *Creature Comforts* of the resources using them in mind.

Accessibility: Consider access by vehicle and foot, and their proximity to ground and air transportation areas.

Guidelines for Establishing Other Search Base Facilities *(Helispots, Spike Camps and Demobilization Check-Out Points)*

Functionality: Designate these other search facilities for service specific functions and objectives.

Safety: Always keep Safety in mind when locating, using and servicing these temporary facilities.

Supervision: Sometimes, crews locate facilities in undesirable areas; therefore, make sure to assign trained and experienced field resources to supervise them.

Special Facilities Planning Guidelines

Try to group the following activities together in a camp.

- Management and plans
- Management and communications
- Latrines, sleeping areas, wash areas

Facilities To Consider:

- Parking
- Fuel storage
- Vehicle maintenance
- Supplies
- Assembly areas
- Sleeping areas
- Toilets
- Heliport
- Base Control
- First Aid
- Kitchen and mess

Which areas need isolation?

- Sleeping area
- Command Post
- Helicopter and helibase

Which areas need ready access to transportation and facilities?

- Management *(CP)*
- Supply
- Equipment area
- Kitchen
- Garbage
- Latrines *(chemical toilets)*

The desired flow of personnel and vehicles through the search base

- Search personnel naturally follow straight lines in camp. Try to minimize pathways through camp to avoid dust or mud.

Reasonable distance between functions and facilities in base.

- Depends upon the complexity of the search.
- Small initial response areas versus large, developed search bases.

Physical factors to consider.
- Physical limitations and capabilities:
    - Size and shape
    - Terrain
    - Existing roads
    - Existing facilities *(i.e., buildings, structures, communications, water, and sanitation facilities)*
    - Sun, dust, mud, etc.

Establishing the water supply.

- Make sure its adequate and safe for the kitchen
- Locate above/upstream of other camp facilities
- Protect the area from contamination with easy to read signs
- Occasionally personnel need to dig out a water source and install plastic pipe or hose

Where to locate the kitchen.

- Level ground
- Good drainage away from the camp area
- Minimal dust
- Adequate water supply
- Shade
- Good lighting
- Cooking, serving and eating areas together
- Access by freezer truck or other cold storage
- Rope off the area to unauthorized personnel

Locating the equipment depot and supply storage areas.

- Adequate space - secured and roped off
- Segregate supplies and equipment by type and condition
- Bins or stalls help in developing a *checkout* and *check-in* system
- Provide parking space for trucks, buses, etc.

Establishing sleeping areas.

- Downstream from kitchen water supply
- Away from dishwashing drainage
- Quiet area away from kitchen, trucks, roads, helibases, latrines, etc.
- Shaded area for night searchers
- Mark or put up signs separating areas for various search units, if desired
- Provide for search manager and overhead team wake-up calls
- Designate and supervise areas for warming fires
- Provide clothes lines
- Provide drinking water

- Look for flat dry ground
- Free of snags and other hazards to safety

Locating the timekeeping or sign-in area.

- Placed near the entrance to the base
- Provide for lights
- Provide tables, seats, shelter and rope off the area
- Avoid dust and noise
- Plainly mark the area for easy identification

Locating the commissary.

- Locate with time recorder

Locating the communications area.

- Away from time keeping, kitchen and equipment areas
- Convenient to the search manager
- If possible, ask the radio technicians or specialists to help you locate the site
- Look for adequate shelter

Locating the first-aid station.

- In a quiet and dust free area
- Look for areas with shade or adequate shelter

Locating the Search Manager and Overhead Team.

- Isolate them away from main base activity
- Make sure to provide tables, chairs, lights, and heat *(if needed)*
- Convenient to communications
- Provide shelter

Locating washup and showering facilities.

- Well drained, sand or gravel
- Adequately lighted
- Away from the kitchen
- Provide hot water, benches, basins, soap, towels, and garbage cans
- Separate facilities for men and women, or arrange a schedule for use at separate times
- Provide clothes lines

Establishing latrines.

- 150 feet from streams and 300 feet from kitchen and sleep areas, as a minimum
- Post direction signs
- Lighted for night use
- Supply with tissue, shovel, and chlorinated lime
- Cover with dirt and level when closing base
- Use chemical toilets whenever possible
- Arrange for service at least once daily
- Locate two latrines near the search command area
- Provide occupied signs or mark them men/women

Handling garbage disposal.

- Distribute garbage receptacles throughout the camp
- If possible use frozen meal boxes for garbage containers
- Haul the garbage out daily
- Check local policy before burning or burying garbage

Handling personnel parking.

- Make vehicles turn around first and park facing the exit
- Keep the turnarounds clear
- Consider vehicles with side opening doors

Consider the following for an assembly area

- Adequate space to assemble people for general announcements
- Provide a bulletin board
- Install a P.A. system, if necessary

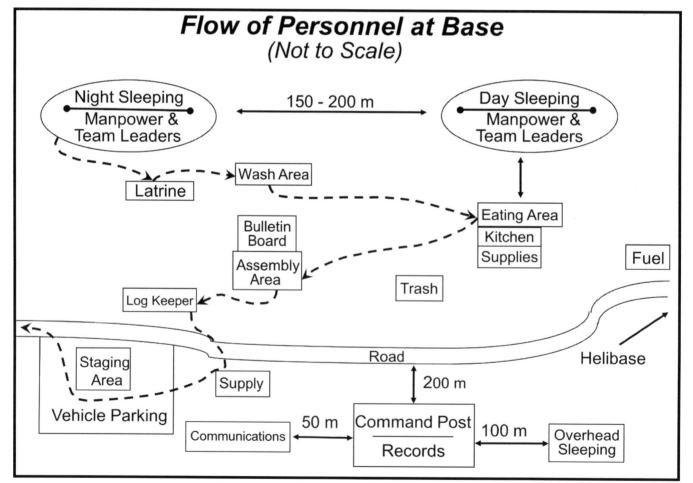

Figure 26-1 SAR Base Personnel Flow

> *"A base camp provides the staging area for personnel and equipment and their logistical support - toilet paper, dry clothing, and the 'three hots and a cot.' The base camp is also the home of the central nervous system of the search in the plans, communication, command, operations, and support facilities."*
>
> — Tim J. Setnicka,
> *Wilderness Search and Rescue*

Search Facilities Safety Guidelines

- Brief all personnel about *in-base* rules, e.g. fires, sanitation, quiet hours, smoking, meals, supplies, area hazards, evacuation plan, etc.
- Identify all hazards in the area and mitigate if possible

    - Flood, flash flood potential
    - Fire potential, both structural and wildland
    - Poison oak, insects *(ticks, yellow jackets, bees, spiders, scorpions)*, snakes, animals
    - Hazardous trees, widowmakers
    - Fuel storage, chemicals
    - Severe weather hazards *(lightning)*

- Produce base maps, showing evacuation routes, and listing base rules
- Establish speed limits
- Use service vehicles equipped with *back up alarms* and guided by personnel on foot
- Test all water sources regularly
- Designate smoking/no smoking areas
- Designate open fire areas and keep adequate fire fighting equipment nearby
- Establish camp security
- Keep a list of camp safety rules current; circulate and post them regularly
- Clearly mark all flammables, store in well shaded supply areas; and as a precaution post and enforce no smoking rules
- Properly store liquid petroleum gas tanks; ensure that only trained personnel handle and light stoves, heaters, lights etc. powered by LPG
- Ensure that all personnel follow appropriate sanitation rules for cooking and washing
- Provide for proper camp hygiene; chemical toilets, latrines, showers, wash areas and monitor or service 2 or 3 time daily
- Ensure proper use and construction of sump and mark or flag sump area well
- Clearly mark, and flag ditches, holes, stumps, or other safety hazards to walking
- Provide for night lighting of camp area and pathways.
- Locate generators so that noise and exhaust never affect personnel
- Properly ground electrical tools and generators
- Locate all electrical cords; inspect for shock potential; and make sure to mark them well
- Secure and anchor tents and shelters for wind, and flag/mark all anchor ropes, guys and braces
- Pick up garbage daily and mark garbage pit areas
- Look out for lightening storms and other weather hazards and follow the appropriate rules
- Maintain a first aid station
- Properly store food

Notes:

External Influences 27

Objectives:

- Describe the external or outside influences that indirectly affect the outcome of a search.

- Develop an effective strategy for dealing with external influences during a search.

Significant External Influences Defined

There are four categories of influences that a Search Manager needs to consider and manage:

1. Relatives, friends of the missing person
2. Media
3. Political entities
4. Parapsychological *(ESP's, seers, witchers, clairvoyants)*

Individuals or groups directly affected by government actions in some way cause external influences. These groups or individuals in turn create pressure and stress on the operational system ultimately trying to cope with the response to an emergency situation. If mismanaged, these non-operational influences begin draining manpower and resources.

Hugh Dougher wrote an article on *Integrating External Influences*, in RESPONSE magazine, 1992. In it he proposed that everyone needs to take a slightly different approach to integrating external influences into the overall strategy.

> *". . . external influences of relatives, media and elected officials can be somewhat superfluous to the search effort and affect the effort sometimes in uncontrolled ways. Further, although they must be managed, they should be kept at arm's length."*

Other search professionals even suggest incorporating these influences as an integral part of the search effort.

> *"...Perceptions influence actions. Relatives, media, and political entities should not be considered external to the incident organization, but rather as valuable special resources. If integrated properly they provide essential support to the search effort".*

The potential significance of integrating external influences, particularly those from the family, makes it important to consider the following recommendations in your overall search organization strategy.

Integrating with the Family

Assign one person to act as the Family Liaison Officer *(FLO)* for the incident organization. This staff position usually falls under the Incident Commander, and needs staffing early in a search operation, preferably about the same time team members initiate contact with the family members. Two important qualifications for this position include the ability to empathize with the family members and sufficient knowledge of search management to explain strategies and tactics to them. Staff assigned to this function, commit to it for the incident's duration. This helps develop the rapport and trust so important in establishing lines of communication, and to reassure relatives of the value in their involvement and input.

Mental Health Professional

The Family Liaison Officer needs to locate and enlist the support of a trained mental health professional such as a psychologist. County mental health agencies usually provide this service. The mental health professionals provide advice to the Incident Commander in family related matters, and more importantly, counsel family members. Mental health professionals meet regularly with the family and try to avoid unannounced appearances. These tend to falsely signal the impending announcement of tragic news to the family (*See Chapter 29 for dealing with Psychological Problems and Stress in Search Management*).

Multiple Subjects

Searches involving multiple subjects greatly increase the complexities of managing family relations. Even with a possible relationship between the missing persons such as best friends, or even marriage, the coalition of family, friends, and miscellaneous others gathering at the incident sometimes brings strangers together in one place.

Suddenly brought together in a tense emotional environment and suffering inadequate rest and food, tempers tend to flare followed by personality conflicts. Relatives of one missing person voice suspicions that the other missing person in the party caused the incident. For example: "John never goes anywhere by himself. If he hadn't been with Mike this never would have happened." Situations like this often turn explosive.

Consider providing separate private spaces for each family. Only, carefully share sensitive missing person behavior profiles in that they may fuel inappropriate accusations. Enlist the help of a mental health professional for counseling in anticipation of psychological conflicts or anger.

Planning Participation

As appropriate for the situation, consider assigning a family representative to a position in the Plans Section. With careful selection and proper supervision, this person becomes a great asset. The family member broadens the staff's perspective and knowledge, provides a communication link between the incident organization and the family, and serves the family as an advocate involved in the decision process. Such involvement increases family confidence and focuses their energy to support incident objectives. Use of this technique also helps minimize unauthorized, and possibly conflicting, search efforts by family members.

Mission Suspension Decision Process

As mentioned before, one of the most difficult and potentially controversial decisions made on a search concerns suspension of the mission. Although the IC ultimately makes this decision, successful resolution depends on a consensus of relatives, media, and interested political entities. The family holds the key to gaining this consensus plus the media and political entities generally follow their lead. If the family disagrees with the decision, the resulting political and media pressures tend to force additional search efforts, regardless of their likelihood of success, or cost.

Obtaining family support depends on trust and confidence. Remember to include the family. Involving relatives in a special pre-suspension planning meeting also attended by incident staff, agency representatives, and other key personnel further establishes this support.

Try to use this next to last meeting as a collective forum and decision making process to bring about a culmination to the search as described in Chapter 24. Present all available information and facts, along with a detailed list of additional tasks staff still needs to complete. At the conclusion of the meeting, in the absence of any significant new information, that termination of the search will take place without notifying the relatives. This strategy involves the relatives in the process and sometimes develops a very positive wrap up for the mission.

Managing Relatives - The General Principles

Never ignore them. Take the initiative and contact them. At the search base, locate them in a comfortable place, preferably somewhere away from the center of activity.

Assign a Family Liaison Officer to assist them and to provide them with regular feedback on the progress of the search. This person needs to posses a real sensitivity to this type of situation and, if possible, assign someone with training in dealing with grief reactions.

Keep them constantly informed on all actions taking place. Never make them come to you for information.

In some cases, people close to the subject want to, or even insist on involving themselves in the search. They feel the need to *contribute* to the effort. This helps them deal with the stress and uncertainty of the situation, and in some cases, guilt. In most cases, sending a relative out to search with a search team turns out badly. Try to find tasks around base camp to keep them busy and involved. In any case, the availability of a relative makes sense for confirming the identification or source of clues.

Make sure to quarter unstable relatives or associates somewhere away from the search base. Idle comments by searchers or accidentally overheard radio messages tend to cause serious reactions.

Maintain an atmosphere of encouragement, while trying not to build up false hopes.

Find out if the relatives or associates want the media contacting them. If not, search managers maintain a moral obligation to keep the media away from them, especially in cases when searchers find the subject dead or in very poor condition.

Brief all searchers as to the situation with relatives or associates, particularly the location and identification of members in the search area or base. Emphasize the need to avoid idle comments.

Consider bringing in specialists to deal with present grief reactions, or keep them on call to assist the relatives, if needed.

General Guidelines for Dealing with Grief Reactions

The following general guidelines deal with family members on the scene of a search and rescue operation involving another family member.

- Provide privacy for the family if possible and gently but firmly keep family members from interfering with SAR operations or endangering themselves.
- Help make them comfortable. Coffee, blankets, etc., present tangible expressions of concern and family and friends greatly appreciate this. Also, look for shock or other physical reactions.
- Provide concrete information to the family. Have the Family Liaison Officer serve as a liaison between the family and the search and rescue operation. This person needs to help the family deal with concrete issues and also help them to face reality in the case of bad news.
- Support the venting of feelings and, if necessary, help channel them within controllable limits. Avoid aggressive confrontation with the irrational beliefs held by the family. Often these beliefs serve as protection against the shock of the loss.
- Support continued professional or paraprofessional help. If the family wants support but appears immobilized by events, make the contact for them. Friends, clergy, or others close to the family offer a lot of help at time like this and even serve well in the liaison role.
- In fatalities, to help avoid additional stress at the scene, suggest that the family leave the area before searchers bring the subject into base camp. Simply advise the family that searchers located the subject and tell them where they took the body. After the family leaves, then remove the subject, thus avoiding a stressful situation for both the search personnel and the family.

The Media

Always exhibit a proactive approach to dealing with the media.

Press coverage provides opportunities for agency publicity, broadcasting of preventive search and rescue *(PSAR)* messages, educating the public related to search management, locating of witnesses and generation of clues.

Preferably fill the Information Officer function with a representative of the lead agency. Most police and sheriff's departments posses a Public Information Officer *(PIO)* or the Department Press Liaison

Officer. This person needs previous experience or training, and when possible the staff needs to help in selecting the position. The Information Officer always acts in a proactive way by contacting the press and in suggesting possible stories, including human interest topics, which highlight techniques or even individual units. The IC also needs to take every opportunity to increase media understanding of search activities and complexities, by facilitating reporter overflights and participation in particular aspects of the search operation.

Managing the Media - The General Principles

Understanding the Media. In SAR, the media educates and informs the public by reporting on how responsible officials handle an incident and by providing a *positive* perspective. In communicating information to the media, use the following basic tenet: KEEP THEM INFORMED. Never make them seek out information. Establish regular and frequent reports to them. Respect their reporting deadlines, such as the 6 pm news. Remember, if SAR officials fail to give the media information, they will always get it from somewhere. The media tends to obtain inaccurate or unflattering information if collecting it on their own accord.

What to Expect from the Media: Media reporting consists of three fairly distinct phases:

1. **Concern for the lost person**. The media shares early feelings of the concern for the subject and shows genuine concern for the IC, SAR personnel and the job at hand.
2. **Accusation.** Occurs when Search and Rescue crews fail to quickly find the subject. Generally the media assumes something went wrong, and starts to hunt for the culprit or culprits. Expect the media to ask, "When are you going to stop screwing up?"
3. **The story behind the news**. In the third phase, the media starts to search for controversy and the story behind the news. What really happened and why, plus the possibilities surrounding a cover-up

Our minds to tend to logically processes these three phases as the news of a SAR incident unfolds. Therefore, always expect the media to seek information that supports these phases.

Characteristics of the Major Media. Three major types of media usually fill the public's desire for information. Each one containing different audiences, different outlets, different deadlines, and different needs.

1. **Print:** Generally only one or two major daily newspapers cover an area. These may also link to various online news outlets and websites. They consistently need pictures and details and work under tight deadlines.
2. **Radio:** In most ares, a number of radio stations provide immediate coverage of incidents. To give their story maximum impact, radio stations usually want the actual voices of the major players.
3. **TV/Video:** Generally, only 2 or 3 news stations exist in an area with any significant news capability and may even stem from distant metropolitan areas. News stations need short film clips to air the story on the afternoon or evening news. The growing trend, however, centers on live coverage whenever a story unfolds in realtime. Often the short video segments will post on a station website after the story initially airs, along with links to other print media and online forums/social media discussions.
4. **Social Media:** Though not a formal news outlet, social media websites fill a more and more important role in people getting information about events. In particular family members and members of the local community will likely share information over various social media outlets. Be proactive and control the flow of information through policies limiting SAR team members use of social media on searches and through official online releases of information.

Chapter 27 — External Influences

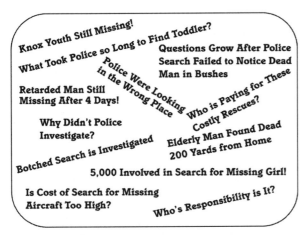

Figure 27-1 Actual Headlines About Searches. Make sure your side of the story gets told !

> *"Reporters are like alligators: You don't have to love them, you don't necessarily have to like them. But you do have to feed them."*
> - A Senior Reagan Administration Official, Economic Summit, Tokyo, 1986.

Pay Attention to the Normal Audience for each Medium.

According to the Pew Research Center *(2014 data)*:

- **Newspapers** almost universally shrink in their paper distribution every year, shifting instead to online publication.
- **Social Media** use for news ranks highest *(61%)* with the millennial generation *(born 1981-1986)* and younger. About half of Generation X *(born 1965-1980)* get their news from online and social media sources. And only 39% of Baby Boomers *(born 1946 - 1964)* use online and social media sources for their news.
- **Television** *(local and national)* provides the other half of the Generation X and 60% of the Baby Boomer generation's news sources. With an ever increasing skew to older generations.
- **Radio**. According to Nielsen *(2013 data)* 9 out of 10 Americans listen to radio at least on a weekly basis.

Managing the Media Response to the Search Incident:

- Always designate one person as the media liaison - a Information Officer *(IO)*.
- Try to confine the media representatives to one location. Although not always possible, less disruption takes place by keeping the media out of the search area.
- *Barring* them from the search area works really well, but arrange regular trips to base *(once or twice a day)* for the media, as a group, to get all the information they need such as; photos, interviews, ask questions and get answers.
- Another useful technique calls for encouraging the media representatives to designate a *pool* reporter or reporting team that represents the interests of the entire group and *shares* with them. The technique works best in situations such as arranging for a media flight over the area, or talking with relatives.
- Brief all searchers as to location of the media and making sure to give them the name of the media liaison. If possible, demand that no one but the media liaison make statements to the media without permission.
- The Search Manager, needs to attend at least one media conference each day. This gives them the opportunity to *get it straight from the source.*
- Give frequent reference and credit to all the organizations involved in the mission. Volunteer organizations, especially, thrive on recognition.

Role of Media
(In the Media's Perspective)

1. **BREAD & BUTTER information**
   (They are a business, don't forget it !)
2. **Rumor Control** *(start or correct it?)*
3. **Inform & educate the public**
4. **Put a face on a Tragedy** *(rate from 1 to 10)*
5. **Evaluate How the Mission is being Handled** - *(Report card to the public)*
6. **Perspective** - *(A third view)*

Figure 27-2 Media Goals

- Take advantage of the opportunity! As SAR experts remember, the media just consists of people. Talk to them.
- Establish fair and uniform rules. The media tends to follow them if scrupulously enforced. Media representatives will wait for any aspect of the story, as long as no one else gets it ahead of time.
- Never, never get into an adversary position regardless of the provocation.
- Establish good access for your media spokesperson and ensure that he/she remains fully informed and credible.
- Whenever possible, deal with reporters individually rather than in groups. This helps the media liaison control the substance of information, and leaves the reporter with a sense that he/she needs to act fairly. Reporters in groups tend to play to each other, often at the expense of the source interviewed.
- Think of the public's interest in your story - that's usually the way a reporter looks at it.
- A unit's information operation needs to use current technology to effectively disseminate information. Never let the news media disseminate information faster than the media liaison.
- Use enough staff to get the job done properly. SAR operations rarely get a second chance to properly re-accomplish something not properly finished the first time.
- Protect your credibility. Make sure not to join forces with an organization that will tarnish the SAR unit's image through poor performance. If forced to appear jointly with them before the media and public, let the media know what type of information/service each organization provides on their own accord.
- Remember to disseminate information to those parts of your own organization that normally dispense information *(e.g., switchboards, dispatchers, higher authorities)*. People tend to turn to other information sources before the media.
- Sometimes the complexity of the incident requires several people answering questions. Make sure they all read off the *same sheet of music*. To accomplish this, clearly identify a single public information officer in charge of information dissemination.
- Not all complex missions get the luxury of a news release. Often events change the situation too rapidly. Consider issuing fact sheets, with quotes for distribution (*from key staff*) whenever appropriate.
- News releases need to stick to only known facts; therefor describe the nature of the mission, but not any aspects still under investigation.

THE MEDIA SERVES IT'S OWN INTERESTS *(Their Audience)*...NOT YOU!
But,....Trust the public.
The common man is smarter than you think!

Guidelines to follow when a Media Liaison gets Interviewed

Be prepared. Always prepare to provide expert opinion to a non-expert and to provide it in the easiest possible way for him/her to understand it. What might they ask? Who, what, where, when, why? Call your PR people for help.

The **best answer** if you lack efficient knowledge to answer a question, "*I do not know.*" Always offer to tell what steps you or the organization intends to take to find out *(if that's appropriate)*. And when you find the answer, keep your promise and tell the questioner and all others interested in the answer.

Avoid answering questions which call for speculation on your part. The media pushes for opinions all the time by asking questions such as; "*Do you think you will find Johnny alive?*" A yes or no answer to this speculation, is virtually impossible to give. Something like "*At this time, crews continue to work all possible leads to find him as soon as possible*" appropriately answers the question. Promise to get facts and then produce them.

Try not to risk off-the-record comments. A reporter's ground rules never match that of the media liaison's.

Answer clearly and to the point. Never *beat around the bush* on important issues.

Start any statement with a direct - calmly expressed

- sentence about the SAR crews intentions and what their expected to produce. Immediately follow that with a description of what action the authorities intend to take in response.

Answer the questions as briefly as possible without coming across short, reticent or uncommunicative. Never attempt to add a light touch. When people talk about a person's life or well being, its not a laughing subject.

Never panic. Admit problems if they exist, but point out positive efforts to correct them.

Keep an open, friendly and helpful attitude.

Use *plain talk*. Talk as if you're talking to a niece or nephew?

Be yourself! Never attempt to change your voice or sound differently. Try not to play-act or act like someone else.

Avoid jargon. Using technical terms such as military or police idioms, confuses the public or leads them to think you're hiding something.

Watch out for emotional *buzz words*. The use of ethnic labels, an inappropriate term, or disparaging characterizations of groups or individuals involved creates a mini-crisis by itself.

Never win a battle at the price of losing a war. In short, try not to start a fight with inquiring reporters. You might win the first round but then lose in the long run.

Try not to make it any worse or better. **Stick to the facts**.

If you tend to lose control of your anger or lack the ability to keep your voice in check during times of stress, let someone else act as spokesperson for most of the media presentation. Then, remain available for answering questions.

If a question offends you or distorts the situation, ask the reporter to reword it, or reword it yourself.

Avoid exaggeration - stick to the facts - try not to give the reporter the impression of trying to manipulate the story or give yourself or your agency a favorable impression.

Talk about the most important facts first. Reporters often write down what they *remember* of what you started with, and then quote that.

Keep calm - try not to lose your cool. If you lose your temper, it becomes the story, not the substance of what you said.

Talk candidly and honestly - if you make a reporter suspicious of your integrity, they always find a way to trip you up.

Sometimes reporters warp your words or take them out of context, but in the long run the reporter's credibility within their organization or with editors suffers. If you think the reporter mistreated you in a story, tell him/her - remind them that you want accuracy and fairness more than you want attention.

Emphasize all positive action taken by the authorities to alleviate the situation.

Never talk down to the public through the reporter; they know it when they hear it and resent it.

Never ever say, *"No comment."* A statement like this means three possible things to a mass audience such as: "I do not know"; "I know but I am hiding the information"; or "Go ask someone else." That someone else might say something a lot worse than whatever subject you try to avoid.

> *The closer you get to the real facts of a situation, the more obvious the errors in all news coverage of that situation.*
> *- Murphy's Law on Truth in Reporting*

Interview Traps:

- If the reporter's questions put you in a negative light, admit it, and then explain all the corrective steps taken.
- Never repeat a reporter's terminology unless you like the words.
- Beware of *false* assumptions, *conclusions* and *facts*.
- Avoid answering hypothetical questions.
- Listen to the whole question before you respond.
- Watch out for the multiple question: ask the reporter to repeat the parts for you and/or pick the part you want to answer.
- Beware of the *speedup* technique in which the reporter shoves the microphone back and forth rapidly between the two of you.
- Look out for the *stall* technique in which the reporter leaves the mike in your face after your answer, hoping for you to say more. Try to look him/her in the eye, smile, say nothing......and wait.

Watch out for these types of questions:

- Leading
- Double-barreled
- Technical
- Hypothetical
- Background
- Off the record
- Pressure or just plain bluff

When meeting the media, use the best possible attitude by saying, *I am glad you asked!* And mean it. Take advantage of this opportunity to present yourself and your organization to the public.

However, on other occasions when confronted by a hostile media, strive for: Do no harm.

PUBLIC EXPOSURE COMES WITH RISK!

The Television Approach

Television presents an emotional medium, not an intellectual one.

Viewers tend to forget the content of your message but remember your style - how you looked, how you behaved, and the quality of your voice.

Check your appearance, and then forget it. The opportunity to change on a moment's notice never happens. Instead, concentrate on what type of questions you think the reporter might ask.

People perceive a person on television quite differently than in person. Remember to sit upright at your desk, or in the chair while preparing to speak *(Never lean backwards, or away from the camera)*.

Look straight ahead, try not to look up for guidance or down to hide.

Concentrate on the reporter's questions. Carefully listen for any bad information built into the questions. Always challenge incorrect information!

PRINT MEDIA TRANSLATES COMPLEX IDEAS BEST

VIDEO LEANS TOWARD ACTION AND ENTERTAINMENT. AS AN INTIMATE MEDIUM. THEY WANT FOOTAGE!

ALTHOUGH CASUAL AND PERSONAL, THE RADIO LIKES STORIES ABOUT PEOPLE. THEY WANT VOICES.

COMMUNITY NEWSPAPERS WANT NEWS THAT DIRECTLY AFFECTS THE COMMUNITY. THEY WANT TO KNOW IF THE SITUATION IMPACTS PART OF THE COMMUNITY NOW OR IN THE FUTURE.

When a Reporter Calls on the Phone:

- Assume the reporter wants information to publish or record and broadcast.
- *Always assume you are on the record.*
- Rules for dealing with the media by phone:
  - Establish what organization called.
  - Establish why they want the information.

- Ask what deadlines the reporter needs to meet.
- Check reporters knowledge...Listen!
- Listen again...make sure you understood the need.
• Then:
  - fill in the background,
  - answer the questions,
  - or, find out and call back.
• If you lack information explain why.
• If possible, ask someone for help.
• Always keep callback promises, provide references and/or research the material.

Dealing with the *Unprofessional* or Unscrupulous Reporter

The public often assumes a much higher level of professionalism from those who work in the media than they actually receive. Often in small communities, part-time students with little or no experience with industry ethics, work for the radio, newspapers and/or websites. They unknowingly, violate your agreement or quote you out of context, or misquote you; or use unscrupulous methods of getting information.

In instances when a reporter divulges untruths or incorrect information, media liaisons happen to posses a means of recourse. Discuss the incident with the reporter first and then with the editor. A good editor never wants this type of behavior in their line of business because it happens when reporting future incidents. Therefore informing them goes a long ways toward addressing the issue. However, if the editor disagrees with you, you may have no further recourse. If this happens, simply advise the editor, that if they want any information in the future, never send that reporter again (*and enforce that rule*).

The Situation from the Media's Point of View

Look at it from their perspective:

• Information unavailable
• Kill the messenger syndrome
• Fears that the media distorts information leading to officials withholding or sanitizing information
• Local, state and national media
• Scientists (*incomprehensible*)
• Conflicting opinions
• Technical/Logistical problems
• DEADLINES

Far too often, the media plays the role of adversary on search missions. This helps no one. To avoid this, PREPLAN all media aspects of the mission. Manage this influence - never let it control you. By meeting and greeting the media, the media liaison opens communication channels with the reporters. Knowing reporters on a first name basis, makes working with them easier than regarding them as adversaries. Building strong relationships with the media also works to the advantage of search crews, by offering the following:

• Assistance in obtaining information, and resources
• Emergency preparedness education
• Funding or donations (*especially to volunteer groups*)
• Public relations

Managing Contacts with Political Entities

Integrating with Political Entities

Some searches generate political interest given the nature of their size, family influence, or press coverage. In these situations, promptly advise the lead agency executive of any such interest and encourage him/her to assume the role of political liaison. This executive and his staff more than likely already posses experience in dealing with political issues, and in working with the concerned official. Both managers and officials usually prefer this arrangement anyway. The officials feel more comfortable in dealing with the higher authority, and executives get the opportunity to present budgetary, staffing, and other management issues in real-time. Once political interest develops, the IC needs to keep the lead agency executive fully informed of any new developments, and include him/her in the routing of all incident generated documents/decisions.

Even after a successful search and finding the missing person, management of the media still creates a major concern. Take the opportunity to talk about the real problems in search and acknowledge the volunteers who devote so much of their time to these life saving efforts. Use the media to give credit and thanks to those that deserve it.

Some situations involve political influence almost immediately:

For example: A politician or VIP happens to go missing.

- Media publicity or family contacts generate the interest of political entities. In either case, the same principles of managing contacts with political entities exists.
- In some cases, an agency's policies dictate how to deal with political contacts.
- Assign one person as the liaison with the interested party or parties.
- Take the initiative and keep them informed. Call them before they call you. Many of the principles used in dealing with the media apply to dealing with political entities as well.
- Recognize that everything becomes a bit more *touchy*. However, effective operational management, yields little need for changes. This type of influence simply heightens the need to perform really well at those things that *show*, such as media briefings, investigation and background checks, searcher briefings and documentation.

General Advice on Dealing With Political Influences

- Instruct searchers on what to say if politicians question them, and where to direct any future questions.
- Instruct searchers to refrain from commenting on the situation.
- Politicians influence the capability of obtaining scarce resources such as; aircraft, military resources, night vision equipment, etc. and transportation if normal efforts fail.
- Politicians also influence establishing long term programs, and getting money or equipment for search and rescue.
- Keep the lines of communication with politicians open at all times, not just during a search. Keep them abreast of your training, programs, needs, mission load and accomplishments *(Get to know your elected officials)*.
- Invite politicians to award programs, specific training sessions, or similar events.
- Remain neutral, make sure not to overtly support candidates for political or public office *(Many U.S. states make it illegal for government agency personnel to support political campaigns)*.
- Always thank politician or government agencies both privately and publicly when they provide the search organization or a search, with something they need.
- If a politician or agency gives an organization money or equipment, invite them and the media to a presentation. Good will goes a long way.
- In dealing with relatives, media or political influences, remember: Honesty reduces rumors.

Para-psychological Influences - This includes ESPs *(Extra Sensory Perception)*, Seers, Clairvoyants, etc.

A major search generally brings out para-psychological influences.

When a search effort extends unsuccessfully over a number of days, friends, relatives and even searchers start to clutch at straws. The availability of these types of influences, eventually cause people to place a strong emphasis on their use.

Even though people believe a charlatan claims to posses psychic powers, they deserve consideration, if for no other reason, than for the balm it provides the family and loved ones of the missing person.

General Guidelines for Handling Psychic Influences

- Determine the person's motives and method by which they learned about the search incident.
- Always escort them into the field. Never leave them without an escort or qualified overhead team member.
- Avoid those who want to charge!
- Never let them talk to family members alone.
- Cautiously observe media contact with these people as an influence on family members.
- With a proper escort, allow them into the field to show you where they think the subject went.
- After several unsuccessful attempts in the field, discourage further dependence on their use.
- Always include them into your overall search strategy.
- Consider their *success* rates *(i.e., other law enforcement agencies who use them)*.
- Never outright dismiss a psychic influence! They could get lucky, or even know something you don't.
- Try not to let these influences drain on your objectives and search planning.

Notes:

Considerations for Rescue & Recovery

Objectives:

- List and discuss the four phases a successful SAR operation.

- Describe why the six step process provides a good template for organizing a rescue or recovery operation.

- Effectively develop an evacuation plan for either a rescue or recovery operation.

An Overview of Rescue / Recovery

Every rescue or recovery mission needs the same underlying structure, or framework as used on a search. The expanding six step cyclic process described in Chapter 15 continues to provide the overall umbrella guidance throughout the operation. Remember, this six step process used in combination with ICS presents a tool for SAR units to use repeatedly in virtually every operational period. As mentioned earlier, the process sets up the blueprint for the redundancy that ensures success.

In the rescue or recovery part of the operation, the six steps provide a very reliable means to organize thinking, apply management principals and continue the Incident Command System or any other management strategy. As this part of an operation unfolds try to answer the following questions:

- When do you begin formulating a rescue plan?
- Is there a potential for special rescue problems and will we know ahead of time?
- When do we identify and notify rescue resources?

How Rescue and Recovery Fits into the Overall Search Effort

All complete SAR operations proceed through the following four phases:

- **Locate**
- **Access**
- **Stabilize**
- **Transport**

Locate: This phase takes anywhere from five minutes to multiple days; like, using a pair of binoculars to locate someone stranded on a rock face, versus hundreds of search crews looking for a missing hunter for five days.

Access: After locating the subject the access phase involves transporting available rescue resources to where they perform their functions. The access phase presents problems in remote areas or in areas requiring specialized skills/equipment e.g. high angle environments, underwater, extreme weather or confined spaces.

Stabilize: Stabilizing means caring for any injuries as well as providing physical comfort and safety of the subject and any other survivors of an incident. This includes potential environmental injury such as hypothermia, or trauma such as a fractured bone. Often, mistakes occur on-scene by concentrating on the casualty only, while their companions potentially suffer from *Post Traumatic Stress* or environmental stresses as a result of the incident.

Transport: Removing the subject to an appropriate facility safely. This involves a range of effort from as simple as leading someone down a trail, to extremely difficult scenarios, such as evacuation from a vertical rock face, or recovery of a body by helicopter hoist.

Review:
The Six Step Incident Response Process:

1. **Size-up the situation**
   - Think about the nature of the rescue
2. **Identify contingencies**
   - Events that possibly make the situation worse
3. **Determine goals and objectives**
   - What searchers need to accomplish in a given time frame
4. **Identify required resources**
   - What type of resources the search requires and the availability of those resources
5. **Build a plan and structure**
   - Complete a Rescue Action Plan.
6. **Take action**
   - Deploy resources and/or wait for sufficient expertise or manpower

Planning - the Key to Effective Rescue and Recovery

The following expands on the **six problem-solving components**:

1. **Size Up:** Gathering all the pertinent information about a situation to effectively and efficiently rescue or recover the subject. Preplanning and the **Vulnerability Assessment** identify not only potential problems and environments, but also the whereabouts of any specialized resources to solve those problems.

- Size up continuously occurs even after notification of resources and links to the next phase.
- Make sure to get the following information:
   - The subject (*physical parameters and condition*)
   - The environment (e.g. terrain, hazards, weather)
   - Availability of resources at the subject's location

Beyond special situations that require an accelerated rescue, conventional evacuation of an injured or incapacitated person involves stabilizing that person, packaging for safe transport and finally evacuation or transport out of the environment.

According to most team protocols, notifying the search base takes place immediately upon contacting the missing subject. Evacuations require an updated status report to call in the appropriate transport resources. In other words, the types of resources used, depends on the condition and location of the missing person. Status usually refers to one of the following:

- No injury - able to walk out on their own
- Slight injury - able to walk
- Slight injury - able to walk with some assistance
- Major injuries - needs considerable attention and assistance
- Major injuries - needs immediate evacuation by air
- Deceased

2. **Identify Contingencies:** Immediately identify contingencies when **notification of the subject's whereabouts** and **condition** comes in (e.g. unhurt, dead, injured). Notification that searchers actually found the subject changes the incident from a search to a rescue or recovery. Ask yourself question such as; whether or not the speed of recovery factors into the evacuation of the subject. The Safety of rescuers also dictates specific strategy and tactics in rescue. What risk management tools will rescuers utilize (*i.e. SARGAR, Military ORM, etc.*)? Daylight or visibility issues create major safety factors for search crews.

3. **Determine Goals and Objectives:** Make sure to base all goals and objectives upon your on-scene assessment (*Time critical, weather factors, air support, subject condition, etc.*).

4. **Identify Required Resources:** During this particular stage, planning crews identify resource

expertise and capabilities. They also contact resources to fulfill primary or backup functions. As early in the operation as possible, try to establish what type of terrain and environment crews need to deal with in the rescue. This obviously dictates which resources respond to the incident.

5. **Build a Plan and a Structure:** After choosing one course of action, formulate at least two alternate plans. Remember, a plan needs flexibility.

- Consider the four elements, *reaching the subject, stabilizing the subject, packaging the subject, and the haul out*, all simultaneously.
- Consider the manpower necessary when a haul-out demands the use of a stretcher/liter *(Stretcher carries require a lot of manpower - see later in this chapter)*

6. **Take Action:** Get the job done. Previous planning steps form the base of a rescue/recovery phase.

- This phase uses all the specialized technology, skills and techniques required to complete the task at hand. The preplan identifies those likely skills and techniques.
- Most often, the action phase receives the most publicity of the whole incident.

The Critique Process: At the end of any rescue/recovery operation make sure to critique the incident *(see Chapter 30, Post Mission & Critique)*. After the first notice, immediately begin planning for rescue or recovery. This helps crews to get ready for, and carry out the mission effectively. Constantly analyze and revise all alternatives based on the following:

- Time elapsed
- Possible subject locations
- Weather
- Hazards
- Availability of rescue/recovery resources
- Reported changes in subject condition
- Availability of medical resources

Rescue and Recovery *Thought Provokers*

- Use technical personnel for technical rescue.
- When searchers find a deceased subject, only evacuate with no risk to the rescuers/recoverers.
- Stabilize the subject before evacuating, if possible.
- Decide on the easiest/safest route, before beginning the actual transportation.
- Appoint someone to serve as route-finder, with a radio and markers, to report potential hazards, problems etc., while selecting the best route of travel.
- Use litter teams of 6-8 personnel. Normally, no more than 20 minutes per shift. The incident needs at least three *(3)* teams *(likely more)*, depending on terrain and conditions. Crews also require additional personnel/resources to carry other equipment.
- A radio carrier brings up the rear.
- A night evacuation requires adequate lighting.
- If traveling across easy ground, make sure carriers walk out of step opposite each other across the liter. Walking in step causes a rhythmic bounce in the stretcher and the motion tends to make the subject ill or very uncomfortable.
- When using a helicopter for evacuation, make sure to:

  - Inform and brief the subject.
  - Prior to the arrival of the helicopter, tie down or secure all belongings such as; equipment, clothing, medical gear etc. In precarious situations, consider the security of the injured subject and rescuers, particularly large aircraft creating severe rotor down drafts. This wind will easily dislodge an unsecured rescuer or dog.
  - Protect *(eyes & head)* subject from wind blast and debris.
  - One crew member who knows the subject's medical condition and treatment, needs to accompany the subject; alternatively, teams need to transfer records of medical assessment and treatment.
  - Make sure to ensure compatibility of all Stretchers*(liters)* with the intended aircraft.

Remember, at this point, searchers turn into rescuers, therefore the safety and comfort of the injured subject needs consideration. After stabilizing the individual, and to ensure patient comfort, remind rescuers to perform some of the following procedures during packaging:

- If conscious, fill their hands with something to grab.
- Apply pressure to and support the bottom of the feet. Litters inevitably bump and jolt the patient around therefor, a patients ability to flex uninjured body parts helps ease any discomfort.
- If conscious, a subject needs the ability to see, as crews transport them to safety. Helicopter hoists and high angle extraction, usually require some kind of eye protection for the subject.

All rescue and recovery operations need to fill out the **Critique of the rescue/recovery portion of the mission** at the end of the incident *(See Post Mission in Chapter 30)*.

Limiting Factors for Rescue / Recovery Operations

In Search and Rescue, *elapsed time*, generally measures the *speed*, or lack of it on a rescue or recovery.

- Do search crews fly a subject out, walk them out or use a ground vehicle?

Ultimately, crews need to take the *Safety* of the subject into consideration and safely, yet quickly, transport a person.

- If the safety of the subject gets compromised in any way, flying, walking, skiing, etc., then transportation stops regardless of any other factors.
- Safety says *yes* or *no* to plans and actions.

The Key to Successful Rescue and Recovery

Teams of rescue personnel throughout the nation frequently receive calls to solve complex problems in a wide spectrum of environments. Managers need to realize that most incidents get solved by well-trained and specialized resources, not just by dedicated responders.

The critical need for specialized skills in every agency, rescue squad, or volunteer unit, pushes these organizations to develop their own training standards, capabilities, and techniques. However, the entire process of rescue *(locating, reaching, stabilizing and evacuation)* needs continuity, and most of all, a consistent foundation in training and planning.

The following list includes common specialized environments and their associated problems during SAR operations:

- Mountains

  - Access
  - Long scree slopes
  - Steep / vertical snow and ice
  - Steep / vertical rock faces
  - Avalanche
  - Glaciers and crevasses
  - Altitude

- Water (*under and over*)

  - Seas and lakes
  - Frozen surfaces (*thin ice*)
  - Coastal white water and surf
  - Whitewater streams and rivers
  - Low-head dams
  - Floods / Flash floods

- Restricted Access

  - Caves
  - Mines
  - Air shafts

- Abandoned wells
- Drainage/irrigation

- Urban/Disaster

  - Building collapse
  - Wide range of special *rescue* conditions

- Weather

  - High winds
  - Snow, rain
  - Excessive heat
  - Excessive cold
  - Low visibility
  - Lightning

- Hazardous Materials

While each of these presents unique problems to the rescuer in the field, the rescue scene manager's job changes very little. Here again, identification and proper use of specialized resources represents the key factor in each case.

Notes:

Managing Psychology and Stress Reactions in Operations Personnel 29

Objectives:

- List and discuss the basic psychological factors that generally complicate search missions.

- Identify the common psychological reactions that occur in the lost person.
- Discuss the primary principles of Crisis Intervention.

- Describe procedures to manage psychological problems under field conditions.

- List the types of stress and link them to search operations.

- Discuss the maintenance of healthy search and rescue personnel.

- Identify symptoms of excessive stress.

The authors wish to thank Jeffrey Mitchell, PhD, for the genesis and revision of this chapter on psychological problems and stress in search management. For many years, Dr. Jeffrey T. Mitchell, Ph.D. of the University of Maryland, Baltimore County has contributed greatly to our understanding of the role of stress in emergency services personnel. He teaches how to use stress to our advantage and how to protect colleagues and ourselves from its harmful effects. He also teaches how to manage the complex psychological problems encountered during searches and other emergency operations *(See the end of this chapter for a brief bio sketch on Jeff and references as well as his suggested further readings on the material covered here)*.

Part I - Search Psychology and Crisis Intervention

> *"A little help, rationally directed and purposefully focused at a strategic time is more effective than more extensive help given at a period of less emotional accessibility."*
> -Lydia Rapoport, 1962. Crisis Intervention Theorist and Associate Professor, School of Social Welfare, University of California.

Introduction

When a person goes missing, and even after the completion and demobilization of a mission, their mental and emotional processes significantly effect the search and the people involved in it. Psychology influences the lost person's behavior and that of his or her family and friends. It exerts itself in the command staff and in the searchers, rescuers and ancillary personnel. Ignoring these mental and emotional processes equates to going into a search without a plan, leadership, equipment and resources. Failing to recognize the importance of this aspect of human health, complicates a crews efforts in assisting the missing person and those closest to them.

Four Main Areas of Psychological Concern on a Search

1. The missing person
2. The missing person's family and friends
3. The public
4. The search mission personnel

The Missing Person

Even before a person goes missing, his or her thoughts, intellectual functions, emotions and personality continuously process. Any of the following contribute to why a person goes missing:

- Distracted
- Emotionally upset or despondent
- Experiencing a diminished self image
- Guilt ridden
- Frightened
- Angry or enraged
- Frustrated
- Feeling rejected
- Mentally confused, impaired
- Stressed
- Overconfident
- Inattentive to details
- Fatigued
- Injured
- Mentally unstable
- Off their medications

Any one of, or a combination of, the factors listed above not only contribute to someone becoming lost, but they also tend to contribute to behaviors which further complicate the search. Lost people tend to run, hide, not respond to attraction tactics, wander aimlessly, take excessive risks, become depressed, self destruct and, although rarely, become a threat to search personnel. Remember! Before a person ever becomes lost, the presence of a psychological profile *(healthy or unhealthy)* already exists. Some elements of their psychological nature help them while others hinder them making it difficult to find them.

Generally, fear and exposure to the elements cause a person's normal psychological state to deteriorate. Part of a SAR members responsibilities include, understanding how a person's psychology works in choosing the most advantageous search tactics, and strategically applying them to find the missing person as fast as possible. Sections of this text on the lost and missing person's behavior help search personnel familiarize themselves with the nature of various classifications of lost or missing persons.

Make sure personnel possess an awareness of the psychological forces impacting the lost person's behavior. Fear, hunger, pain, stress, embarrassment, disorientation, and mental confusion cause people to behave in unintentional ways and tend to threaten their survival. Prolonged isolation and compromised physical health cause deterioration in positive mental attitude and the missing persons will to survive.

If you cool a human brain or heat it up; dry it out or subject it to toxic materials; physically traumatize it, emotionally stress it or take it to an altitude in excess of 10,000 feet unusual human behavior occurs. Under any of these circumstances, a search easily turns into a race against time, and conditions that threaten the mental and physical health of the lost person. The more searchers understand about the psychological reactions of lost people, the more they anticipate lost person behaviors and act decisively to bring the search to a successful conclusion.

Direct psychological support services to the lost person fail to exist as long as the person remains lost with no communications link to the searchers. Every search plan needs a crisis intervention specialist available to communicate directly with a conscious person once searchers find them. Rescuers with wilderness medical training, also trained in crisis intervention, making them the best choice for providing emotional support in the field. In any case, address the emotional needs of the lost person simultaneously with the their physical needs.

Notes on Caring for the Lost Person Once Rescued

- Address medical conditions immediately
- Assure safety
- Treat for hypo or hyperthermia
- Dehydration causes further mental deterioration so treat it appropriately
- Once rescued, speak directly to the person
- Listen carefully to the victims giving them ample opportunity to express themselves
- Accurate, current and timely information helps the well being of the victim
- Never give the provision of bad news about a

friend or colleague in the field unless medically stable
- Give bad news gently, carefully and in brief segments never rushing
- Reassure people that they are safe now
- Establish a private area for the victims as soon a possible
- Provide for medical, social, religious, psychological, shelter, food and other needs
- Never tell victims that *luck* found them because it could have been worse. Statements like this almost never console and usually anger a distressed person
- Gently touch a distressed person on the shoulder or hand if they seem receptive to such contact
- Personnel need to keep calm and speak in a soothing and reassuring voice
- Immediately evacuate a shocked, very silent and withdrawn person from the scene, making them the first priority group for evacuation and intervention
- Although noisy, hysterical or acting out victims stick out in a situation, make them a secondary priority *(although they tend to interfere with the operations)*
- When subjects show no sign of distress at the scene, consider them a third priority for evacuation and keep an eye on them in case they get worse
- Children possess the most vulnerability to psychological harm during a stressful search operation or a disaster and need plenty of reassurance and sometimes physical contact

The Missing Person's Family and Friends

SAR personnel often see the best and the worst of human beings when they get involved in a search. Family and friends of the lost person come into the situation with their own psychological backgrounds. They gather together and suddenly undergo enormous stress with little preparation or experience. They fail to understand the rudiments of search strategy and tactics. Overwhelmed and frightened, family and friends demonstrate anxiousness, confusion and no patients for action and results. Especially searches involving a lost child.

Family and friends lack an understanding for carefully planning and orchestrating the use of the available search resources. Their imagination runs wild and they fear the very worst. They want to stay close to the search area and frequently show up in a base camp or even at the command post. Some family and friends feel a need to involve themselves in the search. Some become loud; others extremely quiet. Some become demanding; others compliant. Some cooperate fully; others demonstrate resistance and resentment. Some demonstrate kindness; others criticize.

Notes on Caring for the Family and Friends of a Missing Person

- Call a local Critical Incident Stress Management team out to base camp to advise and guide the command staff, and to provide crisis support services to the family when needed. CISM team members also help interview distressed family members and friends.
- Assign a competent family liaison to function as an intermediary between the Command and Plans sectors and the loved ones.
- Provide information on search actions taken so far and plans for further action.
- Provide family scheduled briefings so family members know when to expect the next *dose* of information.
- Provide *ACT* information; Accurate, Current and Timely.
- Accurate information helps keep people calm. It also generates feelings of hope in the family members and friends.
- Protect family members and friends from further stress such as the press, curiosity seekers, gory sights and sounds, or exposures to any *horrible aspects* of the incident.
- Try to engage family members in activities that keep them occupied and contributing in the effort. Let them search out buildings like sheds and barns, or search a campground, playground or a known gathering place. Always give them some instructions to carry out these tasks. Encouraging family and friends to cooperate with investigators also helps.

- Ask the family members and friends what they need most. Come up with some suggestions if they fail to think of anything on their own.
- Mobilize any necessary resources such as the Red Cross or clergy members to assist the family and friends.
- Reconnect group members in the same area.
- Listen carefully to loved ones. Sometimes they offer a new insight into the lost person even after the interview ends. Give them an opportunity to express themselves. Provide accurate, current and timely information and reassurance. Never tell them that everything will be okay. Keep yourself calm and your voice soothing and reassuring. Instilling hope is important.
- Manage family and friend's needs as they arise. If receptive, use appropriate touch.
- During a stressful search operation, children become the most vulnerable to psychological harm. Give special care to and afford children, especially siblings or immediate family members of the lost person.
- Protect family members from exposure to weather conditions such as cold, wind, snow and ice, heat, rain, thunder storms, etc.
- Brief family members first before announcing anything to the public.

The Public's Psychological Reaction

Lost people, especially children, capture the interest of the public. A broad range of reactions come from the public. Some barely pay attention, making the search none of their business since they know none of the people involved. The mysterious elements of the case intrigue some individuals. Searches sometimes take on the appearance of a real live mystery played out in newspapers and on radio and television. A few want to criticize the lost person, their loved ones and the search operations. *Arm chair quarterbacks* and *experts* pop up all over the place critiquing every element of the operation.

To seek personal gain, a tiny proportion of the people cause harm. Examples of such depraved behavior include people calling the home of relatives and stating that they deserved the loss, *punishment from God*. Or, they spread disturbing rumors. In some cases, people completely disconnected with the search, call and demand money for the safe return of the missing person.

Other members of the public personally identify with the missing person, putting themselves in the place of the lost person and considering what actions they might take and how they would feel. These individuals become so distraught by their imaginations that resources outside of their own family need to calm them down.

Still other people, not involved with the search, personalizing themselves as if a relative of the lost subject experiencing a tragic loss. Many feel genuine concern and distress and offer prayers and good wishes for the safe finding of the lost person. Some find it necessary to volunteer in any way possible. Repeatedly, large numbers of well meaning, but untrained and inexperienced people show up at a search base camp offering to help. These types of situations place Incident Command in a somewhat uncomfortable position of sorting out if and how the untrained volunteers help in the search effort.

Notes on Managing the Public During a Search Incident

- News bulletins help alert the public to look for the missing person.
- Before releasing any information to the public, verify the accuracy of it.
- Tell the public specifically what to look for. Give accurate descriptions of the lost subject and a number to call with any helpful information.
- Tell the public what searchers need to facilitate the search. In the past, people generously provided boats, all terrain vehicles, snow shoes, cross country skis and four wheel drive vehicles to assist in a search.
- If people need to stay away from certain areas, give them instructions. Try not to divulge specific details of the location in case curious members of the public enter the scene and interfere with the search operations.
- If people spontaneously volunteer and show

up in the base camp, let them search buildings, roads or trails to assist in limiting the search area. Always send teams of two or three to search low probability areas. Never send a solitary volunteer out on a mission.
- Volunteers lacking in physical fitness work best in less strenuous support duties such as preparing meals for the searchers or making phone calls.
- If Incident Command decides to use spontaneous volunteers, someone needs to brief them before assigning any tasks.
- If too many spontaneous volunteers show up at base camp, ask a staff member to thank them for coming out and send them on their way.
- Always act kindly and politely when telling spontaneous volunteers to leave. They mean well and staff needs to notify them without hurting their feelings by an abrupt dismissal.
- If people contributed to the search effort, thank them before their release.
- Brief the media regularly. Sometimes they help keep the public under control. Besides, when the media feels that search personnel failed to properly inform them, they tend to contact less informed people for stories or even worse, make up news reports for distribution to the public.
- If anyone suspects criminal activity in a missing person situation, the media helps to expand the search and sometimes pressure the person to release the subject. This only occurs if accurate and up to date information gets released to the public.

Psychological Impacts on Search Personnel

Search personnel never work in a vacuum, somehow exempt from their own psychological reactions. In fact, each searcher comes into the search mission with their own psychological background. Whether good or bad, it comes with the territory. Humans possess a body, emotions, memories, and an intellect, which provides an integrated *package* on every search.

Most searchers come with upbeat, hopeful, positive mental attitudes and happy personality features when deploying for a search. But, what if one searcher argued with a loved one before setting out for the search or arrives with very little sleep. One searcher's stomach hurts and he/she wont tell anyone for fear of staff asking them to leave. Yet others experience financial difficulties, a recent death in the family, a sick mother, rebelling teenagers, an irritating boss or any number of distracting and worrisome issues in their lives. This psychology comes to work with each searcher when they commit themselves to the mission.

During a search mission, it often becomes necessary for SAR personnel to wear many hats, so to speak, by engaging in numerous activities which transcend the specific areas of expertise and training they posses.

Anxiety, pressure to succeed and, physical exhaustion inevitably take toll on search personnel. Additional psychological pressures also add to a searchers experience by emotional stress and the sometimes traumatic experience of dealing with family and friends of the missing/rescued subject*(s)*.

Critical Incidents and Crisis Intervention

The lost person, family and friends of the lost person, general public, and search personnel all encounter their own psychological reactions to the search situation or *critical incident*. That does not mean that the search mission needs extra levels of chaos. The psychological elements involved with all people in every aspect of a search mission actually help or get mitigated, controlled and directed. Many of the crisis intervention remarks below apply to anyone. Some comments, especially those under the topic of search stress, specifically address the needs of search personnel.

Critical Incidents

Many critical incidents evoke traumatic scenes in the imagination of a lost person or the loved one of a lost person, which in turn, cause powerful emotional reactions *(crisis)* in those people involved with the event. Almost every SAR member remembers their own worst case scenario and categorizes it as a *critical incident*. The following list provides examples of critical incidents:

- Line of duty death of a searcher
- Suicide of a colleague, friend, family member or co-worker
- Serious search related injury
- Multi-casualty events/ disaster / terrorism incidents
- Events with a high degree of threat to the personnel
- Significant events involving children
- Events in which personnel know the victim
- Events with excessive media interest
- Prolonged or negative outcome events or searches where searchers never find the subject
- Any significantly powerful, overwhelming distressing event

Crisis

An acute emotional *reaction* to a powerful stimulus or demand, as well as a state of emotional turmoil, describes a crisis. Two main types of crises exist, maturational and situational. A maturational crises comes about as a result of development, experience, growth or aging as a human being. Retirement, develops into a crisis for some people, as they shift from intense daily work activities to a whole new set of interests and pursuits.

A situational crises consists of an event such as a natural disaster, death, accidents, loss, and damage to property. They also include getting lost or an overdue or unaccounted for friend or relative. Finding a dead person, particularly a child, at the conclusion of a search or some other gruesome outcome consistently generates a crisis reaction in most search personnel. All these examples usually produce a critical incident, at least for those involved in them. Crisis reactions come from a direct response to a critical incident.

General Crisis Concepts

Although every person reacts in their own way to a critical incident, some general concepts apply to most people.

- People fall vulnerable to a crisis at almost any time in their life. But vulnerability to a crisis reaction fails to mean that a person stays in a state of crisis on a regular basis. Thankfully, crisis reactions occur on a very infrequent basis.
- A crisis reaction always puts the person involved in distress, even though others fail to see the crisis event as upsetting.
- Most crises, including search operations, happen suddenly and unexpectedly, making people inadequately and ill prepared to manage them.
- Temporary in nature, most acute crisis reactions subside in 24 to 72 hours.
- The usual coping methods people use to cope on a day-to-day basis tend to fail during a crisis.
- Crisis events produce potentially dangerous or unacceptable behaviors for the victims and the people concerned with their welfare.
- Most distressed people react positively to and appreciate the support provided by others.

Crisis Characteristics

The three main characteristics of any crisis include the following:

1. The relative **balance** that usually exists between a person's **thinking** abilities and **emotions** *gets disrupted*. Causing a lost person to behave in an irrational manner and further endangering them.
2. The **usual coping methods fail** to work in the face of unusual and overwhelming circumstances. When our usual reactions fail to work, we encounter heightened distress and poorly thought out behaviors.
3. **Evidence of mild to severe impairment** in the individual or group involved in the critical incident exists. Even if not in their best interests, a highly distressed person tends to run or hide. In some cases they freeze up entirely and fail to make rational decisions.

A number of factors make a crisis more difficult, or alternatively, easier to manage. The suddenness and intensity of the event, and its duration, influences the difficulties in managing the crisis. Other factors affecting the management of a crisis consist of the age of the person in a crisis and the availability of resources to handle the situation.

Crisis Intervention

The use of common sense lessens emotional turmoil and helps maintain control when a crisis reaction occurs. *Crisis intervention* describes many types of support given to people overwhelmed by the circumstances around them. Crisis intervention offers an *active*, *temporary* and *supportive* process for individuals or groups experiencing an acute state of emotional distress. Some refer to it as *emotional* or *psychological* first aid. Crisis intervention developed over the last century and a half as an organized and systematic approach to assist a distressed person or a group to return to adaptive functions and recover from the crisis reaction. Crisis intervention requires some training but no background in the mental health field to apply it effectively, therefore, any personnel, with the appropriate training, uses it in the field whenever necessary. Searchers usually provide one on one support, the most common form of crisis intervention.

Crisis Intervention Goals

Crisis intervention helps to stabilize both the situation and the intense emotional reactions to the situation, in addition to mitigating the psychological impact of the crisis event. Additionally, crisis intervention attempts to mobilize helpful resources for those in distress and normalize a person's reaction to the situation. Ultimately, crisis intervention aims at restoring people back to their normal functions. Try not to think of crisis intervention as a form of psychotherapy or a substitute for psychotherapy. The use of crisis intervention never cures any physical or psychological condition. It only offers a support process during times of emotional turmoil.

The goals of crisis intervention includes the following:

- Mitigate impact of event *(lower tension)*
- Facilitates a normal recovery processes for normal people with normal reactions to abnormal events
- Restoration to adaptive function

Principles of Crisis Intervention

The seven core principles of crisis intervention follow:

1. **Simplicity:** Keep it simple. People respond to simple not complexity in a crisis.
2. **Brevity:** Keep it short. Staff lacks excessive time during a search mission, sometimes only minutes in most situations. Trained Critical Incident Stress Management team members present at the base camp, tend to spend more time with the family members of the missing person. Search personnel usually receive brief contact *(3-5 total contacts of only a few minutes each is typical)*.
3. **Innovation:** Try to use novel ideas to help. Creatively manage new situations. New circumstances evolve all the time in a search mission. As circumstances alter, crisis intervention services need to adapt.
4. **Pragmatism:** Keep it practical. Constructive suggestions work best. When suggestions to distressed people include the unrealistic, they will lose trust in those trying to help them.
5. **Proximity:** Place support near the person's normal work area. Effective contacts work closer to operational zones or in their homes.
6. **Immediacy:** Provide assistance right away. A crisis demands rapid intervention. The distress and disturbance grows significantly with unexpected and prolonged delays in intervention.
7. **Expectant:** Encourage the person or group in crisis, by making them believe in a manageable situation, and that people always recover from this type of experience. The crisis intervener or searcher assigned to provide crisis support works to set up expectations with reasonably positive outcomes. They also pay careful attention not to instill false hopes or unrealistic expectations.

The Seven Steps to Managing a Crisis Reaction:

Assessment

Every crisis reaction requires a quick assessment before taking action. An assessment covers two important features. First, the *situational assessment* and second, determining the *severity of emotional distress*. A *situational assessment* encompasses what just happened and what continues to occur. The type of person involved and how many. Any unusual aspects of the situation that the crisis worker needs to keep in mind. Situational assessment also takes into consideration whether or not the situation includes any threats to the search staff. It questions the current status of the search mission and who needs help, such as a recently found subject, the family, a relative or friends of a still missing person or search and rescue personnel.

The second portion of the assessment, determining the *severity of emotional distress* felt by those involved in the situation. Looks at the severity of emotional distress and gives us insight into how we need to react and how quickly we need to assist the person, group or search unit. It assesses whether or not so much distress exists that it impairs and individual or groups functions and it they need a medical assessment due to the extreme distress.

- Obtain as much basic information as possible. Like the nature of the stressful event such as; an injured searcher, aviation accident, a crime such as sexual assault or other violent act, sudden death of a loved one, suicidal threat from a teenager, severe illness, fire, flood, property loss, terrorist act, loss of job, physical injury, Alzheimer's patient, psychiatric breakdown, a gruesome find, etc. Look at who needs help, possibly a relative of the missing person? Look at any alcohol or drug involvement? Take into consideration if a history of psychiatric disturbance exists, and make sure to ask witnesses about any possible impairment.
- Any life threatening conditions present *(drug overdose, suicidal or homicidal threat, a weapon, and dangerous weather conditions)*? Some friends and relatives of a missing person react poorly to bad news and possibly experience an out-of-control response. If that occurs, the person needs immediate transport from the base camp or even from the field to a hospital for further evaluation. Often staff needs to call on police services to protect the searchers and the person needing help. Never hesitate to call police, emergency medical services or other forms of assistance when you encounter an emotionally out-of-control person. Always keep yourself and fellow searchers out of danger. If the person makes homicidal or suicidal threats call for back up personnel. In other words, never work alone.
- Analyze the impact of the crisis event occurring and the effect on those directly involved *(mild; moderate; severe)*? Remember severe temperatures, altitude, injury, and toxicity dramatically change a person's behavior. Resolving an environmental situation, sometimes improves the behavior.
- Take into consideration if the symptoms exhibit a typical crisis response or show unusual. Some classic symptoms include; increased heart rate, elevated breathing rate and feeling distressed. Unusual symptoms consist of; hallucinations, chest pain and acting out in a violent rage. The more out of the ordinary the symptoms, the more likely a person needs immediate professional medical or psychiatric assistance.
- Who needs help, just an individual, children, family members, another group, or an entire community for example?
- Determine the type of help needed. Police, emergency medical assistance, hospitalization, family involvement, or crisis worker support only.
- Look at when staff needs to administer help, immediately or possibly delay for a few hours, or even a day. Check and see if the circumstances of the search allow appropriate crisis intervention or not.
- To provide the right help at this time, determine the necessary types of resources to use. Check on the availability of the resources in the midst of the search operations.

Establish Rapport

Accomplish this step simultaneously with the assessment stage.

- Make contact with the individual and introduce yourself as well as anyone else working with you.
- Convey respect for and acceptance of the person. If working with an older adult, use titles like *Mr.* or *Mrs.*

- Assure the person that you want to help.
- Listen carefully to a distressed person.
- Never rush the person.
- Try not to lighten the mood by joking. Distressed people tend to think in concrete terms and usually fail to find the lost person situation as funny. Jokes evoke anger from the person more than understanding and appreciation.
- Demonstrate friendly, kind, and concerned behaviors while at the same time maintaining a professional attitude.
- Use appropriate body positioning and try to get on the same eye level. Especially when working with children.
  - Speak in a calm, confident and controlled manner.

Explore the Crisis Situation

- Ask them if something specific just occurred that upset them, or if the overall search operations upsets them. Encourage the distressed person to talk about how they feel.
- Ask if this particular event or another painful experience happened in the past. Past events make the best predictors, so if the current event occurred before, try to learn a little more about the previous events and how the subject handled them.
- Ask how the person coped with similar experiences in the past. What helped them through previous situations? What made the other situations worse?
- Discuss any potentially dangerous or threatening aspects of the current experience. For example; any serious conflicts between family members present in base camp. Or, a friend or a family member present at base camp who needs medications for a physical condition, but wants to stay and not go home and get it. If the staff fails to ask the right questions, material remains hidden until it shows up in the form of disruptive behavior.
- Use a series of open-ended questions to get the best information from the person. Open ended requests such as; please tell me more about how your son reacted the last time he went missing? Encourage people to say more than a simple yes or no in response to your questions.
- Ask the person to tell his or her own view of the current crisis experience. Get them to describe their relationship with the lost person. Sometimes they give important details that may be helpful in the search.
- Listen carefully and empathetically. Avoid forming judgments. You need to remain objective and open to the conversation so you do not miss important information. Your judgments can "blind" you or keep you from hearing information that could help calm the crisis reaction or alter the search.
- Use reflection of emotional content *("That must have been frightening when you first received the news that he was missing.")* and paraphrase *("If I heard you correctly, you are angry with the investigator because you do not feel that you were listened to earlier today.")*.

Explore the Feelings

- Although some of the emotional distress related to the search is spontaneously discussed when the crisis situation is reviewed, it is important to discuss any emotional features of the situation that may still be hidden. Often guilt feelings, anger, resentment or arguments contributed to the person becoming lost. Knowing the emotional status of the lost person can be quite helpful in finding that person.
- Sometimes it is helpful to apologize for having to ask so many questions. "I am sorry to be asking you so many questions. I do not mean to upset you, but experience in search and rescue has taught us that little things that seem unimportant may actually contribute to our search team's ability to find your loved one."
- Active and intense listening coupled with concern and support for the person is the best technique to gather information about emotional content.
- Try to mentally put yourself into the person's situation. Ask yourself, "What would help me?"

If you cannot relate to their particular situation, you might ask, "If this person was someone I love, what would help my loved one through the situation?" In most cases you will pick something that is supportive and helpful.

Develop Helpful Alternatives

- Ask the person about what usually helps them most in a crisis situation. Also ask if they know what might help them now. Sometimes they will guide you. For example, they might say that their pastor is an important help to them. You can then inquire if it would be helpful to see if the pastor is available to come to the base camp or if they might be transported to place where they could meet with the pastor.
- Ask the person if they need anything right now such as food, water, etc.
- Ask the person if they have tried any thing that has helped them in the past.
- Encourage the person to do some of those things if they have not tried them yet.
- If a person fails to generate any practical stress reducing options associated with waiting while the search teams look in their assigned sectors, on their own, prepare to offer them some suggestions on managing stress.

Develop and Implement a Crisis Action Plan

- Develop a list of possible options based on the assessment of the crisis and the discussion with the distressed person in the previous steps. Most of the time personnel creates a mental list, since time limits them in writing down a plan in a crisis situation. Especially an active search. Make sure to put all possible solutions to the crisis on the list, always including options that, more than likely, get rejected. This helps avoid overlooking potentially helpful solutions. It also helps to identify any potential failure points before going too far along in developing a crisis plan.
- Pick out the best options and develop an action plan with the best chances of success.
- Implement the chosen crisis plan immediately. Delays often allow complications to creep up which then inhibit a successful resolution of the crisis.
- Provide whatever assistance appears necessary to quickly implement the action plan.

Check on the Plan's Success and Follow-up

Never implement an action plan and then stop. The crisis support person needs to constantly monitor the progress of the plan. This way if alterations on a course of action need to occur, personnel immediately identifies them, and implements the appropriate measures. New clues, locating a witness, or a rumor tend to alter the course of a search without warning. Therefor crisis support personnel need to prepare for unexpected developments in the search. Try to avoid getting caught up in a specific plan, and rigidly adhering to it. The possibility exists that the proposed scenario wont work exactly as planned and changes need to occur.

- Check on the success of the plan
- Change or refine the crisis plan if necessary
- Maintain a successful plan until achieving resolution of the crisis reaction or until handing it off to other qualified mental health providers
- Follow-up with the person or group who experienced the crisis event
- If the search or crisis gets resolution, then abandon the plan and close out the crisis intervention
- If evidence of significant and continued impairment exist, then refer the subject/subjects for further assessment and possible professional care

The seven steps of the crisis intervention process reviewed.

1. Assess the situation and the impact on the person*(s)*
2. Establish rapport
3. Explore the crisis situation
4. Explore the feelings and reactions
5. Develop helpful alternatives
6. Develop and implement the crisis plan
7. Check on the plan and follow-up

Concluding Remarks on Search Psychology and Crisis Intervention

Every person involved in any aspect of a search mission brings his or her own psychological background. Search psychology either works as an ally or an enemy in a search. The more people know about psychology, the easier it gets to work with it and control it.

Crisis intervention introduces a set of, relatively easy to learn and apply, tactics to help manage the psychological aspects of any critical incident including search operations. Nobody needs an advanced degree in psychology or social work to use crisis intervention tactics. Peer support personnel such as fellow searchers work on the front line, and often need to mitigate and manage a crisis. Sometimes, under field conditions, they even provide more effective help than mental health professionals. Simple things often make the greatest difference in the lives of others. The best crisis teams consist of a combination of peer support personnel and mental health professionals serving on the team.

The next section focuses on managing search stress for the SAR personnel. The principles and application of crisis intervention discussed in the preceding pages of this chapter help to understand and control the search stress described in the following section.

Part II - Search Stress

Definition of Stress

Stress, better know as, a state of cognitive, emotional and physical arousal, gets caused by exposure to some actual or perceived demand or stimulus in our environment. After arousing someone's intellect, emotions in the body, cause changes to occur in a person's behavior. Stress, at reasonable levels, creates a healthy life, but causes danger in extreme or prolonged situations. When stress gets out of control, it produces a powerful and destructive force. Thus, disrupting a SAR mission and sometimes causing it to fail at achieving any objectives.

Types of Stress

The four main categories of stress:

1. General Stress – routine daily stress of life
2. Cumulative Stress – a build-up of unresolved stress over a lengthy period of time
3. Critical Incident Stress – A normal but painful reaction to a traumatic event
4. Prolonged or abnormal conditions - resulting from an exposure to caused one or more by traumatic events

Stress Related Conditions Caused by Traumatic Experiences

Post-Traumatic Stress Disorder - *(PTSD usually results from an exposure to a severe traumatic event. Additional information on PTSD is presented later in this chapter. But, as seen in the list below, other stress related conditions sometimes arises after a traumatizing experience).* Other conditions resulting from traumatic experiences include, among others:

- Panic attacks - Periodic episodes in which a person feels overwhelmed and that they might die
- Panic disorder – When panic attacks become a repetitive, frequent, and severe pattern.
- Major depression – Persistent sadness, loss of pleasure in formerly interesting things, insomnia, loss of energy, feeling worthless, excessive and inappropriate guilt, loss of concentration and poor decisions
- Extreme fear reactions – Phobic reactions
- Dissociation reactions such as feelings of being in a movie or "outside of oneself"
- Substance abuse including alcohol abuse
- Brief psychotic reactions – the symptoms of a psychotic episode, but symptoms dissipate once the crisis subsides
- Stress related physical diseases
- Some personality disorders
- Other

Normal Stress Pathways

General stress and **critical incident stress** reactions *(numbers 1 and 3 previous page)* refer to normal pathways of stress. General stress occurs as a result of the demands of everyday living. People usually deal with general stress, recover from it and move on in life. General stress creates healthy living as long as it never increases to excessive amounts, or continues for prolonged periods of time. Keep in mind that every searcher comes into a search mission with the general stresses of every day life. If personnel properly rest, eat, and receive adequate information on the search, they tend to focus on and carry out their mission leaving daily stressors in the background, and not letting them interfere with the search operations.

Critical Incident Stress: A normal type of stress consisting of a normal stress reaction in normal people to an abnormal event. A critical incident Stress fails to exist without a critical incident. Despite its normalcy, this stress comes with an unpleasant reaction and pain. The pain of the experience reveals a situation so intense that it demands our attention. Critical incident stress As part of a healthy human drive toward survival, critical incident stress demonstrates a heightened state of arousal that results from an exposure to some powerful traumatic event. This occurs in every search operation when fatigue, poor self care, and mounting operational stressors take over. If accompanied by little leadership and guidance, this sets the stage for every day general stress to come forward and create difficult personal experiences for the searcher.

Signs and Symptoms of Critical Incident Stress

Any severe symptoms, especially those in the physical category, need the attention of a medical or psychological professional. Failure to refer people with severe symptoms for further assessment leads to extremely negative consequences. Always try not to take unnecessary risks with your own health and wellness or that of others by failing to seek out further assessment. If any intense or unusual symptoms arise, make sure to strongly recommend further evaluation. Too many stress symptoms exist to list them all, but the list below presents some of the most common physical, cognitive, emotional and behavioral symptoms *(See Figure 29-1 next page)*.

Physical	Cognitive	Emotional	Behavioral
Nausea	Slowed thinking	Anxiety	Withdrawal
Upset stomach	Impaired decisions	Fear	Running away
Muscle tremors	Impaired problem solving	Guilt	Hiding
Loss of coordination	Disorientation	Grief	Angry outbursts
Profuse sweating	Confusion	Depression	Emotional tirades
Chills	Poor concentration	Sadness	Acting out
Diarrhea	Poor calculations	Feeling lost	Defensive position
Dizziness	Poor memory	Abandoned	Excessive sleeping
Chest pain	Difficulty naming things	Isolated	Hyperactivity
Rapid pulse	Intrusive thoughts	Worry	Hypo activity
Rapid breathing	Distressing dreams	Anger	Startle response
Headaches	Low attention span	Irritability	Emotionally numb
Increased BP	Muscle aches	Emotional shock	Sleep disturbance

Figure 29-1 Critical Incident Stress Signs and Symptoms

Critical Incident Stress Management

Critical Incident Stress Management *(CISM)* makes up a comprehensive, integrated, systematic, multi-tactic form of crisis intervention, that when applied, manages critical incident stress after traumatic events. CISM involves a coordinated program of tactics linking and blending together to alleviate the cognitive, physical, emotional and behavioral reactions following a traumatic event.

A CISM system depends on critical placement of each element before a traumatic event occurs. This makes pre-incident stress education essential for organizations and individuals, and calls for creating practical plans for organizational and individual stress management. CISM teams require proper training along with well developed plans and protocols. Finally, organizations need to put sensible policies in place, to care for their personnel in the aftermath of a critical incident. The absence of stress management policies in an organization demonstrates a lack of support for members or employees when a critical incident strikes.

SAR units need CISM component in place during a search mission also. SAR operations, need on-site support services at the base camp. Always make sure that people eat, receive fluids, adequate rest, provide shelter, and inform and protect them during emergency operations. This creates a good CISM program. In addition, certain conditions call for some one-on-one psychological support. CISM services entail providing appropriate advice and guidance to supervisors when needed. On occasion CISM offers direct support to a lost person, once found, or to that person's family and friends while still waiting, for the activation of Red Cross or other appropriate resources in prolonged operation.

After a critical incident, CISM services include; one-on-one crisis intervention, informational group processes such as Rest, Information Transition Services (RITS) and Crisis Management Briefings (CMB), interactive group processes such as defusing and Critical Incident Stress Debriefing *(CISD)*, spouse support services, follow up services and referrals for those identified as needing more assistance.

Remember, CISM involves a multiple not single tactic approaches to critical incident management. Therefore, individual interventions, group interventions, significant other interventions, organizational interventions and community interventions all fall under the umbrella of CISM.

CISM Teams

Over 500 CISM teams operate in the United States and an additional 500 serve in 28 nations around the world. Typically, a team consist of mental health professionals working as partners with peer support personnel from search organizations, fire services, law enforcement agencies, emergency medical organizations, military personnel, nurses, or employees from schools, businesses and industrial settings. Teams provide voluntary services to their organizations and communities.

Participants on a CISM team require training which consists of a minimum of 3 courses, 2 days each in length. The courses provide skills training in the following areas:

- Assessment of the situation and the severity of impact of an event on those exposed to it
- Developing a strategic plan to manage the incident
- Establishing skills to assist individuals in crisis
- Informational group intervention skills *(Rest, Information and Transition Services for staff and Crisis Management Briefings)*
- Interactive group intervention skills *(Defusing and Critical Incident Stress Debriefing)*
- Follow-up and referral services

CISM Tactics for Controlling Search Stress

Stress management techniques or tactics never apply equally to all people, under all circumstances and at all times. For this reason, teams need a collection of techniques to use for different people under different circumstances. Choosing the right technique for the job, makes the task easier and creates a better chance of success. Likewise, if the right stress management technique gets used, it makes the task easier and enhance the success potential.

Before a Search Incident Occurs

Long before deploying on a search mission, teams need to accomplish the following suggestions:

- Obtain education and information on critical incidents, critical incident stress and the crisis response. Well informed people manage critical incident stress when it strikes better.
- Make sure to put policies and procedures for CISM in place for personnel involved in the Search and Rescue mission.
- Establish a well trained CISM team with the ability to provide a variety of services to individuals and groups under different circumstances. CISM trained peer support personnel *(people actually searching)* provides a major advantage for search organizations. Similar to people trained in wilderness medicine actually on field units involved in a search.

During the Search Mission

- Calm yourself before deploying to a search task. Try breathing deeply. This gives you a few seconds to think about how to approach the situation.
- The controlled action can be helpful in reducing the tension associated with waiting for a search task, but try not to become overwhelmed by the intense stimuli of the activation.
- Take frequent breaks. Brief rest periods coupled with food and fluids helps keep you alert during a mission.
- Actual operation work periods vary from search to search. Therefor a few general rules exist, to help supervisors in charge. Typically run a two hour work period followed by a half hour down time. Intense cold, heat or the intensity of the scene itself, cause alterations in the deployment cycles.
- One half day off after every five days and a full day off after ten consecutive days of search work helps to keep people functional.
- Remind yourself that you posses the skills to carry out the mission.
- A sense of humor helps but know when to use it. Inappropriate use includes: in the presence of the actual victims or their family members.
- Try not to over control your emotions. A brief and controlled discharge of emotions helps more than completely suppressing emotions which possibly hurts more later.

- Limit caffeinated products during search operations work. They tend to elevate stress responses and cause some people to feel agitated and tense.
- Avoid alcohol altogether since it interferes with Rapid Eye Movement *(REM)* sleep patterns. REM sleep helps us to mentally process the traumatic events or pressures of the last few days.
- Eat, even if you do not feel like it. You need energy.
- Avoid too much sugar, foods high in fat content, processed foods and white bread.
- Eat balanced meals with proteins, complex carbohydrates and fruits and vegetables.
- In a prolonged incident, try to limit shifts to 8 hours if possible. If unusual circumstances require longer time commitments, only allow a maximum of 12 hours of work. Search organizations usually practice a formula of alternating between 12 hours on duty, then 12 hours off duty. This helps to maintain a healthy work force.
- Constantly reminding search crews of the time on search missions, helps people to stay oriented and focused.
- Even in unusual circumstances, everyone needs at least four hours of sleep in twenty four hours, but never make four hours in twenty four hours the persistent rule. If it goes on for too many days, health problems tend to arise. Ideally, searchers need 7 to 8 hours of sleep per night.
- Limit exposure to gory sights and disturbing sounds and smells.
- Disengage non essential personnel from the scene as soon as possible.
- Try not to make personnel feel stuck on one assignment indefinitely by rotating them to various duties whenever possible.
- Practice rotating people from high stress operations to moderately stressful work before moving them to rest areas. People also adjust to intense work situations better, when they move from rest to moderately stressful work, and then onto highly stressful work.
- People handling human remains and personal effects experience extremely stressful work. These people need frequent breaks and emotional support. Also, try to give them new assignments as soon as possible.
- Call in supportive resources to assist one's personnel according to the needs expressed by the operations personnel.
- Keep on scene support services from CISM teams, low key and unobtrusive, never interfering with ongoing operations. CISM services in the field need to focus on providing advice to supervisors, and assisting individuals experiencing significant reactions to the emergency services work. Some situations provide direct crisis intervention services to the primary victims and survivors of the incident, until other resources come to assist.

After a Search

- Rest
- Eat nutritious meals
- Exercises that physically exert the body, help reduce distress chemicals. Even walking really helps. Never overdue it though.
- When offered, try to attend interactive group support services such as; a Critical Incident Stress Debriefing by a trained CISM team. This tends to take the *edge off* of a bad incident and help in restoring unit cohesion and unit performance for all the members of one's group. Everyone gets a sense of the *big picture* and comments made by one member of the group often clarify the experience for other members of the group. Keep in mind that group services after search missions provide support not critiques of the event.
- Restore normal routines as soon as possible.
- Keep yourself active. Avoid boredom.
- Encourage personnel to express any personal feelings to people they trust.
- Searches with tragic outcomes, often cause disturbing dreams and memories. They generally decrease over several weeks time, but if they remain intense after three weeks to a month, suggest seeking out CISM team members for assistance and/or a referral for professional care.
- Avoid joking with fellow workers about the tragedy too much. Some individuals remain sensitive to the experience long after the mission ends.

- Try not to engage in unproductive criticism of others. Let the organization's leadership handle mistakes made during the incident, and any corrective action or additional training if required. Constantly bringing up mistakes made by colleagues, never helps individual members of the organization or their fellow search and rescue personnel.
- The intensity of a major event frequently stirs up anger in a person. Try not to take it personally. Usually it subsides in a reasonable time. If not, encourage the angry search member to seek professional help to help get things back under control.
- Focus on the here and now. Telling old war stories of events worse than the current event, never helps people with only the recent search for reference.
- Listen to those who want to talk about their experience.
- Shedding tears after a painful event normally occurs. But frequent uncontrolled crying spells, accompanied by sleep disturbance, and an inability to return to normal duties, indicates that a person needs assistance from a CISM team or a mental health professional.
- Help each other by trying to understand and care for each other. Those who perform the same duties offer the best support. If people come across as careless with the feelings of others, then the opposite rule applies. Meaning, no one potentially hurts you more than one who knows what happens in the field first-hand.

Critical Incident Stress Debriefings

Critical Incident Stress Debriefing *(CISD)* offers one of the most effective ways to assist a homogeneous group of search personnel exposed to a traumatic event. This seven-phase interactive group crisis intervention process, developed in 1983, proved to lower stress symptoms and facilitate the recovery of emergency operations personnel. Close to one hundred studies indicate that when units provide CISD by a trained CISM team, that carefully follows procedures and protocols, they generate very effective outcomes.

Critical Incident Stress Debriefing *(CISD)* consists of a specific, interactive group crisis intervention process provided by a specially trained team. Search experts designed CISD for a homogeneous group, to mitigate the impact of a traumatic event on the group members. Search units benefit greatly from a CISD. A CISD typically occurs several days after the crisis and lasts between one and three hours. The CISD technique depends on CISM. It only works within the context of CISM's comprehensive, integrated, systematic, and multi-faceted approach to crisis intervention. Never consider CISD *psychotherapy,* or a substitute for psychotherapy. CISD, a *support and assessment* service, only guides discussions of a traumatic event.

The team leaders provide information on the typical physical and psychological impact of the event and many techniques used to reduce stress reactions. The leadership makes every effort to normalize these reactions and offer specific suggestions to enhance the group members' stress management capabilities. CISD works as a screening tool for determining if group members need additional support or perhaps a referral for therapy. The CISD enhances a search units cohesion and performance.

The seven phases of CISD:

1. **Introduction**
2. **Fact**
3. **Thought**
4. **Reactions**
5. **Symptoms**
6. **Teaching**
7. **Re-entry**

Successful management of CISD, requires several conditions:

- A homogeneous group
- A concluded critical incident or one beyond most acute stages
- Only group members exposed to the same traumatic event attend the CISD
- CISM teams providing the CISD need proper training and experience

Abnormal, Dangerous or Disruptive Stress Pathways

The other two types of stress *(numbers: 2 - cumulative stress, and 4 - Prolonged or abnormal conditions - resulting from an exposure to one or more traumatic events)* are **not** normal pathways of stress. Both posses the capability of producing considerable disruption in the lives of those who suffer through these conditions. If these types of stress continue without attention they set the stage for deterioration in health and performance.

Cumulative stress, a pathological pathway of stress, consist of an excessive accumulation of unresolved general stress, which tends to develop physical illness and emotional distress. Cumulative stress starts off with a warning phase characterized by four primary symptoms – chronic fatigue, boredom, anxiety and depression. When people ignore the primary symptoms, mild symptoms such as more frequent colds, gastro-intestinal distress, headaches, alcohol use, feelings of intense anger and other physical and emotional symptoms appear. Unresolved cumulative stress escalates into more and more severe symptoms until a person develops persistent physical and emotional problems requiring professional mental health and medical intervention.

Prolonged or abnormal conditions - resulting from an exposure to one or more traumatic events. In the beginning of part two of this chapter, a list of conditions that can arise from an exposure to one or more traumatic events was presented. It would help the reader to review those conditions before reading ahead. On that list is Post Traumatic Stress Disorder (PTSD). As noted earlier it is not the only condition that may come about as a result of an exposure to a traumatic event. But, it is usually considered the worst of the abnormal or permanent conditions that sometimes results from a traumatic experience. Further discussion of PTSD therefore follows.

Post-traumatic Stress Disorder *(PTSD),* one of the most destructive forms of stress, develops from exposure to a significant traumatic event. Events such as, finding the mutilated body of a child potentially causes PTSD. The condition comes about only as a direct result of unresolved critical incident stress. Once diagnosed, the most serious PTSD conditions typically require mental health intervention to overcome. A PTSD diagnosis requires at least the following criteria:

1. It starts with an exposure to a horrible, threatening or disgusting event. Events that initiate a critical incident stress reaction tend to bring about PTSD. If the critical incident stress goes unresolved the PTSD develops. The latest publication (2013) from the American Psychiatric Association on the criteria for PTSD requires an exposure to actual or threatened death, serious injury, or sexual violence.
2. One or more *Intrusion symptoms*. A person sees, hears, smells, tastes or feels some aspects of the event over and over. Or the person experiences distressing dreams and nightmares or struggles with uncontrollable thoughts of the event.
3. A person with PTSD tries to avoid any reminders of the event. The criteria for PTSD require a persistent avoidance of stimuli associated with the trauma, beginning after the traumatic event. Avoidance includes: places, people, conversations, and circumstances.
4. PTSD causes intensified feelings of arousal and reactivity that began with the exposure to the traumatic event and may have worsened after the traumatic event, causing them to experience trouble with sleeping, resting, and relaxing. They also anticipate further harmful events.
5. A PTSD diagnosis requires at least thirty days of symptoms.
6. PTSD produces considerable disruption in normal life pursuits at home and at work. They feel stuck and unable to participate in everyday life like before the traumatic event took place.
7. The disturbance originates from something other than the physiologic effects of a substance *(e.g. medication, alcohol)* or other medical condition.
8. Negative alterations in cognitions and mood associated with the traumatic event beginning or worsening after the traumatic event.

PTSD Symptom Severity

PTSD symptoms can be mild, moderate or severe. Mild symptoms tend to resolve spontaneously over time with or without help. Early assessment and appropriate intervention makes a huge difference in recovery. Extreme traumatic stress reactions or those lasting longer than 3 weeks indicate a greater danger of developing PTSD. If personnel find it difficult to shake off the effects of a search mission in about 3 weeks and if they are having a negative impact on your performance at work or at home, then a CISM team member needs to refer them to someone who can properly assess their condition.

Coping With Prolonged or Abnormal Traumatic Stress Reactions

Never leave your recovery up to others. You are the most important person in your recovery.

- Participate in crisis and stress management programs such as the Critical Incident Stress Debriefing.
- Never wait until symptoms become severe.
- Never self-treat, especially with severe symptoms.
- PTSD does not cause all symptoms. Make sure people receive a professional evaluation to determine PTSD exists or some other condition. Many other physical or emotional conditions tend to cause stress symptoms or accompany PTSD.
- Learn about PTSD. Read books. Take a class.
- Accept appropriate help. Several different types of therapies help people deal with PTSD; most of them working in relatively short periods of time.
- Remember, most people recover from PTSD.
- Tap as many resources as you need.
- You are not alone in your struggle.

Conclusion

Search personnel serve as the most important resource in Search and Rescue. A search manager responsibility includes assuring that all search personnel receive emotional support during the operation. This responsibility for supporting one's personnel, however, never ends upon completion of a mission. A search managers needs to provide continuous access to resources, such as CISM teams, which facilitate the recovery of their personnel and their return to normal life functions.

Author Jeff Mitchell's brief Bio:

Dr. Jeffrey T. Mitchell serves as a SAR Instructor and Clinical Professor of Emergency Health Services at the University of Maryland, Baltimore County. Dr. Mitchell serves as co-founder and President of the Emeritus of the International Critical Incident Stress Foundation. As a Certified Trauma Specialist, Dr. Mitchell holds Diplomat status with the American Academy of Experts in Traumatic Stress.

He consults with the United Nations as a member of the Working Group on Stress Management, and authored over 270 articles and 17 books in the fields of crisis intervention, traumatic stress and critical incident stress management. The Austrian Red Cross awarded him with a Bronze Medal for his support of search and rescue personnel involved in two national tragedies, a major avalanche and a deadly tunnel fire.

Selected References for Further Study

Adler, A., Litz, B.T., Castro, C.A., Suvak, M., Thomas, J.L., Burrell, L. (2008) Group randomized trial of critical incident stress debriefing provided to US peacekeepers. Journal of traumatic Stress, 21, 253-263.

Adler, A., Bliese, P.D., McGurk, D., Hoge, C.W., & Castro, C.A. (2009) Battlemind debriefing and battlemind training as early intervention with soldiers returning from Iraq: Randomized by platoon. Journal of Consulting and Clinical Psychology, 77, 928-940.

American Psychiatric Association (1964). *First Aid for Psychological Reactions in Disasters.* Washington, DC: American Psychiatric Association.

Boscarino, J.A., Adams, R.E. & Figley, C.R. (2011) Mental health service use after the world trade center disaster: Utilization trends and comparative effectiveness. Journal of Nervous and Mental Disease, 199, 91-99.

Caplan, G. (1964). *Principles of Preventive Psychiatry.* New York: Basic Books. Chemtob, C., Tomas, S., Law, W., Cremniter, D. Post disaster psychosocial intervention. *American Journal of Psychiatry*, 134, 415-417.

Deahl, M., Srinivasan, M., Jones, N., Thomas, J., Neblett, C., and Jolly, A. (2000). Preventing psychological trauma in soldiers. The role of operational stress training and psychological debriefing. *British Journal of Medical Psychology*, 73, 77-85.

Dyregrov, A. (1989). Caring for Helpers in Disaster Situations. *Disaster Management,* 2, 25-30.

Everly, G.S., Jr. (1999). Emergency Mental Health: An Overview. *International Journal of Emergency Mental Health,* 1, 3-7.

Everly, G.S., Jr. and Mitchell, J.T. (1999). *Critical Incident Stress Management: A new era and standard of care in crisis intervention.* Ellicott City, MD: Chevron Publishing Corporation.

Everly G. S., Jr., Mitchell J. T. (2008). Integrative crisis intervention and disaster mental health. Ellicott City, MD: Chevron.

Everly, G.S. and Mitchell, J.T. (2013) Critical Incident Stress Management CISM: Key papers and core concepts. Ellicott City, MD: Chevron Publishing.

Flannery, R.B., Jr., Anderson, E., Marks, L. & Uzoma, L. (2000). The Assaulted Staff Action Program (ASAP) and Declines in Rates of Assaults: Mixed replicated
findings. *Psychiatric Quarterly,* 71, 165-175.

Gibson, M. (2006). *Order From Chaos: Responding to Traumatic Events.* Bristol: UK, The Policy Press, University of Bristol.

Jenkins, S.R. (1996). Social Support and Debriefing Efficacy Among Emergency Medical Workers After a Mass Shooting Incident. *Journal of Social Behavior and Personality,* 11, 477-492.

Lindemann, E. (1944). Symptomatology and management of acute grief. *American Journal of Psychiatry,* 101, 141-148.

Mitchell, J.T. and Resnik, H.L.P. (1981). *Emergency Response to Crisis.* Englewood Cliffs, NJ: Robert J. Brady Company, Subsidiary of Prentice Hall.

Mitchell, J.T. (2002). Stress Management. In FEMA staff, *Integrated Emergency Management Course.* Emmittsburg, MD: Emergency Management Institute, Federal Emergency Management Agency.

Mitchell, J.T. (2004). Characteristics of Successful Early Intervention Programs. *International Journal of Emergency Mental Health,* 6, 4. 175-184.

Mitchell, J. T. (2007). Group crisis support: Why it works, when and how to provide it. Ellicott City, MD: Chevron Publishing.

Mitchell, J.T. (2015) Group Crisis Intervention, 5th edition. Ellicott City, MD: International critical Incident Stress Foundation.

Mitchell, J.T. (2004). Managing Crises. In R. Coombs (Ed.), *Addiction Counseling Review: Preparing for Comprehensive, Certification, and Licensing.* Mahwah, NJ: Lawrence Erlbaum Associates.

Mitchell, J.T. and Everly, G.S., Jr., (2001). *Critical Incident Stress Debriefing:* An operations manual for CISD, Defusing and other group crisis intervention *services, Third Edition.* Ellicott City, MD: Chevron

Mitchell, J.T. and Resnik, H.L.P. (1981). *Emergency Response to Crisis.* Englewood Cliffs, NJ: Robert J. Brady Company, Subsidiary of Prentice Hall.

Mitchell, J.T. and Visnovske, W.L. (2015) Crucial Moments: Stories of support in times of crisis.

Middletown, DE: Create Space.

Neil, T., Oney, J., DiFonso, L., Thacker, B. and Reichart, W. (1974). *Emotional First Aid.* Louisville: Kemper-Behavioral Science Associates.

O'Flaherty, J. (1995). *Trans World Airlines: Trauma Response Team, Section Leader Manual.* St Louis, MO: Trans World Airlines, Inc.

Parad, H.J. (1971). Crisis Intervention. In R. Morris (Ed.), *Encyclopedia of Social Work* (vol. 1, pp. 196-202). New York: National Association of Social Workers.

Roberts, A.R. (2000). An Overview of Crisis Theory and Crisis Intervention. In A. Roberts (Ed.) *Crisis Intervention Handbook: Assessment, Treatment, and Research.* New York: Oxford University Press.

Roberts, A. (2005). Bridging the Past and Present to the Future of Crisis Intervention and Crisis Management. In Allen Roberts (*Ed.*) *Crisis Intervention Handbook: Assessment, Treatment and Research. Third Edition.* New York: Oxford University Press.

Slaikeu, K.A. (1984). *Crisis Intervention: A handbook for practice and research. Boston*, MA: Allyn and Bacon, Inc.

Tuckey M. R. (2007). Issues in the debriefing debate for the emergency services. Clinical Psychology Science and Practice, 14, 106-16.

Tuckey, M. R. & Scott, J. E. (2014, on line). Group Critical Incident Stress Debriefing with emergency services personnel: A randomized controlled trial. Anxiety, Stress, and Coping.

Demobilization & Post Mission — 30

Objectives:

- List and discuss the key principles of demobilizing resources in an organized, and preplanned manner.

- List and describe the primary planning components of demobilization.

- Identify the primary legal issue associated with demobilization and getting resources back home safely.

- Describe post mission responsibilities, the tasks necessary to fulfill them, and make sure all personnel contributed critiquing the entire operation.

- Conduct an effective post search critique of the operation.

> A written demobilization plan should be required on any large search, as a function of the plans and support crew. Orchestrating demobilization takes teamwork due to the complex nature of providing a small army with food, shelter, and transportation home.
> - Tim J. Setnicka
> *Wilderness Search and Rescue, 1980*

Demobilization: The Overlooked Function

People tend to make the wrong assumptions when it comes to Demobilization. Never think of it as the mirror image of mobilization. This function makes sure all the responding resources get back safely to the same places they came from. When mobilizing for a search, a number of individuals from different places direct, coordinate, and provide transportation to get search and rescue resources to a single point. All too often, when the search terminates, the search staff tells all resources on hand, to put it simply, to go home. Unfortunately, both safety and liability issues accompany demobilization efforts. In some cases, demobilization requires some timely and crucial management decisions.

Timing. When searchers initially check into base camp, staff need to collect information regarding each person's place of origin, method of travel, and travel times. A simple way of accomplishing this task consists of collecting and organizing travel manifests. All units need complete records showing places of origin, method of transportation to search area, their home unit, and unit leader. Logistics capabilities always need assessment. Therefore additional record keeping personnel always helps to catalog logistic capabilities and obtain additional information.

Formal demobilization planning needs to begin within the first-half of the expected duration of the mission.

Demobilization needs a written plan: A good written plan includes release priorities, release procedures and processing activities, who, by name, the responsibilities of each searcher, and a schedule.

Control: A search staff needs total control over resources, which they exercise from base camp to home base. In addition to the obvious need for control to ensure safety and cost effectiveness, availability issues spring up with units away from home and whether or not a new assignment in their own area materializes. Many unforeseen delays occur and priority adjustments only happen with thorough and rigid control.

Communications: Every mission needs adequate, rapid communications among all key personnel and facilities involved in the demobilization effort. Make sure that demobilization communications differs from those involved in the ongoing search effort, if possible *(i.e. different frequency, high band vs. low band, command and control, separate frequencies)*.

Staffing: Staff the demobilization organization to fit the needs of the plan. Always consider both facilities and personnel. The more complex the operation the greater the need for highly qualified facilitating personnel. Staff early and adequately.

Teamwork: Demobilization invariably functions better as a team effort. Demobilization planning and execution calls for total involvement of the entire overhead team.

Safety and Cost Effectiveness: Tired people make mistakes and often lose patience. Adequate rest prior to demobilization takes on added importance for searchers with long travel times. Never sacrifice safety and cost effectiveness for speed. Account for each searcher and make sure no one gets left in the field. Keep all resources in base camp until confirming priorities and transportation arrangements.

The Demobilization Plan

Plan Preparation: The Demobilization Coordinator in close coordination with search overhead personnel prepare the demobilization plan.

Termination *(sudden)* vs. Suspended *(scaled down)*.

- Each of these requires different demobilization approaches.
- Sometimes priorities of release differ.
- Difficulty in coordination and organization depends on sudden termination or scaled down operations.

Demobilization Plans need the following components:

- **General Information:** Includes orientation information and general discussion of the demobilization procedure followed by staff for each search. Sometimes this includes information on the overall situation or even specific instructions.
- **Responsibilities:** Spells out the responsibility for the plan initiation and specific responsibilities by name for various implementation activities. It establishes a chain of command and outlines the activities at each location or processing point. Then determines the personnel in charge at each location or processing point.
- **Release Priorities:** The search manager determines release priorities depending on the situation <u>and</u> by the logistics function depending on transportation availability. Avoid late night releases for travel. Always try to release resources in *good condition* - rested, showered, fed, etc.

    - Example Release Priorities: Aircraft first, then volunteer vs. paid personnel; and the overhead team leaves last.

- **Release Procedures:** This section spells out all the various steps in the release procedures *(e.g. Plans: to support services, to bus loading area, to showers, to home)*. Be specific!
- **Organization and Flow Charts:** Include: forms used, anticipated travel or standby times, routes and methods of travel, procedures to take place at each stop and any other instructions useful in preventing confusion.
- **Directory:** Telephone directory, maps, routes of travel.

Legal Considerations

Consider these following situations:

- A team assisting with the search effort for 36 hours, finds the subject and terminates the mission. No formal demobilization took place, everyone just dispersed. On the way home, the

driver of the team vehicle falls asleep, drives off the road, killing himself and 3 other team members, injures 4 others, and destroys the truck.
- Same situation, but this time the driver crosses the center line, and a head-on collision results, killing a family of 5. Several team members die and several receive injuries, in addition to the unit vehicle getting totaled.
- On the way home, the team stops at a *road house* for a few beers. Later that evening, an accident occurs as a result of fatigue and alcohol, causing death and injury.

QUESTION: In the above situations, who holds the liabillity? Would formal demobilization make a difference?

RECOMMENDATION: Ensure that drivers leave base camp well rested. Offer all personnel a chance to sleep and eat. State in the demobilization plan that the search manager assumes no liability if personnel consume alcohol en route home.

Too often, little or no planning takes place for demobilization, or it comes too late. Things simply fizzle away. Often times this result in incomplete information, missing equipment, poor image of the agency in charge by the responders and many other problems, including legal.

Post Mission

Responsibility

A Search Manager always provides effective critiques of the entire search operation.

- Always critique a suspended mission when personnel fail to find the subject.
- As a minimum, a person's own self-critique helps to review and improve the preplan.

The Critique

A process intended to identify the lessons learned from an exercise or actual event. The following list fails to meet the requirements of a critique:

- A public session intended to lay blame on those who made mistakes.
- A finger-pointing session.
- A forum intended to permit adversaries to embarrass each other.

Critique Objective

To completely review a mission from start to finish. Personnel need to conduct the critique as soon as the mission ends to determine the following:

- **WHY/HOW** the search occurred?
- **HOW** to prevent searches like it in the future.
- **ASSESS** the effectiveness and efficiency of the entire search operation. What went well? What did not? Why or why not?

Elements of the Critique

- Gathering of key mission personnel immediately after the search operation ends.
- Written comments on the search operation suggesting corrections and improvements.
- Analyze the corrections recommended:
  - Decide which corrections to accept.
  - Make changes in the plan.
  - Make changes in facility arrangements.

Critique Considerations

- Compile all necessary information and statistics related to the mission. Consider the search planning maps, logs, missing person questionnaire, debriefing summaries, etc.
- Select a critique format and organize your presentation.
  - Location for holding the critique
  - Who participates in the critique
  - Ask yourself about the need for a Board of Inquiry *(gross mistakes, liability etc.)*
  - Consider using maps, slides, photos

"Only a Fool learns from his own mistakes. A wise man learns from the mistakes of others."
-- Otto von Bismark

Helpful Hints

- Prepare a chronological listing or sequence of time and events
- Assess the positive and put together a step-by-step list of improvements in chronological order
- Provide a mission report for everyone at the critique
- Submit an initial report to critique members, and let them read it to identify any questions Prepare a list of these questions in advance
- Record the critique proceedings
- Examine the search plan

  - Look at whether or not the preplan worked effectively
  - Take into consideration the objectives and their appropriateness
  - Look at the effectiveness of the organization
  - Analyze whether or not the strategy/tactics execution and procedures worked
  - Look at the type of equipment and resources used and whether or not they worked appropriately for the job
  - Identify special problem areas
  - Determine if communication problems existed
  - Look at the efficiency of the whole mission
  - Check the SOPs for effectiveness and completeness
  - Review the investigation *(any criminal activity involved)* and if so, remember, all clues also serve as evidence

Controlling the Oral Critique

- Controller sets the tone by saying what went right
- Limit number of people commenting
- Limit time allotted to speakers
- Control the person who never really understood the Mission or search, but likes their own voice
- Control the person who sees only the negative side of things

Critique Techniques

- Honestly, seek improvements, not faults
- Send the results of the critique to interested parties

> *"If one man calleth thee a donkey, pay him no mind. If two men calleth thee a donkey, get thee a saddle."*
> --Yiddish Proverb

Remember, to always speak honestly, with an open mind. Truth, fact and reality from your perception never mean anything. The perceptions of the other *players (e.g., cooperating organizations, volunteers, the media, etc.)* dictates how they respond and act during future missions. Always find out their perceptions.

Critique Follow-Up

- <u>Revise</u> your search plan as appropriate
- Hold follow-up meetings with organizations, units, or agencies needing to make improvements
- Share information
- Commit to improvements with specific assignments

NOTE: Often all of these considerations get overlooked. As the Search Manager, your job continues until finishing the paperwork.

Post Mission Tasks

Final paperwork

- Mission Report: Include all information on the decision-making process as well as the results
- Media Release: Always give credit to <u>all</u> the units involved
- Appreciation Letters to Volunteers: This goes a long way to insure both a willingness to respond again, and a sense of sincere appreciation

Claims

- Make sure to include proper documentation
- Types of claims *(usually only for volunteers)*:

- Injury
- Property loss/damage
- Expendable supplies
- *Out-of-pocket* expenses

Replace equipment

- In preparation for the next mission, immediately replace any used or damaged equipment

Critique

- Make the critique a requirement and try to conduct it as soon as the mission ends
- When team leaders lack the opportunity for a critique, integrate it with the debriefing *(Puts more emphasis on a need for a well done debriefing)*

Follow-up tasks

- Determine what personnel needs to accomplish and then assign jobs with a definite completion date
- Make a final report and distribute it to everyone that needs to know
- Review the Plan

> *"The trouble about man is twofold. He cannot learn truths which are too complicated; and he forgets truths which are too simple."*
> --Rebecca West

Notes:

Acronyms Used In Search and Rescue

AA - Agency Administrator
ACA - Area Command Authority
ACO - Aircraft Coordinating Officer
AFRCC - Air Force Rescue Coordination Center
AHJ - Authority Having Jurisdiction
AMDR - Average Maximum Detection Range
AMS - Aeromedical Services
AOBD - Air Operations Branch Director
AREP - Agency Representative
BOLO - Be On the Look Out
CAP - Civil Air Patrol
CISD - Critical Incident Stress Debriefing
CP - Command Post
CTSP - Computer Technical Specialist
DEMOB - Demobilization Unit Leader
DPIC - Deputy Incident Commander
ECC - Emergency Coordination Center
EMS - Emergency Medical Services
EOC - Emergency Operations Center
ETA - Estimated Time of Arrival
FCC - Federal Communications Commission
FLIR - Forward Looking Infrared
FOGSAR - Field Operations Guide for Search & Rescue
FRS - Family Radio System
GIS - Geographic Information Services
GPS - Global Positioning System
GSUL - Ground Support Unit Leader
HAZMAT - Hazardous Materials
IAMSAR - International Aeronautical Maritime SAR
IAP - Incident Action Plan
IC - Incident Commander
ICP - Incident Command Post
ICS - Incident Command System
IMT - Incident Management Team
INTD - Intelligence/Investigations Branch Director
INTO - Intelligence/Investigations Officer
IPP - Initial Planning Point
ISRID - International SAR Incident Database
IT - Information Technology
JFO - Joint Field Office
JIC - Joint Information Center
LED - Light Emitting Diode
LKP - Last Known Point
LPB - Lost Person Behavior
LPQ - Lost Person Questionnaire
LSC - Logistics Section Chief
LZ - Landing Zone

MEDL - Medical Unit Leader
MGRS - Military Grid Reference System
MPQ - Missing Person Questionnaire
NAD - North American Datum
NCIC - National Crime Information Center
NGO - Non-governmental Organization
NIMS - National Incident Management System
NOTAM - Notice to Airman advisory
OP - Operational Period
OPBD - Operations Branch Director
OPS - Operational Section
OSC - On-scene Coordinator
OSC - Operations Section Chief
Pden - Probability Density
PIO - Public Information Officer
PL - Private Line
PLB - Personal Locator Beacon
PLS - Point Last Seen
POA - Probability of Area
POC - Probability of Containment
POD - Probability of Detection
POS - Probability of Success
POV - Personally Owned Vehicle
PPE - Personal Protective Equipment
PSC - Plans Section Chief
PSR - Probability Success Rate
RADO - Radio Operator
RCC - Rescue Coordination Center
Rd - Average Range of Detection
RS - Rescue Specialist
SAP - Search Action Plan
SAR - Search and Rescue
SEND - Satellite Emergency Notification Device
SM - Search Manager
SMC - Search Mission Coordinator
SOP - Standard Operating Procedure
SR/TL or TL - SAR Team Leader or Team Leader
SRTM - Search and Rescue Team Member
SUBD - Support Branch Director
TFR - Temporary Flight Restriction
UC - Unified Command
USCG - United States Coast Guard
UL - Unit Leader
US&R - Urban Search and Rescue
UTM - Universal Transverse Mercator
WGS - World Geodetic Survey

Notes:

Reference Bibliography & Sources of Information on Search

Allan, S. E., & Blough, D. S. (1989). Feature-based Search Asymmetries in Pigeons and Humans. *Perception & Psychophysics*, (46), 456-464.

Australian emergency manual: leadership. (1997). Dickson, A.C.T.: Emergency Management Australia.

Automated Mutual-Assistance Vessel Rescue System - Home. (n.d.). Retrieved January 31, 2017, from http://www.amver.com/.

Air Force Rescue Coordination Center. (n.d.). Retrieved January 31, 2017, from http://www.1af.acc.af.mil/Units/AFRCC.aspx

Bailey, R. G. (2009). Ecoregions of the United States. *Ecosystem Geography*, 93-114. doi:10.1007/978-0-387-89516-1_7

Benkoski, S. J., Monticino, M. G., & Weisinger, J. R. (1991). A survey of the search theory literature. *Naval Research Logistics*, 38(4), 469-494. doi:10.1002/1520-6750(199108)38:4<469::aid-nav3220380404>3.0.co;2-e

Blough, P. M. (2001, September). Cognitive Strategies and Foraging in Pigeons. from http://www.pigeon.psy.tufts.edu/avc/pblough/

Bounds, J. M. (1984). Managing Search Missions: Comments on Probability of Detection. *Response*, 3(1), 15-20.

Bownds, J. M. (1991). *Mountain searches: effectiveness of helicopters*. United States: National Association for Search and Rescue.

Bownds, J. M. (1981). *Desert searches: effectiveness of helicopters*. Tucson, AZ: University of Arizona.

Bounds, J., Ebersole, J., Lovelock, M., & O'Connor, D. (1991). Re-examining The Search Management Function. Part I. *Response*, 10(1), 12-28.

Bounds, J., Ebersole, J., Lovelock, M., & O'Connor, D. (1991). Re-examining The Search Management Function. Part II. *Response*, 10(2), 16-20.

Bounds, J., Ebersole, J., Lovelock, M., & O'Connor, D. (1992). Re-examining The Search Management Function. Part III. *Response*, 11(3), 12-15.

Bounds, J., Ebersole, J., Lovelock, M., & O'Connor, D. (1992). Re-examining The Search Management Function. Part IV. *Response*, 11(4), 10-14.

Charnes, A., & Cooper, W. W. (1958). The Theory of Search: Optimum Distribution of Search Effort. *Management Science*, 5(1), 44-50. doi:10.1287/mnsc.5.1.44.

Chiacchia, K. B., Houlahan, H. E., & Hostetter, R. S. (2015). Deriving Effective Sweep Width for Air-scent Dog Teams. *Wilderness & Environmental Medicine*, 26(2), 142-149. doi:10.1016/j.wem.2014.10.004

Colwell, M. (1992). New Concepts for Grid Searching. *Search and Rescue Technical Publications Series*, 1(1).

Colwell, M. (1997). Trail-based Probability of Area: A Terrain-based Approach to POA Estimation. *Response*, 15(4), 7-13.

Colwell, M. (1992). Sound Sweep: A New Tool for Search Teams. *Search and Rescue Technical Publications Series*, 1(2).

Cooper, D. C., (2005). *Fundamentals of Search and Rescue*. Sudbury, MA: Jones and Bartlett and the National Association for Search and Rescue.

Cooper, D. C., Frost, J. R., & Robe, R. Q. (2003, December). Compatibility of Land Search Procedures with Search Theory. Retrieved from https://www.uscg.mil/hq/cg5/cg534/nsarc/LandSearchMethodsReview.pdf

Cooper D.C., Frost J.R.: Sweep Width Estimation for Ground Search and Rescue; Appendix A: Selected Inland Search Definitions. (2003, December). Retrieved from https://www.uscg.mil/hq/cg5/cg534/nsarc/DetExpReport_2004_final_s.pdf

Cooper, D.C., LaValla, P., & Stoffel, R. (1990). *Search and rescue fundamentals: basic skills and knowledge to perform search and rescue* (3rd ed.). Olympia, WA: Emergency Response Institute and National Rescue Consultants.

Cornell, E. H., & Heth, C. D. (1995). *Distance Traveled during Urban and Suburban Walks Led by 3 to 13-Year-Olds: Tables for Search Managers*. Dept. of Psychology, University of Alberta.

Cornell, E. H., Heth, C. D., Kneubuhler, Y., & Sehgal, S. (1996). Serial Position Effects in Children's Route Reversal Errors: Implications for Police Search Operations. *Applied Cognitive Psychology*, 10(4), 301-326. doi:10.1002/(sici)1099-0720(199608)10:4<301::aid-acp383>3.3.co;2-1

Cornell, E. H., & Hill, K. A. (2006). The Problem of Lost Children. *In Children and their environments: learning, using and designing spaces*. New York, NY: Cambridge University Press.

Dougher, H. (1992). Integrating External Influences. *Response*, 11(3), 26-27. NASAR.

Erwin, C. (1994). *SAR Vulnerability Assessment* (Rep.). Olympia, WA: Emergency Response Intitute, Inc.

Federal Aviation Administration. (2017, February 15). Retrieved February 15, 2017, from http://www.faa.gov/

Foster, E. (n.d.). Search and Rescue Satellite Aided Tracking. Retrieved February 26, 2017, from http://www.sarsat.noaa.gov/

Freedman, D., Pisani, R., Purves, R., & Adhikari, A. (1991). *Statistics* (Second ed.). New York, NY: W.W. Norton & Company.

Frost, J.R. (1998). *Search Theory Enhancement Study: Interagency Committee on SAR Research and Development Working Group* (Rep.) Fairfax, VA: Soza and Company, Ltd.

Frost, J.R. (1998). *What's Missing from Ground Search Theory?* (Rep.) Fairfax, VA: Soza and Company, Ltd.

Frost, J.R. (1998). *Search Theory Enhancement Study: Interagency Committee on Search and Rescue Research and Development Working Group* (Rep). Fairfax, VA: Soza and Company, Ltd.

Frost, J. R. (1998). *The Theory of Search. A Simplified Explanation.* (USA, USCG, Office of Search and Rescue). Fairfax, VA: Soza & Co. Ltd and USCG.

Frost, J.R. (1999). Principles of Search Theory - Part I: Detection. *Response*, 17(1), 7-15.

Frost, J.R. (1999). Principles of Search Theory - Part II: Effort, Coverage and POD. *Response*, 17(2), 8-15.

Frost, J.R. (1999). Principles of Search Theory - Part III: Probability Density Distributions. *Response*. 17(3), 1-10.

Frost, J.R. (1999). Principles of Search Theory - Part IV: Optimal Effort Allocation. *Response, 17*(3), 11-23.

Fuller, G., Johnson, E., & Koester, R. J. (2000). *Man-trackers & dog handlers in search & rescue: basic guidelines and information.* Charlottesville, VA: DbS Productions.

Goodman, R., & Cowan, B. (1996). William Syrotuck Symposium. In The "POC" Factor. Denver, CO: *Response 96.* NASAR.

Gorden, R. L. (1987). *Interviewing: strategy, techniques, and tactics.* Homewood, IL: Dorsey Press.

Hanfland, K. A., Keppel, R. D., & Weis, J. G. (1997). *Case management for missing children homicide investigation.* Washington, D.C.: Homicide Investigation and Tracking System, Attorney General of Washington.

Harbaugh, J. W., Doveton, J. H., & Davis, J. C. (1977). *Probability Methods in Oil Exploration.* New York: Wiley and Sons.

Heth, C., & Cornell, E. H. (1998). Characteristics of Travel by Persons Lost in Albertan Wilderness Areas. *Journal of Environmental Psychology, 18*(3), 223-235. doi:10.1006/jevp.1998.0093

Hill, K. A. (1996). [Distances Traveled and Probability Zones for Lost Persons in Nova Scotia]. Unpublished raw data.

Hill, K.A. (1992). Analyzing Lost Person Scenarios. *Response, 11*(1), 23-27.

Hill, K.A. (1995). How Many Clues Do You Need? Applying Information Theory to Land Search. *Response, 14*(3), 6-8.

Hill, K., & Gale, R. (1998). *Managing the Lost Person Incident.* Chantilly, VA: National Association for Search and Rescue.

Hill, K.A. (1992). Analyzing Lost Person Scenarios. *Response, 11*(1), 23-27.

Hoffman, J. E. (1979). A two-stage model of visual search. *Perception & Psychophysics, 25*(4), 319-327. doi:10.3758/bf03198811

IAMSAR manual: International Aeronautical and Maritime Search And Rescue manual. (2006). London: IMO/ICAO.

Incident Command System: national training curriculum. (1994). Boise, ID: National Interagency Fire Center.

International aeronautical and maritime search and rescue manual: volume I-II-III. (1998). Montréal: IMO/ICAO.

International aeronautical and maritime search and rescue manual: incorporating 2001, 2002, 2003, 2004, 2005, 2006 and 2007 amendments. (2008). London: IMO and the ICAO.

Kelley, D. E. (1973). *Mountain Search for the Lost Victim.* Montrose, CA: Kelley.

Koester, R. J. (2014). *Incident Command System Field Operations Guide for Search & Rescue: (ICS-FOGSAR).* Charlottesville, VA: DbS Productions.

Koester, R. J., Cooper, D. C., Frost, J. R., & Robe, R. Q. (2005). *Sweep Width Estimation for Ground Search and Rescue (USA, Coast Guard, National Search and Rescue Committee).* Alexandria, VA: Potomac Management Group, Inc. (https://www.uscg.mil/hq/cg5/cg534/nsarc/DetExpReport_2004_final_s.pdf)

Koester, R. J. (2008). *Lost Person Behavior: a search and rescue guide on where to look for land, air, and water.* Charlottesville, VA: dbS Productions.

Koester, R. J., Gordon, R., & Wells, T. (2010). *The Development of a Detection Index for Sound and Light: Search and Rescue Institute of New Zealand POD Experiments, Design of an international best practice experiment* (Rep.). Christchurch, NZ: Search and Rescue Institute New Zealand.

Koester, R. J., Chiacchia, K. B., Twardy, C. R., Cooper, D. C., Frost, J. R., & Robe, R. Q. (2014). Use of the Visual Range of Detection to Estimate Effective Sweep Width for Land Search and Rescue Based On 10 Detection Experiments in North America. *Wilderness & Environmental Medicine*, 25(2), 132-142. doi:10.1016/j.wem.2013.09.016

Koester, R. J., & Stooksbury, D. E. (1995). Behavioral profile of possible Alzheimer's disease patients in Virginia search and rescue incidents. *Wilderness & Environmental Medicine*, 6(1), 34-43. doi:10.1016/s1080-6032(13)80007-5

Koester, R. J. and Stooksbury, D. E. (1992). Lost Alzheimer's Subjects - Profiles and Statistics. *Response*. 11(4), 20-26.

Koopman, B. O. (1946). *Search and Screening*. Washington, DC: Operations Evaluation Group.

Koopman, B. O. (1999). *Search and Screening: general principles with historical applications*. Alexandria, VA: Military Operations Research Society.

LaValla, P., Stoffel, R., Erwin, C., & Pargeter, R. A. (1991). *Blueprint for Community Emergency Management: a text for managing emergency operations*. Olympia, WA: Emergency Reponse Institute.

LaValla, P., Stoffel, R., & Jones, A. S. (1997). *Search is an Emergency: a text for managing search operations*. Olympia, WA: Emergency Response Institute.

Lavalla, P. H. (1989). Robability of Detection (POD) *Research and Other Concepts for Search Management* (Ed.). Olympia, WA: Emergency Response Intitute, Inc.

Lawson, N. (n.d.). Rescue Standards - Straightjacket or Salvation. *Response*, 5(5), 21-23.

Lovelock, D. (1991). *The Influence of Clues on the POAs* (Rep.).

MacInnes, H. (1984). *International Mountain Rescue Handbook*. London: Constable.

Mattson, R. J. (1975). *Establishing Search Priorities* (Rep.).

McCue, J. R. (2010). Helicopter Visual Search Effectiveness (Unpublished master's thesis). Embry-Riddle Aeronautical University.

National Response Plan (NRP). (2005). Washington, D.C.: Press Office, U.S. Dept. of Homeland Security.

O'Donnell, S. (1987). *The Comparative Rate of Searching by Police Aircraft and Men on Foot*. London: Home Office, Scientific Research and Development Branch.

Richardson, H. R., & Discenza, J. H. (1980). The United States Coast Guard Computer-Assisted Search Planning system (CASP). *Naval Research Logistics Quarterly*, 27(4), 659-680. doi:10.1002/nav.3800270413

Robe, R. Q., & Frost, J. R. (2002). *A Method for Determining Effective Sweep Widths for Land Searches: Procedures for Conducting Detection Experiments*. (USA, USCG, National Search and Rescue Comittee). Alexandria, VA: Potomac Management Group, Inc.

Rock, I. (1995). *Perception*. New York: Scientific American Library.

Schneider, W., & Shiffrin, R. M. (1977). Controlled and automatic human information processing: I. Detection, search, and attention. *Psychological*

Review, 84(1), 1-66. doi:10.1037//0033-295x.84.1.1

Setnicka, T. J., & Andrasko, K. (1980). *Wilderness Search and Rescue*. Leicester: Cordee.

Shea, G. (1988). Formula for the Field: A Simple Method for Shifting Probability of Area. *Response*, 7(3), 20-24.

Shiffrin, R. M., & Schneider, W. (1977). Controlled and automatic human information processing: II. Perceptual learning, automatic attending and a general theory. *Psychological Review*, 84(2), 127-190. doi:10.1037//0033-295x.84.2.127

Shimp, C. P. (1976). Organization in Memory and Behavior. *Journal of the Experimental Analysis of Behavior*, 26, 113-130.

Simons, D. J., & Chabris, C. F. (1999). Gorillas in Our Midst: sustained inattentional blindness for dynamic events. *Perception*, 28(9), 1059-1074. doi:10.1068/p2952

SOLAS: consolidated text of the International Convention for the Safety of Life at Sea, 1974, and its Protocol of 1988: articles, annexes and certificates. (2009). London: International Maritime Organization.

Spencer, C., & Blades, M. (2006). *Children and their Environments: learning, using, and designing spaces*. Cambridge, UK: Cambridge University Press.

Stoffel, R. C. (Ed.). (1987). *Helicopter Operations and Personnel Safety*. Olympia, WA: Emergency Response Intitute, Inc.

Stoffel, R., Swombow, C., & Wilfong, R. (2005). *The handbook for managing land search operations*. Cashmere, Wa.: Emergency Response International, Inc.

Stoffel, R. C. (2006). *The Textbook for Managing Land Search Operations*. Cashmere, WA.: Emergency Response International, Inc.

Stoffel, R., & Stoffel, B. C. (2013). *SAR Skills for the Emergency Responder*. Cashmere, WA: Emergency Response International, Inc.

Stone, L. D. (2007). *Theory of Optimal Search*. Linthicum, MD: INFORMS.

Swombow, C. (1996). The Searching Science. *Police Science and Technology Review*, (4), 27-32.

Syrotuck, W. G., & Syrotuck, J. A. (2000). *Analysis of lost person behavior: an aid to search planning*. Mechanicsburg, PA: Barkleigh Productions.

Syrotuck, W. G. (1974). *Some grid search techniques for locating lost individuals in wilderness areas*. Westmoreland, NY: Arner Publication.

Syrotuck, W. G. (1975). *An introduction to land search probabilities and calculations*. Westmoreland, NY: Arner Publications.

Treisman, A. M., & Gelade, G. (1980). A feature-integration theory of attention. *Cognitive Psychology*, 12(1), 97-136. doi:10.1016/0010-0285(80)90005-5

Treisman, A., & Gormican, S. (1988). Feature Analysis in Early Vision: evidence from search asymmetries. *Psychological Review*, 95(1), 15-48. doi:10.1037//0033-295x.95.1.15144.

United States national Search and Rescue Supplement to the International Aeronautical and Maritime Search and Rescue Manual. (2000). Washington, D.C.: The National Search and Rescue Committee.

USA, USCG, National Search and Rescue Committee. (2007). *The United States National Search and Rescue Plan*. Retrieved from https://www.uscg.mil/hq/cg5/cg534/manuals/Natl_SAR_Plan(2007).pdf

Ullman, S. (1997). *High-level vision: object recognition and visual cognition.* Cambridge, MA: The MIT Press.

Wartes, J. (1988). *Washington Explorer Search and Rescue: team member training manual.* Tacoma, WA: Washington Explorer Search and Rescue.

Wartes, J. (1993). *Explorer Search and Rescue Team Leader Training Manual.* Olympia, WA: Emergency Response Intitute, Inc.

Wartes, J. (1974). *An Experimental Analysis of Grid Sweep Searching* (Rep.). Sunnyvale, CA: Western region ESAR..

Washburn, A. R. (2014). *Search and Detection.* Monterey, CA: Operations Research Department, Naval Postgraduate School.

Wolfe, J. M., Cave, K. R., & Franzel, S. L. (1989). Guided search: An alternative to the feature integration model for visual search. *Journal of Experimental Psychology: Human Perception and Performance,* 15(3), 419-433. doi:10.1037//0096-1523.15.3.419

Young, C. S., & Wehbring, J. (2007). *Urban Search: Managing Missing Person Searches in the Urban Environment.* Charlottesville, Va: dbS Productions.

Searching With Dogs

Search and Rescue Dogs: Training Methods. (1991). New York: Howell Book House.

Bryson, S. (1979). The Shepards Vs The Hounds: Air scenting vs. Tracking in the Search Dog's Function. *Search and Rescue Magazine,* (Spring), 6-8.

Bryson, S. (1984). *Search Dog Training.* Pacific Grove, CA: Boxwood Press.

Bulanda, S., & Bulanda, L. (2014). *Ready!: Training the Search and Rescue Dog.* Irvine, CA: I-5 Publishing.

Button, L. (1990). *Practical Scent Dog Training.* Loveland, CO.: Alpine Publications.

Doran, J. (1980). *Search on Mount St. Helens.* Bellevue, WA: Imagesmith.

Graham, H. (1994). Probability of Detection for Search Dogs or How Long is Your Shadow. *Response,* 13(1), 9-12.

Greatbatch, I., Gosling, R. J., & Allen, S. (2015). Quantifying Search Dog Effectiveness in a Terrestrial Search and Rescue Environment. *Wilderness & Environmental Medicine,* 26(3), 327-334. doi:10.1016/j.wem.2015.02.009

Hardy, M. (1993). How to Develop and Train a Water Search Dog Team. *Response.* 12(1), 18-27 & 34.

Holt, A. B. (1995). Bloodhounds: An Underutilized Resource. *Response.* 14(2), 22 -27.

Johnson, G. R. (2003). *Tracking Dog: Theory & Methods.* Mechanicsburg, PA: Barkleigh Productions.

Koenig, M. (1987). Wilderness Search Strategy for Dog Handlers. *Response.* 6(2), 28-35.

Pearsall, M., & Verbruggen, H. (1982). *Scent, training to track, search, and rescue.* Loveland, CO: Alpine Publications.

Reed, L. F. (1979). How the Bloodhounds Do It. *Search and Rescue Magazine.* (Spring), 12-13.

Sessions, J. (1991). Managing Stress in Dog Teams on Searches. *Response.* 10(4), 12-15.

Syrotuck, W. G. (2000). *Scent and the Scenting Dog.* Mechanicsburg, PA: Barkleigh Productions..

Williams, S. (1995). Desert Searching with Dogs. *Response.* 14(3), 3-5.

Tracking

Taylor, A., & Cooper, D. C. (2014). *Fundamentals of Mantracking: the step-by-step method.* New York, NY: Skyhorse Publishing.

Graham, H., & Graham, J. (1985). Constructing a Footprint. *Response*, 4(4), 13-14.

Kearney, J. (1978). *Tracking: a blueprint for learning how.* El Cajon, CA: Pathways Press..

Robbins, R. (1977). *Mantracking: introduction to the step-by-step method.* Montrose, CA: Search and Rescue Magazine.

Speiden, R., & Fuller, G. (2013). *Foundations for Awareness, Signcutting and Tracking.* Christiansburg, VA: Natural Awareness Tracking School, LLC.

Notes:

Made in the USA
Middletown, DE
09 September 2024

60043708R00278